KU-706-942

The World Book

Home Medical Encyclopedia

Volume Two
Medical Reference

I–Z

The World Book Home Medical Encyclopedia

Reprinted 1981
Revised edition 1984

Filmset in Great Britain by Filmtype Services Ltd, Scarborough
ISBN 0 7166 5501 2
(Library of Congress Catalog Number 79-56907)
Printed and bound in Spain
by TONSA, San Sebastian
Dep. Leg. S.S. 360-80

I

Iatrogenic disorder is any disorder brought about as a result of medical treatment.

Ichthyosis is a skin disorder in which the skin becomes dry and scaly, like the skin of a fish. The condition develops either shortly after birth, or between the ages of one and four years. There is no cure for ichthyosis, but a doctor may prescribe ointments to keep the skin soft and supple.

Icterus. *See* JAUNDICE.

Icterus gravis neonatorum. *See* HAEMOLYTIC DISEASE OF THE NEWBORN.

Ictus is a sudden convulsion or seizure, such as may occur at the start of a stroke or an attack of epilepsy. *See* STROKE.

Identical twins are two individuals that have developed from the splitting of a single fertilized egg. *See* TWINS.

Idioglossia is a speech defect characterized by unintelligible pronunciation. The condition may be caused by severe DEAFNESS in infancy, or it may occur after a STROKE.

Idiopathic describes a disorder or condition that occurs for no known reason. Many forms of epilepsy and high blood pressure are described as being idiopathic.

Idiosyncrasy is an unusual and possibly eccentric pattern of behaviour in an individual. Medically, the term is used to describe an unusual reaction to a drug, such as hypersensitivity, or no reaction at all even to a larger than normal dosage.

Ileitis is inflammation of the ileum, the lower part of the small intestine. Symptoms of the disorder include abdominal pain, often with vomiting or diarrhoea, and sometimes blood or mucus in the stool. Malnutrition may result if severe ileitis persists.

Q: *What causes ileitis?*

A: Infections such as traveller's diarrhoea, cholera, typhoid, salmonella poisoning, viral infections, and tuberculosis may cause ileitis. Acute inflammation of the ileum can also result from food poisoning. Chronic inflammation can occur with COELIAC DISEASE, CROHN'S DISEASE, or tuberculosis.

Q: *What is the treatment for ileitis?*

A: Drugs are sometimes effective. One form of treatment is to remove the portion of the intestine that is affected. Another is to allow the ileum to heal by surgically by-passing the diseased part.

Ileostomy is an opening into the small intestine that is created surgically by bringing a part of the small intestine (ileum) to the outside surface of the body at the abdomen. An ileostomy may be required as a temporary measure to by-pass the intestine, during the treatment of intestinal obstruction. A permanent ileostomy is necessary following removal of the large intestine.

Q: *How are the contents of the ileum collected?*

A: The patient must wear a special kind of bag over the ileostomy to collect the liquid that drains from the ileum.

Q: *What problems might an ileostomy patient have to deal with?*

A: The three main possible problems are skin irritation, odour, and leakage. The skin becomes irritated if it comes into contact with the faeces, or if the patient develops an allergy to the materials of the appliance. Special pastes and ointments can be applied to protect the skin, but the most effective way to prevent irritation is to ensure that the bag fits well over the ileostomy. A secure fit also eliminates any unpleasant odour.

One of the functions of the large intestine is to absorb water from the faeces as they pass along the intestine. An ileostomy patient is unable to reabsorb this fluid, and may become dehydrated. Supplements of salt in the diet and extra fluids are necessary.

Q: *Can an ileostomy patient lead a normal life?*

A: Yes. Many patients with ileostomies are

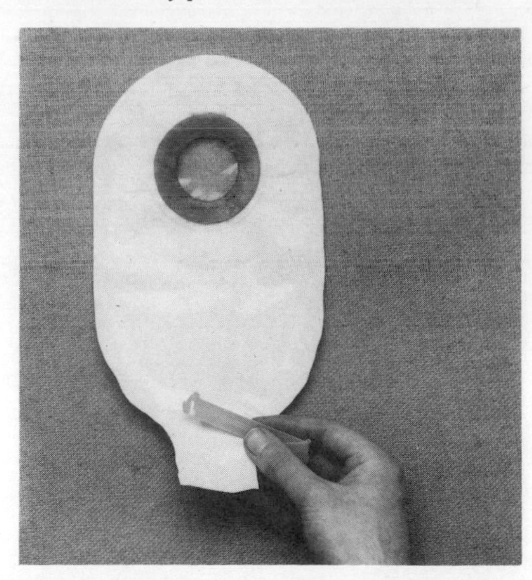

Ileostomy drainage bags fix securely over the stoma and collect the contents of the ileum.

young adults. Once they become adjusted to the minor social inconvenience of an ileostomy, they can lead a normal life. The various ileostomy associations can give sound, practical advice to new patients.

See also COLOSTOMY.

Ileum is the section of the small intestine that extends from the jejunum to the beginning of the large intestine (colon). It is about 3.9 metres (13 feet) long. (*See* DIGESTIVE SYSTEM.)

Disorders of the ileum, such as chronic ILEITIS, produce malnutrition if they continue for a long time. Tumours of the ileum are rare, but a MECKEL'S DIVERTICULUM may occur as a congenital anomaly.

Ileus is an obstruction of the small intestine. It causes pain and vomiting. Paralytic ileus is an obstruction caused by muscle paralysis that leads to abdominal distension. This commonly occurs after an abdominal operation or peritonitis.

Immersion foot, also known as trench foot, is a serious condition resembling FROSTBITE. If neglected, it can lead to GANGRENE, particularly in a person suffering from arteriosclerosis, diabetes mellitus, or hypothyroidism.

Immersion foot is caused by exposure of the feet to wet, cold conditions, and especially to icy water, for a prolonged period of time.

Immunity is the body's ability to resist invasion by any ANTIGEN (a disease organism, poison, or foreign substance). In defence, the body produces antibodies. These destroy or neutralize antigens. Antitoxins, a type of antibody, nullify poisons produced by invading organisms (such as bacteria). The next time that the same organisms invade the body, the defence system recognizes and rapidly destroys them (*see* ANTIBODY). Other foreign substances are dealt with by WHITE BLOOD CELLS (leucocytes). These attack and "swallow up" the invading bacteria, and dispose of it as pus. The role of the leucocytes in the immunity system is not fully understood, but current medical opinion is that one type of white blood cell, the lymphocytes, produce antibodies.

There are two types of immunity: passive immunity and active immunity (*see* IMMUNIZATION).

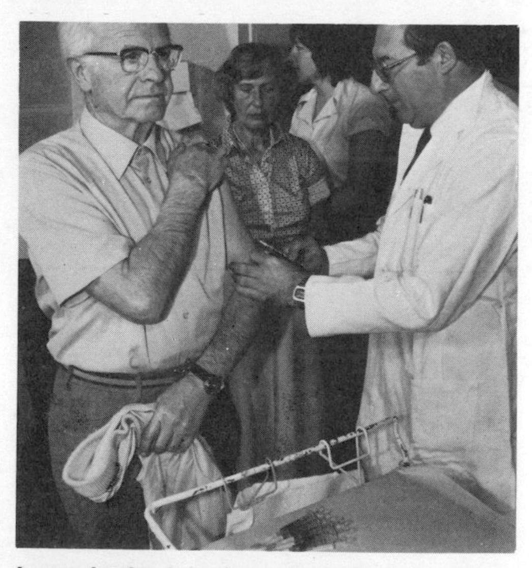

Immunization injections can be given quickly and with relatively little discomfort.

A talk about Immunization

Immunization is the production of IMMUNITY to various specific diseases and disorders. Such immunization is also known as inoculation or VACCINATION.

Like the body's natural defence system, the immunity gained by immunization may be divided into two types: passive immunity and active immunity.

Q: What is passive immunity?

A: Passive immunity following immunization is only temporary and it helps the body to fight a disease possibly contracted. Such immunity to specific diseases is usually provided by injecting gamma globulin containing antibodies from an immunized person or animal. SERUM SICKNESS may occur as a reaction to immunization for passive immunity.

Q: What is active immunity?

A: Active immunity provided by immunization is long-lasting in effect and may even be permanent. The immunization stimulates the body's own natural immunity mechanism, and is a precautionary measure to prevent the body contracting a particular disease.

Active immunity is usually provided in one of three ways: (1) by injecting a dead organism of the disease (as against diphtheria, influenza, tetanus, and whooping cough); (2) by injecting a weakened live organism of the disease (as against measles, mumps, tuberculosis, and yellow fever); or (3) by introducing a weakened, live virus through a scratch in the skin (as against smallpox). Some vaccines, such as that against poliomyelitis, can also be taken by mouth.

Q: Does active immunity give total protection?

A: Unfortunately not. But if the disease is

IMMUNIZATION, advised for children

NAME AND DOSE	REACTIONS	NOTES
Diphtheria 3 injections at 5, 6, and 12 months. Further injection at age 5.	Rare. Sometimes local soreness.	Usually given with tetanus and pertussis as Triple Antigen. Small dose used for older children and adults preceded by Schick Test for previous immunity or severe reaction.
Tetanus 3 injections at 5, 6, and 12 months. Further injections at age 5 and 10 years.	Rare. Sometimes local soreness.	Usually given with diphtheria and pertussis as Triple Antigen. Further boosters following cuts or animal bites. Antitetanus serum available for injuries in unvaccinated persons.
Whooping cough (Pertussis) 3 injections at 5, 6, and 12 months.	Rare. Sometimes local soreness. Very rarely fever; vomiting.	Usually given with tetanus and diphtheria in Triple Antigen. Not advised if there is a history of allergy or convulsions in family, or cerebral palsy.
Tuberculosis Single injection at birth or age 13.	Small lump may ulcerate for some weeks.	Known as BCG, and given at birth if tuberculosis in family. Later in life given after a negative Tuberculin skin test.
Poliomyelitis 3 oral vaccine doses at 5, 6, and 12 months (with Diphtheria, Whooping cough, and Tetanus injections). Further doses at age 5 and 10 years.	Rare.	Usually given with Triple Antigen. Not advised during bout of diarrhoea; when taking corticosteroid drugs; in first three months of pregnancy.
Measles 1 injection at 15 months.	Sometimes fever; rash within 8-10 days, for 3-4 days.	May be combined with mumps and/or rubella. Not given to persons taking corticosteroid drugs; suffering from leukaemia or tuberculosis; or during pregnancy.
Mumps Single injection at any age: only if recommended by a doctor.	Rare.	May be combined with measles and/or rubella. Not given to persons with serious illness; allergy to eggs; or during pregnancy. Advised for adult males who have not had the disease, after test to confirm absence of the disease.
German measles (Rubella) Single injection at age 11, for girls only.	Infrequently slight fever; rash; aching joints.	May be combined with mumps and/or measles. Not given to persons taking corticosteroid drugs; suffering from leukaemia or tuberculosis; or during pregnancy.

contracted, the effects are much milder than they would otherwise be.

Q: Are there any risks in immunization for active immunity?

A: Statistically, the risks are few. Some people may have allergies to specific vaccines. Rarely, the whooping cough vaccine may lead to brain damage.

Q: Why are babies immunized?

A: Diseases such as whooping cough and measles can lead to pneumonia, severe brain damage, permanent disability, or even death.

Immunosuppressive drugs or treatments suppress the natural immune mechanism of the body. They are used to treat AUTOIMMUNE DISEASE, or after organ TRANSPLANT SURGERY to prevent the body rejecting the foreign tissue of the transplanted organ.

Immunotherapy is a method of treating a patient by conferring passive immunity, usually by injecting gamma globulin containing antibodies that act on a particular infection or by immunizing a patient with his or her own tumour cells. The term sometimes refers to treatment with IMMUNOSUPPRESSIVE drugs.

Impacted describes body structures that are pressed so closely together that normal movement or growth is impossible.

Imperforate describes any structure in which a natural opening is abnormally closed.

Impetigo is an infectious skin disease that is usually caused by staphylococcus or streptococcus bacteria. It is common among children, and may appear as a complication of an existing skin condition such as eczema or ichthyosis. Chronic impetigo in older persons is known as ecthyma.

Q: Why is impetigo common among children?

A: The body's immunity is less well developed in children. Frequent colds with a runny nose move staphylococci from the nose onto the face. Nose-blowing and scratching beneath and around the nose produce minor abrasions on the skin, which allow the bacteria to enter. Other areas, such as the hands and legs, may also become infected.

Q: What are the symptoms of impetigo?

A: Small blisters appear on the skin. These rapidly break down to form pale, crusty, oozing areas that spread. The condition may be complicated by further infection from streptococcus bacteria.

Q: How is impetigo treated?

A: Medical advice should be sought promptly because the infection can spread rapidly to other people. Doctors usually prescribe an antibiotic cream; any crusts should be soaked off with warm water before the cream is applied. If the condition recurs, it may be necessary to use antibiotic cream in the nose, and antiseptic solution in the bath to kill bacteria on the skin.

Q: Are there any complications of impetigo?

A: Yes. If additional streptococcal infection breaks out on the area affected by impetigo, it can cause the kidney disorder acute NEPHRITIS.

Impotence is a man's inability to produce, or maintain, a penile erection. For this reason, an impotent man cannot have sexual intercourse. The condition may be short-lived or may last for a long time. Brief bouts of impotence may follow depression and illnesses, such as influenza, or after taking drugs or alcohol, but in these cases the man can expect a swift return to former potency. Impotence is not the same as INFERTILITY or STERILITY.

Q: What causes impotence?

A: Impotence usually has a psychological origin. There may, however, be a physical cause, such as certain diseases or disorders; for example, Cushing's syndrome, hypopituitarism, polyneuritis, a stroke, diabetes mellitus, or alcoholism. Impotence may also occur as an after-effect of certain surgical procedures, and the patient should be informed of this before such an operation.

Q: How is impotence treated?

A: Where the impotence has a psychological basis, a doctor may arrange for the problem to be discussed with a sex therapist or marriage counsellor. The patient's sexual partner should be involved in such discussion and any consequent treatment.

Where impotence is the result of a physical disease or disorder, the underlying cause must be treated first. Unfortunately impotence caused by some physical disorders may be permanent.

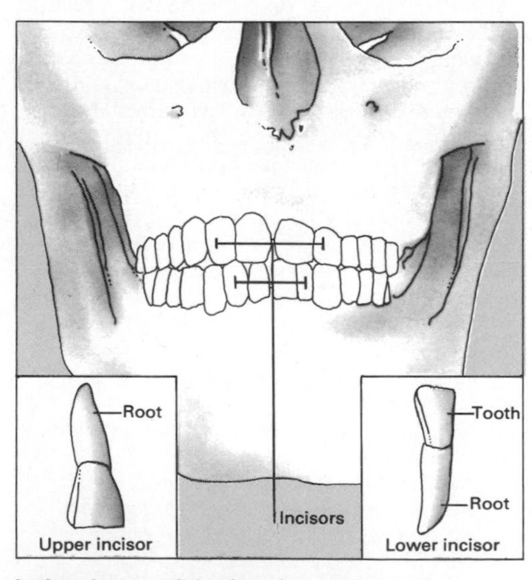

Incisor is one of the four front teeth in the upper and lower jaws of the adult.

Incision is the cut a surgeon makes at the beginning of an operation. The position of the incision is chosen to cause as little damage to the surrounding structures as possible, and to ensure that the tissues will heal strongly.

Incisor is a chisel-like front tooth used for cutting. There are four incisors at the front of each human jaw. *See* TEETH.

Incontinence is the lack of voluntary control of the bladder or bowels, particularly in an adult. Voluntary control of the bladder during the daytime is not achieved until about the age of two years, and at night may not occur until some years later.

Q: What can cause incontinence of the bladder?

A: Any neurological disorder that interferes with normal sensations from the bladder can prevent control of the sphincter muscle that normally closes it. Such disorders include spina bifida, damage to the spinal cord, multiple sclerosis, and nerve degeneration that occurs with conditions like diabetes mellitus and strokes, or senility. This type of incontinence is also common in attacks of epilepsy.

Incontinence may also result from partial obstruction caused by enlargement of the prostate gland (prostatomegaly) and from disorders of the muscle that controls the outflow of urine; such a muscle disorder may follow an operation or cancer. Some women develop STRESS INCONTINENCE because of prolapse (a displacement) of the womb, which presses on the bladder and changes its anatomy so that urine escapes when the woman coughs or laughs. Incontinence may also result from an injury to the spinal cord that prevents impulses between the brain and bladder.

Q: What can cause incontinence of the bowels?

A: In young children, lack of bowel control may simply be resistance to toilet training. But in older children it may be a sign of a serious psychological disorder.

Faecal incontinence is common in the senile, as is constipation. Failure to control the bowels may also be associated with neurological disorders, such as a stroke, multiple sclerosis, or the polyneuritis associated with diabetes mellitus. The condition may follow damage to the sphincter muscle that closes the anus following childbirth or an operation for anal fistula or fissure. Another factor can be cancer of the rectum or simply severe diarrhoea.

Q: How is incontinence treated?

A: The treatment of any form of incontinence must be directed toward the cause. Special bags may be used for urinary incontinence, but faecal incontinence is more difficult to control; absorbent pads have to be worn in waterproof underpants.

A new treatment involves electrical stimulation of the muscles that close the exit from the bladder and rectum.

Incrustation is the formation of crusts or scabs on the skin. *See* SCAB.

Incubation period is the time between exposure to an infectious illness and the appearance of the first symptoms. It is not the same as QUARANTINE. *See* INFECTIOUS DISEASES.

Incubator is a life-support system used in hospitals for rearing premature or seriously ill newborn babies. It is a ventilated, boxlike apparatus in which the atmosphere can be kept sterile and at constant temperature and humidity.

An incubator is also any device used to promote the growth of organisms placed inside it.

Indian hemp is another name for cannabis or marijuana. *See* MARIJUANA.

A talk about Indigestion

Indigestion is incomplete or imperfect digestion. But the condition is poorly defined, and it can vary according to situation and person. Acute indigestion is unpleasant and the chronic form is debilitating. Chronic indigestion is sometimes a symptom of a more serious disorder, such as hiatus hernia, a gall bladder disorder, or a peptic ulcer. It is common during the later stages of pregnancy.

Q: What are the symptoms of indigestion?

A: Usually the person experiences vague abdominal discomfort, and feels generally bloated. Burping may bring temporary relief. The symptoms may be severe enough to produce ill-defined pain that may or may not vary in intensity. Sometimes the feeling of discomfort increases, the patient feels nauseated, and vomits. The symptoms usually last for only about two hours, although a bout of indigestion can last many weeks.

In addition to these symptoms, there may be HEARTBURN. This produces a burning sensation beneath the breastbone that is sometimes accompanied by a bitter taste of fluid rising up into the mouth.

Q: What causes indigestion?

A: Indigestion is usually caused by GASTRITIS (inflammation of the lining of the stomach), often brought on by overeating or an excess of alcohol. Smoking aggravates the condition. A person who has irregular meals, drinks too much strong coffee, and is anxious or depressed, often develops mild gastritis. The bloated feeling and flatulence may encourage AEROPHAGIA, the habit of swallowing air, which increases the indigestion symptoms. Obesity also aggravates the condition. Chronic indigestion can also be a warning symptom of cancer.

Q: When should an indigestion sufferer consult a doctor?

Incubators provide a germ-free environment to help premature newborns survive.

A: If the symptoms are severe enough to interfere with normal life, or to disturb sleep, a doctor should be consulted within twenty-four hours.

Q: Is an upset stomach the same as indigestion?

A: An upset stomach is usually an acute form of indigestion lasting only a few hours and may, in severe forms, be accompanied by diarrhoea and vomiting. This is likely to be a form of GASTROENTERITIS or acute GASTRITIS.

Q: How is indigestion treated?

A: Treatment depends on the cause of the indigestion. Many patients find that the symptoms improve after a light, easily digestible meal, or a glass of milk. Others find that an antacid medicine or tablets bring relief, particularly from heartburn.

In cases of excessive acid production, the doctor may prescribe a new ANTIHISTAMINE that decreases acid production. If anxiety, depression, and tension seem to be the main reasons for the indigestion, the doctor may prescribe tranquillizers or antidepressant drugs. Definite physical causes are treated in the appropriate way.

Induction means causing or producing. The term has several medical applications. In one meaning, induction is the artificial initiation of childbirth. Labour is induced either by surgically rupturing the membrane around the foetus, or by injecting the mother with drugs (*see* PREGNANCY AND CHILDBIRTH).

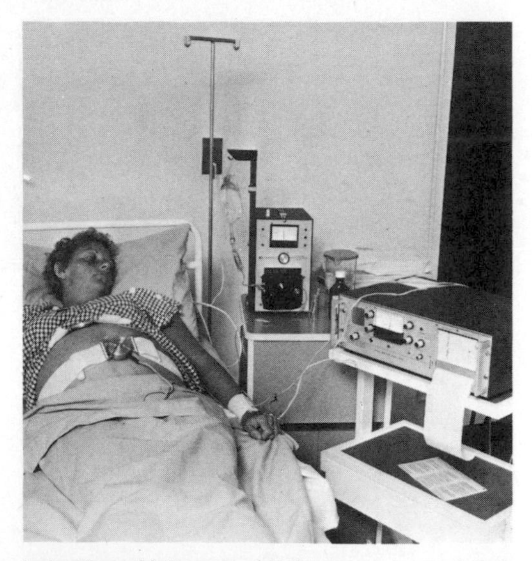

Induction of labour in childbirth can be assisted by complex monitoring equipment.

Induction is also used to describe the beginning of anaesthesia. It may refer to the intravenous injection of a short-acting barbiturate, or the initial inhalation of an anaesthetic gas.

In psychology, induction is a logical process of learning. The term also describes feelings reflected in another person; for example, grief in one person can induce sympathy in another.

Induration is an unusual area of hardness or firmness in a body tissue. The term may refer to bruising, scarring around a wound, or the hardened tissue surrounding an abscess.

Industrial diseases are disorders that are caused by exposure to various toxic substances and microorganisms that are used in industrial processes. *See* OCCUPATIONAL HAZARDS.

Infantile paralysis. *See* POLIOMYELITIS.

Infarction is an area of dead tissue in an organ that has had its blood supply cut off due to blockage in a blood vessel, usually an artery, supplying it. The seriousness of the condition depends on where the infarction occurs.

Q: What causes a blockage in a blood vessel?

A: Thrombosis (blood clotting) in an artery creates a blockage and may be caused by ARTERIOSCLEROSIS or damage to the vessel. A blood clot from another part of the body may become trapped in an artery; this is known as an EMBOLISM.

Q: What are the symptoms of an infarction?

A: These depend on which part of the body is affected. If the infarction is in the heart muscle (myocardial infarction), the patient's symptoms may vary from severe pain radiating from the centre of the chest to the left arm, the neck, shoulders, back, and jaw to a feeling of mild indigestion (*see* CORONARY HEART DISEASE). If the infarction is in the brain the patient suffers a stroke. In both instances, there are no alternative blood supplies, and the tissues die. If the infarction is in the leg, the patient experiences acute cramp-like pain and the leg becomes white and cold. If the patient does not receive immediate surgery, GANGRENE rapidly sets in. An infarction in the kidney produces blood in the urine (haematuria).

Q: Can an infarction be treated?

A: No. Once the tissue has died, it cannot be replaced. It can gradually heal and form scar tissue. Treatment is aimed at preventing an embolism from developing and causing an infarction. Emergency surgery can replace part of the femoral artery with a graft or plastic tubing, but if

INFECTIOUS DISEASES

Disease	Incubation (days)	Quarantine (days)	Infectivity (days)	Duration (days)
Chickenpox	14-21	21	−1 - +6	6-8
Diphtheria	2-5	7	14-28 (until clear)	Until clear
Dysentery (bacillary)	2-7	7	7-21 (until clear)	3-5
German measles (rubella)	14-21	21	7 before rash appears until 5 after	5
Glandular fever	4-14	5+	Not known	7-21
Influenza	1-3	Not necessary	When symptoms appear until 7 after	3-5
Measles	8-14	14	4 before rash appears until 7 after	6-8
Meningitis	3-5	5+	2	Varies
Mumps	14-28	28	7 before symptoms appear until 9 after	10-14
Poliomyelitis	4-13	21	Last part of incubation period and first week of acute illness	10-15
Roseola	2-5	5	Varies	5-7
Scarlet fever	2-5	Until clear	Beginning of incubation period until 14-21 after symptoms appear	7-10
Typhoid fever and Paratyphoid	7-21	Until clear	Until clear	14-21
Whooping cough (pertussis)	7-21	21	21	42

the tissues have already died (gangrene), amputation is the only treatment.

Infection is the invasion of the body by disease-producing organisms. There are five main types of infective organisms: (1) viruses (*see* VIRUS); (2) BACTERIA; (3) fungi (*see* FUNGAL DISORDERS); (4) PROTOZOA; and (5) WORMS. Infection may enter the body in the air that is breathed; in food or water that is eaten or drunk; directly through the skin; or from another part of the body in which the organism produces no ill effects (*see* CONTAGIOUS DISEASES).

Infectious diseases are those diseases that are transmitted from one person to another, possibly causing an epidemic. For this reason, such diseases are also called COMMUNICABLE DISEASES. CONTAGIOUS DISEASES are caught by direct physical contact with the diseased.

The table on this page lists common infectious diseases, each of which has a separate article in the A-Z section of this book.

There are many other less common infectious diseases, and the following also have articles in the A-Z section of this book: AMOEBIC DYSENTERY; BORNHOLM DISEASE; BRUCELLOSIS; CHOLERA; ENCEPHALITIS; HAND-FOOT-AND-MOUTH DISEASE; HEPATITIS; RABIES; SMALLPOX; TOXOPLASMOSIS; TUBERCULOSIS; TYPHUS; VENEREAL DISEASES; YAWS; YELLOW FEVER.

Infectious mononucleosis (glandular fever) is an acute infectious disease. *See* GLANDULAR FEVER.

Inferiority complex is a state of mind in which a person believes himself or herself to be inferior to others. *See* COMPLEX.

A talk about Infertility

Infertility is the inability to produce offspring. It is not the same as STERILITY, because an infertile person may have no physical disorder of the reproductive system.

Many couples are temporarily infertile. The likelihood of becoming pregnant on any one occasion is only about one per cent. However, over a period of two years, ten per cent of couples are infertile.

Fifty per cent of women under the age of thirty who have regular intercourse can become pregnant within six months. Nearly eighty per cent may be pregnant within a year, the remaining ten per cent within two years. Older women usually take longer.

Q: What should a couple do if they believe they are infertile?

A: Taking into consideration the above statistics, it is advisable for a couple to delay any kind of investigations for at least a year. During this time they can work out the exact OVULATION day of the woman. To do this, the woman takes her temperature first thing in the morning before having anything to eat or drink. Fourteen days before the onset of menstruation, the temperature rises by about 0.5°C (1°F). The rise in temperature occurs twenty-four hours *after* ovulation. If a temperature chart is kept for three to four months, a woman can estimate the day of ovulation.

The ovum is ready for FERTILIZATION for twenty-four hours. It is not known for certain how long a sperm can survive in the womb, but it is thought to be up to three days.

Q: Why are some couples infertile?

A: A SEXUAL PROBLEM, such as complete ignorance about the mechanics of intercourse, is a more common factor than is realized. Other sexual difficulties that disrupt fertility include FRIGIDITY and IMPOTENCE.

Sometimes a woman who ovulates only occasionally has a partner with a low sperm count. This means the chance of fertilization is greatly reduced.

In fifty per cent of infertile couples, both partners are affected because of some physical reason. In the remaining fifty per cent, half the men and half the women are physically incapacitated.

Q: What conditions can make a man infertile?

A: Apart from sexual problems, infertility results if a condition or disorder affects (1) the total number of sperm produced during ejaculation; or (2) the number of viable, or normal, sperm produced. Such disorders include any infection of the sexual organs, for example, epididymitis; venereal disease; prostatitis; mumps; or a blockage of the vas deferens (sperm duct).

The temperature of the testicles affects the production of sperm. Undescended testicles are too warm to function. In the same way, some obese men become temporarily infertile in hot environments, or from wearing tight underpants that hold the testicles too close to the body. More rarely, varicose veins of the spermatic cord, known as varicoceles, increase the blood flow of the testicles, and keep them too warm. Other causes of infertility include certain chromosome abnormalities, Klinefelter's syndrome, cystic fibrosis, certain drugs, and irradiation of the testicles.

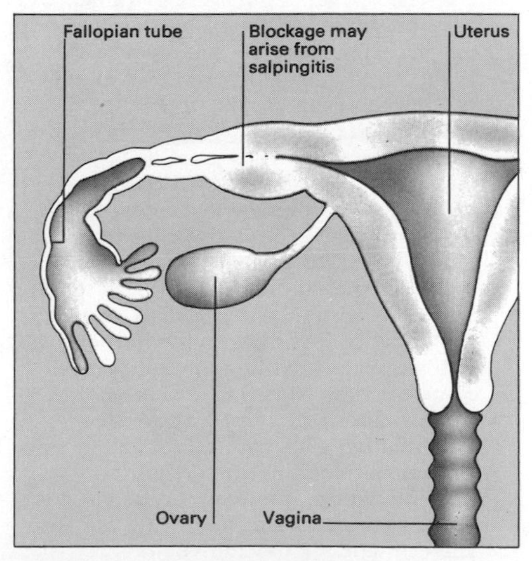

Infertility in women may be caused by a blockage in the fallopian tube.

Q: How is a man's fertility assessed?

A: A doctor examines the man's testicles and then the prostate gland during a rectal examination. A sample of semen is collected and examined within two hours using a microscope to determine the sperm count. If any abnormality is noticed, the test is repeated two or three times to ensure an accurate diagnosis.

Q: How is infertility in a man treated?

A: General attention to health is essential. If the man is overweight, he must diet to lose weight. He should not smoke and should moderate his drinking, if necessary. Loose underpants often help to increase the number of sperm produced, and sometimes the doctor recommends bathing the testicles in cold water twice a day. If the sperm count is low, abstinence from sexual intercourse three to four days before the expected day of ovulation should increase the number of sperm ejaculated.

Infections of the reproductive organs must be treated; a varicocele can be removed by a minor operation. If no sperm are being produced, or if there is a blockage in the vas deferens, it is seldom possible to cure the condition, although sometimes an operation can unblock the sperm duct. Undescended or retractile testicles have to be treated during childhood.

Sexual problems, such as impotence or premature ejaculation, need sympathetic discussion with a sex therapist or the family doctor.

Q: What conditions make a woman infertile?

A: Infertility in women results if a condition or disorder affects (1) ovulation; (2) the movement of the ovum along the fallopian tube; (3) the ability of the fertilized ovum to implant in the wall of the womb; or (4) normal sexual intercourse.

Ovulation may be disrupted by anxiety, or one of various hormone disorders. A hormone imbalance may occur for a few months following a course of contraceptive pills. Illnesses such as tuberculosis or diabetes mellitus affect ovulation, and it is also thought that obesity, smoking, and alcohol affects it. An ovarian cyst also disrupts ovulation.

The movement of the ovum is restricted by any infection of the fallopian tube, including salpingitis, venereal diseases, or an abscess. The lining of the tube becomes scarred, and even if an egg is successfully fertilized, an ECTOPIC PREGNANCY is likely.

Disorders that affect the womb include endometriosis, endometritis, polyps, and fibroids. In some women, a congenital anomaly results in a deformed womb.

The presence of an intact hymen or VAGINISMUS may indicate problems with techniques of sexual intercourse. Dyspareunia (painful intercourse) may indicate a gynaecological infection.

Sometimes cervical secretions kill the sperm even when intercourse is successful.

Q: *How is infertility in a woman assessed?*

A: Some tests can be carried out at home, for example, the temperature test for the day of ovulation described above. A gynaecological examination is necessary to see if there is any local infection in the vagina, cervix, or fallopian tubes. It is usual for a doctor to check general health with a chest X-ray, blood test, and urine sample. A cervical smear is taken to eliminate the possibility of local infection due to cervicitis as well as cancer.

A postcoital test may have to be done. Vaginal secretions are examined two to three hours after intercourse to make sure that the sperm are still moving vigorously, and are not being killed by the secretions.

If the results of these tests are normal, a D AND C operation is usually performed to examine the lining of the womb. This may be followed by a salpingogram to show the shape of the womb and the condition of the fallopian tubes.

Q: *How is infertility in a woman treated?*

A: Anxiety is a cause of infertility among many couples who have not been able to have children for a few years. Medical investigations often act as a form of psychotherapy, which has led some infertile couples to conceive even before treatment begins.

If an infection is discovered during the investigations, it is promptly treated. However, repair operations on already scarred fallopian tubes are rarely successful. Adjustment of a womb abnormality is also difficult, but is sometimes successful.

Hormone disorders are easier to treat. Ovulation can be stimulated with a drug called clomiphene, combined with a small dose of oestrogen. Care is taken to prevent multiple pregnancy.

In a technique introduced in Britain during the late 1970s, infertile women have become pregnant after having a fertilized ovum implanted in the womb. The ovum is taken from the woman at ovulation, fertilized in a laboratory by sperm taken from the husband, and then replaced in the woman's womb. This has yet to become popularly successful.

Q: *How successful are treatments for infertility?*

A: Of those couples who seek treatment, twenty per cent of the women conceive before treatment is started. A further twenty per cent become pregnant within two years of treatment. It is important, however, that each partner follows the doctor's advice. Conception may occur after years of infertility. This may happen after the adoption of a child, but there is no scientific explanation for it.

Infestation is the harbouring of animal parasites, such as ticks, mites, and fleas, on the skin or in the hair, or worms in the body tissues or organs.

Inflammation is a localized reaction of body tissue to injury or disease. Inflammation may result from physical damage, infection or surgery, or exposure to electricity, chemicals, heat, cold, or radiation. It may also occur in

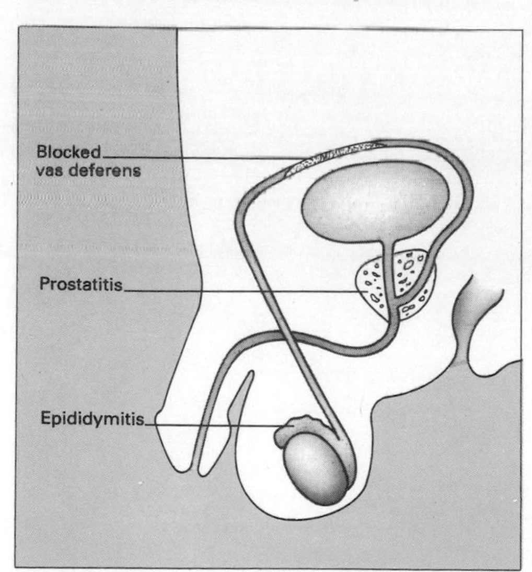

Infertility in men may arise from prostatitis, epididymitis, or a blocked vas deferens.

AUTOIMMUNE DISEASE and with cancer.

Q: What are the symptoms of inflammation?

A: The affected area becomes swollen and painful, and the skin becomes red and warm. If the inflamed area is large, there may also be a slight rise in body temperature, headache, and a loss of appetite. As the body repair processes start to heal and replace injured tissue, the inflammation gradually disappears. However, a collection of pus may remain. This usually discharges through the skin, with the final disappearance of all the symptoms. If the pus is not discharged, it acts as a barrier to healing. In this case, a tough capsule may form around the pus, causing an ABSCESS.

Occasionally, chronic inflammation may occur. Some infections, such as tuberculosis, act slowly, and the process of healing keeps pace with the damage. If this happens, fibrous tissue may form around the centre of infection. The fibrous tissue may cut off the blood supply, so that the central area of affected tissue dies. If this occurs internally, a chronic abscess is formed; if it involves the body surface, an ulcer or festering sore results.

Q: How does the body respond to inflammation?

A: After the initial injury or infection, damaged tissue releases a chemical, probably a HISTAMINE, that causes the blood vessels in the area to expand and leak. This increased blood flow causes redness and warmth. The escape of fluid from the blood vessels causes the swelling. Pain is partly caused by compression of the nerve endings that accompanies the swelling, and partly by irritation of the nerve endings by substances causing or resulting from the inflammation.

The inflow of blood carries additional WHITE BLOOD CELLS and ANTIBODIES. These remove damaged tissue and attempt to destroy any invading micro-organisms by engulfing them. However, in engulfing the micro-organisms, the white blood cells themselves may be destroyed. Pus is composed of dead white blood cells.

Q: How is inflammation treated?

A: Because inflammation is a natural healing process, it is advisable to interfere as little as possible. The injured area should be washed and a mild antiseptic applied. Any foreign bodies or chemicals should be carefully removed or washed away. The inflamed part should be rested. A doctor should be consulted if the area of inflammation is extensive; if it becomes extremely painful; if it persists for a long time; or if an abscess or a festering sore forms.

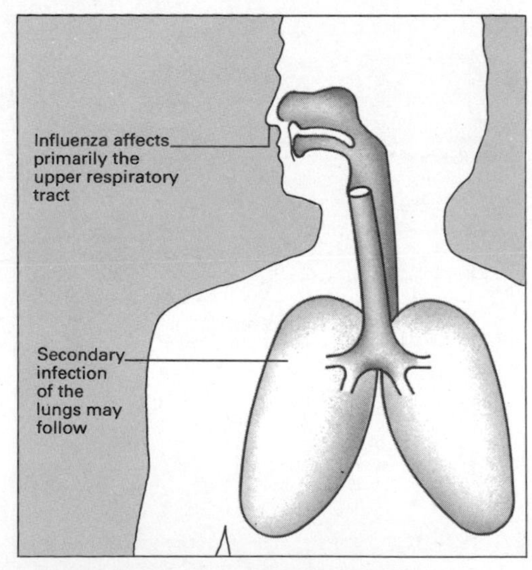

Influenza is a viral infection that may lead to secondary infection of the lungs.

A talk about Influenza

Influenza is an acute viral infection caused by any of several closely related viruses. There are three major groups of these viruses, designated A, B, and C. Infections with the influenza A virus tend to be more severe and to last longer than those caused by the milder B and C viruses. Major influenza epidemics are usually caused by a strain of the influenza A virus.

Q: What are the symptoms of influenza?

A: After an incubation period of about two days there is a sudden onset of shivering, sometimes with a chill; headache; weakness and fatigue; aching in the muscles and joints; a sore throat; and a dry, painful cough. At the beginning of the illness there may also be vomiting and an aversion to light and noise. Initially, the body temperature may rise to about 40°C (104°F), dropping to between 38°C (102°F) and 39°C (103°F) for two or three days, then settling at between 37.5°C (100°F) and 38°C (102°F).

As the illness progresses, the cough may become less dry and painful because of the production of sputum. If no complications develop, the fever generally lasts for about five days. Recovery is usually rapid and without relapse, although it may be accompanied by some weakness and depression.

Q: Can influenza have any complications?

A: Yes. Influenza lowers the body's resistance to infection. This makes the patient vulnerable to invasion by other organisms that may cause secondary infections, especially of the throat, sinuses, and ears, such as laryngitis, sinusitis, and otitis media. With such relatively minor complications, the original symptoms of influenza are intensified, and may be accompanied by bronchitis and a persistent cough. Pneumonia may also occur.

Q: How is influenza treated?

A: Influenza should be treated as any other fever. The patient should go to bed as soon as symptoms appear, and should remain there until a complete recovery has been made. The patient should drink plenty of fluids, especially while there is a fever. Aspirin may help to relieve muscle and joint pains, and to reduce fever. The patient should be isolated, both to prevent the spread of infection and to reduce the risk of secondary infections. If any complications develop, a doctor should be consulted. Antibiotics are often prescribed, but these are of no value against influenza itself, although they may be useful for treating secondary infections.

Q: Can influenza be prevented?

A: Injections of dead influenza virus may confer immunity to that particular strain of influenza. The vaccination is neither immediately nor totally effective: it confers immunity about seven days after injection and protects about 70 per cent of those immunized. But the influenza virus tends to change and produce new strains, so vaccination with one strain does not give immunity to all of them. For this reason, vaccinations must be given each year as new strains develop. Experiments have been performed using a modified live virus, but these have not proved as effective as vaccinations with the dead virus.

The drug amantadine hydrochloride, has proved useful in preventing respiratory infections due to A_2 strain of influenza virus. Amantadine hydrochloride should not, however, be used by pregnant women.

Q: How does influenza spread?

A: Influenza is an infectious disease, that may cause an epidemic. It is spread by inhaling infected droplets in the air, which are produced by coughing and sneezing. Influenza may occur at any time of the year, but is most common during winter.

Infra-red treatment is the use of infra-red radiation to treat various disorders. Infra-red is invisible heat radiation beyond the red end of the visible spectrum. Infra-red treatment may be used by physiotherapists for muscle disorders and rheumatic diseases, or to help in relieving the pain caused by minor muscle damage, such as sprains and strains. A device called an infra-red thermograph, which detects and photographs infra-red rays, may be used in the diagnosis of some disorders, particularly breast cancer. *See* THERMOGRAM.

Infusion is the introduction of a sterile fluid into a vein. Drugs may be administered by this method, and it may also be used to maintain the balance of salts within the body.

Infusion is also a method of extracting chemicals by soaking a substance, usually a plant, in water.

Ingrown toenail is a tendency for the edge of a toenail to grow into the adjacent soft tissue, producing infection and inflammation. This condition most commonly develops on the big toe from a combination of factors, including tight shoes; the tendency to cut the nail in a semicircular shape; and, in many people, having nails with an inverted U-shape rather than a flat surface, so that the edges point down into the toe.

Q: What is the treatment for an ingrown toenail?

A: The first essential remedy is to wear

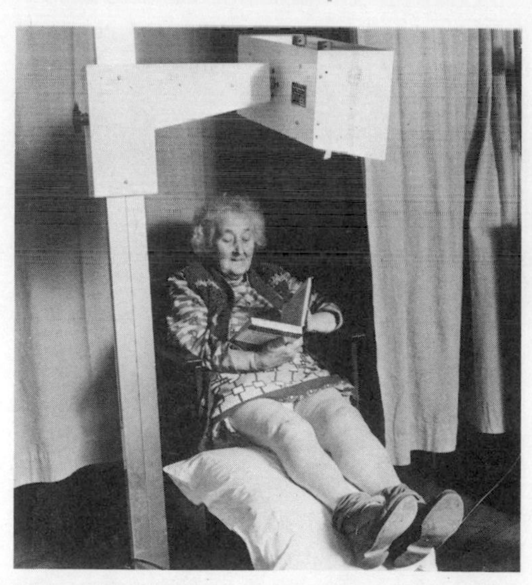

Infra-red treatment may be used to relieve pain from osteoarthritis of the knees.

loose-fitting, round-toed shoes to remove pressure from the nail. The toenail should be cut straight across and not in a curve. The toe should be thoroughly cleaned at least twice a day, when the edges of the nail can be gently lifted. Regular cleaning helps to reduce minor infection, and a small plug of cotton, soaked in surgical spirit, can be used as an antiseptic.

If these simple measures fail to control the infection, and PARONYCHIA (chronic infection) develops, then antibiotic creams and lotions may be tried. If infection still persists, a surgical operation may be performed to remove the side of the nail and part of the skin of the toe.

Inguinal describes anything pertaining to the groin. For example, the inguinal glands are lymph nodes situated in the groin.

Inhalation therapy is the drawing in of breath, vapour, gas, smoke, drugs, or powder into the lungs to treat various respiratory disorders.

Inherited disorders are abnormalities that may be passed on from parents to children. *See* CONGENITAL ANOMALIES; HEREDITY.

Inhibition is the prevention or restraint of some bodily activity by another bodily process. For example, fear may inhibit gastric secretions.

In psychiatry, inhibition refers to the restraints against performing antisocial acts. For example, in adults, anger at another person seldom leads to violence as it usually does in children; most adults are inhibited against violence. In this sense, inhibition is different from repression: inhibition may be a conscious or an unconscious process; repression is always unconscious and automatic.

See also AUTONOMIC NERVOUS SYSTEM; PERISTALSIS.

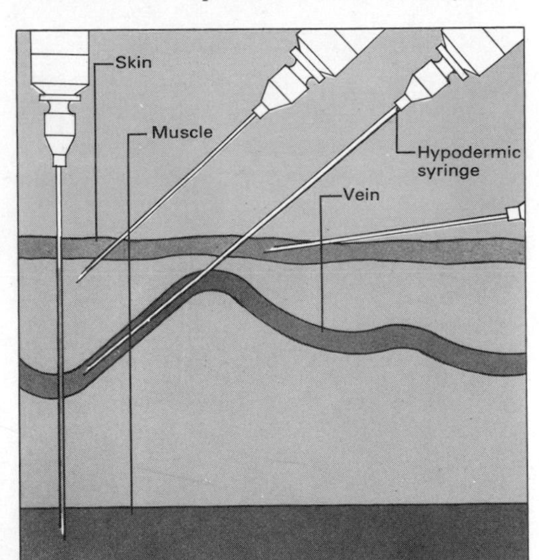

Injections can be given in many ways, including intramuscularly and intravenously.

Injection is a method of forcing a fluid into the body. It is usually performed using a needle and a syringe, but may also be done using compressed air. An injection may be intradermal, in which fluid is injected into the superficial skin layers; subcutaneous, injected between the skin and underlying muscle; intramuscular, into a muscle; intravenous, into a vein; intra-arterial, into an artery; epidural, around the nerves of the spinal cord; intrathecal, under the meninges of the brain; or intra-articular, into a joint.

Inner ear is the part of the ear that consists of the cochlea, semicircular canals, and auditory nerve. *See* EAR.

Innocent. *See* BENIGN.

Inoculation is a method of IMMUNIZATION in which a micro-organism or toxin is injected into the body to produce immunity.

Insanity is a legal term for any mental disorder that results in a person being unaware of the consequences of his or her actions, and in not being held responsible for them. Various legal procedures may be necessary before a person can be certified as legally insane and before medical treatment for a specific mental disorder can be started. *See* MENTAL ILLNESS.

Insect bites. *See* First Aid, pp.514-515.

Insecticide is any substance that kills insects. Many insecticides are also poisonous to animals and human beings. The newer insecticides lose their potency and are destroyed more quickly, so that long-term hazards are less likely.

Insidious describes any condition that comes on so gradually that the affected person is unaware of its onset. Cancer is often insidious, whereas the onset of influenza is sudden or acute.

Insomnia is the inability to sleep, or difficulty in sleeping, resulting in long periods of wakefulness. Some people require less sleep than others, and the inability to sleep continuously through the night is not an illness in itself. Because of great individual differences in sleep patterns, what one person considers to be insomnia another may regard as normal.

Q: What causes insomnia?

A: Insomnia may be a symptom of almost any disease or disorder. Physical causes of insomnia include overeating, hunger, cold, heat, noise, excessive tea or coffee before going to bed, or an uncomfortable bed. Pain is a common cause of insomnia, and a cough, particularly when combined with a fever, often causes difficulty in sleeping. Persistent insomnia is often caused by anxiety or depression.

Q: How is insomnia treated?

A: It is important to ensure that there is a warm, comfortable bed in a quiet room. Pain should be treated with painkillers, such as paracetamol or aspirin. A hot bath, a warm, milky drink, or a light snack may also help. Some people find that plenty of physical exercise during the day and a short walk before going to bed make sleeping easier.

If sleeplessness is caused by anxiety or depression, it may help to discuss the problems with a doctor who may then prescribe sleeping drugs for a short period during the initial treatment of depression. Sleeping drugs should not be taken without consulting a doctor.

See also SLEEP; SLEEP PROBLEMS.

Insufflation is the blowing of a fluid, gas, or powder into a body cavity. Insufflation may be used in the treatment of inflammations of the external tube of the ear, and as a method of unblocking the Eustachian tube in the treatment of middle ear diseases.

Insulin is a hormone produced by the ISLETS OF LANGERHANS, clusters of cells within the pancreas, a gland situated behind the stomach. Insulin controls the use of glucose, fats, and lipids by the body. An excess of insulin, sometimes caused by a pancreatic tumour, causes HYPOGLYCAEMIA (a low level of sugar in the blood), and a lack of insulin produces hyperglycaemia, which is a symptom of DIABETES MELLITUS.

Insulin can now be made synthetically by GENETIC ENGINEERING, but is also made from the pancreases of cattle or pigs. In the treatment of diabetes mellitus it is given by injection, as quick-acting soluble insulin, or slowly, in combination with zinc or other substances, so that only one or two injections a day are necessary. The strength of insulin is expressed in units of activity in each ml (cc), and is given in syringes calibrated in units.

Integument. *See* SKIN.

Intelligence quotient (IQ) is an index of intelligence based on the results of a variety of tests of verbal, writing, and mathematical ability, together with physical performance at set tasks. Standard intelligence tests include the Babcock-Levy, Binet, and Stanford-Binet tests, although most of these have been superseded by the Wechsler test.

The IQ of a child taking a test is compared with others of the same age in percentage terms. For example, a child may score between 90 and 110 per cent of what would be expected of someone of his or her age group, and so is said to be of normal average intelligence. Any score above 110 ranges from superior intelligence to near genius or genius, whereas a score below 90 ranges from dull normal to profoundly mentally retarded. Tests for adults are different from those for children, and are not otherwise age-related.

Q: Are IQ tests always accurate?

A: No. There are many reasons why such tests may be inaccurate. Much depends on the way a child has been educated and on his or her social and cultural background.

Intercostal means situated between the ribs.

Intercourse. *See* SEXUAL INTERCOURSE.

Interferon is a protein substance that is produced by body cells to help to combat virus infection by preventing the growth of viruses. Research is now under way into methods of stimulating interferon production by the body. Interferon may be produced by GENETIC ENGINEERING. Initial enthusiasm for it in the treatment of cancer has not been fulfilled.

Intermittent claudication is pain or cramp in the calf muscle during exercise. Relieved by rest, the pain recurs when the muscle is again exercised.

Q: What causes this form of pain?

A: The cramp-like pain is the result of an inadequate blood (and therefore oxygen) supply to the calf muscles, caused by a disorder of the blood vessels. The disorder is usually ARTERIOSCLEROSIS, or may follow blockage of an artery by an embolus (clot of blood or other material from elsewhere in the body), or by BUERGER'S DISEASE (chronic inflammation

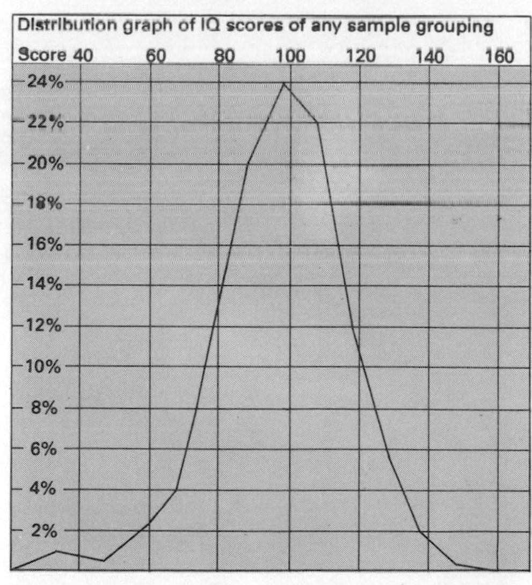

IQ (intelligence quotient) levels in any given group can be represented by this graph form.

of the blood vessels). Occasionally, intermittent claudication occurs following an injury to the leg and subsequent blood vessel damage.

The condition commonly develops in smokers, and in those with diabetes mellitus. The symptoms become worse if the patient becomes anaemic or develops HYPOTHYROIDISM.

Unless the onset is sudden because of an embolus or thrombosis, there is a gradual deterioration in blood supply to the muscles. The symptoms tend to become worse, and, finally, any form of activity causes pain.

Q: *Are there any dangers in intermittent claudication?*

A: Yes. The condition is a sign of poor blood supply to the leg, and other tissues also suffer, possibly resulting in gangrene of the toes and feet. Sudden blockage of the blood vessel may lead to an INFARCTION (area of dead tissue) and gangrene in the muscles and the gradual deterioration may result in peripheral NEURITIS (inflammation of nerves).

Q: *How is intermittent claudication treated?*

A: It is essential that a patient who smokes should stop smoking, because this may prevent any further progress of the condition and allow him or her to lead a relatively normal life without further discomfort. A doctor may prescribe a drug that makes the blood vessels widen (vasodilator), but such drugs are seldom successful because the disease of the arteries prevents their expansion.

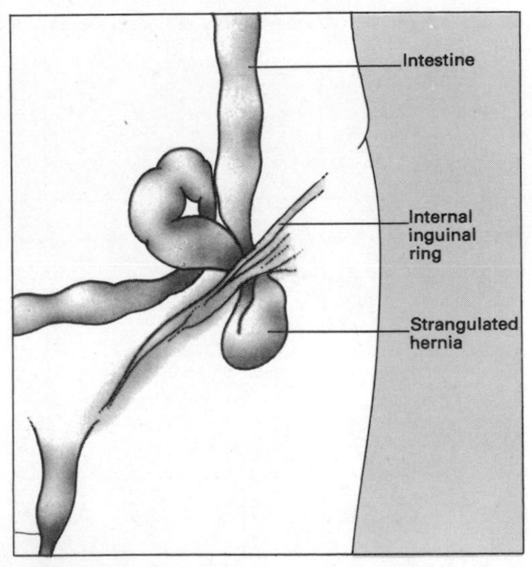

Intestinal obstruction may be caused by a strangulated hernia and requires surgery.

If the symptoms are severe and the patient is suffering from considerable incapacity, surgery is indicated. An arteriogram locates the diseased section, and arterial surgery is performed to graft in a new segment of artery or plastic tubing. This treatment often gives complete relief from symptoms.

Intersex is an individual with both male and female characteristics. *See* HERMAPHRODITE.

Intertrigo is the soreness and inflammation that occur between layers of skin which rub together; it is a form of DERMATITIS. The skin becomes soft and peels off to expose reddened, sore areas that are vulnerable to infection. Intertrigo usually occurs in the creases of the neck, beneath large breasts, and in the groin. In obese people, intertrigo may also occur in the abdominal creases.

Treatment involves dieting and exercise to lose weight, and keeping the skin clean and dry, with frequent washing and powdering.

Intestinal flu, also called gastric flu, is a popular name for viral GASTROENTERITIS.

Intestinal obstruction is a complete or partial blockage of the intestine. It may occur at any time and for a variety of reasons. An intestinal obstruction interferes with the normal passage of the products of digestion through the digestive system.

Q: *What are the symptoms of an intestinal obstruction?*

A: The first symptom is usually abdominal pain, followed by swelling (distention) of the abdomen. The swelling is more marked if the obstruction occurs in the lower parts of the intestine. There may also be constipation and failure to pass internal gas. Vomiting may occur, although not for some hours after the initial symptoms, unless the obstruction is in the small intestine.

Q: *What causes an intestinal obstruction?*

A: There are various conditions that may cause an intestinal obstruction. Some are comparatively simple to treat, such as an accumulation of hard faeces or infestation with parasitic worms. Others are more serious, such as tumours, a strangulated hernia, or intestinal adhesions.

Q: *How is an intestinal obstruction treated?*

A: The treatment depends on the cause of the obstruction. If the large intestine is obstructed and the symptoms are not severe, there may be time for various tests, such as SIGMOIDOSCOPY and X-ray examination following a barium enema. If the symptoms are acute, an urgent surgical operation is required.

Surgery is not always necessary, but other treatments are given only if the cause is comparatively simple to treat or if the intestine can overcome the obstruction without the need for surgery. For example, if the obstruction is caused by the twisting of the intestine around an adhesion or a scar, it may untwist on its own without treatment. In all such cases the stomach is kept empty by sucking fluid up a gastric tube, and intravenous fluids are continued until it is certain that either the obstruction has disappeared or that surgery is necessary.

See also ADHESION; CROHN'S DISEASE; DIVERTICULITIS AND DIVERTICULOSIS; HERNIA; HIRSCHSPRUNG'S DISEASE; INTUSSUSCEPTION; MECKEL'S DIVERTICULUM; MECONIUM; VOLVULUS.

Intestine is the part of the digestive tract that extends from the outlet of the stomach to the anus. It is commonly called the gut, or bowel.

The intestine has two parts: the small intestine and the large intestine (the terms refer to their diameters, not to their lengths). The small intestine is the longer of the two, made up of the short DUODENUM and the JEJUNUM, which make up about two-fifths of the small intestine; and the ILEUM, which makes up three-fifths.

The large intestine is made up of the CAECUM (with the appendix), and the COLON, which ends at the RECTUM.

The contents of the intestine are moved by a series of muscular contractions and relaxations known as peristalsis. In the small intestine, food is digested and absorbed and the excess waste products and water pass into the large intestine. In the large intestine, excess fluid is reabsorbed, and bacterial action on the faeces produces some of the essential vitamins B and K for the body. *See* DIGESTIVE SYSTEM.

The intestine is covered by the peritoneum which, in many places, combines to form a membrane (the mesentery). The mesentery allows the ileum and parts of the colon freedom of movement and position while, at the same time, holding the intestine in the correct position. Blood vessels and nerves as well as many lymphatic vessels and lymph nodes occur in the mesentery. The veins in the mesentery join the hepatic portal vein that carries blood to the liver.

Intoxication is a state of being poisoned. The term is commonly applied to the condition produced by an excess of alcohol, but it can also refer to poisoning by drugs, and the confusion and delirium caused by fever.

Intradermal means within the skin layer. For example, rashes that occur within the substance of the skin are termed intradermal rashes.

Intramuscular means within a muscle. For example, an intramuscular injection is one in which a solution of a drug is injected directly into a muscle.

Intrauterine device (IUCD, IUD) is a plastic or metal and plastic device that can be inserted into the womb (uterus) as a form of contraceptive. The intrauterine contraceptive device is more correctly called an IUCD rather than an IUD. (In medical terminology, IUD can also mean intrauterine death.)

There are at least four main kinds of intrauterine contraceptive device, most of which are in the shape of a double S, the figure 7, the letter T, or are like a ram's horn.

Q: How does an IUCD work?

A: The way an IUCD works is not exactly known. It is now thought that the principal effect takes place within the womb, either by creating an environment hostile to sperm or to the blastocyst, or by interrupting the process during attachment of the blastocyst.

One type of IUCD is activated by the hormone progestagen and is usually effective for a year, after which it should be changed. Other types should be changed every two years or are effective indefinitely.

Q: Does an IUCD cause pain or discomfort?

A: In general, no. But unfortunately, pain and heavy periods may occur for several months after an IUCD is inserted. Some IUCD's have been known to puncture the lining of the womb and cause heavy bleeding or haemorrhage. This form of contraception does not suit every woman,

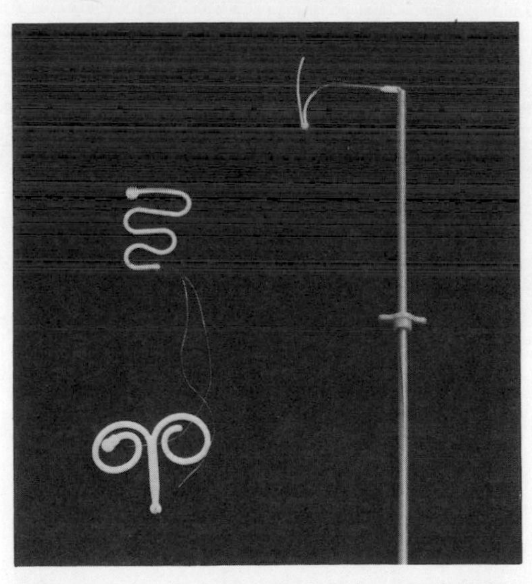

IUDs of various shapes; the one on the right is attached to the introducing instrument.

and should be considered only on a doctor's advice.

See also CONTRACEPTION.

Intravenous means within a vein. For example, an intravenous injection is made directly into a vein.

Intravenous cholangiogram is a special X-ray of the gall bladder and bile ducts taken after an intravenous injection of an iodine salt that contains a radiopaque solution. *See* CHOLANGIOGRAM.

Intravenous pyelogram (IVP) is a special X-ray of the kidneys taken after an intravenous injection of an iodine salt that forms a radiopaque solution.

Introvert is a personality type characterized by an introspective attitude, as opposed to an extrovert, who has an outgoing and sociable personality.

See also EXTROVERT.

Intussusception is a form of intestinal obstruction in which one section of the INTESTINE telescopes into the next section, like the finger of a glove being turned inside-out, and is drawn increasingly farther in by the action of the intestinal muscles. Most intussusceptions occur in children.

Q: What causes intussusception?

A: In most cases, the cause is not known. It has been suggested that intussusception occurs most often in children who have had a recent infection that causes a swelling of lymphoid tissue in the intestinal wall. The body treats the swelling as part of the intestinal contents and pulls it along by the action of the intestinal muscles. Occasionally a polyp, tumour, or MECKEL'S DIVERTICULUM may cause intussusception in adults.

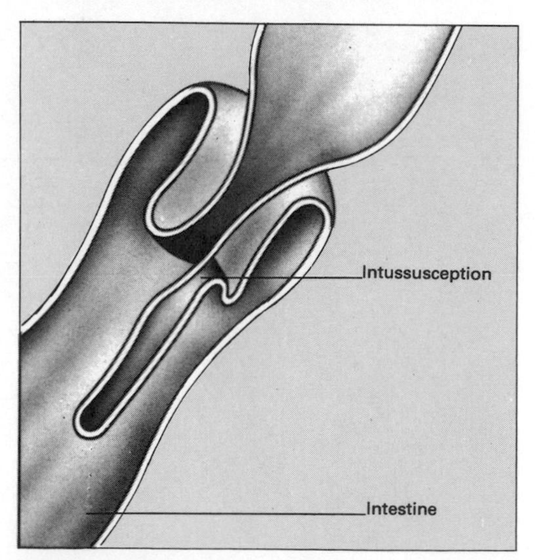

Intussusception is an obstruction caused when a part of the intestine folds in upon itself.

Q: What are the symptoms of intussusception?

A: In children, intussusception usually occurs suddenly, with severe pain, vomiting, and pallor. The affected child may draw up the knees and scream with the pain. As the attacks become more severe, the straining to expel faeces may cause blood and mucus to be passed from the rectum. But between attacks, the child may be calm and relaxed and may appear to have recovered.

Q: What is the treatment for intussusception?

A: Immediate hospitalization is vital. The patient is first given a barium enema, to prove the diagnosis. The pressure of the enema sometimes restores the affected parts of the intestine to their normal positions. But if this does not happen, a surgical operation is necessary.

In vitro is a term applied to reactions that occur outside a living body. For example, drugs are often tested in vitro ("in glass") before being tested on a living body.

In vivo is a term applied to reactions that occur within a living body.

Iodine is a non-metallic element. It is essential in the human diet for the correct functioning of the THYROID GLAND. Lack of iodine in the diet leads to the formation of a GOITRE and HYPOTHYROIDISM.

Q: Is iodine used in medical treatment?

A: Yes. Iodine salts may sometimes be given in the early treatment of hyperthyroidism (THYROTOXICOSIS), excessive activity of the thyroid gland. Iodine dissolved in an alcoholic solution or combined with povidone (povidone-iodine) is used as an antiseptic skin preparation before surgical operations or to clean wounds. Iodine preparations are also used as a diagnostic aid in special X-rays, such as a cholecystogram (of the gall bladder), intravenous pyelogram (of the kidney), and arteriogram (of an artery).

Radioactive iodine is used in the diagnosis of thyroid gland disease as well as in investigations of liver, lung, and kidney disorders. The preparation loses half its radioactivity within eight days. In larger doses, it may also be used in the treatment of hyperthyroidism and cancer of the thyroid gland.

Ionizing radiation is any radiation that causes substances to break up into ions (charged atoms or molecules). Gamma rays and X-rays are two examples of ionizing radiation. *See* RADIATION.

IQ is an abbreviation of intelligence quotient. *See* INTELLIGENCE QUOTIENT.

Iridectomy is an operation to remove part of the iris in the eye. It is most commonly performed as a treatment for acute GLAUCOMA to reduce the build-up of fluid pressure in the eyeball. An iridectomy may also be done to create an artificial pupil.

Iris is the coloured ring that surrounds the pupil of the eye. The iris is positioned in front of the lens and behind the cornea. Within the iris are muscle groups that by contracting or relaxing regulate how much light passes through the pupil. In bright light, some muscles of the iris relax and the pupil becomes smaller; in dim light, these muscles contract and the pupil becomes larger to admit as much light as possible.

Q: What determines the colour of the iris?

A: Eye colour, produced by pigment cells in the iris, is an inherited characteristic. (*See* HEREDITY.)

Q: What disorders can affect the iris?

A: The iris can become inflamed (iritis, choroiditis, or uveitis). A cleft iris is a congenital anomaly known as a COLOBOMA. An albino has very little pigmentation in the iris, and so the eyes look pink because the small blood vessels are visible.

Iritis is inflammation of the iris of the eye. The iris appears muddy in colour and smaller than usual. The pupil is also small and it changes size slowly in reaction to light variations, and so vision tends to be blurred. The eye waters continually. Pain in and above the eye, sensitivity to light (photophobia), redness, and soreness are other symptoms.

Iron is a metallic chemical element. It occurs in HAEMOGLOBIN, the constituent in red blood cells that carries oxygen, and so iron is an essential element in the human body. Iron is also present in enzymes (substances that produce chemical change) associated with respiration and in myoglobin, an important protein in muscle. The body gets its iron from foods. Those rich in iron include liver, eggs and lean meat. Pregnant women need more iron than do other adults. Growing children also need more iron to help to build new body tissue.

Q: What happens if there is insufficient iron in the body?

A: Iron deficiency ANAEMIA occurs. The condition may be caused by a gradual loss of iron from the body because of a bleeding peptic ulcer, menstrual problems, or bleeding from a cancer. Iron deficiency may be caused by a sudden and severe haemorrhage.

Q: How is iron deficiency treated?

A: The body is able to absorb iron, in almost any form, when taken orally. If iron deficiency does not improve after iron has been taken orally, as may happen in conditions in which there is absence of acid in the stomach, then iron may be given by intravenous or intramuscular injection. Adverse side effects from taking a normal dose of iron are rare but, occasionally, a patient has constipation or diarrhoea with mild symptoms of indigestion.

Irradiation is the application of any form of radiation to a tissue or substance. In medical treatment, irradiation may be in the form of X-rays, radioactive particles, heat, or ultraviolet light. *See* RADIATION.

Irrigation is the washing out of a body cavity or a wound with water or an antiseptic fluid.

Irritable bowel syndrome. *See* MUCOUS COLITIS.

Ischaemia is a decreased blood supply to a particular part of the body. It is caused by spasm or disease in the blood vessels.

The condition most commonly develops in ARTERIOSCLEROSIS. This may result in cramp (*see* INTERMITTENT CLAUDICATION) in the legs, or ANGINA PECTORIS if it affects the heart, or a mild STROKE (transient ischaemia), if it affects the brain. Such strokes may be followed by complete recovery, because there is sometimes no brain damage.

Ischaemia may also result from acute blockage of an artery either following injury or because of a blood clot (*see* EMBOLISM). Some tissues die much more quickly than others when they become ischaemic. The brain survives for only about five minutes whereas the kidneys can continue to function for one to two hours.

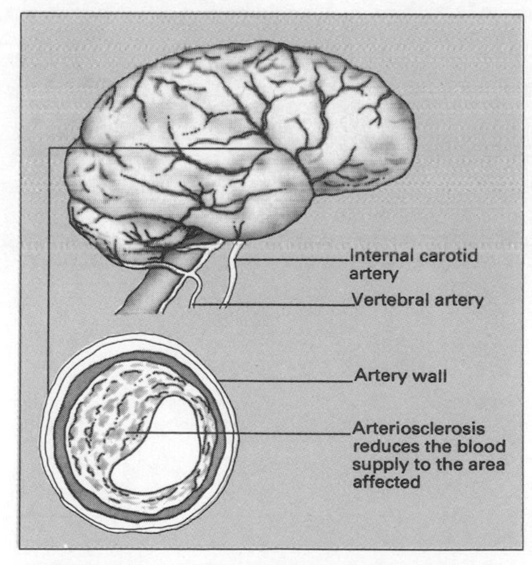

Ischaemia is a reduced blood supply. When it occurs in the brain, it causes a mild stroke.

Ischiorectal abscess is an infection between the ischium bone of the pelvis (part of the hip-bone) and the adjacent area of the intestine, more usually the anus than the rectum. The abscess is painful, with local swelling and extreme tenderness. An ischiorectal abscess requires surgical treatment.

Ischium is one of the three bones that form the pelvis. It joins the ILIUM near the hip joint and the PUBIS at the front. The ischium is a strong bone with a protuberant lower part, which is covered by a fluid-filled cavity (bursa) that counters pressure. This is the area that supports the body when sitting.

Ishihara's test is a method of detecting colour blindness. *See* COLOUR BLINDNESS.

Islets of Langerhans are clusters of cells within the pancreas, a gland located behind the stomach.

Q: What is the function of the islets of Langerhans?

A: They secrete insulin and glucagon. The most important is INSULIN, which reduces the level of glucose in the bloodstream by helping to convert glucose to glycogen. GLUCAGON increases the level of glucose in the blood.

Q: What happens if the islets of Langerhans fail to function normally?

A: The production of the pancreatic hormones is upset, resulting in various disorders. Lack of insulin causes DIABETES MELLITUS.

Rarely, a tumour of the pancreas may cause overproduction of insulin, causing HYPOGLYCAEMIA; or excess glucagon, producing HYPERGLYCAEMIA.

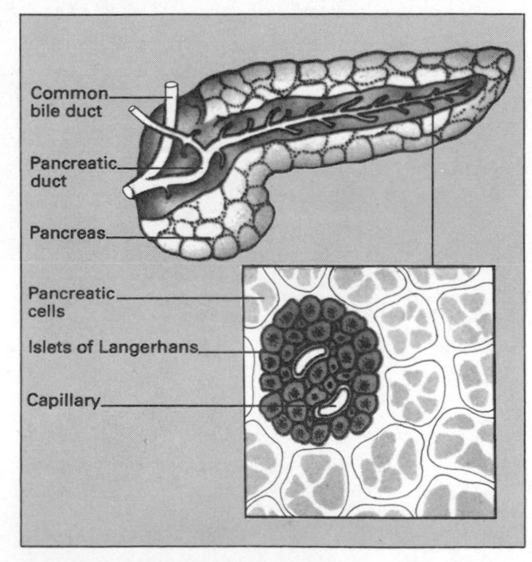

Islets of Langerhans are pancreatic cells that secrete insulin and glucagon.

Recurrent attacks of PANCREATITIS damage the islets of Langerhans and may cause diabetes mellitus.

Isolation has various medical meanings. The most common use of the term describes the situation of a patient who is kept apart from other people to prevent the spread of an infectious disease, such as smallpox. A patient may also be kept in isolation during the treatment of various diseases, such as leukaemia, in which the treatment itself reduces the patient's resistance to infection.

Isolation also describes the extraction and identification of bacteria or viruses that cause a particular disease.

In psychiatry, isolation describes a patient's state of loneliness or solitude.

Isotonic describes anything, particularly muscles, that have equal tone or tension. An isotonic solution is a solution of salts in water that closely matches the body's normal fluids in strength.

Isotope is an individual form of a chemical element that differs from others like it only in the composition of the nucleus of its atoms. All isotopes of a single element have similar chemical properties. But all their physical properties may vary; for example, some isotopes are radioactive. Radioactive isotopes are used in the investigation and diagnosis of many disorders. They are also used in treatment, for example, to destroy cancerous tumours.

See also RADIOLOGY.

Itching, known medically as pruritus, is a symptom that is produced by a disturbance to the nerve endings just under the skin. The reasons for itching are not fully understood. Some people feel itching sensations much more easily than others, and an itching skin condition such as measles can cause much more distress in one patient than another.

Q: What conditions may cause itching?

A: Itching may be a symptom of dry skin following sunburn or ICHTHYOSIS. There are many other skin disorders that may be accompanied by itching, including ECZEMA, URTICARIA, SCABIES, and LICHEN PLANUS. Generalized itching, which is often worse when the person is tired or warm in bed, may occur for no obvious reason. Various investigations may be carried out to discover if the cause is URAEMIA, or a liver disorder such as JAUNDICE or CIRRHOSIS. Sometimes continued itching or itching that stops and starts again is a symptom of underlying anxiety or depression. Occasionally, a malignant disease, such as HODGKIN'S DISEASE, produces itching for some months before the disease itself appears. Rarely itching occurs during pregnancy, when it may be accompanied by urticaria.

Q: Why do areas of itching occur?

A: Itching in one spot may be caused by sensitivity to chemicals or materials. Examples include perfume behind the ears, nickel on jewellery, or clothing made of wool or an artificial fibre.

Local itching around the anus (pruritus ani) may be associated with the slight moist discharge from a HAEMORRHOID (piles), following diarrhoea or, quite commonly, as a form of allergy to anaesthetic ointments used in the treatment of haemorrhoids. In children, anal itching, particularly at night, may be caused by THREADWORM.

Itching of the vulva (pruritus vulvae) may occur with any form of local infection, such as VULVITIS or VAGINITIS; or it may be associated with skin infections, such as MONILIASIS (thrush). Genital itching is a common symptom of DIABETES MELLITUS and may occur with LEUKOPLAKIA, a condition that develops before cancerous changes in the vulva.

Q: How is itching treated?

A: Areas of irritation that occur after sunburn or dry skin from any cause may be helped with soothing creams and lotions, such as calamine. If the itching persists a doctor may carry out investigations to discover the cause and prescribe the appropriate treatment.

Antihistamine and antipruritic drugs and creams may aid in controlling the symptoms and sometimes the doctor may prescribe corticosteroid creams or ointments to be used for a short time.

IUCD. *See* INTRAUTERINE DEVICE.

IUD. *See* INTRAUTERINE DEVICE.

IVP. *See* INTRAVENOUS PYELOGRAM.

J

Jacksonian epilepsy is a form of epilepsy in which only one half of the brain is involved, generally because a scar or a tumour there acts as a focal point for irritation. As a result, when a grand mal attack (a major seizure) occurs, only limited areas of the body are affected at first: for example, one side of the face or one hand. The seizure may then progress and affect the whole of one side of the body before finally causing loss of consciousness and the typical convulsions. Sometimes, however, the attack remains localized and the patient does not lose consciousness. *See* EPILEPSY.

Jaundice, known medically also as icterus, is a condition characterized by a yellowing of the skin and the whites of the eyes. It is a symptom, not a disease in itself. The yellow colour is caused by an excess in the body of the BILE pigment bilirubin. Normally, bilirubin is formed by the breakdown of haemoglobin during the destruction of worn-out red blood cells. It is then excreted by the liver into the bile via the bile ducts.

Q: What causes an excess of bilirubin in the body?

A: An excess can be caused by (1) overproduction of bilirubin; (2) the failure of the liver to metabolize bilirubin or to excrete it; or (3) a blockage of the bile ducts.

Overproduction of bilirubin may be caused by the destruction of an excessive number of red blood cells (haemolytic anaemia). The liver cannot then excrete bilirubin fast enough. This occurs in malaria, thalassaemia, and haemolytic disease of the newborn.

Mild jaundice occurs as a common and normal condition in newborn babies, because at birth there is a deficiency in the enzyme that helps to excrete bilirubin. Rarely, this enzyme deficiency can also cause jaundice in adults. But in babies, the condition disappears within a few days as the enzyme is formed.

Jaundice may also result from diseases of the liver such as hepatitis or cirrhosis.

If the bile ducts become blocked, bile

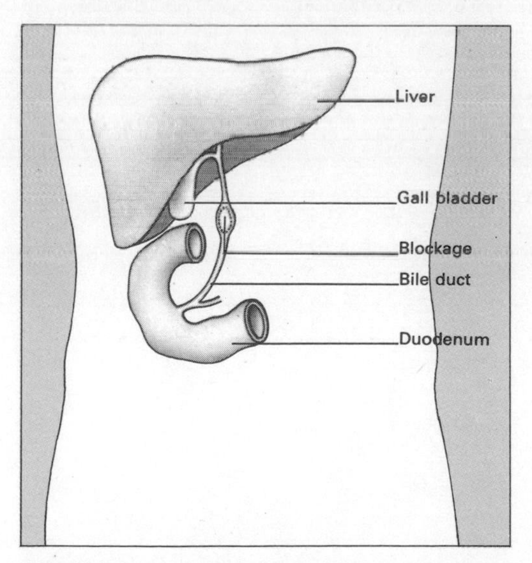

Jaundice is a symptom of many disorders, one of which is blockage of a bile duct.

cannot be excreted, and jaundice occurs. The ducts may be blocked by (1) inflammation and infection (cholangitis); (2) a gallstone (cholelithiasis); or (3) cancer of the pancreas or the common bile duct. Occasionally, drugs such as chlorpromazine may inhibit bilirubin excretion by the liver.

Q: What other symptoms can occur with jaundice?

A: Other symptoms depend on the specific cause of the jaundice. In many forms of the condition, bilirubin is excreted in the urine, which becomes dark brown in colour. If the excretion of bile is obstructed, stools are almost white and the digestion of fat is impaired. If the condition has been present for some time, intense itching may occur due to excess bile in the skin.

Q: How are the causes of jaundice diagnosed?

A: Diagnosis requires special blood tests, in which a doctor determines whether the liver is diseased, whether the bilirubin is being correctly metabolized by the liver cells, and whether there is any abnormal weakness in the red blood cells. The urine is examined for bilirubin, and the faeces for pale coloration (which would indicate an obstruction to bile excretion). It is sometimes necessary to perform a liver BIOPSY to examine cells under a microscope.

Jaw is the name of each of the two large bones in which the teeth are embedded. Each jaw represents two bones that fuse before birth: the mandibles join in the front to form the chin, and the maxillae form most of the roof of the mouth and contain the two sinuses that open into the nose.

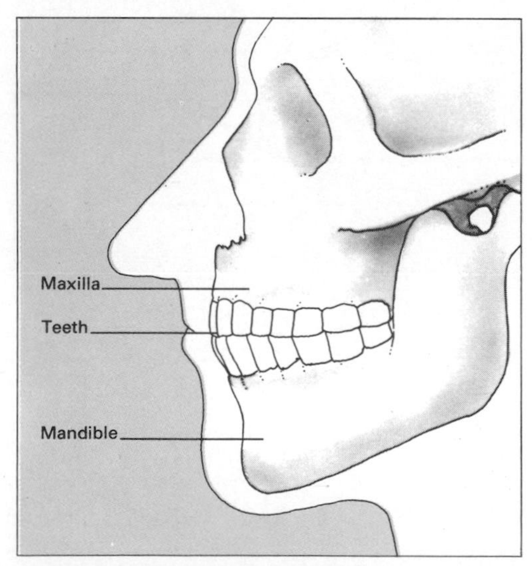

Jaw, the framework of the mouth, is formed by the maxilla and mandibular bones.

The upper jaw is stationary and the lower jaw is hinged from it at small hinge joints situated in front of the ears. Powerful cheek muscles pull the lower jaw up to the upper jaw for biting. For chewing, the muscles move the lower jaw backward and forward or from side to side.

Q: What medical problems can occur with the jaw?

A: Because the hinge joints are small, the most common jaw problem is dislocation, resulting in the inability to close the mouth. A sudden blow is the usual cause, but dislocation may occur from yawning while leaning with the chin on one hand. Careful manipulation by a doctor replaces a dislocated jaw.

Fractures of the jaw may require dental and facio-maxillary surgery to reposition either jaw in the correct biting position. Because the upper jaw extends upward as far as the floors of the eye sockets, fractures of the maxilla may also cause a change in the position of the eye, resulting in visual problems.

Minor arthritis in a jaw joint causes a clicking sensation, and sometimes pain when the jaw is moved up and down.

Infection of the jaw may follow dental disorders, and may cause inflammation of the nasal sinuses (sinusitis) or, rarely, inflammation of the bone (osteomyelitis).

Q: How can a person eat with a fractured jaw?

A: A person with a fractured jaw cannot eat solid food: it is impossible to bite. The broken jaw is usually wired to the other jaw to re-establish the correct biting position. For this reason, all food has to be sucked through a straw. Great care must be taken to ensure that choking and vomiting do not occur, because a person whose jaws are wired together cannot expel the vomit and may choke to death. A doctor may advise the patient to carry wire cutters to use in such an emergency.

Jejunum is part of the small intestine. It is about 1.2 metres (four feet) long and connects the duodenum and the ileum. Enzymes in the small intestine continue the breakdown of food (from the stomach), which can then be absorbed through its wall into the lymphatic vessels and the hepatic portal vein.

COELIAC DISEASE is a disorder of the mucous lining of the jejunum.

See also INTESTINE.

Jet lag is the disorientation in the normal biological CIRCADIAN RHYTHM that is experienced by a person who travels quickly from one time zone to another of more than four hours' difference. The greater the time difference, the more serious is the disorientation. Because of jet lag, a person may feel sleepy during the day, alert during the night, and hungry at inconvenient hours. The body temperature may no longer be synchronized with day and night requirements.

Q: What is the best way to deal with jet lag?

A: The body may take a long time to adjust to a new circadian rhythm, possibly as many as ten days. If the stay in the new time zone is to be short, it is often advisable not to adapt, but to retain the familiar rhythm, even at the expense of unusual hours. On a business trip this generally means that at least some working hours fall within commercial times. A longer visit requires adaptation, which may mean taking sedatives for a few nights to ensure enough sleep.

Jigger (or chigger, or chigoe) is the common name of the burrowing flea, *Tunga penetrans*, which occurs in tropical India, Africa, and America. The female flea burrows under the skin, generally of the legs and feet and especially between the toes, where it causes intense local itching. A swelling forms where the insect lays its eggs, and the swelling often becomes ulcerated and infected. Treatment is to open the swelling with a sterilized needle to remove the jigger and the eggs and then to apply antiseptic cream.

Dirt that enters the skin as the jigger burrows its way in may cause tetanus.

Joint is medically defined as an area in the body at which two bones are in contact. At a joint, the bones may be freely mobile under the control of muscles, ligaments, and tendons; they may be only slightly mobile; or they may be fixed so as to be immobile.

Q: What are mobile joints?

A: At a typical mobile joint, the ends of the bones are covered with tough cartilage and lined with a membrane (the synovial membrane) containing a small amount of lubricating fluid. The joint has stabilizing ligaments limiting the directions and the extent to which the bones can be moved.

Q: Are there different kinds of mobile joints?

A: Yes, there are several different kinds. A hinge joint acts like a hinge: examples include the elbow and the fingers. A ball-and-socket joint, in which the rounded end of one bone fits inside a concave socket of the other, allows good rotation: examples are the shoulder and the hip. A saddle joint allows sliding movement in two directions: the ankle and thumb are saddle joints. A plane joint permits only slight sliding movement, as in the wrist bones. An ellipsoid joint allows circular and bending movements but no rotation: the fingers have ellipsoid hinge joints. A pivot joint, allowing rotation and no other movement, is found solely between the two top vertebrae of the neck.

Mobile joints are more complex than the slightly mobile or immobile joints.

Q: What are slightly mobile joints?

A: At a typical slightly mobile joint, the bones have a layer of cartilage between them and are held firmly together by strong ligaments. Such joints are found between the pubic bones (symphysis pubis) and the discs between the vertebrae of the spine.

Q: What are immobile joints?

A: Immobile joints occur where two bones are fused or fixed together before or shortly after birth. Examples are the ilium, pubis, and ischium, which together form the pelvis, and the many flat bones that combine to make up the skull.

Joint disorders. There are many conditions that may involve joints: degenerative conditions, such as osteoarthritis; inflammatory conditions, such as rheumatoid arthritis; conditions involving the membranes surrounding the joints, such as synovitis; generalized disorders involving the joints, such as gout; damage to the joint involving dislocation or complicated fracture; congenital disorders, including congenital dislocation of the hip and clubfoot; and, sometimes,

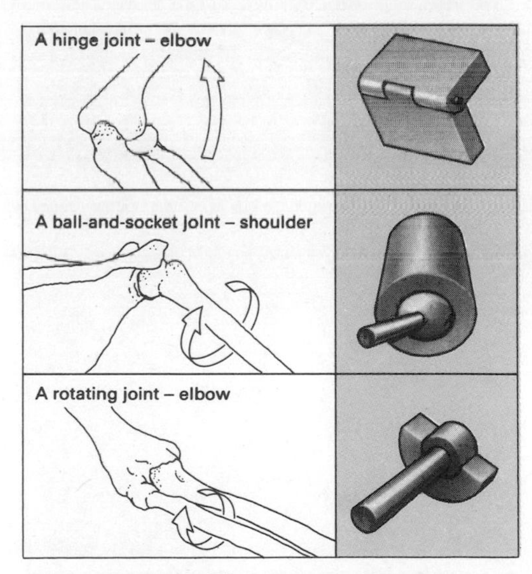

Joints of several different types allow the human skeleton freedom of movement.

disorders of the cartilage, such as a slipped disc and a torn cartilage in knee disorders.

Each of the following joint disorders has a separate article in the A-Z section of this book:

ANKYLOSING SPONDYLITIS	GOUT
ANKYLOSIS	HAMMERTOE
ARTHRITIS (including rheumatoid arthritis and osteoarthritis)	OSTEOARTHROPATHY
ARTHRODESIS	OSTEOARTHROSIS
BURSITIS	OSTEOCHONDRITIS
CAPSULITIS	PERTHES' DISEASE
CERVICAL SPONDYLOSIS	POLYARTHRITIS
CLUBFOOT	RHEUMATIC FEVER
DISLOCATION	SLIPPED DISC
FROZEN SHOULDER	SPONDYLITIS
	SPONDYLOLISTHESIS
	SPONDYLOSIS
	SUBLUXATION
	SYNOVITIS

Jugular vein is any one of four veins in the neck. They are: the internal jugular veins, one on each side of the neck; and the external jugular veins, one at the front of the neck and the other at the side of the neck.

K

Kahn test is a blood test for detecting the presence of the venereal disease syphilis. *See* SYPHILIS; WASSERMANN TEST.

Kala-azar. *See* LEISHMANIASIS.

Kaolin, or china clay, is a naturally occurring form of aluminum silicate used medically in many antidiarrhoeal mixtures.

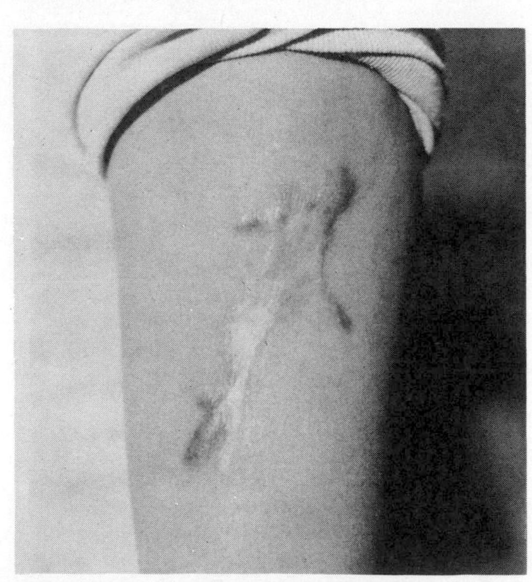

Keloid scar occurs when the body's healing process overresponds following an injury.

Keloid is a mass of excessive fibrous tissue that develops at the site of a scar. Black people are more likely to form keloids than are people of other races.

Keratitis is an inflammation of the cornea, the transparent membrane that forms the front of the eye. If the condition occurs suddenly, it causes pain, sensitivity to light (photophobia), and watering of the eye. If keratitis develops gradually, only minor discomfort may result. Opaque patches in the cornea can cause the patient's vision to blur.

Q: What causes keratitis?

A: Keratitis is often a symptom of a more general disorder. Virus infections, such as TRACHOMA (chronic conjunctivitis) or herpes simplex, may infect the cornea. Bacterial infection may follow any eye wound. Keratitis is also a consequence of congenital syphilis or, rarely, tuberculosis. Occasionally a form of keratitis occurs in middle-aged women with ROSACEA. A deficiency of vitamin A causes dryness of the cornea which makes it more susceptible to infection.

Q: How is keratitis treated?

A: Further damage to the cornea can be prevented with eye drops containing the drug atropine to dilate the pupil. Corticosteroid drugs reduce the inflammation. It is essential for the eyes to be examined by an ophthalmologist.

Kernicterus is a serious form of haemolytic disease of the newborn, a condition in which brain damage occurs. *See* HAEMOLYTIC DISEASE OF THE NEWBORN.

Kernig's sign may be seen as a result of a neurological test in which the patient lies flat on the back after bending the knee. The doctor then tries to straighten the leg. If the patient unconsciously resists, it may indicate irritation of a nerve where it passes out of the spine, as may occur with a slipped disc or meningitis.

Ketones are substances formed by the body during the breakdown of fats and fatty acids into carbon dioxide and water. Acetone is an example of a ketone.

Excessive amounts of ketones are formed when fat is used, instead of sugar, for providing energy. This condition, called ketosis, occurs during starvation and, sometimes, during high fevers when large amounts of heat energy are needed. It may also happen in diabetes mellitus, when the body has difficulty in using sugar normally.

Ketosis. *See* KETONES.

Kidney is one of a pair of organs located at the back of the abdomen, against the strong muscles next to the spine, and behind the intestines and other organs. The adrenal glands lie on the top of the kidneys.

Each kidney weighs about five ounces (150 grams) and is about 10 cm (four inches) long in the average adult. Its inner side forms the renal pelvis, which collects urine as it is formed and passes it out of the kidney to the bladder via the ureter. The inner side is also joined to the artery and vein that carry blood to and from the kidney.

Q: What is the function of the kidneys?

A: The kidneys filter out water and also unwanted substances in the blood. These substances are produced by the normal working of the body. They are excreted by the kidneys in the form of urine. The kidneys also keep the salts and water of the body in the correct balance.

Q: How do the kidneys work?

A: Blood passes through each kidney under high pressure. The blood is filtered by the glomeruli, special structures in the kidney containing clusters of capillaries that collect water, salts, and unwanted substances. The filtrate passes along a fine tube, the nephron (of which there are approximately one million in each kidney), which reabsorbs any of the water, glucose, and salts that the body still requires and allows the rest to pass into the pelvis of the kidney as urine.

See also p.14.

Kidney dialysis (medically known as haemodialysis) is a method of filtering unwanted substances from the blood using a machine that acts as an artificial kidney. It is used for patients whose own kidneys are damaged or malfunctioning.

Q: How does a kidney dialysis machine work?

A: Blood from an artery passes into the dialysis machine and over a thin sheet of membrane that acts as a filter for unwanted substances. The purified blood is then fed back into one of the patient's veins.

A variety of machines are available, some of which are small and safe enough to be used by the patient at home. The most modern machine is portable.

Q: Are there any problems in using such a machine?

A: Yes. Many of the problems are associated with maintaining sterility, but most of these have been overcome by the use of machines with disposable parts. It can be difficult to find suitable veins and arteries in the patient, but it is now possible to implant a small plastic tube (called a shunt) in the blood vessels that can be connected to the machine.

Q: How often should dialysis be performed?

A: It is usually necessary to perform dialysis for periods of four to six hours, three times a week, in hospital, at a special dialysis centre set up for the purpose, or at the patient's home.

Q: When may kidney dialysis be used?

A: Dialysis is used to treat acute or chronic kidney failure. In acute renal failure, dialysis continues until the kidneys recover their normal function. In chronic renal failure, dialysis continues either for the rest of the patient's life or until a kidney transplant is performed.

See also KIDNEY; KIDNEY DISEASE; TRANSPLANT SURGERY.

Q: Can dialysis be carried out without the use of a machine?

A: Yes. Peritoneal dialysis does not require a machine. It is performed by inserting a sterile plastic catheter into the abdominal cavity and irrigating the peritoneum with an isotonic solution that extracts the unwanted substances from the blood.

A talk about Kidney disease

Kidney disease. The body depends on the kidneys to excrete many waste products and to maintain the correct balance of water and salts, and any kidney disorder interferes with these important functions.

Q: What are the symptoms of kidney disease?

A: The symptoms of kidney disease depend on the underlying cause. They are often

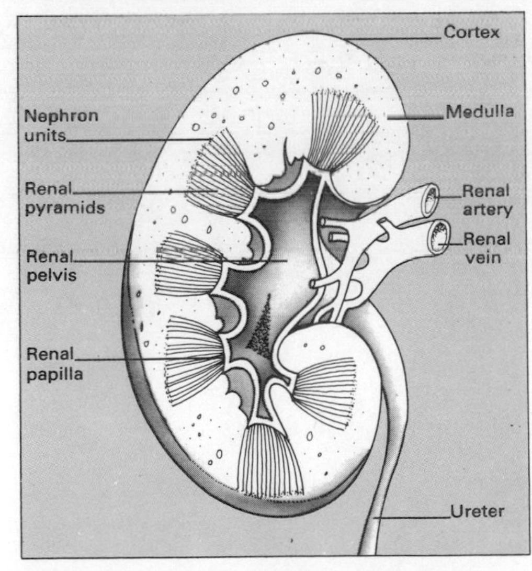

Kidney filters body fluids within the nephron units and expels wastes via the ureter.

mild and vague until a late stage in the disease. Kidney disease may cause an increased amount of urine to be formed, leading to abnormally frequent urination (polyuria). Or the formation of urine may be diminished, leading to abnormally infrequent urination (oliguria).

Some kidney diseases, such as acute nephritis, may cause blood in the urine (haematuria). Other symptoms of kidney disease include acute abdominal pain (colic); and generalized oedema, which is swelling due to the accumulation of water in the body tissues.

If both kidneys stop working completely, waste products accumulate in the body and poison the patient. This can be fatal and requires urgent medical attention.

Q: What causes kidney disease?

A: Kidney disease may be caused by many factors, such as injury; infection; cancer; or disorders in other parts of the body. In some cases, kidney disease may occur without apparent cause.

The kidney may be damaged in a serious accident, causing a rupture of its surrounding capsule and leading to severe haemorrhage. The damaged kidney may have to be surgically removed (nephrectomy). Rarely, the kidney may be damaged by radiotherapy treatment carried out for cancer. This may eventually result in high blood pressure and kidney failure.

Stones may form in the kidneys (nephrolithiasis) and cause kidney damage. This may occur without apparent cause, or it may be due to an underlying metabolic disorder. Occasionally, microscopic crystals form in the kidney substance itself (nephrocalcinosis). These may occur for the same reasons as do stones, or, rarely, in babies who are given excessive amounts of vitamin D.

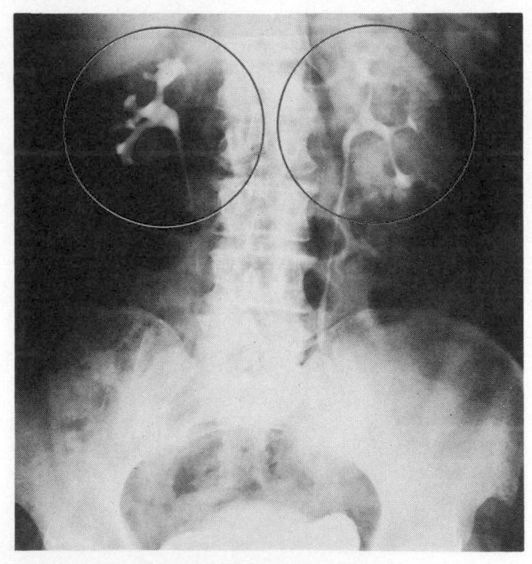

Kidney disease may be detected with an intravenous pyelogram, a form of X-ray.

The kidney may become infected and inflamed. This may result in various kidney diseases, such as nephritis; glomerulonephritis; or pyelonephritis. Infection of the kidneys often results from the spread of infection from the bladder.

Cancer of the kidney may occur in the renal pelvis, the collecting area for urine, or in the kidney itself (hypernephroma). The latter is most common in adults, but a nephroblastoma (Wilms' tumour) may occur in young children.

Many disorders in other parts of the body have an effect on the kidney. High blood pressure gradually damages the kidneys. Because of such damage, high blood pressure often continues to be a problem after the original cause has been found and treated. Various hormone disorders, such as parathyroid gland hyperactivity, Cushing's syndrome, and diabetes insipidus, affect kidney function. Diabetes mellitus not only causes sugar in the urine (glycosuria) but may eventually cause damage to the glomeruli or to the blood supply to the kidney. A stone in the ureter may cause urinary obstruction. This may result in reverse pressure of the urine into the kidney, producing distention and progressive loss of function (hydronephrosis).

Q: What tests are carried out to diagnose kidney disease?

A: Suspected kidney disease can be investigated in various ways. Chemical testing of the urine detects the presence of any abnormal substances, such as protein (albuminuria), sugar (glycosuria), or haemoglobin (haemoglobinuria). The concentration of salts and urea also can be determined. Examination of urine through a microscope may detect blood (haematuria) or white blood cells resulting from infection. Tests that measure the amount of urea and creatinine (two waste products that should be excreted by the kidney) in the blood help detect kidney disease.

The kidneys also may be given either an INTRAVENOUS PYELOGRAM (IVP), a retrograde pyelogram, or an ULTRASOUND test. These procedures outline the urine collecting system and help to detect abnormalities of kidney size and shape.

An ARTERIOGRAM shows the blood supply to the kidney; and occasionally a renogram, using radioactive iodine, is carried out.

Finally, if the diagnosis still is in doubt, a renal biopsy may be performed, using a long needle to obtain a small sample of kidney tissue for examination with a microscope.

Q: How are kidney diseases treated?

A: The treatment of kidney diseases depends on their cause, and may involve the skilled care of a nephrologist, a specialist in kidney diseases.

For details of individual kidney disorders, *see* ALBUMINURIA; CALCULUS; DIABETES MELLITUS; GLOMERULONEPHRITIS; GLYCOSURIA; HAEMATURIA; HAEMOGLOBINURIA; HYDRONEPHROSIS; NEPHRITIS; NEPHROTIC SYNDROME; NOCTURIA; OLIGURIA; POLYURIA; PYELONEPHRITIS; URAEMIA.

Kidney stone. *See* CALCULUS.

Kleptomania is a compulsive and uncontrollable desire to steal. The stolen objects often have little intrinsic value. It is a form of mental illness and may be a symptom of depression in which the stealing continues, in an obvious manner, until the patient is caught. In such cases there is probably an unconscious desire to be caught and to receive appropriate treatment.

Klinefelter's syndrome is a genetic disease seen in males, caused by the presence of one or more extra (female sex) X chromosomes. It is not true hermaphroditism. It is not usually diagnosed until after puberty, at which time the male breasts may become enlarged and the testicles remain small. Varying degrees of mental retardation may also be present. There is no specific treatment.

See also HERMAPHRODITE.

Knee is the hinge joint between the lower end of the thigh-bone (femur) and the upper end of the shin-bone (tibia). The front of the knee is covered by the lower tendon of the quadriceps femoris, a massive group of muscles that extend to the top of the thigh. The broad tendon that attaches this muscle to the front of the tibia contains the patella (kneecap). The patella forms a protective shield in front of the knee joint, behind which pass the main artery, vein, and nerve of the leg.

There are strong ligaments on each side of the knee which prevent its dislocation outward or inward. Inside the joint are two ligaments (cruciate ligaments) that protect the joint from dislocation forward or backward. There are also two semilunar cartilages attached to the outer edges of the internal surface of the joint on top of the tibia.

When the leg is extended to straighten it at the knee, the bones work together so that they lock into a rigid structure.

See also KNEE PROBLEMS.

Kneecap. *See* PATELLA.

Knee jerk may be seen as the result of a neurological test in which the tendon of the large muscle in front of the thigh (quadriceps femoris) is tapped with a small hammer just below the kneecap (patella). This produces an involuntary kicking movement of the leg. The manner and speed with which the reaction takes place help a doctor to diagnose certain neurological disorders. *See* REFLEX.

Knee problems. The knee is a complex joint capable of a large range of movements and it has to support the full weight of the body. For this reason, it is particularly vulnerable to injury, degenerative changes, and joint disorders. With increasing age, degeneration of the knee joint through osteoarthritis becomes more likely. It occurs particularly in those who are overweight or who have a previous history of knee injury. A form of bursitis (housemaid's knee) occurs particularly in persons who have to kneel frequently or continually while working.

Damage to the semilunar cartilages within the knee joint is a common occurrence that often results from excessive rotation when "locking" the leg straight (*see* KNEE). Sometimes the surface lining the knee can degenerate (osteochondritis), and a fragment can break off inside the joint. This causes pain, further damage, and a tendency for the knee

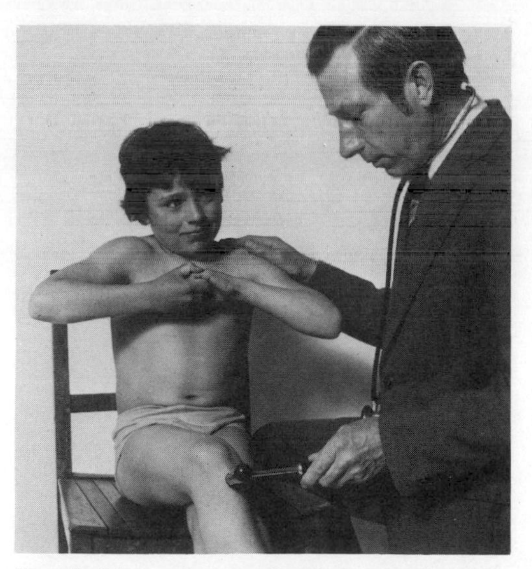

Knee jerk is a reflex reaction that is obtained by tapping the knee just below the patella.

to lock, thereby preventing the leg from being fully extended.

Occasionally, the quadriceps muscle (which passes over the knee) ruptures and causes an unstable knee joint. This condition is usually associated with a sudden strain, but sometimes there is little obvious reason. This is particularly likely to happen in the elderly.

See also BOW-LEGS; BURSITIS; JOINT DISORDERS; KNOCK-KNEE; MENISCUS; PATELLA.

Knock-knee (medically known as genu valgum) is a disorder in which the lower legs are curved outward so that the knees touch each other and the ankles are apart. This condition commonly occurs in childhood as a normal stage of development between the ages of about two and a half and four years. As the child continues to grow, the legs gradually straighten.

Koilonychia is a deformity of the nails. The nail becomes thin and the normal curve of the outer surface is reversed, giving the nail a spoon-shaped appearance. This uncommon condition may occur in patients with iron-deficiency anaemia.

Koplik's spots are a sign of measles. They are tiny red spots with white centres that appear on the palate, inside the cheeks, and on the tongue; they may also occur on the internal surface of the eyelids.

See also MEASLES.

Korsakoff's syndrome is a form of mental illness. It is commonly found in brain-damaged patients suffering from ALCOHOLISM, but it may also accompany other forms of brain damage, for example, cerebral tumours, head injuries, and minor strokes.

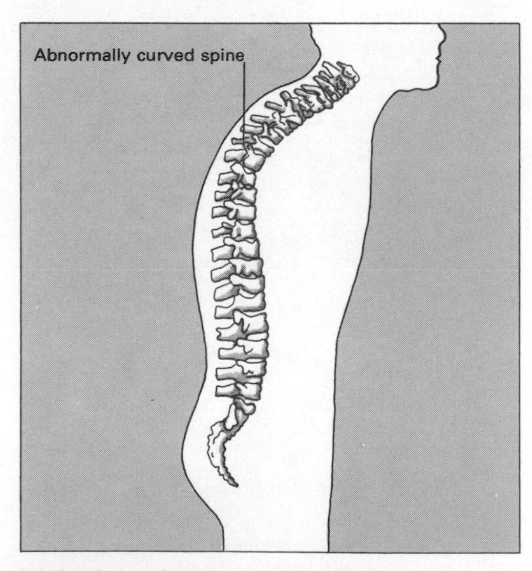

Kyphosis produces a stooping posture by exaggerating the spine's posterior curve.

Q: What are the symptoms of Korsakoff's syndrome?

A: The patient is unable to remember recent events and tends to invent plausible accounts of what he or she has been doing during the past few days or weeks. Memory for distant events is normal and any skills learned in the past can be performed with ease. This is in contrast to the patient's ability to learn a new skill which, being difficult to remember, is consequently difficult to perform.

Q: What is the treatment for Korsakoff's syndrome?

A: The treatment depends on the cause. Alcoholism should be treated appropriately, and large amounts of B vitamins often produce a slow improvement.

See also ALCOHOLISM.

Küntscher nail is a tubular metal nail that is inserted into the centre of a bone in the treatment of a fracture.

Kwashiorkor is a form of severe malnutrition in children. There is a characteristic loss of pigmentation of the hair giving it a reddish-brown appearance. The children have dry, scaling, pale skin, as well as a protuberant abdomen, and they fail to grow normally. There is also often swelling (oedema) of the feet and legs. Severe cases may lead to extreme emaciation.

Kymograph is an instrument that records movements such as blood pressure changes, muscle contractions, respiratory movements, or changes in pressure in the intestine. The recording is called a kymogram.

Kyphosis is either an excessive curvature of the spine, such as that of a "hunchback," or a more gradual, but still abnormal, curvature. It commonly affects the spine behind the chest, but may affect the lower or upper spine if there is an excessive amount of bending forward.

It is frequently associated with scoliosis (sideways curvature of the spine), and with bone disorders that affect the vertebrae, osteoporosis in the elderly, ankylosing spondylitis, and a form of osteochondritis that affects the bones of the spine.

See also LORDOSIS; SCOLIOSIS.

L

Labial describes anything pertaining to the lips, either of the mouth or vulva.

Labium is a lip or edge of a body structure. The term is used to describe the thick edge of a bone, the cervix (neck) of the womb, or one of the lips of the mouth. *See* VULVA.

Labour is the process of childbirth by which the baby and placenta (afterbirth) are delivered. *See* PREGNANCY AND CHILDBIRTH.

Labyrinth is the inner ear, consisting of the three semicircular canals and the cochlea. *See* EAR.

Labyrinthitis is inflammation of the inner ear. Labyrinthitis is accompanied by extreme dizziness and vomiting, and sometimes causes deafness.

Bacterial or viral infection may spread to the inner ear from a middle ear infection (OTITIS media); occur with MENINGITIS; or follow an operation on the ear, such as FENESTRATION or STAPEDECTOMY. The disorder requires urgent treatment from a specialist in ear diseases.

Laceration is a tear in any tissue in the body. It may be external or internal. External lacerations are often caused by a cut from a sharp object (for EMERGENCY treatment, *see* First Aid, p.582). Internal lacerations may occur when an organ is damaged by a violent blow, and an emergency operation is often necessary.

Lacrimal apparatus is the anatomical name for the structures in each eye that produce and distribute tears. The lacrimal gland lies in a notch in the upper, outer corner of the bony eye socket. The tears it secretes are carried in twelve small ducts to the surface of the eyeball. They are washed across the eye by the action of blinking. Two ducts at the inner corner of the eye drain the tears into the lacrimal sac and then into the nose.

Lacrimation is the medical term for the production of tears by the lacrimal gland of the eye. *See* LACRIMAL APPARATUS.

Lactation is the secretion of milk from the female breasts, and the period of lactation is the length of time for which breast-feeding continues.

Q: *What makes the breasts start producing milk at the end of pregnancy?*

A: Throughout pregnancy, the breasts develop and increase in size in response to increased amounts of the hormones oestrogen, progesterone, and chorionic gonadotrophin (the chorion is the membrane that encloses the foetus). These hormones are produced by the placenta, the organ of chemical interchange between mother and foetus. The increase in breast size is caused partly by the larger number of ducts that form in the breast and partly by an increase in the amount of fatty tissue.

Milk is not formed until after the baby is born. Milk production is stimulated by the hormone PROLACTIN produced by the pituitary gland at the base of the brain, which in turn is stimulated by changes that take place at the onset of labour.

But "first milk" or COLOSTRUM, a fluid rich in fat and proteins, is secreted near the end of pregnancy. It contains antibodies from the mother that help to protect the baby against disease. As soon as the baby is born, the mother's hormone levels drop rapidly, prolactin secretion starts, and milk is produced. *See* PREGNANCY AND CHILDBIRTH.

Q: *Why does milk secretion sometimes occur before the baby starts sucking?*

A: The contraction of the breast tissue to expel milk is partly a reflex to the baby sucking and partly a response to the presence of the hormone OXYTOCIN (also secreted by the pituitary gland). This hormone may be produced in response to the mother's emotional reaction when she hears the baby crying. Oxytocin also causes contraction of the womb, and this accounts for an increase in vaginal flow when breast-feeding takes place.

Q: *How may lactation be stopped?*

A: If the woman does not want to breast feed, firm binding of the breasts is usually sufficient to stop lactation after the birth of the baby. If milk appears later, further oestrogens should be given.

The problem is more difficult if lactation needs to be stopped once it has started. A combination of oestrogens, restricted fluid intake, and a firm brassiere may stop lactation.

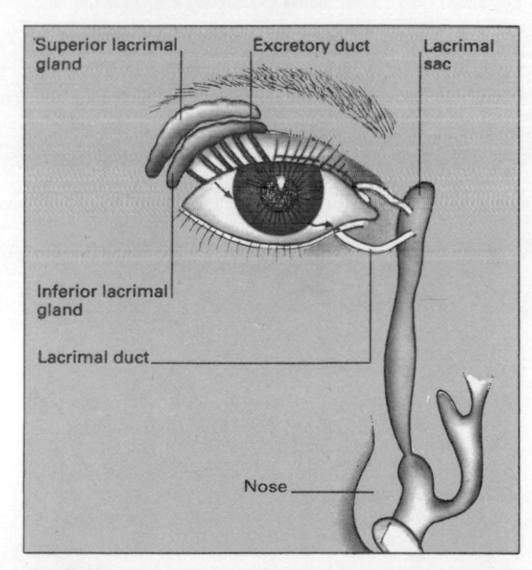

Lacrimal apparatus is the structure from which tears flow to wash over the eyes.

Q: *Are there any dangers in using oestrogens to stop lactation?*

A: Yes, although risks are small and probably affect only women who are over the age of thirty-five, those who smoke, or those who have had an operation, such as a Caesarean section. There is also a slightly increased risk of venous thrombosis because of the effect of the oestrogens.

Q: *Can anything be done if lactation does not begin?*

A: Little can be done because the reasons for failure to start lactation are not fully understood.

Q: *Are there any problems that may occur during lactation?*

A: Yes. Gradual failure of lactation, once it has started, is usually caused by a combination of the mother's fatigue and anxiety as well as lack of sufficient fluid. This may occur when the mother returns home from hospital, and it is relatively easy to treat.

Other problems include engorgement of the breasts, failure to produce sufficient milk, or MASTITIS (inflammation of the breasts). Infection of the breast ducts usually results from a cracked nipple, but it may occasionally be a complication of PUERPERAL FEVER, a condition that can develop after a woman has given birth. Part of a breast becomes tender, swollen, and inflamed, and a sudden fever occurs, often starting with a shivering attack. A doctor may prescribe antibiotics and painkilling drugs. If possible, breast-feeding should continue because this empties the affected area. If an abscess forms, it will have to be incised.

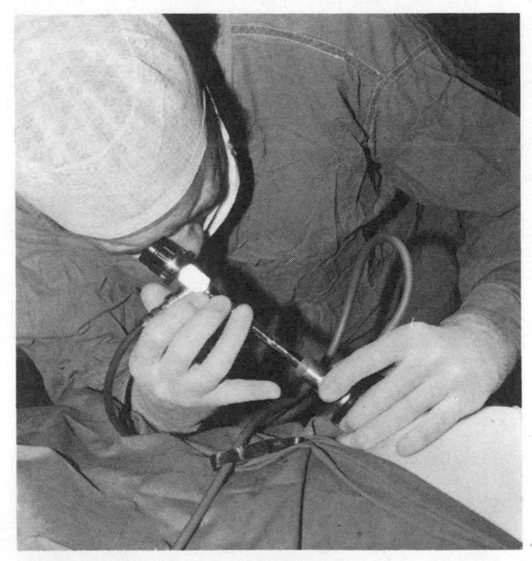

Laparoscope is used under general anaesthetic to illuminate and explore the inner abdomen

Lactic acid is a colourless substance produced by the fermenting action of bacteria on milk or milk sugar (lactose). It occurs in sour milk and certain other foods. It is also produced during glucose and fat metabolism in the human body.

Lactose is a sugar found in milk. In the human digestive system, it is broken down into simpler substances by an enzyme (lactase) in the small intestine.

Lameness. *See* CLAUDICATION.

Laminectomy is a surgical operation in which a plate of bone (lamina) is removed from the back of one or more vertebrae to expose the spinal cord. It is performed during any operation on the spinal cord.

Lance is a double-edged surgical knife. The term is also used for a minor surgical operation in which a lance is used to open an abscess or boil.

Langerhans' islands. *See* ISLETS OF LANGERHANS.

Lanolin is a pale yellow fatty substance obtained from the grease of sheep's wool. It is used in various skin preparations because it mixes with oils and with water to produce ointments that penetrate the skin and so help in the absorption of drugs.

Lanugo is the fine, downy hair that covers a foetus.

Laparoscopy is an examination of the interior of the abdomen with a lighted tube called a laparoscope. Laparoscopy is also known as peritoneoscopy.

Q: *How and why is laparoscopy performed?*

A: The examination can be carried out under local or general anaesthesia. A small incision is made, usually next to the navel; the instrument is then passed through the peritoneum, the membranous sac that lines the abdominal cavity. Carbon dioxide or nitrous oxide gas is passed into the peritoneal cavity through a needle to swell the abdomen and make it possible to examine the organs.

Disorders such as cancer, CROHN'S DISEASE, and cysts of the ovary can be diagnosed using this technique.

Q: *Can any operations be performed with a laparoscope?*

A: Yes. A surgeon can take a small piece of tissue for microscopic examination (biopsy), or perform a STERILIZATION operation in a woman.

Q: *Is laparoscopy a safe procedure?*

A: Yes, the examination is relatively safe and simple to perform.

Laparotomy is a surgical operation to open the abdomen. It may be performed to inspect the internal organs (exploratory laparotomy), or as a preliminary to further surgery.

Laryngectomy is an operation to remove the voice box (larynx), usually performed in the treatment of cancer. An opening is made in the windpipe (TRACHEOTOMY) so that the patient can breathe, and many of the nearby lymph glands are removed at the same time if they are malignant.

Q: *Can a patient with a laryngectomy talk?*

A: Not immediately, and never normally as before. But a patient with no larynx can learn OESOPHAGEAL SPEECH, in which sounds are produced in the oesophagus.

Laryngitis is inflammation of the vocal cords. It may be acute or chronic.

Q: *What causes acute laryngitis?*

A: Any sudden respiratory infection, such as the COMMON COLD or INFLUENZA, or infection of the back of the throat, such as TONSILLITIS or PHARYNGITIS, can cause acute laryngitis. Diphtheria used to be a common cause of laryngitis, but is now extremely rare in Western countries.

Overuse of the voice, heavy smoking, and habitual alcohol consumption all tend to produce a hoarse voice made rapidly worse by any minor infection.

Q: *What are the symptoms of acute laryngitis?*

A: The voice is husky and sometimes disappears completely (aphonia). Talking may cause pain in the throat.

Q: *What is the treatment for acute laryngitis?*

A: It is essential to attempt to stop talking for at least forty-eight hours. Steam inhalations may help, and treatment of the causative condition, such as tonsillitis, may be necessary.

Q: *Are there any complications of acute laryngitis?*

A: Yes. In babies and young children, the infection may occasionally spread to the windpipe (tracheitis) and bronchi (bronchitis) causing a syndrome called laryngotracheobronchitis, or croup. This is a potentially serious complaint and often needs treatment in hospital. The child usually has a high fever and a barking cough.

In adults the condition is seldom serious. It usually interferes with normal speech for about one week.

Q: *What are the symptoms and causes of chronic laryngitis?*

A: The chief symptom is continued hoarseness, accompanied by a slight cough and a tendency for the voice to become weaker with use. Drinking alcohol, smoking, and overuse of the voice are all factors that can produce these symptoms.

Q: *How is chronic laryngitis diagnosed and treated?*

A: The diagnosis is made by a throat specialist, who examines the vocal cords to make sure that there is no other cause for the hoarseness.

See also HOARSENESS.

Laryngoscopy is the examination of the interior of the voice box (larynx) using an instrument called a laryngoscope.

In the technique known as indirect laryngoscopy, the laryngoscope consists of a rod with a small mirror at one end. It is passed down the throat and gives a reflected view of the larynx.

In direct laryngoscopy, performed under a general anaesthetic, the laryngoscope is a rigid, illuminated tube which is passed down the throat to give a direct view of the larynx.

Larynx is the structure in the front of the neck that is commonly known as the voice box. It extends from the root of the tongue to the entrance of the windpipe (trachea). Until puberty, the larynx of a male person differs little in size from that of a female. At puberty, it enlarges considerably in males but only slightly in females.

The "box" that makes up the larynx consists of nine cartilages that are connected by ligaments and membranes, and are moved by several muscles. The largest of the cartilages, the thyroid cartilage, protrudes at the front of the neck to form the Adam's apple.

Q: *What are the functions of the larynx?*

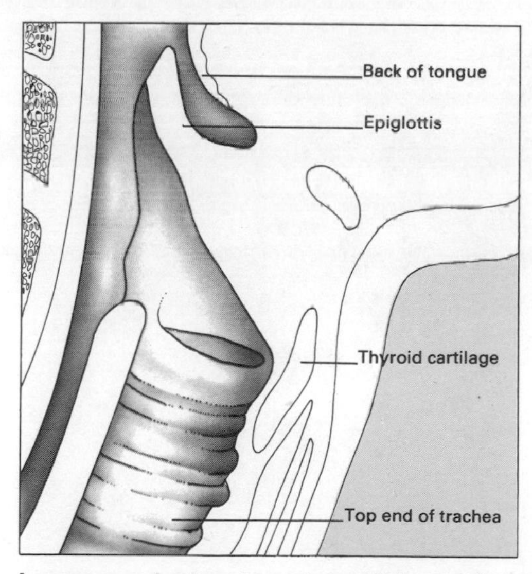

Larynx, or voice box, is made up of nine cartilages joined by ligaments and a membrane.

A: It forms part of the airway to the lungs; the epiglottis, one of the cartilages, closes it during swallowing. The other main function is the production of speech. The two vocal cords, at rest, are open to allow breathing. For speech the cords are pulled close together and vibrate when air passes between them.

Q: What disorders can affect the larynx?

A: LARYNGITIS may occur as an inflammation on its own or as part of respiratory infections such as the common cold or bronchitis. The vocal cords may be damaged by overuse, such as through public speaking, which may cause small swellings producing prolonged hoarseness. Cancer and other tumours may occur; treatment of laryngeal cancer is by surgical removal (larygectomy) or radiotherapy.

Laser is a device that amplifies light to produce an extremely intense beam. Such a beam can be used in very much the same way as a surgical scalpel and has the added advantages of being transmissible through fibre-optic endoscopes to many parts of the body in which surgery would ordinarily entail an external incision; of being totally aseptic; and of incidentally being able to cauterize minor blood vessels instantly at the surgical site, reducing shock. Used in conjunction with a microscope, many surgical techniques are now commonplace using lasers that would otherwise require superhuman finesse by surgeons. This is true particularly in laser treatment for a detached retina.

Used in a slightly more diffuse form, the laser can be utilized to "vaporize" unhealthy cells within the body, and so prevent cancer even as the first signs appear. This form of treatment is especially common in connection with the condition in women known as pre-cancer of the cervix.

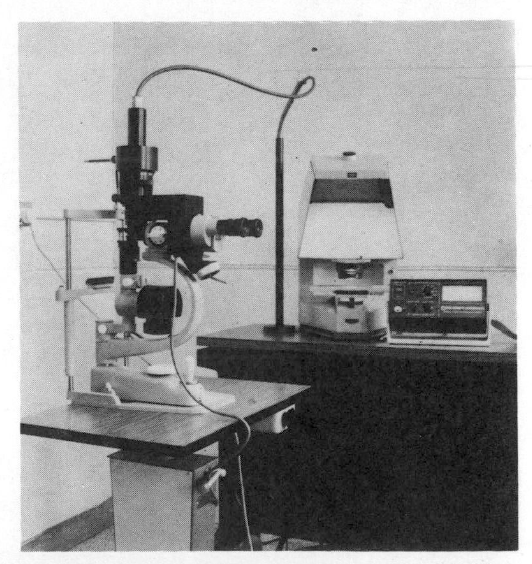

Laser apparatus can be used to perform highly accurate and specialized surgical procedures.

Lassa fever is an acute viral illness that is often fatal. It is most common in West Africa, but cases have occurred elsewhere. The onset of the symptoms is usually gradual, with high fever, headache, severe muscle pains, loss of appetite, an abnormal decrease in the number of white blood cells, and a slow pulse rate. These symptoms may last for one or two weeks, after which there is a slow recovery, or there may be a deterioration. In about half of all cases, these initial symptoms are followed by confusion, coma, and death.

Q: How is Lassa fever treated?

A: There is no cure for Lassa fever. The treatment involves complete bed rest and careful monitoring of all the bodily functions. The patient must be isolated to ensure that the infection does not spread to other people. Injections of GAMMA GLOBULIN from a person who has recently recovered from Lassa fever may be given, both to the patient and to anyone who may have come into contact with the illness.

Laughing gas is the common name for the anaesthetic gas nitrous oxide. *See* NITROUS OXIDE.

Lavage is the washing out of a body cavity. Gastric lavage is the washing out of the stomach with water, sodium bicarbonate, or some other fluid.

Laxatives are any substances that cause emptying of the bowel. They are often used in the treatment or prevention of CONSTIPATION.

Q: What substances are used as laxatives?

A: There are three main groups of laxatives. Those most commonly used act by irritating the bowel wall, causing a contraction and forcible expulsion of the faeces. But continued use of this kind of irritant laxative leads to a gradual loss of effectiveness. Senna, cascara sagrada, and phenolphthalein are examples of this group and are found in many commercial preparations.

The second group of laxatives acts by attracting water from the body into the intestine, increasing the volume of faeces. Milk of magnesia, Epsom salts (magnesium sulphate), and Glauber's salts (sodium sulphate) are common examples. More recently, vegetable substances that swell when they are swallowed have been used.

The third group is called bulk laxatives, and they include bran, vegetable fibre, and general roughage. Bulk swells the contents of the large intestine and acts as a stimulant to defecation as well as resulting in a bulkier stool. The diet of many people in Western countries is deficient in these substances. This may lead to constipation as well as other disorders.

Q: *What are the dângers in using laxatives?*

A: Laxatives should be used only in cases of severe and prolonged constipation and under a doctor's orders. Laxatives that act by irritating the bowel may become habit-forming so that the bowel may not function well without the irritant stimulus. In order to produce a laxative effect, gradually increasing doses have to be used. If they are taken over a prolonged period of time, the bowel wall may become damaged.

Other kinds of laxatives are safer to use, but may need to be taken in larger amounts than is first realized.

Q: *Should laxatives be used to treat any form of constipation?*

A: No. Laxatives should never be used if constipation suddenly occurs or is accompanied by abdominal pain or fever. In such a case, there may be an INTESTINAL OBSTRUCTION or APPENDICITIS and laxatives are likely to make the condition worse. A doctor should be consulted.

L-dopa is another name for the drug levodopa. *See* LEVODOPA.

Lead poisoning occurs most commonly in children, who absorb it more easily than do adults. Recently, children with high levels of lead in them have been shown to have lowered intelligence and behaviour problems. Drinking water supplied through lead pipes, and old paint containing lead chewed by children are common causes — but the main one is lead in petrol. Poisoning is also not uncommon among workers in the lead industry: lead is excreted very slowly from the body. The UK, like the USA and Japan, is to ban lead in petrol.

Q: *What are the symptoms of lead poisoning?*

A: The symptoms of chronic lead poisoning appear gradually and include fatigue; headache; irritability; dizziness; and breathlessness, caused by anaemia. If the intestine becomes involved, there may also be constipation, nausea, and severe abdominal pain. Nerve damage and permanent brain damage may also result.

Acute lead poisoning causes severe cramp, vomiting, black or bloody diarrhoea, acute abdominal pain, convulsions, delirium, and coma. The first sign is a metallic taste in the mouth, then signs of burns in the throat and oesophagus.

The diagnosis of lead poisoning is confirmed by the presence of anaemia with excessive amounts of lead in the blood and urine.

Q: *How is lead poisoning treated?*

A: Acute lead poisoning requires emergency medical treatment. Initially, the stomach is often washed out. Special drugs, called CHELATING AGENTS, help to remove lead from the tissues. This lead is then excreted by the kidneys in the urine.
If lead poisoning has caused anaemia, a special diet with supplementary iron may be prescribed. Any brain damage requires expert psychological assessment and help.

Q: *Can lead poisoning be prevented?*

A: Yes. By stopping its use in petrol; by treating soft water in lead pipes; by the use of lead-free paint; and by using protective clothing in the lead industry.

A talk about Learning disabilities

Learning disabilities are a group of disorders that interfere with a child's ability to learn. They may, therefore, cause a child to do poorly in school, or not to do as well as the child otherwise might.

There are many types of learning disabilities. A learning-disabled child may, for example, have difficulty concentrating, memorizing, or co-ordinating certain kinds of physical movements. A learning disability may also interfere with a child's ability to speak, spell, understand spoken language,

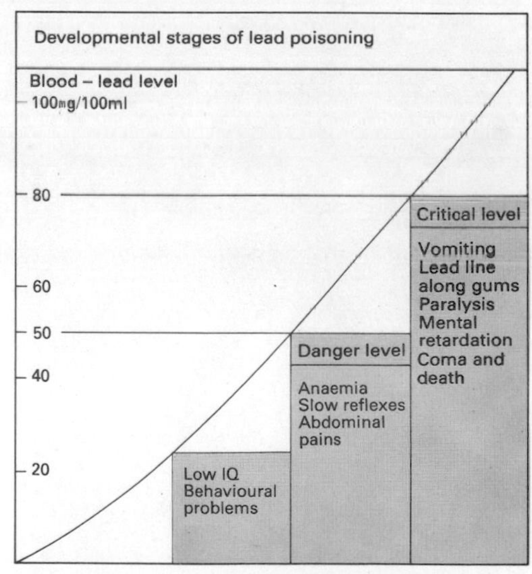

Lead poisoning is at a critical level when there is 80mg lead content per 100ml of blood.

or solve mathematical problems.

Q: *What are the causes of learning disabilities?*

A: Finding the exact cause of a child's learning disability is not always easy. Researchers believe, however, that most learning disabilities result from damage to major nerves leading to the brain or from minor damage to the brain itself. The nervous-system damage interferes with the ability to receive and use information transmitted from the disabled child's senses to his or her brain. Many children suffering from a learning disability nevertheless tend to be of average or above-average intelligence, and they do not seem to have an unusual incidence of abnormal hearing or vision.

Q: *What might cause nerve or brain damage?*

A: Such damage can occur before birth, during the birth process, or after birth. Damage before birth can result from poor nutrition and illness in the mother, which may affect the foetal nervous system. Certain injuries during pregnancy, particularly those involving the abdomen or pelvis, can also result in nervous-system damage to the unborn child. In addition, some hereditary defects in the mother or the father, or both, can cause nerve or brain damage before birth.

During the birth process, nerve or brain damage can occur if labour is prolonged or particularly difficult, causing temporary lack of oxygen supply to the brain.

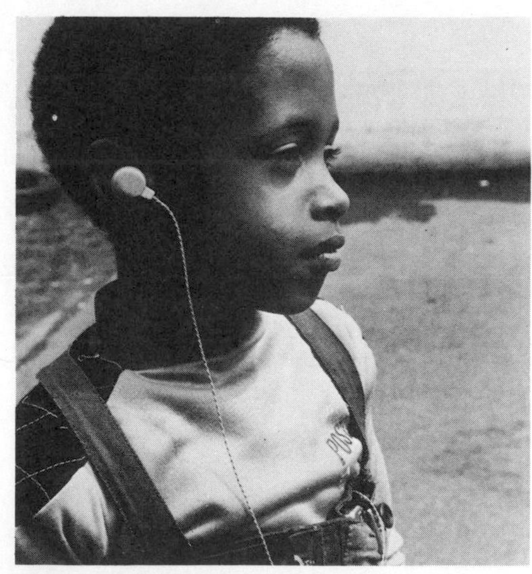

Learning disabilities can sometimes be overcome by specialized equipment.

Nerve or brain damage after birth can result from many causes, including injuries to the skull or spinal cord, malnutrition, inherited chemical imbalances, or disease. Research suggests that certain chemicals, especially lead, may also contribute to learning disabilities after birth.

Q: *Can a learning disability be present when there is no damage to nerves or to the brain?*

A: Yes. Although research into this phenomenon continues, scientists are generally of the opinion that a learning disability can come about without nervous-system damage. Scientists have found, for example, that continued absence of various early learning experiences, such as hearing language or handling objects, can result in certain learning disabilities in children.

Q: *What are the symptoms of a learning disability?*

A: The symptoms of a learning disability depend on the type of disorder involved. The symptom of one type of learning disability, DYSPHASIA, is a child's difficulty in speaking or in understanding oral language. DYSLEXIA, on the other hand, shows itself as a difficulty in reading and writing. DYSGRAPHIA, a third type of learning disability, is likely when a child is unable to control the finger muscles used in writing.

Still other types of learning disability interfere with a child's power to concentrate or to behave in a socially acceptable manner. Such a child is considered to suffer from hyperactivity, or HYPERKINESIS. Hyperactive children—who are more often boys than girls—tend to speak and to act impulsively and boisterously. These children are also usually impatient. Their conduct, whether at home or at school, is generally looked upon by peers and adults as disruptive and uncontrolled.

Other learning disabilities display themselves as a lack of distinguishing left from right or of distinguishing between letters of the alphabet that have some similarities in form, such as *b* and *d*.

Q: *How are learning disabilities diagnosed?*

A: The parent is usually the first person to suspect that a child has a learning disability. The parent usually alerts the family doctor.

Upon examination, the doctor may refer the child to other specialists for further testing and evaluation. The specialists may include a neurologist, a psychologist, a child psychiatrist, an eye specialist, an ear specialist, and a speech therapist. In addition, one or more of these may recommend that a social worker become involved in the evaluation of the child to try to determine if some factor in the home environment is contributing to, or even causing, the child's learning disability. Some schools provide for the diagnosis and treatment of children with learning disabilities.

Q: How are learning disabilities treated?

A: The kind and extent of treatment of a child with a learning disability depends on the individual diagnosis. In sum, there is no one form of treatment that seems to work well with all of the various types of learning disabilities. Doctors and educationists therefore continue to study the effectiveness and safety of many of the treatment methods presently used.

Leech is a bloodsucking parasite that was formerly used in medicine, until the early twentieth century when it was abandoned, as a means of bloodletting.

Infestation with leeches is called hirudiniasis, and it can result in a considerable blood loss. It is rare.

Q: What is the treatment for hirudiniasis?

A: If a leech is still on the skin surface, a lighted cigarette, match, or salt applied to the leech causes it to release its hold. The wound should be washed with an antiseptic, and a sterile dressing applied. If a leech is attached internally, expert medical attention is required.

Various repellent substances are available to protect against leeches.

Left-handedness, a tendency to use the left hand in preference to the right, is found in about eight per cent of people. In most people, the left side of the brain is "dominant," and controls the right side of the body; in left-handed people, the right side of the brain is dominant. Left-handed people are usually left-footed also, and they may stutter or suffer from dyslexia if they are forced to write with the right hand.

Legionnaire's disease is a potentially fatal bacterial disorder, named from an outbreak at the 1976 American Legion conference in Philadelphia, where 182 got the illness and 29 died. Previously it was unknown. It is seldom transmitted from one person to another. The illness is mild in some people; others become seriously ill with pneumonia causing breathlessness and confusion. Early treatment with the antibiotic Erythromycin is effective.

Leiomyoma is a benign (noncancerous) tumour of smooth muscle, commonly called a fibroid when it occurs in the womb. Leiomyomas may also occur in the gastrointestinal tract where they generally produce no symptoms, although occasionally they cause an INTESTINAL OBSTRUCTION.

Leishmaniasis is a group of infectious diseases of the skin and internal organs caused by various protozoan parasites of the genus *Leishmania.* Leishmaniasis is usually transmitted by sandflies.

There are two main types of leishmaniasis: visceral leishmaniasis, also called kala-azar; and cutaneous leishmaniasis, also called Delhi boil or oriental sore. Various forms of leishmaniasis are endemic to tropical and subtropical regions throughout the world.

In American leishmaniasis, one of the two varieties of leishmaniasis of the skin, the ulcers form in a similar way to those of oriental sore. But the ulcers usually form in the nose and throat and tend to be more destructive; also they commonly become infected. This can cause serious complications and may even be fatal. American leishmaniasis may last for several years.

Q: How is cutaneous leishmaniasis treated?

A: Many cases of oriental sore and some of American leishmaniasis heal spontaneously and do not require treatment. When spontaneous recovery does not occur, the treatment is similar to that for visceral leishmaniasis: with antimony drugs, or amphotericin B for resistant infections only, and antibiotic drugs to treat secondary infection.

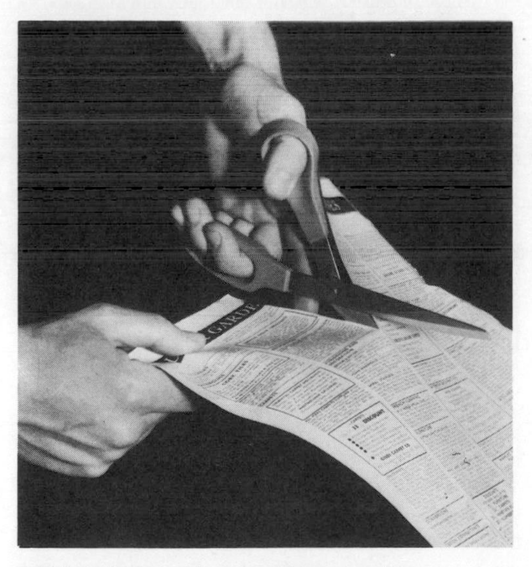

Left-handed people sometimes need to use specially adapted utensils and equipment.

Lens is a curved piece of transparent material that causes light rays passing through it to converge or diverge. The lens in the eye is a transparent, colourless, biconvex disc that helps to focus light onto the retina (for details, *see* EYE). Glass lenses are used in CONTACT LENSES, SPECTACLES, and various medical instruments.

Leontiasis is a thickening of the tissue or bones of the face. It causes considerable swelling and an alteration in appearance, giving a lionlike expression. Leontiasis may be a symptom of LEPROSY or it may be caused by an underlying bone disease (leontiasis ossea), which is probably a form of PAGET'S DISEASE OF BONE.

Leprosy is a slowly progressive infection caused by the bacterium *Mycobacterium leprae*. The disorder is common in Central and South America, in the Far East, in tropical countries of Asia and Africa, and in some of the Pacific Islands.

Leprosy is not infectious in adults unless they have been in close contact for long periods. But it is infectious in children, and they should be kept out of contact.

There are two main forms of leprosy, tuberculoid leprosy and lepromatous leprosy. Often, both occur in the same patient.

Q: What are the symptoms of tuberculoid leprosy?

A: Tuberculoid leprosy appears as an infection around nerve endings, causing gradual loss of feeling and also the appearance of pale areas on the skin where sensation is disordered. The nerves may be felt as thickened, tender rope-like structures. This may lead to paralysis producing WRIST DROP OR FOOT DROP, and sometimes local areas of ulceration because of the lack of normal sensation.

Q: What are the symptoms of lepromatous leprosy?

A: The normal pigmentation in some areas on the skin is lost and becomes slightly reddened, because of inflammation. There are usually many such areas scattered symmetrically across the body, and the edges merge into the normal skin so that they may not be obvious in a pale-skinned person. Occasionally there is thickening of the skin of the face, often involving the ears, to produce the "lion face" (LEONTIASIS).

As the disease progresses, the membranes of the nose, mouth, and throat may ulcerate producing distorted lips and loss of cartilage in the nose.

Q: How does leprosy progress?

A: The progress is extremely variable. Patients with tuberculoid leprosy often overcome the infection without much damage. Lepromatous leprosy progresses slowly, with increasing episodes of fever, enlargement in the size of affected skin areas, eye infection (IRITIS), lymph gland enlargement and, sometimes, involvement of the testes (ORCHITIS). Reactions like this ultimately lead to death.

Q: How is the condition diagnosed and treated?

A: For a doctor, diagnosis is simple, and can be confirmed by examining a biopsy of the edge of an affected skin area or nerve.

Drugs such as DAPSONE are successful in the treatment of leprosy, but must be used initially in small doses. The drug may otherwise cause the symptoms to become worse, with pain in the nerves. Treatment must be given for at least two years, generally longer.

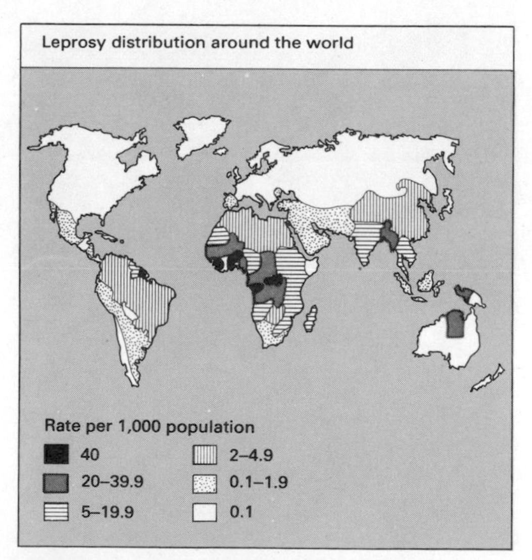

Leprosy, now an easily treatable disease, is still endemic in some parts of the world.

Leptospirosis is an infectious disease caused by spirochaete bacteria of the group called leptospira. It is passed on to humans from dogs, pigs, or rats that are carriers of the disease. There are about 130 kinds of leptospira bacteria.

Q: How is leptospirosis transmitted?

A: A human becomes infected with bacteria through direct contact with the animal's urine or with water or soil contaminated by it. The infection penetrates scratches on the skin or may enter through the mucous membranes of the mouth or vagina. Infections occur most commonly in sewer workers, veterinary surgeons, and farmers, but anyone can catch leptospirosis by swimming in contaminated water.

Q: What are the symptoms of leptospirosis?

A: After an incubation period of up to three weeks, there is sudden onset of severe headache, muscular aching (myalgia) with shivering attacks (rigor), and fever that may last about a week. The whites of the eyes often become red and inflamed.

The fever then settles slowly, and about ten days later the symptoms return with neck stiffness and mental confusion. The patient has a dislike of bright lights (photophobia), caused by a mild or severe form of MENINGITIS.

In severe forms of the illness, JAUNDICE and bleeding occur, mental confusion is common, and urinary output is greatly reduced resulting in uraemia (a toxic condition caused by failure of the kidneys). Death may result.

Q: How is leptospirosis diagnosed and what is the treatment?

A: The leptospira bacteria may be cultured from a sample of the patient's blood, urine, or spinal fluid. The blood may also contain antibodies that indicate the presence of leptospira.

Leptospirosis is a serious illness and the patient must be admitted to a hospital for antibiotic treatment.

Lesbian is a woman who has a sexual preference for women, and practises lesbianism, the female form of homosexuality.

Lesion is any damaged or abnormal area of tissue, such as a wound, injury, or an area altered by infection.

Lethargy is a feeling of fatigue and listlessness, both physical and mental. It may occur for no particular reason, or following any illness or operation. Continued lethargy, for no obvious reason, is abnormal and a doctor should be consulted.

Leucocyte. *See* WHITE BLOOD CELL.

Leucocytosis is an increase in the number of white blood cells (leucocytes) in the blood. It is a normal response to infection and also to bodily damage, such as that caused by surgery or by an accident. An increase in abnormal leucocytes may occur in conditions such as GLANDULAR FEVER, LEUKAEMIA, and some forms of ANAEMIA.

Leucopenia is a reduction in the normal number of white blood cells (leucocytes) in the blood. It may occur in any acute virus infection or in forms of chemical poisoning, with agranulocytosis.

See also AGRANULOCYTOSIS.

Leucotomy is the cutting of the nerve fibres that lead from the middle to the front part of the brain. It is usually known as lobotomy.

A talk about Leukaemia

Leukaemia is a malignant disease of the white blood cells (leucocytes), which play a key part in the body's defence mechanism against infection. It is a type of cancer that affects the bone marrow and other blood-forming tissues throughout the body. The cause of leukaemia is not known, but seems to be associated with a failure of the developing leucocytes to mature.

Normal mature leucocytes cannot reproduce and are replaced at the ends of their lives. Leukaemic cells, however, have the ability to reproduce but do not develop sufficiently to act as a defence against infection. As leukaemia progresses, the leukaemic cells displace normal leucocytes, leaving the patient extremely vulnerable to infection.

There are several forms of leukaemia, both acute and chronic, which are classified according to the type of leucocyte affected. The major types of leucocytes involved in leukaemia include lymphocytes, polymorphonuclear leucocytes, and granulocytes.

Q: What forms of acute leukaemia are there?

A: There are two main forms of acute leukaemia: acute lymphoblastic leukaemia (ALL), and acute myeloblastic leukaemia (AML). ALL affects lymphocytes and occurs usually in children. AML affects the cells that form polymorphonuclear leucocytes and is more common in adults.

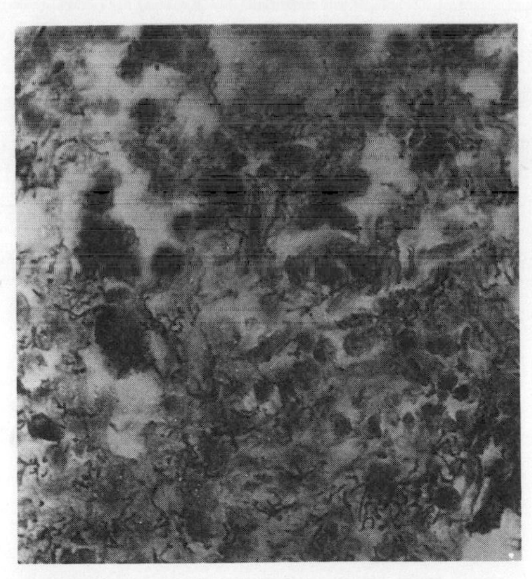

Leptospira bacteria can be seen as small irregular lines in this picture of blood.

Leukaemia

Q: What are the symptoms of the acute leukaemias?

A: The symptoms of both forms of acute leukaemia are similar. The patient usually has a sudden high fever and a severe throat infection. There may also be nosebleeds, bruising under the skin, and pain in the joints. In some patients, the onset of symptoms is slower, with lethargy, anaemia, and increasing weakness.

Q: What forms of chronic leukaemia are there?

A: There are two main forms of chronic leukaemia: chronic myeloid leukaemia (CML), and chronic lymphocytic leukaemia (CLL). CML affects immature polymorphonuclear leucocytes, and usually occurs after the age of thirty five years. CLL affects lymphoid tissue and lymphatic cells, and usually occurs in men over the age of fifty years.

Q: What are the symptoms of the chronic leukaemias?

A: The symptoms of both forms of chronic leukaemia are similar. The onset is usually slow, with increasing fatigue, lethargy, and weakness. The patient may also lose weight and suffer from loss of appetite. The course of the illness is also slow and may last for several years without causing major problems. However, there may be various complications, such as anaemia; bleeding under the skin; recurrent fever; and the formation of nodules and ulcers under the skin.

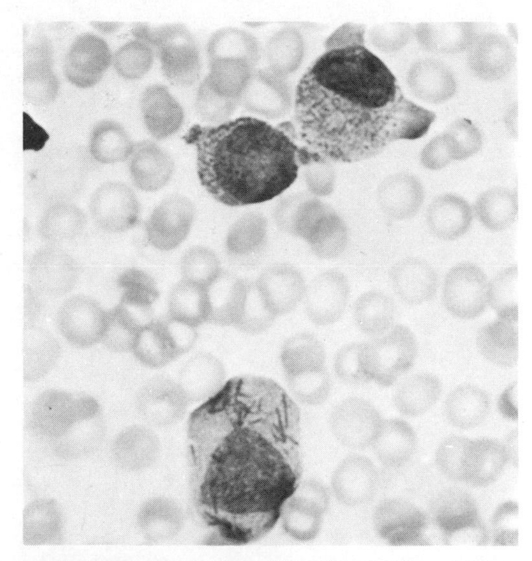

Leukaemia affects the white blood cells, which are displaced by leukaemic cells.

Q: How is leukaemia diagnosed?

A: The specific diagnosis of leukaemia requires a blood test and a bone marrow BIOPSY. Leukaemia is confirmed by the presence of large numbers of abnormal leucocytes in the blood, and the typical leukaemic cells in the bone marrow. With the chronic leukaemias, the patient may be unaware of the disease, and a diagnosis is often made only when the patient is examined for another reason, such as a routine check-up.

Q: How is leukaemia treated?

A: The treatment of acute and chronic leukaemia is often similar, but it is dependent on varying factors involved in each case. The aim of treatment is to suppress the reproduction of leukaemic cells. CYTOTOXIC DRUGS, which prevent cell multiplication, are used for this purpose. The rapidly-dividing leukaemic cells are more susceptible to these drugs than are normal leucocytes.

The treatment of the acute leukaemias usually involves the use of several cytotoxic drugs together. Once the number of leukaemic cells has been reduced, CORTICOSTEROIDS and only one or two cytotoxic drugs need be used to maintain the improvement. With the chronic leukaemias, cytotoxic drugs and corticosteroids may also be used. In some cases, blood transfusion may be necessary.

Research into leukaemia is very active. Several new drugs are being tested and many of the latest techniques are available only in leukaemia research centres. For this reason, a patient with any form of leukaemia should obtain advice and treatment from an expert in this field.

Q: Can leukaemia be cured?

A: No cure has yet been found for most forms of leukaemia. A large number of children treated for ALL have survived for over five years without any further symptoms, and may be cured. Most patients (about eighty per cent) can resume normal life for some time before a relapse occurs. The problem is to ensure that every leukaemic cell has been destroyed.

AML is invariably fatal, but the symptoms can be controlled and the patient's life extended, especially the period of useful life. The prognosis for those with the chronic leukaemias is largely dependent upon the age at which the disease occurs; as with AML, the symptoms can be controlled and life extended. Patients with CML are more likely to die as a result of leukaemia than are those with CLL, because CML usually starts at an earlier age.

Leukoderma is the loss of the normal skin pigmentation, resulting in the appearance of pale patches. This may occur temporarily following the treatment of any skin infection, such as DERMATITIS. Leukoderma may also be caused by handling chemicals that remove the pigment from the skin. Less commonly it may be caused by LEPROSY. VITILIGO is a form of leukoderma for which the cause is unknown.

Leukoplakia is a condition in which thickened white patches develop on the tongue and inside the cheeks or other mucous membranes, such as those of the vulva or penis. It is a disorder of the cells of the mucous membrane that may be a prelude to cancer.

Q: What causes leukoplakia of the mouth and how is it treated?

A: Smoking, drinking alcohol, and chronic irritation from damaged teeth or badly fitting dentures are thought to be some of the causes. The causes should be eliminated or treated and small lesions removed by surgery.

Q: How is leukoplakia of the vulva treated?

A: Itching irritation of the vulva may be the symptom that makes a woman consult a doctor. An examination may reveal the white patches of leukoplakia. The area should be examined regularly to see if there are any malignant changes. In the rare cases in which cancer is thought to be developing, parts of the vulva may be surgically removed.

Levodopa (L-dopa) is a drug used in the treatment of PARKINSON'S DISEASE. It is thought to increase the amount of dopamine, a chemical necessary for the normal working of brain tissue which is lacking in this disorder. Initial small doses of levodopa are usually increased to larger doses, which may produce toxic symptoms. These include loss of appetite and nausea with, occasionally, abdominal pain, constipation, and diarrhoea. Lowered blood pressure may cause a feeling of faintness and dizziness, often accompanied by excessive sweating and palpitations. The patient may also show neurological symptoms such as involuntary chewing and twisting movements of the limbs.

Psychiatric problems such as drowsiness, depression, and (sometimes) paranoia and hallucinations, may also arise. Even less commonly, there are problems with passing urine and, in men, sexual problems.

Q: How are the toxic effects of levodopa treated?

A: The toxic effects of levodopa are seldom a major problem if the dosage of the drug is increased slowly. A small temporary reduction in dosage causes the symptoms to disappear.

Q: Are there any conditions in which levodopa should not be used?

A: Yes. Care must be taken with patients who have a psychiatric history or the eye disorder glaucoma, or who are taking certain other drugs, such as MAO inhibitors for depression. Persons with disease of the heart, liver, or kidneys are more likely to develop toxic effects. Levodopa should not be taken by pregnant women.

LGV is an abbreviation of lymphogranuloma venereum, a venereal disease. *See* LYMPHOGRANULOMA VENEREUM.

Libido is a psychological term for the conscious or unconscious sexual drive, the desire of an individual for another person. The form and force of psychosexual libido depends, in part, on cultural conditioning and psychological education. It also depends on biological effects produced by the sex hormones.

Libido may be increased by visual and sensory impulses, and reduced by fear, anxiety, or depression. Sexual drive and desire can be altered by hormonal changes that occur during the menstrual cycle and by hormone disorders, such as HYPOPITUITARISM.

Lice are a group of parasitic insects that live on various animals, including humans. There are three main types of lice that infest human

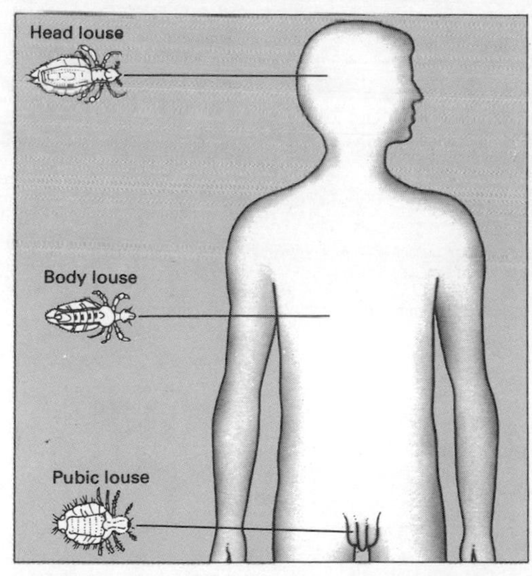

Lice of three main kinds infest the head hair, the body hair, and the pubic hair.

beings: the two varieties of *Pediculus humanus*, which live in the hair or on the body, and the crab louse, *Phthirus pubis*, which lives in the pubic hair. The head louse belongs to the same species as the body louse, but it confines itself to the scalp.

Q: *What symptoms do head lice cause?*

A: Often there are no symptoms, although in severe cases there is itching of the scalp, which can cause secondary infection through scratching with dirty fingernails. Crusting and oozing then occur, similar to that of impetigo.

Head lice are most common among schoolchildren because of the frequency with which they put their heads together during work projects and games. If one child is infected, then all the other children are likely to be infected.

Q: *How is the condition diagnosed and treated?*

A: In severe cases, the lice can be seen. But in most children, the diagnosis is made after finding small, shiny, pearl-coloured eggs (nits) attached to the hairs.

Treatment involves careful washing of the hair with a medicated shampoo, prescribed by a doctor. After washing, the hair should be combed to remove any nits. The procedure should be repeated a week later and, on each occasion, the shampoo should be left to dry on the hair before it is washed off the next morning.

Q: *What symptoms indicate the presence of crab lice?*

A: There is intense itching in the pubic area and possible secondary infection in scratch marks. In severe infestations, the hair in the armpits, eyebrows, and eyelashes may also be involved.

Q: *What is the treatment for crab lice?*

A: The diagnosis is made in the same way as for head lice by finding nits on the hairs or lice on the body. Treatment involves washing the body from the neck downward with a special solution each day for three days, and leaving it to dry. Prolonged treatment may cause dermatitis. The patient's sexual partner should also be treated.

See also RELAPSING FEVER; TYPHUS.

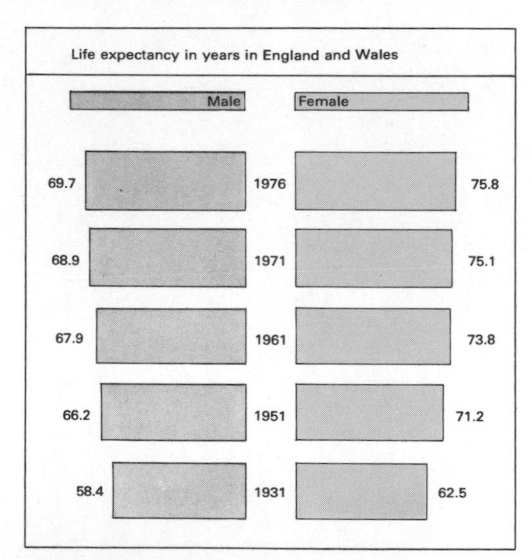

Life expectancy has steadily increased as general health standards have improved.

Lichen planus is a skin inflammation of sudden onset that usually starts at the wrists and spreads to the trunk. The condition may last many weeks or months.

Q: *What are the symptoms of lichen planus?*

A: The skin lesions are small, slightly raised purple or red areas that glisten. They occur on the front surfaces of the forearms, trunk, and shins. In severe cases, the lesions may occur anywhere on the body. The lesions itch and are often surrounded by scratch marks. They may even occur in the mouth, or on the vulva or penis. Occasionally, the nails may be involved, resulting in ridging and splitting.

Sometimes the symptoms subside within three months; the patches lose their shiny colour and become brown and scaly, before disappearing. In some patients, the condition lasts for many years.

Q: *What is the treatment for lichen planus?*

A: As the cause is not known, there is no specific treatment, although usually the lesions can be kept under control with creams or lotions containing corticosteroid drugs.

Life expectancy is the length of time for which, according to statistics, an individual may expect to live. In Britain, the life expectancy of a child born between 1975 and 1980 is estimated to be 73.1 years.

Ligament is a supporting band of fibrous tissue that holds a joint or body organ in place. Ligaments give support and at the same time allow movement.

Ligation is the application of a ligature. *See* LIGATURE.

Ligature is a thread made of catgut, silk, nylon, or steel that is used to tie round and close a blood vessel or any body tube.

See also SUTURE.

Lightening is the sensation of reduced abdominal swelling or distension that usually occurs during pregnancy about two to four weeks before the onset of labour. *See* PREGNANCY AND CHILDBIRTH.

Limping, or lameness. *See* CLAUDICATION.

Lipaemia is the presence in the bloodstream of large amounts of the fatty substances called LIPIDS (which include cholesterol). There is strong evidence that extremely high levels of such substances, the condition called hyperlipaemia or hyperlipidaemia, is a factor in the cause of ARTERIOSCLEROSIS and therefore of coronary heart disease, strokes, and disorders of peripheral arteries.

Q: What causes an increase of the fatty substances in the blood?

A: There is a normal increase in the lipids (particularly triglycerides) after any meal. For this reason, in a medical test the level of lipids is measured after a patient has been fasting for at least eight hours.

Hyperlipaemia detected in this way may be caused by such disorders as HYPOTHYROIDISM, DIABETES MELLITUS, and a rare condition present at birth called XANTHELASMA, in which the body is unable to metabolize cholesterol normally.

More commonly, hyperlipaemia is associated with a combination of factors, such as a mild inherited tendency towards the condition, cigarette smoking, a diet containing excessive amounts of animal fats, lack of physical exercise, and obesity.

Q: What is the treatment for high lipid levels?

A: Treatment of any specific cause found may reduce the level of lipids. But, more usually, treatment is directed at the individual's life-style. A doctor may recommend special drugs and a diet low in animal fats and carbohydrates. The person should stop smoking, reduce weight if obese, and exercise regularly.

Lipid is any one of a group of fats or fatlike substances that occur in the body. Lipids include TRIGLYCERIDES and cholesterol as well as fatty substances that are combined with sugars and phosphates.

Lipids are easily stored in the body, where they are an important part of cell structure and a source of reserve energy.

Lipoma is a benign (noncancerous) tumour that is made up of fat cells. Lipomas commonly occur under the skin and may be felt as diffuse, soft swellings, particularly over the shoulders and trunk. They seldom cause problems, but can be removed surgically.

Lips, the fleshy structures round the mouth, are where the normal skin of the face joins the mucous membrane that lines the mouth.

See also CHEILOSIS; HARE-LIP.

Lisp. *See* SPEECH DEFECTS.

Listlessness is a vague feeling of lack of energy, fatigue, and other symptoms suggestive of mild depression. Listlessness is similar to LETHARGY.

Lithiasis. *See* CALCULUS.

Lithium is a metallic chemical element used medically as lithium carbonate or lithium citrate in treating MANIC-DEPRESSIVE ILLNESS.

Litholapaxy is an operation to remove a stone (calculus) from the bladder without making an incision. First a surgeon makes a cystoscopic examination of the bladder, and then crushes the stone by LITHOTRITY. The fragments are flushed out immediately.

See also CALCULUS; LITHOTOMY.

Lithotomy is an operation to remove a stone (calculus), usually from the bladder or salivary glands, through a surgical incision.

See also CALCULUS; LITHOLAPAXY.

Lithotrity is the use of a special instrument, called a lithotrite, to crush a stone (calculus) in the bladder or urethra.

See also LITHOLAPAXY.

Little's disease is a form of CEREBRAL PALSY in which the legs are particularly affected. It is often accompanied by epilepsy, writhing movements of the limbs (athetosis), and mental retardation.

A talk about the Liver

Liver is the largest and most complex organ in the body. Most of it lies in the right upper side of the abdomen under the diaphragm and ribs, and it extends across to the left side of the body, overlying the upper part of the stomach.

The liver in the average adult weighs about

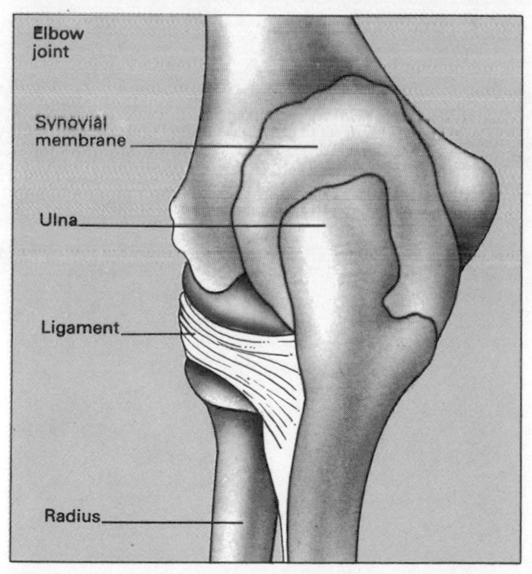

Ligaments bind together the bones at a joint, such as at the elbow.

1.5 kilos (three pounds). It is covered by a rough, fibrous capsule. The gall bladder and its ducts lie beneath the right side of the liver.

The products of digestion are absorbed by capillaries in the intestinal wall and carried in the hepatic portal vein to capillaries within the liver. The liver is composed of up to 100,000 branched and interconnected cells (lobules). Each lobule is surrounded by capillaries from the hepatic portal vein and the hepatic artery. More than a litre (two to three pints) of blood passes through the liver each minute. The blood leaves along the hepatic vein to join the inferior vena cava and pass to the heart.

See also DIGESTIVE SYSTEM; GALL BLADDER.

Q: What is the function of the liver?

A: The cells of the liver process digested food, storing as much of it as is required and converting the remainder into substances the body needs. For example, the sugar glucose is converted into glycogen and stored in the liver until the body needs extra energy.

The liver stores vitamins (except vitamin C) until they are required, and its reserves can last for many months. Iron and several other minerals are also stored in the liver. Liver cells also manufacture PROTEINS and LIPIDS.

Liver cells also recycle various substances, such as haemoglobin, that are needed by the body. In addition, the liver destroys many poisonous substances that may be absorbed into the body and acts as an organ of excretion. BILE salts and bilirubin are formed in the liver and pass into the bile ducts, to be excreted into the duodenum or stored in the gall bladder. Unwanted proteins are destroyed and changed into urea, which is carried in the bloodstream to the kidneys and excreted in the urine.

All these metabolic processes produce a considerable amount of heat that helps to maintain the body's normal temperature.

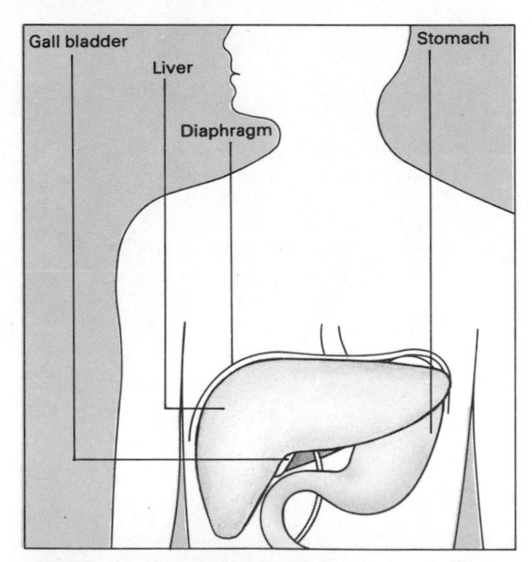

Liver is the largest organ in the body and lies below the diaphragm protected by the rib cage.

Q: What disorders may affect the liver?

A: The liver is a complex organ that can be disrupted by a number of disorders, of which the major causes include infection; poisoning; excessive alcohol; metabolic abnormalities; obstruction; and deficiency diseases. Many disorders do not produce any symptoms until they have reached an advanced stage because the liver has large reserves that can be used if it is damaged.

Infection of the liver may cause it to become swollen, and may produce a dull ache in the upper right part of the abdomen. Usually, however, pain does not occur with liver disorders. Instead, the first symptom of many disorders is JAUNDICE, which occurs when the bile pigment bilirubin accumulates in the blood. This may be caused by an inability of the liver to metabolize bilirubin, or by an obstruction to the flow of bile from the liver to the intestines.

Abdominal swelling, resulting from fluid in the peritoneum (ASCITES), may be caused by obstruction of the hepatic portal vein. Such obstruction may also cause varicose veins to form at the lower end of the oesophagus and burst, causing blood to be vomited (HAEMATEMESIS) and blood in the faeces (MELAENA). The sudden blood loss and influx of protein into the intestines may cause hepatic encephalopathy.

Other causes of this disorder include CIRRHOSIS and acute viral HEPATITIS, which are themselves caused by infection or poisoning. The symptoms include confusion; flapping movements of the hands; and lack of co-ordination (ataxia). The patient may lapse into a coma, which may be fatal.

Cancer of the liver may also occur. Liver tumours are usually malignant and result from the spread of cancer from other parts of the body (metastasis). Occasionally a primary tumour may occur in the liver, called a hepatoma. Hepatomas are usually associated with cirrhosis, caused either by alcoholism or by nutritional deficiency.

See also BUDD-CHIARI SYNDROME; CHOLANGITIS; HAEMOCHROMATOSIS; HYDATID CYST; LEPTOSPIROSIS; MALARIA.

Liver fluke. *See* FLUKES.

Loa loa, or loiasis, is a form of filariasis transmitted by the flies of the genus *Chrysops,* which occur in Central and Western Africa.

Lobectomy is an operation to remove a lobe from any organ, usually of the lung.

Lobotomy is a surgical incision into the rounded, projecting part (lobe) of an organ. The term usually refers to a psycho-surgical operation known in full as a prefrontal lobotomy, in which nerve fibres leading to the frontal lobes of the brain are severed. The operation may be performed in the treatment of severe forms of mental illness, such as schizophrenia and obsessive or compulsive neuroses. But it is done only for the most disabling disorders, and only after all other forms of treatment have failed.

Prefrontal lobotomy may cause adverse and irreversible side effects, such as disturbed reasoning and a blunting of the emotions. The operation is now rare.

Lochia is the vaginal discharge that occurs for three to four weeks after childbirth. During the first few days the discharge is mainly bright red blood that gradually becomes reddish-brown in colour, to brownish-yellow and then to white over the next three weeks. The amount of lochia varies.

Lockjaw. *See* TETANUS.

Locomotor ataxia is a loss of muscular co-ordination caused by advanced syphilis. *See* TABES DORSALIS.

Logorrhoea, also known as logomania, is extremely rapid speech that may be incomprehensible and over which the speaker seems to have little or no control. In a mild form, logorrhoea may occur with anxiety. But, in a more serious form, obsessive talkativeness is a symptom of MANIA and, occasionally, SCHIZOPHRENIA.

Longsightedness (hyperopia, or hypermetropia) is a disorder of vision in which distant objects are seen clearly, but closer objects appear blurred. The blurring occurs because light rays from nearby objects are not focused normally on the retina, either because the refractive power of the eye lens is too strong, or (more commonly) because the eyeball is not long enough from front to back. Longsightedness may be inherited or it may develop after the age of 40 as the lens of the eye becomes less elastic (presbyopia). Corrective SPECTACLES or CONTACT LENSES may be prescribed to restore normal vision.

Lordosis, also known as hollow back or saddle back, is an excessive curvature of the spine with the bend towards the front. The condition affects the lumbar region (between the ribs and the pelvis), and is the opposite in deformity of KYPHOSIS or hunchback.

Q: *What causes lordosis?*

A: Lordosis commonly occurs in obese people with weak back muscles and heavy abdomens. It may also develop in pregnant women. And any hip deformity, such as that caused by osteoarthritis, tends to make the body lean forward, which may produce lordosis.

Q: *How is lordosis treated?*

A: Treatment must be directed toward the cause; this is the only way of encouraging the spine to return to normal shape.

Loss of appetite is known medically as anorexia. It is a common symptom in most illnesses and usually precedes the onset of nausea. The patient's appetite returns when he or she recovers from the illness.

Q: *Are there any more serious causes?*

A: Yes. Loss of appetite in the elderly must always be taken seriously if it continues for more than a week or two.

It is more commonly a symptom that occurs with depression, and may be accompanied by a slight loss of weight. In younger patients, loss of appetite may also be related to psychological factors, and may occur with alcoholism, because of chronic gastritis (inflammation of the stomach).

Females more commonly than males suffer from ANOREXIA NERVOSA, a serious

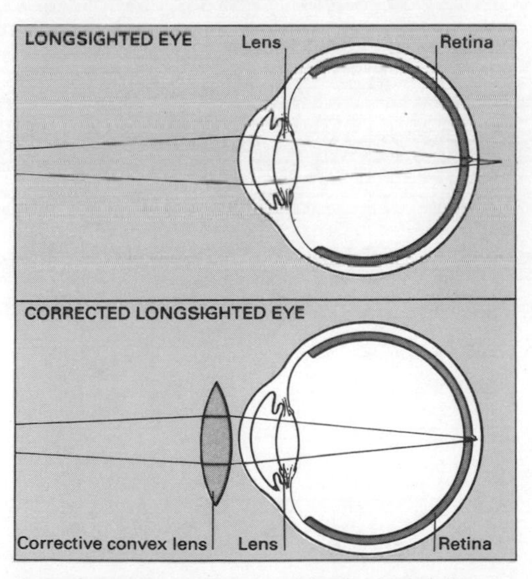

Longsightedness occurs when the lens fails to focus light at one point on the retina.

disorder that may not be detected until weight loss has been considerable.

Q: How is loss of appetite treated?

A: In most cases, the cause is obvious and the treatment is directed toward the main problem; the appetite then improves in due course. But any patient who has lost his or her appetite for more than two weeks should consult a doctor in case there is a more serious underlying cause.

Loss of hearing. *See* DEAFNESS; HEARING DISORDERS.

Loss of memory. *See* AMNESIA.

Loss of sensation. *See* NUMBNESS.

Loss of sight. *See* BLINDNESS.

Loss of weight. Like loss of appetite, loss of weight occurs with many acute or prolonged illnesses and may be one of the obvious signs of the disorder. Continued loss of weight for no obvious reason must always be considered a serious symptom.

Q: What may cause unexplained loss of weight?

A: ANOREXIA NERVOSA may be a cause particularly in young girls and women, but in older people an underlying chronic disorder, such as tuberculosis or cancer, must always be considered. Hyperthyroidism (overactivity of the thyroid gland) increases the body's rate of metabolism and this may cause unexplained loss of weight. Depression and anxiety are also commonly accompanied by weight loss.

Q: How should weight loss be treated?

A: If the cause of weight loss is not obvious and is rapid or continues for more than a month, the individual must consult a doctor. A thorough physical examination, with various tests and X-rays, may have to be carried out to discover if there is any serious cause.

See also WEIGHT PROBLEMS.

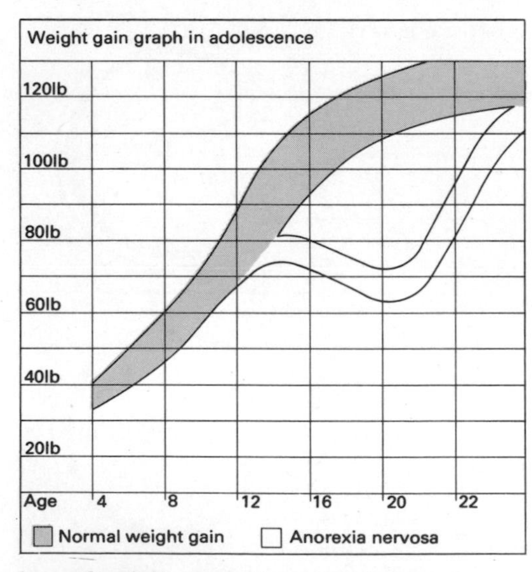

Loss of weight caused by anorexia nervosa and normal weight gain is contrasted.

Louse. *See* LICE.

Low back pain. *See* LUMBAGO.

Low blood pressure (hypotension) is a condition in which the blood pressure is below normal or reduced. Most doctors in the English-speaking world consider low blood pressure to be a symptom of some other disorder. But, in many parts of the world, low blood pressure is itself considered to be a disorder that can cause various symptoms, including depression, lethargy, and fatigue.

This strikingly different attitude is probably the result of different methods of medical training. In a patient recovering from influenza, for example, low blood pressure may accompany the depression and the lower than normal temperature that usually occurs with this disorder. In other words, the symptoms may not be caused by the low blood pressure itself.

Q: What conditions may be accompanied by low blood pressure?

A: Like high blood pressure, slightly low blood pressure may be a particular person's normal pressure. Provided there are no other symptoms and the individual feels well, the low blood pressure can be considered a chance variation from average, probably associated with a prolonged life expectancy. But if low blood pressure occurs in an individual whose blood pressure is normally higher, it may be caused by some recent illness. In this case, it should be only temporary and should improve spontaneously. Some kinds of drugs, particularly antidepressants, may cause low blood pressure.

A more serious possible cause of low blood pressure is peripheral neuritis, in which the autonomic nervous system is affected so that blood accumulates in the veins of the legs because of the absence of the normal nervous response that causes the veins to contract. Disorders such as diabetes mellitus, tabes dorsalis, and Parkinson's disease may result in low blood pressure. Patients who have had a coronary THROMBOSIS or who are in a state of shock also have low blood pressure.

Q: What are the symptoms of low blood pressure?

A: Frequently there are no symptoms and the condition is found at a routine physical examination. The person may feel dizzy and a sudden change in position, such as standing up quickly, may cause fainting. Serious low blood pressure may bring on the symptoms of shock, pallor, and a feeling of coldness.

Q: How is low blood pressure treated?

A: There is a spontaneous improvement in most individuals, although treatment of the cause helps the return to normal. Drug treatment that may cause the low blood pressure should, if possible, be discontinued. Patients with peripheral neuritis are more difficult to treat. An improvement may be made by an increase in blood volume, achieved by additional salt in the diet and, sometimes, with corticosteroid drugs.

Low blood sugar. *See* HYPOGLYCAEMIA.

LSD is an abbreviation of lysergic acid diethylamide. It is a drug that, even in minute doses, produces disturbances of the autonomic nervous system and the brain. It may produce apprehension, hallucinations, and various states of anxiety and depression. Persons who take LSD claim that it may also produce elation and heightened perception.

One possible result of taking LSD is a flashback. This is an episode in which an unpleasantness experienced while on LSD is reproduced when the person has not taken the drug, with all the upsetting symptoms of the original experience. For example, a person on LSD may become frightened in a crowd, and he or she may later feel exactly the same when in a crowd again, even though the drug has not been taken.

LSD is not a truly addictive drug. But experimenting with it can be dangerous, especially for those who are not mentally or emotionally stable, and long term damage may be done. Some LSD takers have developed a persistent psychosis.

LSD has been used medically in psychological research into various forms of mental illness, such as psychotic disorders, as well as in the treatment of chronic alcoholism.

See also DRUG ADDICTION.

Lues is a medical term for SYPHILIS.

A talk about Lumbago

Lumbago is low backache, in the lumbar region of the spine. It is an extremely common symptom and can be caused by various conditions. These may be related directly to the spine, or they may originate elsewhere in the body with pain being referred to the lumbar region.

Q: What spinal conditions may cause lumbago?

A: The ligaments holding the lumbar vertebrae may become strained when the muscles are weakened or the spine has an abnormal curvature. This produces deep pain that is made worse by movement. It may occur with LORDOSIS or SCOLIOSIS caused by poliomyelitis, or be caused by differences in the lengths of the legs. Occasionally, particularly in women, the vertebrae are not formed correctly so that there is partial dislocation of the spine (spondylolisthesis).

Lumbago can result from bone problems that affect the spine, such as ankylosing spondylitis in young men, or osteoporosis, osteoarthritis, or cancer of the vertebrae in the older age groups.

A SLIPPED DISC can cause low back pain. If the disc puts pressure on the sciatic nerve, the condition is made worse by the addition of sciatica, in which there is pain down one or both the legs.

Q: What other conditions may cause lumbago?

A: Lumbago may result from muscular disorders such as fibrositis, or slightly strained or torn muscles. Generalized muscle disorders, such as polymyalgia rheumatica in the elderly, may also cause lumbago.

Kidney disorders can frequently produce backache. Gynaecological disorders such as painful periods (dysmenorrhoea) are often accompanied by dull, persistent lumbago.

Occasionally, shingles is preceded by considerable pain in the lower back

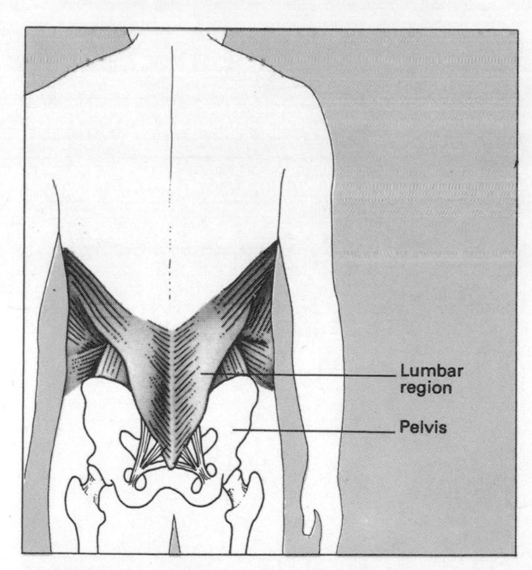

Lumbago is a term used to describe pain in the muscles of the small of the back.

before the typical rash appears.

Lumbago is a common symptom with depression, but all other causes must be eliminated before the backache can be considered to be of psychological origin.

Q: How is lumbago treated?

A: A doctor decides on the appropriate treatment after diagnosing the cause. Diagnosis may require a full physical examination accompanied by appropriate blood tests, spinal X-rays, and, if necessary, a kidney X-ray (IVP).

A firm mattress, heat, and exercises to strengthen the back muscles and, if obesity is producing chronic strain of the spinal ligaments, a weight-reducing diet, all help. Painkilling drugs and those that produce muscle relaxation help to relieve many forms of lumbago; antirheumatic drugs, such as indomethacin, may be prescribed if bones and ligaments are involved. Manipulation may help if lumbago is of sudden onset and caused by spinal problems, and a surgical corset is also sometimes required to give the spine support and limit movement.

If all treatments fail and pain continues, it may be necessary to consider some form of surgical operation to stabilize the spine. This may be the only way to deal with a slipped disc or spondylolisthesis, for example.

If lumbago persists, its psychological aspects must be considered and antidepressive treatment may be needed. It is understandable if patients wish to try some form of unorthodox treatment, such as acupuncture, although it is essential to make sure first that the condition does not require surgery.

See also BACKACHE.

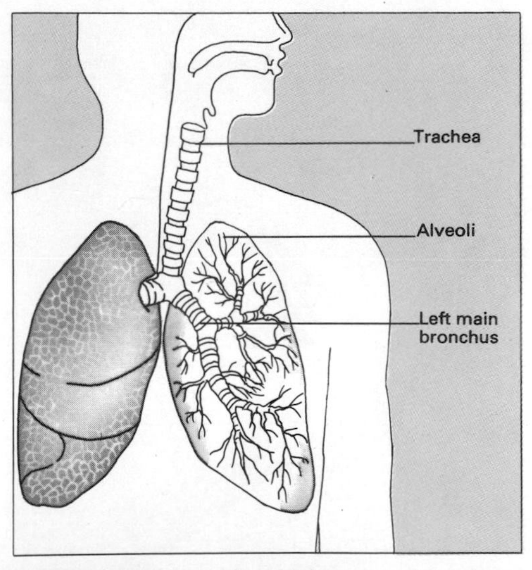

Lungs are the ogans in which oxygen from the air is transferred to the bloodstream.

Lumbar puncture is the insertion of a long needle to extract cerebrospinal fluid from around the nerves below the spinal cord in the lumbar region.

Lump is any abnormal swelling. Most lumps are benign (noncancerous), but some are malignant (cancerous) and for this reason anyone with a persistent unexplained lump should consult a doctor without delay. *See* BUBO; CYST; FIBROMA; GANGLION; HERNIA; LIPOMA; NEUROMA; OSTEOMA; TUMOUR; VON RECKLINGHAUSEN'S DISEASE.

Lumpy jaw is a form of actinomycosis, a chronic fungus infection of the mouth, jaw, face, and neck. *See* ACTINOMYCOSIS.

Lung is the organ concerned with respiration (breathing). There are two lungs, sited within the thorax (chest cavity), a protective cage formed by the ribs and breastbone in front and the spine at the back. Between the lungs lies the heart, major blood vessels, and the oesophagus.

Air enters the body through the nose and mouth and passes into the throat. From there it enters the larynx and then into the trachea (windpipe) which divides into two bronchi, each of which leads to a lung.

Inside the lungs, oxygen in the air breathed in enters the bloodstream. At the same time, carbon dioxide leaves the blood and enters the lungs to be breathed out.

Q: What is the internal structure of the lungs?

A: The right lung, consisting of three lobes, is slightly larger than the left lung which has only two lobes. Each lobe is further divided into segments.

As the two main bronchi enter the lungs they divide into five narrower bronchi, one for each lobe. These bronchi then divide and subdivide into narrower and narrower tubes, called bronchioles. The bronchioles terminate in tiny and extremely thin-walled air sacs called alveoli. The oxygen-carbon dioxide exchange takes place through the moist walls of the alveoli.

The lungs and the inner surface of the thorax are covered by a thin membrane called the pleura. A small amount of lubricating fluid on the pleura allows the lungs and rib-cage to move against each other without friction.

The bronchi and bronchioles are lined with cells that keep them moist. These cells have small hairlike projections that sweep mucus and debris to the trachea, and eventually to the oesophagus.

See also LUNG DISORDERS.

Lung cancer is the presence of a malignant (cancerous) tumour in the lung. The tumour usually forms in a bronchus (one of the tubes that carries air to and from the lungs), although it may grow in the alveoli that form the lung tissue itself. It is a serious disorder, usually not detected until the disease has already spread and it is too late for effective treatment. Most people who contract lung cancer are heavy cigarette smokers. Compared with a nonsmoker, a heavy smoker (more than twenty cigarettes a day) a 20 times greater chance of developing lung cancer. Regular chest X-rays may increase the chance of early detection.

Q: What are the symptoms of lung cancer?

A: Cancer of the bronchus does not always produce symptoms until it has been present for some time. The first symptom is usually a cough, with only a little sputum which may be blood-stained (haemoptysis). This may be followed by pneumonia or collapse of a segment of the lung (atelectasis) caused by partial blockage of the bronchus. The later symptoms include weight loss and increasing weakness and lethargy. Breathlessness is a feature and is usually caused more by general weakness than by damage to the lung tissue.

Q: How is lung cancer diagnosed and treated?

A: The diagnosis may be made by chest X-ray as well as by the detection of cancer cells in the sputum. It can be confirmed by means of bronchoscopy, which enables a surgeon to determine the exact position of the tumour. Unfortunately, treatments for lung cancer are not likely to be successful. The average survival time for an untreated patient is less than a year, and even with treatment only ten per cent survive for five years.

Fewer than a quarter of patients have a tumour that can be treated with surgery (either lobectomy or pneumonectomy). The usual alternative treatments are radiotherapy and the use of cytotoxic drugs, although such drugs are seldom effective.

Q: How can lung cancer be avoided?

A: Because of the association between cigarette smoking and lung cancer, the best way to avoid the disease is not to smoke. If smoking is stopped, the chance of developing lung cancer drops at a steady rate.

See also CANCER.

Lung disorders. The lungs have great reserves of capacity for air. Disorders of slow onset may therefore not cause symptoms until they have progressed for some time and caused considerable damage.

Disorders of the lung include those affecting: (1) the trachea and bronchi (the tubes that carry air in and out of the lungs); (2) the bronchioles (the narrower tubes within the lungs); (3) the lung fabric itself, where the exchange of oxygen and carbon dioxide takes place between the air and blood; and (4) the surrounding pleura and ribcage (thorax). Each of the disorders listed has a separate article in the A-Z section of this book.

Area affected	Possible disorder
Trachea and bronchi	ABSCESS of the lung BRONCHIECTASIS (scarring of bronchi preventing proper drainage of mucus) BRONCHITIS (inflammation of the bronchi) CANCER of the bronchus TRACHEITIS (inflammation of the windpipe)
Bronchioles	ASTHMA CYSTIC FIBROSIS (formation of abnormally sticky mucus)
Lung fabric	ACTINOMYCOSIS (fungal infection of the lung) ATELACTASIS (complete or partial collapse of the lung) EMBOLISM (blockage of an artery)

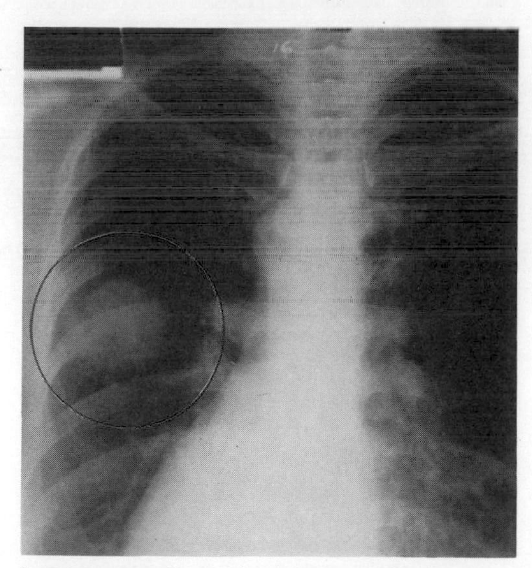

Lung cancer: the malignant growth can be seen on the left of the X-ray photograph.

Lung function tests

Area affected	Possible disorder
Lung fabric	EMPHYSEMA (destruction and enlargement of lung's air sacs)
	LUNG CANCER
	PNEUMOCONIOSIS (from inhaled dust)
	PARAGONIMIASIS (flukes)
	PNEUMONIA
	TUBERCULOSIS
Pleura and thorax	EMPYEMA (pus in the pleural cavity)
	HAEMOTHORAX (blood in the pleural cavity)
	LUNG CANCER
	PLEURISY (infection of the pleura)
	Epidemic PLEURODYNIA (Bornholm disease, a virus disorder)
	PNEUMOTHORAX (air in the pleural cavity)
	TIETZE'S SYNDROME (inflammation of the cartilage)
	TUBERCULOSIS

Lung function tests (pulmonary function tests) assess the condition and functioning of the lungs. They may be used as part of an investigation into a respiratory disorder. The various tests help a doctor to diagnose a condition and determine its severity; they may also establish whether a particular treatment is effective. Some lung function tests can be performed using simple equipment, such as a spirometer and a peak flow meter. Other tests, such as the analysis of gases in exhaled air and the measurement of oxygen and carbon dioxide levels in the blood, require sophisticated equipment and a detailed analysis of the results.

Lung function test is carried out on a piece of apparatus called a respirometer.

Lung machine. *See* HEART-LUNG MACHINE.

Lupus erythematosus (LE), one of a group of disorders known as the collagen diseases, takes two distinct but unrelated forms: discoid or cutaneous lupus erythematosus (DLE) and systemic lupus erythematosus (SLE). Both conditions affect the skin; SLE is probably an autoimmune disease.

Collagen is a fibrous insoluble protein in connective tissue. Both DLE and SLE affect the connective tissue, but are of unknown cause or causes. It is often difficult to distinguish between the two conditions; much confusion has arisen because the skin lesions are the same in both diseases. But other features are completely distinctive.

Q: What are the symptoms of DLE?

A: DLE is a chronic skin disorder that occurs most commonly in middle-aged women. It produces thickened, slightly scaly, reddened patches on the face, cheeks, and forehead. The characteristic is known as "butterfly rash." The patches sometimes spread to the scalp and cause hair loss. Sunlight makes the condition worse, so in some patients it virtually disappears during the winter months. Nearly all patients with DLE remain in good health apart from the skin disorder. It is exceptionally rare for patients with DLE to develop SLE.

Q: How is chronic DLE treated?

A: Patients with DLE should wear hats and sunlight barrier creams to protect their skins. Also, the use of corticosteroid skin creams may be helpful. Ultimately, some of the lesions heal on their own.

In severe cases, chloroquine (a drug used to treat malaria) may be beneficial. But, because chloroquine sometimes has an effect on the eyes, it should be used with great caution.

Q: What are the symptoms of SLE?

A: The patient may have a similar kind of butterfly rash as in DLE. There may also be fever, arthritis and signs of problems with lung and heart function.

Unlike DLE, SLE, also known as disseminated lupus erythematosus, is a generalized condition that may affect not only the face, but many tissues of the body, especially the kidney.

Q: How is SLE diagnosed and treated?

A: A knowledge of the patient's history combined with discovery of abnormalities in blood tests will help diagnosis. Treatment with corticosteroids may help.

Luxation. *See* DISLOCATION.

Lymph is the clear fluid that is drained from around the body's cells into the lymphatic system. It carries away bacteria and waste products.

See LYMPHATIC SYSTEM.

Lymphadenitis is inflammation of a lymph node, which causes it to swell. It is a normal reaction to any nearby infection. For example, any infection of the upper respiratory tract is accompanied by swelling of the tonsillar glands and other glands in the neck.

Lymphadenoma is a malignant (cancerous) tumour that affects the lymph nodes. *See* HODGKIN'S DISEASE.

Lymphangitis is inflammation of the lymphatic vessels. It occurs, to a certain extent, with LYMPHADENITIS. It may also develop in serious infections of the skin, for example in a septic wound, when red lines can be seen in the skin running from the wound to the nearest lymph nodes. This is a serious sign and requires urgent medical treatment.

Lymphatic leukaemia. *See* LEUKAEMIA.

Lymphatic system is a network of thin-walled vessels found throughout the body which drains fluid (lymph) from between the body cells into the bloodstream. The lymph vessels contain small valves, similar to those in veins, which prevent the backflow of lymph.

Rounded bean-shaped structures called lymph glands are situated at frequent intervals along the lymph vessels.

Most of the lymph vessels eventually converge to form the thoracic duct, a major lymph vessel that runs alongside the descending aorta. It connects to one of the main branches of the superior vena cava, a main vein carrying blood to the heart.

Lymphatic vessels are important to the mechanism by which fats are processed by the body. Vessels draining the small intestine collect the digested fat and pass it directly into the main blood circulation so that it bypasses the liver.

See also LYMPH GLAND.

Lymph gland, or node, is a small bean-shaped structure that forms part of the LYMPHATIC SYSTEM. Lymph glands are found throughout the body, particularly in places where lymph vessels unite.

The lymph glands have three main functions: (1) to filter out and destroy foreign substances such as bacteria and dust; (2) to produce some of the white blood cells called lymphocytes; and (3) to produce antibodies to help in the body's IMMUNITY system.

Specialized lymphoid tissue, similar to lymph glands, includes the tonsils, adenoids, and areas of the body such as the Peyer's patches in the wall of the small intestine.

Lymphocyte is one of the two main types of WHITE BLOOD CELLS. Lymphocytes are made in the lymph nodes, bone marrow, and thymus gland. They are concerned with the formation of antibodies and IMMUNITY.

See also LEUKAEMIA.

Lymphogranuloma venereum (LGV) is a venereal disease caused by bacteria related to those that cause psittacosis and trachoma. Symptoms include enlargement of the lymph nodes in the groin and the appearance of small ulcers on the surrounding skin.

Lymphoma is any form of growth connected with lymphoid tissue. A growth of this kind occurs, for example, with HODGKIN'S DISEASE.

See also LYMPHOSARCOMA.

Lymphosarcoma is a kind of malignant (cancerous) LYMPHOMA. Its symptoms are very similar to those of lymphatic LEUKAEMIA.

Lysol is an antiseptic solution of cresols and soap used as a general disinfectant. Lysol cannot be used to disinfect wounds because it is damaging to the skin.

M

Macula is the medical term for either a flat blemish or spot on the skin, or the part of the retina of the eye containing the FOVEA, on which light is focused.

Madura foot is a chronic fungus infection that occurs most commonly when fungi spores enter a wound in the foot.

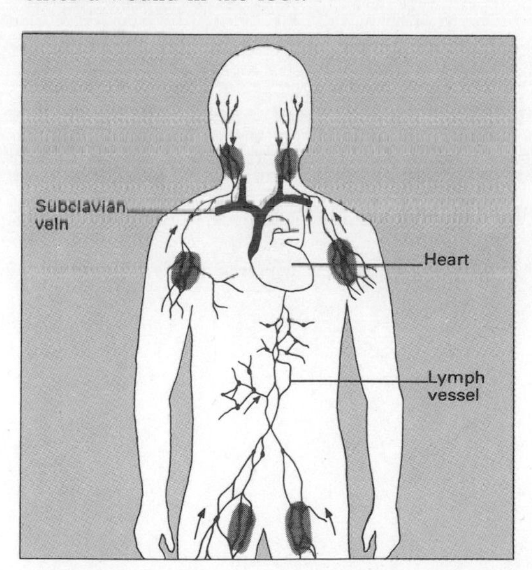

Lymphatic system drains fluid from around body cells back into the circulation.

Magnesia, Milk of, is a suspension of magnesium hydroxide in water. It is used as a mild LAXATIVE or to treat indigestion.

Magnesium sulphate, commonly known as Epsom salts, is generally used as a LAXATIVE.

Magnesium trisilicate is a chemical compound of magnesium oxide, silicon dioxide, and water. It is used as an antacid in various preparations for treating indigestion.

Maidenhead. *See* HYMEN.

Malaria is a serious disease caused by a PROTOZOA called plasmodium. The disease is transmitted by the anopheles mosquito. The female mosquito bites an infected human and sucks the blood into its stomach, where the protozoa develop; when the mosquito next bites a human, these protozoa are injected into the bloodstream and reach the liver. Finally, they are released back into the blood to infect the red blood corpuscles; when these burst, further red blood corpuscles are infected and a recurring cycle of symptoms is started. The most severe form of malaria is called malignant tertian malaria (because the symptoms recur every three days) and is frequently fatal. It is caused by the parasite *Plasmodium falciparum.* The other three, milder forms are caused by *P. vivax*, *P. ovale*, and *P. malariae.*

Q: What are the symptoms of malaria?

A: After an incubation period of two to five weeks, there is a sudden attack of shivering followed by a high fever of at least 40°C (104°F). This is often accompanied by confusion, headache, and vomiting that lasts for several hours. These symptoms may occur at intervals of two to three days, depending on the type of malaria, and, if the disease is not treated, they will recur at irregular intervals throughout the person's life.

Q: How is malaria diagnosed and treated?

A: The diagnosis is made by examination of a blood sample, which reveals the presence of malarial parasites.

Initial treatment with the drug CHLOROQUINE may have to be supplemented by using QUININE or other drugs.

Q: What measures can be taken to prevent malaria?

A: Any person travelling to a malaria-infected area must take antimalarial drugs, usually chloroquine or primoquine, every week, throughout the stay and for one month after returning to a nonmalarious area.

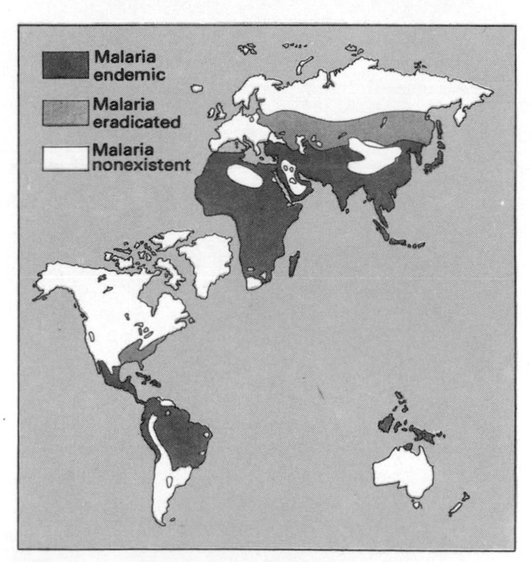

Malaria still persists in areas of uncleared swampland where the carrier mosquitos breed.

Malignant describes any condition or disorder that has a tendency to become worse.

See also BENIGN.

Malnutrition describes the physical deterioration of the body caused by following a diet that is deficient in nutrients, or by disorders in which the body fails to absorb nutrients.

See also ANOREXIA NERVOSA; KWASHIORKOR; NUTRITIONAL DISORDERS; SPRUE.

Malocclusion is the failure of the teeth of the upper and lower jaws to meet correctly. It may cause problems with biting and chewing, but can usually be corrected with a brace on the teeth and proper orthodontic care.

See also DENTAL DISORDERS; ORTHODONTICS.

Malpresentation describes an abnormal position of a foetus in the womb, possibly making natural delivery difficult. *See* PRESENTATION; PREGNANCY AND CHILDBIRTH.

Malta fever. *See* BRUCELLOSIS.

Mammogram is a specialized X-ray examination of breast tissue that is performed to investigate unidentified lumps in the breast.

See also THERMOGRAM.

Mammoplasty is an operation to change the size and shape of the breasts. In reduction mammoplasty, the breasts are made smaller by removing some tissue. To increase the size of the breasts, an inert fluid-filled bag is implanted behind each breast.

Mandible is the lower jawbone. *See* JAW.

Mania is a form of mental disorder characterized by emotional excitement and lack of self-control, often resulting in rapid, irregular speech, overactivity, and violent behaviour.

Mania is also an uncontrollable desire to do something: for example, dipsomania is an abnormal and excessive desire to drink alcohol.

See also DEPRESSION; MANIC-DEPRESSIVE ILLNESS.

Manic-depressive illness is a form of mental

disorder that affects at least one per cent of the population. The first attack most commonly occurs in early middle-age, and it is more likely to occur in women than in men.

There are apparently two forms of this disorder: (1) the type in which depression is the only form of illness – periods of normal mood and behaviour are followed by a prolonged downswing of depression; and (2) the less common form in which mania alternates with depression.

Q: How is manic-depressive illness treated?

A: Hospitalization, with drug treatment and, sometimes, electroconvulsive therapy (ECT), is needed for severe cases.

The controlled use of lithium often prevents recurrences of mania. If it is combined with an antidepressant drug, given on maintenance therapy, it helps to lessen the mood swings of manic-depressive illness.

See also DEPRESSION; MANIA.

Mantoux test is a method of determining whether a person has at some time been infected by tuberculosis. A positive reaction generally indicates that the person has acquired partial immunity to the disease. A negative reaction indicates lack of immunity.

See also HEAF TEST; TINE TEST.

MAO inhibitors (monoamine oxidase inhibitors) are a group of drugs that are used in the treatment of DEPRESSION, particularly if other antidepressant drugs have not been effective.

Q: What adverse reactions can occur with the use of MAO inhibitors?

A: These drugs make the body destroy adrenaline, noradrenaline, and similar substances at a slower rate than usual. In a patient taking an MAO inhibitor, any drug or food that contains adrenaline-like substances or that stimulates the body to form adrenaline may cause a sudden and dramatic rise in blood pressure. This results in a severe headache and the danger of rupturing a blood vessel which, in turn, could lead to a stroke. For this reason, a psychiatrist may be wary of prescribing such drugs to a patient with a history of stroke, high blood pressure, or heart or liver disease.

Apart from these serious side effects, MAO inhibitors cause few of the other side effects that are associated with other antidepressant drugs.

Q: What precautions should be taken by patients taking MAO inhibitors?

A: Patients must obtain from the prescribing doctor a list of foods that must be avoided while taking MAO inhibitor drugs and for at least two weeks afterwards. These foods contain substances that may form adrenaline-like factors; they include cheese, broad beans or their pods, protein and yeast extracts, and alcohol.

Patients taking MAO inhibitor drugs are advised not to take any additional drugs without consulting their doctor.

Marburg disease is a rapidly fatal form of virus ENCEPHALITIS that was first imported from Africa to research laboratories at Marburg, West Germany. The disease cannot be cured. Treatment involves complete isolation to prevent the spread of infection, and injections of GAMMA GLOBULIN prepared from a patient who has recently recovered from the disease.

Marijuana is a drug made from the dried leaves or flowers of the cannabis plant. It is usually smoked in cigarettes and is regarded as only mildly addictive. Other names for marijuana include cannabis, Indian hemp, kif, bhang, and dagga. The possession or use of marijuana is illegal in most Western countries.

Q: What are the effects of taking marijuana?

A: Mild drowsiness is often accompanied by an increased awareness of colour, sounds, and taste, which fluctuates in accordance with complex mood changes.

Many people who smoke marijuana tend to become listless and may have difficulty in concentrating. Physical inertia is commonly accompanied by loss of appetite, loss of weight, and a general lack of care about physical appearance.

Q: Is there any harm in smoking marijuana?

A: When marijuana is smoked occasionally by an otherwise well-adjusted individual there appears to be little harm.

Continued frequent use of marijuana, however, produces physical changes, and, sometimes, a true state of addiction. Physical changes include loss of weight, loss of sex drive, and a reduced sperm count in men.

Q: Can the use of marijuana lead to other, more serious forms of drug abuse?

A: It is unlikely that marijuana leads to dependence on any other drug. But the social situation in which illegal drugs are used means that marijuana smokers can be in association with persons who use "hard" drugs such as heroin and cocaine. This creates the opportunity to experiment with the other drugs.

See also DRUG ADDICTION.

Marrow is the soft, central part of bone. There are two types of marrow: (1) red marrow and (2) yellow marrow. *See* BONES.

Masochism is a psychiatric term for a feeling of sexual satisfaction derived from being hurt. It is named for the Austrian novelist von Sacher-Masoch. It is manifested in many minor ways, for example, lovers' bites. But in its severer forms, such as whipping, it can cause physical harm and suffering. A doctor may recommend psychiatric counselling.

See also SADISM.

Massage is a therapeutic treatment in which the muscles are rubbed and manipulated for the relief of local pain and for relaxation. It is often used to remove excess fluid and to break up small adhesions under the skin.

Mastectomy is an operation to remove a breast. A partial mastectomy is the removal of one section of the breast, simple mastectomy is the removal of the whole breast, and radical mastectomy is the removal of the breast as well as some of the underlying muscle and the lymph glands in the armpit.

Q: Why is a mastectomy performed?

A: The operation is performed to remove breast tumours. Simple and radical mastectomies are performed as treatments for breast cancer, where the tumour is malignant and there is a danger of cancerous cells invading other parts of the body.

Q: Is any further treatment given for breast cancer?

A: Yes, sometimes, but this depends on the type and stage of the cancer. If the cancer is localized in the breast tissue, further treatment may not be required. Radiotherapy and chemotherapy are often used in conjunction with the operation.

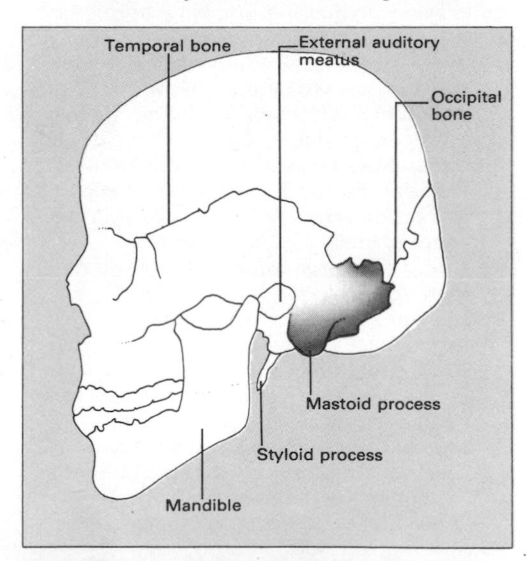

Mastoid is a projecting bone on the skull that is located behind the ear lobe.

Q: What problems may occur after a mastectomy?

A: As fluid may gather under the wound, drainage tubes are normally left in place for a few days. Apart from the physical discomfort associated with the operation, a woman who has had a breast removed also has to face major psychological problems. Discussion with a doctor may help to relieve anxiety but, frequently, a talk with another woman who has had the same operation is most helpful. She knows and understands the underlying fears and anxieties that are likely to arise. The woman will learn to insert an artificial breast (prosthesis) in her brassiere. Her husband is often also given counselling to help to restore her confidence.

Mastitis is inflammation of the breast. It may be acute (occurring suddenly) or chronic (long-lasting).

Q: What causes acute mastitis?

A: Acute mastitis is caused by an infection, which occurs most commonly during lactation after childbirth when the breast is swollen with milk. Infection usually enters through a cracked nipple.

Q: How is acute mastitis treated?

A: If possible, breast-feeding should be continued, because this keeps the breast ducts clear. Firm bandaging of the breast and a reduction in the amount of fluid consumed help to reduce any excessive swelling (engorgement). A doctor may prescribe antibiotic drugs and painkillers until the infection is under control.

Occasionally, these treatments fail and an abscess starts to form. In such cases, breast-feeding must be stopped and the abscess incised and drained.

Q: What is chronic mastitis?

A: It is not an infection. It is caused by hormones in the body that affect the breast tissues so that they become swollen and tender. It is quite common just before a menstrual period and, in women who generally suffer from premenstrual tension, it can last from several days to two weeks. Chronic mastitis frequently occurs in women who are approaching menopause. This form of the disorder ceases after menopause is complete.

Q: How is chronic mastitis treated?

A: A firm, well-fitting brassiere may be all that is necessary. If the discomfort persists, fluid-removing (diuretic) pills are frequently helpful. The regular use of hormones is sometimes necessary.

Mastoid is a part of the temporal bone that is located behind the ear. The mastoid is filled with air cells arranged like a honeycomb that communicate with the middle ear. *See* MASTOIDITIS.

Mastoiditis is an infection of the mastoid bone behind the ear. It is usually caused by the spread of an infection from the middle ear, which occurs if a middle ear infection is inadequately treated. The symptoms include fever, a throbbing earache, a discharging ear, and deafness. In some patients the bone behind the ear may be painful.

Early treatment with antibiotic drugs cures most patients, and is essential to prevent damage to the mastoid bone. If bone damage has occurred, or if the infection does not respond to antibiotics, part of the mastoid bone may be surgically removed (MASTOIDECTOMY) to prevent deafness.

Masturbation is the stimulation of one's own genitals to produce an ORGASM.

Q: Why do people masturbate?

A: Masturbation is a normal activity when it reduces sexual tension if, for cultural or social reasons, sexual intercourse is not possible. It is usually practised for the first time in early puberty, boys tending to start at an earlier age than girls. Full sexual maturity and regular sexual intercourse reduces the need for, and the frequency of, masturbation. Masturbation continues, however, as a common outlet for sexual relief, particularly during times of marital stress or illness, following the break-up of a marriage, and in people who have never had sexual intercourse.

Q: Is masturbation harmful?

A: Blindness, mental illness, and impotence are still sometimes believed to be the consequences of masturbation: there is absolutely no evidence to support these theories. The anxiety and feeling of guilt, aroused because the person feels that he or she is doing something wrong, are much greater problems.

Maxilla is the upper jawbone. *See* JAW.

Measles, also known as rubeola morbilli, is a highly contagious virus disease that causes fever and a characteristic rash. It occurs most commonly before adolescence and one attack usually confers immunity for life. The incubation period varies between eight and fourteen days. Measles is contagious during a period that lasts from four days before until five days after the rash appears. The quarantine period is fourteen days from the date of last contact with measles.

Q: What are the symptoms of measles?

A: The initial symptoms include fever, which may reach 40°C (104°F); a sore throat; coughing; and a running nose. These symptoms usually last for about four days. About two days before the rash breaks out, small white spots (Koplik's spots) may appear inside the mouth and eyelids. These usually fade when the rash appears. The characteristic rash of measles is blotchy and orange-red in colour. It usually appears first behind the ears, then spreads to the face and neck. About twenty-four hours after its first appearance, the rash has usually covered the whole body. During the next three or four days, the rash and fever gradually disappear, although the cough may persist for an additional ten to fourteen days.

Q: How is measles treated?

A: There is no cure for measles. Treatment is directed at reducing the fever, and preventing the development of complications such as otitis media, sinusitis, bronchitis, and, rarely, encephalitis.

Q: Can measles be prevented?

A: Yes. A vaccine of a mild form of the measles virus will protect 97 per cent of children against the disease. They should be vaccinated no earlier than twelve months but no later than fifteen months.

Meckel's diverticulum is a small pouch near the end of the ileum. It is the remains of a branch of the gut that extended into the umbilical cord in the foetus. It is present in about two per cent of the population.

See also DIVERTICULUM.

Meconium is the greenish brown, thick faeces that a baby passes in the first few days after birth. It consists mainly of the cell debris and bile that a baby swallows in the womb.

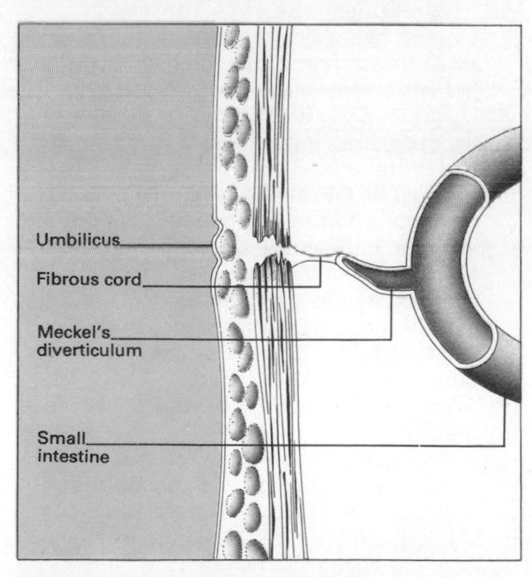

Meckel's diverticulum is a pouch in the wall of the intestine that may become inflamed.

Medical insurance

Medical insurance. The two main benefits provided by medical insurance are (1) the payment of an income when the insurer's normal income is lost because of illness, and (2) the payment of medical fees and other expenses incurred by the insurer.

Q: What forms of state medical insurance benefits may be obtained?

A: In the U.K., the weekly National Insurance contributions that are paid partly by employers and partly by employees entitle all employed people to sickness benefit. This benefit does not cover the cost of prescription charges, unless the individual concerned has a certificate of exemption or is included in one of the categories of people who are automatically exempt from prescription charges. These categories include children, the elderly, and those with low incomes.

The system of medical certification for illness was changed in 1983: a person who is unwell now fills in a form supplied by the employer for self-certification of sickness. This is valid for a week, after which a doctor's certificate is required. Patients thus do not need a doctor's certificate for really minor illnesses. The employer continues to pay the employee at the usual rate, and reclaims the sickness benefit through standard procedures from the Department of Health and Social Security. The system is easier for everyone.

Q: Can this sickness benefit be obtained indefinitely?

A: In exceptional cases, yes. However, anyone who claims sickness benefit for more than a few weeks will have his or her case reviewed by a medical board (appointed by the Ministry for Social Security), and it may be necessary for the patient to appear before this board. The hospital or GP will be asked to supply a detailed report on the patient's condition.

Those in financial difficulty may apply for Supplementary Benefit on a form supplied by the Social Security office. In certain cases, a Disablement Allowance will be paid for those who are permanently incapacitated.

Q: What forms of medical insurance exist in industry?

A: All companies have some form of accident insurance in case an employee is injured while at work or at the place of work. In addition to this compulsory accident insurance, certain trade unions provide their members with private sickness benefit and can arrange for their members to be treated at a trade union hospital.

Many companies offer their executives private medical insurance as one of the benefits of employment. Certain trade unions now offer similar benefits to their members.

Q: How do private medical insurance schemes work?

A: The largest private medical insurance companies are the British United Provident Association (BUPA) and the Private Patients' Plan (PPP). The Western Provident Association (WPA) and Lloyd's of London also operate medical insurance schemes. There are slight differences between all of these schemes.

Generally, the benefit obtained depends on the premium, the amount of money that is paid into the scheme each year. At the highest premium rate all medical expenses in the most expensive hospitals are covered, but the benefit for consultations and medical tests outside hospitals is usually less than the fees that are charged.

Individual premiums are usually lower if insurance is obtained through a company scheme.

Q: What points should be considered when choosing private medical insurance?

A: Most medical insurance schemes are complicated, and it is often wise to discuss the matter with a friend who has experience of one or other of the schemes. It is important to read the details of each scheme carefully, and to understand exactly which medical expenses the insurance covers.

Many of the available insurance schemes provide comprehensive cover for in-patient hospital treatment, but will only pay a proportion of the fees for any out-patient consultations and treatment. Also, not all the schemes provide cover for medical tests and investigations that are carried out outside a hospital.

Very few insurance schemes provide cover for fees charged for private treatment by GPs, although specialists' fees are usually covered.

All private medical insurance schemes stipulate a maximum amount of benefit that a patient can claim in any one year. For expenses above this amount, which may be incurred by a long-lasting serious illness, the patient is not insured.

Even under the most comprehensive and expensive schemes there are always certain expenses, such as drugs obtained outside a hospital, that are not covered.

Q: Is it advisable to obtain medical insurance when travelling abroad?

A: Yes. Although there are reciprocal arrangements for health care between most European countries, the procedure for obtaining treatment is often difficult. It is sometimes necessary to pay the full cost of treatment, and claim a reimbursement later.

Private medical insurance schemes generally provide cover for medical expenses incurred abroad up to certain limits, but people travelling to North America, or to non-European countries that do not have special health agreements with the U.K., should obtain additional insurance.

Medical social worker, formerly an almoner, is a trained member of a hospital staff who is concerned with the social welfare of patients. The duties of a medical social worker include helping with the claiming of any relevant Social Security benefits, and ensuring that adequate arrangements are made for the patient's convalescence at home, when the services of a health visitor, district nurse, or home help may be required.

Medical tests are physical examinations that ascertain the state of a person's general physical health or confirm a provisional diagnosis. The following is a list of medical tests, each of which has a separate entry in the A-Z section of this book.

AMNIOCENTESIS
ANGIOGRAM
AORTOGRAM
ARTERIOGRAM
AUDIOGRAM
BARIUM
BASAL METABOLIC RATE
BIOPSY
BLOOD PRESSURE
BODY TEMPERATURE
BRONCHOGRAM
CAT SCANNER
CERVICAL SMEAR
CHOLANGIOGRAM
CYSTOGRAM
CYSTOSCOPY
ECHOCARDIOGRAM
ECHOGRAM
ELECTROCARDIOGRAM (ECG)
ELECTROENCEPHALOGRAM (EEG)
ELECTROMYOGRAM (EMG)
ENDOSCOPY
GASTROSCOPY
GENETIC COUNSELLING
GLUCOSE TOLERANCE TEST
HEAF TEST
INTELLIGENCE QUOTIENT (IQ)
INTRAVENOUS PYELOGRAM (IVP)
ISHIHARA'S TEST
KAHN TEST
LARYNGOSCOPY
LUNG FUNCTION TESTS
MAMMOGRAM
MANTOUX TEST
MYELOGRAM
ORAL CHOLECYSTOGRAM
PALPATION (breast examination)
PHONOCARDIOGRAM
QUICK'S TEST
RINNE'S TEST
SCHICK TEST
SEDIMENTATION RATE (ESR)
SPINAL TAP
TINE TEST
TSH TEST
TUBERCULIN TEST
ULTRASOUND TECHNIQUES
URINALYSIS
VENOGRAM
WASSERMANN TEST
WIDAL'S TEST

Mediterranean anaemia. *See* THALASSAEMIA.

Mediterranean fever is a type of intermittent fever that is usually caused by brucellosis. *See* BRUCELLOSIS.

Medulla is the inner part of a structure in the body, in contrast to the outer part (which is called the cortex).

Megacolon is an extremely enlarged colon that usually results from HIRSCHSPRUNG'S DISEASE, which is a congenital abnormality of the large intestine. Rarely, a megacolon may be caused by chronic constipation or by damage to the intestinal wall, as may occur with ULCERATIVE COLITIS and DIVERTICULITIS.

Megaloblast is a large, immature type of cell that is found in the bone marrow. It forms abnormal red blood cells, particularly those associated with PERNICIOUS ANAEMIA.

Megalomania is an unrealistic and unshakable belief that one is of great importance, usually associated with the conviction that others do not recognize this importance. It is also known as delusion of grandeur. *See* MANIA.

Meibomian cyst. *See* CHALAZION.

Melaena are faeces that are black and tar-like. The condition is caused by the action of intestinal enzymes on blood, which may come from bleeding anywhere in the intestine.

Melancholia. *See* DEPRESSION.

Melanin is the dark pigment that is found in the skin, hair, and the CHOROID of the eye.

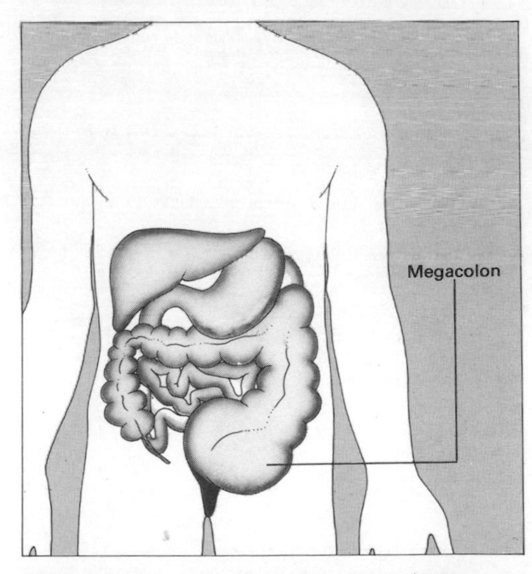

Megacolon usually affects the whole of the large intestine above the part without nerves.

See also CHLOASMA; MELANOMA; MELANURIA; MELASMA.

Melanoma is a dark, pigmented lesion. A cancerous pigmented tumour is called a malignant melanoma. Most malignant melanomas arise from pigment cells in normal skin; a few may develop from pigmented moles. They are extremely rare in children. People who have been exposed to strong sunlight throughout their lives are more likely to develop malignant melanomas than those who have not. Pigmented growths on the legs, particularly in women; under the nails; on the palms of the hands and soles of the feet; or on the mucous membranes inside the mouth are particularly likely to become malignant. Malignant melanomas may also occur in the pigmented choroid layer of the eyeball.

Q: What are the symptoms of a malignant melanoma?

A: Most melanomas do not produce any definite symptoms, especially when they are in the early stages of development. For this reason a doctor should be consulted when any naevus, whether pigmented or not, forms a scab; bleeds; becomes surrounded by an inflamed area; becomes larger; or changes colour.

Q: How is a malignant melanoma treated?

A: It is usually necessary for the malignant melanoma to be removed surgically. If it has spread, it may also be necessary to remove any lymph glands affected.

Chemotherapy may be used if a malignant melanoma is situated on a limb. CYTOTOXIC DRUGS are usually injected into an artery to give a high concentration of the drug in the affected area. By the time the drug has reached the rest of the body, it has been greatly diluted; this method keeps any adverse effects to a minimum.

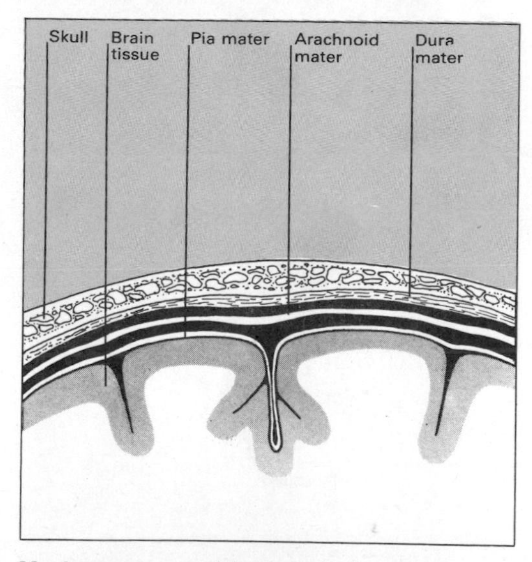

Meninges surround the brain in three layers: pia mater; arachnoid mater; and dura mater.

Melanuria is abnormally dark urine. It is found in cases of jaundice; haemoglobin in the urine (haemoglobinuria); certain malignant melanomas; and some rare congenital metabolic disorders, such as porphyria.

Melasma is pigmentation of the skin in which brown patches occur on the forehead and cheeks. It affects some women who take contraceptive pills or who are pregnant. In such women the condition is called chloasma. Melasma is increased by sunlight. The skin patches fade naturally when the woman stops taking the pills or after childbirth.

Membrane is a thin tissue layer that covers the surface of an organ, lines the inside of a tube or cavity, or separates one organ from another.

Memory, loss of. *See* AMNESIA.

Menarche is the onset of menstruation at puberty. *See* MENSTRUATION.

Menière's disease is a disorder of the inner ear arising from changes in the pressure of fluid within the ear's semicircular canals. It is commonest in those over the age of forty, and in 25 per cent of patients it will eventually affect both ears.

Q: What are the symptoms of Menière's disease?

A: Symptoms include attacks of dizziness, vertigo, nausea, vomiting, and sudden increases of deafness in the affected ear. The attacks occur in bouts, with periods of months or even years between them. They last several hours, and often leave a continued buzzing (TINNITUS) in the ear.

Q: How is Menière's disease treated?

A: There is no single effective method of treatment. Acute attacks are treated with antinausea drugs, and others drugs may reduce the frequency of the attacks. If treatment with drugs is ineffective, surgery may be necessary.

Meninges are the three membranes that cover the surface of the brain and spinal cord and follow the nerves for a short distance outside the central nervous system.

See also MENINGIOMA; MENINGITIS; SUBARACHNOID HAEMORRHAGE; SUBDURA.

Meningioma is a tumour that arises from the MENINGES, usually those around the brain and most commonly those above the CEREBELLUM. Multiple meningiomas may occur in VON RECKLINGHAUSEN'S DISEASE. They are usually benign (noncancerous) but may occasionally form a SARCOMA.

Meningitis is inflammation of the membranes (meninges) that cover the brain and the spinal cord. The symptoms of meningitis usually appear suddenly (acute meningitis) but, in some forms of the disorder, the onset of symptoms may be gradual. If untreated, acute meningitis is rapidly fatal.

Q: What are the symptoms of meningitis?

A: Acute meningitis is often preceded by a minor, influenza-like infection or by a sore throat. After one or two days, there is a sudden onset of a severe headache, vomiting, fever, and mental confusion. In severe cases, the patient goes into a coma. The patient may also have a stiff neck; be unable to straighten the leg after bending it at the hip joint (Kernig's sign); and be abnormally sensitive to light (photophobia). Some infections that cause meningitis, such as meningococcal meningitis, may produce skin rashes.

If the onset of meningitis is gradual, the symptoms are similar to those of the acute form, but develop over a period of one or two weeks.

Q: What causes meningitis?

A: Meningitis may be caused by a wide variety of viral, fungal, protozoan, or bacterial infections.

Q: How is meningitis treated?

A: The treatment of meningitis depends upon the cause. But meningitis may be fatal if treatment is not started in the early stages; immediate hospitalization is necessary. A lumbar (spinal) puncture is then performed and the cerebrospinal fluid examined to determine the cause of the meningitis.

Most patients with acute bacterial meningitis respond well to treatment with powerful antibiotics. Intravenous infusions may also be necessary if the patient is dehydrated.

The treatment of protozoan and viral meningitis depends upon the symptoms. Patients with viral meningitis usually recover, but they may be extremely ill during the early stages of the disorder.

Meniscus is a thin, crescent-shaped cartilage that is attached to the upper end of the shinbone (tibia) within the knee joint. There are two menisci: the lateral meniscus and the medial meniscus. Collectively, they are called the semilunar cartilages. They form an important part of the mechanism by which the knee is locked to produce a strong and stable straight lower limb (*see* KNEE).

The most common disorder that affects the meniscus is tearing of the cartilage. It is a common sporting injury and usually occurs when the knee is twisted violently while in a half-bent position. There is usually pain as soon as the cartilage is torn. The victim often falls down and is unable to straighten the leg. The following day the knee is usually swollen and painful. The swelling may disappear after resting the knee for one or two weeks. But when normal activity is resumed, the knee may give way or may suddenly lock so that the leg cannot be straightened normally. The usual treatment is to remove the cartilage surgically (meniscectomy).

A talk about Menopause

Menopause is the end of menstruation. By popular usage, the term has come to be synonymous with CLIMACTERIC. Menopause is a combination of physical and psychological changes.

Q: At what age does menopause usually occur?

A: Menopause occurs most commonly between the ages of 45 and 55 years, but it may occur earlier or later without there being any abnormality. As a general rule, the younger a woman was when she began to menstruate, the older she will be at the start of menopause.

Menstruation ceases at any age after the surgical removal of the womb (hysterectomy). But the symptoms of menopause occur only if both ovaries as well as the womb are removed and menopause has not already taken place naturally.

Q: How does menstruation cease?

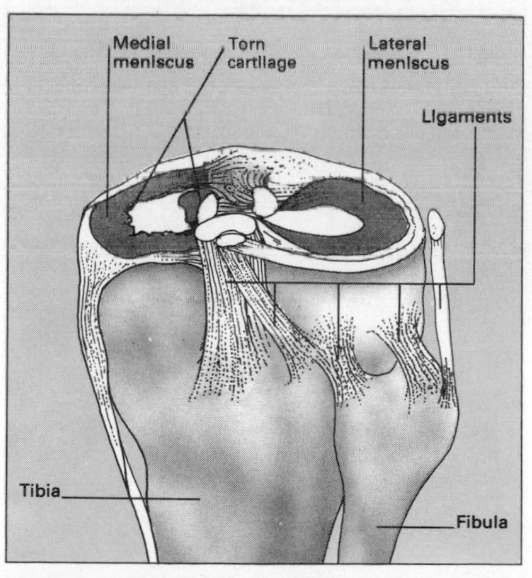

Meniscus cartilage is composed of strong fibres; it helps to lock the leg straight.

A: This varies greatly from woman to woman. Some women menstruate normally and regularly, then stop suddenly. But in most women, menstruation becomes irregular during menopause. The periods themselves may be shorter than usual, and the interval between them may vary from about two weeks to ten weeks. The periods may be heavy or light.

Any bleeding that occurs more than six months after the last period, even if it seems like a normal period, should be regarded as abnormal and reported to a doctor.

Q: What are the symptoms associated with menopause?

A: The most common symptoms are hot flushes, sweating, palpitations, depression, irregular menstruation, fatigue, headache, and sleeping difficulties.

Q: Do all women suffer from menopausal symptoms?

A: No. In many women the symptoms are absent or extremely mild. But most women do have some symptoms, although many do not consider the problems serious enough to consult a doctor. It is often difficult to be sure that the symptoms are associated with menopause and not with other problems. For example, headaches are common at any age and depression may have various other causes.

Q: Why do menopausal symptoms occur?

A: The symptoms are caused by hormonal changes that occur gradually over several years. In a woman of childbearing age, the ovaries secrete the oestrogen hormones in response to FOLLICLE-STIMULATING HORMONE (FSH) from the pituitary gland. At the approach of menopause, the ovaries become less responsive to FSH and secrete less oestrogen. As a result, the pituitary gland produces more FSH to try to maintain oestrogen levels.

As a direct result of these hormonal changes, ovulation becomes infrequent, periods become irregular and menopause finally occurs. However, the pituitary gland still secretes large amounts of FSH, which affect the blood vessels in the skin, causing them to dilate. This in turn produces the hot flushes, sweating, palpitations, and headaches, all common menopausal symptoms.

The hormonal changes also cause the breasts and womb to become smaller after menopause. The lining of the vagina becomes thinner and drier, and the muscles that support the womb become weaker, so that a PROLAPSE may occur.

Q: How can the symptoms of menopause be treated?

A: Medical treatment is not usually necessary. A doctor may be able to help by explaining what happens during menopause and by dispelling the anxieties that a woman may have about loss of femininity and the expectation of years of depression and unhappiness.

If treatment is after all necessary, the doctor may prescribe a mild tranquillizer or an antidepressant. If the hot flushes are severe, drugs may be prescribed to reduce the sensitivity of the blood vessels.

Sometimes these treatments are ineffective, in which case hormone replacement therapy (HRT) may be recommended. This involves giving small doses of oestrogen, with or without progesterone, by mouth, injection, or implantation of an oestrogen-containing pellet. HRT increases the amount of oestrogen, thus adjusting the hormonal balance by decreasing the FSH.

Q: What other changes may occur after menopause?

A: Apart from gradual reduction in size of the breasts and womb, the vagina and the vulva also change. These changes may cause discomfort and pain during sexual intercourse. If this occurs, oestrogen-containing suppositories or creams, used regularly, restore the thickness and moistness of the vaginal lining.

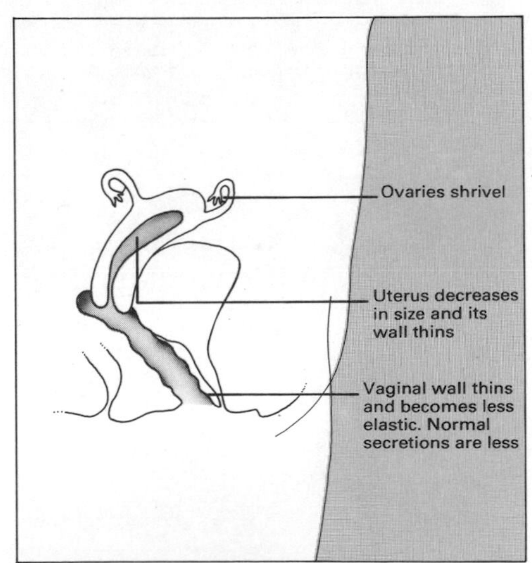

Menopause is accompanied by changes in the female reproductive system.

Q: Should a woman still have regular gynaecological examinations after menopause?

A: Yes. Regular gynaecological examinations, including a CERVICAL SMEAR test, are as important after menopause as before it.

Q: Is there any change in attitudes to sex after menopause?

A: This varies among individual women. Most women do not notice any change in their sex drive. Some find that their sex drive is increased after menopause, when the risk of an unwanted pregnancy has definitely disappeared. However, women who become depressed find that often their sex drive is reduced.

Q: What form of contraception should be used during menopause?

A: A doctor should be consulted about contraception during menopause. Contraceptive pills are inadvisable for women over the age of forty years. An intrauterine contraceptive device (IUD) or a diaphragm with a spermicidal cream or jelly probably give the best protection (*see* CONTRACEPTION). Contraceptive measures should be used for at least six months and, sometimes, up to one year after menopause to make sure that periods have finally stopped, and that the woman is no longer fertile.

Menorrhagia is the medical term for heavy periods; that is, regular menstruation that involves greater than normal blood flow and that usually lasts longer than normal. *See* MENSTRUAL PROBLEMS.

A talk about Menstrual problems

Menstrual problems may occur at any time between menarche (when periods first begin) and MENOPAUSE (when they end).

During puberty, many girls have irregular periods. But as a rhythm becomes established, problems become less common, and the absence of periods (AMENORRHOEA) is usually a sign of pregnancy or of a psychological problem.

The most common problem during the early years of menstruation is pain (*see* DYSMENORRHOEA), and in later years there may be feelings of irritation and depression, breast tenderness, and ankle swelling because of PREMENSTRUAL TENSION. Also, fluid retention may occur for a few days before menstruation.

Bleeding between periods may occur at any time, but is most common during the few years before menopause. If it persists, you should consult a doctor. Heavy periods (*see* MENORRHAGIA) or irregular periods (*see* METRORRHAGIA) also commonly occur.

A threatened MISCARRIAGE may simulate a menstrual problem when in fact it is caused by a pregnancy.

Q: What conditions cause abnormal menstrual bleeding?

A: Heavy periods may be caused by various conditions that affect the womb, such as ENDOMETRIOSIS, ENDOMETRITIS, FIBROIDS, or SALPINGITIS. Occasionally, general disorders, such as hypothyroidism or thyrotoxicosis, CIRRHOSIS of the liver, and blood disorders involving a reduction in clotting ability, may cause abnormal menstrual bleeding. More frequently, heavy periods are associated with the hormone imbalance related to menopause or, less frequently, to an OVARIAN CYST.

At any age, one of the most common causes of abnormal bleeding is psychological disturbance because of ANXIETY, DEPRESSION, or SEXUAL PROBLEMS.

Q: How is abnormal menstruation treated?

A: Treatment depends on the cause. A woman experiencing this problem should consult a doctor. A diagnosis will be made after physical and gynaecological examinations. If necessary, it will include a CERVICAL SMEAR test and a vaginal swab to discover if any infection is present. A pregnancy test reveals if pregnancy is the cause of lack of menstruation.

Menstrual problems	Associated symptoms
Amenorrhoea	Absence of menstruation. Commonly due to pregnancy, menopause, and emotional disturbance.
Dysmenorrhoea	Pain starting just before or with menstruation.
Ectopic pregnancy	A missed period followed by severe pain. Fallopian tube may rupture. Internal haemorrhage may result.
Menorrhagia	Prolonged and heavy periods.
Metrorrhagia	Bleeding between periods. Possibility of uterine fibroids or cancer of the uterus.
Premenstrual tension	Irritability, depression, fatigue, headaches, breast tenderness, abdominal swelling.

Menstrual problems can usually be easily identified and treated by a doctor.

Menstruation

If no physical cause can be found for the absence of menstruation, a hormonal disturbance may be the cause. This is frequently of a temporary nature and no treatment is needed. However, if there is no return of natural menstruation, a doctor may prescribe hormones that usually produce a type of menstruation.

Q: *What are other treatments if diagnosis is uncertain or hormone therapy is unsuccessful?*

A: A diagnostic D AND C (dilation and curettage) is a simple and minor operation that allows a general gynaecological examination as well as a microscopic examination of the lining of the womb. Often this simple operation is in itself sufficient to return menstruation to normal. The woman does not need to remain hospitalized for more than a day.

If abnormal bleeding continues, either because of hormonal disturbance, fibroids, or cancer, a HYSTERECTOMY (surgical removal of the womb) may have to be performed. But this operation is becoming less common. Hysterectomy induces menopause. Troublesome symptoms occur only if the ovaries are removed as well as the womb.

Menstruation is the shedding of the lining of the womb (endometrium) that occurs regularly in women between menarche (the beginning of menstrual periods) and menopause (the end of periods). It produces a vaginal bleeding that lasts for three to seven days and occurs every twenty-four to thirty-four days – the length of the menstrual cycle. About half-way through the cycle, an egg is released from an ovary in a process called OVULATION. The egg travels along the fallopian tube to the womb.

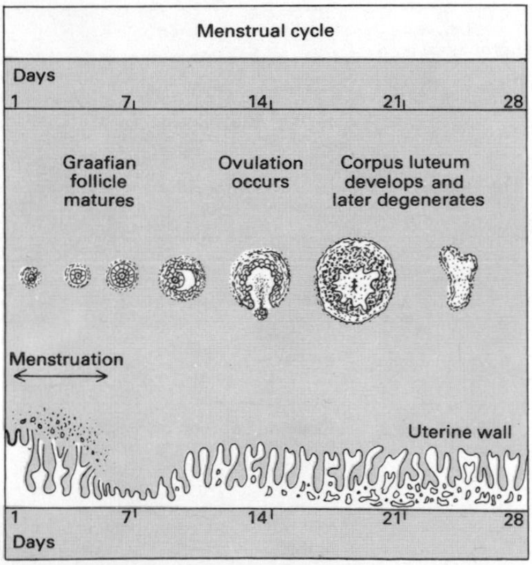

Menstruation normally occurs during the first five days of the menstrual cycle.

Q: *How is the length of a menstrual cycle calculated?*

A: The menstrual cycle is the time between the first day of one period and the first day of the next, including the days when bleeding occurs.

Q: *Are all menstrual cycles the same?*

A: No. Most women have a slight variation, within a day or so, in the length of their menstrual cycles, and each woman's cycle can also vary from month to month. The cycle tends to be the same length, usually about twenty-eight days, but some women have a cycle that is consistently longer or shorter than this.

Q: *Is menstruation always the same?*

A: Like the menstrual cycle, the period may have slight variations in individual women. Bleeding is usually heavier in the first day or two and then becomes lighter for the next two or three days.

Q: *How does the body control menstruation?*

A: Regularity of menstruation is a complex balance between the levels of hormones produced by the ovaries (oestrogens and progesterone) and those produced by the pituitary gland at the base of the brain, the follicle-stimulating hormone (FSH) and the luteinizing hormone (LH). FSH stimulates the ovary to produce oestrogen in the first half of the menstrual cycle. Oestrogen causes a thickening of the lining of the womb. In mid-cycle, a sudden increase in LH causes ovulation and production of progesterone, which alters the womb lining in preparation for a fertilized egg.

Fertilization produces an embryo that stimulates another hormone to maintain the womb lining. If fertilization does not take place, the womb lining is shed as the menstrual flow, and the cycle of events begins all over again.

Q: *How are the hormones from the pituitary gland involved in menstruation?*

A: As the production of oestrogen increases from the ovaries, its rising concentration diminishes the level of FSH from the pituitary by a mechanism known as a "feedback." The pituitary gland then releases LH.

The feedback of the various hormones is detected by the hypothalamus in the brain. The hypothalamus can also be affected by other factors, such as emotions, anxiety, or depression, and the effects of other hormones in the bloodstream.

Q: Why do menarche and menopause occur?

A: The onset of menstruation is associated with the hormonal changes of puberty, and the final end of menstruation is caused by aging of the ovaries. But in neither case is the exact mechanism fully understood.

Q: What care should a woman take during menstruation?

A: There is no need to restrict any activities during menstruation unless the blood flow is extremely heavy. Absorbent pads (sanitary napkins) or internal tampons may be worn. Sanitary napkins are more obtrusive and may cause vulval soreness, but they are more absorbent than tampons. Tampons left in the vagina for a long time may produce offensive discharge because of vaginitis. Menstrual blood has no harmful effects on the woman or anything that it may touch.

Q: At what age may a girl use internal tampons?

A: This depends on her size. It is often advisable to attempt to insert the first tampon when she is not menstruating, because the technique is sometimes difficult to learn.

See also AMENORRHOEA; MENOPAUSE; MENSTRUAL PROBLEMS.

Mental defect is a deficiency of one or several areas of brain function. It may be a general lack of intelligence (mental retardation), or it may affect only one type of mental ability without affecting the overall level of intelligence.

A talk about Mental illness

Mental illness is an abnormality of thinking or behaviour without any obvious physical cause. Mental illness is a relative term. It refers to the behaviour of those who deviate from what is normally expected of them by others. Because of this and also because the normal range of behaviour is so wide, it is often extremely difficult to establish that a person is mentally ill. If the abnormality is so great or if the history of the disorder is obviously one of profound mental disturbance, then a doctor may be able to make a diagnosis. Diagnosis and treatment are made easier if a patient consults a doctor voluntarily.

Q: What types of mental illness may occur?

A: There are several different ways of classifying mental illness, none of which is completely satisfactory. One of the most widely used systems of classification divides mental illness into three main categories: (1) psychoses, (2) neuroses, and (3) personality disorders.

In addition to these main categories are sexual disorders, mental retardation, and the dementias.

Q: What are psychoses?

A: Psychoses are gross disturbances of mental functioning and behaviour accompanied by a distintegration of the personality and loss of contact with reality. Psychoses are characterized by persistent delusions and hallucinations. The patient usually has no insight into the disorder. Psychoses are thought to be caused by a chemical or hormonal disorder that affects the brain in genetically vulnerable individuals. The main psychoses are schizophrenia; manic-depressive illness; and paranoia.

Q: How are psychoses treated?

A: Psychoses may be treated with tranquillizers, such as chlorpromazine and haloperidol, which may be combined with electroconvulsive therapy (ECT). Because many patients with psychotic disorders do not realize that they are mentally ill, such treatment often has to be given after compulsory admission to hospital. Treatment of psychoses is not always effective, although the symptoms can usually be alleviated. Some patients respond well and become normal for long periods. However, the condition may return at any time after treatment ceases.

Group therapy can help many patients bring their difficulties out into the open.

Q: What are neuroses?

A: Neuroses are an exaggeration of the normal responses to the stresses of life. In a patient with a neurosis, the reaction interferes with normal activities. Unlike a psychotic patient, however, a person with a neurosis is aware of the disorder and usually seeks medical help. Anxiety, depression, hypochondria, hysteria, obsession, and phobias are all neuroses.

Q: How are neuroses treated?

A: The treatment of neuroses is often difficult. Symptoms, such as hysteria, may be controlled with tranquillizing drugs. If such treatment is given early in the disorder, the symptoms may disappear spontaneously. However, it is usually necessary to combine drug treatment with PSYCHOTHERAPY or behaviour therapy.

Q: What are personality disorders?

A: There are several different types of personality disorders:(1) personality pattern disturbances, including schizoid (shy and seclusive), cyclothymic (alternations of depression and elation), and paranoid behaviour (delusions of persecution); (2) personality trait disturbances, which have a single dominant characteristic, such as compulsiveness; and (3) psychopathic personality disturbances, which are marked by antisocial behaviour without feelings of guilt. ALCOHOLISM and DRUG ADDICTION are also considered to be personality disorders.

Q: How are personality disorders treated?

A: Most personality disorders need expert psychiatric treatment, which may involve behaviour therapy using desensitization methods that expose the patient to the conditions inducing the disorder.

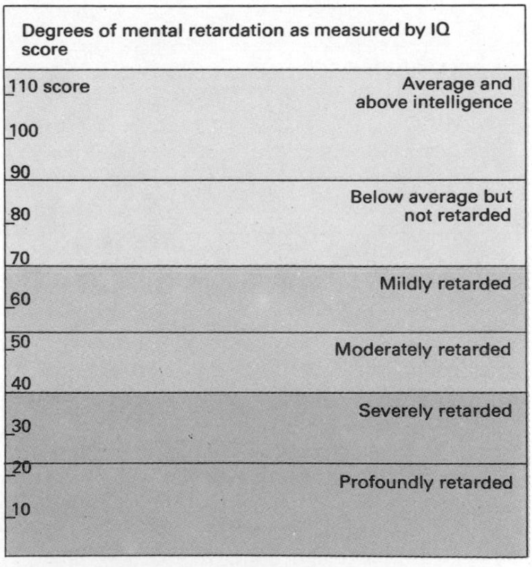

Q: Can mental illness occur in children?

A: Yes. Apart from mental retardation and certain types of MENTAL DEFECT, children may also become depressed. AUTISM is a rare condition that some psychiatrists believe to be a form of juvenile schizophrenia.

Q: How can the community and the family help a patient who is mentally ill?

A: It is important that the family, friends, and the family doctor are aware that some forms of mental illness, such as schizophrenia and manic-depressive psychosis, are more common in certain families. An awareness of this possibility means that treatment can be started early, even if it requires compulsory admission to hospital.

Provisions should be made for those who are so mentally ill that they are a danger to themselves or to others. Most patients with depression are aware of their condition and realize the need for treatment. However, those with a psychotic illness may not be aware of their disorder, and compulsory admission to hospital is needed. A doctor will be able to give advice about the necessary procedures.

Most people with hysterical or mildly paranoid personalities are able to adapt to normal life, although their behaviour may seem strange.

Co-operation between hospitals, the family, and the community means that fewer patients are compulsorily detained for psychiatric treatment than previously. Many patients are encouraged to lead as normal a life as possible while under overall supervision of a psychiatrist or a social worker, which may include some form of psychotherapy.

See also ANOREXIA NERVOSA; DEMENTIA; HOMOSEXUALITY; MASTURBATION; MENTAL RETARDATION; PERSONALITY DISORDERS; SEXUAL PROBLEMS.

Degrees of mental retardation as measured by IQ score

IQ score	Degree
110 score, 100, 90	Average and above intelligence
80, 70	Below average but not retarded
60	Mildly retarded
50, 40	Moderately retarded
30	Severely retarded
20, 10	Profoundly retarded

Mental retardation (shaded) is graded by IQ. A person below 90 is educationally subnormal.

Mental retardation is subnormal intelligence. It may be caused by lack of brain development, or brain damage from injury or illness.

Q: What causes mental retardation?

A: In most cases the cause is unknown but the normal variation in intelligence that occurs in the population can produce persons with below average as well as above average intelligence. Several rare inherited disorders, such as phenylketonuria, Tay-Sachs syndrome, and von Recklinghausen's disease may cause mental retardation.

Chromosomal abnormalities (of which Down's syndrome, mongolism, is the most common) and antenatal infection (such as German measles) may also result in brain damage. Smoking and alcoholism during pregnancy and various disorders, such as pre-eclampsia and placenta praevia, may reduce the blood flow to the developing foetus. This may produce a mild form of foetal malnutrition that may affect development of the brain.

Brain damage may occur at birth. It may, for example, be caused by asphyxia or haemolytic disease of the newborn. Premature babies, especially if their birth weight is less than 1.5kg (3lb), are more likely to be mentally retarded during infancy and childhood. Such damage may be caused by a serious head injury; a serious infection, such as meningitis; or poisoning, especially with heavy metals such as lead. Chronic malnutrition, such as kwashiorkor, can also prevent normal brain development, thereby reducing intelligence.

In many cases of mild mental retardation, social and economic factors are more significant than medical causes. These factors include poverty, social isolation, and cultural deprivation during early childhood. It has also been shown that if an infant is separated from its mother for a continuous period during its first year of life, mental retardation may result. If the separation lasts for longer than six months, the mental retardation may be irreparable.

Q: How is mental retardation assessed?

A: In some cases, mental retardation may be detected at birth or soon afterward. For example, Down's syndrome is usually apparent at birth. However, mental retardation, particularly if it is mild, is often detected first by the parents, who may notice that their child has problems with feeding; lacks normal responses, such as smiling; or is slow in learning to crawl or walk. In such cases, the parents should consult a doctor, who will examine the baby to try to find a cause. The examination usually includes a full neurological investigation, sometimes with an electroencephalogram (EEG), skull X-rays, hearing tests, and vision tests. From these, a doctor may be able to give the parents an indication of the degree of the child's retardation and the problems that they may encounter. Many parents find it difficult to accept that their child may be mentally retarded, and, even if they suspect that this may be the case, refrain from seeking expert confirmation. Professional advice, however, is essential if the child's learning potential is to be developed as fully as possible, and will help the parents to cope with the strain and responsibility of bringing up a mentally retarded child.

An accurate assessment of an infant's intelligence is impossible. When the child is about three years old, an intelligence test may be given. This can give a reasonable indication of the severity of mental retardation, which may help the parents to plan for the child's future.

Mental retardation is generally classified as mild, moderate, or severe. Individuals are assessed according to their degree of subnormality and their potential for learning social, occupational, and academic skills.

Children with mild retardation (with an INTELLIGENCE QUOTIENT in the range of 50-70) can usually be taught to do simple mathematics, to read and write, and to perform uncomplicated tasks. Those with severe retardation may have difficulties with speech, co-ordination, bladder control, and bowel control. The most severely retarded seldom learn to walk and usually remain incontinent, needing lifelong supervision.

Q: Can mental retardation be prevented?

A: In some cases it is possible to prevent mental retardation. At present, however, it is not possible to prevent most cases of mental retardation. If any inherited disorder has occurred in the family of either of the potential parents, a genetic counsellor may be able to give advice about the likelihood of retardation in their children. Some chromosomal abnormalities can be detected by testing fluid from the womb during pregnancy (amniocentesis). If this indicates that the baby will be retarded, an abortion can be performed if the parents wish it.

The possibility of brain damage caused by malnutrition of the foetus can be reduced by stopping smoking before pregnancy, and by skilled antenatal care during pregnancy.

Tests for phenylketonuria are performed routinely within ten days of birth. If these are positive, a special diet will prevent brain damage. Early diagnosis and treatment of hypothyroidism prevents cretinism.

Q: Are there other problems that are associated with mental retardation?

A: Yes. Cerebral palsy and epilepsy, which are also caused by brain damage, often occur in the mentally retarded. The drugs that are used to control epilepsy may further impair mental functioning.

It is difficult to teach mentally retarded persons about safety precautions, and so they are more likely to be hurt in accidents.

Q: How can the mentally retarded be helped?

A: Skill, patience, and understanding from the parents, doctors, and educators who specialize in teaching the mentally retarded can enable retarded children to be educated to their fullest capabilities.

The severely retarded often have other disorders, such as spina bifida and hydrocephalus, cerebral palsy, or congenital heart disease. Such disorders may prevent them from being educated to the fullest extent, and they may need lifelong hospital care.

Home care of the mentally retarded is extremely demanding on other members of the family, even with the support and encouragement of relatives and friends. Societies that have a special interest in a particular disorder can often give expert advice, and may be able to put parents in contact with others who have similarly retarded children.

Menthol is an alcohol that is obtained from the oils of several kinds of mint. It may be used alone or in steam inhalations to treat sinusitis and bronchitis. Menthol is often combined with camphor or eucalyptus to produce creams, lotions, and ointments.

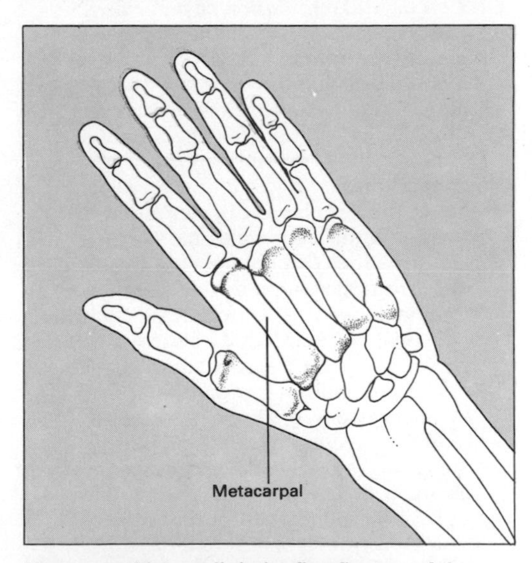

Metacarpal bones link the five fingers of the hand with the small bones of the wrist.

Meprobamate is a tranquillizing drug that is used mainly to treat mild anxiety.

Meprobamate may produce loss of appetite, nausea, vomiting, diarrhoea, and headaches. Large dosages may cause dizziness, drowsiness, lack of co-ordination, and a decrease in blood pressure.

Mercury is a liquid metallic substance that is commonly used in thermometers and other instruments. Some mercury compounds are still used in antiseptics and eye ointments, but teething powders containing mercury are no longer used as they were found to be a cause of PINK DISEASE.

Mercury poisoning may occur from pollution of food (*see* MINAMATA DISEASE), from the use of mercury in industrial processes that may be inhaled, or from skin contact over a period of time. If mercury has been swallowed, treatment must include washing out the stomach and swallowing an egg white to absorb the mercury.

Mescaline is an alkaloid that is the active hallucinogenic substance of the peyote or peyotl cactus (*Lophophora williamsii*). The effects of mescaline are similar to those of LSD and include visual and auditory hallucinations, distortions of time sense, feelings of anxiety or even persecution, and feelings of elation. Not all of these effects necessarily occur, because the reaction to mescaline varies considerably among individuals, as well as in the same person at different times.

See also DRUG ADDICTION.

Mesentery is a membrane-like fold of tissue attached to the back of the abdominal wall. It supports the intestines and contains the blood vessels, nerves, and parts of the lymphatic system that connect with the intestines.

Metabolism is the sum of all the chemical and physical processes that occur within the body. It includes the repair and replacement of dead or damaged tissues, and the production of energy.

Metabolism involves two basic processes: anabolism and catabolism. Anabolism is the synthesis of complex substances from simpler ones, which occurs during the growth of body tissues. Catabolism is the reverse process: the breakdown of complex substances into simpler substances. The BASAL METABOLIC RATE is a measure of the body's energy expenditure when at complete rest.

Metacarpal is any one of the five bones that form the structure of the palm of the hand.

See also HAND.

Metastasis is the spread of a disease from one

part of the body to another. The term usually refers to the spread of cancer, although metastasis may also occur in some infections, such as endocarditis and tuberculosis.

In cancer patients, cells that have separated from a primary tumour may spread through the lymphatic system, into the veins, or, more rarely, into an artery. These cells (metastases) may also spread across the surface of a structure, such as the peritoneum lining of the abdomen or the pleura surrounding the lungs. Occasionally, metastases result from surgery, and may be found in the scar of the wound through which a tumour has been removed. *See* CANCER.

Metatarsal is any one of the five bones that form the main part of the arch of the FOOT. *See* BUNION; HALLUX VALGUS; METATARSALGIA.

Metatarsalgia is pain in the front of the foot. The most common cause is a form of flatfoot in which the arch between the bases of the big and little toes is deformed, and the heads of the metatarsal bones rest on the ground. This pressure on the bones produces pain, causes the skin to thicken, and may eventually cause the toes to curl. Metatarsalgia may also be caused by pressure on a nerve (neuralgia), or by a stress fracture, which can occur after prolonged walking or running.

Resting the injured foot and wearing a soft-soled shoe is usually the only treatment required while the fracture heals. Prolonged physiotherapy to strengthen the underlying muscles may be effective in patients under the age of forty years. But if the pain is severe, it may be necessary to wear a plaster cast for about one month.

Methadone is a synthetic painkiller similar to morphine. It may be used as a cough suppressant and in the treatment of heroin addiction. Methadone blocks the effects of heroin withdrawal and, although methadone itself is addictive, it is thought to be easier to withdraw from than is heroin. Use of methadone in heroin withdrawal should be under expert medical supervision in a centre that specializes in control of drug addiction.

Methamphetamine is a stimulant drug that has effects similar to those of amphetamine. *See* AMPHETAMINE.

Methaemoglobin is a compound form of HAEMOGLOBIN that prevents the haemoglobin in red blood cells from carrying adequate amounts of oxygen to the body tissues. The presence of methaemoglobin is usually caused by poisoning with aniline dyes, potassium chlorate, or various other chemicals, including nitrites in drinking water. But it may also be caused by a hereditary deficiency of the substance that helps convert methaemoglobin to haemoglobin.

Methyl alcohol. *See* ALCOHOL.

Metropathia haemorrhagica is bleeding from the womb for which a cause cannot be found. *See* MENSTRUAL PROBLEMS.

Metrorrhagia is the medical term for bleeding from the womb, either during menstruation or at other times. *See* MENORRHAGIA; MENSTRUAL PROBLEMS.

Microbes are microscopic living organisms. The term is often applied to any organism that causes disease. *See* GERMS.

Microcephalic describes an individual whose head is disproportionately small in comparison with the rest of the body. The abnormally small head, present at birth, is usually associated with mental retardation.

Microsurgery is any surgical technique that requires the use of a microscope and specially adapted instruments. It is used for operations that require extreme delicacy, as in surgery of the ears, the eyes, or the brain.

Micturition is the medical term for the act of passing urine. *See* BLADDER DISORDERS; URINE.

Middle ear is the part of the ear that transmits sounds from the outer ear to the inner ear (*see* EAR).

Midwife, or nurse-midwife, is a person skilled in caring for women in normal pregnancy, during labour, and following childbirth.

A talk about Migraine

Migraine is a recurring severe headache, often affecting only one side of the head and accompanied by a variety of other symptoms. It occurs more commonly in women than in

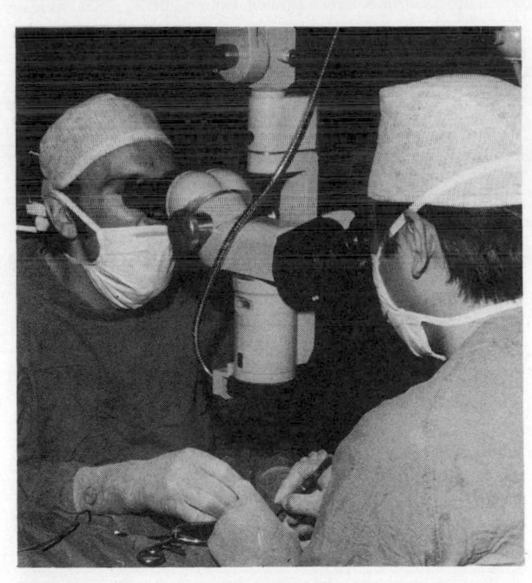

Microsurgery permits surgeons to perform operations of extreme delicacy.

men and usually first appears between the ages of ten and twenty years.

Q: *What are the symptoms of migraine?*

A: The initial symptoms are usually mild fatigue and depression. These may be accompanied by visual disturbances with irregular, flashing patterns of light; temporary blindness in one half of the visual field (hemianopia); or double vision (diplopia) because of eye muscle weakness. Sometimes there is also weakness or loss of sensation in a limb (hemiparesis or hemi-anaesthesia).

The symptoms may last a few minutes and disappear before the beginning of the typical throbbing headache. The pain is frequently accompanied by nausea and vomiting, aversion to light (photophobia), and sensitivity to noise.

The headache may last several hours, or even a day or two, before disappearing and allowing the individual to fall asleep and then to awake refreshed. Migraine attacks may occur daily or as infrequently as once every few months.

Q: *What causes migraine?*

A: The cause is not known, although about half of all migraine sufferers have another member of the family who has similar headaches. Sometimes there is an association with certain foods, such as chocolate, cheese, or cured meats, suggesting an allergy. The initial symptoms result from a narrowing of the blood vessels that supply the brain, followed by an expansion that produces the headache.

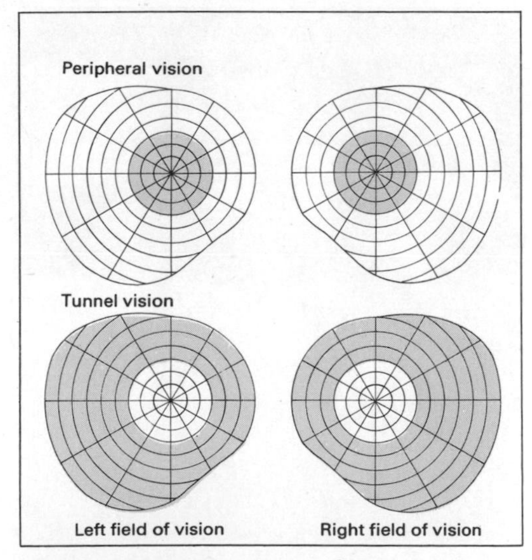

Migraine: shaded area of this diagram shows areas of defective vision.

Q: *Does migraine last for life?*

A: Usually migraine becomes less frequent with increasing age, and is relatively uncommon after the age of fifty. Some people, however, continue to suffer from migraine into old age.

Q: *Can migraine occur in young children?*

A: Yes. A child may not complain of a headache, but suffer from recurrent attacks of malaise accompanied by nausea and vomiting. The child may be able to describe the first symptoms of distorted vision and flashing lights, which can be extremely frightening if neither the child nor the parents understand what is happening.

Q: *Can anything increase the likelihood of migraine?*

A: Yes. Apart from certain foods that may cause migraine in some individuals, there are other factors that may bring on the symptoms. Many women experience a migraine a day or two before menstruation and the headache is associated with premenstrual tension. Some people develop a migraine when they are under emotional stress or after a period of stress, typically during the weekend. Some people find that particular wines can produce a migraine, probably because of a combination of alcohol and other wine ingredients.

Q: *Why does alcohol cause migraine?*

A: It is not known why alcohol causes migraine. But there is a particular kind of migraine, sometimes called a cluster headache, in which a one-sided headache is accompanied by a running nose and a sore, reddened eye on the affected side. Several attacks occur within a few days and then there is a prolonged period without headaches. This type of migraine is more common in middle-aged men and may be triggered by alcohol.

Q: *How is migraine treated?*

A: The usefulness of drugs is limited and many people learn to cope without them. Some migraine sufferers merely go to bed in a darkened room until the headache passes. Painkilling drugs, such as aspirin, are useful in relieving the headaches.

The drug ergotamine may be prescribed for acute attacks. It must be taken at once in the dosage prescribed. It works effectively if sucked, but it can also be given by injection, especially if nausea or vomiting is occurring.

Q: *Can migraine be prevented?*

A: If attacks occur frequently, treatment of premenstrual tension or anxiety and depression may produce an improvement.

If this does not work, a doctor may prescribe one of the drugs that can be effective in preventing migraine.

Migraine sufferers should learn to keep track of things and conditions that normally precede their attack. Steps can then be taken in the future to prevent similar attacks.

Miliaria is an intensely irritating, fine red rash on the body, especially round the waist, and in the bends of the knees and elbows. *See* PRICKLY HEAT.

Milk is the secretion from the female breast that feeds a newborn baby. Human breast milk contains the right balance of ingredients, such as water, organic substances, antibodies, enzymes, and mineral salts, for the infant's well-being, although human milk varies in quantities of nutritive ingredients week by week during lactation. An alternative is cow's milk, modified by processing. Untreated cow's milk should not be fed to babies.

See also LACTATION.

Milk of magnesia. *See* MAGNESIA, MILK OF.

Milk teeth are the first, temporary set of teeth to appear. They are also called deciduous teeth. The teeth are present, hidden in the jaws, in a newborn baby and they begin to grow through the gums by the end of the first year. A child has twenty milk teeth. *See* TEETH.

Milroy's disease is an inherited disorder in which there is an absence of lymph vessels in one part of the body, such as an arm or a leg. There is generalized swelling of the area that becomes worse in hot weather; when the limb is allowed to hang down unsupported; or, in women, before menstruation.

Treatment is to wear a tight stocking or bandage and to take precautions against skin infections, because any resultant scarring may be increased by the swelling. Operations to remove the swollen tissues are seldom successful.

See also LYMPHATIC SYSTEM.

Minamata disease is a form of MERCURY poisoning that first occurred in the late 1950s among the population of Minamata Bay, Japan, after eating fish contaminated by mercury compounds discharged into the bay by local industry. Symptoms included trembling, weakness, and anaemia, as well as mental disturbances. Death occurred in the severest cases.

Mineral oil (liquid paraffin) is a preparation of light petroleum oils sometimes used in medicine. The oil is used on the skin and as a lubricant for catheters (tubes passed into the body to inject or remove fluid) and surgical instruments. Taken internally, mineral oil acts as a laxative and is used in the treatment of chronic constipation.

Minerals are inorganic elements or compounds. Minerals in the diet are important to good health. Various elements are essential parts of body cells, including calcium, chlorine, copper, fluorine, iodine, iron, magnesium, manganese, phosphorus, potassium, and sodium. The chief mineral salts in the body are chlorides and phosphates. Some minerals are incorporated into body tissues, but others are excreted.

See also DIET.

Miotic is any substance that makes the pupil of the eye constrict. Pilocarpine and eserine are miotics.

Mirror writing is writing formed from right to left (instead of left to right) so that it appears normal when seen reflected in a mirror. Mirror writing commonly occurs in left-handed children who are attempting to write with their right hand. Learning problems can be avoided if the trait is recognized and help is obtained for the child.

See also LEARNING DISABILITIES.

Miscarriage is the spontaneous termination of pregnancy before the embryo or foetus can live independently. In medical terminology, miscarriage and ABORTION have the same meanings. The usual reason for a miscarriage is a defect in the embryo or foetus that prevents its natural development. This defect may be inherited, caused by injury to the mother, or the result of infectious illness. The first symptom of a threatened miscarriage in a pregnant woman is vaginal bleeding, and

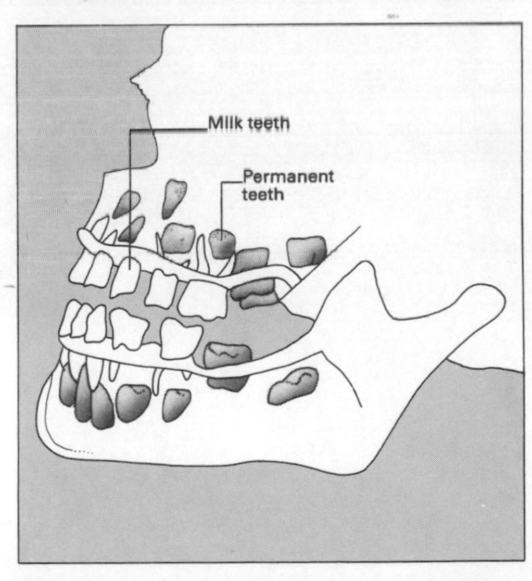

Milk teeth begin to be replaced by permanent teeth when a child is about five years old.

this requires immediate medical attention. A miscarriage is most likely to occur in the third or fourth month of pregnancy. Expulsion of a foetus from the womb after approximately the twenty-eighth week of pregnancy is known as a stillbirth if the foetus is dead, and as a premature birth if the foetus is alive.

See also ABORTION.

Mites are minute arachnids related to spiders. They are classified as Acarina and there are many different species. Some species can transmit diseases to humans. One group, the House Dust Mite, may cause allergic symptoms similar to hay fever.

See also ALLERGY; RICKETSIA; SCABIES; TICKS.

Mitral valve disease is a disorder of the heart caused by damage to the valve between the upper chamber (atrium) and the lower chamber (ventricle) on the left side of the heart. The opening in the valve may be narrower than normal (mitral stenosis) or wider than normal (mitral incompetence). Commonly these conditions result from scarring caused by RHEUMATIC FEVER, or, rarely, they may be present at birth.

Q: What are the symptoms of mitral stenosis?

A: The first symptoms are usually shortness of breath during exercise and, sometimes, episodes of breathlessness at night because the lungs become congested with blood. The symptoms begin gradually, because it takes many years for the scarring to take place. As scarring worsens, the symptoms become more severe so that acute breathlessness may occur on the slightest exertion, and there may be signs of heart failure because of back pressure of blood into the right side of the heart. Signs may include a bluish tinge to the lips (cyanosis) and swollen ankles (*see* CONGESTIVE HEART FAILURE).

Many patients develop a rapid irregular heartbeat called atrial FIBRILLATION. Sometimes the shortness of breath is accompanied by coughing attacks that may produce bloodstained sputum (haemoptysis).

Q: What is the treatment for mitral stenosis?

A: Initially, a doctor may prescribe diuretic drugs and digoxin to help to control the heart failure. If atrial fibrillation has recently occurred, beta-blocking drugs or a controlled electric shock (cardioversion) may restore normal heart rhythm.

Moderately severe or severe mitral stenosis may be treated by surgery. The valve can be enlarged by cutting the scarred tissue (valvotomy), or replaced with an artificial valve or one obtained from a pig's heart.

Q: What are the symptoms of mitral incompetence and how is it treated?

A: The symptoms are less severe than those of mitral stenosis, but increasing fatigue and shortness of breath commonly occur. Usually drug treatment with diuretics and digoxin is sufficient to control the symptoms. However, if this fails, the damaged valve can be replaced by surgery, as in mitral stenosis.

Molar is a broad tooth at the back of the mouth used for chewing and grinding. An adult has twelve molar teeth, with three upper and three lower molars on each side of the mouth. The back four molars are also known as wisdom teeth. *See* TEETH.

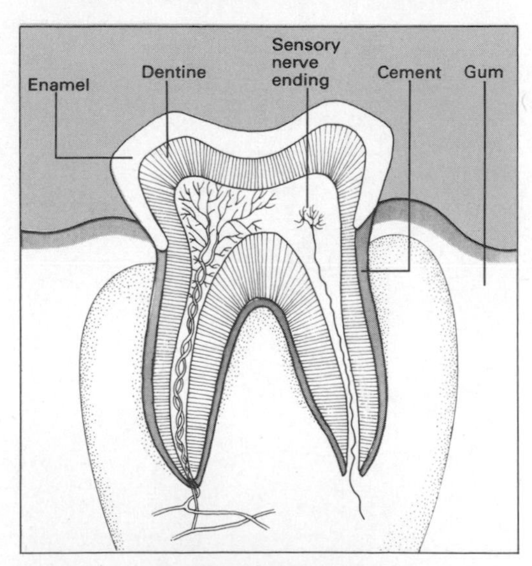

Molar is a large, deep-rooted tooth at the back of the jaw used for chewing and grinding.

Mole is a coloured area or spot on the skin. Moles vary in size, may be flat or raised, and may have various shades of colour or pigmentation. Some are covered with hair.

Moles are formed from cells containing the dark pigment melanin. Some may be present at birth, although many develop during childhood or early adult life. A mole that is present at birth is usually called a birthmark.

Q: Do moles require treatment?

A: Treatment is not necessary unless the mole is disfiguring, for example, a large hairy mole on the face. Treatment may also be necessary if the mole is situated where clothing irritates it, such as around the waist, possibly resulting in infection and inflammation. Moles can usually be removed, under a local anaesthetic, by plastic surgery.

Q: Can moles become cancerous?

A: Yes, but this is extremely rare. A mole that changes in size, colour, or shape should be examined by a doctor. Bleeding moles may be malignant (cancerous), and they should be reported to a doctor at once.

See also MELANOMA.

Molluscum contagiosum is a virus skin infection that is often caught in swimming pools, or through sexual intercourse. Small, firm, pearly warts commonly occur in one region of the trunk, near the armpit or groin, and may spread elsewhere on the body. They usually disappear spontaneously after a few months, but a doctor may treat them by freezing, cautery, or applying a caustic.

Molluscum fibrosum. *See* VON RECKLINGHAUSEN'S DISEASE.

Mongolism. *See* DOWN'S SYNDROME.

Moniliasis, also called candidiasis and thrush, is an infection caused by the microorganism *Candida albicans,* a yeast fungus that is normally found in the intestine and on the skin. A change in environment, for any reason, can allow the microorganism to increase in number and cause the infection.

Q: What environments encourage moniliasis?

A: Antibiotic treatment for some other condition, such as bronchitis, kills many of the bacteria normally present on the skin and in the intestine. This allows the fungus to grow and cause moniliasis. Altered hormone levels in the body, such as those that occur during pregnancy and in women who take contraceptive pills, also make it easier for monilial fungi to grow. The infection may accompany other disorders, such as diabetes mellitus, leukaemia, or conditions that require treatment with corticosteroid drugs, all of which alter the body's immunity to monilia.

Q: Which parts of the body are affected by moniliasis?

A: Moniliasis mostly affects areas of the body that are moist and warm. In babies, the mouth is a common area for thrush, where moniliasis results in small white patches on a red, inflamed background. Similar conditions occur in the vagina, and this is a common area for the infection in women.

There are various areas on the skin that can commonly become infected. These are the groin, around the anus, beneath the breasts (particularly in heavily built women), and in folds of skin in people who are obese.

Moniliasis may occur as a form of nappy rash in babies when the buttocks are allowed to remain moist with urine.

Q: Can moniliasis occur elsewhere?

A: Yes. It may infect the nail folds, particularly in those whose hands are often in hot water, and this can form a kind of PARONYCHIA. Occasionally, moniliasis can invade the body to infect the lungs, the intestine, or the urinary tract; this occurs particularly in those who are seriously ill or who have undergone prolonged treatment with powerful antibiotics.

Q: Can moniliasis be sexually transmitted?

A: Yes. Inflammation of the end of the penis (balanitis) may occur in uncircumcised men after intercourse with a woman with moniliasis. Both partners must be treated (*see* BALANITIS).

Q: How is moniliasis treated?

A: Skin infections are treated with fungicidal creams or lotions, and vaginal infections may be treated with pessaries. The rare internal forms of moniliasis have to be treated with potent fungicidal drugs, under the care of a doctor.

Q: Are there any serious complications with moniliasis?

A: Serious complications only arise when moniliasis invades the body, and these are rare. Commonly, however, moniliasis recurs after treatment. In this situation, it may be necessary to give fungicidal drugs by mouth to kill any excess of monilia in the intestine.

Monoamine oxidase inhibitors. *See* MAO INHIBITORS.

Monocyte is a type of white blood cell that has a single nucleus and a relatively large amount of surrounding cytoplasm. *See* WHITE BLOOD CELL.

Mononucleosis. *See* GLANDULAR FEVER.

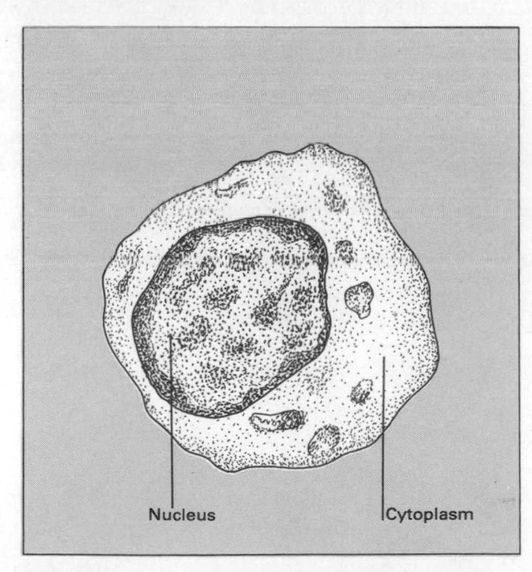

Monocyte is a type of white blood cell that contains a large nucleus and cytoplasm.

Monoplegia is paralysis of one limb. *See* PARALYSIS.

Morbidity is the state of being ill. The term is also used to describe the proportion of sick people in a particular community.

Morbilli is a medical word for MEASLES.

Morning sickness affects about fifty per cent of women in early pregnancy. They experience nausea and vomiting, usually beginning about the sixth week of pregnancy and finishing by the twelfth week. A headache often occurs with morning sickness, and a feeling of dizziness and exhaustion. The symptoms usually occur in the morning, but may be present at any time during the day.

Q: What causes morning sickness?

A: Morning sickness probably results from an increased sensitivity of the vomiting centre in the brain, caused by the hormonal activity of early pregnancy. These hormones also have an effect on the gastrointestinal tract, so that the movement of faeces along the colon is slowed down. As a result, some food and gastric secretions remain in the stomach in the morning.

Q: How is morning sickness treated?

A: Many women find that nausea can be prevented by eating a few biscuits and drinking a glass of milk first thing in the morning. This is because the gastric secretions are absorbed by the food.

If this simple measure fails, a doctor may prescribe an antinausea drug to be taken before going to bed at night. B complex vitamins may also be prescribed.

Q: Can morning sickness ever be serious?

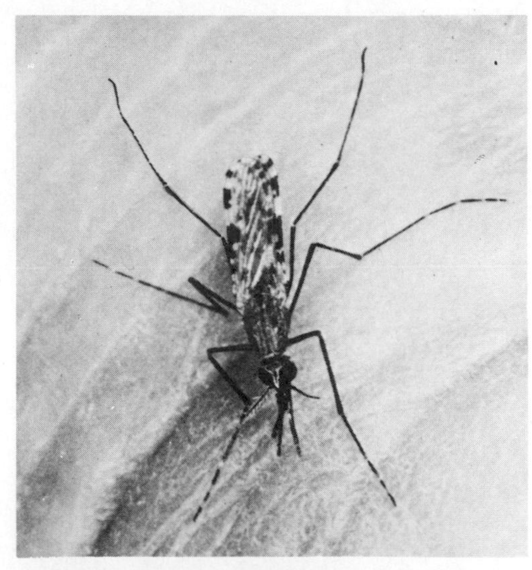

Mosquito can carry the infective organisms that cause malaria and yellow fever.

A: Yes. In a few women, vomiting and nausea occur so frequently that loss of weight occurs.

Rarely, a condition of excessive vomiting known as HYPEREMESIS gravidarum occurs. Continued vomiting produces dehydration, and the condition requires hospital treatment with intravenous infusions of glucose, antinauseant drugs, and sedation.

Morphine is an ALKALOID drug derived from the opium poppy. It is a powerful painkiller and cough suppressant. Morphine relieves anxiety as well as inducing contentment and even happiness in patients suffering from severe pain. It is also used in the treatment of acute heart failure and shock. Prolonged use of morphine can result in psychological and physical dependence.

Morphine is seldom prescribed in tablet form because, although it may be absorbed through the intestine, its action is slow and uncertain. Morphine is injected to produce a predictable result, and rapid action follows an intravenous injection. The drug is often prescribed for patients with terminal cancer.

Morphine should not be prescribed for the elderly or the very young, because they are particularly sensitive to the drug's effects. Nor should it be used in those who have lung disease, such as asthma, because of its depressant effect on breathing.

See also METHADONE; OPIATE.

Mosquito is a bloodsucking insect. It can carry parasites that cause diseases in human beings. There are many species of mosquitoes. Those of the Anopheles group carry MALARIA; the Aedes mosquito carries YELLOW FEVER and DENGUE fever, as well as viruses that cause encephalitis in some tropical countries; and the Culex mosquito carries a form of filaria that causes ELEPHANTIASIS.

Infections transmitted by mosquitoes can be prevented by spreading the breeding grounds of the mosquito with a thin film of oil; this prevents the larvae, which grow in water, from breathing. Insecticides sprayed at night and the use of mosquito nets over beds provide personal protection, and insect repellant creams may be effective during the day.

Motion sickness is nausea and vomiting caused by violent or repeated movement of the body. Motion sickness may be preceded by sweating, yawning, and fatigue. It is more common in children and often disappears with age as the organ of balance (the semicircular canals within the ear) becomes less sensitive to movement. Airsickness, carsickness, and seasickness are all examples of motion sickness. It may be caused by any form of transport, as well as by amusement rides at fairs or playgrounds.

Q: How can motion sickness be prevented?

A: A person who suffers from motion sickness should take antinausea drugs before starting any journey, but not if they are driving. During the journey, the person should lie with the head slightly raised, preferably in the part of the vehicle that experiences the least movement.

Small amounts of food and drink should be taken at regular intervals, but alcohol should be avoided.

Motor describes any body structure that is concerned with movement. For example, a motor nerve carries the "instructions" that make a muscle move.

Motor neuron disease is a group of similar disorders of unknown origin that cause degeneration of the nerve cells in the spinal cord or brain and affect muscle activity. There is increasing muscle weakness and wasting, usually beginning in the hands and feet and spreading to involve the shoulders and buttocks. It usually affects adults in late middle age.

The type of motor neuron disease called amyotrophic lateral sclerosis is usually fatal within three years, whereas progressive muscular atrophy may last for as long as twenty years. The condition known as progressive bulbar palsy affects the throat muscles and causes difficulty with talking, chewing, and swallowing. Death often occurs within a year or two from pneumonia.

There is no effective treatment for motor neuron disease, although physiotherapy may help to maintain mobility.

See also MUSCULAR DISORDERS.

Mountain sickness. *See* ALTITUDE SICKNESS.

Mouth is formed by the bone structure of the jaws. The upper part is formed by the upper jawbone (maxilla) and the lower part by the lower jawbone (mandible). The entrance to the mouth is surrounded by the skin and muscles that form the LIPS, and the interior contains the GUMS, PALATE, TEETH, and TONGUE. The MUCOUS MEMBRANE, the soft skin lining the mouth, is kept moist by the secretions of the SALIVARY GLANDS and heals rapidly if damaged.

See also CHEILOSIS; CLEFT PALATE; DENTAL DISORDERS; GINGIVITIS; HARE LIP; LARYNGITIS; MOUTH ULCER; SORE THROAT; STOMATITIS; TONSILLITIS.

Mouth breathing is breathing through the mouth when the nose is blocked, perhaps as a result of an infection, such as a cold or an injury to the nose, such as a fracture. In children, mouth breathing is often caused by swollen ADENOIDS.

Mouth breathing may also cause SNORING and disturbed sleep. The mouth may also become dry, which increases the probability of gum infection. Treatment is not necessary to stop a person breathing through the mouth, if the cause is obvious. Normal breathing is resumed when the cause disappears.

Mouth-to-mouth resuscitation is a form of artificial respiration in which the victim's lungs are inflated with air breathed out by the rescuer. For details, *see* First aid, p.518.

Mouth ulcer is an open sore that affects the mucous membrane that lines the inside of the mouth. It is known medically as aphthous ulcer. It is possibly caused by a virus that normally lives in the body cells without causing symptoms. But in the presence of a disorder, such as a common cold, ulcers form. Throat drops and ointments may help mouth ulcers to heal. A doctor may prescribe tablets that can be sucked for rapid healing.

MS. *See* MULTIPLE SCLEROSIS.

Mucopurulent describes a discharge from the body that contains both mucus and pus. Such a discharge may occur as mucus from the nose, sputum from the lungs, or fluid from the anus in disorders that involve inflammation of the colon or rectum, such as ulcerative colitis and diverticular disease.

Mucous colitis, also called spastic colon and irritable bowel syndrome, is a recurrent intestinal disorder in which there are bouts of abdominal pain with diarrhoea or constipation in an apparently healthy person. There is an abnormality of the muscular action that passes food along the colon, and this causes the constipation or diarrhoea.

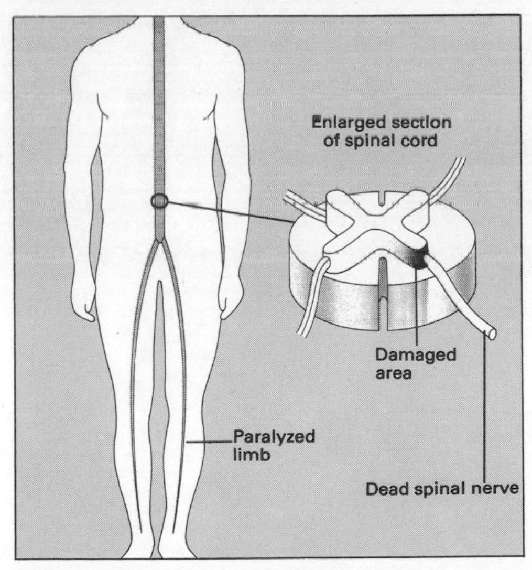

Motor neuron disease affecting the spinal nerves results in leg paralysis.

Q: What causes mucous colitis?

A: Mucous colitis may develop during emotional stress, such as studying for examinations, or anxieties associated with work or domestic problems. There is a tendency for it to occur in individuals who are obsessional, but it may also appear for no apparent reason. Sometimes a food allergy may be involved.

Q: What are the symptoms of mucous colitis?

A: The disorder first appears in young adults and it is variable, with long periods in which there are no symptoms. Abdominal pain may occur as a dull ache over one area of the colon or, occasionally, there may be intermittent colic that is relieved by a bowel movement. Sometimes there is constipation or a form of diarrhoea in which frequent small amounts of faeces with a thin tape-like or pellet-like appearance are passed. The faeces may be covered with mucus. Diarrhoea is often the principal symptom, usually occurring first thing in the morning or immediately after a meal. The rest of the day may be free from pain or diarrhoea. The person may feel tired and mildly depressed. Weight loss is unusual.

Q: How is mucous colitis diagnosed and treated?

A: A doctor makes a diagnosis after excluding other possibilities, such as gastroenteritis, ulcerative colitis, amoebic dysentery, or other intestinal disorders that cause abdominal pain and diarrhoea. If necessary, the doctor may arrange for faecal analysis, sigmoidoscopy, and a barium enema to make sure there is no underlying disease of the intestine.

Once the doctor has made the diagnosis, the patient can be reassured that there is no serious disorder. This reassurance combined with a diet containing additional bulk (such as bran or methyl cellulose) and the use of antispasmodic drugs usually produce an immediate improvement.

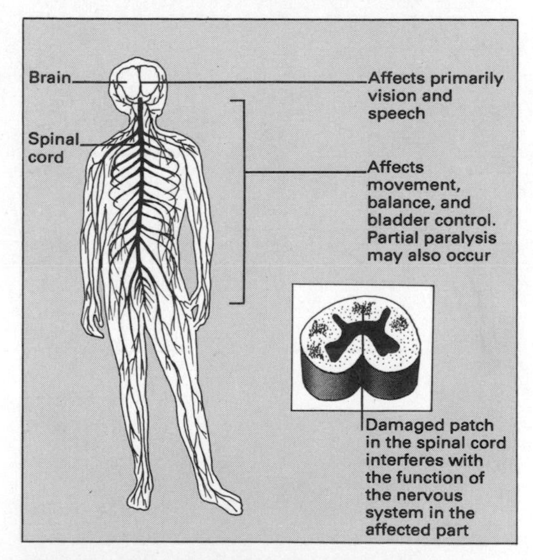

Multiple sclerosis is slow damage of areas of nervous tissue causing progressive paralysis.

Mucous membrane is a thin layer of cells containing glands that secrete a sticky fluid called MUCUS. Mucous membranes line the internal passages and cavities of the body, such as the bladder, bronchial tubes, intestine, mouth, and vagina.

Mucus is a clear, slime-like fluid that is continually secreted by glands within any of the body's mucous membranes. Mucus acts as a protective lubricant barrier.

Multipara is the medical term for a woman who has had two or more pregnancies that lasted for more than twenty weeks. A grand multipara is a woman who has had six or more children.

Multiple sclerosis, or disseminated sclerosis, is a disorder of the brain and spinal cord in which scattered areas of damage to nerve cells occur. The nerve damage results in a great variety of symptoms, sometimes followed by recovery or marked improvement. Further damage may occur at irregular intervals over many years, causing increasing disability in some, but not all, patients.

The cause of multiple sclerosis is not known, but it may be associated with some kind of altered immunity to a virus infection.

Q: What are the symptoms of multiple sclerosis?

A: The first symptoms usually occur between the ages of twenty and forty and are slightly more frequent in women. The onset is usually gradual and may include slight, temporary weakness in one arm or leg; tingling or numbness in a limb or on one side of the face; double vision (diplopia) because of a weakness of an eye muscle; blurred vision (amblyopia); or frequently pain in one eye because of neuritis affecting the optic nerve (retrobulbar neuritis). Other symptoms that may occur at the same time or in later attacks include incontinence of urine; unsteady gait (ataxia); giddiness (vertigo); and sometimes emotional disturbance with sudden tears or laughter, depression, or cheerfulness.

As the disorder progresses, these symptoms recur along with various others that involve the nervous system. They tend to last longer and may not disappear completely, so that the patient may be left with a limp, a hesitation in speech or a flickering movement of the eye.

Some patients are never disabled by their symptoms, but in others the symptoms may be severe enough to confine them to bed, and make them unable to walk or maintain bladder control. As the disorder progresses, recovery from each attack is less complete. The patient may be left with stiff limbs, often accompanied by intermittent, painful spasms of the muscles. Eventually, urinary or lung infections may occur, and one of these complications usually causes death.

Q: *What is the treatment for multiple sclerosis?*

A: There is no treatment for this disorder. A few patients have a rapid, progressive disease with frequent relapses that lead to death within one or two years. Others may have only one or two minor problems followed by complete, spontaneous recovery without further trouble. Most patients, however, have recurring symptoms for fifteen to twenty-five years, and may then stabilize.

The diagnosis is made on the basis of a history of the recurrent attacks and a doctor's examination of the patient. Prompt administration of corticosteroid drugs may produce a rapid improvement in symptoms, but does not affect the progress of the disorder.

Physiotherapy, massage, and treatment of any infection all help to maintain reasonable health. It is important to keep up the morale of the patient.

Mumps, also called epidemic parotitis or infectious parotitis, is a virus infection that causes painful inflammation and swelling of the salivary glands. Mumps is most common among children, but it may also affect adults.

Q: *How long is the incubation period and quarantine for mumps?*

A: The incubation period is between fourteen and twenty-five days; usually twenty-one days. Quarantine should last for twenty-eight days after the last contact. The disorder is infectious for about two days before the swelling appears and for three days after the swelling goes down or for a total of ten days, whichever is longer.

See also INFECTIOUS DISEASES.

Q: *What are the symptoms of mumps?*

A: There is usually an initial period of one to two days of headache, malaise, and fever. This stage is followed by a sudden rise in temperature to about 40°C (104°F), which accompanies the onset of painful swelling of the salivary glands. The parotid glands in front of the ears are the glands most commonly involved in the early stage, but swelling may spread to the glands under the jaw. The swollen glands are tender to touch and may cause difficulty in opening the mouth. The extent of the swelling may vary from day to day. Only one side may be affected. The acute stage of the illness usually lasts five to six days, with a gradual reduction in the swelling as the patient improves.

Mumps in adults may cause inflammation of the pancreas; of the testicles in men, which may lead to sterility; or of the ovaries in women.

Q: *What is the treatment for mumps?*

A: There is no cure for mumps. Therapy is directed toward making the patient comfortable, reducing fever, and ensuring adequate fluid intake. Painkilling and sedative drugs may be prescribed.

Q: *Can mumps be prevented?*

A: Yes. A vaccine containing a mild, living virus is available and it may be used to immunize children at the age of twelve to fifteen months. It is not often recommended in the U.K. except for adults who have not had the disease. Occasionally, mumps vaccine produces a mild illness. It is thought that immunity lasts for life and the vaccine certainly protects about 95 per cent of children.

Münchausen's syndrome is a mental disorder in which the patient persuades doctors that he or she has a real physical disease when no

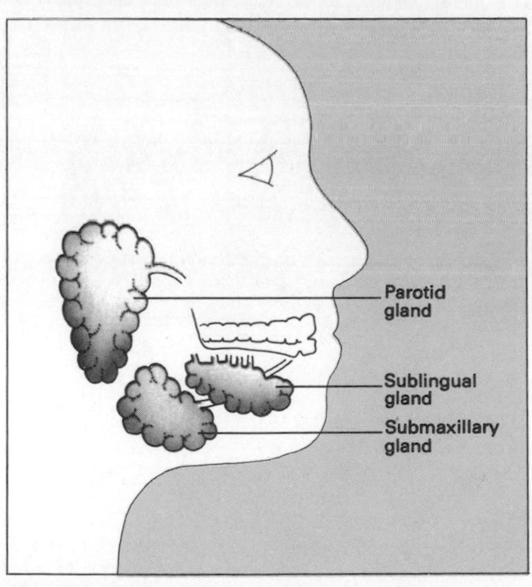

Mumps usually affects the parotid salivary glands but can cause other inflammation.

disease is present. It can be regarded as an extreme form of malingering. The disorder is named after Baron Karl F. H. von Münchausen, who was known for his tall tales of courage and skill on the battlefield, none of which were true.

Patients with Münchausen's syndrome are skilled at mimicking the physical signs and symptoms of a disorder, such as myocardial infarction, appendicitis, and cerebral tumour. Such pretended complaints may lead to hospital admission, multiple tests, and even surgical operations to try to determine the cause of the "disorder." Despite having a definite desire for medical treatment, the patient may be unaware of his or her underlying need for sympathy and care.

Murmur. *See* HEART MURMUR.

Muscle is a tissue composed of fibres that can contract and relax to produce movement in a part of the body. There are three kinds of muscles: striated, smooth, and cardiac.

Disorders that can affect muscles or are associated with muscular disorders include: CUSHING'S SYNDROME; FRIEDREICH'S ATAXIA; HYPERTHYROIDISM (THYROTOXICOSIS); HYPOTHYROIDISM; LUPUS ERYTHEMATOSUS; MUSCULAR DYSTROPHY; MYALGIA; MYASTHENIA GRAVIS; MYOCARDITIS; MYOSITIS; MYOTONIA CONGENITA; and TETANY.

Muscle relaxants are drugs of two main types, those that relax muscles and those that relieve painful muscle spasms.

Drugs of the first type are used in general anaesthesia to produce complete relaxation of the muscles before surgery, and may be short-acting or long-acting. Drugs of the second type are used to relieve the muscle spasms that sometimes occur in spastic conditions, such as those following a stroke, or in some muscle and rheumatic disorders.

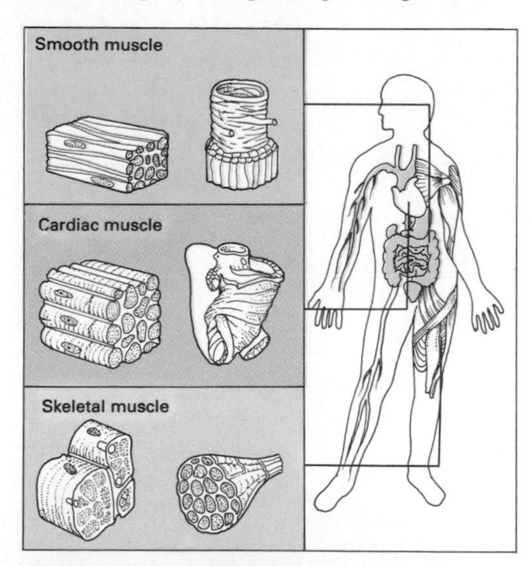

Muscle may be smooth (involuntary); specialized (cardiac); or striped (skeletal).

Muscular dystrophy is the name of a group of progressive disorders the symptoms of which include weakness and gradual wasting away of muscles. There are various classifications of these disorders, but the terms most usually applied to the three main types are: pseudohypertrophic muscular dystrophy, facioscapulohumeral muscular dystrophy, and limb-girdle muscular dystrophy.

There is no specific treatment but physiotherapy can help in the slowly progressive forms of muscular dystrophy. Corrective surgery can also be considered as treatment for the slowly progressive forms.

Mutation is a sudden change in some characteristic. In genetics, mutation describes a permanent change in one of the genes of a chromosome (*see* HEREDITY).

Mute describes someone who is unable to speak. A person may lose the power of speech following a stroke (the condition called aphasia) or disease or injury to the vocal cords.

See also DEAFNESS.

Myalgia is pain in a muscle. Such pain may occur after excessive physical exercise. Myalgia may also develop during any acute virus illness and is an indication of mild inflammation of the muscles (myositis). It is frequently associated with inflammation of fibrous tissue (fibrositis).

The pain is usually made worse by movement and the muscles are frequently tender. Treatment with mild painkilling drugs and the application of heat is usually effective.

See also RHEUMATIC DISEASES.

Myasthenia gravis is a disorder that affects the nerve impulses that control the movement of muscles. It is a form of AUTOIMMUNE DISEASE. The muscles become weak, although temporary recovery slowly takes place if affected muscles are rested.

Q: What are the symptoms of myasthenia gravis?

A: The onset is often sudden, producing a drooping eyelid (ptosis) and double vision (diplopia) because of weakened eye muscles. These symptoms may be accompanied by difficulty in swallowing or speaking. Weakness of a limb may occur, particularly after the limb has been exercised. On some days the symptoms may not be noticeable, whereas on others they may become severe. Occasionally, the muscles involved in breathing become affected, producing the risk of asphyxiation.

Q: How is myasthenia gravis diagnosed and treated?

A: A doctor may suspect the presence of myasthenia gravis and the diagnosis can be confirmed by the improvement that takes place after use of a drug that helps to improve nerve transmission to the muscles. In many patients the surgical removal of the thymus gland is curative (*see* THYMUS).

Some patients improve naturally, and in these no treatment is required.

Mycetoma is a chronic fungal infection that produces festering swellings, often on the feet. *See* ACTINOMYCOSIS; MADURA FOOT.

Mycobacteria are a group of microorganisms, two of which cause leprosy and tuberculosis.

See also BCG.

Mycosis is any infection caused by a fungus, such as actinomycosis and blastomycosis.

Mydriatic is any substance that makes the pupil of the eye dilate.

Myelin is a fatty substance that forms a sheath around many of the body's nerves.

Myelocele is an opening in the lowest part of the spine that exposes the underlying spinal cord. Myelocele is the most serious form of spina bifida. *See* SPINA BIFIDA.

Myelogram is an X-ray of the spinal cord. It is used in the diagnosis of spinal tumours, slipped discs, and other spinal problems.

Myeloid leukaemia. *See* LEUKAEMIA.

Myeloma is a malignant (cancerous) tumour of the bone marrow. The tumour usually occurs first in one bone, but soon spreads to many other bones (multiple myelomatosis). The bones of the skull, ribs, spine, and pelvis are usually involved, although myelomas may occur in any bone. Myelomatosis is most common in the elderly.

Q: What are the symptoms of myelomatosis?

A: Backache or pain in the affected bone is a common symptom, although fatigue and shortness of breath caused by anaemia may be noticed first. The patient's resistance to infection is lowered, allowing chest and urinary infections to develop. The tumours weaken the bones, and fractures commonly occur.

Q: How is myelomatosis diagnosed and treated?

A: Many patients with myelomatosis produce an abnormal type of gamma globulin (Bence Jones protein) that can be detected in the urine. The presence of this protein, anaemia, and a high ESR (red blood cell sedimentation rate) all suggest multiple myeloma. The diagnosis can be confirmed by a bone marrow biopsy, in which a sample of bone marrow is examined using a microscope.

Treatment with chemotherapy, corticosteroids, and radiotherapy may greatly prolong the patient's life, but the disease is eventually fatal. Treatment of secondary infection with antibiotics and blood transfusion for severe anaemia improve the patient's general health and vitality.

Myocarditis is inflammation of the heart muscle. The symptoms are often vague and mild at first. Fatigue, shortness of breath, and sometimes palpitations (rapid, irregular heart beat) occur. Heart failure may develop and sometimes blood clots in the heart. The clots (emboli) may travel in the blood circulation to other parts of the body and cause strokes or sudden obstruction of an artery to a limb, resulting in gangrene.

Q: What causes myocarditis?

A: Various infections can affect the heart muscle, either because of the infection or the toxins that it produces, such as those from diphtheria. Many other conditions, such as disseminated lupus erythematosus, and rheumatic fever, can also involve the heart.

Various chemicals and some drugs, particularly those used in the treatment of cancer, can damage the heart muscle. Care must also be taken during radiotherapy of lung cancer to insure that the heart does not become inflamed.

Q: How is myocarditis diagnosed and treated?

A: A doctor makes an initial diagnosis from the symptoms and confirms it with an electrocardiogram (ECG) and other

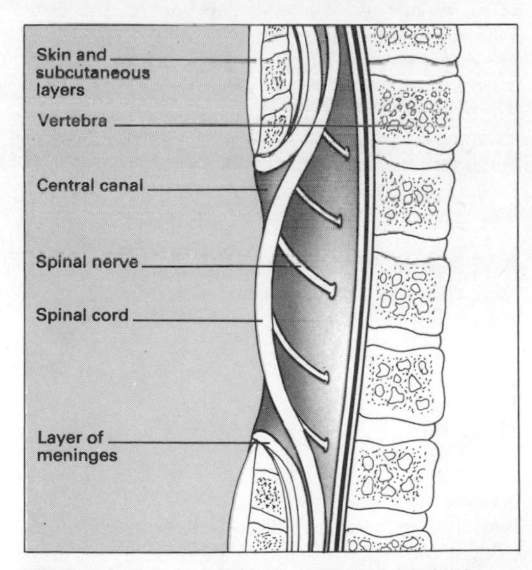

Myelocele is a condition in which the spinal cord protudes through the vertebrae.

heart investigations. Treatment is directed at the cause, once it has been discovered. The patient must have complete rest, oxygen if necessary, and corticosteroid drugs.

Myoclonus is a brief spasm of muscular contraction that may involve a group of muscles, a single muscle, or even only a number of muscle fibres. Often the contractions occur rhythmically, producing a regular twitching of the affected muscle. If myoclonus involves several muscles, it may be sufficiently violent to cause the person to fall over. The treatment depends on the cause, but there is a variety of antispasmodic drugs that may help to reduce the likelihood of myoclonus.

Myoma is a muscle tumour. Most myomas are benign, although a few may become malignant (SARCOMA).

Myopathy is any muscular disorder that results in weakness and degeneration of the muscle tissue that is not caused by a defect in the nervous system. The muscular dystrophies are classified as myopathic disorders. *See* MUSCULAR DYSTROPHY.

Myopia is the medical term for shortsightedness. *See* SHORTSIGHTEDNESS.

Myositis is inflammation of the muscles. It may be caused by injury, infection, exposure to cold, or parasitic infestation.

Myotonia congenita is a rare, inherited muscular disorder in which muscles relax slowly after contraction. This causes stiff movements; for example, difficulty in relaxing the grip after shaking hands. The throat muscles may be affected, causing difficulty in speaking or swallowing. There is no cure, but drug treatment can control the disorder.

Myringotomy is surgical perforation of the eardrum, usually performed under a general anaesthetic. This is done for acute otitis media or when the middle ear is filled with thick mucus (glue ear). This may occur following antibiotic treatment for otitis media, and may cause deafness.

See also MASTOIDITIS.

Myxoedema. *See* HYPOTHYROIDISM.

Myxovirus is a family of viruses that includes those that cause mumps and influenza.

N

Naevus. *See* BIRTHMARK.

Nail is the hard semitransparent tissue that covers the upper surfaces of the fingers and toes. It is also the medical term for a metal rod used in orthopaedic surgery to stabilize a fracture.

Fingernails and toenails are dead tissue, without nerves or blood supply. They are a modification of skin, and they grow from a groove that is overlapped by a fold of the skin, the nailfold. The semicircular paler area near the base of the nail is called the lunula. The thin outer layer of skin adjacent to the nail is known as the cuticle.

Fingernails grow at an average rate of about one fiftieth of an inch (0.5mm) per week; toenails grow at about a fourth of this rate. The rate of growth may be altered by the season of the year, any acute illness, or damage to the nail bed.

Q: What conditions affect the nails?

A: Bitten fingernails are commonly a sign of anxiety. Ridging or grooving on the nails is evidence of altered growth because of illness or damage to the nail bed. The nail bed may become infected with tinea or monilia (both fungal diseases), causing deformity of the nail with discoloration and splitting. The nails of psoriasis patients are frequently pitted and often split easily. A similar condition may be seen in patients with rheumatoid arthritis. Nails can also be affected by certain hormone deficiencies.

See also CLUBBING; INGROWING NAIL; KOILONYCHIA; ONYCHOGRYPHOSIS; PARONYCHIA.

Nappy rash is inflammation of a baby's skin in the area covered by the nappy. The red inflamed area round the buttocks and genitalia may ooze and crust. Nappy rash is usually caused by faecal bacteria reacting with the urine to produce ammonia. The longer a baby lies in a wet, dirty nappy the stronger the ammonia becomes. The rash may be aggravated by the nappy's moisture, monilial infection and also the chemical effect of any detergents or soaps left in a nappy that has not been properly rinsed after washing. Nappies may be kept free from bacteria by soaking them in a sterilizing solution or boiling them.

Q: What is the treatment for nappy rash?

A: Frequent changing of the nappy is essential. Exposure to the air without any covering is the surest way to heal the skin. The urine in the nappy must be able to evaporate, so plastic pants should not be worn until the rash has disappeared. Various soothing applications, such as calamine lotion, zinc compound cream, or petroleum jelly, are effective, and should be applied frequently after careful washing of the inflamed area. If the area becomes infected, a doctor may prescribe antibiotic or antifungal creams.

Narcoanalysis is a form of psychotherapy in which a patient is questioned while under the influence of sedative or hypnotic drugs that help to reduce the patient's conscious and unconscious resistance to questioning.

Narcolepsy is a syndrome characterized by recurrent and overpowering attacks of sleep at unexpected or inappropriate moments. It usually happens after a sudden burst of emotion, but may also occur without warning, or after the psychic or sensory awareness of an impending attack (the aura). The sleep pattern is shallow, and the normal need for sleep is not disturbed. Narcoleptic people sometimes also suffer from cataplexy, an emotional seizure that causes the victim to fall to the floor without losing consciousness.

Narcotics, or more correctly narcotic ANALGESICS, is a term that refers to the naturally occurring opiates morphine and codeine; derivatives of these substances; and totally synthetic compounds that produce effects similar to morphine and codeine. The term narcotics, when properly used, does not include sedatives or hypnotics such as the barbiturates.

See also DRUG ADDICTION; DRUGS.

Nares is the medical name for the nostrils, the external openings of the nose.

Nasal describes anything pertaining to the nose.

Nasopharynx is the small space, above the soft palate at the back of the roof of the mouth, that connects the nasal cavities with the throat. Also known as the postnasal space, it contains the ADENOIDS and the openings of the two Eustachian or auditory tubes that lead to the ears. The nasopharynx is closed during swallowing by the muscles of the soft palate.

Natural childbirth is a term that describes several methods of childbirth in which the mother actively co-operates and consciously enjoys the birth and delivery of her baby. Natural childbirth reduces, and occasionally makes it possible to avoid altogether, the need for painkilling drugs or anaesthesia and makes the delivery a more natural event.

There are many myths about childbirth that can produce anxiety in a woman when she discovers that she is pregnant. Her whole attitude to pregnancy may be modified by increasing fears based on these myths.

Q: How can these anxieties about labour be changed?

A: Antenatal classes explain what is happening at the various stages of pregnancy and exactly what happens during labour. It is explained that the hard effort that is necessary during labour is similar to that needed for any athletic sport, a mixture of physical and psychological stress. The basis of the instruction in the classes is to teach the woman how to help herself and her attendants during labour.

Q: In what ways can a woman help during labour?

A: Muscular tension can be lessened by special exercises, such as breathing in a manner that relaxes. In the first stage of labour, before the neck of the womb is open, breathing during contractions should be a series of deep breaths that become rapid and more shallow as the pains increase, and return to slower, deeper breathing as the pains lessen. This difficult stage, which is often lengthy and tiring for the mother, can be made easier by applying gentle pressure to the area over the sacrum bone. Such pressure shifts the weight of the body from the spinal column to the pelvis.

In the second stage of labour, when the foetus is being expelled from the womb and down through the pelvis, the breathing pattern is different. Rapid, short puffing breaths are taken and then the breath is held for a few moments while the mother pushes down with her abdominal muscles during contraction.

The obstetrician indicates when to "push," and this pattern of puffing and pushing alternates until the baby is expelled from the birth canal. During this second stage, if the father is present, he can help by supporting the mother's back with his arm and holding her legs bent.

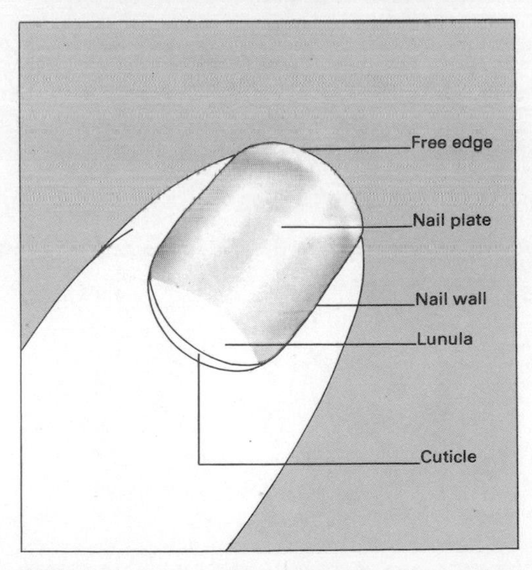

Nail injuries, especially to the nail wall or to the cuticle, can be extremely painful.

The third stage of labour is the expulsion of the placenta. This is not a lengthy process and the woman should be asked to give a further push or cough as the placenta is expelled.

Q: *What are some methods of natural childbirth?*

A: There are many different methods of natural childbirth, often called after the doctor who first advocated the particular regimen. Examples are the Leboseyer, Lemaze, and Dick-Read methods.

Whatever method is taught, it is essential for the woman to realize that everything is being done to help her and that some labours are much more difficult than others, even when perfectly normal. Many women do need painkilling drugs, but this is not a sign of failure on the part of the mother or of the method. Other problems may arise so that the obstetrician may use forceps, vacuum extraction, or perform a Caesarean section.

Q: *Can all women be helped by learning one of the methods of natural childbirth?*

A: Unfortunately not. Some women find it impossible to overcome their fears about labour and are not helped by antenatal classes that teach natural childbirth methods.

See also PREGNANCY AND CHILDBIRTH.

Naturopathy is an alternative method of treatment using diet, herbal medicines, and physical treatments such as hydrotherapy and exercise. Conventional drugs are not used.

Naturopathy has a long history and has recently been enjoying a revival. But nature cures are considered to be outside the sphere of normal medical practice. Naturopathists believe that nature treatments are the only way to deal with disease.

Q: *What sort of remedies do naturopathic practitioners use?*

A: Herbal remedies are common, and many can be effective. Most aperients (senna, cascara, and other vegetable laxatives) are of herbal origin. Digitalis and quinidine, which are derived from plants, are used in orthodox medicine to treat heart conditions; peppermint may be prescribed for digestive disorders; and extracts of the poppy (opium and morphine) are commonly prescribed by doctors as painkillers. Other herbal remedies are still being discovered or reintroduced into medical practice as the basis for their action becomes understood. Naturopathic practitioners have used many of them for centuries.

Q: *What other forms of treatment are used in naturopathy?*

A: Faith healing is used by some naturopathic practitioners, and, it would seem, healing can take place whether the patient believes in it or not. Many patients have reported remarkable improvements, but the benefits of natural healing have not yet been scientifically proven.

Nausea is the sensation of feeling sick in the stomach. Many conditions can cause nausea, which is a preliminary symptom before vomiting. Nausea may also accompany any sudden shock, either from a physical cause, such as an accident, or emotional shock, such as revulsion on seeing something unpleasant.

Q: *What physical conditions cause nausea?*

A: Any digestive disorder, particularly acute or chronic gastritis, may be accompanied by nausea. Probably the most common cause is eating too much rich, fatty food, or drinking too much alcohol, particularly on an empty stomach. Nausea may precede vomiting in MOTION SICKNESS and is a frequent symptom of early pregnancy (*see* MORNING SICKNESS).

Q: *How is nausea treated?*

A: The treatment of nausea depends on the cause. A severely nauseated person may be more comfortable lying down in a quiet place, possibly with head and shoulders raised. Anyone with persistent nausea should consult a doctor.

Navel. *See* UMBILICUS.

Nearsightedness. *See* SHORTSIGHTEDNESS.

Neck is any narrow region between two parts of an organ or body, although the term usu-

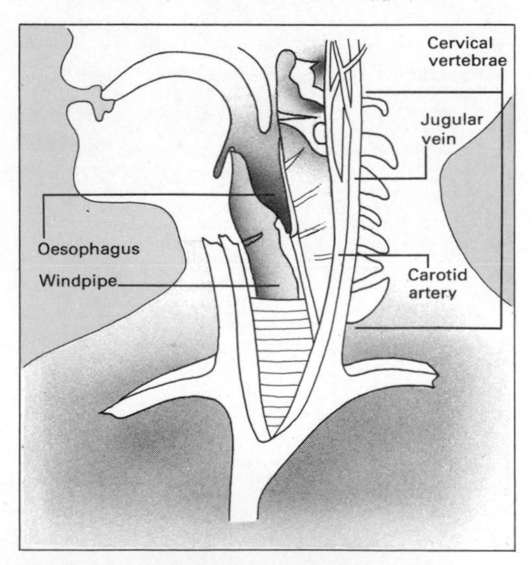

Neck contains many arteries, veins, nerves, and muscles supported by cervical vertebrae.

ally applies to the part of the body between the shoulders and the head.

The neck is a flexible structure that supports the head and contains major blood vessels and separate tubes for air and food. The seven bones in the neck, called cervical vertebrae, form the upper part of the spine. The two top cervical vertebrae, the atlas and axis, are pivoted to allow rotation of the head.

Strong muscles on each side of the spine partly protect the structures in the front part of the neck. These structures include the oesophagus, the trachea (windpipe), and the larynx (voice box). The carotid arteries and jugular veins in the neck carry blood to and from the head and brain. There is also a series of lymph glands that guard against the entry of infection from the throat. The salivary parotid glands, below the ears and adjacent to the jaw, produce saliva. The thyroid gland, just below the larynx in front of the trachea, produces hormones that control the body's metabolism.

See also SLIPPED DISC; STIFF NECK.

Necrosis is the death of a small area of tissue within an organ. It may occur as a result of an accident, such as a burn, or of a disease, such as tuberculosis. Necrosis often follows obstruction of an artery that supplies a particular area of tissue, as in GANGRENE.

Neisseria is a group of bacteria that includes the organisms that cause GONORRHOEA and one of the common forms of bacterial MENINGITIS.

Nematodes is the scientific name for ROUNDWORMS; *see also* WORMS.

Neonatal describes any event occurring in the first four weeks after birth. *See* ANTENATAL.

Neoplasm is the medical name for any new growth, but in common usage it frequently refers to a tumour. Doctors distinguish between malignant (cancerous) neoplasms and benign (noncancerous) neoplasms.

See also CANCER.

Nephrectomy is an operation to remove a diseased kidney. A partial nephrectomy is performed when only part of the kidney is diseased.

A nephrectomy may be necessary if there is a kidney tumour such as HYPERNEPHROMA; if the kidney is severely damaged by disease, for example, HYDRONEPHROSIS, or a CALCULUS (stone); or following an accident in which the kidney is badly damaged. Recovery from the operation is quick, and the remaining kidney increases in size to cope with the increased demands on it.

Nephritis is a general term for any inflammation or infection of the kidney. The condition may involve the kidney's filtration unit (glomerulus) producing GLOMERULONEPHRITIS. Or nephritis may involve the tubules within the kidney, causing problems in reabsorption of water and salts (interstitial nephritis). Inflammation affecting the drainage area of the kidney, with damage to the kidney pelvis and surrounding tissue, leads to PYELONEPHRITIS.

Disease of the kidney tissue may be an allergic reaction, or may be caused by blood vessel disorders, or the result of high blood pressure (hypertension). Certain drugs may also damage the kidneys. Kidney damage may follow a rise in the level of calcium in the blood associated with parathyroid gland disorders or other disorders, including gout. Damage can also be caused by poisoning with lead or by radiation.

See also NEPHROTIC SYNDROME; PYELITIS; URAEMIA.

Nephrolithiasis is the formation of stones (calculi) in the kidney.

Q: Why do kidney stones form?

A: Stones may form if there is obstruction of the normal urine flow, as in HYDRONEPHROSIS. They may result from an excess of certain chemicals in the bloodstream, such as uric acid in gout and calcium in parathyroid gland disorders.

Q: What are kidney stones made of?

A: There are three common forms of stones: those formed from uric acid; those that are calcium oxalate; and mixed stones composed of calcium, magnesium, and ammonium phosphates. *See* CALCULUS.

Q: What are the symptoms of nephrolithiasis?

A: Often there are no symptoms until the stone moves from its usual position.

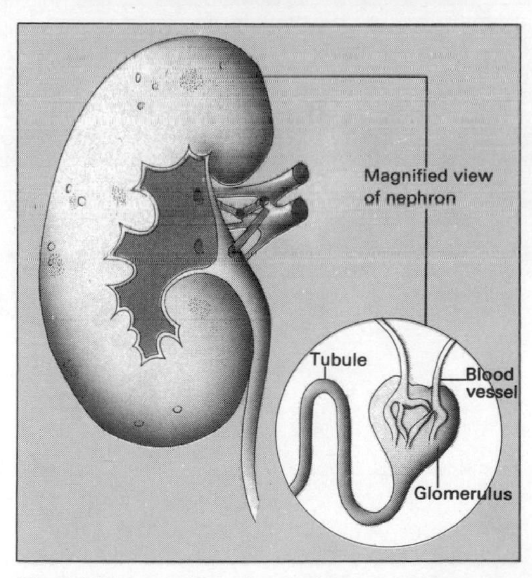

Nephritis may affect the nephrons or other parts of the kidney, such as the pelvis.

Rarely, large stones can form in the kidney (staghorn calculi), causing kidney damage without any obvious symptoms.

When a stone moves from the pelvis of the kidney into the ureter (the tube that carries urine to the bladder), there are severe spasms (renal colic) of pain from the lower back to the groin, with vomiting and sweating. There may also be blood in the urine (haematuria).

Q: *How is nephrolithiasis diagnosed and treated?*

A: A history of pain and haematuria suggests a stone, and its presence can usually be detected by an X-ray. An INTRAVENOUS PYELOGRAM (IVP) reveals where the stone is causing an obstruction.

A small stone may eventually pass down the ureter and out through the bladder. But large stones either remain in the kidney (and may have to be removed surgically) or become stuck in the ureter. A special instrument can be used to extract the stones stuck in the ureter during CYSTOSCOPY (an examination of the bladder). If this measure fails, surgery has to be done to remove the stone.

An acute attack of pain requires urgent treatment with strong painkilling and antispasm drugs prescribed by a doctor. Large quantities of fluid should be drunk, because this helps to make the stone pass down the ureter. All the urine that is passed must be filtered through a fine cloth so that the stone can be seen. It is usual to have an X-ray a few weeks later to make certain that a second stone has not stuck in the ureter.

Q: *Apart from pain, what are the dangers of kidney stones?*

A: The stone may obstruct urine flow and cause hydronephrosis or frequent attacks of PYELONEPHRITIS (inflammation of kidney substance).

Q: *Why do some people develop stones more easily than others?*

A: Apart from the reasons already mentioned, stones may develop from drinking water with a high concentration of salts. Stones more commonly occur in hot climates as the urine is more concentrated. It is necessary for people to drink plenty of fluid in tropical countries.

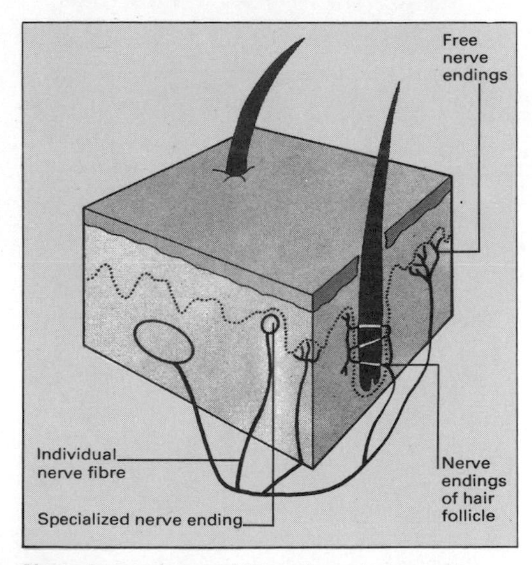

Nerve is a number of fibres bundled together that carries electrical impulses.

Nephrosis is any disorder of the kidney that is caused by degeneration and not by inflammation, for example, HYDRONEPHROSIS (obstructed outflow) and the NEPHROTIC SYNDROME (degenerative kidney change). It may also occur with AMYLOIDOSIS and some forms of poisoning.

Nephrostomy is an operation to drain urine from the pelvis of the kidney, usually performed because the ureter is blocked by a stone or a tumour.

Nephrotic syndrome is a kidney disorder in which too much protein is excreted in the urine. This results in decreased protein in the blood, OEDEMA (swelling of the body tissues), and disturbances of body fats. In rare cases the disorder may be present at birth or occur spontaneously in early childhood.

Q: *What are the symptoms of nephrotic syndrome?*

A: Symptoms include fatigue, weakness, and loss of appetite. A physical examination by a doctor may reveal a sudden or slow accumulation of fluid in the body tissues.

Q: *What causes nephrotic syndrome?*

A: Acute or chronic GLOMERULONEPHRITIS may result in the disorder. Also, any abnormality that causes an increase in the back pressure of blood in the veins leaving the kidney produces congestion in the kidney tissue. This can happen in heart failure or following a thrombosis in the renal vein.

Nephrotic syndrome may be a result of some systemic disease such as POLYARTERITIS NODOSA, AMYLOIDOSIS, DIABETES MELLITUS, MALARIA, OF MYELOMA (bone marrow tumour). It may also be caused by an allergic reaction to drug treatment (*see* SERUM SICKNESS). The cause of the most common form of nephrotic syndrome in children is not known.

Q: *What is the treatment for nephrotic syndrome?*

A: Nephrotic syndrome requires careful and skilled attention from a specialist in kidney disease, with repeated tests to assess the effect of treatment. The more serious causes make treatment difficult, and the outcome is more likely to be fatal. Corticosteroid drugs are particularly useful for treating children and chemotherapy is sometimes effective. DIURETIC drugs to increase urine flow reduce the swelling of oedema.

Nephrotomy is a surgical operation to cut into kidney tissue. It is sometimes performed as part of the treatment for a kidney stone (NEPHROLITHIASIS).

Nerve is a part of the body's "communications system," which carries messages between the brain and spinal cord and various other parts of the body. It consists of bundles of nerve fibres covered with a sheath of connective tissue and sometimes by a layer of fatty cells (myelin). Nervous impulses are transmitted by a weak electrical current that results from chemical changes taking place through the nerve wall. The final transmission, from one nerve to another or from a nerve to another structure, is carried out by a chemical reaction.

Sensory nerves collect information from the body and transmit it in the form of electrical impulses to the central nervous system for action. Other nerves pick up the impulses at nerve junctions (synapses) and trigger appropriate responses. For example, specialized nerve endings in the skin may detect a sensation such as cold, and pass the information to the brain. The brain may cause other nerves to stimulate shivering.

Motor nerves cause movement through the action of muscles. A reaction to intense heat, for example, causes the brain to stimulate motor nerves that cause the part of the body to be jerked away from the source of heat.

The main nerves are named according to the region from which they branch off. There are twelve pairs of cranial nerves, and thirty-one pairs of spinal nerves. The spinal nerves consist of eight pairs of cervical nerves, twelve pairs of thoracic nerves, five pairs of lumbar nerves, five pairs of sacral nerves, and one pair of coccygeal nerves.

See also AUTONOMIC NERVOUS SYSTEM; NERVOUS SYSTEM.

Nervous breakdown is a nonmedical term for any form of incapacitating mental illness. *See* MENTAL ILLNESS.

Nervous diseases. *See* MENTAL ILLNESS; NEUROLOGICAL DISORDERS.

Nervous system is a network of millions of interconnected nerve cells (neurons) that receive stimuli, co-ordinate this sensory information, and cause the body to respond appropriately. The individual nerve cells transmit messages by means of a complicated electrochemical process.

The nervous system is comprised of two main divisions: the central nervous system (CNS), which consists of the BRAIN and the SPINAL CORD; and the peripheral nervous system (PNS), which consists of spinal nerves and cranial nerves. These nerves link the CNS with the body's receptors and effectors.

Q: What are receptors and effectors?

A: The receptors include the various sensory cells and sense organs, whose function is to respond to various types of stimulation. For example, eyes respond to light, and ears respond to sound.

The effectors are all of the parts of the body, such as muscles and glands, that respond to instructions from the CNS.

Q: What are the functions of the CNS?

A: The CNS integrates the information from the PNS and sends instructions to various parts of the body so that appropriate responses are made to continually changing conditions. The brain is also involved in the processes of thinking, learning, memory, and intelligence.

Q: What are the functions of the PNS?

A: The PNS signals changes in the environment, as registered by the receptors, to the CNS. The instructions from the CNS to different parts of the body are also carried by the PNS.

Anatomically, the autonomic nervous system (ANS) is part of the PNS. However, in terms of function, the ANS

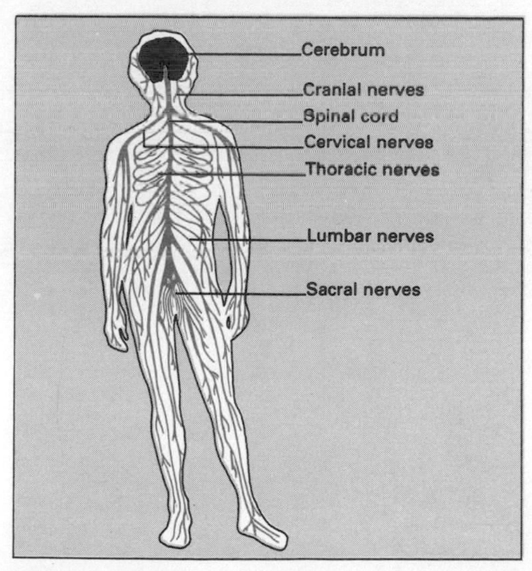

Nervous system runs throughout the body and relays information to the brain.

can be considered as a separate system. The ANS is concerned with controlling the body's involuntary activities, such as the beating of the heart, intestinal movements, and sweating. The actions of the ANS can be modified by the CNS, but it also has a degree of independence.

Nettle rash. *See* HIVES.

Neuralgia is any form of pain along a nerve. Pressure on a nerve, such as from a slipped disc in the neck, may produce continuous pain in the shoulders and arms. Neuralgia may also occur as a result of inflammation, as may occur in shingles (herpes zoster). The pain may persist in the trunk area after the attack because of scarring around the nerve endings. This condition is known as post-herpetic neuralgia.

Another type of neuralgia is known as metatarsalgia, in which the bones in the foot press on a nerve. Trigeminal neuralgia is a rare and acute form involving severe spasms of pain in the nerve endings of the face (*see* TRIGEMINAL NEURALGIA).

Q: How is neuralgia treated?

A: Treatment is directed at finding the cause, which may be difficult because some causes are not well understood. Painkilling and muscle relaxant drugs frequently give relief until the cause can be identified and treated. If drugs are not effective, some types of neuralgia may be treated surgically.

Neurasthenia is a term, no longer in use, that describes a condition in which a person complains of lack of energy, loss of appetite, and, frequently, loss of weight; it is often accompanied by insomnia, fatigue, and a feeling of inadequacy. These are usually symptoms of DEPRESSION, but they may signal the onset of any chronic illness. The symptoms may have an underlying physical cause, and a doctor should be consulted. The doctor may suggest psychotherapeutic help.

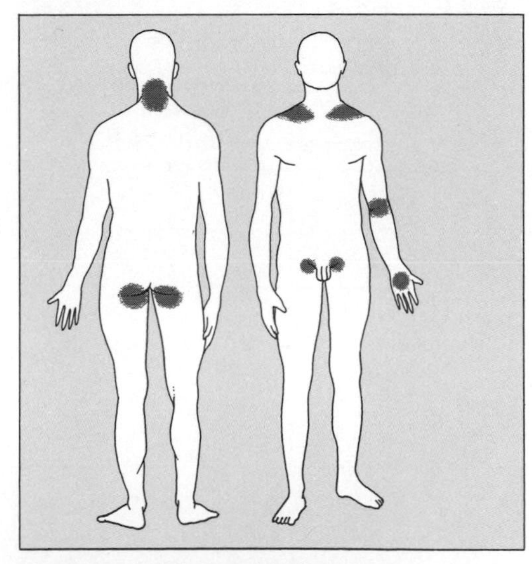

Neurodermatitis is a skin disorder that most commonly affects the sites shown.

Neuritis is inflammation of a nerve. If neuritis affects many nerves, the condition is called polyneuritis. *See* POLYNEURITIS.

Neurodermatitis is a skin disorder in which recurrent irritation occurs for no obvious reason. It causes an intense desire to scratch, resulting in inflammation and possibly infection. Continued scratching may lead to local thickening of the skin, which may develop a brownish pigmentation.

Q: What causes neurodermatitis?

A: An allergy, eczema, and congenital dry and scaly skin may be contributory factors. But anxiety, mental tension, and emotional disturbances are probably the main causes. The condition is more common in women than in men and in families with a history of allergy. Before diagnosing neurodermatitis, a doctor makes sure that there are no other skin conditions such as scabies, lichen planus, or local vaginal or anal infections that may produce irritation in those areas.

Q: How is neurodermatitis treated?

A: Corticosteroid creams usually give relief and an antipruritic drug may be prescribed to combat itching.

Neurofibroma is the swelling of a peripheral nerve, caused by a thickening of the nerve sheath or connective tissue. If a neurofibroma occurs in soft tissue, such as that of the mouth or stomach, there may be only slight symptoms. But neurofibromas that develop on nerves leaving the skull or spine, or on nerves adjacent to bones, may cause loss of sensation or paralysis as a result of pressure on the nerve. *See* VON RECKLINGHAUSEN'S DISEASE.

Neurofibromatosis is a disorder in which pigmented areas form on the skin. It is associated with multiple neurofibromas. *See* NEUROFIBROMA; VON RECKLINGHAUSEN'S DISEASE.

Neuroglia is the connective or supporting tissue between nerve cells within the central nervous system of the brain and spinal cord.

Neurological disorders. There are many disorders that affect the nervous system. The brain is concerned with both physical control of the body and with mental activities, such as reasoning. For disorders of mental activity, *see* MENTAL ILLNESS.

The following table lists some disorders of

the nervous system according to the structures involved. Each disorder has a separate article in the A-Z section of this book.

Structure	Disorder
Meninges (membranes surrounding the brain and spinal cord)	MENINGIOMA (a tumour of the meninges) MENINGITIS (inflammation of the meninges) SPINA BIFIDA (a congenital defect of the spinal canal)
Central nervous system (brain and spinal cord)	ALZHEIMER'S DISEASE (presenile dementia) BRAIN DISORDERS CEREBRAL HAEMATOMA ENCEPHALITIS (inflammation of the brain) ENCEPHALITIS LETHARGICA (epidemic encephalitis) EPILEPSY EXTRADURAL HAEMORRHAGE (external bleeding around the brain) GLIOMA (tumour of supporting cells of the brain) HYDROCEPHALUS (build-up of fluid within the brain) KORSAKOFF'S SYNDROME (generalized brain dysfunction) MICROCEPHALY (incomplete brain development) MIGRAINE MOTOR NEURON DISEASE (degeneration of brain cells) POLIOMYELITIS STROKE SUBARACHNOID HAEMORRHAGE (bleeding around the meninges) SYRINGOMYELIA (cavity formation in spinal cord) TABES DORSALIS (brain dysfunction due to syphilis)
Peripheral nervous system	BELL'S PALSY (facial paralysis) NEUROFIBROMA (a tumour of the connective tissue of a nerve) POLYNEURITIS (inflammation of several nerves) RETROBULBAR NEURITIS (inflammation of the optic nerve) TRIGEMINAL NEURALGIA (facial pain) VON RECKLINGHAUSEN'S DISEASE (multiple tumours of the nerve sheaths)

Neurology is the study of the nervous system and its disorders.

Neuroma is a tumour that is made up of nerve cells. A mature nerve cell cannot reproduce, and so cannot form a tumour. But the connective tissue (neuroglia) that supports the nerve cells can form tumours.

Some neuromas occur singly, others may be found throughout the body with pigmented patches on the skin. This condition is called VON RECKLINGHAUSEN'S DISEASE.

Neuropathy is a general term for any disorder of the peripheral nerves, including the autonomic nervous system. For example, pressure on one of the peripheral nerves in the hand (the median nerve) may cause CARPAL TUNNEL SYNDROME.

See also POLYNEURITIS.

Neurosis is a term used to describe a mental disorder that has no physical cause and that does not produce gross disturbances of the mental processes. *See* MENTAL ILLNESS.

Neurosurgery is the specialized branch of surgery that deals with the nervous system.

Neurotic is a person who is suffering from a NEUROSIS or in whom emotions overcome the normal steadying effect of reason.

Neutropenia is a decrease in the number of neutrophils, the most common white blood cell. It may be caused by any of several factors, but most commonly results from a viral infection.

See also AGRANULOCYTOSIS.

Niacin is the chemical name for one of the vitamin B complex. It is also called nicotinic acid. *See* VITAMINS.

Nicotinamide is a derivative of niacin or

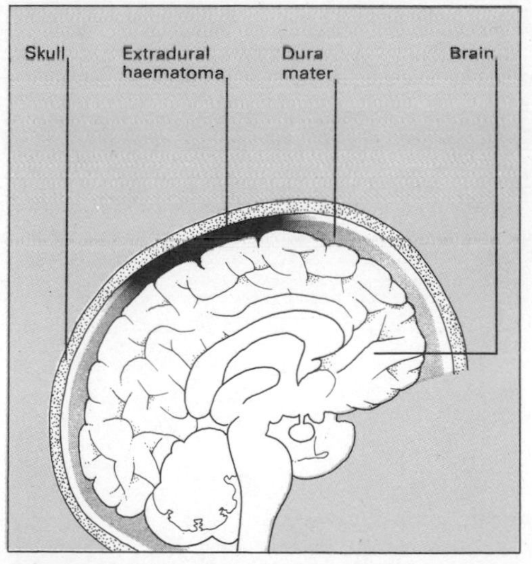

Extradural haematoma is bleeding between the dura mater and the skull.

nicotinic acid, and is a member of the vitamin B complex. *See* VITAMINS.

Nicotinic acid is an alternative name for niacin, one of the vitamin B complex. *See* VITAMINS.

Night blindness is an eye disorder in which vision is abnormally impaired in dim light or at night. It is caused by a deficiency of visual purple (rhodopsin) in the light-sensitive rods of the retina at the back of the eye. Visual purple is decreased if there is a dietary deficiency of vitamin A – its principal component. Another cause may be the slow regeneration of visual purple after exposure to bright lights, which causes the supply to be used up. Night blindness may also occur in other eye disorders, such as retinitis pigmentosa, choroidoretinitis, glaucoma, and xerophthalmia.

Q: How is night blindness treated?

A: Night blindness caused by vitamin A deficiency can be treated with therapeutic dosages of the vitamin, sometimes in the form of halibut liver oil. Treatment of the cause of the disorder may improve the condition, but there is no treatment for retinitis pigmentosa. Some types of damage to the retina, such as retinitis pigmentosa, are usually irreversible.

Nightmare is any frightening dream. Nightmares are most common in young children, who may find difficulty in distinguishing between fantasy and reality.

Frightening mental stimulation may also cause night terrors, in which a child wakes screaming but cannot remember the cause. Gentle reassurance is all that is usually needed to help the child return to sleep. Night terrors follow a specific pattern.

Q: Why do adults have nightmares?

A: Nightmares sometimes occur in adults who are depressed or anxious about something with which they feel incapable of dealing. Such nightmares are often accompanied by the physical signs of fear, such as palpitations and sweating, and may wake the individual. Antidepressant drugs may help those whose nightmares result from depression.

Nightmares may also result from a traumatic experience, such as a serious accident, or a death in the family.

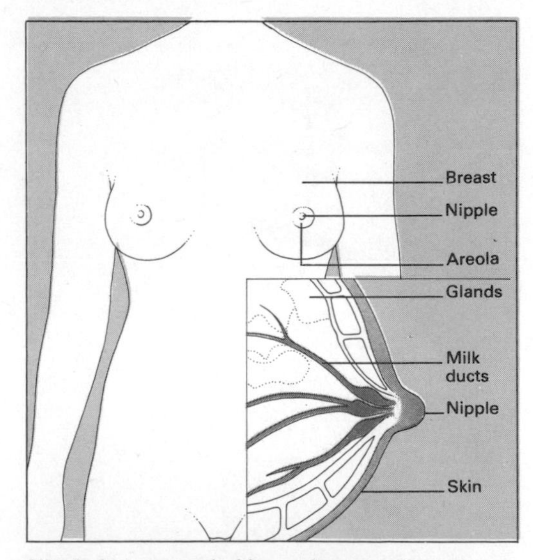

Nipple is surrounded by a pigmented areola and contains ducts from the mammary glands.

Night sweat is profuse sweating during sleep. It is common in children and normal when caused by vigorous activity before going to bed. Night sweats, in both adults and children, may also be caused by a chronic disease in which the body temperature rises during the night and falls during the following morning. Some diseases that may cause night sweats include tuberculosis, brucellosis, malaria, and, occasionally, cancer. The treatment of night sweats depends upon the cause. Most cases are harmless and require only fewer bedclothes and a change of night clothes. However, if night sweats persist, it is advisable to consult a doctor.

Night terror is a severe form of nightmare in which a child wakes up screaming and extremely frightened. It may be accompanied by SLEEPWALKING. *See* NIGHTMARE.

Nipple is the raised area in the centre of the breast. It is surrounded by a disc-shaped pigmented area called the areola. In a woman, about twenty milk ducts join in the nipple, and it is from these that milk is secreted by a mother who is breast-feeding a baby. *See* LACTATION.

Any bleeding from the nipple should be discussed immediately with a doctor, because it may indicate breast cancer. Skin diseases can also affect the nipple; the most serious of these is a moist, red eczema called PAGET'S DISEASE OF THE NIPPLE.

Nit is the egg of a louse. Nits may be seen as small white spots on the hair of an infested person. *See* LICE.

Nitrate is a salt of nitric acid. Some nitrates, such as glyceryl trinitrate, cause the blood vessels to dilate, and are used to treat angina pectoris. Others, such as potassium nitrate (saltpetre), are used as food preservatives.

Nitrous oxide is a colourless gas with a faint, characteristic odour that is used as a general anaesthetic in minor operations. However, in combination with another anaesthetic, it can be used for major surgery. Recovery from nitrous oxide anaesthesia is often accompanied by a period of confusion, during which the patient alternates between tears and laughter. For this reason, nitrous oxide is commonly called laughing gas.

Nocturia is the need to pass urine at night. It is differentiated medically from involuntary urination at night (nocturnal enuresis).

Nocturia commonly occurs in the elderly because the kidneys are less able to concentrate urine, and it becomes necessary to empty the bladder once or twice a night. In pregnant women, nocturia results when the enlarged womb presses on the bladder.

Nocturia may be a symptom of DIABETES MELLITUS, PROSTATE PROBLEMS, or a kidney disorder, such as chronic NEPHRITIS, NEPHROTIC SYNDROME, or PYELONEPHRITIS. Nocturia often occurs in HEART FAILURE or liver disease when there is OEDEMA (fluid retention).

Treatment depends on the cause. Assessment may involve kidney function measurements and other tests.

Nocturnal enuresis. *See* BED-WETTING.

Nonspecific urethritis (NSU) is inflammation of the urethra (the tube through which urine passes from the bladder) that is not known to be caused by a specific organism. It may be caused by various infections, including a viral infection similar to trachoma and the protozoan infection trichomoniasis. Nonspecific urethritis is a form of venereal disease and can be transmitted only by sexual contact.

Q: What are the symptoms of nonspecific urethritis?

A: The main symptoms in men are pain on urination and a discharge from the penis that is usually worse in the morning. In severe cases, urination is extremely painful, and there may be a thick white discharge similar to that in gonorrhoea.

Most women show no symptoms. Rarely, there may be mild pain during urination, a slight vaginal discharge, and pain during sexual intercourse. In most women, the only sign of nonspecific urethritis is infection of the neck of the womb (cervicitis).

Q: How is nonspecific urethritis treated?

A: Nonspecific urethritis is usually treated with an antibiotic drug; tetracycline is the most effective. Treatment lasts for two or three weeks. Alcohol should not be drunk for at least two weeks after the start of treatment, and sexual intercourse should be avoided until a doctor considers that the patient is cured.

Q: Can nonspecific urethritis cause any complications?

A: Yes. A relapse may occur before the patient is cured. This is especially likely if the patient has had sexual intercourse or has drunk alcohol during treatment.

Nonspecific urethritis may also cause EPIDIDYMITIS, PROSTATITIS, or SALPINGITIS. The most serious possible complication is REITER'S DISEASE, which may cause inflammation of the iris of the eye (iritis) and swelling of the joints (arthritis).

Noradrenaline is a hormone that is secreted by the sympathetic nervous system. Produced at nerve endings, it is the main chemical transmitter from sympathetic nerves to smooth muscle, heart muscle, and glands. It is also produced by the central part (medulla) of the adrenal glands, from which it passes into the bloodstream. Noradrenaline is a hormone that prepares the body for "fight or flight" in situations of stress. Circulating in the blood, it constricts the blood vessels and so reduces the blood flow to the brain, intestine, liver, and kidneys; relaxes the pupils of the eyes; and soothes movement of the smooth muscle of the gut. Another of its actions, when a large dose is given, is to stimulate the release of glucose from the liver, causing a rise in blood sugar level.

Noradrenaline can be released by stimulating the nerves or by the action of drugs such as amphetamines. It is given by intravenous infusion to treat shock.

See also ADRENAL GLAND; ADRENALINE; PHAEOCHROMOCYTOMA; SHOCK.

Nose, an external protrusion in the centre of the face, is the major organ of smell, and has an internal part that extends, backward, as two channels, through the front of the skull. It extends as far as the nasopharynx at the

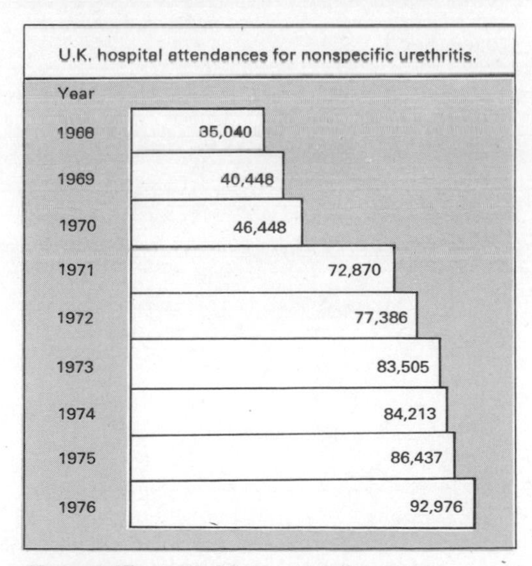

Nonspecific urethritis is spreading more quickly than other venereal diseases.

upper, back part of the throat. The two channels from the nostrils are separated from each other by a thin partition bone called the nasal septum. On each side are openings into air spaces within the cheekbones, the maxillary sinuses, and there are connections with the two sinuses in the frontal bone of the skull located at the top of the nose. There are other, smaller sinuses in the centre of the skull (*see* SINUS).

The external nose is formed by two small nasal bones, which can be felt at the bridge of the nose, and pliable cartilage covered with more mobile areas of skin that form the flare of the nostrils.

Q: *What are the functions of the nose?*

A: The nose has several functions. The hairs at the entrance filter out large dust particles, and the adenoids at the back of the nose combat disease organisms. The mucous membrane lining the nose warms and humidifies the air before it passes into the throat. And at the top of the nose, adjacent to the frontal sinuses, sensitive endings of the olfactory nerve detect smells. In addition, the cavities of the nose and sinuses help to give the voice its characteristic resonance.

Q: *What disorders may affect the nose?*

A: The COMMON COLD is the most usual infection that affects the nose, although an allergy such as HAY FEVER or VASOMOTOR RHINITIS may be another cause of a running nose. A nosebleed may occur spontaneously, or following infection or an accident. Chronic nasal infections produce CATARRH and a postnasal drip. The skin on the surface of the nose may become swollen and reddened, a condition known as RHINOPHYMA.

A blow to the front of the face may break the nose bones and damage the cartilage. Often the structures return to their natural positions after healing and, provided the nasal septum is straight, no permanent damage results. If, however, the nose is deformed, it should be set in the correct position by surgery. Sometimes the nasal septum is deformed, either as a result of a congenital anomaly or following an accident (*see* DEVIATED NASAL SEPTUM).

Occasionally small, soft swellings called polyps occur in the nose, causing obstruction to one or both nostrils. These may result from an allergy or a chronic infection. They can usually be removed under local anaesthetic.

It is usual for the sense of smell to deteriorate with age and to be lost whenever the nose is blocked, either because of infection, injury, or on the rare occasions when a foreign body is pushed into a nostril. Smoking may also reduce the sense of smell.

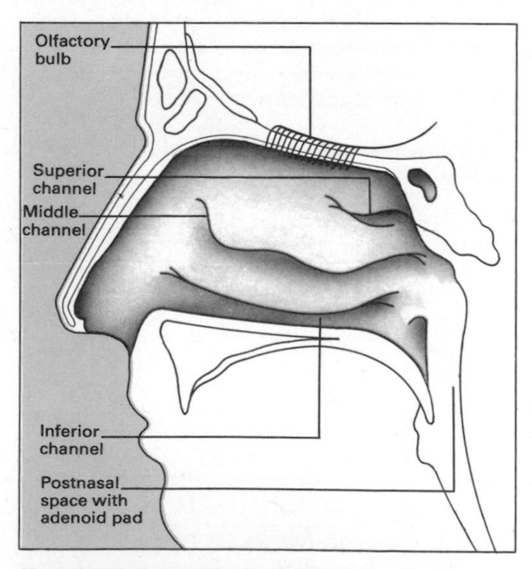

Nose is a large cavity in the skull lined with mucosa, communicating with the throat.

Nosebleed. For EMERGENCY treatment, *see* First Aid, p.590. Bleeding from one or both nostrils may occur for various reasons. Causes include an accident; an infection, such as the common cold; the result of a blood disorder, such as HAEMOPHILIA or LEUKAEMIA, or a side effect of taking anticoagulant drugs; because of repeated picking of the nose with the fingernails; or high blood pressure. Some nosebleeds happen spontaneously for no apparent reason.

Q: *Why do nosebleeds occur spontaneously?*

A: Spontaneous nosebleeds that occur in the elderly may be associated with deterioration of the blood vessels in ARTERIOSCLEROSIS, and are not really linked with high blood pressure (hypertension), as is commonly believed. Spontaneous nosebleeds are also common at puberty, particularly in boys, when they are thought to be caused by an expansion of the blood vessels in the nose from the stimulus of the sex hormones.

Q: *How should a nosebleed be treated?*

A: There are two procedures to be followed, depending on the age of the victim. The individual can sit in a chair with the head bent over a bowl and with a finger pressed to the bleeding nostril for at least ten minutes. Following an accident, and particularly with elderly people, lay the victim down with the head and shoulders supported on pillows or cushions, and see that the nostril is compressed. An ice pack on the bridge of the nose helps to reduce the blood flow.

If these simple measures fail to work, consult a doctor.

Q: How is a persistent or recurring nosebleed treated?

A: If the nosebleed is caused by a ruptured blood vessel, an E.N.T. specialist may be able to cauterize it with chemicals or by electricity, thus stopping the bleeding. If this is not possible, the nose can be packed with adrenaline-soaked gauze for at least twenty-four hours. It is rarely necessary to do more than this, although occasionally the victim needs a blood transfusion and a further operation to stop the bleeding.

Nostril is one of the two external openings of the nose. *See* NOSE.

Nucleus is a central point of a body around which matter is concentrated. For example, every body cell has a nucleus, which contains CHROMOSOMES and various other minute structures (*see* CELL) that control its activity.

The term nucleus is also used to describe a collection of nerve cells in an area within the brain.

Nucleus pulposus is the central part of an intervertebral disc; it is surrounded by a ring of tough, fibrous cartilage. At birth, the nucleus pulposus is a soft, jelly-like material, but with increasing age it is gradually replaced with fibrocartilage of the surrounding ring and thus loses much of its elastic quality. *See* DISC; SLIPPED DISC.

Nullipara is the medical term for a woman who has never given birth. The term covers those whose pregnancy has been terminated naturally or under medical supervision.

Numbness is complete or partial loss of sensation in an area of skin.

There are many conditions that may cause numbness and most of them involve the nervous system. Intense cold also produces numbness of the hands and feet and other skin areas, particularly in persons with poor peripheral circulation. Numbness may also be a symptom of an acute emotional upset, like hysteria. TINGLING may occur with numbness.

Q: What are the neurological causes of numbness?

A: Neurological causes of numbness include those caused by pressure on a nerve, such as sciatica, spondylosis (a degenerative condition of the spine), carpal tunnel syndrome (a disorder in the wrist), as well as polyneuritis. Other causes of numbness may involve the central nervous system as a result of a stroke or multiple sclerosis, syringomyelia (a disorder of the spinal cord), tabes dorsalis, or locomotor ataxia (a disorder of the nervous system). Numbness may also be caused by a deficiency of vitamin B_{12}, resulting in polyneuritis and degeneration of the spinal cord.

Q: How is numbness treated?

A: The treatment depends on a correct diagnosis of the cause. This can be made only by a doctor, who should be consulted when any numbness persists.

Nutrition is the sum total of the processes of eating, digesting, and assimilating food to obtain the carbohydrates, proteins, vitamins, and minerals necessary to maintain growth and health. *See* DIET; MALNUTRITION.

A talk about Nutritional problems

Nutritional problems may develop if food does not contain the essential nutrients or if a disorder interferes with the normal digestion or absorption of food.

Q: What are the likely causes of nutritional deficiency?

A: Nutritional disorders occur because of either a deficiency of the correct nutrients in food needed to maintain normal working and repair of the body, or a failure of the body to assimilate the correct nutrients. Everyone needs a certain balance of trace elements, vitamins, and other nutrients in his or her diet to maintain normal body activities.

There can also be too much of a nutrient in the diet, such as excessive

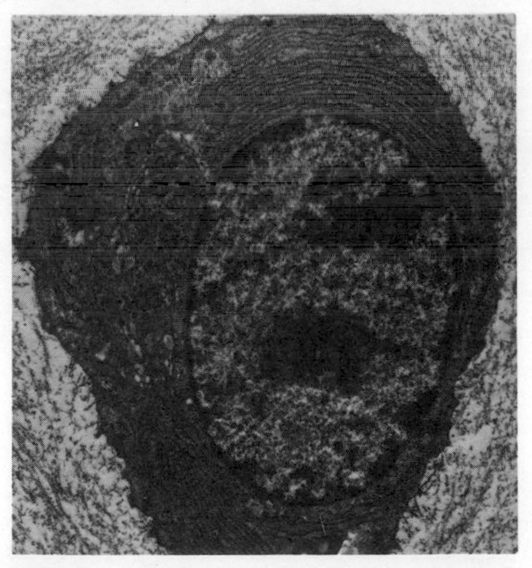

Nucleus of a cell controls and co-ordinates its chemical activity.

carbohydrate, resulting in such problems as obesity. Much of the excess is stored in the body as fat.

Q: Why do nutritional disorders occur?

A: Nutritional disorders will result from excessive fasting, from failure to eat the correct food during times of increased need, such as pregnancy and lactation, and during childhood, when growth is most rapid. Nutritional disorders also result from a voluntary or psychological refusal to eat some or all foods, as with total vegetarians and in anorexia nervosa; or from an increased intake of food, as occurs in any chronic disorder. This is particularly noticeable when it is accompanied by a fever or loss of protein from the body because of burns or wounds.

Q: Are there any other medical causes of nutritional disorders?

A: Yes. Medical causes of nutritional disorders include liver disease (cirrhosis), malabsorption from the intestine because of conditions such as Crohn's disease (inflammation of the ileum) and sprue (malabsorption). Other medical causes include genetic anomalies (such as phenylketonuria), and disorders that sometimes develop following gastro-intestinal surgery during which part of the intestine is removed or by-passed (such as gastroenterostomy).

Q: What are some symptoms of nutritional disorders?

A: The symptoms depend on which nutrient the body lacks. For example, lack of iron produces anaemia and nail deformity (koilonychia); lack of calcium causes osteomalacia (bone softening); and deficiencies of protein, carbohydrate, and fat result in weight loss. *See* DEFICIENCY DISEASE; VITAMINS.

Q: How are nutritional disorders prevented and treated?

A: Where there is no underlying medical problem, nutritional disorders can be prevented by eating a varied, well-balanced diet. This is especially important for pregnant women, who need a good, balanced diet because it also provides for the nutritional demands of the foetus.

A person suffering from a nutritional disorder usually recovers quickly when the diet improves, unless there is an underlying disease. A doctor can help in planning an appropriate diet.

When a nutritional disorder is well advanced and serious, it may be necessary to hospitalize the patient and to supply a diet of protein concentrates given by gastric tube or intravenously.

Q: What disorders other than obesity are caused by an incorrect diet?

A: It is probable that conditions such as appendicitis, constipation, diverticular disease, and mucous colitis are aggravated by a diet rich in refined carbohydrates and containing little vegetable fibre. It cannot be emphasized enough that roughage is an important ingredient of any balanced diet. A diet rich in saturated fats causes an increase in the levels of cholesterol and fats in the blood, exposing the person to the risks of arteriosclerosis.

Many people drink too much alcohol and eat too little food. Alcohol is a common substitute for energy foods and is the cause of many health problems. In some parts of the world, people drink large quantities of herbal teas that can cause cirrhosis and liver cancer.

Some food fads cause nutritional disorders if they are indulged in. VEGANS may develop vitamin B_{12} deficiency with pernicious anaemia.

See also KWASHIORKOR; MARASMUS.

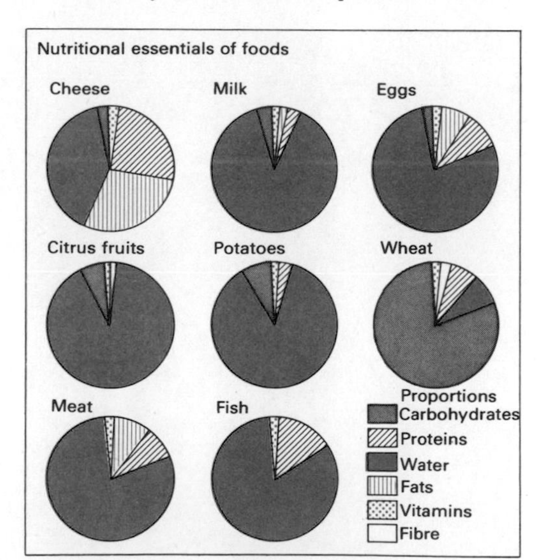

Nutrition is the process by which the body extracts and uses food constituents.

Nymphomania is an abnormally excessive desire in females for sexual intercourse. It may sometimes be associated with an inadequate personality development. Such a personality is unable to sustain a deep, lasting commitment and is able only to support superficial and transient relationships.

Nystagmus is a disorder that involves

involuntary eye movements. The eyes move rapidly and constantly from side to side or, less commonly, up and down or rotationally.

Q: What causes nystagmus?

A: Congenital nystagmus may be caused by an eye defect such as a cataract, coloboma, or severe nearsightedness (myopia). It often affects albinos, and also miners who have worked for long periods in badly-illuminated conditions. It can be an indication of a disorder of the organ of balance (such as labyrinthitis or Ménière's disease) or of the centre in the brain associated with balance (for example, caused by a brain tumour or a stroke). Other causes include motion sickness, drugs such as alcohol or barbiturates, chorea, and multiple sclerosis.

Q: How is nystagmus treated?

A: The treatment of nystagmus is directed at the cause.

Obesity is the condition of being overweight because of excess body fat. Strictly, the term obesity is used to denote a body weight that is twenty per cent or more over the average for a person's age, build, sex, and height. The degree of obesity can be determined by measuring the thickness of the fat over the muscles of the fold in front of the armpit. *See* WEIGHT PROBLEMS.

Obsession is a state of anxiety in which an individual is preoccupied with an idea or an action to the exclusion of all else. The action or idea may bring no benefit to the individual, but he or she is nevertheless abnormally concerned by it.

Q: Is obsession a form of mental illness?

A: Everyone has or has had mild obsessions about something or somebody, and it could be argued that obsession is an essential factor in creativity. But obsession in a pathological form that interferes with normal life is a form of mental illness and should be treated. When the obsession totally controls the behaviour of a person, he or she is said to be suffering from an obsessional neurosis. Psychoanalysts identify some people as obsessional types because they are controlled by anxiety. In such cases obsession is considered to be a personality disorder, or a feature of one.

Q: What forms does obsession take?

A: An obsession may be impulsive, inhibitory, or compulsive. Impulsive obsession is characterized by some form of action and can become a MANIA. Inhibitory obsession usually takes the form of a phobia, in which the individual cannot do something because of a fear that is often irrational.

In compulsive obsession, the individual may become extremely anxious if he or she is unable to carry out the obsessional desire. For example, a person may feel compelled to wash his or her hands constantly in the belief that they will never be clean. Other people may develop an obsession for locking doors. They may return again and again to make sure the door is locked before leaving, or find themselves unable to leave home for fear that the door can never be locked properly. This may be because the person feels vulnerable to hurt or harm.

Q: Can obsessions be treated?

A: Treatment is difficult. In mild cases, the use of tranquillizers can sometimes be helpful. Psychotherapy or psychoanalysis is seldom successful; behaviour therapy may help some people. The symptoms frequently lead to depression, which makes the obsession worse. Treatment of the depression with antidepressant drugs or electric shock therapy, or, occasionally, pre-frontal lobotomy, sometimes improves the condition.

Obstetrics is the branch of medicine that is concerned with pregnancy, labour, and the period just after childbirth (*see* PUERPERIUM). Obstetricians also specialize in GYNAECOLOGY.

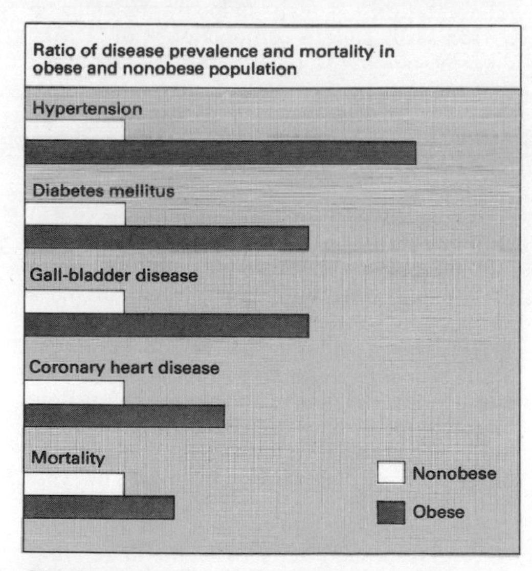

Obesity can seriously increase the incidence of certain diseases in a population.

Obstruction (for respiratory obstruction, *see* First Aid, p.518) is a blockage of an internal structure.

Occlusion is the state of being closed. This may be normal, as in the occlusion of the small gaps, called fontanelles, in the skull of a baby that occurs at about the age of eighteen months. An occlusion may also be abnormal, for example, when it is caused by an obstruction. Occlusion also refers to the way in which the teeth of the upper and the lower jaw fit together when the jaws are closed.

See also MALOCCLUSION.

Occult blood is blood that is present in such small amounts that it can be detected only by careful analysis. For example, minor bleeding in the intestines may not produce any obvious change in the faeces, but a simple chemical test on the faeces can detect the occult (hidden) blood.

Occupational hazards are any aspects of a person's work that may cause a disorder. Many occupations or ways of life carry the risk of particular diseases or disorders. For relevant information, *see* ACTINOMYCOSIS; ALCOHOLISM; ANTHRAX; ASBESTOSIS; ASPERGILLOSIS; BENDS; BRUCELLOSIS; BYSSINOSIS; CANCER; DEAFNESS; DERMATITIS; DUPUYTREN'S CONTRACTURE; HEATSTROKE; LEPTOSPIROSIS; MINAMATA DISEASE; PNEUMOCONIOSIS; PSITTACOSIS; RADIATION; RAYNAUD'S PHENOMENON; RINGWORM; STRESS; TUBERCULOSIS.

Occupational therapy is any activity, either physical or mental, that is performed to promote a patient's recovery. Occupational therapy, under the supervision of a registered therapist, is an integral part of treatment and rehabilitation. It can help by teaching a person skills and, in conjunction with physiotherapy, helping to restore muscles and joints that are damaged or wasted.

Odontitis is inflammation of the teeth. *See* PERIODONTITIS.

Oedema is a localized or general swelling caused by the build-up of fluid within body tissues. Excess fluid may be a result of (1) poor circulation of the blood; (2) a failure of the lymphatic system to disperse the fluid; (3) various diseases and disorders; or (4) a combination of factors.

Other causes of oedema include salt retention caused by disease of the heart or kidneys, or a reduction in the amount of protein in the blood, which may occur as a result of cirrhosis, chronic nephritis, or toxaemia of pregnancy (eclampsia). Localized oedema may result from injury or infection.

Q: How is oedema treated?

A: The treatment depends on the underlying cause of the oedema. Diuretic drugs, which make the kidneys eliminate excess salt and water, often produce an immediate improvement. Oedema caused by varicose veins and pregnancy can be prevented by wearing elastic stockings. Oedema of the ankles, from any cause, may be helped by lying down with the feet raised.

See also ANKLES, SWOLLEN.

Oedipus complex is a psychoanalytical term for the sexual love of a son for his mother, often accompanied by feelings of jealousy toward the father. The female counterpart is the Electra complex. *See* COMPLEX.

Oesophageal speech is a method of producing viable speech, after the surgical removal of the voice box (larynx), by vibrating air in the oesophagus instead.

Oesophagus, also known as the gullet, is a muscular tube about 25cm (10 inches) long that extends from the pharynx at the back of the throat to the stomach. In the neck, the oesophagus lies behind the trachea, and enters the thorax behind the aorta and heart to join the top of the stomach.

The oesophagus conveys food and drink from the pharynx to the stomach. This is achieved partly by gravity and partly by peristalsis (rhythmical waves of muscular contractions). When a person breathes in, air is directed to the larynx and the trachea. At the same time, however, saliva is able to run down the oesophagus. Where the oesophagus and the stomach join, there is a ring of muscle (the lower oesophageal sphincter) that prevents the stomach contents from passing back up the oesophagus.

See also ACHALASIA; DYSPHAGIA; HEARTBURN; HIATUS HERNIA.

Oestrogen is the collective name for several female sex hormones produced mainly by the ovaries but also by the adrenal glands.

At the onset of puberty, oestrogens stimulate the development of pubic hair and of secondary female sex characteristics, such as rounded hips and breasts. Oestrogens also play an essential part in the hormonal control of menstruation, being partly responsible (with progesterone) for the cyclical changes in the lining of the womb.

Oestrogens have a number of medical uses. For example, synthetic oestrogens are a component of most types of contraceptive pill, and are also used in the treatment of menstrual disorders and in hormone replacement therapy (HRT) at menopause.

In men, synthetic oestrogens are used in the treatment of cancer of the prostate gland.

See also HORMONES.

Olecranon is the part of the bone of the forearm (ulna) that sticks out at the back of the elbow. With the bone of the upper arm (humerus), the olecranon forms part of the elbow joint. *See* ELBOW.

Olfactory means relating to the sense of smell.

Oliguria is the excretion of abnormally small amounts of urine. It may occur as the result of a high fever, poisoning, or SHOCK, or it may accompany excessive fluid loss from sweating, vomiting, or diarrhoea. Oliguria may also be a symptom of a kidney disorder such as NEPHRITIS, PYELONEPHRITIS, or URAEMIA. If oliguria is persistent, a doctor must be consulted.

Omentum is a loose fold of the membrane (peritoneum) that hangs from the stomach and covers the front of the intestines. It protects the intestines and helps to seal any damage to the intestinal wall, so helping to prevent infection.

Onchocerciasis is the infestation with the parasitic worm *Onchocerca volvulus.* It occurs in regions of Africa, Mexico, and South America. The larvae of the worms are transmitted by the bite of infected black flies of the genus *Simulium.*

Oncology is the study of tumours. It involves the development of improved surgical techniques, radiotherapy, and chemotherapy for the treatment of malignancies.

Onychia is inflammation of the nail bed. *See* PARONYCHIA.

Onychogryposis is a deformity of the nails in which they become thickened and curve inward. It occurs most commonly on the nail of the big toe as a result of pressure from ill-fitting shoes. Onychogryposis may also be caused by repeated injury to the nail bed, or by fungal infections, such as RINGWORM.

Oophorectomy is the surgical removal of an ovary. It is usually performed when there is a cyst or a tumour in the ovary. It may also be necessary if a fertilized ovum has become implanted on the ovary (*see* ECTOPIC PREGNANCY). If there is a benign cyst in the ovary, a partial oophorectomy may be performed.

When a woman over 45 years of age has a HYSTERECTOMY, both ovaries are usually removed; this is called a bilateral oophorectomy. A bilateral oophorectomy may also be performed as part of the treatment for breast cancer.

Oophoritis is inflammation of an ovary. It may be caused by mumps, or other virus organisms. It may be secondarily related to SALPINGITIS, or an infection in the pelvis, such as appendicitis. The symptoms of oophoritis are pain as well as excessive menstruation. Most patients respond to treatment with antibiotics; severe cases may require surgery.

Ophthalmia is any inflammation of the eye. Ophthalmia neonatorum affects newborns; the conjunctivae are contaminated during birth, usually because the mother has gonorrhoea. Early treatment with antibiotic drugs avoids the onset of blindness.

Sympathetic ophthalmia is inflammation of one eye as a reaction to injury of the other eye. This disorder is rare, and it can usually be treated with drugs.

Electric ophthalmia is caused by prolonged exposure to intense light. Symptoms are pain, sensitivity to light, and excessive watering of the eyes.

See also CONJUNCTIVITIS; EYE DISORDERS; TRACHOMA.

Ophthalmic describes anything pertaining to the eye.

Ophthalmoplegia is paralysis of some or all of the muscles of the eye. It may affect one or both eyes, and may come on gradually or occur suddenly. External ophthalmoplegia is paralysis of the muscles on the outside of the eye that control movement of the eyeball. Internal ophthalmoplegia makes the pupil dilated and immobile.

Q: What causes ophthalmoplegia?

A: Ophthalmoplegia may occur temporarily with migraine or the muscle disorder myasthenia gravis. It may also occur in an advanced or acute stage of thiamine (vitamin B_1) deficiency; or with polyneuritis, particularly when associated with diabetes mellitus. It can also be caused by pressure on nerves that supply the optic muscles, whether from an aneurysm, brain tumour, or brain infection such as meningitis. Ophthalmoplegia can also occur with multiple sclerosis. External ophthalmoplegia is a result of hyperthyroidism (thyrotoxicosis); fatty tissues in the eye socket swell and press on the eyeball, which makes the eye bulge outward and eventually paralyzes the eye muscles.

Q: What are the symptoms of ophthalmoplegia?

A: Ophthalmoplegia in one eye causes double vision (diplopia), because the affected eye is immobile while the other eye is free to move. Internal ophthalmoplegia impairs vision because the pupil is unable to react to variations in the amount of light reaching the eye, and the lens is unable to adjust to focus at different distances.

Q: How is ophthalmoplegia treated?

A: The cause of the condition must be found and treated. However, if only one eye is affected, temporary relief from the distress of double vision can be obtained by wearing a patch that covers the paralyzed eye.

Ophthalmoscope

Ophthalmoscope is an instrument for examining the interior of the eye. It has lenses, a mirror, and a light that shines a bright beam through the patient's pupil. Using an ophthalmoscope, a doctor can examine the retina, optic nerve, and the eye's network of blood vessels, in the diagnosis of specific eye disorders and some physical conditions.

Opiate is any drug that contains opium or one of its constituents, morphine or codeine.

Opisthotonus is a severe form of body spasm in which the back, head, and legs arch backward. It is a symptom of strychnine poisoning and severe forms of TETANUS.

Opium is the dried secretion from the unripe seed pods of the opium poppy (*Papaver somniferum*). It has a bitter taste and a characteristic smell. Opium contains more than twenty alkaloid drugs, including MORPHINE, CODEINE, and papaverine. The effects of opium are similar to those of morphine and, like morphine, it produces physical dependence. Heroin is a semisynthetic derivative of opium. The medical use of opium and its constituents morphine and codeine, is strictly controlled by law.

See also DRUG ADDICTION.

Optic describes anything concerned with the eye or vision.

Oral describes anything pertaining to the mouth.

Oral cholecystogram is an X-ray examination of the gall bladder. It is used to diagnose gallstones and chronic inflammation of the gall bladder (cholecystitis). The patient is given a fat-free meal on the evening before an examination, and is then deprived of solid food. The following morning, the patient swallows an iodine-containing compound. Several hours later, a series of X-rays are taken of the gall bladder. The iodine compound becomes concentrated in the gall bladder and makes abnormalities such as gallstones visible on X-rays. The patient is then given a fatty meal, and more X-rays are taken. Absorption of fats from the meal causes the gall bladder to contract, and permits the bile ducts to become visible.

An oral cholecystogram gives a definite result in most cases. However, if the gall bladder and the bile ducts cannot be seen on the X-rays, an intravenous cholecystogram may be necessary.

Oral contraception. *See* CONTRACEPTION.

Oral surgery is surgery performed on the mouth. It may be performed by a dental surgeon to treat diseased or impacted teeth, gum disorders, or disorders of the underlying bone. Oral surgery is sometimes necessary in the treatment of a MALOCCLUSION.

An otolaryngologist, who specializes in disorders of the ear, nose, and throat, may perform oral surgery to treat cancer of the jaw, mouth, or tongue. Some disorders of the salivary glands, such as tumours or stones, may also require oral surgery. Fractures of the jaw and face usually require surgery.

Orbit is the bony socket that surrounds and protects the eye. It is considerably larger than the eye, the space being filled with loose fat so that the eye is free to move. Six muscles that move the eye are attached to the orbit at one end, and to the outer coat of the eyeball at the other. There is a hole at the back of the orbit through which the optic nerve and blood vessels pass.

See also EYE.

Orchidectomy is the surgical removal of a testicle. It may be necessary if there is a tumour of the testicle, or if the testicle has become twisted, as may occur with an undescended testicle (*see* CRYPTORCHIDISM). The removed testicle may be replaced with a synthetic substitute for cosmetic purposes.

Orchiopexy is surgical fixation of an undescended testicle in its correct place in the scrotum. In some forms of this operation, the testicle and the scrotum are temporarily attached to the inner side of the thigh.

Orchitis is inflammation of the testicles. It occurs most commonly as a complication of MUMPS, but it may also be caused by injury to the testicles, or by the spread of infection from elsewhere in the body, such as occurs in EPIDIDYMITIS. One or both testicles may become enlarged and extremely painful. Fever, nausea, and vomiting may also occur. These symptoms may be relieved by the

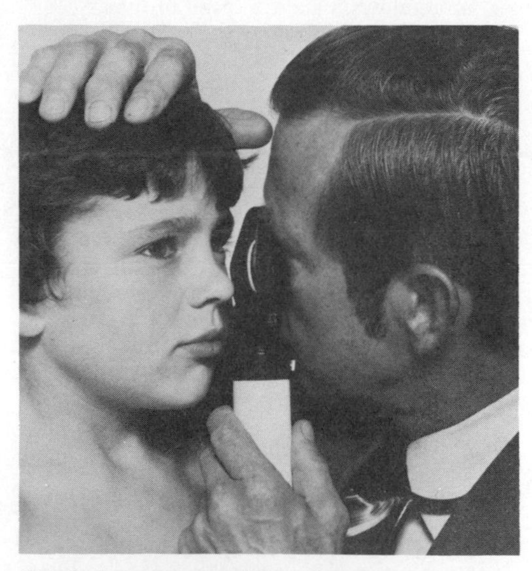

Ophthalmoscope enables a doctor to examine the interior of the eyes.

application of ice packs and the use of painkillers. The scrotum should also be placed on a cotton wool pad, which should be supported by adhesive tape stretched between the thighs. The inflammation usually subsides within a few days.

Orgasm is a pleasurable sexual climax. In men it is accompanied by the ejaculation of semen and by rhythmic contractions of muscles in the genital area. In women, orgasm is accompanied by contractions of the vagina.

An orgasm does not necessarily always occur during sexual intercourse, but continual failure to attain orgasm is, in most cases, caused by psychological factors.

Ornithosis. *See* PSITTACOSIS.

Orthodontics is the branch of dentistry that is concerned with the prevention and correction of abnormally positioned teeth. Orthodontic treatment is usually performed during childhood, when the jaw is still developing and when the gradual restraint of certain teeth can prevent development of a MALOCCLUSION.

Orthopaedics is a specialty of medical science concerned with the treatment of disorders of bones and joints. Orthopaedic surgery is the surgical prevention or correction of bone deformities. Orthopaedics also includes the study and treatment of rheumatic disorders and disorders of muscles or nerves that may aggravate or cause orthopaedic conditions.

Orthopnea is breathlessness that occurs in any position other than standing or sitting upright. The term commonly means difficulty in breathing when lying down. *See* BREATHLESSNESS.

Orthoptics is a technique used to correct defects in the muscles that control the alignment of the eyes. It involves a set of eye exercises to co-ordinate the movements of the two eyes. Orthoptic training is beneficial in the treatment of strabismus (squint).

Ossicle is any small bone. The term usually refers to one of the three small bones in the middle ear: the malleus, incus, or stapes. *See* EAR.

Ossification is the formation of bone. It occurs normally during the development of a foetus, when bone is formed from cartilage. It continues during childhood, and the final stage in bone formation, the ossification of the growing ends of bone, occurs during adolescence.

Abnormal ossification may develop within tissues that have been damaged, particularly in muscles, ligaments, and sometimes tendons. Bone formation may occasionally occur in a frozen shoulder (a form of tendinitis) in the muscle of the shoulder blade, but is more frequent in metabolic disorders associated with raised CALCIUM levels in the blood.

Osteitis is inflammation of bone that involves the marrow. It causes periostitis, a swelling and local tenderness of the periosteum, the membrane that surrounds the bone. For practical purposes, osteitis and osteomyelitis can be considered to have the same causes and treatment. *See* OSTEOMYELITIS.

Osteitis deformans. *See* PAGET'S DISEASE OF BONE.

A talk about Osteoarthritis

Osteoarthritis is a chronic disorder involving the joints. It is a degenerative change in the joints and should properly be called osteoarthrosis. It is not caused by inflammation. The degenerative changes take place because of the rubbing of the joint surfaces, causing a wearing away and disintegration of the tissues.

There is usually some additional factor that speeds up this process. The factors include unusual stresses on the joint, such as those resulting from obesity or bow-legs; disorders that damage the joint cartilage, such as rheumatoid arthritis and osteochondritis (bone and cartilage inflammation); or damage to the joint surfaces from a fracture or torn cartilage. Other factors are disorders of the joint, such as congenital dislocation of the hip, and the slowing down of the normal repair processes that take place in old age.

Q: Which joints are most likely to be affected by osteoarthritis?

A: The joints that carry the body's weight are most likely to develop osteo-

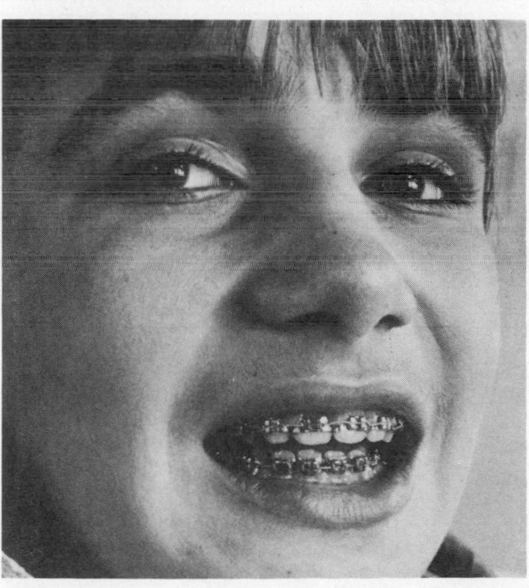

Orthodontic disorders can be treated with the use of highly specialized teeth braces.

arthritis. For example, repeated injuries to an athlete's hips, knees, or ankles are likely to result in osteoarthritis in those joints in later life. Repeated attacks of gout or of septic arthritis can also cause osteoarthritis.

Q: *What happens to the joint in osteoarthritis?*

A: The slippery cartilage that lines the joint surface is gradually worn away, exposing the underlying bone. The bone becomes smooth and its edges become rough, with small areas of bony formation, known as osteophytes. The surrounding ligaments and membranes also become thickened because of the recurrent slight strains that occur in an osteoarthritic joint.

Q: *What are the symptoms of osteoarthritis?*

A: There is gradually increasing pain, with restriction of movement. The amount of pain varies from time to time; additional strains or unexpected movements make the condition worse. In most joints, this process is accompanied by a grating that can sometimes be heard and usually felt.

Q: *How is osteoarthritis diagnosed?*

A: A doctor makes the diagnosis after an examination of the joint is confirmed by X-rays. Swellings adjacent to the end joints of the fingers (Heberden's nodes) are common.

Q: *What is the treatment for osteoarthritis?*

A: Osteoarthritis is increasingly common with age, and treatment is directed toward improving general health. This includes encouraging weight loss if the patient is overweight, and teaching exercises designed to strengthen surrounding muscles and maintain movement of the joint when it is not bearing weight. The emphasis should be on either resting without strain (not too much walking or standing), or on taking exercise without strain. Hot pads often give relief if a joint has become acutely painful. If necessary, canes, crutches, or walking frames can be used.

Morale can be maintained with encouragement from the doctor. During the initial stages, aspirin or some other painkilling drug may be prescribed. Various antirheumatic drugs, such as indomethacin and ibuprofen, may be used.

Q: *Does surgery help in osteoarthritis?*

A: Yes. There are many surgical procedures that are helpful in the treatment of osteoarthritis. Arthrodesis, an operation to fix the joint in one position, can be done to prevent further pain. The ankle is often fixed in this way.

Other operations include removing some of the membranes around the joint or forming a new joint, as is done in treatment for hallux valgus deformities.

In recent years total replacement of a joint has become possible by the insertion of a plastic and metal artificial joint. This has been done successfully in finger joints, hip joints, and knee joints.

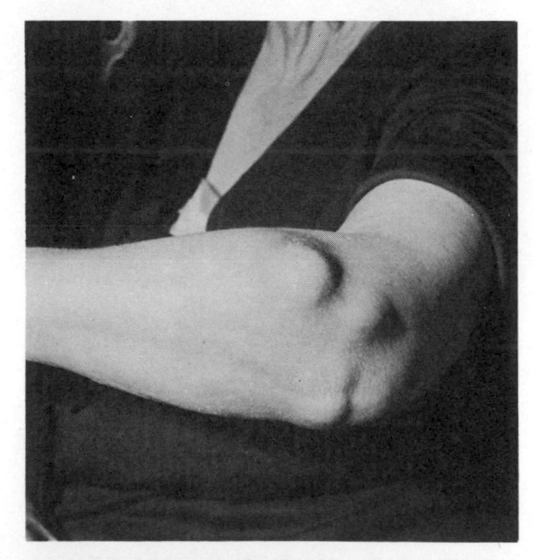

Osteoarthritis gradually destroys the cartilage of the joint, producing overgrowths of bone.

Osteoarthropathy is any disease of the joints and bones. Usually the joints become damaged as a result of some other disorder. For example, nerves in the joints, which normally give a sense of position and are responsible for the sensation of pain, may be affected by inflammation (peripheral neuritis).

Some causes of these conditions include tabes dorsalis (damage to the lower spinal cord); neuritis associated with diabetes mellitus; and syringomyelia, another spinal cord disease. Repeated damage results in a thickening or enlargement of the joints, instability of movement, and osteoarthritis of the joint.

Chronic hypertrophic pulmonary osteoarthropathy is the medical term for CLUBBING of the fingers and toes in persons with chronic lung or heart disease.

Osteoarthrosis. *See* OSTEOARTHRITIS.

Osteochondritis is inflammation of bone and cartilage; in most cases, it leads to degeneration of these tissues (osteochondrosis). There are two forms of the disorder, osteochondritis dissecans and osteochondritis deformans juvenilis. Their causes are not known.

Q: What are the symptoms of osteochondritis dissecans and how is it treated?

A: The disorder usually affects young adults, who have recurrent attacks of mild pain, usually in the knee joint. Fluid in the area may increase, followed by sudden and recurrent locking of the joint.

What probably happens is that the blood supply to the local bone and cartilage is affected and causes a piece of cartilage and underlying bone to break off and move into the joint. This loose fragment causes the sudden locking and resulting pain.

The condition is usually diagnosed late. Bone and cartilage may heal if the joint is kept in a cast for eight to ten weeks. But an operation to remove the fragment is the best form of treatment.

Q: What are the symptoms of osteochondritis deformans juvenilis and how is it treated?

A: This disorder, also known as PERTHES' DISEASE, occurs in children. It usually affects the thoracic spine, the top of the thigh-bone (femur), the wrist, and the foot. The bone becomes softened and may easily be deformed by pressure or accident. The usual symptom is pain over the bone, and the damage can be seen on an X-ray. The disorder is relatively harmless, but may ultimately lead to osteoarthritis of the joint.

If the condition is diagnosed early, the joint can be rested in a cast so that further deformity does not occur. This is particularly important when the condition affects the hip joint.

Osteoclastoma is a bone tumour that is usually benign (noncancerous), although it invades the tissues surrounding the bone. This disorder commonly affects young adults and involves the bones on either side of the knee joint. There is pain with the swelling of the bone, and possibly fractures.

Treatment is the removal of the tumour by surgery, even if the surrounding joint and tissue have to be destroyed. Radiotherapy is used for treatment of areas such as the spine that are difficult to reach by normal surgical techniques. *See* OSTEOSARCOMA.

Osteogenesis imperfecta, or fragilitas ossium, is an inherited disorder in which the bones are abnormally brittle and may break easily, often causing deformities. The condition may be associated with a blue coloration of the whites of the eyes and with chronic, progressive deafness (OTOSCLEROSIS).

A child with osteogenesis imperfecta may die in early life. Otherwise, there is a tendency for slight improvement with age.

Osteology is the study of the structure and function of bones. It also involves the study of all the diseases and disorders that affect bones.

Osteoma is a benign (noncancerous) tumour of bone. It usually forms on the skull or long bones. Most osteomas cause local thickening of bone and do not produce any symptoms. They can be left alone or removed if they are unsightly or obstruct a blood vessel. But an osteoid osteoma, a rare benign tumour of bone, can cause severe and deep pain. It is treated by surgical removal of the tumour, which gives immediate relief from pain.

Osteomalacia is a softening of the bones in an adult, similar to rickets in children. In persons with osteomalacia, the basic structure of the bone remains unaltered.

Q: What are the symptoms of osteomalacia?

A: Common symptoms are aching and painful bones, as well as fractures. Softened bones may also bend under the weight of the body.

Q: What causes osteomalacia?

A: Osteomalacia is also called adult rickets because it usually results from a lack of vitamin D and calcium in the diet. Other causes include kidney failure and intestinal disorders. *See* RICKETS.

Q: How is osteomalacia diagnosed and treated?

A: Diagnosis depends on bone X-rays and blood tests to determine calcium and phosphorus levels. The possibility of conditions with similar symptoms, such as osteoporosis, hyperparathyroidism, and Cushing's syndrome, must first be eliminated.

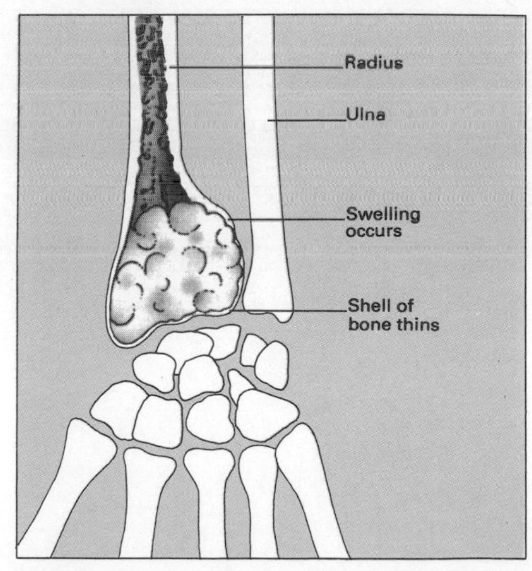

Osteoclastoma is a benign tumour of giant cells within the bone marrow causing swelling.

Osteomyelitis

Osteomyelitis, or osteitis, is inflammation of bone, including the marrow. It is usually caused by a bacterial infection.

There are two kinds of osteomyelitis: acute and chronic. Children most commonly suffer from acute osteomyelitis. Chronic osteomyelitis usually follows an acute attack and rarely occurs on its own. It can, however, be caused by tuberculosis.

Q: *Why does acute osteomyelitis occur?*

A: In acute osteomyelitis, bacteria may be carried by the bloodstream from another area of infection to the bone. It may be the result of a septic tooth, a boil, or an ear infection. It can also reach the bone through an injury such as an open fracture. There is frequently a history of recent minor injury or knocks to the bone. The growing end of the bone is the area most frequently infected.

Q: *What are the symptoms of acute osteomyelitis?*

A: Children may have several days of fever and general illness before suffering from local bone pain. But in both adults and children bone involvement is followed by a sudden increase in temperature, sometimes with vomiting, and local tenderness of the bone with painful movement of nearby joints. Swelling occurs and the skin becomes red.

Q: *How is acute osteomyelitis diagnosed and treated?*

A: X-rays seldom help diagnosis in the early stages, but a white blood cell count shows the type of response the body is making to acute infection, helping a doctor to diagnose osteomyelitis and begin treatment immediately. Massive doses of antibiotics, usually one of the penicillin drugs, are given for at least two months and the bone is immobilized in a splint. Careful assessment by an orthopaedic surgeon or doctor is necessary to ensure that an abscess has not formed. If an abscess is found, antibiotics are given and surgery performed to remove the abscess. If pus has formed, it is sometimes necessary to drain the bone by drilling holes in it.

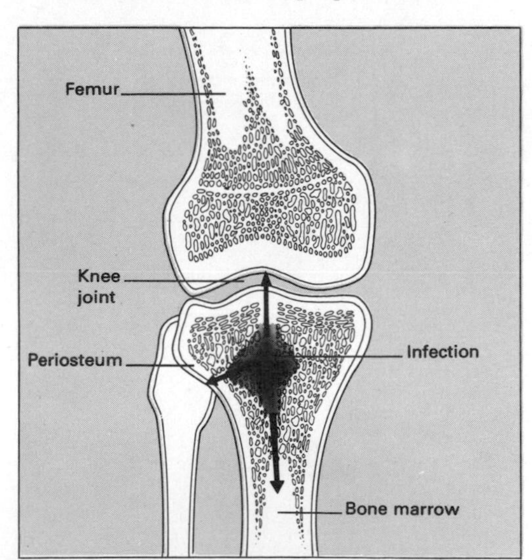

Osteomyelitis is an infection of the bone marrow that can spread to the periosteum.

Q: *What are the symptoms and treatment of chronic osteomyelitis?*

A: The usual symptom is pain and a discharge of pus. The bone abscess usually discharges through the skin, although sometimes pain and swelling occur over the bone and the patient has a mild fever. An X-ray confirms the diagnosis, and surgery is performed to remove any fragments of dead bone that can encourage continued infection. Complete cleansing of the area is more important than the use of antibiotics.

Brodie's abscess is a form of chronic osteomyelitis that occurs without a previous acute attack. The main symptom is deep, intense bone pain. The treatment is the same as for any other form of chronic osteomyelitis.

Q: *What other forms of osteomyelitis may occur?*

A: Tuberculosis may spread to bone, producing a "cold" abscess in which there is swelling without heat or redness to the skin, but with local pain. The patient usually experiences a slight fever, loss of weight, and general malaise. The diagnosis is confirmed by a combination of X-rays, blood tests, a Mantoux test (a test for tuberculosis infection), and the examination of pus from the abscess.

Treatment consists of antituberculous drugs, splinting of the bone, and an operation to remove the abscess.

It is important that a search be carried out for other possible areas of tubercular infection, especially in the lungs and kidneys. People who have had contact with the patient, particularly children, must be examined to prevent spread of the disorder.

Osteopathy is a system of physical treatment developed by the American physician Dr Andrew Taylor Still (1828–1917). Dr Still taught that the body is able to deal with any disorder provided any underlying defect in its structure is corrected. These defects are diagnosed in a conventional manner, if necessary by the various tests and examinations used in conventional medical practice. The defects are treated by both manipulation of the spine and other bones and by conventional medical and surgical techniques to correct the underlying structural problem. Osteopaths are seldom qualified doctors; GPs may not therefore feel able to refer patients to one.

Q: How do osteopaths help their patients?

A: An osteopath can sometimes help a patient suffering from a functional disorder for which orthodox medicine has proved less effective. The osteopath makes a careful assessment of the patient's condition, finally arriving at a diagnosis on which to base treatment. X-rays help to locate any abnormality, especially if it is in the spine.

Treatment of spinal disorders consists of a combination of manipulation and encouraging movement of the spine by gently turning the body or pulling it in certain directions. The osteopath is skilled in the art of manipulating the vertebrae of the spine by sensitive finger pressure. Similar methods are used in the treatment of other parts of the body.

Q: What conditions respond to osteopathy?

A: The main value of osteopathy is in the treatment of orthopaedic and rheumatic disorders, but it can be used to treat a much wider range of functional disorders. Many people consult an osteopath only for treatment of backache, sciatica, or shoulder pain caused by osteoarthrosis in the neck. However, osteopaths may treat many conditions from headache to painful periods (dysmenorrhoea) in which muscle spasm is, in part, a cause.

Q: Can osteopathy prevent the development of certain conditions?

A: Yes. Osteopathy can, in some cases, prevent the recurrence of backache or sciatica, because the treatment keeps the spine in the correct alignment. An osteopath may also notice minor faults before symptoms have developed and can often prevent the occurrence of a disorder by manipulation.

Osteoporosis is a disorder in which both calcium salts and bone fabric are lost. It is different from OSTEOMALACIA, in which only calcium is lost from the bone.

Q: What are the symptoms of osteoporosis?

A: There may be no symptoms. But the individual may lose height because of a collapse of the vertebrae and suffer from increasing kyphosis (bending forward of the spine). There may also be a vague, generalized backache because the vertebrae, in becoming thinner, tend to compress the surrounding nerves. Bones fracture more easily, causing more acute and severe pain. Such severe pain is caused by a compression fracture of one of the vertebrae, commonly in the midspine. Other bones, such as the hip, may fracture more easily than usual in the elderly.

Q: What causes osteoporosis?

A: The cause of osteoporosis is not precisely known, but it is probably caused by some kind of hormonal imbalance. It occurs most commonly in the elderly and more often in women than in men. The disorder may accompany Cushing's syndrome (overactivity of the adrenal glands) or hyperparathyroidism (overactivity of the parathyroid glands), or occur following prolonged bed rest.

Q: How is osteoporosis diagnosed and treated?

A: The diagnosis is usually made on the basis of the physical appearance of the patient and using X-rays to reveal that the bones are less dense than normal.

In most cases, treatment is not necessary because osteoporosis is part of the normal aging process. However, if there is severe pain, a back brace or support of some kind may have to be worn until the pain subsides.

Osteoporosis that is rapidly progressive may have to be treated with doses of vitamin D and additional calcium to help maintain bone formation and strength. Anabolic hormones, derived from male sex hormones, may help maintain the

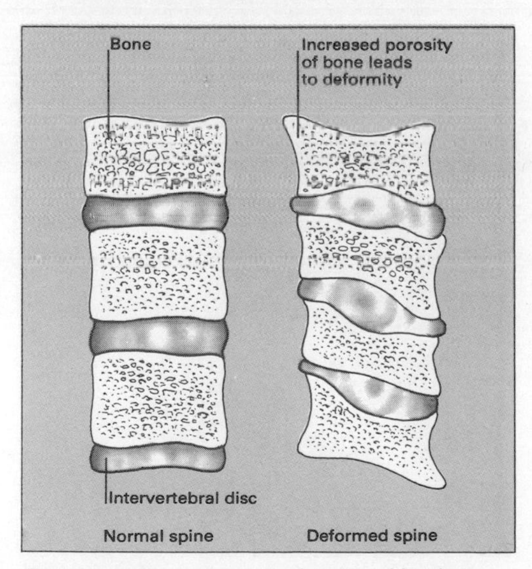

Osteoporosis weakens the bone and leads to deformities mainly in weight-bearing bones.

bone structure. Women may be given female sex hormones, and this treatment has been shown to prevent further osteoporosis. But oestrogen treatment may have adverse effects on menstruation and cause the breasts to swell and ache.

Osteosarcoma is a malignant (cancerous) bone tumour that usually arises on either side of the knee joint or on the upper end of the armbone. The disorder is most common in the first twenty years of life, but may occur at any age with PAGET'S DISEASE OF BONE, in which the bones become thickened and soft.

Q: What are the symptoms of osteosarcoma?

A: There is local pain and swelling with an increased sensation of warmth, similar to that accompanying osteomyelitis (infection and inflammation of bone).

Q: How is an osteosarcoma treated?

A: Intensive radiotherapy is usually attempted first. If this fails, amputation of the affected limb must be considered. This operation is followed by chemotherapy to combat the spread of the tumour to the lungs and other tissues. These modern forms of treatment have improved life expectancy considerably. In the past, osteosarcoma was generally fatal.

See also OSTEOMA.

Osteotomy is an operation in which a bone is cut, enabling a surgeon to reposition it. An osteotomy may be performed to lengthen or shorten a leg, or to correct bowed or bent legs. It may also be done to reset a fracture.

An osteotomy may be carried out in hip operations to alter the position of the thigh-bone, and can be of help in the treatment of osteoarthritis of the hip. But total replacement of the hip joint with an artificial joint is often more effective.

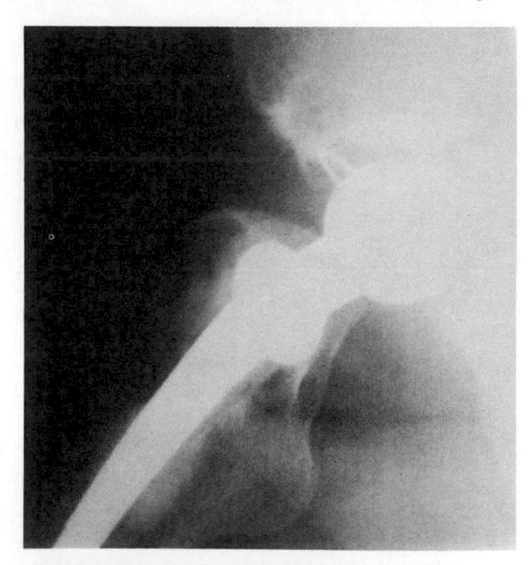

Osteotomy is required to implant an artificial hip joint (white) into the thigh-bone.

Otalgia. *See* EARACHE.

Otic preparations are substances used in the treatment of external OTITIS and as an aid in removing wax (cerumen) from the ear.

A talk about Otitis

Otitis is inflammation of the ear. Inflammation of the outer ear is called otitis externa; inflammation of the middle ear is otitis media; and inflammation of the inner ear is called LABYRINTHITIS. Infection of the external ear flap (pinna) may be caused by otitis externa or by any skin disorder.

Q: What are the symptoms of otitis externa?

A: The symptoms include itching, pain in the ear, a slight discharge, and deafness. Occasionally the infection is localized and a boil forms. This condition is called furunculosis.

Q: What causes otitis externa?

A: It is often caused by a combination of bacterial and fungal infections. Such infections may result from scratching the ear; from swimming; or from excessive sweating. Otitis externa is more common in people with ECZEMA, and in those with diabetes mellitus.

Q: How is otitis externa treated?

A: The dead skin, pus, and wax should be removed by a doctor. Antibiotics and antifungal preparations may be prescribed to treat the infection. In some cases, it may be necessary to pack special dressings into the ear until the infection is cured.

Q: How can otitis externa be prevented?

A: The ears should be kept dry by wearing earplugs when swimming. A doctor may also advise the use of alcohol ear drops after swimming. The ears should not be scratched.

Q: What are the symptoms of otitis media?

A: The main symptoms are severe earache, deafness, and fever. There is an accumulation of pus in the middle ear that may build up to such an extent that the eardrum ruptures, thereby releasing the pus and relieving the earache. Young children may also have diarrhoea, abdominal pain, and vomiting.

Q: What causes otitis media?

A: It is most commonly caused by the spread of infection from the back of the nose, along the Eustachian tube, and into the middle ear. This may occur with the common cold; tonsillitis; or any infection that affects the upper part of the respiratory system, such as influenza, measles, or whooping cough. Less commonly, otitis media may be caused by sudden pressure changes (*see* BAROTRAUMA) or by an infection such as SINUSITIS. It may also occur after a TONSILLECTOMY or following rupture of the eardrum.

As a result of infection, there is increasing secretion from the membranes that line the middle ear. These secretions block the Eustachian tube and cause an increase in pressure, resulting in earache.

Q: *How is otitis media treated?*

A: In the early stages of otitis media, before the eardrum has burst, antibiotics are usually effective. A doctor may also prescribe painkillers, and nose drops to relieve the congestion at the lower end of the Eustachian tube. Antihistamine, taken in the form of tablets, may help to relieve blockage. Rarely, it may be necessary to perforate the eardrum surgically (*see* MYRINGOTOMY).

If the eardrum has ruptured and is discharging pus, the ear should, in addition, be kept clean and dry until the eardrum has healed.

Q: *Can otitis media cause any complications?*

A: Yes. The infection may spread to the mastoid bone, causing mastoiditis. Occasionally, treatment kills the infection but the pus may be unable to escape because the Eustachian tube is blocked. Such obstructions may be caused by enlarged adenoids and may result in continued deafness. In adults this condition may be treated by passing a tube into the nose and blowing clear the Eustachian tube. In children it is usually treated with a myringotomy and the insertion of a drainage tube. If the obstruction is not treated, permanent deafness may result.

Q: *What precautions should be taken in connection with otitis media?*

A: Any minor respiratory infection may result in otitis media, particularly in children, whose adenoids and tonsils may become swollen. To prevent this from happening, antihistamines may be prescribed at the first signs of a cold or throughout the winter. If these are ineffective, a doctor may recommend that the adenoids be removed surgically.

A child who is recovering from otitis media should not be allowed to swim until a doctor has given permission. It is also advisable to have the child's hearing tested after the condition has been treated to make sure that there is no residual deafness resulting from GLUE EAR.

Otolaryngology. *See* OTORHINOLARYNGOLOGY.

Otology is the study of the ear.

Otomycosis is a fungal infection of the outer ear. The condition may be associated with monoliasis (thrush) or aspergillosis, a mould infection. It is a form of otitis externa, and is common following swimming or working in hot, humid conditions. *See* OTITIS.

Otorhinolaryngology is the study of the ear, nose, and throat, including their functions and their disorders.

Otorrhoea is a discharge from the ear. It may be caused by inflammation of the external ear (otitis externa), or a perforated eardrum. Any ear discharge should be reported to a doctor. *See* OTITIS.

Otosclerosis is a disorder of the middle ear that leads to progressive deafness. It is one of the main causes of deafness in young adults. Otosclerosis is caused by the gradual build-up of extra bony tissue around one of the small bones (the stapes) in the middle ear. As a result, the stapes cannot vibrate, thus preventing the transmission of sound from the eardrum to the inner ear. In some persons with otosclerosis, there is a family history of deafness. Otosclerosis usually affects one ear before the other, but eventually both ears become affected. *See* DEAFNESS.

Q: *What are the symptoms of otosclerosis?*

A: The major symptom is progressive

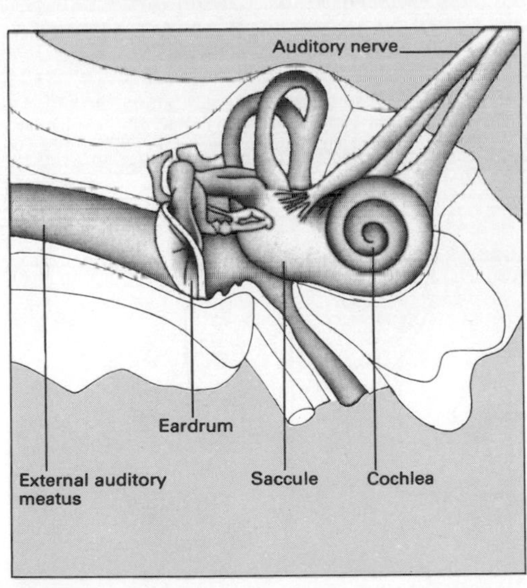

Otitis can affect any part of the ear, producing inflammation, swelling, and pain.

deafness. There may also be noises in the ear (tinnitus), and the whites of the eyes may be slightly blue in some patients. The symptoms often become worse during pregnancy.

Q: How is otosclerosis treated?

A: Surgery is usually the most effective treatment. Fenestration, which is an operation to make an artificial opening into the inner ear, has largely been replaced by stapedectomy, in which the stapes bone is replaced by a synthetic substitute. This operation usually restores normal hearing. However, the patient should avoid exposure to loud noises because the sound vibrations may damage the artificial stapes.

Otoscope is an instrument for examining the ear. It provides a light source that enables the ear canal and the eardrum to be inspected.

Ovariectomy. *See* OOPHORECTOMY.

Ovaritis. *See* OOPHORITIS.

Ovary is a female organ that produces eggs and sex hormones. The two ovaries, each about the size of a walnut, lie on each side of, and usually slightly behind, the womb (uterus). They are attached to the womb and the inner walls of the abdomen by ligaments, which give them a mobility that many other internal organs do not have. This mobility may allow one or both ovaries to take up a slightly different position.

The surface of each ovary is covered by a thick layer of connective tissue called the tunica albuginea. Inside, the ovary is composed of many thousands of cells that have the potential to form ova (eggs) and a firm structure of connective tissue. Before puberty, the ovaries are small and soft. After menopause they shrivel in size.

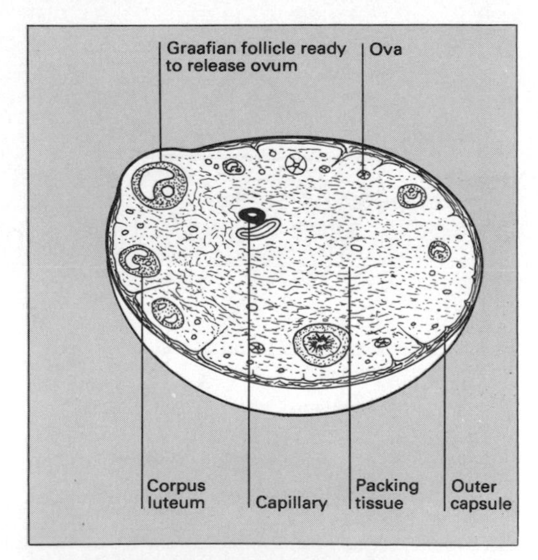

Ovary has hundreds of ova, one of which is released during each menstrual cycle.

The ends of the FALLOPIAN TUBES, with their long, finger-like extensions, overhang the ovaries. In a woman of childbearing age, they collect an ovum (egg) when one is released every month.

Q: How many eggs does an ovary produce?

A: The ovaries usually produce one mature egg each month throughout the fertile life of a woman, beginning at menarche (the start of menstrual periods) and ending at menopause. During this time, the ovarian tissue is under regular rhythmical control by hormones from the PITUITARY GLAND at the base of the brain. *See* MENSTRUATION; OVULATION.

Q: What disorders can affect an ovary?

A: Inflammation of the ovaries, called OOPHORITIS, usually accompanies SALPINGITIS (infection of the fallopian tubes), but may result on its own from MUMPS.

Tumours of the ovary are usually CYSTS and most frequently occur in women over thirty-five years of age. About 95 per cent of these tumours are benign (noncancerous). In a younger woman, a follicle may sometimes develop into a cyst and be discovered during gynaecological examination. It is usually worth waiting to see if the cyst is still present after menstruation.

Q: What symptoms may an ovarian tumour or cyst cause?

A: Frequently there are no symptoms, unless the tumour has grown so large that it causes abdominal swelling or presses on the bladder to cause frequent passing of urine.

Ovarian tumours are commonly discovered during a routine gynaecological examination. They seldom cause pain unless they twist or are malignant (cancerous) and the cancer has already spread to involve adjacent tissues. *See* CANCER.

Cysts can be caused by an imbalance of the hormones from the pituitary gland, so that the ovary is subjected to a constant abnormal stimulus. This may produce a condition in which there is INFERTILITY, infrequent menstruation, and an abnormal growth of body hair (Stein-Leventhal syndrome).

Q: How is a ovarian tumour treated?

A: A laparoscopy, an examination of the inside of the abdomen with a lighted tube, X-ray, ultrasound scanning, and sometimes exploratory surgery may be done to confirm the presence of an ovarian tumour. Such examinations may confirm that the tumour is neither a FIBROID nor a swelling of a fallopian tube that sometimes follows salpingitis.

If an ovarian tumour is found, the ovary is generally totally or partially removed (*see* OOPHORECTOMY).

Q: Can ovarian tumours or cysts produce complications?

A: Yes. A cyst may occur in early pregnancy because of an increase in the size of the corpus luteum and this may occasionally remain, causing problems of obstruction later in pregnancy.

A tumour can cause the ovary to twist on its ligaments, resulting in severe abdominal pain. There may also be abdominal pain if the cyst ruptures or there is bleeding into the cyst.

Overweight and underweight. *See* WEIGHT PROBLEMS.

Ovulation is the release of a mature OVUM (egg) from an OVARY. It occurs about every four weeks in the middle of the menstrual cycle, approximately fourteen days before the next menstrual period. After ovulation, the ovum passes along a fallopian tube to the womb.

The development of an ovum is under hormonal control. Follicle-stimulating hormone (FSH) from the pituitary gland stimulates the ovum to mature within the ovary. On approximately the fourteenth day of the menstrual cycle there is a sudden increase in the amount of luteinizing hormone (LH), and ovulation occurs.

See also MENSTRUATION.

Ovum is a mature female reproductive cell, also known as an egg. Ova are formed in the ovaries, pass down the fallopian tubes, and enter the womb. Usually, one ovum matures each month, although not necessarily in alternate ovaries. If a SPERM fertilizes the ovum, it develops into an EMBRYO. If the ovum is not fertilized, it degenerates and passes out of the body at MENSTRUATION.

Oxycephalic describes the shape of a skull in which the top part appears unusually high and pointed. A newborn baby's head is often slightly pointed because of the moulding of the skull during childbirth, but it returns to a normal shape within a few weeks.

An oxycephalic skull may also occur as a form of congenital anomaly, which can be associated with syndactyly (webbing of the fingers). The anomaly is caused by the skull bones joining together earlier than normal, but it can be corrected surgically to prevent the possible development of mental retardation or blindness.

Oxygen is an odourless, colourless gas that makes up about twenty per cent of normal air. It is an essential component for respiration in animals and plants. *See* OXYGEN THERAPY; RESPIRATION.

Oxygen tent is a pliable, plastic sheet that is held by a frame above and around a patient's bed and is tucked in below the mattress to produce an enclosed atmosphere. Humidified oxygen is blown into the tent; the patient can then move freely in an atmosphere containing a much higher proportion of oxygen than normal.

The patient can be fed through openings in the side that can be sealed, and medical treatment, such as intravenous transfusions, can be given without difficulty.

Oxygen therapy is the administration of oxygen to patients. Oxygen gas is supplied from a high-pressure cylinder that has a valve to allow the release of oxygen at low pressure.

Q: What disorders are treated using oxygen therapy?

A: Any condition that causes decreased transfer of oxygen to the blood in the lungs may be helped by oxygen therapy. These conditions include heart failure; reduced circulation, as occurs in acute shock and a heart attack; pneumonia; and chronic bronchitis with emphysema. Oxygen is often given to newborn babies to assist their respiration in the first few minutes after birth.

Q: How is oxygen therapy given?

A: Oxygen is most commonly given through a mask that fits over the patient's nose and face. An alternative and more

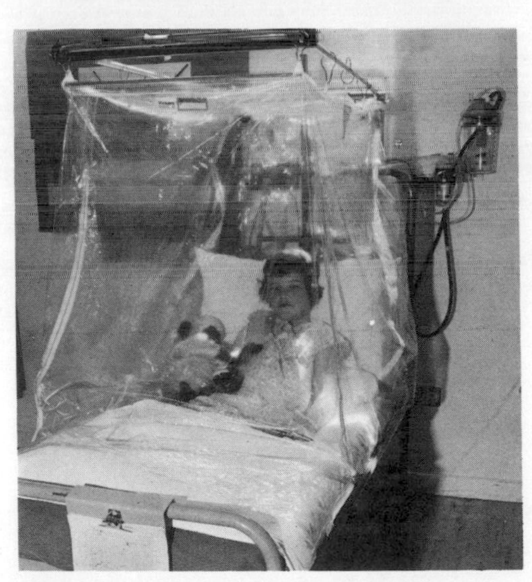

Oxygen tent is an airtight chamber with a raised oxygen composition maintained inside.

comfortable way is to administer oxygen through small plastic tubes inserted into each nostril and held in place by a lightweight apparatus like a pair of spectacles. A patient who requires oxygen therapy for some period of time is generally enclosed in an OXYGEN TENT.

Hyperbaric or high-pressure oxygen therapy is administered in centres that have a special chamber in which oxygen pressure can be increased to about three times normal. It is used in the treatment of gas gangrene and carbon monoxide poisoning, and in some radiotherapy treatments for cancer.

Q: *Are there any other situations in which oxygen is used?*

A: Yes. Oxygen is administered routinely in most operations as an aid to anaesthesia. It enables the anaesthetist to give a larger dose of an anaesthetic gas, such as nitrous oxide, without the risk of anoxia (lack of oxygen).

Q: *Are there hazards in using oxygen?*

A: Under medical control there are few hazards. Retrolental fibroplasia, which causes blindness in premature infants, is produced by high oxygen concentration. Also oxygen toxicity is a hazard for both adults and children when a high concentration of oxygen prevents the correct ventilation of the lungs.

Oxyhaemoglobin is a combination of haemoglobin (the red colouring matter in blood) and oxygen. Haemoglobin combines with oxygen in the lungs, and the resultant oxyhaemoglobin carries oxygen to the tissues. Oxyhaemoglobin gives the bright red colour to arterial blood.

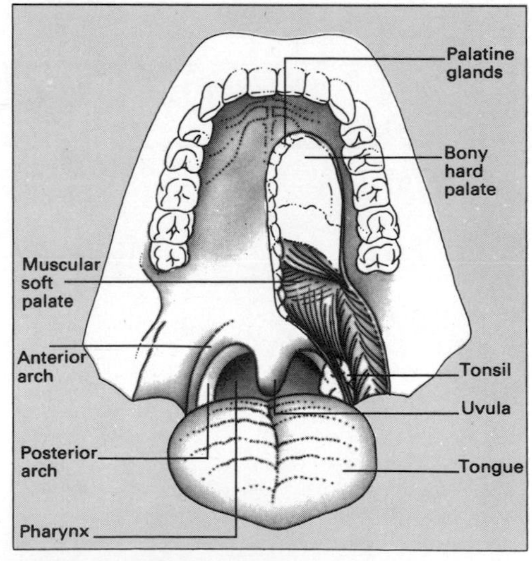

Palate, the roof of the mouth, has hard parts at the front and is soft at the back.

Oxytocin is a hormone that is produced by the HYPOTHALAMUS in the brain and is stored in the rear lobe of the PITUITARY GLAND. It stimulates the womb to contract during childbirth, and also stimulates the breasts to produce milk (lactation). A baby sucking at the nipple causes oxytocin to be released reflexly, which in turn increases lactation.

Oxytocin can be synthesized. Synthetic oxytocin may be given intravenously to induce labour. This is usually done only when labour is unusually slow, and administration of the drug is carefully supervised by an obstetrician. Induction of labour by this method is usually a safe procedure if carried out by an experienced obstetrician. Rarely, however, labour may not begin, or, if too much oxytocin is given, the contractions of the womb may be too strong and may endanger the baby.

Oxyuriasis is infestation with the threadworm *Enterobius vermicularis,* which thrives in the large intestine. *See* ROUNDWORMS.

P

Pacemaker is the area of the heart, called the sinoatrial node, that starts the rhythmical contraction of the heart by an electrical impulse.

See also CARDIAC PACEMAKER.

Paediatrics is the branch of medicine that is concerned with the growth, development, and diseases of children.

Paget's disease of bone, or osteitis deformans, is a bone disorder of unknown cause in which there is a slow progressive thickening of several bones, most often the pelvis, the lower limbs, and the skull. Elderly people are most commonly affected. Some new forms of therapy are effective, but the condition is seldom severe enough to need treatment.

Q: *What are the symptoms of Paget's disease?*

A: There may be thickening of the skull, and the leg bones may bend because of gradual softening as well as thickening. Pain may be noticed in the legs. The diagnosis commonly is made during a routine examination of an elderly person, or from the X-ray investigation of some other condition.

Q: *Are there any complications of Paget's disease?*

A: Yes. Bones affected by Paget's disease fracture more easily than others and, rarely, form osteosarcomas.

See also BONE DISORDERS; HYPERPARA-

THYROIDISM; LEONTIASIS; MYELOMA; OSTEOPOROSIS; OSTEOSARCOMA.

Paget's disease of the nipple is a rare type of cancer of the mammary ducts. It begins superficially in the ducts, causing the nipple to become red and crust-like. If the condition is discovered and treated before it penetrates beyond the ducts, the survival rate is very high. The treatment is the same as for other types of breast cancer. *See* CANCER.

Pain is a sensation of physical or mental anguish or suffering caused by aggravation of the sensory nerves. The body is seldom able to adjust to pain stimuli, and pain is usually a symptom of inflammation or pressure.

Many pains can be relieved with commercial preparations. However, if a pain persists a doctor should be consulted. Even the most severe pains can be treated with strong ANALGESICS (painkilling drugs).

See also ANAESTHETICS; CORDOTOMY; COLIC; HEADACHE; HYPERAESTHESIA; HYPESTHESIA; MIGRAINE; PHANTOM LIMB; TIC DOULOUREUX.

Painkilling drugs. *See* ANALGESICS.

Palate is the roof of the mouth. It consists of two parts. The front part, the hard palate, is made up of the base of the two upper jawbones (maxillae) and the palatal bones of the skull. The back part, the soft palate, is fleshy and, at its midline, forms a small projection (the uvula). The soft palate consists of muscle. The whole of the palate is covered with a mucous membrane.

See also CLEFT PALATE.

Paleness. *See* PALLOR.

Palliative is a drug or a treatment that relieves the symptoms of a condition without producing a cure.

Pallor, or paleness, is a lack of normal skin colour. It may result from fatigue, cold, low blood pressure, or constriction of the blood vessels in the skin. Pallor may also be a symptom of various disorders such as ANAEMIA, CUSHING'S SYNDROME, and HYPOTHYROIDISM. The pallor of those who are ill is usually caused by the loss of the slight skin pigmentation that normally comes from exposure to the wind and the sun.

See also ALBINO.

Palm is the front part of the hand that extends from the wrist to the bases of the fingers. *See* HAND.

Palpation is a diagnostic method in which the hands are used to make an examination. Self-palpation of the breasts is recommended to women as a method of detecting a lump in the breast while it is still in the early stages of development and, therefore, easier to treat.

Palpitation is a rapid, violent, regular or irregular heartbeat. Palpitations are most commonly caused by anxiety, fear, excessive smoking, or by drinking too much coffee. They may also be caused by heart disease, anaemia, and hyperthyroidism.

See also HEART DISEASE.

Palsy. *See* BELL'S PALSY; CEREBRAL PALSY; PARALYSIS; PARKINSON'S DISEASE.

Pancreas is a large, soft, and irregular gland about 12-15 cm (5–6 inches) long that lies on the back wall of the abdomen, behind the stomach, and extends horizontally from the duodenum to the spleen. The area next to the duodenum is thicker than the rest and commonly is called the head. This is joined to the main part, the body, before reaching the thinner part, the tail, adjacent to the spleen. The pancreas has a large blood supply, mainly from the splenic artery, as well as many nerves from the autonomic nervous system.

Two ducts, the main pancreatic and accessory pancreatic ducts, join together and leave the head of the pancreas to join with the common bile duct just before it penetrates the duodenal wall, forming the ampulla of Vater, protruding into the duodenum.

Q: What are the functions of the pancreas?

A: The main part of the gland produces enzymes essential for digestion. Also lying within the structure of the pancreas are many microscopic areas, the ISLETS OF LANGERHANS, which are part of an endocrine gland manufacturing the hormones insulin and glucagon.

Pancreatic juice contains enzymes, activated by intestinal juice, that digest proteins, carbohydrates, and fats. The pancreatic enzymes trypsin and chymo-

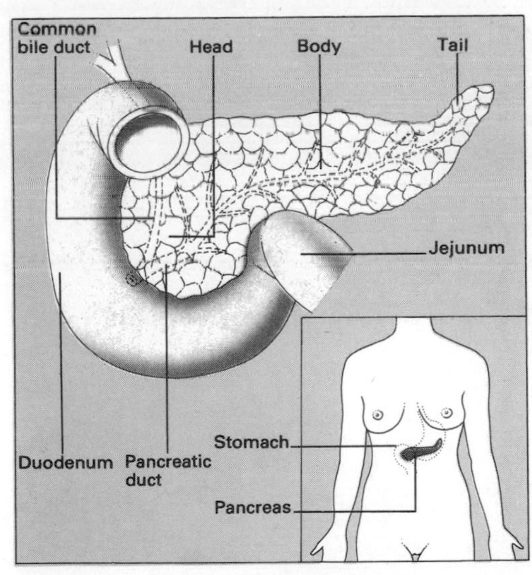

Pancreas is the gland that releases the essential hormone insulin into the blood.

trypsin digest protein; amylase digests starches and other carbohydrates; and lipase changes fats into glycerol and fatty acids. Pancreatic juices are produced partly by nervous stimulation, but mainly as a reaction to hormone secretion in the upper part of the small intestine activated by food from the stomach.

See also CAT SCANNER; CYSTIC FIBROSIS; DIABETES MELLITUS; GLUCAGON; INSULIN.

Pancreatic cystic fibrosis is an inherited disorder that affects the pancreas, lungs, and sweat glands. *See* CYSTIC FIBROSIS.

Pancreatin is a preparation made from the pancreatic enzymes of animals. Pancreatin tablets are prescribed for patients who are unable to digest food properly because of a deficiency in natural pancreatic secretions, which may be caused by disorders of the pancreas, for example, CYSTIC FIBROSIS and PANCREATITIS.

Pancreatitis is an inflammation of the pancreas. It may be acute or chronic.

Q: *What are the symptoms of acute pancreatitis?*

A: Severe upper abdominal pain, often accompanied by backache, vomiting and fever with the onset of shock are the usual symptoms. The pain may continue for several days, or even weeks, before gradually decreasing. Concentration of the enzyme amylase is frequently increased in the blood and this, accompanied by a high white blood cell count, usually suggests acute pancreatitis.

Q: *What causes acute pancreatitis?*

A: The cause is often unknown, but it is commonly associated with drinking excessive alcohol. Attacks may also be associated with infection of the gall bladder and bile ducts (cholecystitis). Acute pancreatitis also can be associated with the passage of a gallstone into the duodenum, causing a temporary blockage of the pancreatic duct and back pressure of the enzymes. Damage is caused to the pancreatic cells, and an acute inflammation is set up. This may occur after abdominal surgery, particularly on the stomach or gall bladder. Virus infections, particularly mumps, may start an attack.

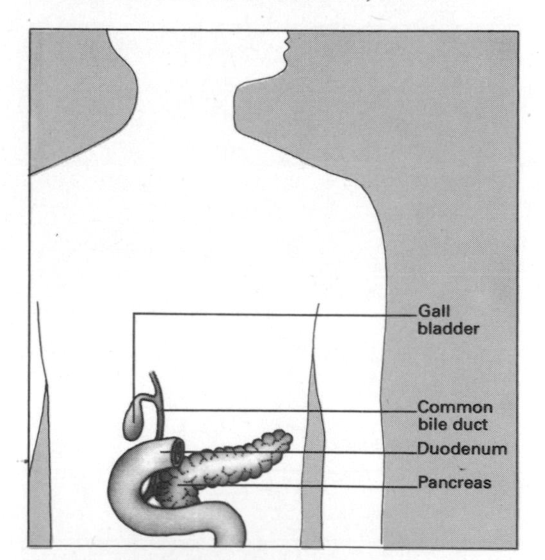

Pancreatitis is often associated with infection of the gall bladder.

Q: *How is acute pancreatitis treated?*

A: Urgent hospitalization is necessary to confirm the diagnosis.

Treatment includes intravenous infusions, evacuation of the stomach, and large doses of painkilling drugs until the condition improves. Disturbances in the salts, particularly calcium, is probable, so calcium may be added to the infusion. Insulin may have to be given if there is an acute onset of diabetes mellitus. Antibiotics may be administered if there is evidence of bacterial infection.

Acute pancreatitis may recur as further acute attacks or as chronic pancreatitis. It can also be fatal.

Q: *What are the symptoms of chronic pancreatitis?*

A: The main symptoms are either intermittent or continuous upper abdominal pain of varying intensity and often accompanied by backache. During the moments when pain is most severe, there may be nausea and vomiting. Continued symptoms, caused by increasing damage to the pancreas, reduce the output of the digestive enzymes. This may result in the malabsorption of food, with excessive fat in the faeces (steatorrhoea). Some patients develop diabetes mellitus.

Q: *What causes chronic pancreatitis?*

A: Chronic pancreatitis may occur as a milder form of acute pancreatitis for the same reasons. But it is also associated with alcoholism, chronic cholecystitis or, less commonly, cancer in the pancreatic duct.

Q: *How is chronic pancreatitis treated?*

A: Treatment may include removal of the gall bladder (cholecystectomy) if gallstones are thought to be the cause. But, most importantly, the patient must avoid drinking alcohol. Abstention usually is followed by loss of pain and improvement in general health. A low fat diet may be necessary, and PANCREATIN may be given to help digestion. Vitamin supplements, especially of folic acid and vitamins A, D, B_{12}, and K, are particularly important if malabsorption is taking place.

Pandemic describes any disease, such as malaria, that affects many people over a large region or continent. *See also* EPIDEMIC.

Panophthalmitis is an inflammation of the entire eye. It can be a complication of any serious eye disorder, such as choroiditis, or result from infection following an eye injury. Panophthalmitis requires immediate treatment, or blindness may result.

Papilla is a small protuberance from the surface of a tissue. Papillae occur in many parts of the body. They are particularly numerous on the surface of the tongue, where specialized papillae contain the taste buds.

Papilloedema is an eye disorder in which the optic nerve is swollen and inflamed at the point where it joins the eye. The causes include: (1) any condition, such as a tumour, aneurysm (swelling of an artery) or subarachnoid haemorrhage, that causes an increase of pressure within the skull; or (2) certain medical conditions such as a sudden dangerously high blood pressure, meningitis or lead poisoning. Treatment of papilloedema is directed at the cause.

Papilloma is a benign (noncancerous) tumour of the skin, mucous membranes, or glandular ducts. Small papillomas may occur in the ducts of the breast and cause bleeding from the nipple. Chronic laryngitis may cause papillomas to grow on the vocal cords. In some people, multiple papillomas occur on the skin around the neck and armpits.

See also WART.

Pap test, or Papanicolaou test, is a procedure carried out for the early detection and diagnosis of cancer cells in the cervix of the womb. *See* CANCER; CERVICAL SMEAR.

Papule is a small, solid, raised spot on the skin. *See* RASH.

Paracentesis is a minor surgical procedure in which a needle is passed into a body cavity to remove fluid. It is usually performed under a local anaesthetic for diagnostic purposes, or to remove excess fluid.

Paracetamol is a mild pain-relieving (analgesic) and fever-reducing (antipyretic) drug. Its effects are similar to those of aspirin, although paracetamol is less effective in treating inflammation and rheumatic conditions. It does not produce some of the undesirable side effects that aspirin may cause, such as internal bleeding, but an overdose can cause liver damage, and kidney damage may result from prolonged large doses. Paracetamol should therefore not be used by patients with a disorder of the liver or kidneys.

Paraesthesia is a sensation, such as a tingling or disordered sensation of heat and cold that occurs without an apparent cause. It may be caused by nerve damage, either from pressure or NEURITIS, or by stroke in which part of the brain is damaged.

Paragonimiasis is infestation with small parasitic flukes of the genus *Paragonimus,* which form cysts in the lungs. Humans become infested by eating raw or undercooked crabs that contain larval flukes. When in human beings, the larval flukes usually migrate to the lungs by penetrating the intestine and the diaphragm. In the lungs the larval flukes grow into mature adults and produce eggs. Some of the larval flukes may mature in other parts of the body, such as the abdomen or the brain.

Q: What are the symptoms of paragonimiasis?

A: The major symptoms include persistent spitting of blood, breathlessness, and chest pains. There may also be clubbing of the fingers.

Q: How is paragonimiasis treated?

A: Treatment with drugs that kill the flukes is effective in most cases, but surgery may be needed to remove some of the adult flukes.

Paralysis is the temporary or permanent loss of the ability to move either a limb or the whole body, usually also accompanied by a loss of sensation. Paralysis is generally the result of muscle or nerve disturbance.

Q: How does nerve disturbance cause paralysis?

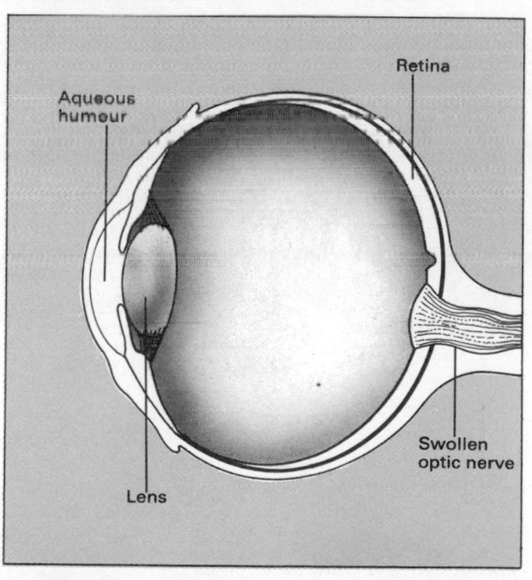

Papilloedema is swelling and inflammation of the optic nerve where it enters the eyeball.

A: Usually paralysis is caused by damage to a peripheral (surface) nerve or to the central nervous system. The results of damage to a peripheral nerve are different from those due to damage to the central nervous system, brain, and spinal cord. Weakness may be caused by muscle disease.

Damage to a peripheral nerve causes complete loss of ability to move that muscle, or muscles, and consequent wasting away. Damage to the central nervous system produces weakness or loss of use of a group of muscles, such as those of an arm or leg, but without wasting away. The affected muscles may make the limb feel stiff, if it is forcibly moved, because of an increased tone. This is known as spasticity.

Q: How is paralysis treated?

A: Treatment depends on the cause and can be started only when a doctor and a neurologist have made a diagnosis.

Physiotherapy can be employed to train muscles that can still move and to maintain a full range of movement of joints, as well as to prevent stiffness. This may be helped by the use of electrical equipment, such as shortwave diathermy (high-frequency heat treatment) and hydrotherapy pools.

Paralysis of speech may require speech therapy, but if swallowing is involved a tracheotomy may be necessary in order to insert a tube into the windpipe.

Peripheral nerve injuries can be helped by nerve transplants, orthopaedic operations to immobilize a joint (arthrodesis), or the transplant of the tendon of a working muscle to aid paralyzed muscles.

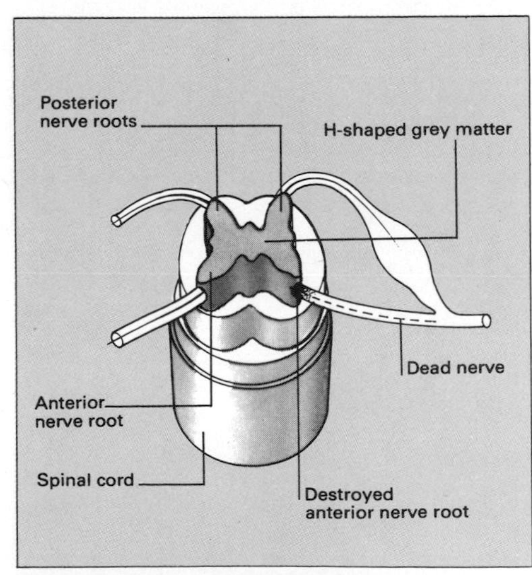

Paralysis may result from the destruction of anterior nerve roots in the spinal cord.

See also BABINSKI'S REFLEX; BULBAR PARALYSIS; CEREBRAL HAEMORRHAGE; CEREBRAL PALSY; DYSARTHRIA; DYSPHAGIA; EXTRADURAL HAEMATOMA; HEMIPARESIS; MENINGIOMA; MOTOR NEURON DISEASE; MULTIPLE SCLEROSIS; MUSCLE; MYASTHENIA GRAVIS; NEUROLOGICAL DISORDERS; NEUROMA; PALSY; POLIOMYELITIS; POLYNEURITIS; STROKE; SUB-ARACHNOID HAEMORRHAGE; SYRINGOMYELIA.

Paralysis agitans. *See* PARKINSON'S DISEASE.

Paralytic ileus is a form of intestinal obstruction caused by paralysis of the muscles of the intestinal wall. It is a failure of the normal muscular contractions (peristalsis) that pass food along inside the intestine. The abdomen becomes swollen, and this condition results in symptoms of constipation, abdominal pain, and vomiting.

Q: What conditions produce a paralytic ileus?

A: A paralytic ileus most commonly occurs as a result of disturbance to nerves and tissue unavoidable in an abdominal operation. But it can also occur with peritonitis and severe chemical upsets, such as those coinciding with kidney failure, diabetic coma, and extreme loss of body potassium salts accompanying diarrhoea or associated with an operation. It may also be the result of disturbance to the autonomic nervous system associated with an injury to the spine; of drugs used to prevent spasm; or of treatment for high blood pressure.

Q: How is a paralytic ileus treated?

A: Hospitalization is necessary. The patient's stomach is kept empty with a tube to prevent further vomiting and is given intravenous fluids to supply necessary salts, water, and glucose. After two to three days, peristalsis restarts and the patient can be allowed to sip fluid before returning to a normal diet within the next three or four days.

See also ILEUS.

Paranoia. *See* MENTAL ILLNESS.

Paraphimosis is a condition in which the foreskin of the penis is retracted and cannot be returned to its normal position. It occurs when the foreskin is inflamed (*see* BALANITIS) so that the normal circulation of blood is constricted. As a result, the bulbous end of the penis (glans penis) becomes swollen and painful.

Q: How is paraphimosis treated?

A: With the patient under a general anaesthetic, the foreskin usually can be pulled back into position quite easily.

However, it is probably best if the surgeon performs a circumcision to prevent the condition from recurring.

See also PHIMOSIS.

Paraplegia is paralysis of the lower half of the body. It is usually caused by injury, damage, or disease of the spinal cord. *See* PARALYSIS.

Paraquat is a very poisonous agricultural spray. If it is swallowed, emergency medical treatment is needed to prevent damage to the heart, lungs, and kidneys, which may be fatal.

Parasite is any organism that lives at the expense of another (host) organism. Ectoparasites, such as lice, fleas, and mites, live on the outside of their hosts. Endoparasites, such as flukes and intestinal worms, live within their hosts. Some parasites carry, or themselves cause, diseases.

See also ENTAMOEBA HISTOLYTICA; FLUKES; GIARDIASIS; WORMS.

Parasympathetic nervous system is one of the two divisions of the AUTONOMIC NERVOUS SYSTEM; the other division is the SYMPATHETIC NERVOUS SYSTEM. Parasympathetic nerve fibres occur in some of the cranial nerves of the brain, and in the sacral nerves of the lower end of the spinal cord. Parasympathetic nerves connect with many parts of the body, including the eyes, the internal organs, and the intestines. The effects of the parasympathetic nervous system include constriction of the pupils, slowing of the heart rate, contraction of the bladder, increasing the rate of digestion, and constriction of the bronchi.

See also VASOMOTOR RHINITIS.

Parathormone is the hormone produced by the parathyroid glands. It controls the level of calcium in the blood and, indirectly, reduces the level of phosphate. It works by releasing calcium from the bones, increasing calcium absorption from food in the intestine, and reducing calcium excretion by the kidneys. At the same time, the excretion of phosphate from the body is also increased. The rise in the calcium level reduces the secretion of parathormone. This "feedback" mechanism has the effect of maintaining a constant level of calcium in the blood.

Parathyroid glands secrete PARATHORMONE, which controls the level of calcium in the blood. The four parathyroid glands are embedded, two on each side, in the thyroid gland tissue situated in the lower part of the front of the neck.

Q: Can anything go wrong with the parathyroid glands?

A: Yes. Lack of parathormone (hypoparathyroidism) often occurs if the parathyroid glands are accidentally damaged or removed during a partial THYROIDECTOMY. More rarely, the parathyroid glands fail to secrete parathormone, or there may be resistance of the body tissues to the stimulating action of parathormone. Excessive secretion of parathormone (hyperparathyroidism) may also occur for no obvious reason.

Q: What are the symptoms of hypoparathyroidism?

A: Lack of parathormone (hypoparathyroidism) leads to an abnormally low level of calcium in the blood (hypocalcaemia), the major symptom of which is TETANY. This is a condition in which there is twitching and spasm of the muscles. *See* CALCIUM.

Q: What are the symptoms of hyperparathyroidism?

A: Excess production of parathormone (hyperparathyroidism) leads to a high level of calcium in the blood, and a serious drainage of calcium from the bones. Symptoms include weakness, nausea, and constipation. These may be accompanied by thirst and the frequent passing of urine.

Kidney stones (nephrolithiasis) are a common complication, and bone disorders with the formation of cysts may develop if the condition is not treated.

Q: How is hyperparathyroidism treated?

A: After a careful assessment and diagnosis has been made by a doctor, a surgeon may be asked to operate and remove the parathyroid glands.

Paratyphoid is a form of enteric fever that is caused by certain bacteria of the genus *Salmonella*. For symptoms and treatment of

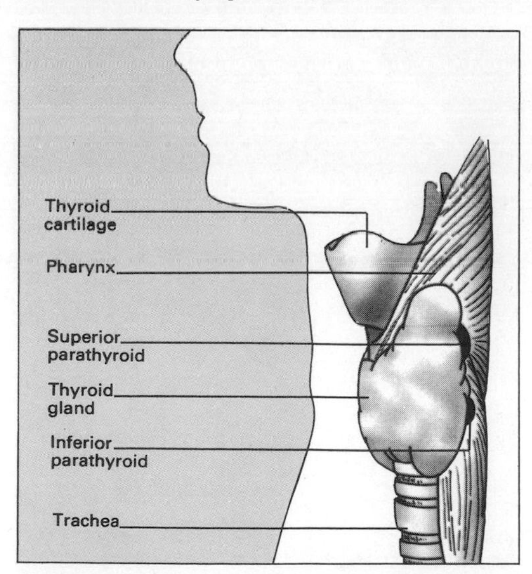

Parathyroid glands are embedded within the tissue of the thyroid gland in the throat.

paratyphoid, *see* TYPHOID FEVER.

Paresis is weakness of the muscles. It may be caused by damage to the central nervous system. *See* PARALYSIS.

Parietal describes the two parietal bones which form the roof and sides of the skull. Parietal also describes the wall of a body cavity; for example, the parietal pleura is the membrane that lines the chest wall.

Parkinson's disease is a chronic disorder of the nervous system characterized by tremors, slow movements, and generalized body stiffness. It occurs most commonly in the middle-aged and elderly. Parkinson's disease does not affect mental faculties, although these may appear to be impaired if the patient's speech is affected. The disease is also known as paralysis agitans or shaking palsy, and is named after the English physician James Parkinson (1755–1824). Parkinsonism is the term that denotes the symptoms of Parkinson's disease.

The cause of Parkinson's disease itself often is not known, although parkinsonism may be caused by several factors. In some patients, parkinsonism is thought to be caused by arteriosclerosis, in which there is degeneration of the brain cells that control body movements. Parkinsonism also may be caused by encephalitis; a brain tumour; brain damage; or poisoning, either from drugs such as reserpine, or from chemicals such as manganese and carbon monoxide.

Q: What are the symptoms of Parkinson's disease?

A: The onset of symptoms usually is gradual and their progress is slow. The initial symptoms include an occasional trembling of one hand and increasing clumsiness of the same arm. As the disorder progresses, both sides of the body become affected, movements become slow and stiff, and the patient may drool. The face assumes a blank and mask-like expression, with the eyes fixed and unblinking, because of rigid face muscles. Speech may also be impaired.

In the later stages there may be continual hand tremors with "pill rolling" movement of the fingers, the arms may be held in a bent position, and the body may be bent forward in a permanent stoop. The patient also may walk slowly with shuffling steps, and then start to run to prevent falling forward. This characteristic gait is called festination. The patient's handwriting may become small and illegible, and speech may become so slurred as to be unintelligible.

Q: How is Parkinson's disease treated?

A: There is as yet no cure, but the symptoms can be controlled in many cases. Drug treatment with levodopa (L-dopa), particularly when combined with carbidopa, can control the symptoms in some patients and enable them to resume a normal life for several years. Some patients respond to treatment with the drug amantadine, either by itself or combined with L-dopa.

If treatment with L-dopa or amantadine is ineffective, atropine-like drugs may be used. However, these tend to cause adverse side effects, such as constipation, a dry mouth, and retention of urine.

Occasionally, the surgical destruction of a small area of the brain may alleviate the symptoms. Such surgery usually is effective against the tremors.

Paronychia is inflammation of the skin that surrounds a nail. The affected area becomes red and swollen, and may discharge pus. Acute paronychia may be caused by a bacterial infection, often with staphylococcus, or by a viral infection, usually with the herpes simplex virus. Chronic paronychia occurs most commonly in those who have their hands in water for long periods of time. It is usually caused by monilia, which is a fungal infection. Chronic paronychia may damage the nail bed, which may result in distorted, ridged nails.

Q: How is paronychia treated?

A: The treatment of acute paronychia usually involves a combination of antibiotics and minor surgery, in which the inflamed area is drained of pus.

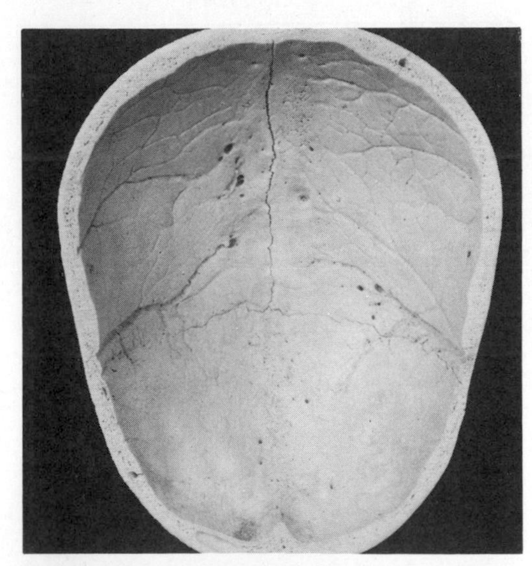

Parietal bones are the two bones that form the sides and roof of part of the skull.

Paronychia that is caused by a viral infection usually responds to treatment with antiviral drugs that are applied directly onto the affected area. Chronic paronychia may be treated with anti-fungal creams. It is advisable to keep the hands dry by wearing rubber gloves when the hands are in water.

Parotid gland. *See* SALIVARY GLANDS.

Parotitis is an inflammation of the parotid glands, the salivary glands in the neck, in front of the ears. It is most commonly caused by MUMPS, but may occur with any virus infection of the salivary glands. It also can be caused by a bacterial infection resulting from a stone in the salivary duct (sialolithiasis) or by mouth infections (stomatitis), particularly in elderly people who are seriously ill and dehydrated. *See* SALIVARY GLANDS.

Paroxysm is a sudden increase in severity of the symptoms of a disease. The term also is used to denote a sudden spasm or convulsion.

Paroxysmal tachycardia is a sudden increase in the heart rate, for no obvious reason, to 150-200 beats a minute. The average rate during an attack is around 180. A large quantity of urine may be passed afterwards.

Q: What causes paroxysmal tachycardia?

A: Frequently the cause is not known, but the origin seems to be a sudden increase in the number of electrical stimuli starting the atrium of the heart, producing a rapid, regular contraction of the ventricles. This may occur in young people without any sign of heart disease, but arteriosclerosis is usually the cause in elderly people.

Q: How is paroxysmal tachycardia treated?

A: An acute attack should be treated by a doctor, but hospitalization may be necessary. Recurrent attacks may require treatment with drugs, and some patients are taught to hold their breath while trying to breathe out. This may stop an attack.

See also TACHYCARDIA.

Parrot fever. *See* PSITTACOSIS.

Parturition is another word for childbirth. *See* PREGNANCY AND CHILDBIRTH.

Patch test is a skin test that is used to identify the specific cause of an allergy. A small amount of the suspected causative agent (allergen) is applied to the skin and covered with adhesive tape, which is removed after two days. If the skin is red and swollen, the patient is allergic to the substance that was applied.

Patella, or kneecap, is a small, disc-shaped bone about 5cm (2 inches) in diameter that lies in the tendon of the quadriceps femoris muscle in front of the knee joint. The inner surface that forms the front of the knee joint is covered by cartilage.

Q: What disorders can affect the patella?

A: Softening of the cartilage (chondromalacia) may occur in young adults, causing an aching pain deep in the knee, which is made worse by walking. This usually heals without treatment.

Recurrent dislocation of the patella usually starts in adolescence when the individual keeps the knee slightly bent for too long and the patella slips sideways, causing severe pain and an inability to straighten the leg. The patella usually can be relocated without a general anaesthetic. Recurring dislocations can be cured by surgically repositioning the tendon.

The tendon of the patella can be ruptured by violent exercise and requires surgery to repair it. A fracture may result from a direct blow: treatment, by operation or plaster cast, depends on how it is broken and the patient's age.

See also KNEE PROBLEMS.

Pathogen is any organism or substance that can cause a disease.

Pathognomonic describes anything that is typical of a particular disease. *See* SYMPTOMS.

Pathology is the study of the changes that occur in the body as the result of a disorder, with particular reference to the underlying cause.

Paul Bunnell test is a blood test for detecting GLANDULAR FEVER.

PCP. *See* PHENCYCLIDINE.

Pectoral refers to the chest.

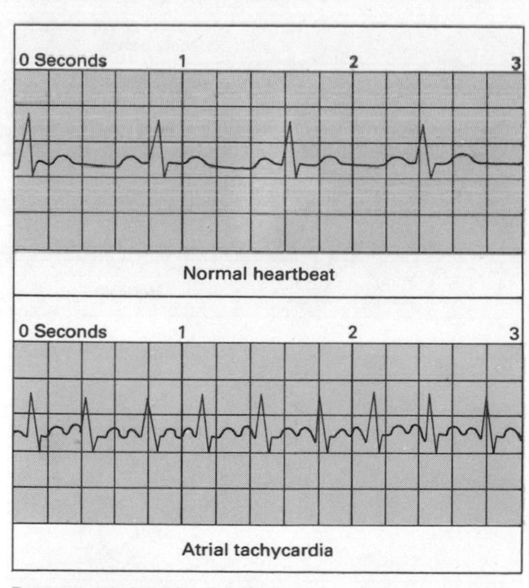

Paroxysmal tachycardia can increase a normal heartbeat of 80 to 180 beats per minute.

Pediculosis is an infestation with lice. *See* LICE.

Pellagra is a deficiency disease that is caused by a lack of niacin (nicotinic acid), one of the vitamin B complex. Pellagra most commonly occurs in those whose staple diet is corn. Pellagra also may result from alcoholism; CIRRHOSIS of the liver; and malabsorption of food, which is often caused by chronic diarrhoea.

Q: What are the symptoms of pellagra?

A: Initial symptoms include a smooth, red tongue, a sore mouth, and ulceration of the inside of the cheeks. The skin on the neck, chest, and back of the hands may become brown and scaly. Often there is nausea, vomiting, and diarrhoea. There may also be insomnia, depression, confusion, and rapid changes of mood.

Q: How is pellagra treated?

A: Pellagra is treated by giving a balancing diet with niacin supplements.

Pelvimetry is measurement of the dimensions of the pelvis, either by physical examination or by X-rays or by both. Pelvimetry is used to determine whether the pelvis is wide enough for normal childbirth.

Pelvis is a basin-shaped cavity. There are two such cavities in the body. The pelvis of the kidney collects urine and funnels it into the ureter, the tube that leads to the bladder (*see* KIDNEY). But the term pelvis usually refers to bones in the lower part of the body that support the spine and connect to the legs at the hip joints.

The pelvis consists of two hip-bones, each composed of the pubis, ilium, and the ischium. These join in front of the pubic bone (symphysis pubis) and are attached at the back to the sacrum by the two sacroiliac joints. The coccyx, a small bone at the lower end of the spinal column, is attached to the sacrum.

The wide wings of the two hip-bones form the upper extremities of the pelvis and are known as the false pelvis. They sweep down to a narrower part called the true pelvis.

A female's pelvis is wider than a male's, and the entrance to the true pelvis is usually circular in shape. This allows childbirth to take place with ease.

Q: What structures does the pelvis contain?

A: The side walls of the pelvis contain muscles that help movement of the thighs. The bottom of the pelvis is made up of ligaments and muscles (the pelvic floor) that support the bladder and rectum and, in a female, the vagina and womb. The false pelvis supports the large and small intestine, which intertwine above the contents of the true pelvis.

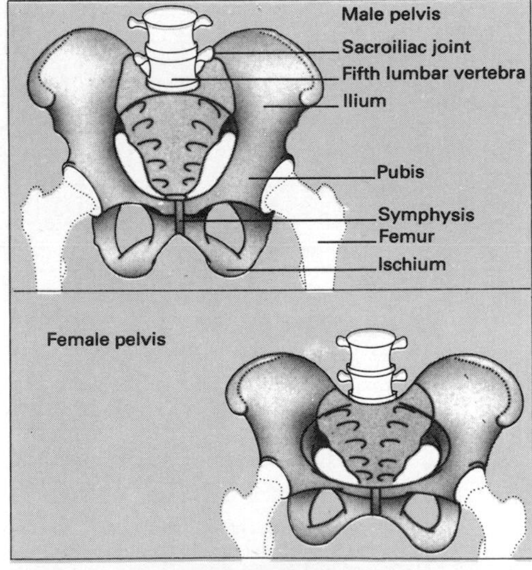

Pelvis of a woman is wider than a man's and the opening is shaped for easy childbirth.

Pemphigus is the general name for a variety of skin diseases characterized by successive outbreaks of large, fluid-filled blisters. It can result from a type of IMPETIGO caused by a staphylococcal infection.

In adults there are two rare forms of pemphigus that may be a form of AUTOIMMUNE DISEASE. They produce blisters in the mouth and on exposed mucous membrane, as well as on the skin.

It is difficult to distinguish between pemphigus and a similar disorder called pemphigoid, which occurs mainly in the elderly and produces itching of the skin followed by blistering.

Q: How are pemphigus and pemphigoid treated?

A: Pemphigus due to impetigo is treated with antibiotics, but the general treatment of other forms of pemphigus and pemphigoid is with corticosteroids to relieve and control the symptoms. Both diseases are, at present, incurable.

Penicillin is one of a group of antibiotics that once were extracted from moulds of the genus *Penicillium,* but now are synthesized. The basic penicillin is called penicillin G.

Over-use of penicillins can result in their becoming ineffective because of the development of resistant bacterial strains. But, penicillin G is still effective against many of the common bacterial infections, and it can be modified to produce a number of more effective penicillins, such as ampicillin, amoxycillin, and cloxacillin. Some of these derivatives are effective against a wider range of organisms than is penicillin G, and some are effective against bacteria that have developed a resistance to penicillin G.

Q: How do penicillins work?

A: The penicillins work mainly by killing bacteria while the bacteria are multiplying, but penicillins also inhibit the growth of bacteria to some extent.

Q: Can the penicillins produce adverse side effects?

A: Yes. All of the penicillins carry the risk of producing allergic reactions. However, these usually do not occur until a patient has had several courses of penicillin treatment. An allergic reaction may produce skin rashes, swelling of the throat, fever, and swelling of the joints. Rarely, ANAPHYLAXIS may occur, which may be fatal.

People who are allergic to one type of penicillin are allergic to all types, and usually to a similar group of antibiotics, the cephalosporins. Such people should warn their doctors so that other antibiotics are prescribed instead.

Penis is the male organ used for passing urine and for sexual intercourse. It is cylindrical in shape and is attached by its base to the front and sides of the pubic arch.

Q: How is the penis constructed?

A: The urethra, the tube for the passage of urine or semen, is surrounded by special tissue and ends in an external swelling called the glans. It lies on top of two tubular and honeycomb-like areas of erectile tissue. The glans at the end of the penis is particularly sensitive and, in an uncircumcised penis, is covered by a protective FORESKIN.

Q: How does the penis function as a sexual organ?

A: The erectile tissue becomes distended with blood, thus making the penis erect and hard. The blood is unable to drain out through the veins due to their being temporarily closed by special muscles. An erection results from physical or psychological sexual stimulation, and it enables the male to insert the erect penis into the female's vagina during sexual intercourse. It is at the stage of greatest sexual excitement (orgasm) that the semen is released into the vagina.

An erection ceases when the veins open so that the blood is able to flow back into the general circulation of the body.

Q: What disorders can affect the penis?

A: Inflammation of the glans (balanitis) may cause narrowing of the foreskin (phimosis) or cause it to act in a constrictive manner if it is pulled back (paraphimosis). *See* BALANITIS.

Venereal diseases, such as the chancre of syphilis or chancroid, form ulcers or cause infections of the urethra (urethritis). *See* GONORRHOEA; NONSPECIFIC URETHRITIS.

Small cysts (sebaceous cysts) may form on the skin of the penis and occasionally cancer can occur. On rare occasions, erections may be prolonged and painful (priapism).

Q: How is cancer of the penis recognized and treated?

A: Cancer of the penis occurs most commonly in elderly males who have not been circumcised and whose low standard of personal hygiene has caused repeated mild attacks of balanitis. A small ulcer that bleeds easily is the first sign that cancer may be present.

Cancer of the penis is treated either by amputating the end of the penis, or by radiotherapy.

See also CIRCUMCISION.

Pep pills are drugs that contain amphetamine. They produce a feeling of well-being and excitement, but are addictive. *See* AMPHETAMINES; DRUG ADDICTION; METHAMPHETAMINE; STIMULANTS.

Pepsin is an enzyme that starts the digestion of proteins in the stomach by breaking down the large protein molecules into smaller molecules, called peptides. In the small intestine, the peptides are further broken down by other enzymes into molecules (amino acids) that are small enough to be used by the body.

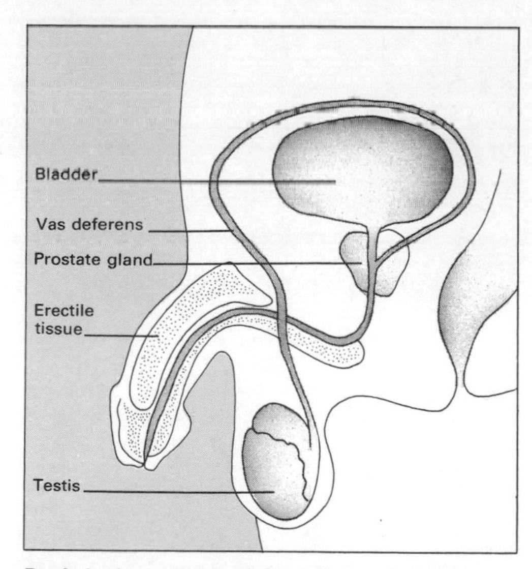

Penis is the outlet both for urine and, during sexual intercourse, for semen.

A talk about a Peptic ulcer

Peptic ulcer is an eroded area in the stomach (when it is called a gastric ulcer) or in the first part of the duodenum (a duodenal ulcer). Peptic ulcers are caused by the combined action of pepsin and hydrochloric acid in the digestive juices of the stomach. They are more common in men than in women.

Q: *Why do peptic ulcers occur?*

A: Acute peptic ulcers occur suddenly, and usually are the result of an excess of alcohol, aspirin, or other drugs.

Sometimes they are called "stress ulcers," because they are considered to be related to periods of intense stress, such as those occurring with shock, severe burns, or accidents. This form of peptic ulcer heals rapidly.

Chronic peptic ulcers develop slowly and for a variety of reasons. It seems likely that there is an alteration in the normal protective action of the mucus and its underlying cells that prevents digestive juices from digesting the stomach itself. Why this occurs is often not known, but it is possible that continued anxiety and smoking in an individual with an inherited tendency to form ulcers can cause a peptic ulcer. The condition is made worse by certain drugs.

Q: *Can peptic ulcers occur in places other than the stomach and duodenum?*

A: Yes. Acid-secreting cells in a MECKEL'S DIVERTICULUM can become active, sometimes producing a peptic ulcer.

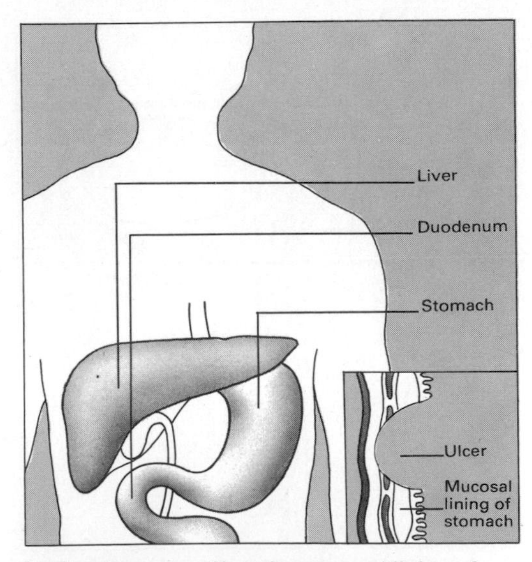

Peptic ulcer may affect the mucosal lining of the stomach, or occur in the duodenum.

Peptic ulceration also may develop in the small intestine after a gastroenterostomy has been performed for a peptic ulcer. Or an ulcer may form in the lower end of the oesophagus (gullet) in a patient with a HIATUS HERNIA.

Q: *How is a peptic ulcer diagnosed?*

A: A barium meal test (*see* BARIUM) is the usual way of diagnosing a peptic ulcer; it reveals an ulcer, if it is present, in more than 90 per cent of patients. Endoscopy, using a FIBRESCOPE, can be done and a biopsy (sample of tissue for analysis) taken to exclude the possibility of cancer if this is suspected or if an ulcer is taking a long time to heal. The duodenum can also be examined, and this may detect an ulcer not revealed by a barium X-ray.

Q: *What are the symptoms of a peptic ulcer?*

A: Pain in the abdomen is the most common symptom of a peptic ulcer, but its frequency varies. There may be long periods when the ulcer is active and symptoms are present, followed by several months during which there are no symptoms.

The pain of peptic ulcer usually is high in the abdomen and often is described as a gnawing, deep ache accompanied by a feeling of hunger or nausea. It is relieved by taking bland food, milk, or ANTACID drugs, but is made worse by alcohol and by fried or spicy foods.

Pain from duodenal ulcer starts about two hours after a meal and is relieved by antacids or more food. The pain commonly wakens the patient in the night, and the symptoms go on for several weeks before gradually disappearing.

A gastric ulcer may be aggravated by eating, because of the sudden production of acid in the stomach, although the pain seldom wakens the patient. Pain may be relieved by vomiting.

These are the typical symptoms, but there is a great variation. In the elderly, pain may persist without relief from food or anticids.

Q: *How is a peptic ulcer treated?*

A: Most patients can be treated at home. Frequent small meals and snacks keep the stomach full, helping to absorb the acid.

For many years, a variety of strict diets, usually containing bland foods and milk, were used; the patient was advised to avoid coffee, tea and cola drinks. But these regimens are no longer essential: modern medical treatment is effective and patients have far fewer restrictions upon what they eat and drink. Fried foods are often blamed for ulcer pain because they increase the secretion of acid by the stomach. Some drinks, particularly alcohol, aggravate the symptoms.

Smoking should be prohibited. Any drugs that are known to aggravate peptic ulceration should, if possible, be stopped. Antacids and drugs to prevent gastric secretion and reduce the speed of emptying the stomach also are effective. Cimetidine reduces gastric secretion and produces rapid relief of symptoms with healing of the ulcer. Carbenoxolone, another type of drug, gives rapid improvement of symptoms. Tranquillizers are sometimes used to reduce stress and tension, and sleeping pills given to ensure a good night's sleep.

Hospitalization is rarely necessary; the pain, in most patients, is usually relieved by the use of drugs and bed rest at home. Admission to hospital is needed only if the family doctor or the specialist considers that complications such as pyloric stenosis, bleeding, or ulceration into the pancreas, causing continuous pain, is occurring.

Surgery (vagotomy or partial GASTRECTOMY) may be performed if the ulcer produces complications.

Q: Can complications occur with a peptic ulcer?

A: Yes. One complication of peptic ulcer is pyloric stenosis, an obstruction of the exit of the stomach. Pyloric stenosis results from a combination of scarring at the exit of the stomach or first part of the duodenum and inflammation produced by an active ulcer. Vomiting of large volumes of fluid, often with food from the previous day, is a common symptom. In severer cases, a partial gastrectomy is needed (*see* PYLORIC STENOSIS).

Bleeding is a common complication of peptic ulcer and the patient may vomit blood (haematemesis) or produce the dark black stools of melaena. Sudden massive blood loss causes weakness and fainting, and all patients who experience this symptom should be hospitalized. Blood transfusion, bed rest, and antacid drugs form the initial stage of treatment but, if the bleeding continues, emergency surgery may be necessary.

Another complication of a peptic ulcer is continuous pain. Pain may be constant and severe, often producing intense backache, if the ulcer penetrates through the stomach wall to involve the pancreas or liver. Medicinal treatment seldom is effective and surgery must be performed.

A peptic ulcer may perforate, suddenly producing severe, intense abdominal pain, often spreading to the shoulders and sometimes accompanied by vomiting. It is a form of PERITONITIS and requires immediate surgery.

Percussion is a diagnostic procedure in which a doctor places a finger over the part of the body to be examined and taps it sharply with a finger of the other hand. The sound and sensation felt enables a doctor to determine the size, position, and consistency of underlying body structures.

Physiotherapists may use a slightly different technique of percussion to vibrate the underlying tissues. This technique can help to free excessive mucus, so that it can be coughed up by the patient.

Perforation is a hole that is made in a part of the body, or the process of making such a hole as part of a surgical procedure.

Perfusion is a technique in which fluid is passed through a blood vessel or a part of the body, either for investigating or for treating a disorder. Occasionally, the terms perfusion and infusion are used interchangeably.

Perfusion may be used in the treatment of some types of cancer, such as cancer of the liver. A special CATHETER is passed along an artery to the area involved, and cancer-killing (cytoxic) drugs are perfused through the catheter. This technique allows a high concentration of a drug to be introduced to a localized area.

Periarteritis nodosa. *See* POLYARTERITIS NODOSA.

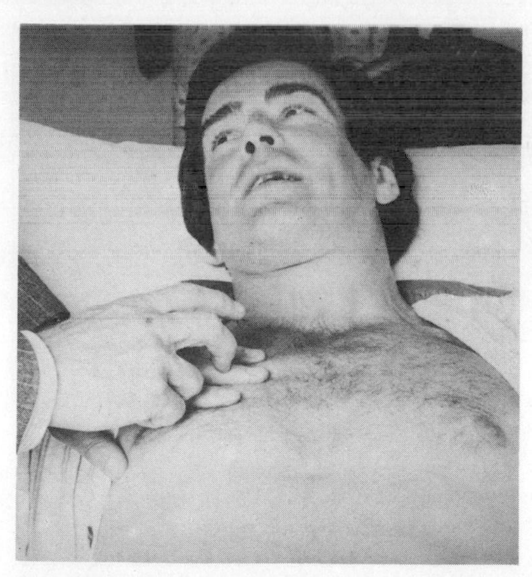

Percussion is a procedure commonly used in examinations of the heart and lungs.

Pericarditis is an inflammation of the membranous sac that surrounds the heart (pericardium). A wide variety of disorders may cause pericarditis. It may be associated with RHEUMATOID ARTHRITIS, systemic LUPUS ERYTHEMATOSUS, and URAEMIA. It also may occur as a complication of cancer of adjacent structures, such as the lungs or oesophagus. Usually however, pericarditis occurs without an apparent cause or due to an infection.

Q: *What are the symptoms of pericarditis and how is it treated?*

A: In most cases, there is pain in the centre of the chest, which may vary in intensity and which may be worsened by movement or coughing. Other common symptoms of pericarditis include fever, breathlessness, coughing, and a rapid pulse rate. The treatment of pericarditis is directed toward the underlying cause. In the early stages of the disorder, painkillers are usually prescribed. Antibiotics may be necessary if pericarditis is caused by an infection. Various other treatments may be necessary if complications develop.

Q: *Can pericarditis cause complications?*

A: Yes. The most common complication is an accumulation of fluid in the pericardium. This causes pressure on the heart and a rapid pulse rate. One type of pericarditis, called constrictive pericarditis, causes scarring and thickening of the pericardium. This may result in progressive heart failure, with increasing breathlessness, enlargement of the liver, and OEDEMA.

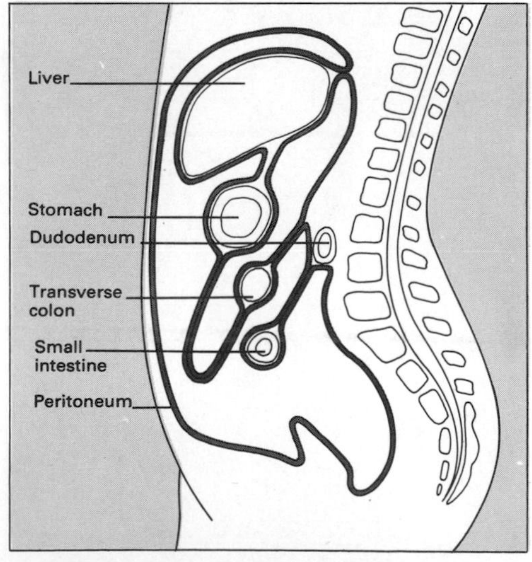

Peritoneum allows movement of the internal organs within its lubricated folds.

Pericardium is the bag-like structure that surrounds the heart. It consists of two layers, between which is a small amount of fluid. This fluid enables the heart to beat almost without friction. The inner layer of the pericardium is soft and membranous. The outer layer is thicker and fibrous, and helps to protect the heart.

Perimetry is a method of examining the area the eye can see (visual field) when it is focused on a central point. This point is marked in the middle of a blank screen. A small light or disc is moved inward from many points on the edge of the screen, and the point where the patient first sees it is charted.

Perinephric describes any tissues that surround the kidney.

Perineum is the area between the anus and the lower edge of the pubis at the front of the pelvis. In a female, it includes the opening of the vagina and the surrounding vulva, as well as the firm fibrous tissue area between the back of the vagina and the anal opening. In a male, the area is composed of the fibrous tissue behind the bag of skin that contains the testicles (scrotum). The tissue of the perineum heals easily. This is particularly important in a woman following childbirth, when the tissues may be damaged or deliberately cut (episiotomy) to enable the baby's head to pass through.

Periodontitis is a gum condition in which the mucous membrane, gums, and underlying bone become thin, and the teeth become loose. It usually follows an infection of the gums (GINGIVITIS).

Q: *What are the symptoms of periodontitis?*

A: Apart from loose teeth, the gums are swollen and there is often a discharge of pus from around one or more of the teeth. The breath smells foul (halitosis).

Q: *How is the condition treated?*

A: Skilled dental care is needed to remove the tartar from the teeth and treat the gingivitis. Improved oral hygiene, with regular brushing of the teeth, is necessary to avoid a recurrence of the condition.

Period pain. *See* DYSMENORRHOEA.

Periods. *See* MENSTRUATION.

Periosteum is a thin, fibrous membrane that covers the entire surface of the bones, except at the joints. It consists of a dense outer layer that contains nerves and blood vessels, and an inner layer which contains cells that help to form new bone. The periosteum plays an essential part in bone nutrition and healing.

Periostitis is an inflammation of the membrane that covers the bones (periosteum). It may occur after a bone fracture when the healing break becomes infected. It is usually caused by an infection of the bone, such as OSTEOMYELITIS; or, rarely, by SYPHILIS.

Peripheral means situated at the outer part of an organ or structure.

Peristalsis is a series of involuntary muscle contractions that move food along the intestines. In the stomach, peristalsis produces a churning action aiding digestion. Occasionally, reverse peristalsis may occur, causing vomiting.

Peritoneum is the membrane that lines the abdominal cavity and surrounds the abdominal organs, such as the intestines, liver, spleen, womb, and bladder. In some places it forms the MESENTERY, which supports the intestines. The peritoneum also secretes a fluid that lubricates the abdominal organs.

Peritonitis is an inflammation of the peritoneum, the membrane that lines the abdominal cavity. It usually accompanies an infection but, rarely, it may occur with conditions such as rheumatoid arthritis and disseminated lupus erythematosus.

Q: What causes peritonitis?

A: Peritonitis most commonly is caused by infection of an abdominal organ, such as appendicitis, cholecystitis, or diverticulitis, or following perforation of a peptic ulcer or inflamed appendix. It may be associated with SALPINGITIS or following an abdominal operation.

Q: What are the symptoms of peritonitis?

A: The chief symptom is severe generalized abdominal pain, in which the patient wants to lie still and may complain of aching shoulders caused by referred pain from an irritated diaphragm. Usually there is a fever and a rapid pulse rate. Vomiting often occurs as the result of the onset of a PARALYTIC ILEUS.

Q: How is peritonitis treated?

A: The patient is hospitalized and treatment is started with intravenous fluids, and antibiotics given in the infusion. Emptying of the stomach through a nasogastric tube is usually needed.

A surgical operation is required if a cause such as appendicitis or ruptured peptic ulcer is found.

Q: Are there any possible complications of peritonitis?

A: Yes. If treatment is not started immediately, death may result.

An abscess may form in the pelvis, particularly following salpingitis, or under the diaphragm (subphrenic abscess). Both may require surgical draining after the initial stage of peritonitis has settled.

Tuberculous peritonitis always develops because of tuberculosis elsewhere in the body. It may begin like acute peritonitis, but the onset is usually more gradual, with an increasing amount of fluid (similar to ascites). It requires antituberculous treatment.

Peritonsillar abscess. *See* QUINSY.

Pernicious anaemia, or Addison's anaemia, is a condition that results from a failure of the body to absorb vitamin B_{12}. It occurs because of a deficiency of a special substance (called an intrinsic factor) secreted by the stomach. The intrinsic factor normally combines with the extrinsic factor, vitamin B_{12}, to form a substance that can be absorbed by the body.

Q: What are the symptoms of pernicious anaemia?

A: The symptoms commonly are the combination of a slow onset of ANAEMIA, with tiredness, slight breathlessness, and a sore, red tongue. There may be symptoms of peripheral neuritis as well as loss of position sense and a slight staggering gait. Depression and mental disturbances suggestive of paranoia also may occur.

Q: How is pernicious anaemia treated?

A: Once the diagnosis has been made, treatment with injections of vitamin B_{12} produces a cure. The injections have to be continued on a monthly basis for the rest of the patient's life.

Patients with pernicious anaemia have a much greater chance of developing cancer of the stomach, and so a barium meal X-ray or gastroscopy (examination of the stomach) should be performed on all patients at the onset of treatment and repeated at regular intervals.

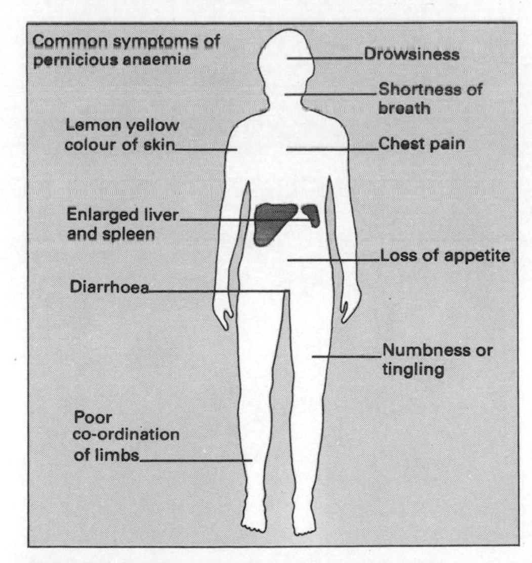

Pernicious anaemia results in a variety of symptoms affecting the whole body.

Peroneal means concerning the FIBULA bone in the lower leg, or the outer side of the leg next to the fibula. For example, the peroneal muscles are attached to the fibula.

Personality disorders are disorders of personal, social, and sexual relationships that are characterized by the individual's lack of awareness of the effects of his or her behaviour on others.

Q: How do personality disorders occur?

A: Personality disorders develop in childhood and later life, and become apparent in the abnormal ways in which a person reacts to other people. The person is usually unaware that his or her behaviour is abnormal, and attributes conflicts of temperament to faults in the other person. This causes feelings of frustration and often anxiety, and the development of a rigid personality unable to adapt to or learn from others.

Q: What are the different kinds of personality disorders?

A: Psychopathic personalities are concerned only with the achievement of their desires, and commonly respond with deceit or physical aggression if these desires are frustrated. Punishment has no deterrent effect. Alcoholism, sexual deviation, and violent criminal activity may occur.

Paranoid personalities have delusions about other people's feelings, and often interpret casual remarks as criticism of themselves. Obsessive personalities are highly conscientious and perfectionist, often intolerant of others and mentally inflexible. Hysterical personalities constantly seek attention and affection, and make impossible emotional demands in personal relationships.

There are many other forms of personality disorders, many of which are difficult to cope with but do not necessarily prevent a person from playing a part in normal social life.

Q: How are personality disorders treated?

A: Treatment is difficult and is often not effective. Benefits may result from a relationship with a mature, affectionate person who can be firm and understanding. Group therapy may enable an individual to realize the destructive effects of the behaviour of other people with similar problems.

See also MENTAL ILLNESS.

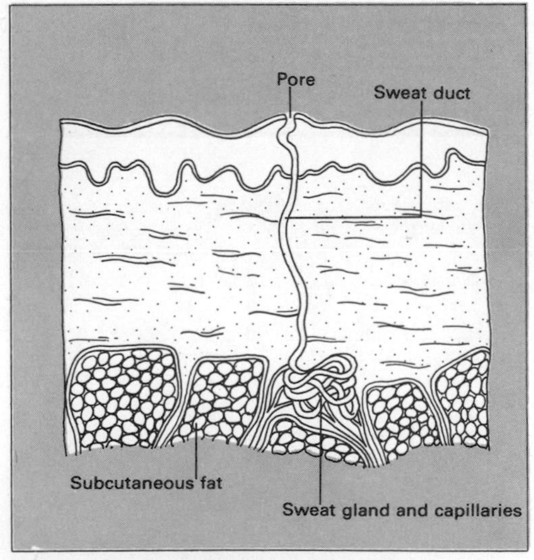

Perspiration is produced by sweat glands in the skin and is secreted through the pores.

Perspiration is the production of sweat by the sweat glands. The main constituents of sweat are water, sodium chloride (common salt), urea, lactic acid, and potassium salts.

In cold weather, perspiration is minimal. In extreme heat, about 1.5 litres (3 pints) of sweat per hour may be lost. Persons who have become acclimatized to heat may lose up to 4 litres (8.5 pints) per hour; it takes about six weeks to become acclimatized. During this period, the sweat glands gradually increase the amount of sweat, and decrease the amount of salts in the sweat, thereby preserving salts in the body.

Q: How do the sweat glands work?

A: A sweat gland consists of a coiled structure that lies deep within the skin, and a duct that passes through the skin layers to the surface. The coiled structure is well supplied with blood by capillaries. It absorbs fluid from the capillaries and surrounding cells and passes this to the surface through the duct. Some of the salts are reabsorbed in the duct, but when sweating is profuse, large amounts of salts may be lost.

The sweat glands are controlled by the AUTONOMIC NERVOUS SYSTEM. This is connected to the hypothalamus in the brain, which is part of the body's heat-regulating mechanism. Sweating also is influenced by the hormones ADRENALINE and NORADRENALINE, which can cause the cold sweats of fear.

Q: What are the functions of perspiration?

A: The main function of perspiration is to cool the body by evaporation. The other function of perspiration is the elimination of waste products, such as urea.

Q: What conditions may affect perspiration?

A: Perspiration may cease completely in the final stages of heatstroke. This is caused by a breakdown of the body's heat-regulating mechanism. Without emergency treatment, it may be fatal.

Increased sweating may occur with fever, irrespective of its cause, and in conditions that raise the metabolic rate, such as HYPERTHYROIDISM. CYSTIC FIBROSIS causes an excessive concentration of sodium chloride in the sweat.

Some people sweat excessively, particularly from the soles of the feet, palms of the hands, and the armpits. This condition is known as hyperhidrosis, and may be aggravated by stress. Bromhidrosis is a condition in which the sweat has an unpleasant odour. This is caused by the breakdown of a mixture of sweat and dead skin cells by bacteria.

Perthes' disease is a chronic disorder (OSTEOCHONDRITIS) of the head of the femur (the ball part of the ball-and-socket hip joint), which degenerates because of an inadequate blood supply to the developing bone. The cause of the disorder is not known. It is most common in boys aged between five and ten years old, and usually affects only one of the hip joints. At this age the bone is not fully developed.

Q: What are the symptoms of Perthes' disease?

A: Movement of the affected joint may be limited, resulting in a limp. There may also be pain in the thigh and groin.

Q: How is Perthes' disease treated?

A: Most forms of treatment involve reducing the pressure on the affected hip. A weight-relieving caliper is often advised but may have to be worn for about two years. In some cases femoral osteotomy is performed. Children with the disease may develop osteoarthritis of the hip during adult life.

Pertussis. *See* WHOOPING COUGH.

Pes cavus is a condition in which the arches of the feet are abnormally high. In most cases there is no obvious cause, or it may be inherited. Other causes that have been identified include various muscular and neurological disorders, such as spina bifida or poliomyelitis in early infancy.

Q: What are the symptoms of pes cavus?

A: There are often no symptoms. However, pes cavus causes the weight of the body to be borne on the front part of the feet. The weakness of the small muscles of the foot leads to clawing of the toes and formation of calluses over the heads of the metatarsals, and corns on the toes.

Q: How is pes cavus treated?

A: Most cases require treatment by a chiropodist and the wearing of pads under the metatarsal heads. If these measures fail, surgery may be necessary.

Pes planus. *See* FLATFOOT.

Pessary is a soluble tablet that dissolves at body temperature. It is inserted into the vagina to treat local vaginal infections or, occasionally, as a method of contraception.

A pessary is also a mechanical apparatus used to support the womb when PROLAPSE is occurring.

Petechia is a small red spot in the skin that is caused by a minute haemorrhage of a blood capillary. Petechiae may be caused by blood clotting defects; coughing, particularly in whooping cough; disorders of the blood vessels; or bacterial ENDOCARDITIS. They may also appear in certain fevers, such as TYPHUS.

Pethidine is the international, nonproprietary name for a synthetic painkiller with similar effects and uses as MORPHINE. Pethidine has less sedating action than morphine, and has no cough-suppressant effects; it is also less constipating than morphine. Like morphine, pethidine is addictive.

The main use of pethidine is as a painkiller. It may also be used in the treatment of colic caused by gallstones or kidney stones, because of its antispasmodic effect. Pethidine may be combined with other drugs, such as antihistamines, as a form of pre-anaesthetic medication.

Q: Can pethidine produce adverse side effects?

A: Yes. Pethidine may cause dizziness, drowsiness, sweating, nausea, vomiting, and a dry mouth. Occasionally, it may also cause retention of urine, palpitations, and convulsions.

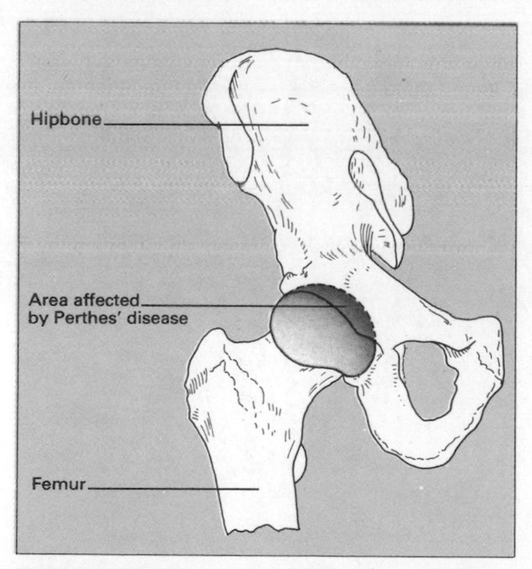

Perthes' disease disrupts the blood supply to the epiphysis of the femur, causing distortion.

Petit mal is a mild form of epileptic attack in which there is a momentary loss of awareness, but no convulsions. *See* EPILEPSY.

Petroleum jelly is used in medicine to prevent dressings from sticking to the skin, and as a base for various ointments.

Pets and disease. The fur and feathers of many species of pet, particularly cats, may cause an ALLERGY. Animal fleas may live temporarily on man but do not cause more irritation than the occasional bite. Anyone handling animals should be immunized against TETANUS, as any animal bite may become infected with tetanus. Warm-blooded animals may carry RABIES.

There are many diseases that may be caused in humans by different varieties of pets. Birds may cause PSITTACOSIS and an allergic lung disease known as bird fancier's lung. Cats may cause CATSCRATCH FEVER, rabies, TOXOCARIASIS, and TOXOPLASMOSIS. Dogs may cause a rare form of LEPTOSPIROSIS, rabies, a HYDATID CYST, toxocariasis, and toxoplasmosis. Tortoises or terrapins may cause SALMONELLA.

Peyer's patch is a collection of lymph nodules that occur mainly in the ileum of the small intestine. *See* LYMPHATIC SYSTEM.

Phaeochromocytoma is a tumour of the central part (medulla) of the adrenal glands. The adrenal gland medulla secretes the hormones ADRENALINE and NORADRENALINE. A phaeochromocytoma causes excessive amounts of these hormones to be produced.

Q: *What are the symptoms of a phaeochromocytoma?*

A: The excessive amounts of adrenaline and noradrenaline cause attacks of palpitations, nausea, and severe headaches. These may be accompanied by a feeling of great anxiety. The patient also may be pale and sweating, the pulse may be rapid, and the blood pressure may be high. These attacks may occur at any time or they may be triggered by emotional stress, a change of posture, or pressure on the abdomen.

It may be necessary to perform urine tests and to take X-rays for the diagnosis of a phaeochromocytoma. This is because there are usually no indications of the condition, apart from high blood pressure, unless the patient is examined during an attack.

Q: *How is a phaeochromocytoma treated?*

A: The tumour is removed surgically only after the patient's hormone levels have been controlled with drugs.

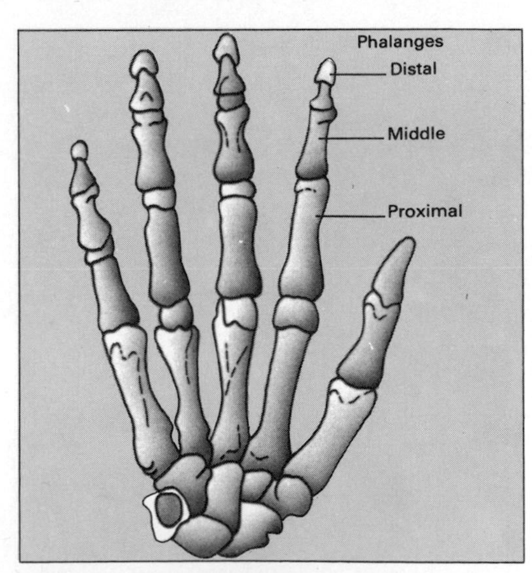

Phalanx is any of the fourteen small bones that form the phalanges of the fingers.

Phalanx is the term given to any one of the bones of the fingers or toes. The thumbs and big toes each have two phalanges; the other fingers and toes each have three.

Phallus is another term for the PENIS.

Phantom limb is the illusion that a limb is still present after it has been amputated. It is a common symptom following an amputation, but usually disappears within a few months. Treatment with tranquillizers and antidepressant drugs may be needed.

Pharmacology is the study and research of drugs, their chemistry, effect on the body, and dosage.

Pharmacopoeia is an authorized book on drugs that contains information on their preparation, effect, dosages, and legal requirements of purity, strength, and quality.

Pharyngectomy is an operation to remove the pharynx, usually to treat cancer (*see* PHARYNX). The operation involves not only the removal of the pharynx (the larynx is also usually removed at the same time), but also its reconstruction using other tissues. This is a complex and highly skilled technique which often requires several operations to complete.

Pharyngitis is an inflammation of the pharynx. It is one of the most common of all disorders. Usually it comes on suddenly (acute pharyngitis), although some people have a persistent form of the disorder (chronic pharyngitis) which may be caused by smoking, drinking, persistent breathing through the mouth, or POSTNASAL DRIP. The symptoms of pharyngitis include a sore throat and discomfort or pain on swallowing.

Q: *What causes acute pharyngitis?*

A: Acute pharyngitis is most commonly caused by a common cold virus.

However, the cause can be the streptococcus bacterium, in which case the infection is known as a "strep throat". The condition is sometimes associated with inflammation of the larynx (laryngitis), inflammation of the mouth (stomatitis), glandular fever, tonsillitis, or nasal conditions, such as sinusitis. In rare cases, diphtheria or leukaemia may be the cause.

Q: Are there any particular problems associated with acute pharyngitis?

A: No, apart from those associated with any infection of the back of the throat and nose, such as laryngitis and otitis media (inflammation of the middle ear).

Q: Why do some people continually suffer from a chronic sore throat and discomfort on swallowing?

A: Chronic pharyngitis, like chronic laryngitis, may occur in those who smoke too many cigarettes or drink too much alcohol. It may also be caused by POSTNASAL DRIP resulting from chronic nasal inflammation. However, often a definite cause cannot be found.

The condition can often be cleared up by improved oral hygiene, giving up smoking, and through the use of antiseptic gargles. If the chronic inflammation is caused by respiratory tract allergies, the sore throat may clear up when the allergies are properly controlled.

Pharynx is the part of the throat situated behind the arch at the back of the mouth, and which connects together the mouth, nose, and larynx. It includes (1) the nasopharynx, the space just above the soft palate which joins up with the back of the nose and which contains the adenoids and openings of the Eustachian tubes; (2) the tonsils and the back of the tongue; and (3) the back of the throat.

Q: What conditions may affect the pharynx?

A: Infection may cause inflammation (PHARYNGITIS). Infections include glandular fever, tonsillitis, and adenoid problems. More rarely, Vincent's angina, syphilis, or diphtheria may cause inflammation, and occasionally it may result from cancer.

Phencyclidine, or **PCP,** is an anaesthetic drug that commonly is used in veterinary medicine. It was originally made as an anaesthetic for humans but was considered unsuitable because of its adverse side effects, such as hallucinations and agitation.

See also DRUG ADDICTION.

Phenobarbitone is a barbiturate drug (*see* BARBITURATES). Its main uses are as an anticonvulsant in the treatment of epilepsy and as a tranquillizer.

Patients undergoing long-term treatment can become tolerant to phenobarbitone. Care must be taken when withdrawing its use, particularly with epileptics. It should be prescribed with caution for the elderly, and for persons with cirrhosis of the liver or kidney disease. Combining alcohol or an antihistamine with phenobarbitone is hazardous and may produce a powerful and dangerous sedative, possibly leading to coma, respiratory failure, or death.

Phenol is another name for carbolic acid. *See* CARBOLIC ACID.

Phenylketonuria (PKU) is an inherited congenital anomaly that causes the accumulation of the substance phenylalanine in the blood. Normally an enzyme breaks down phenylalanine into amino acids. In about one in 10,000 people, this enzyme is missing. The chief symptoms are gradual mental deterioration, accompanied by irritability, vomiting, and convulsions. However, about one week after birth, when the baby has had protein in the diet, the heel is pricked and a PKU test (Guthrie test) performed. If phenylalanine is detected, further blood tests are taken. A special phenylalanine-free diet must be maintained throughout the child's growing life. Regular blood tests are made. In adulthood it may be possible to revert to a normal diet, except during pregnancy.

Phimosis is a condition in which the foreskin of the penis is so tight that it cannot be pulled back over the tip of the penis (glans).

Q: What problems occur with phimosis?

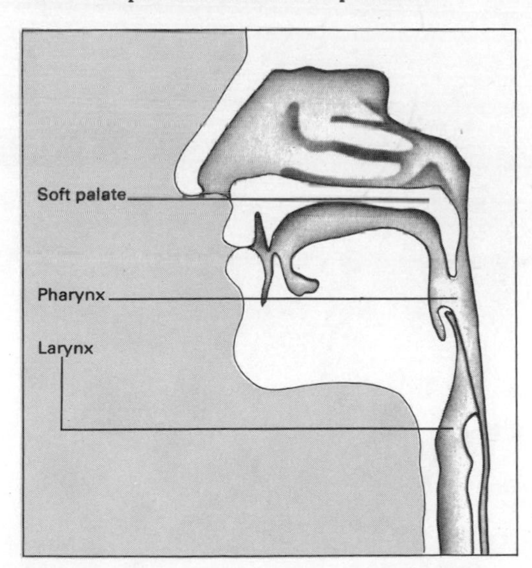

Pharynx serves as a passageway for air from the nasal cavity to the larynx.

A: During urination, the foreskin can be seen to bulge. The stream of urine is narrow and comes out slowly. In serious cases, the back pressure of the urine may damage the kidneys (hydronephrosis).

Q: What causes phimosis?

A: (1) It may occur following repeated infections (*see* BALANITIS). (2) At birth, the foreskin and tip of the penis are joined together. Separation of the two parts occurs gradually during the first few years of a child's life. Repeated attempts to forcibly pull back the foreskin before it is ready may cause phimosis where none had existed before.

Q: What is the treatment for phimosis?

A: The condition usually is corrected by circumcision. *See* CIRCUMCISION.

Phlebitis is an inflammation of a vein. *See* VENOUS THROMBOSIS.

Phlebolith is a chalky deposit in a vein. It results from a blood clot (thrombus) that has been present for so long that it has become calcified. It seldom causes symptoms as it usually occurs in abdominal veins. It does not usually require treatment.

Phlebothrombosis. *See* VENOUS THROMBOSIS.

Phlebotomus is a genus of bloodsucking flies. Some species transmit infections to humans; for example, *Phlebotomus sergenti* is one of the species that transmits LEISHMANIASIS.

Phlebotomy, or venesection, is the cutting of a vein.

Phlegm is thick MUCUS that is secreted by the mucous membranes of the nose, throat, or bronchial tubes.

Phlyctenule is a small blister that occurs most commonly on the conjunctiva of the eye. Symptoms include redness, swelling, pain, and sensitivity to bright lights (photophobia). Phlyctenules are common in children, and are thought to be an allergic reaction to an infection elsewhere in the body. Locally applied corticosteroid preparations and antibiotics are usually prescribed.

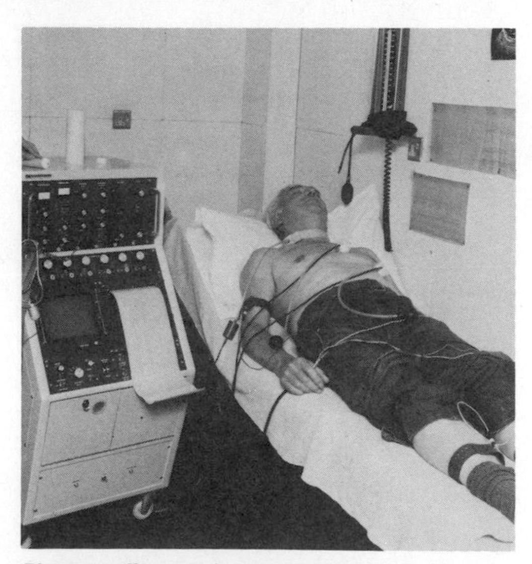

Phonocardiogram is a record of the sounds that the heart produces as it beats.

Phobia. *See* MENTAL ILLNESS.

Phonocardiogram is a graphic recording of heart sounds that is obtained using several microphones placed on the chest.

Photophobia is an abnormal sensitivity to bright light. It is a symptom of migraine, high fever, measles and German measles, and will occur with any form of acute brain infection, such as meningitis or encephalitis. Photophobia may accompany any infection of the eye. It is a common problem in albinos.

Phthirus pubis is the scientific name for the crab louse. It mainly infests the hair of the pubic region, but may also be found in the armpits, eyebrows, and eyelashes.

See also LICE.

Phthisis is a medical term for wasting. *See* WASTING.

Physiology is the study of the physical and chemical workings of animals and plants. It is closely associated with anatomy.

Physiotherapy describes the various techniques used by a specialist (a physiotherapist) for the relief of pain; improvement of joint and muscle function; and repairing, through training, damaged parts of the body.

See also DIATHERMY; ULTRASOUND TECHNIQUES.

Pica is the generally harmless desire to eat substances not considered food, such as coal, earth, and dried paint. Some pregnant women suffer from pica.

PID is an abbreviation for prolapsed intervertebral disc, commonly known as a slipped disc. *See* SLIPPED DISC.

Pigeon chest is a prominence of the breastbone (sternum), thought to be caused by a congenital abnormality, or respiratory illnesses in children. It does not require treatment.

Pigeon toed (toeing in) describes the condition in which a person walks with the feet turned inward. Most infants begin walking in this way because it aids balance. If there is no improvement after six months, a doctor should be consulted.

Piles. *See* HAEMORRHOIDS.

"Pill," the. *See* CONTRACEPTION.

Pilonidal sinus is a small duct containing dead hairs that sometimes forms a dermoid cyst. If such a cyst becomes infected, it must be removed surgically. Pilonidal sinuses are most commonly found over the sacrum above the anus; young hairy males are most commonly affected.

Q: How is an infected pilonidal sinus treated?

A: The infection is allowed to subside. The infected tissue often requires surgical drainage and ultimately removal of the sinus tissue. This eliminates the cause of the recurrent infection.

Pimple, or spot, is a small skin eruption containing pus. Pimples can occur anywhere on the body but are most common on the face. *See* ACNE.

Pineal body is a small structure that is situated in the centre of the brain. Its function is not known. Rarely, a tumour forms in the pineal body and may cause the early onset of puberty in boys.

Pink disease, or acrodynia, is a disorder caused by mercury compounds in baby teething powder, now withdrawn from the market. *See* MERCURY.

Pink eye is a form of conjunctivitis, usually caused by bacterial or viral infections. *See* CONJUNCTIVITIS.

Pinna is the visible external part of the ear. It consists of skin over cartilage. *See* EAR.

Pins and needles is a sensation of tingling related to a nerve disorder. *See* TINGLING.

Pinta is a chronic skin infection that is caused by a spiral-shaped bacterium called *Treponema carateum,* which is similar to the bacterium that causes syphilis and yaws. Pinta is transmitted by physical contact. After an incubation period of between one and three weeks, a small nodule appears on the skin. This gradually enlarges and becomes surrounded by other nodules. The lymph glands in the affected area also may swell. After about a year, blue patches develop, usually on the face and the limbs. These patches gradually fade, leaving scars. Pinta can be cured with penicillin.

Pinworm is a small, parasitic nematode worm that infests the intestine. Some authorities use the term to refer to the worm *Enterobius vermicularis* (*see* OXYURIASIS), and some to refer to the worm *Strongyloides stercoralis* (*see* STRONGYLOIDES).

Pituitary gland, or hypophysis, is a small gland about the size of a pea, situated at the base of the brain. It is connected by a short stalk to the hypothalamus, which helps regulate body temperature, blood pressure, fluid balance, weight, and appetite. The gland is protected by a circle of bone, called the pituitary fossa, in the centre of the skull just behind the point at which the two optic nerves join.

The pituitary gland is made up of two parts, the anterior or front lobe and the posterior or rear lobe.

Q: How does the pituitary anterior lobe function?

A: This is the most important of the glands that secrete hormones directly into the bloodstream. It produces hormones that stimulate other endocrine glands to manufacture their individual hormones. The level of these hormones is carefully regulated by special areas in the hypothalamus that are sensitive to the blood level of a variety of hormones and accordingly regulate the pituitary gland, sending chemical messages down the connecting stalk.

Q: What hormones does the anterior pituitary lobe produce?

A: The anterior lobe produces a number of hormones. They are: thyroid stimulating hormones (TSH) to control the production of the thyroid gland hormones, THYROXINE and triiodothyronine; adrenocorticotropic hormone (ACTH) to stimulate the cortex of the adrenal gland to produce hydrocortisone and other CORTICOSTEROIDS; follicle-stimulating hormone (FSH) and luteinizing hormone (LH) that control the testes and ovaries; growth hormone (GH) that maintains normal growth until adult life; and PROLACTIN, which helps lactation.

Q: How does the posterior lobe of the pituitary gland function?

A: The hypothalamus produces the two hormones oxytocin and vasopressin (antidiuretic hormone). These are stored in the cells of the pituitary's posterior lobe. The production of these hormones

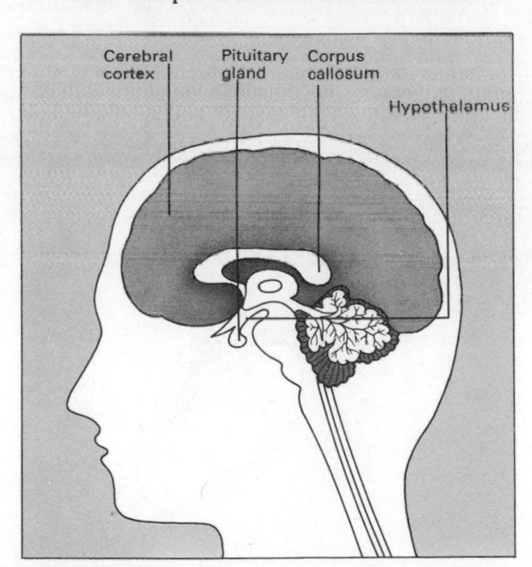

Pituitary gland, attached to the base of the brain, controls many endocrine secretions.

is carefully monitored by the same kind of "feedback" system that works in the anterior pituitary lobe.

Q: *What do vasopressin and oxytocin control?*

A: Vasopressin controls the excretion of water by the kidneys. An increase in vasopressin causes an increased reabsorption of water by the kidney tubules. A lack of vasopressin results in diabetes insipidus. Oxytocin stimulates the pregnant uterus to contract.

See also ACROMEGALY; ADDISON'S DISEASE; CUSHING'S SYNDROME; DWARFISM; GIGANTISM; HYPOPITUITARISM; HYPOTHYROIDISM; INFERTILITY.

Pityriasis rosea is a skin condition that starts with a slightly oval, pink, scaly area on the skin about an inch in diameter. It develops into a rash on the trunk, but rarely on the face. It causes mild itching, and the rash persists for six to eight weeks when it disappears spontaneously. The cause is unknown.

PKU. *See* PHENYLKETONURIA.

Placebo is a harmless substance without any medicinal effect. Although placebos are chemically inactive, many patients feel better after taking them.

Placenta is the specialized organ formed by a fertilized ovum (embryo) after it has attached itself to the lining of the womb. After the first few weeks of pregnancy it acts as an endocrine gland secreting chorionic gonadotropin, a hormone, to maintain the pregnancy.

The disc-shaped placenta is made up of twenty to forty smaller areas, called cotyledons. One side of the placenta is connected to the wall of the mother's womb; the other side is connected with the membrane containing the amniotic fluid that surrounds the embryo or foetus. The umbilical cord provides a direct link between the placenta and the developing baby, because it contains blood vessels that connect the centre of the placenta to the abdomen of the foetus.

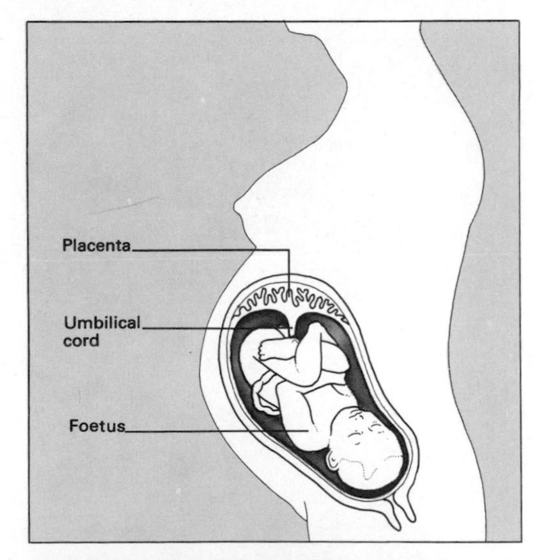

Placenta reaches full maturity by the 34th week of pregnancy, then slowly degenerates.

By the time the fully developed foetus is ready to be born, the placenta weighs about 0.5kg (1lb), and measures about 25cm (10in) across. The placenta is expelled shortly after the birth of the baby as part of the afterbirth.

Q: *How does the placenta work?*

A: The mother's blood flows through the uterine wall and an exchange of the substances that the foetus needs (such as food and oxygen) and those that have to be excreted (such as carbon dioxide and urea) takes place between the placenta and the uterine wall through a thin film of cells. Thus, there is no direct contact between the foetal and maternal blood circulations.

Q: *What abnormalities can affect the placenta?*

A: The umbilical cord may be attached to one side of the placenta, instead of to its centre. Or one or more of the cotyledons may lie apart from the main body of the placenta. There also can be abnormalities of the cord, or of the shape of the placenta. Sometimes, the placenta is situated in front of the foetus so that the exit from the womb is partly or completely blocked. This is known as a placenta praevia, and it is a serious complication of pregnancy. In most cases of placenta praevia it is necessary to perform a Caesarean section (*see* CAESAREAN SECTION).

Q: *Does the placenta have any other functions?*

A: Yes. Early in pregnancy, it produces the hormone called chorionic gonadotropin, which it also makes together with increasing amounts of oestrogen and progesterone to maintain pregnancy after the third month, when the ovaries cease to make the major contribution of these hormones.

Q: *Are there any conditions that may damage the placenta?*

A: Yes. Conditions in the mother such as high blood pressure, chronic nephritis, diabetes mellitus, and pre-eclampsia (toxaemia of pregnancy) damage the blood vessels and reduce the efficiency of the placenta. This increases the risk of intrauterine death of the foetus, and reduces the rate at which the foetus grows.

Recent research has shown that smoking also damages the placenta, resulting in smaller-than-average babies who have a greater chance of early death.

Q: What happens to the placenta before and during normal labour?

A: There is some deterioration in the way the placenta functions during the last two weeks of pregnancy. This probably is a factor in causing the onset of labour.

Once labour has started, the mother's blood supply to the placenta stops during contractions of the womb, and returns when the muscles relax. During the final minutes of labour, the restricted blood flow probably causes a slight increase in the carbon dioxide level in the foetal bloodstream. This acts as an additional stimulus for the baby to start breathing through the lungs immediately after birth.

The placenta is delivered in the third stage of labour. It should be examined to make sure that it is complete. If a piece of placenta is left in the womb, it can cause a postpartum haemorrhage. *See* PREGNANCY AND CHILDBIRTH.

Plague (bubonic plague; black death) is a severe, potentially fatal infection that is caused by the bacterium *Yersinia pestis* (also called *Pasteurella pestis*). It occurs primarily in wild rodents but can be transmitted to humans. There are two main forms of plague that affect humans: bubonic plague, which results from the bite of an infected animal flea; and pneumonic plague, which results from inhaling droplets breathed by infected people. Both forms of plague are now rare.

Q: What are the symptoms of bubonic plague?

A: After a variable incubation period, which is usually between two and five days, there is a sudden onset of repeated shivering attacks, and the patient's body temperature rises to over (40°C) 104°F. The lymph glands become swollen and painful (buboes), and the patient may become delirious. The death rate in untreated patients is more than fifty per cent, with most deaths occurring within about five days.

Q: What are the symptoms of pneumonic plague?

A: After an incubation period of about two days there is a sudden onset of high fever; chills; and headache. There also may be increasing breathlessness, and coughing with foamy, bloodstained sputum. Most untreated patients die within about two days.

Q: How is plague treated?

A: Immediate treatment can be life-saving. Both forms of plague are treated with large doses of antibiotics, such as tetracycline, streptomycin, or chloramphenicol. The patient must be isolated to prevent the spread of infection. Prompt treatment usually improves the symptoms rapidly and enables most patients to survive the infection.

Q: How can plague be prevented?

A: Prevention is based on rodent control and the use of insect repellents to reduce the number of fleas. All people travelling to districts of countries in Asia with known plague should be immunized. Anybody who has been in contact with an infected person should be treated with antibiotics immediately.

Plantar reflex is the movement of the big toe when the outer side of the sole is stroked, causing it to point down. This reflex indicates that the nervous system is reacting normally. The opposite response is called the Babinski reflex, a pointing up of the big toe when the outer side of the sole is stroked. The lack of a plantar reflex and the presence of the Babinski reflex indicates a disorder of the nervous system, although this abnormal response is seen in all infants less than one year old.

Plantar wart (verruca) is a contagious wart. *See* WART.

Plaque has two medical meanings. (1) As a skin complaint, it is a group of eruptions that form a plate or patch on top of the skin. (2) Plaque as a dental disorder is an accumulation of hard material on the teeth that can

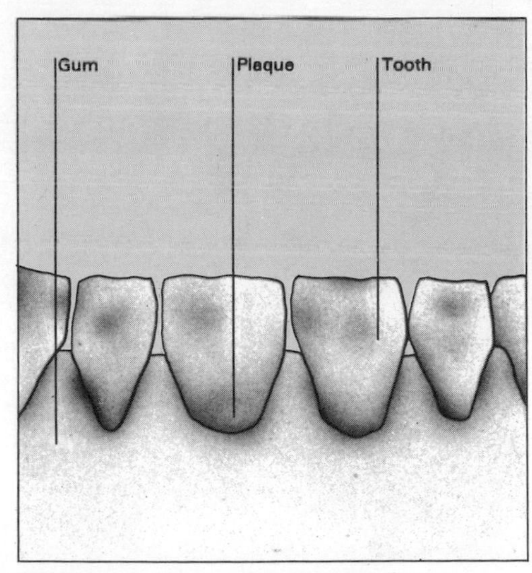

Plaque accumulates on teeth that are not cleaned regularly, and causes gum disorders.

cause gum disorders, such as GINGIVITIS and PYORRHOEA.

Plasma is the fluid part of the blood in which the blood cells and the platelets are suspended. It consists of water in which many chemicals are dissolved, including proteins, salts, sugars, nitrogenous wastes, and carbon dioxide. Plasma is different from SERUM, which is the fluid that remains when blood has clotted; serum is plasma without fibrinogen and the other components of a blood clot.

Plasma is the main medium for the transportation of substances throughout the body. It carries nutritive substances to the body structures and removes their waste products. Plasma also makes possible chemical communication within the body by transporting hormones.

Plasma may be given by transfusion to patients who have lost serum through burns. It also may be used to treat shock, or disorders in which protein is lost from the body, such as ASCITES and NEPHROSIS.

See also PLASMA FRACTIONS.

Plasma fractions are the different proteins that can be extracted from the blood plasma and used to treat various disorders. For example, gamma globulin can give temporary protection against some diseases, such as measles; antihaemophilic globulin may be used to prevent bleeding in haemophiliacs; and albumin may be used in the treatment of NEPHROSIS and liver CIRRHOSIS.

Plasmodium is a genus of PROTOZOA, certain species of which cause MALARIA. The species that are known to cause malaria are *Plasmodium falciparum; Plasmodium malariae; Plasmodium ovale;* and *Plasmodium vivax.* These parasitic microorganisms are carried by the Anopheles mosquito and infect the red blood cells in humans.

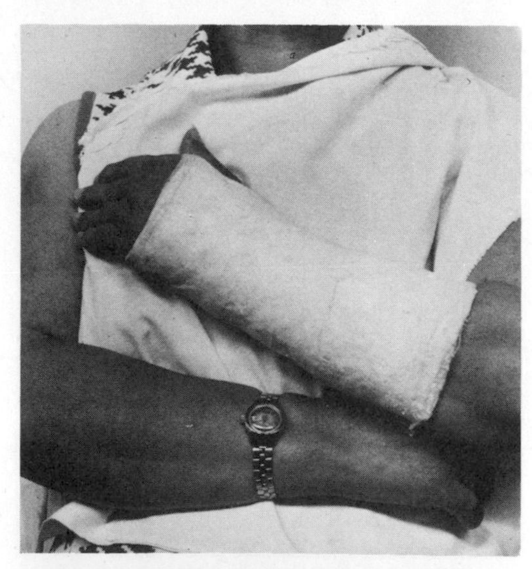

Plaster of Paris is a gypsum cement used to make a stiff bandage to immobilize limbs.

Plaster of Paris is a form of gypsum which, when mixed with water, forms a paste that hardens rapidly. It can be applied in cotton bandages and used to immobilize fractured limbs.

Plastic surgery is a special treatment concerned with restoring and restructuring damaged surface features. If the treatment is carried out merely to improve the patient's appearance, it is known as cosmetic surgery.

Platelet is a minute particle that is suspended in the blood plasma. Platelets also are known as thrombocytes. They are formed by the fragmentation of large cells in the bone marrow. Platelets play an essential part in the clotting of blood.

Plating is the application of bacteria to a culture medium in a shallow dish. Plating also refers to a surgical technique in which a metal plate is screwed onto a fractured bone.

Pleura is the membrane that surrounds each lung and lines the internal surface of the chest cavity. There are two pleurae, one around each lung. Each pleura consists of two layers: the parietal layer, which lines the chest cavity; and the visceral layer, which covers the surface of the lung. The space between the layers is known as the pleural cavity. It contains a small amount of fluid that lubricates the two layers, thereby facilitating the movements of the lung during breathing.

See also EMPYEMA; HAEMOTHORAX; PARACENTESIS; PLEURISY; PNEUMOTHORAX.

Pleurisy is an inflammation of the pleura. Most commonly it is caused by infection of the pleura or of the underlying lung, as may occur with PNEUMONIA. Pleurisy also may be caused by a pulmonary INFARCTION; an injury that penetrates the pleura; the spread of disease from elsewhere in the body, such as cancer; or as a complication of a generalized disease, such as kidney failure (*see* URAEMIA).

Q: What are the symptoms of pleurisy?

A: The onset is usually sudden, with localized pain near the area of inflammation that may be aggravated by breathing, coughing, or movement. If the part of the pleura that covers the diaphragm is affected, the pain may be referred to the shoulder on that side. There may also be rapid, shallow breathing and, if pleurisy is caused by infection, the patient may have a fever.

As the condition develops, the pain usually ceases because fluid forms in the pleural cavity and separates the inflamed surfaces of the pleura. If a large amount of fluid forms (pleural effusion), the underlying lung may collapse, causing breathlessness.

Q: How is pleurisy treated?

A: Treatment is directed toward the underlying cause. Initially, painkillers may be given and, if the patient has a fever, antibiotics may be prescribed. When a definite diagnosis has been made, the appropriate treatment can be given, such as anticoagulants for a pulmonary infarction.

Q: Can pleurisy cause complications?

A: Yes. Injury to the pleura or lung cancer may cause bleeding into the pleural cavity (haemothorax). Pleurisy that is caused by infection may result in an accumulation of pus in the pleural cavity (EMPYEMA). This may require antibiotic treatment or surgical drainage. Pleural effusions that are caused by cancer tend to recur. They may need treatment with cytotoxic drugs.

Pleurodynia is a sharp pain in the muscles of the chest wall that is similar to, but which is not caused by, pleurisy. Pleurodynia may be caused by FIBROSITIS.

Pleurodynia, epidemic, commonly known as Bornholm disease or Devil's grip, is an infection caused by one of the Coxsackie viruses. Children are most susceptible to the disease, especially in the summer and autumn.

The symptoms include pain in the region of the diaphragm, fever, headache, nausea, general discomfort and tenderness and swelling of the muscles. The illness lasts two to seven days and is followed by tiredness and depression that may persist for several weeks.

A doctor usually recommends that the patient is given strong painkilling drugs, confined to bed, and encouraged to drink plenty of fluids.

Plexus is a network of nerves, veins, or arteries. The solar plexus is a collection of nerves that lies behind the stomach.

Plumbism. *See* LEAD POISONING.

Pneumoconiosis is a general term for any lung disorder that is caused by the inhalation of dust particles. It is an occupational disorder. There are three main types of pneumoconiosis: (1) simple pneumoconiosis results from the deposition of inert dust in the lungs and is apparently harmless (for example, iron, tin, and carbon dust do not seem to cause any adverse effects); (2) irritant dusts, such as silica and asbestos, can cause SILICOSIS or asbestosis, and these diseases cause scarring and gradual destruction of the lung tissue; (3) organic dusts may cause a form of allergic reaction. For example, BYSSINOSIS is caused by cotton fibre dust.

Q: What are the symptoms of pneumoconiosis?

A: Simple pneumoconiosis seldom produces any symptoms. Coal dust, however, may cause scarring and destruction of lung tissue similar to that caused by silica and asbestos.

Pneumoconiosis that results from irritant dusts may cause increasing breathlessness, coughing, and spitting of blood. Asbestosis may lead to lung cancer.

The main symptom of pneumoconiosis that is caused by organic dusts is asthma. In some cases this may be complicated with bronchitis.

Q: How is pneumoconiosis treated?

A: There is no cure for this condition. It is essential that a person change jobs at the first suspicion of pneumoconiosis. It is impossible to remove the dust particles once they have reached the lungs, and lung deterioration is likely to continue for some time after a person has stopped inhaling the dust. Dust suppression and regular medical examinations are essential.

Pneumonectomy is the surgical removal of a lung. A partial pneumonectomy, which also is known as a lobectomy, is the removal of a section of a lung. A pneumonectomy most commonly is performed in the treatment of lung cancer. A partial pneumonectomy may be necessary in some cases of TUBERCULOSIS; BRONCHIECTASIS; or a lung abscess.

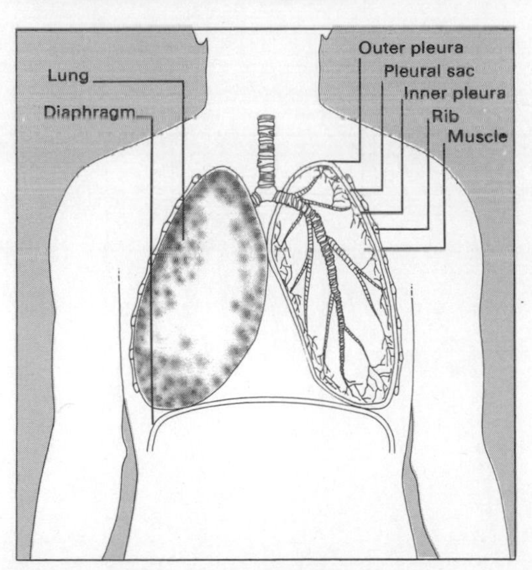

Pleura is a membrane that folds around the lungs and lines the inside of the thorax.

Pneumonia

Pneumonia is infection lungs by bacteria, viruses, or fungi. In rare cases, it may be aggravated by inhaled matter or worm infestations. If infection spreads down the bronchioles, it is known as bronchopneumonia. If only one lobe of the lung is involved, it is called lobar pneumonia.

Q: What kinds of infection cause pneumonia?

A: The common bacterial infections include *Hemophilus influenzae*, pneumococcus, and haemolytic streptococcus. Mycobacterium tuberculosis is now rare in Western countries. Antibiotic resistant staphylococcus is particularly dangerous and must be treated in a hospital.

Viruses include influenzas, chickenpox, measles, and Coxsackie. Similar pneumonia infections are produced by *Mycoplasma pneumoniae* and psittacosis. Fungal pneumonia may be caused by *Histoplasma capsulatum, Coccidiodes immitis*, or blastomycosis.

Q: What are the symptoms of pneumonia?

A: In bacterial pneumonia, the patient develops the symptoms of a cold followed by a sudden shivering attack, sputum that is often bloody, and a high fever (40°C; 104°F) with rapid respiration and pulse rate. The patient often feels pain due to pleurisy. Vomiting and diarrhoea may occur; confusion is common.

In other forms of pneumonia, especially among elderly patients, the symptoms develop slowly with clear evidence of bronchitis and a worsening cough, often with bloodstained sputum. Headache, muscle aches, and cyanosis (blue tinged lips because of poorly oxygenated blood) are common. Progress depends on the individual's resistance to the type of infection. In elderly or weak patients death may occur. Children or babies show few symptoms suggesting a chest infection. But the child obviously is ill, and may collapse.

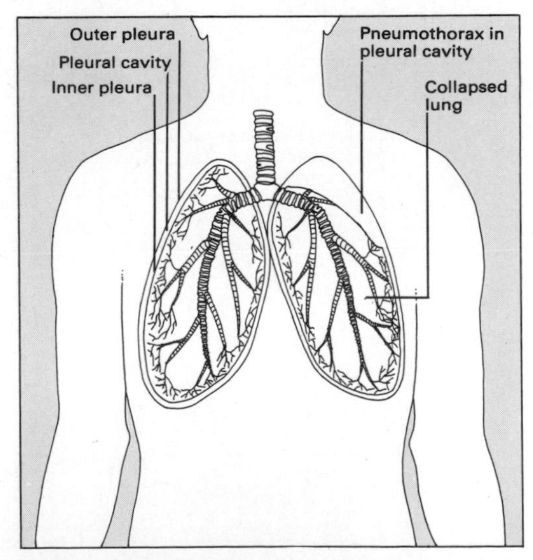

Pneumothorax is air in the pleural cavity that can cause a lung to collapse.

Q: How is pneumonia diagnosed and treated?

A: Diagnosis follows a doctor's examination and, usually, a chest X-ray. A specimen of the sputum is examined and cultured to identify the infective organism. Sometimes a white bood cell count may help to determine whether the infection is caused by bacteria or by a virus.

Antibiotics are used in the treatment of bacterial and fungal infections.

Breathing exercises and percussion to shake the chest wall encourage the patient to cough up sputum. If the sputum is thick and sticky, steam inhalations may also help. A seriously ill patient may need oxygen therapy. Painkilling drugs are prescribed if the patient has pleurisy.

Most patients suffering from mild forms of pneumonia can be treated at home with rest, antibiotics, and breathing exercises.

See also PLEURISY.

Pneumonitis is an inflammation of the lungs. It may be a symptom of several diseases, such as PNEUMONIA and PNEUMOCONIOSIS.

Pneumothorax is a condition in which there is air in the pleural cavity, the space between the lungs and the chest wall. It prevents the normal expansion of the lungs, thereby impairing breathing.

Q: What causes a pneumothorax?

A: The most common cause of a pneumothorax is a penetrating injury of the chest wall. This is known as a traumatic pneumothorax. Rarely, injury may cause a life-threatening form of traumatic pneumothorax in which a flap of tissue acts as a valve that allows air to be drawn into the chest, but not to be blown out again. The pressure within the chest rises rapidly and causes both lungs to collapse. This condition is known as a tension pneumothorax.

A spontaneous pneumothorax is caused by air leaking from the lungs. This may be the result of an underlying disorder, such as EMPHYSEMA, or by a congenital weakness of the lungs.

Q: What are the symptoms of a pneumothorax?

A: The symptoms of a pneumothorax vary greatly. A traumatic pneumothorax is always serious, because of damage to the chest wall. The main symptoms are breathlessness and pain. A tension pneumothorax causes extreme breathing difficulty, and may be rapidly fatal.

The symptoms of a spontaneous pneumothorax range from slight breathlessness on exertion to the sudden onset of severe chest pains and extreme breathing difficulty.

Q: How is a pneumothorax treated?

A: A patient with a traumatic pneumothorax requires hospitalization so that the air in the pleural cavity can be removed by insertion of a needle into the chest wall. Then the injury is treated. A tension pneumothorax requires emergency medical treatment; the rapid removal of air from the pleural cavity may be lifesaving.

Most patients with a small, spontaneous pneumothorax do not require treatment because the air is gradually reabsorbed. Occasionally, the condition may recur, in which case surgery may be necessary.

Pock is an old word for a pustule, a small elevation of the skin filled with pus or lymph.

Pockmarks are small scars left after the healing of pustules. They may occur if any spot becomes infected and leaves a scar, such as may result in chickenpox if the spots are scratched. *See* PUSTULE.

Podagra. *See* GOUT.

Poisoning (for EMERGENCY treatment, *see* First Aid, p.562) is the taking into the body by eating, inhaling, injecting, or absorbing through the skin any substance that damages or prevents the normal working of the body.

Poker back, a rigid, slightly bent spine, is probably the result of the rheumatic disorder ANKYLOSING SPONDYLITIS.

Polio. *See* POLIOMYELITIS.

Polioencephalitis is an inflammation of the grey matter of the brain. It may be caused by encephalitis. It also may occur as a complication of vitamin B_1 deficiency (BERI-BERI), when it produces acute mental disturbances similar to those of KORSAKOFF'S SYNDROME.

See also ENCEPHALITIS.

Poliomyelitis, also called infantile paralysis, is an infection of the nervous system caused by one of the three polio viruses. It occurs throughout the world. The disease is common in the summer months in temperate climates, and all year round in the tropics. Epidemics can occur, but the risk of an epidemic is lessened by improved sanitation and immunization of children with oral vaccine.

Q: How long does poliomyelitis take to develop and what are its symptoms?

A: There is an incubation period of three days or more, followed by feverish illness. A sore throat and headaches develop over a period of one to two (and occasionally five) days. Most people recover after this stage without further symptoms. Ten per cent, however, suddenly develop severe headaches, fever, muscle pains, and neck stiffness, suggestive of meningitis. There is a tingling sensation in the limbs, and increased weakness and paralysis.

Throat and respiratory poliomyelitis may be fatal. Many patients suffering from paralysis during the illness regain most, or all, movement in time, but in severe cases paralysis may remain.

Q: How is poliomyelitis treated?

A: Mild cases require bed rest. Severe cases need isolation and complete rest, with slight sedation and painkilling drugs. With respiratory paralysis, artificial respirators and a TRACHEOSTOMY are necessary. A physiotherapist regularly moves the patient's joints to prevent stiffness. Extra fluids are given to prevent dehydration. The patient may have to be fed through a tube into the stomach, and a catheter is needed if the bladder is paralyzed.

Poliomyelitis is much easier to prevent than to treat. Infants should be given three doses of oral Sabin live attenuated virus vaccine (OPV), with boosters at five years, and when recommended by a doctor.

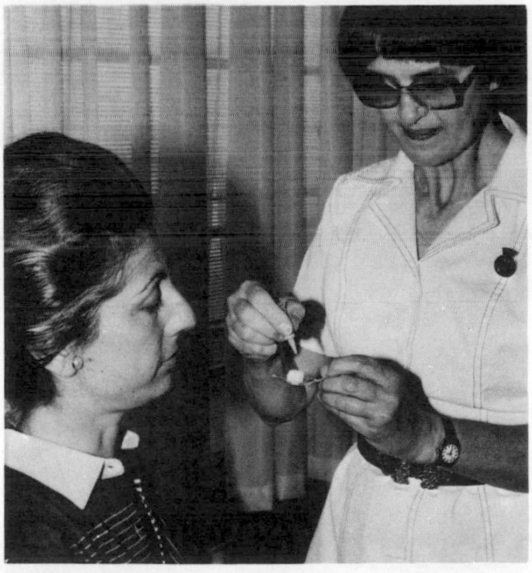

Poliomyelitis vaccine can be given orally on a lump of sugar.

Epidemic poliomyelitis is unlikely in vaccinated communities.

Pollen is the powderlike substance produced by male flowers which fertilizes other plants.

Polyarteritis nodosa is a rare, potentially fatal inflammation of the small arteries. It often results in arterial thrombosis and death of the surrounding tissue. The cause of polyarteritis nodosa is not known. However, in some cases the onset of the disorder may be associated with bacterial infection or with certain drugs, such as sulphonamide. Polyarteritis nodosa usually occurs in persons between the ages of 25 and 50 years, and is more common in men than in women.

Q: What are the symptoms of polyarteritis nodosa?

A: The symptoms of this disorder are extremely variable. The most common symptoms include fever, recurrent abdominal pain, weight loss, peripheral neuritis, asthma, hypertension, oedema, and fatigue. The muscles and joints may ache, and nodules and ulcers may appear on the skin. The kidneys also may be affected, causing high blood pressure, swelling of the ankles, and, ultimately, kidney failure.

Q: How is polyarteritis nodosa treated?

A: There is, as yet, no cure for this disorder, which is fatal in most cases. However, the symptoms can be controlled and the life can be prolonged by treatment with large doses of CORTICOSTEROIDS. In some cases, parts of the intestine may die, resulting in PERITONITIS. Such cases usually require surgery.

Polyarthritis is any form of arthritis that affects several joints at the same time. *See* OSTEOARTHRITIS; RHEUMATOID ARTHRITIS.

Polycystic kidney is a congenital anomaly of the kidney in which some of its tissue fails to join up with the drainage tubules for urine. It leads to the formation of cysts that contain urine. Polycystic kidney may occur in several members of a family. A kidney transplant is the only treatment.

Polycythaemia is an excess of red cells in the blood. Polycythaemia vera is a rare disease of the part of the bone marrow that produces red blood cells. The number of red cells and the total volume of blood increases gradually over several years. The cause of polycythaemia vera is not known. The disorder cannot be cured but, by removing blood regularly from the veins (phlebotomy) and treatment with radioactive phosphorus, life can be prolonged.

Polydactylism is a congenital abnormality in which there are extra fingers and toes.

Polymorph is an abbreviation of polymorphonuclear leucocyte, a type of WHITE BLOOD CELL.

Polymyalgia rheumatica is an uncommon form of rheumatism that affects the elderly, usually those over sixty years of age. It is more common in women than in men. Polymyalgia rheumatica is characterized by pain and stiffness in the neck, shoulders, and back. There also may be a persistent headache. Patients often feel unwell, but rarely are seriously ill. The cause of the condition is unknown, but it is thought to result from a type of arterial inflammation. If the arteries in the eye become inflamed, the patient may suddenly become blind.

Treatment with corticosteroid drugs is rapidly effective and must be continued for several months.

Polyneuritis is damage or inflammation of the nerves. Damage to one nerve (mononeuritis) or to several nerves in more than one area (mononeuritis multiplex) are closely related disorders.

Polyneuritis may be caused by injury; viral infection; toxic poisoning; industrial poisoning; vitamin B_{12} deficiency; alcoholism; diabetes mellitus; or cancer, most commonly of the lung. Symptoms may be mild, producing tingling or altered sensation in the affected area, or severe, affecting respiration. In most cases of polyneuritis, patients make a complete and spontaneous recovery, although some may require physiotherapy or corticosteroid treatment.

See also FRIEDREICH'S ATAXIA.

Polyp is a growth or tumour on a mucous membrane. It grows on a short stalk. Polyps are usually benign (noncancerous). They may occur anywhere in the body, but are most common in the nose, the cervix of the womb, within the uterine cavity, and in the rectum.

Polyps within the colon or large intestine may become malignant. A condition in which there are many intestinal polyps (familial polyposis) commonly develops into cancer.

Polyuria is the frequent passing of large amounts of urine. It is a typical symptom of diabetes and kidney disease, such as chronic NEPHRITIS.

See DIABETES.

Pompholyx is a type of eczema that produces highly irritating blisters on the hands and feet. The cause is unknown. The condition lasts for one to two weeks, but commonly recurs.

The blisters break into small open sores that gradually heal. Treatment with soothing corticosteroid creams reduces the irritation until natural healing takes place. It is important to keep the area clean and dry to prevent secondary infection.

Pore is a minute opening in the skin which allows matter to pass through. *See* SKIN.

Porphyria is a group of congenital disorders of the metabolism or regulation of the body.

Porphyria is characterized by excessive secretions of porphyrins in the blood or liver. Porphyrins are nitrogen-containing organic compounds that are needed to unite with iron and the protein globin to form HAEMOGLOBIN.

There are two main types of porphyria: those that occur within the red blood cells, and those that involve the liver.

Q: *What are the symptoms of porphyria in the red blood cells?*

A: The symptoms occur most commonly in children, and may be very severe. They include blisters, red teeth, and purple or pink urine. If the skin is exposed to the sun, the blister formations may progress to a stage of scarring. The condition may be fatal, but in its mildest form the patient needs only to avoid sunlight.

Q: *What are the symptoms of porphyria in the liver?*

A: There may be severe abdominal pain, vomiting, and abdominal swelling. These may be accompanied by neurological disorders, such as epileptic seizures.

Q: *How is porphyria treated?*

A: Children with porphyria must avoid sunlight. In adults, the precipitating cause, usually drugs, must be discovered and avoided. Relatives of a person with porphyria should also be examined. Treatment with painkilling drugs may be necessary, and also dietary treatment.

Portacaval shunt is an artificially-produced junction between the hepatic portal vein and the inferior vena cava.

Portal vein is a vein that carries blood between two organs.

Port-wine stain, or port-wine mark, is a flat, purplish-red birthmark formed by abnormal blood vessels. *See* BIRTHMARK.

Postnasal drip is a discharge from the back of the nose down the back of the throat.

Q: *What are the symptoms of postnasal drip?*

A: One or both nostrils may be intermittently blocked. There may be a slight coughing of sputum as a result of the irritating effect of the discharge.

Q: *How is postnasal drip treated?*

A: Consult a doctor, because the treatment depends on diagnosing the cause. Continued use of nasal drops and sprays may only aggravate the condition, and for this reason they should not be used without medical supervision.

See also CATARRH.

Postpartum describes anything that occurs within six weeks after the birth of a baby.

Post-traumatic describes any medical condition that occurs as a result of or following an injury.

Postural drainage is a method used by physiotherapists and surgeons to position a patient so that gravity assists in the drainage of a congested area.

Pott's disease is tuberculosis of the spine. It mainly affects children and adults up to the age of forty. The disorder produces destruction of a vertebra by tuberculous osteitis (inflammation of the bone). Collapse of a vertebra results in the compression of the spinal cord and nerves. Pott's disease gives the individual the typical hunchback appearance of kyphosis. Paralysis may also occur.

Treatment includes curing the infection with antituberculosis drugs, relieving the spinal cord from pressure, removing any pus or bone, bed rest, adequate diet, and careful exercise.

See also KYPHOSIS.

Pott's fracture is a fracture of the ankle. The break involves the tibia (shin-bone) or fibula (the second of the two long bones in the lower leg), or both. The ankle joint can be dislocated, and the ligaments are torn.

Pott's fracture is a common injury. It is usually treated by manipulation into the correct position under general anaesthesia and immobilization of the ankle in a plaster cast for about six weeks. With severe fractures, the broken bones are operated on.

Poultice is a heated dressing that is applied to the skin to relieve congestion, inflammation, or pain, or to encourage a boil to discharge.

Poultices are seldom effective. They lose

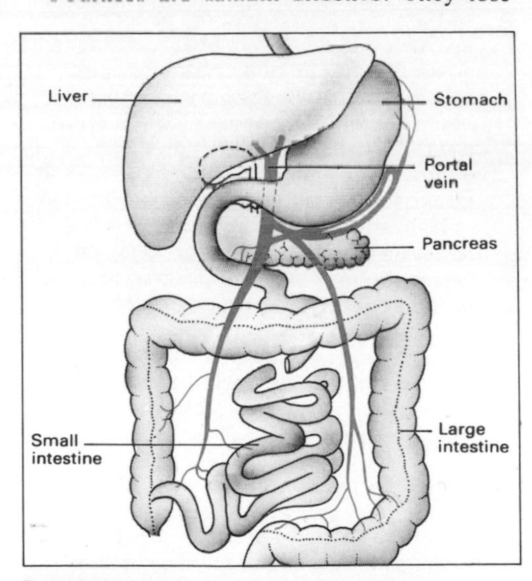

Portal vein receives the final products of digestion and transports them to the liver.

heat rapidly, damage the skin by making it moist, and may cause burns.

Prednisone and another corticosteroid drug, prednisolone, are synthetic preparations that have actions similar to the naturally occurring steroid hormone cortisol, which is formed by the adrenal glands.

Prolonged use of prednisone, like all corticosteroids, causes loss of calcium from the bones (osteoporosis), a tendency to develop diabetes mellitus, and the likelihood of developing a peptic ulcer. There is reduced resistance to infection, and the skin becomes thin and heals more slowly than normal.

Prolonged high dosage of prednisone may produce a typical moonface, acne, and an increase in body fat. If prednisone has been taken for a long period of time, the dosage must be reduced slowly so that the adrenal glands start producing cortisol again. *See* CORTICOSTEROIDS.

Pre-eclampsia is a condition that sometimes occurs late in pregnancy. Symptoms include: high blood pressure; swelling (oedema) of the legs, hands and, to a lesser extent, the face; and protein in the urine (albuminuria). It sometimes is called toxaemia of pregnancy, although there is no evidence to suggest that it is caused by a toxin. In fact, the cause of pre-eclampsia is not known. But the condition is more likely to occur in women who already have high blood pressure, who suffer from chronic nephritis, or who are expecting their first baby. Antenatal care is essential if pre-eclampsia is to be detected in its early stages.

Q: How is pre-eclampsia treated?

A: In the very early stages, the patient is instructed to take additional rest. She is advised not to lie on her back because this causes the womb to press on the blood vessels that supply it. She is given mild sedatives, and a strict diet plan emphasizing high protein and normal salt intake to prevent any further weight gain.

If these measures are not successful, the woman may be admitted to hospital, where she may be given drugs to reduce blood pressure. If these are not effective and tests show that the baby is not getting enough oxygen, labour is induced.

Q: What complications may occur with pre-eclampsia and how are they treated?

A: The most serious complication is ECLAMPSIA, in which convulsions and coma may occur in the woman. The more common complications are those that affect the foetus. The blood supply to the womb is reduced, and foetal growth is slowed. There is an increased likelihood of intrauterine death.

Prefrontal leucotomy. *See* LEUCOTOMY.

A talk about Pregnancy and childbirth

Pregnancy and childbirth. A normal pregnancy lasts about 265 days, although pregnancies naturally vary in duration.

Q: Can a woman always be sure that her estimated date of confinement is correct in the first place?

A: No. A woman whose periods have always been irregular is unlikely to reach an accurate date for delivery based on calculation. This is because the date of ovulation, and thus fertilization, probably occurred about two weeks before a period was due. It is possible for bleeding to occur during pregnancy, lasting one or two days. However, it may make a woman think she has menstruated and become pregnant a month later than was actually the case.

Q: What are the early symptoms of pregnancy?

A: Often, the earliest sign is the absence of a period (amenorrhoea). This may be accompanied by a feeling of heaviness in the breasts, slight nausea first thing in the mornings (morning sickness), and frequency of urination.

Q: What tests and examinations are carried out to confirm pregnancy?

A: A PREGNANCY TEST can be performed using a sample of urine, after the period has been overdue for eight days. If this is positive, it is relatively certain that the woman is pregnant. If the test is negative, it should be repeated in a week's time.

Once the period is more than three weeks overdue, a gentle vaginal examination usually reveals an enlargement of the womb. This, combined with other symptoms suggestive of pregnancy, may confirm pregnancy without a pregnancy test.

Q: How are the common problems of the first three months of pregnancy treated?

A: Morning sickness affects about fifty per cent of women. A doctor may prescribe antinauseant drugs to be taken at night. Eating biscuits before getting out of bed in the morning helps to control mild nausea. Breast tenderness is relieved by wearing a firm brassiere that gives good support. HYPEREMESIS gravidarum is a severe form of morning sickness.

Q: What information is required, and what examinations and tests are carried out by the obstetrician?

A: It is most important for the woman to

give the full history of any previous pregnancies or abortions she may have had.

She will also be asked about any illnesses or disorders she may have had. Chronic nephritis, diabetes mellitus, high blood pressure, and rheumatic valve disease of the heart all can cause problems during pregnancy. If there is a family history of diabetes mellitus, there is a possibility that the patient could develop mild diabetes while under the stress of pregnancy.

A complete physical examination includes weighing, breast examination, blood pressure test, urine test, cervical smear, and vaginal examination. At each subsequent visit blood pressure, weight, and urine are monitored, and the obstetrician checks the ankles for signs of oedema. The growth of the womb is checked each visit after the fourteenth week of pregnancy. The obstetrician can tell this by feeling the abdomen.

Finally, some laboratory tests are made on a sample of the woman's blood. These include a haemoglobin test to detect anaemia, and tests for blood group and Rhesus (Rh) factor and for signs of previous infections such as German measles (rubella).

The obstetrician usually discusses the findings of the examinations and tests with the patient to reassure her that the pregnancy is normal, and to emphasize the importance of regular antenatal examinations. At first these are generally given on a monthly basis, unless there is some abnormality present. But later in pregnancy the visits become more frequent, usually occurring every two weeks from the twenty-eighth week of pregnancy, and weekly from the thirty-sixth until delivery.

Q: *Should a pregnant woman keep to a special diet or take extra care in early pregnancy?*

A: No. Unless she has a condition such as nephritis, only a normal diet and regular exercise are needed. But she must not smoke nor drink more than two glasses of alcohol a day: these can affect the baby.

Q: *May sexual intercourse continue throughout pregnancy?*

A: Yes. In general, intercourse may take place as usual. If there is a history of spontaneous abortion, however, the obstetrician probably will advise avoiding intercourse during the first three months at around the time when a period would normally have occurred.

Q: *What tests and examinations may be carried out during the middle three months of pregnancy?*

A: Using ultrasonic equipment, the obstetrician usually can detect foetal life by the end of the second month of pregnancy. There is no danger for either the mother or foetus in this technique. Scans also detect potential problems and can accurately assess the progress of a pregnancy, in cases where there is doubt, after the fourth month.

Amniocentesis involves taking a sample of fluid from around the foetus by inserting a needle into the womb, under

Jan.	1	2	3	4	5	6	7	8	9	10	11	12	13	14	15	16	17	18	19	20	21	22	23	24	25	26	27	28	29	30	31	Jan.
Oct.	**8**	**9**	**10**	**11**	**12**	**13**	**14**	**15**	**16**	**17**	**18**	**19**	**20**	**21**	**22**	**23**	**24**	**25**	**26**	**27**	**28**	**29**	**30**	**31**	**(1**	**2**	**3**	**4**	**5**	**6**	**7**	**Nov.**
Feb.	1	2	3	4	5	6	7	8	9	10	11	12	13	14	15	16	17	18	19	20	21	22	23	24	25	26	27	28				Feb.
Nov.	**8**	**9**	**10**	**11**	**12**	**13**	**14**	**15**	**16**	**17**	**18**	**19**	**20**	**21**	**22**	**23**	**24**	**25**	**26**	**27**	**28**	**29**	**30**	**(1**	**2**	**3**	**4**	**5**				**Dec.**
Mar.	1	2	3	4	5	6	7	8	9	10	11	12	13	14	15	16	17	18	19	20	21	22	23	24	25	26	27	28	29	30	31	Mar.
Dec.	**6**	**7**	**8**	**9**	**10**	**11**	**12**	**13**	**14**	**15**	**16**	**17**	**18**	**19**	**20**	**21**	**22**	**23**	**24**	**25**	**26**	**27**	**28**	**29**	**30**	**31**	**(1**	**2**	**3**	**4**	**5**	**Jan.**
April	1	2	3	4	5	6	7	8	9	10	11	12	13	14	15	16	17	18	19	20	21	22	23	24	25	26	27	28	29	30		April
Jan.	**6**	**7**	**8**	**9**	**10**	**11**	**12**	**13**	**14**	**15**	**16**	**17**	**18**	**19**	**20**	**21**	**22**	**23**	**24**	**25**	**26**	**27**	**28**	**29**	**30**	**31**	**(1**	**2**	**3**	**4**		**Feb.**
May	1	2	3	4	5	6	7	8	9	10	11	12	13	14	15	16	17	18	19	20	21	22	23	24	25	26	27	28	29	30	31	May
Feb.	**5**	**6**	**7**	**8**	**9**	**10**	**11**	**12**	**13**	**14**	**15**	**16**	**17**	**18**	**19**	**20**	**21**	**22**	**23**	**24**	**25**	**26**	**27**	**28**	**(1**	**2**	**3**	**4**	**5**	**6**	**7**	**Mar.**
June	1	2	3	4	5	6	7	8	9	10	11	12	13	14	15	16	17	18	19	20	21	22	23	24	25	26	27	28	29	30		June
Mar.	**8**	**9**	**10**	**11**	**12**	**13**	**14**	**15**	**16**	**17**	**18**	**19**	**20**	**21**	**22**	**23**	**24**	**25**	**26**	**27**	**28**	**29**	**30**	**31**	**(1**	**2**	**3**	**4**	**5**	**6**		**April**
July	1	2	3	4	5	6	7	8	9	10	11	12	13	14	15	16	17	18	19	20	21	22	23	24	25	26	27	28	29	30	31	July
April	**7**	**8**	**9**	**10**	**11**	**12**	**13**	**14**	**15**	**16**	**17**	**18**	**19**	**20**	**21**	**22**	**23**	**24**	**25**	**26**	**27**	**28**	**29**	**30**	**(1**	**2**	**3**	**4**	**5**	**6**	**7**	**May**
Aug.	1	2	3	4	5	6	7	8	9	10	11	12	13	14	15	16	17	18	19	20	21	22	23	24	25	26	27	28	29	30	31	Aug.
May	**8**	**9**	**10**	**11**	**12**	**13**	**14**	**15**	**16**	**17**	**18**	**19**	**20**	**21**	**22**	**23**	**24**	**25**	**26**	**27**	**28**	**29**	**30**	**31**	**(1**	**2**	**3**	**4**	**5**	**6**	**7**	**June**
Sept.	1	2	3	4	5	6	7	8	9	10	11	12	13	14	15	16	17	18	19	20	21	22	23	24	25	26	27	28	29	30		Sept.
June	**8**	**9**	**10**	**11**	**12**	**13**	**14**	**15**	**16**	**17**	**18**	**19**	**20**	**21**	**22**	**23**	**24**	**25**	**26**	**27**	**28**	**29**	**30**	**(1**	**2**	**3**	**4**	**5**	**6**	**7**		**July**
Oct.	1	2	3	4	5	6	7	8	9	10	11	12	13	14	15	16	17	18	19	20	21	22	23	24	25	26	27	28	29	30	31	Oct.
July	**8**	**9**	**10**	**11**	**12**	**13**	**14**	**15**	**16**	**17**	**18**	**19**	**20**	**21**	**22**	**23**	**24**	**25**	**26**	**27**	**28**	**29**	**30**	**31**	**(1**	**2**	**3**	**4**	**5**	**6**	**7**	**Aug.**
Nov.	1	2	3	4	5	6	7	8	9	10	11	12	13	14	15	16	17	18	19	20	21	22	23	24	25	26	27	28	29	30		Nov.
Aug.	**8**	**9**	**10**	**11**	**12**	**13**	**14**	**15**	**16**	**17**	**18**	**19**	**20**	**21**	**22**	**23**	**24**	**25**	**26**	**27**	**28**	**29**	**30**	**31**	**(1**	**2**	**3**	**4**	**5**	**6**		**Sept.**
Dec.	1	2	3	4	5	6	7	8	9	10	11	12	13	14	15	16	17	18	19	20	21	22	23	24	25	26	27	28	29	30	31	Dec.
Sept.	**7**	**8**	**9**	**10**	**11**	**12**	**13**	**14**	**15**	**16**	**17**	**18**	**19**	**20**	**21**	**22**	**23**	**24**	**25**	**26**	**27**	**28**	**29**	**30**	**(1**	**2**	**3**	**4**	**5**	**6**	**7**	**Oct.**

Estimated date of delivery can be calculated from the first day of the woman's last period. Find the latter date (in light type) and the delivery date is below it (in heavy type).

local anaesthetic. This procedure may be carried out if there is any possibility of a congenital foetal abnormality, such as Down's syndrome. It also can detect developmental disorders of the nervous system, as well as other abnormalities.

Q: *What is "quickening," and at what stage can it be felt?*

A: Quickening describes the first movements of the foetus in the womb felt by the mother. A woman undergoing her first pregnancy usually feels it between the eighteenth and twentieth weeks. In subsequent pregnancies, however, when the mother is aware of what to expect, she may feel it about two weeks earlier.

Q: *What are the common problems of the latter half of pregnancy?*

A: Many minor problems may affect a woman as pregnancy progresses, although few are serious.

(1) *Backache.* This is extremely common because the ligaments that normally hold the joints in place are affected by hormones which cause them to become more stretched and relaxed.

The woman is advised to wear low-heeled shoes and to place a firm board under her mattress (or under her side of it). Muscle strengthening exercises and instruction on how to hold the body properly help to relieve backache. Occasionally, it is necessary to wear a lumbar support corset.

(2) *Headaches.* A common symptom, these may be associated with fatigue and the additional stress and anxiety placed upon a woman during pregnancy. They are generally not serious and seldom need more than simple treatment.

(3) *Constipation.* This is a common complaint throughout pregnancy, caused by the production of the hormone progesterone. This hormone has a relaxing effect on the intestinal tract. The condition is often improved by adding increased bulk to the diet, such as bran and fresh vegetables, as well as by drinking additional fluids.

(4) *Increased frequency of urination.* This occurs not only in the early days of pregnancy, but also toward the end because of increased pressure on the bladder.

Painless increase in urination is seldom anything to worry about. If there is any discomfort, however, it should be reported to the obstetrician because urinary infections, such as CYSTITIS, can occur during pregnancy.

(5) *Heartburn.* The production of the hormone progesterone during pregnancy causes relaxation of the muscle at the lower end of the oesophagus (gullet). This allows the acid contents of the stomach to pass back into the oesophagus.

The symptoms can be improved by taking frequent small meals, and by avoiding a large meal before going to bed. ANTACID medicines often can help, as can raising the head and shoulders at night.

(6) *Ankle swelling.* This is a common symptom caused by the effect of

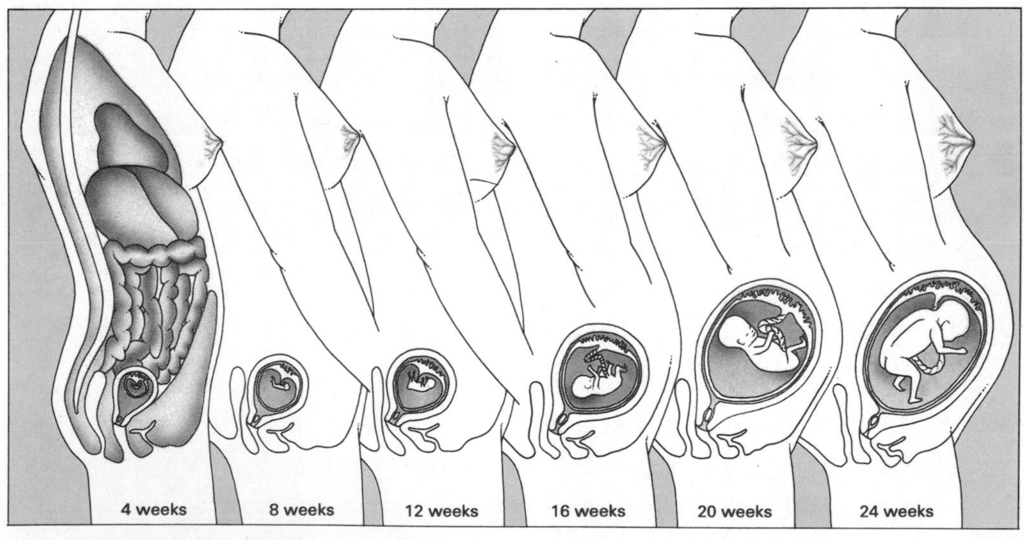

At 4 weeks the foetus's heart has developed, and by 8 weeks it has nearly all the organs.

After week 12 the mother's breasts enlarge, and the abdomen swells.

progesterone on the blood vessels, as well as by the pressure and weight of the pregnant womb on the veins that carry blood from the legs. Varicose veins may aggravate the condition.

To treat swollen ankles, the feet should be raised above the level of the pelvis as often as possible during the day, and the foot of the bed should be raised at night.

(7) *Varicose veins and haemorrhoids.* Varicose veins may occur as a result of increased pressure (improving after the birth). The enlarged womb presses on the veins of the pelvis and obstructs the blood flow from the legs to the heart. Haemorrhoids (piles) are a similar condition, usually caused by the pressure set up in the anal area by the straining action of constipation.

During pregnancy, women with varicose veins may wear elastic stockings to prevent aching. Haemorrhoids can be relieved with ointments preventing constipation.

(8) *Insomnia.* Sleeplessness commonly occurs in the last few weeks of pregnancy. Insomnia may be caused by the large abdomen, backache, or vigorous foetal movements. If necessary, the obstetrician may prescribe a mild sedative.

(9) *Palpitations and sweating.* These symptoms are similar to those experienced during MENOPAUSE and are caused by the effects of the hormones on the mother's body during pregnancy. They are seldom severe.

Q: *What regimen of diet and exercise should be followed in the latter half of pregnancy?*

A: During the second half of pregnancy, the mother should pay particular attention to diet. The foetus requires increased nourishment, but the woman must avoid excessive weight gain.

First-class proteins (such as those in eggs, milk, fish, and meat), together with vegetable proteins, are particularly important.

Energy requirements are supplied mainly by carbohydrates in the diet. These should be adjusted to fit in with the protein and the small amount of fat that makes up the remainder of the diet.

Fresh fruit and vegetables are an essential part of the diet because they supply vitamins and the bulk that helps to prevent constipation. The obstetrician often prescribes small doses of supplementary vitamins and iron.

Milk contains protein, calcium, and phosphorus, the minerals responsible for bone formation. But milk is not essential as long as the diet includes meat and cheese.

Regular exercise is an essential part of maintaining good health. Routine antenatal exercises are an essential part of maintaining physical and psychological well-being.

Q: *When should a pregnant woman start attending antenatal classes?*

A: The timing depends on the recommendation of the individual obstetrician, but it is usual to defer antenatal classes until the last three months of

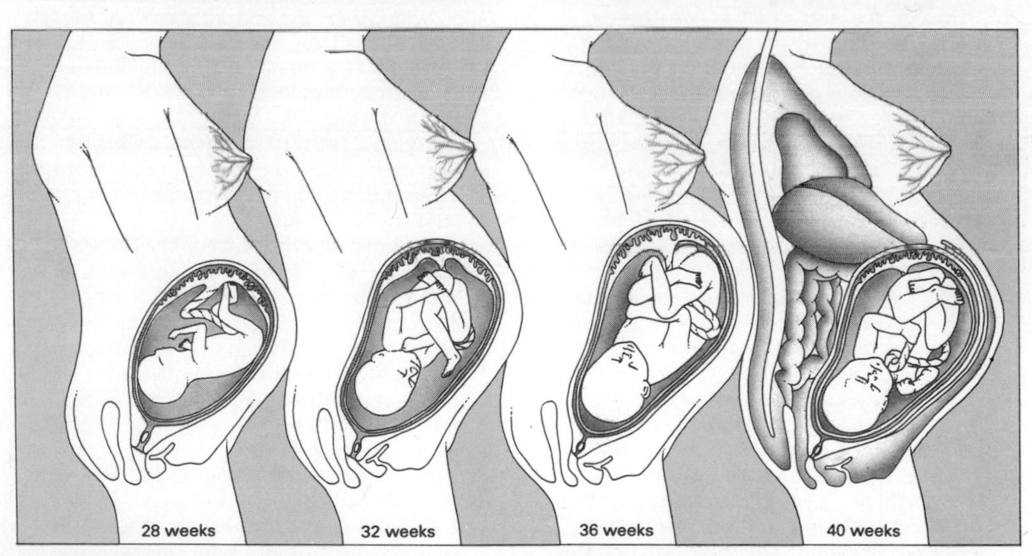

At 28 weeks the foetus usually settles in the womb with the head pointing down.

The womb continues to enlarge, until about two weeks before delivery it "lightens".

pregnancy. Usually a series of eight to twelve weekly classes are attended by the same group of prospective parents. They are told about the normal development of the foetus, the progress of pregnancy, and the stages of labour.

The class also is shown exercises to strengthen the back and pelvic muscles, as well as special methods of breathing which may be of assistance during the various stages of labour. The women are asked to practise these exercises at home.

At least one class is devoted to the care of the newborn baby: how to bathe and dress the baby, as well as how to change a nappy. Often a mother who has just had a baby returns to the class to demonstrate baby care, bringing her own infant with her.

It is usual, at some point during antenatal classes, to discuss the problems that may arise in labour, and the kind of action that the obstetrician may take.

Q: *What is "lightening", and when can it be expected to occur?*

A: Lightening is the sensation of increased physical comfort that is experienced when the foetus has descended into the lower part of the womb, in the pelvic cavity, thus relieving pressure on the upper abdominal area. It usually occurs about the thirty-sixth week, but, in women who have had babies before, it may not occur until labour starts.

Q: *What special tests or examinations are carried out by the obstetrician during the last three months of pregnancy?*

A: Provided the pregnancy is developing normally, the only special tests needed are a reassessment of the level of haemoglobin in the blood to check for anaemia, a repetition of the antibody test for the Rh (rhesus) factor, and sometimes a test of the urine to ensure that there is no infection. The obstetrician usually performs an internal, gynaecological examination about the thirty-seventh week of pregnancy. This is done to assess the size of the pelvis to ensure that there is enough room for the foetus to be born.

Q: *Why may pregnancy end prematurely, and is this a problem?*

A: In many cases the cause of premature birth is not known. Factors that may contribute to prematurity include pre-eclampsia, twins, and antepartum haemorrhage. If premature rupture of the membranes occurs, without the onset of labour, it usually is advisable to keep the woman resting in bed until at least the thirty-fourth week of pregnancy, when labour may be induced.

The main problem of premature labour is that it produces an immature baby who will require specialized care.

Q: *What are the problems associated with prolonged pregnancy?*

A: There is a gradual deterioration in the placenta toward the end of pregnancy. Even at forty-two weeks, however, the placenta may be capable of providing a mature foetus with all the nourishment it needs. But there is a greater likelihood of foetal death occurring, so the obstetrician may induce labour if the woman is considered to be more than a week overdue, and if the circumstances are favourable for induction.

Q: *Is infection serious during pregnancy?*

A: German measles (rubella) is a serious infection when contracted by a woman in early pregnancy. It greatly increases the risk of congenital anomalies in the foetus. Infection with a type of herpes virus may be fatal to the foetus. Any infections should be reported to the obstetrician.

Q: *What is the onset of labour?*

A: During the final two or three weeks the woman may notice the occasional, irregular, but firm contraction of her womb. The abdomen hardens, but no discomfort is felt. If this is confused with the actual onset of labour, it is termed a false labour. Labour commences when regular, powerful contractions occur every twenty to thirty minutes accompanied by a dull ache or pain in the lower abdomen and back.

Sometimes there is a "show" of blood and mucus from the vagina as the plug of mucus which blocks the cervix during pregnancy breaks apart and the cervix starts to open.

Rupture of the membranes (bag of waters), followed by a rush of clear fluid from the vagina, may occasionally be the first sign of labour.

As soon as the contractions are occurring every ten to fifteen minutes, or the membranes have ruptured, the patient should go to the hospital. She should take a suitcase that has already been packed with some clothing for the baby, and a dressing gown, nightdress, and nursing brassiere, as well as toilet articles for the mother.

Q: *What occurs during labour, and how can the mother help?*

A: Labour is divided into three stages. The first stage continues, with regular contractions of increasing frequency, until the cervix of the womb is fully open (dilated). The second stage includes the passage of the baby through the pelvis, until it is delivered. The third stage is the expulsion of the placenta and membranes from the womb.

The first stage of labour varies greatly in duration, but commonly takes between five and ten hours. It is shorter in women who have previously had a baby.

At first, contractions may occur only every twenty to thirty minutes, each one lasting for ten to fifteen seconds. As the contractions become more frequent and longer in duration, the cervix progressively dilates. It is during these contractions that the breathing methods, learned in the antenatal classes, are useful. Usually during this first stage of labour, the membranes rupture.

Eventually the contractions occur every two to three minutes, and the woman feels the urge to push. This sensation may be accompanied by a dull, deep backache. This is the beginning of the second stage of labour. The second stage is one of hard, physical effort with contractions coming every one to two minutes, and each one lasting at least thirty seconds. The second stage seldom continues longer than two hours, and is frequently over in less than an hour. Before it commences, the obstetrician usually carries out a careful, sterile gynaecological examination to ensure that the cervix is fully dilated, and to assess the position of the foetal head.

During the second stage of labour the foetal head is pushed further down into the pelvis. When it reaches the pelvic floor, the back of the head turns round to the front of the pelvis. The foetus's chin is pressed down onto its chest. As the foetus extends the head from this bent position upward, the mother's vulva is extended and stretched open. The head is "crowned" at the moment when the vulva is stretched round the greatest circumference of the foetal head.

During this stage, the mother can help by taking a deep breath prior to the contraction, and forcibly trying to expel the baby through the pelvis by "bearing down" during the contraction. It is most comfortable if she can keep her knees bent, and her head and shoulders raised. This exercise and position is taught in the antenatal and natural childbirth classes.

As the foetal head is crowned, the obstetrician may decide to cut the skin at the back of the vulva (episiotomy) so that the foetal head can be delivered more easily, and to ensure that the vagina does not tear. A neat cut is easier to repair than a ragged laceration. Once the head comes through, the rest of the body follows quite rapidly.

Just after being born, the baby's mouth is sucked clear of mucus so that breathing can take place easily, and the eyes are cleaned. The umbilical cord is clamped, tied and cut, and the baby is wrapped in a towel. The baby often is handed to the mother so that she can enjoy her first moments with her child.

The third stage of labour usually is over within thirty minutes. Contraction of the womb is helped by an injection of ergometrine given to the mother as the baby is delivered. There is slight vaginal bleeding as the obstetrician gently manoeuvres the placenta out of the womb. All that is required of the mother at this stage is a final, gentle push.

While waiting for the placenta to be expelled, the obstetrician may inject a local anaesthetic, stitch up the episiotomy, and repair any minor damage to the vagina that has occurred during delivery of the baby.

Q: What can the woman's partner do to help during labour?

A: During the first stage of labour, which may last some hours, he can accompany his partner while she walks up and down in her room or the corridor of the hospital. During contractions, he can apply gentle pressure with his hands to her back and remind her to breathe

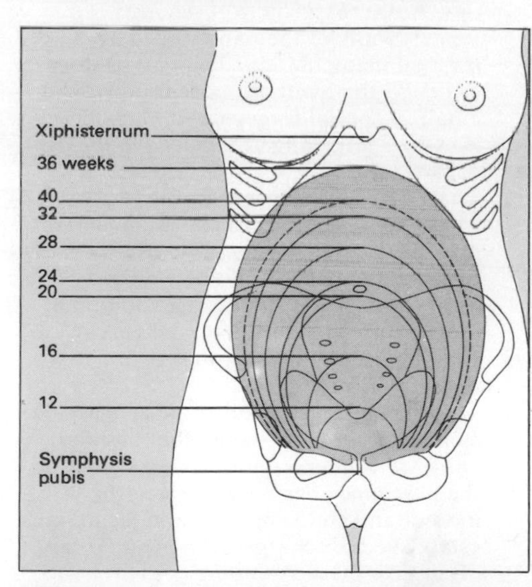

The womb rises steadily during pregnancy, reaching its greatest height at week 36.

correctly. In the second stage, while in the delivery room, he can provide encouragement to his partner. He also can help to support her neck and legs when she is trying to expel the foetus.

Q: *How can pain be reduced during labour?*

A: Painkilling drugs can be given during labour if requested. Inhalation of a special gas or an epidural anaesthetic causes only slight discomfort, and allows the woman to remain conscious throughout labour. A skilled anaesthetist is required to give the epidural injection.

Occasionally, quite severe headaches may occur for two or three days after delivery. From time to time, general anaesthesia is needed during labour.

Q: *What can the obstetrician do if labour is not normal?*

A: Sometimes the obstetrician decides, before labour commences, that a normal delivery would be too risky. This may occur with a placenta praevia, abnormalities of the pelvis or, sometimes, if the woman has previously had a Caesarean operation. In such cases, the obstetrician performs a Caesarean operation just before the baby is due.

Sometimes, problems occur once labour has already started, such as foetal distress, or prolonged labour. To deal with these problems the obstetrician either performs a Caesarean, if labour still is in the first stage, or helps the delivery by carefully applying forceps around the baby's head. In this way, the baby is gently, firmly, and steadily pulled out. A MALPRESENTATION requires repositioning of the baby's head by internal manipulation. This can be done either by the hand or, more usually, with a pair of special forceps.

Q: *Are there any dangers involved in the use of forceps?*

A: There is a slight chance that the foetus will be damaged or bruised as a result of pressure exerted by the forceps. The risks of foetal damage should be weighed against the risks of not using additional methods to help a difficult delivery.

Q: *How long is it necessary to stay in hospital?*

A: This depends on the obstetrician's advice as to whether both the mother and the baby are well enough to return home. If the pregnancy has been normal, the mother and child are well, and lactation is established, discharge from hospital can often take place within forty-eight hours of delivery.

Q: *What can the mother do to help in her physical recovery after labour?*

A: It is usual to allow twenty-four hours of rest after labour. The mother can help to get her figure back to normal with exercises to strengthen the muscles of the pelvis, abdomen, and back. Care should be taken not to do these too strenuously at first. The ligaments of the joints are still soft, and excessive exercise could cause joint strains.

Q: *Why is it sometimes necessary to induce labour artificially, and how is it done?*

A: Labour is induced if either the health or life of the mother or foetus is at risk. It may be recommended for a variety of reasons: pre-eclampsia; a pregnancy that has continued for more than a week or ten days past the expected date of delivery; a placenta praevia in which the placenta is obstructing the passage of delivery; a maternal problem such as diabetes mellitus; or rhesus incompatibility of the blood, which could lead to haemolytic disease of the newborn.

Labour is usually induced by artificially rupturing the membranes that surround the baby (amniotomy). Intravenous oxytocin may be given to help the uterus contract. Occasionally, drugs alone, by mouth or by injection, bring on labour. The procedure is carefully monitored, and an induced labour should follow the pattern of a normal labour.

Q: *Are there any things that a woman should avoid during pregnancy and the puerperium?*

A: Yes. All drugs, including aspirin, must be avoided during early pregnancy unless they have been prescribed by a doctor. This is primarily to reduce the chances of congenital malformation in the foetus. There also is evidence that drugs, such as marijuana, heroin, and cocaine, can cause problems in babies soon after they are born. Drug addiction must be stopped before labour takes place.

Mothers who smoke cigarettes are more likely to go into premature labour than those who do not. Their babies also tend to be born smaller than average, greatly increasing the chances of the baby dying.

Some drugs may adversely affect the mother. For example, many commonly used drugs aggravate the symptoms of heartburn during the latter months of pregnancy and should be avoided.

Pregnancy test is a urine test to confirm whether or not a woman is pregnant. It is about 95 per cent accurate in women whose periods are two to three weeks overdue. Most tests will not produce a reliable result until the period is at least eight days overdue.

Premature birth describes any birth before the thirty-seventh week of pregnancy or a baby whose birth weight is less than 2.5kg (5.5lb). About two thirds of premature births occur before the thirty-sixth week of pregnancy. Low birth weight does not necessarily result from a short pregnancy: it may be a result of reduced intra-uterine growth during the full length of pregnancy, caused by conditions such as pre-eclampsia.

Some premature babies are perfectly healthy and well-developed. Those who are not fully developed are placed in an incubator, and require the specialist care of a hospital. This may include frequent feeding by spoon or dropper if the baby is unable to suck, and injections of vitamin K to prevent bleeding.

Premedication is a drug or combination of drugs that is given to a patient before a general anaesthetic. It produces a state of mild drowsiness and dries the secretions in the mouth and the bronchi, the main airways to the lungs.

Premenstrual tension, or syndrome, consists of various symptoms that, in some women, occur regularly for several days before each menstrual period. Symptoms vary in severity and include irritability, depression, fatigue, headaches, breast tenderness, and a feeling of abdominal swelling. There may also be running nose, asthma, migraine, and backache. Premenstrual tension can also make women anxious, intolerant, and prone to accidents.

Q: *What causes premenstrual tension?*

A: The cause is thought to be a hormonal disturbance, accompanied by retention of water within the body tissues.

Q: *Can premenstrual tension aggravate any other problems?*

A: Yes. Depression, from causes other than premenstrual tension, tends to be increased. Women who suffer from epilepsy may have convulsions only during this time. Any marital problems may be made worse if the wife's irritability is increased.

Q: *What treatments can help premenstrual tension?*

A: A doctor may prescribe a diuretic (water-removing) drug. This is often quite effective and may also be combined with medication to help depression. Tranquillizers help to combat irritability, but make fatigue worse.

If these simple treatments are not successful, hormone preparations of progesterone sometimes give relief from the symptoms. In some cases, a doctor may prescribe the contraceptive pill.

Q: *Do many women suffer from premenstrual tension?*

A: Yes. At least one in ten women has the symptoms in a severe form, and a further two in ten have them to a lesser extent. Many other women experience some of the symptoms from time to time. Premenstrual tension becomes more common with increasing age, and the more pregnancies a woman has had. It disappears after the menopause.

Premolar is a bicuspid tooth, which is well adapted for grinding food. There are two pairs of premolars in each jaw, located between the canine teeth and the molars.

Prenatal. *See* ANTENATAL.

Prepatellar bursitis, commonly called housemaid's knee, is an inflammation of the bursa in front of the kneecap. *See* BURSITIS.

Prepuce. *See* FORESKIN.

Presbyopia is longsightedness that occurs as a normal process of aging. As a person becomes older, the lens of the eye loses its elasticity so that the muscles that adjust it become less effective. Distant vision remains unaltered, but the ability of the eye to focus on close objects is impaired. Spectacles usually correct the condition.

Presenile dementia is a degenerative process of the brain that results in loss of memory and inability to care for oneself. It begins before the onset of old age. *See* ALZHEIMER'S DISEASE.

Presentation is an obstetric term used to indi-

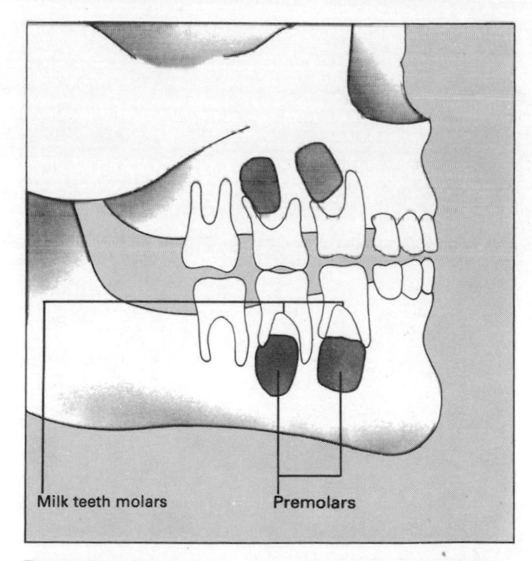

Premolars begin to form at about the age of 2, and are complete at about the age of 6.

cate which part of a foetus is positioned lowest in the womb, just above the cervix. The position of the baby's body is called the "lie".

The normal presentation is occipital, meaning that the back of the head is just above the cervix. *See* MALPRESENTATION; PREGNANCY AND CHILDBIRTH.

Priapism is a persistent, painful erection of the penis without sexual stimulus. It is caused by blockage of the veins in the penis. It is sometimes caused by local infection, leukaemia, or sickle cell anaemia. Sometimes, blood can be extracted from the penis. Anticoagulant drugs also may help.

Prickly heat, or miliaria, is an intensely irritating, fine red rash. The irritation is caused by the body's inability to produce sweat because the sweat glands have become blocked by dead skin cells.

Calamine lotion may give some relief, and light cotton clothing should be worn.

Primapara is the medical term for a woman who has had one pregnancy lasting at least twenty-eight weeks, producing a baby or twins, either stillborn or alive. *See* MULTIPARA.

Procaine hydrochloride is one of the safest and least toxic local anaesthetics. However, excessive amounts of procaine or an allergy to it may be associated with lowered blood pressure and possibly fatal cardiac arrest.

Procidentia. *See* PROLAPSE.

Proctalgia is pain in the anal region without obvious cause. Proctalgia fugax is an intermittent pain in the anal region, commonly occurring at night.

Proctitis is inflammation of the rectum and anus. The main symptoms are pain in the rectal region and a frequent desire to pass faeces. Defecation is painful and may be accompanied by diarrhoea and the passing of blood and mucus. This often is followed by tenesmus (spasm of the local muscles) and pain. The symptoms may be controlled with antispasm and painkilling drugs. But hospitalization may be necessary for thorough investigations to be carried out.

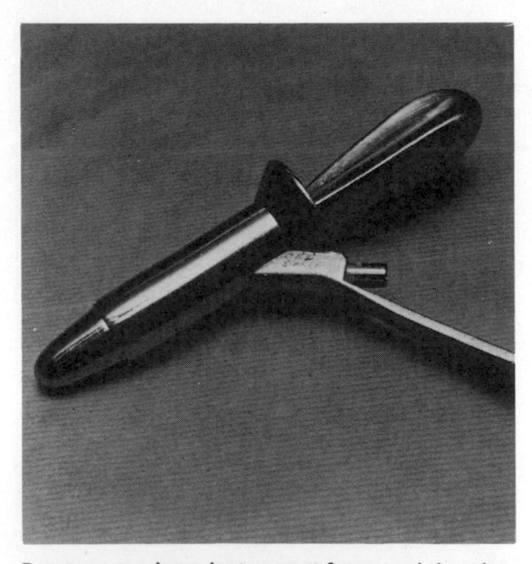

Proctoscope is an instrument for examining the rectum to detect certain disorders.

Proctology is a medical specialty concerned with disorders of the anus and rectum.

Proctoscope is a metal or plastic tubular ENDOSCOPE, often containing a light, that is used to examine the rectum.

Prodromal means any early, minor symptom or sign of disease that occurs before the onset of the actual condition.

Progesterone is a female sex hormone produced by the corpus luteum in an ovary during the second half of the menstrual cycle. It prepares the lining of the womb for the reception of a fertilized ovum (egg). Preparations called progestogens have similar effects to progesterone and are used in some contraceptive pills.

See also MENSTRUATION; OESTROGEN.

Progressive muscular atrophy is a form of MOTOR NEURON DISEASE in which there is increasing wasting of the muscles resulting from degeneration of the spinal cord. The exact cause of the condition is unknown. There are several similar conditions occurring at different ages which are characterized by muscular weakness that worsens gradually over several years. There is no treatment.

Prolactin is a hormone that is produced by the front lobe of the PITUITARY GLAND in women. It stimulates the glands in the breasts (mammary glands), thereby starting milk production (lactation) at the end of pregnancy and sustaining it after childbirth. Prolactin has this effect only when certain hormones, such as OESTROGEN, PROGESTERONE, and OXYTOCIN, are also present.

Prolapse is an abnormal, downward displacement of a part of the body. Examples include prolapse of the rectum, in which the membranes that line the rectum protrude through the anus; and prolapse of the womb (uterus), in which the supporting ligaments become so weak that the womb is displaced into the vagina. Prolapse of the rectum is relatively uncommon, and may be the result of an underlying disorder or a congenital abnormality.

Q: How is prolapse of the rectum treated?

A: This seldom is a problem when it occurs in infants, providing a doctor is consulted. By applying gentle pressure to the protruding tissue, it generally can be pushed back inside, and the condition usually is self curing in a matter of weeks.

In the elderly, prolapse of the rectum is a more serious matter. If it recurs frequently, or if it is not possible to push it back, an operation may have to be done to remove the prolapsed tissues. Alternatively, a circle of wire or nylon can be placed around the anus to tighten the opening.

Q: Why does prolapse of the womb occur?

A: The cause is a gradual slackening of the ligaments that support the walls of the vagina and the womb. This usually happens because the ligaments are stretched during childbirth; they also become weakened after menopause because of lack of hormone production. Although prolapse of the vagina may occur without prolapse of the womb, the two usually occur together.

Q: What are the symptoms of prolapse of the womb?

A: The main symptom is a sensation of "something falling out of the vagina." This is sometimes accompanied by a deep ache in the lower abdomen. If the prolapse is severe, the neck of the womb (cervix) sticks out of the vagina, between the labia; this is known as a procidentia.

Other symptoms include incontinence of urine on coughing, laughing, or lifting weights (stress incontinence); and, occasionally, difficulty in defecating. The prolapse may be accompanied by a vaginal discharge.

Q: How is a prolapse of the womb treated?

A: The best treatment is a surgical operation to shorten the ligaments that support the womb, and to stitch the top of the vagina back into a secure position. This operation usually is accompanied by removal of part of the cervix.

If an operation cannot be performed, a plastic ring (pessary) can be inserted into the vagina to hold the womb in place.

Q: Is there any way in which a woman can prevent a prolapse of the womb from occurring?

A: Yes. Care during childbirth is essential so that the second stage of labour does not last too long (*see* PREGNANCY AND CHILDBIRTH). After childbirth, the woman should strengthen the muscles and ligaments surrounding the womb by doing postnatal exercises, as recommended by a physiotherapist.

Prone is the position of the body when lying face downward.

Prophylactic is any agent that is used to prevent disease, for example, immunization in childhood or the use of antimalarial drugs.

The term prophylactic also describes any chemical or physical device used to reduce the risk of contracting a venereal disease.

Proptosis is a forward bulge, especially of the eye. It is the main feature of EXOPHTHALMOS.

Prostaglandins are a series of closely related substances that act on many types of tissue throughout the body, such as the heart or the uterus, causing contraction or relaxation of muscle. They are called by letters (like E) with subgroups such as E_1 and E_2.

Prostatectomy is an operation to remove the prostate gland. This may sometimes be done through the penis (transurethral prostatectomy), or in an abdominal operation. Prostatectomy always results in sterility.

See also PROSTATOMEGALY.

Prostate gland is a walnut-sized organ that is part of the male urogenital system. It lies beneath the bladder and surrounds the urethra, the tube that carries urine from the bladder. The prostate gland produces secretions that maintain the vitality of SPERM.

Prostate problems generally cause difficulties with urination, because the prostate gland surrounds the urethra (the tube that carries urine from the bladder). A gradual enlargement of the prostate gland (benign prostatomegaly) normally occurs with increasing age. But enlargement also may be caused by cancer of the prostate. Inflammation of the prostate (prostatitis), caused by an infection, tends to occur in younger men.

Q: What symptoms occur with prostate problems?

A: The symptoms caused by benign

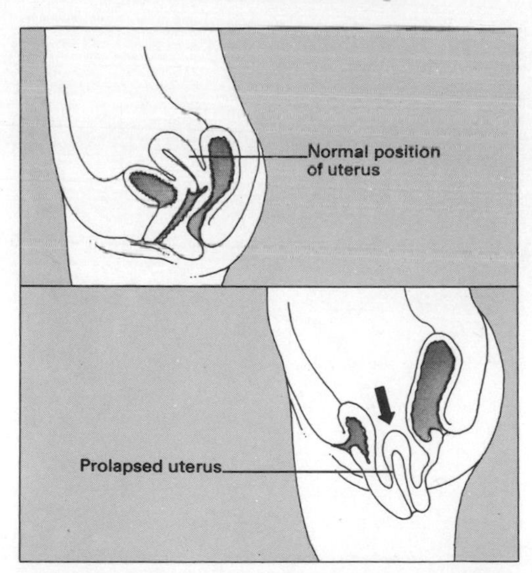

Prolapse (severe) of the uterus occurs when the muscles in the pelvic floor give way.

prostatomegaly, prostatitis, and cancer are all similar. There is increased frequency of passing urine, combined with a feeling that the bladder is not empty, even immediately after urination. Sometimes there is extreme urgency as well as slight discomfort on passing urine (dysuria) or, alternatively, the patient is unable to pass urine even when he has the opportunity. Usually he has to urinate several times at night (nocturia), and occasionally there is blood in the urine (haematuria).

Sometimes the patient cannot pass urine at all. This may occur gradually over a matter of a few weeks (chronic retention), with backflow of excess urine leading to kidney failure (uraemia). Or it may occur suddenly, as a painful acute retention of urine. Any form of retention needs urgent treatment.

Q: How are prostate problems treated?

A: Treatment depends on the cause. *See* PROSTATITIS; PROSTATOMEGALY.

Prostatic hypertrophy is enlargement of the prostate gland. *See* PROSTATOMEGALY.

Prostatitis is inflammation of the prostate gland. It may occur as the result of a venereal disease, nonspecific urethritis, or infection spreading from the intestine, or it may develop after an examination of the inside of the bladder (cystoscopy).

Prostatitis causes symptoms similar to those of other prostate problems. Painful and frequent passing of urine (dysuria) is a common symptom if the infection is acute.

Prolonged treatment with antibiotics may be necessary, and the patient usually is advised to avoid sexual intercourse until the infection is cured.

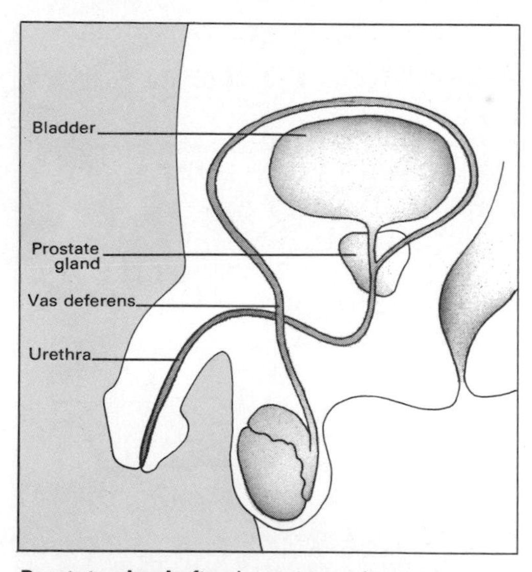

Prostate gland often becomes enlarged in men past middle age, and impedes urination.

Prostatomegaly is an increase in the size of the prostate gland. It normally occurs in men over the age of fifty years and slowly, but steadily, develops so as to cause the minor symptoms of prostate problems. This condition is known as benign prostatomegaly and often needs no treatment. But if the symptoms become severe or are caused by cancer, medical treatment is necessary.

Q: Can complications arise from benign prostatomegaly?

A: Yes. Complications arise from back pressure of the urine and poor drainage from the bladder. These may result in (1) retention of urine, and bleeding from a dilated vein, which causes blood in the urine (haematuria); (2) urinary infection and the formation of bladder stones (calculi) due to incomplete emptying of the bladder; and (3) damage to the kidney, causing hydronephrosis and uraemia.

Q: How is benign prostatomegaly treated?

A: Surgical removal of the prostate gland (PROSTATECTOMY) is the only way of curing the symptoms. Occasionally it may be necessary to reduce the pressure caused by retention of urine by catheterizing the patient for a few days before the operation.

Q: What is the treatment for prostatomegaly caused by cancer?

A: In the early stages of the disorder, an operation to remove the prostate gland often cures the condition. In later stages, particularly if the man is elderly and the cancer has spread, treatment with female hormones (oestrogens) or removal of the testes is often effective. It can prevent further spread and development for many years, as well as reduce the size of the gland and lessen the symptoms.

Prosthesis is the medical term for the replacement of any part of the body by an artificial substitute. Some external prostheses are used for purely cosmetic reasons. *See* REPLACEMENT SURGERY.

Prostration is a dangerous state of physical and mental exhaustion that occurs as a result of excessive fatigue, heatstroke, or illness.

The victim should be placed in the recovery position (*see* First Aid, p.573) and someone should remain with him or her until professional medical help arrives. It is essential to find the cause of prostration so that appropriate treatment can be given.

Protein is one of a class of complex nitrogenous compounds that are built up from simpler amino acids. Proteins are an essential part of the fabric of every living cell in the body.

Human proteins are formed in the liver from amino acids derived from the digestion of protein-containing foods (such as meat and fish). The principal proteins produced in the liver are albumin and globulin, which pass in the bloodstream to various cells, which can make their own complex proteins from them.

Proteins are formed from about twenty different amino acids, and the body is able to synthesize most of these. A total of eight essential amino acids cannot be made by the body, and so they must be obtained from the diet. Complex proteins, such as the red blood pigment haemoglobin, may contain minerals. Other important proteins include the enzymes that are necessary for the normal metabolic activities of the body.

See also AMINO ACID; GAMMA GLOBULIN.

Prothrombin is a soluble protein that is an essential factor in blood clotting. When bleeding occurs it is changed into an insoluble form and assists clotting. Its formation in the liver is slowed by ANTICOAGULANT drugs. The Prothrombin time test distinguishes between normal blood and that of a person being treated with anticoagulants, by the time of reaction.

Protozoa are the simplest single-celled organisms to be classified as animal. Some species can cause infectious diseases. *See* AMOEBIC DYSENTERY; MALARIA; SLEEPING SICKNESS.

Proximal describes a part of the body that is closer than some other part to a central point. The part that is farther away is referred to as being distal.

Prurigo is a skin condition in a patient who has been suffering from severe itching (pruritus). Small, firm lumps appear on areas of the skin associated with crusting and sometimes obvious scratch marks.

Pruritus. *See* ITCHING.

Pseudocyesis is the medical term for a false pregnancy.

Pseudomonas is a group of bacteria. *Pseudomonas aeruginosa* can infect human beings, causing pneumonia, endocarditis, or urinary infections. Treatment of pseudomonas infections is often difficult. Few antibiotics are capable of killing the bacteria.

Psittacosis, also called ornithosis and parrot fever, is a rare form of pneumonia caused by a microorganism (*Chlamydia psittaci*) carried by birds. It is usually caught by inhaling dust from faeces or feathers of infected birds. The disorder is infectious and can be transmitted from one person to another by means of airborne droplets (produced by coughing).

Q: What are the symptoms of psittacosis?

A: The infection usually takes between one and three weeks to develop and may begin suddenly or slowly as an influenza-like illness with fever, aching muscles, and malaise accompanied by a cough. The cough produces a small amount of sputum that may become bloodstained as the illness progresses.

Without treatment, the illness lasts for about two weeks with a gradual improvement followed by a further month of malaise, weakness, and often mild depression.

Usually the disorder is fairly mild, but occasionally it can be severe and even fatal in the elderly, if untreated.

Q: How is psittacosis treated?

A: The tetracycline group of antibiotics are usually used in treatment, producing a rapid improvement within two days. The patient should be kept isolated in bed until the fever has subsided. Strong cough mixtures, oxygen, and other forms of treatment for pneumonia may be needed.

Psoriasis is a chronic skin condition that is found in about one per cent of the population. The cause is unknown, but heredity probably is the most important factor; children of an affected parent have a one in four chance of developing the condition. Psoriasis may appear for the first time soon after a streptococcal throat infection. The condition usually occurs in persons between the ages of ten and twenty-five and, although it may disappear for short periods of time, long periods of freedom from it are rare.

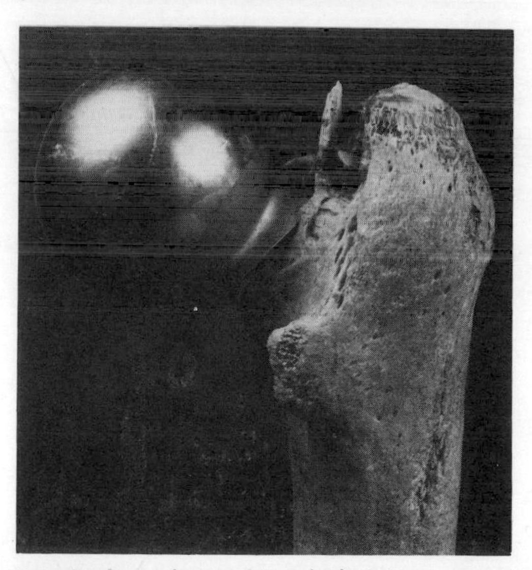

Prosthesis can be used to substitute an artificial part for the head of a femur.

Q: What are the symptoms of psoriasis?

A: A typical lesion of psoriasis is an oval, slightly raised area covered with dry, silvery scales overlying a red area of skin. The size, extent, and distribution of the lesions varies considerably. They may be scattered all over the body, including the scalp, or there may be only one or two rather large lesions, with normal skin elsewhere on the body. The pattern of distribution may be influenced by hormonal changes that occur at puberty, at menopause, or during pregnancy.

Some drugs, such as chloroquine, aggravate the condition. The lesions can join together into extensive areas of scaling skin. Lesions on the scalp do not affect hair growth, and it is unusual for the lesions anywhere on the body to cause more than the mildest irritation.

The condition is often improved by sunlight, and it is noticeable that psoriasis is more common in temperate regions than in the tropics.

Q: Are there any complications with psoriasis?

A: Yes. In about a quarter of the patients, the fingernails become pitted, ridged, or discoloured. The nails also may break much more easily than normal.

A form of arthritis sometimes occurs in patients suffering from psoriasis. Any joint may be affected, but commonly it is those of the fingers and lower spine. This produces a condition similar to a mild form of RHEUMATOID ARTHRITIS.

Q: What is the treatment for psoriasis?

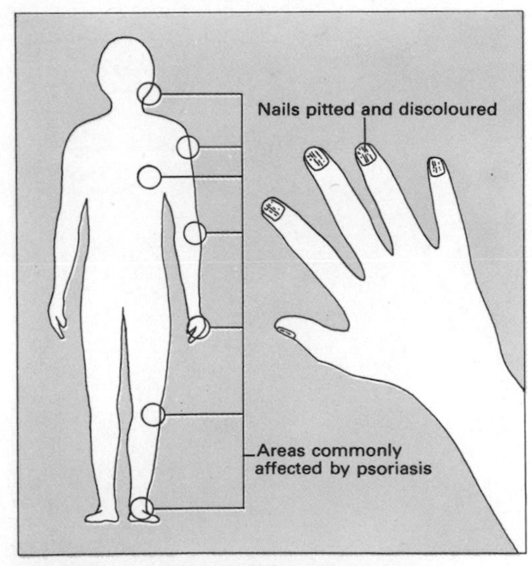

Psoriasis is a skin condition that commonly affects certain parts of the body.

A: Most doctors start by prescribing a simple course of ointments, such as those containing coal tar and salicylic acid. If these prove ineffective, the drug dithranol may help, but dithranol may stain the skin brown and cause allergies. Psoriasis of the scalp may be treated with various shampoos and creams to separate the scaly skin from the hair.

For more severe cases, corticosteroid creams are applied under a layer of polythene at night. This treatment generally is successful for a short time. The use of cytotoxic drugs is sometimes advisable in patients who have extensive and severe psoriasis. This treatment should be given only under the close supervision of a dermatologist.

Ultraviolet light is of benefit to patients with psoriasis, and treatments involving sunlight, or artificial ultraviolet light, produce an improvement. Recently a new form of treatment has been instituted using psoralens, drugs that increase the skin's sensitivity to light. The administration of psoralens is followed by courses of exposure to ultraviolet light (PUVA treatment).

Many patients with psoriasis become extremely depressed by their condition. It is therefore important for the doctor to keep up their morale because of the social anxieties created by this condition.

Psychedelic describes a mental condition that involves visual hallucinations and an abnormal intensification of feelings, usually induced by drugs such as lysergic acid diethylamide (LSD) or mescalin. *See* DRUG ADDICTION.

Psychiatry is the medical specialty that deals with mental illness, also called psychiatric illness.

Psychoanalysis is a method of treating mental illness devised by Sigmund Freud. An alternative method of treatment based on similar theories of human behaviour was devised by Carl Jung, and is known as analytical psychology.

Psychology is the study of behaviour. Human psychology attempts to measure development, change, normality and abnormality. A psychologist, who is not necessarily a doctor, is trained to make these comparative assessments.

There are various subspecialties within the field of psychology. Educational psychologists assess the mental, social and emotional development, and intelligence, especially applied to education. Clinical psychologists are trained in psychotherapy and assess those with mental illnesses.

Psychomotor seizure is a form of convulsion, usually caused by temporal lobe epilepsy. *See* EPILEPSY.

Psychoneurosis is a mental disorder that has mental but not physical symptoms, unlike a psychosomatic disorder. Psychoneurosis is an ill-defined term, however, and is often used interchangeably with NEUROSIS.

Psychopathy is a form of personality disorder in which there is emotional instability without a specific mental disorder. Psychopathic behaviour is amoral and antisocial, with a lack of concern for the welfare of others. *See* MENTAL ILLNESS.

Psychopharmacology is the study of the effects of drugs on the mind.

Psychosis is a mental disorder in which paranoia, persistent delusions, hallucinations, and a loss of contact with reality are prominent features.

Psychosomatic disorders are illnesses in which emotions and mental disturbances are thought to produce or aggravate physical symptoms. Symptoms produced by overactivity of the sympathetic nervous system include sweating and palpitations, fainting and nausea, and some skin conditions. Stress and anxiety may cause or aggravate asthma, migraine, and peptic or duodenal ulcers.

Psychotherapy. *See* MENTAL ILLNESS.

Ptomaine poisoning is an old term for a type of food poisoning that was thought to be caused by the bacterial decomposition of proteins forming ptomaine (a poison). It was later discovered that the digestive processes usually destroy ptomaine before poisoning can occur.

Ptosis is the dropping or drooping of an organ such as the stomach (gastroptosis), kidney (nephroptosis) or, especially, the eyelid. Stretched ligaments, obesity, or lack of muscle tone are responsible for most ptoses. *See* HORNER'S SYNDROME.

Q: Can ptosis be treated?

A: Abdominal ptoses can sometimes be treated by wearing a surgical belt which helps to strengthen the abdominal muscles. Ptosis of the eyelid improves with treatment of the underlying cause. In some cases, a special contact lens can be worn to hold up the drooping lid.

Puberty is the period between childhood and adolescence when hormonal body changes produce development of the secondary sexual characteristics. *See* ADOLESCENCE.

Pubis, also called the pubic bone or os pubis, is the smallest of the three bones at the lowest part of the front of the pelvis. The three bones, including the ischium and ilium, together form the innominate bone. The midline joint, made up of strong ligaments and a disc of fibrocartilage, is known as the pubic symphysis. Toward the end of pregnancy, the cartilage in a woman's pubic symphysis softens to allow the pelvis to widen for childbirth.

Puerperal fever, also called childbirth fever, is any fever causing a temperature of 38°C (100.4°F) or over that lasts for more than twenty-four hours within the first ten days after a woman has had a baby.

Puerperal fever resulting from streptococcal infection of the womb used to be a common cause of maternal death after childbirth. Now, puerperal fever is rare because of high standards of hygiene in maternity wards.

Q: What causes puerperal fever?

A: The most common causes are influenza; tonsillitis, and infections of the urinary and genital tracts. In a few cases, fever results from a breast infection that occurs during lactation.

Q: How is puerperal fever diagnosed and treated?

A: After a careful examination, an obstetrician uses a swab to take a sample from the vagina and submits this, and a specimen of urine, for bacteriological tests. A blood test to detect anaemia, and whether white blood cells show reaction to bacterial infection is taken. The patient is occasionally isolated to prevent the spread of infection to other patients.

Once the tests have been made, treatment with antibiotic drugs usually lasts for at least a week, or until the patient's condition improves.

Puerperium is the recovery time after the

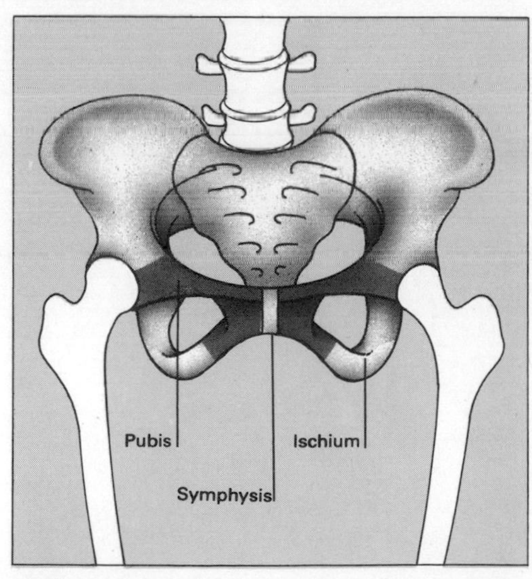

Pubis, a bone at the front of the pelvis, protects the urinogenital internal organs.

delivery of a baby. This period is generally considered to end with the obstetrician's postnatal examination at about six weeks.

Q: What particular care should a mother take during puerperium?

A: During puerperium, a healthy mother and baby have to deal with each other, for the first time, as individuals. If the woman has never been a mother before, she is naturally anxious about handling, washing, and feeding the baby. It is during this time that nurses can help to build up her confidence by showing her how to do things in the correct way, and by reassuring her that the baby's crying is not necessarily caused by hunger or pain. The reassurance helps a great deal toward the woman's recovery.

During the first twenty-four hours, it is often advisable to rest in bed. After this time, however, the woman is encouraged to get up and walk around. This helps to prevent deep vein thrombosis.

Routine care includes observations of the lochia (vaginal discharge) as well as vulval swabbing with antiseptic solutions to keep the area clean and to help the healing of any lacerations or cuts. If there are any stitches in the perineum, these may cause discomfort, and a rubber ring is more comfortable when sitting.

There may be problems with passing urine in the first twenty-four hours, caused by swelling around the urethra (exit tube from the bladder) as a result of labour. Occasionally, it is necessary to pass a catheter into the bladder in order to release the urine. It is usually necessary to give laxatives to produce normal working of the bowels.

A transient depression, in which tears mix with laughter, commonly occurs a few days after delivery. These are known as the "blues" and usually pass within twenty-four to forty-eight hours. They result from the combination of excitement, fatigue, and anxiety that is mixed with the happiness of having a baby.

Q: Are there any serious conditions that may develop during the puerperium?

A: Yes. Occasionally a woman who has had pre-eclampsia develops the more serious condition of eclampsia. This can usually be prevented by careful obstetric care.

PUERPERAL FEVER occurs in about two per cent of women during the ten days after delivery.

Depression may occasionally become increasingly severe and, in five to ten per cent of women, may require medical treatment. Increasing fatigue and a feeling of futility, combined with despair at her own inadequacy in dealing with the baby are sufficient symptoms for the mother or her family to discuss the matter with the doctor. Occasionally, a true psychotic illness occurs that requires admission to hospital.

A postpartum haemorrhage is a serious complication that may result from infection of the genital tract or retention of part of the placenta in the womb. This needs urgent treatment in the hospital.

Q: What physical changes take place in the mother during the puerperium?

A: During this time, lactation begins and the mother's body undergoes considerable change. First, a large amount of body fluid is lost, followed by a gradual tightening of the ligaments and tendons that have become softened by the effect of hormones during pregnancy. The womb gradually becomes smaller and produces less lochia, which also changes in colour. The mother notices that she is returning to her original weight and shape.

Q: May sexual intercourse be resumed during the puerperium?

A: Deep sexual intercourse should not be resumed within the first month of the puerperium to avoid the possibility of introducing infection into the womb. Contraception should consist of the sheath and contraceptive creams until the postnatal examination by the obstetrician, when some other form of contraception may be recommended.

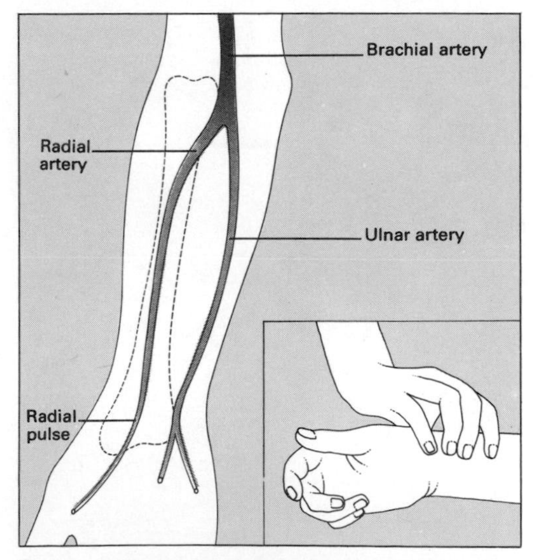

Pulse can be felt by depressing the radial artery onto the radius bone just above the wrist.

Pulled muscle is a common term for a muscle that has been slightly damaged by a sudden rupture of fibres within the muscle tissue.

The pulled muscle causes pain and stiffness that gradually improves over a number of days. Treatment with painkilling drugs, heat and massage, and exercises that fully stretch the muscle help to prevent it from tearing again when it is used.

Pulmonary describes anything to do with the lungs. *See* LUNG.

Pulmonary function tests. *See* LUNG FUNCTION TESTS.

Pulpitis is inflammation of the pulp of a tooth, usually caused by infection of the central cavity. *See* TOOTHACHE.

Pulse is the rhythmical expansion and contraction of an artery that can be felt near the surface of the body. The rate and regularity of the pulse is an indication of the pumping action of the heart and varies with age and activity. The pulse rate of a young baby is about 110 beats per minute; for a resting adult it is about seventy beats per minute. A trained athlete at the extreme of physical effort may have a pulse rate of up to 180 beats per minute, with a resting pulse rate of less than sixty beats per minute.

Irregularities of the pulse may occur in even a healthy young person when the rate varies slightly with breathing (sinus arrhythmia) or occasionally misses a beat.

Ectopic beat (missed beat) occurs more frequently in persons who smoke or those who have some underlying form of heart disease. Rapid pulse rates are known as TACHYCARDIA and slow pulse rates as BRADYCARDIA. Totally irregular pulse rates are usually caused by atrial FIBRILLATION.

Q: Where is the best place to feel the pulse?

A: The most convenient place to feel for the pulse is over the radial artery just before it passes into the wrist. This pulse may be detected by gently pressing down onto the tissues about 2.5cm (1 inch) above the base of the thumb. An alternative place is just in front of the ear, where the temporal artery passes to the forehead.

Patients who have collapsed from shock or undergone cardiac arrest do not have detectable pulses in these places. The only place that a pulse can be felt is over the carotid artery where it passes up the neck alongside the Adam's apple.

Punch drunk is an imprecise term used to describe a form of chronic brain damage usually caused by repeated minor injuries to the head. The repeated damage produces multiple concussions, minor haemorrhages, and loss of brain substance that results in a gradual physical and mental deterioration.

Q: What symptoms are shown by a person who is punch drunk?

A: The condition develops gradually with slurring speech, staggering gait, and dementia. There is a lack of tolerance to alcohol and outbursts of aggression occur.

PUO is an abbreviation of pyrexia (fever) of unknown origin. The term is commonly used by doctors when a patient has had an undiagnosed fever for longer than a week.

Pupil is the circular opening in the centre of the coloured area (iris) of the eye. Light passes through the pupil to the back of the eye (retina). The pupil contracts in bright light and when the eye is focusing on a near object. It dilates in dim light, when the eye is focusing on a distant object, and at times of excitement or emotion. The ability of the pupil to change size is known as the pupil reflex. The size of the pupil is controlled by muscles in the iris, which are supplied by nerves in the autonomic nervous system. An abnormal pupil reflex can indicate a neurological disorder.

Q: What can go wrong with the pupil?

A: Disorders that affect the iris, such as IRITIS, can make the pupil irregular in shape. If iritis causes the iris to stick to the lens, pupil reflex is absent.

Constriction of the pupil may be caused by old age, over-sensitivity to light (PHOTOPHOBIA), HORNER'S SYNDROME, or drugs. Dilation of the pupil may be caused by blindness or poor sight, GLAUCOMA, paralysis of the nerve that controls eye movements (oculomotor

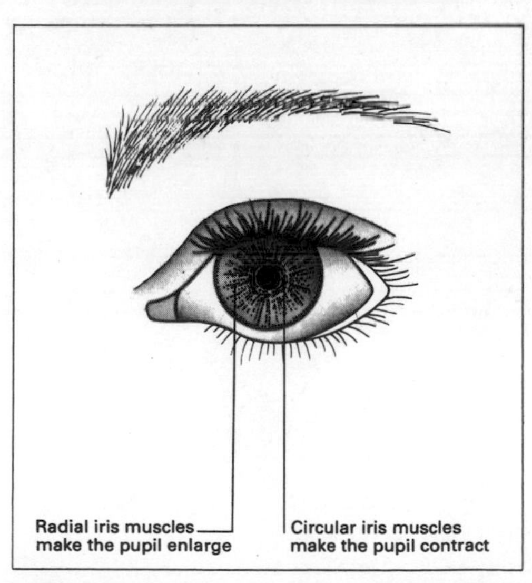

Pupil of the eye becomes larger or smaller as the iris muscles relax and contract.

nerve paralysis), or drugs, such as cocaine. ARGYLL-ROBERTSON PUPIL is failure of the pupil to adjust to the intensity of light but a normal pupil reaction, when focusing. ADIE'S SYNDROME is a congenital anomaly in which one pupil adjusts more slowly than the other.

Q: How are pupil disorders treated?

A: Most disorders of the pupil improve with treatment of the underlying cause. Miotic drugs, such as pilocarpine, constrict the pupil; mydriatic drugs, such as atropine and homatropine, act as pupil dilators.

Pupil reflex is the constriction of the pupil of the eye in response to light. *See* PUPIL.

Purgative is any substance that increases bowel movement. *See* LAXATIVES.

Purpura is a skin discoloration caused by bleeding (haemorrhage) into the skin. A small haemorrhage is called a petechia and a large one, as in a bruise, is called an ecchymosis. Purpura may result from fragility of the blood vessels or a blood disorder.

Q: What causes fragility of the blood vessels?

A: Fragility of the blood vessels usually is inherited, although it seldom is serious. In a more serious inherited form of the disorder, there are obvious abnormalities of the blood vessels in the lips, mouth, and fingers, a condition known as inherited telangiectasia.

Prolonged treatment with drugs such as aspirin and cortisone may also result in purpura. Scurvy (caused by lack of vitamin C) is another disorder that causes purpura. A rare, but serious, cause of purpura is an allergy (Henoch-Schönlein purpura), which may follow a streptococcal infection that damages the blood vessels.

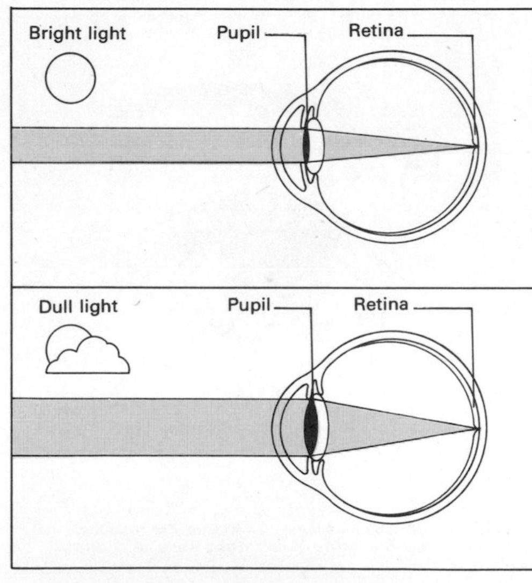

Pupil reflex automatically regulates the amount of light entering the lens of the eye.

Q: What defects of blood clotting cause purpura?

A: Various clotting defects can cause purpura. They include haemophilia, THROMBOCYTOPENIA (deficiency of platelets in the blood that help coagulation), and liver disorders in which the level of prothrombin (a protein necessary for blood clotting) is lowered. Drugs also may cause clotting defects. Examples include heparin or warfarin (used in the treatment of thrombosis) and phenylbutazone (used in the treatment of rheumatoid or arthritic disorders).

Q: What are the symptoms of purpura and how are they treated?

A: There may be purple or reddish spots on the skin. Other symptoms may vary from very minor bleeding under the skin to major areas of bruising and haemorrhage into tissues, such as the pleural membranes surrounding the lungs, the back of the eye, or the intestines. Repeated bleeding may cause anaemia.

Treatment of purpura must depend on the accurate diagnosis of the cause. Serious conditions, such as allergic purpura, need urgent hospitalization, with specialized investigation and care.

Purulent. *See* PUS.

Pus is the thick liquid produced by inflammation in abscesses and other infected areas. It contains white blood cells, cellular debris, and fluid. The white blood cells gather in the area to fight infection; the fluid drains from the damaged tissue.

Pustule is a small, pus-containing area just under the skin.

Pyelitis is an infection of the pelvis of the kidney. *See* PYELONEPHRITIS.

Pyelogram is an X-ray of the kidneys made using special iodine-containing dyes, which are opaque to X-rays. There are two main methods of obtaining a pyelogram: intravenous pyelography (IVP) and retrograde pyelography. In retrograde pyelography, a small tube is inserted into one or both of the ureters using a cytoscope (*see* CYTOSCOPY). The dye is then forced along the tube to the kidneys.

See also INTRAVENOUS PYELOGRAM.

Pyelonephritis is an inflammation of the kidney and the renal pelvis, which is the hollow cone into which urine flows from the kidney. The onset of pyelonephritis may be sudden (acute pyelonephritis) or gradual (chronic pyelonephritis).

Acute pyelonephritis usually is caused by

the spread of infection from the bladder. Occasionally, it may be caused by the spread of infection through the bloodstream. Chronic pyelonephritis causes destruction and scarring of the kidney tissue as a result of an untreated bacterial infection. Both forms of pyelonephritis are associated with an obstruction to the flow of urine.

Q: What are the symptoms of acute pyelonephritis?

A: Usually, there is a sudden onset of pain in the lower back, fever with chills, nausea, and vomiting. Urination may be painful (DYSURIA) and more frequent than usual.

Q: How is acute pyelonephritis treated?

A: Acute pyelonephritis is treated with antibiotics and an increased fluid intake. Surgery may be necessary if an obstruction is present.

Occasionally, the treatment eliminates the symptoms without destroying the infection. Such a symptomless infection is rare in men.

Q: What are the symptoms of chronic pyelonephritis?

A: The disorder progresses over several years with recurrent attacks of acute pyelonephritis. Usually, there are no symptoms between attacks. Chronic pyelonephritis may cause HIGH BLOOD PRESSURE, and eventually kidney failure with URAEMIA and a large output of urine.

Q: How is chronic pyelonephritis treated?

A: Treatment involves removal of any obstruction, which may require surgery and a prolonged course of antibiotics. Treatment for high blood pressure and uraemia also may be necessary.

Pyemia is a serious condition in which septicaemia (blood poisoning) occurs from a pus-forming area and produces multiple abscesses throughout the body.

Q: What are the symptoms of pyemia?

A: The symptoms of pyemia are violent shivering because of sudden chill with high rises in temperature, followed by sweating. Frequently, jaundice develops, as well as abscesses in various areas of the body, such as the liver, lungs, and kidneys.

Q: How is pyemia treated?

A: The development of pyemia requires urgent hospitalization with full investigations to find the cause. Large doses of antibiotics must be given for some weeks to ensure recovery. Abscesses may have to be lanced.

Pyloric stenosis is a narrowing of the exit (pylorus) from the stomach to the duodenum that causes a partial obstruction. It also is known as pyloric obstruction.

Q: What causes pyloric stenosis?

A: Congenital hypertrophic pyloric stenosis occurs in about one in 500 babies and is four times more frequent in boys than girls. It is a genetic disorder.

Pyloric stenosis in adults is caused by spasm or scarring of the pyloric muscle. This is commonly associated with a peptic ulcer, often because of the scarring from repeated ulceration.

Q: What are the symptoms of congenital hypertrophic pyloric stenosis?

A: The symptoms usually start in the second week of life with occasional vomiting after feeds. Within a few days, there is vomiting after every feed. It is termed projectile vomiting, because the milk is ejected out of the mouth with a characteristic violence. The baby is constipated and hungry and rapidly becomes dehydrated if the vomiting continues.

Q: How is congenital hypertrophic pyloric stenosis treated?

A: The usual treatment is an operation that is performed after the baby has been given intravenous fluids to correct any dehydration and to replace salts that may have been lost. The thickened muscle around the pylorus is cut. Drug treatment helps only in milder cases.

Q: What are the symptoms of pyloric stenosis in an adult?

A: Vomiting may occur with any peptic ulcer, but in pyloric stenosis large quantities of fluid are brought up. A partial obstruction is indicated if the

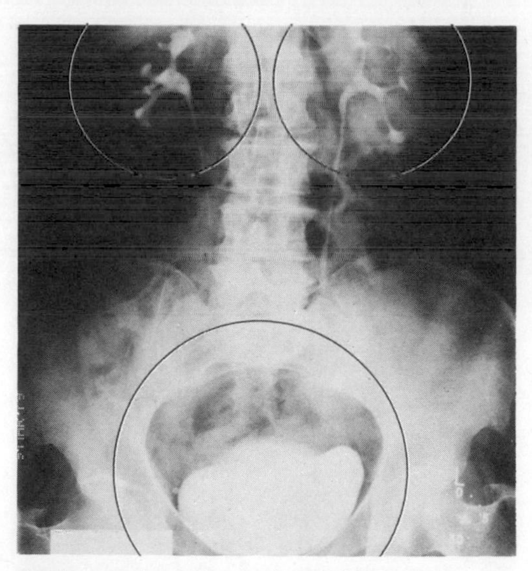

Pyelogram is an X-ray of the kidneys taken after injection of an iodine compound.

vomit contains food eaten six to twelve hours previously.

The patient may complain of a feeling of fullness and, if vomiting is frequent, there will be a loss of weight and sometimes dehydration. Once suspected, the stomach is emptied and a barium meal X-ray taken. A gastroscopy, an examination of the inside of the stomach, helps to confirm the diagnosis.

Q: *How is the adult form of pyloric stenosis treated?*

A: Because it is not always certain whether the stenosis is caused by spasm or scarring, a trial of medical treatment with antispasm drugs, as well as treatment for peptic ulcers, is given. The course may be continued if the symptoms improve and frequent small meals can be eaten. If the symptoms remain, a surgeon will operate to remove part of the stomach (partial GASTRECTOMY) or to create a new opening from the stomach to the intestine (GASTROENTEROSTOMY).

Pyloroplasty is an operation to relieve the obstruction of PYLORIC STENOSIS by cutting through the pyloric muscle.

Pylorospasm is a spasm of the pyloric muscle at the exit from the stomach, causing the symptoms of PYLORIC STENOSIS.

Pylorus is the narrow exit from the stomach into the duodenum. It contains a circular muscle called a sphincter. The pyloric sphincter helps to control the gradual emptying of the stomach.

Pyogenic is any condition that produces PUS.

Pyorrhoea is a discharge of pus from any part of the body, such as from a boil. The term most commonly is applied to a discharge of pus from the gums.

Pyrexia. *See* FEVER.

Pyridoxine (vitamin B_6) is essential to the body for the formation of proteins from amino acids. It is found in many foods, particularly eggs, cereals, meat, and fish. Pregnant women and those taking contraceptive pills need more vitamin B_6 than usual.

Pyrogen is any substance that produces a fever.

Pyrosis. *See* HEARTBURN.

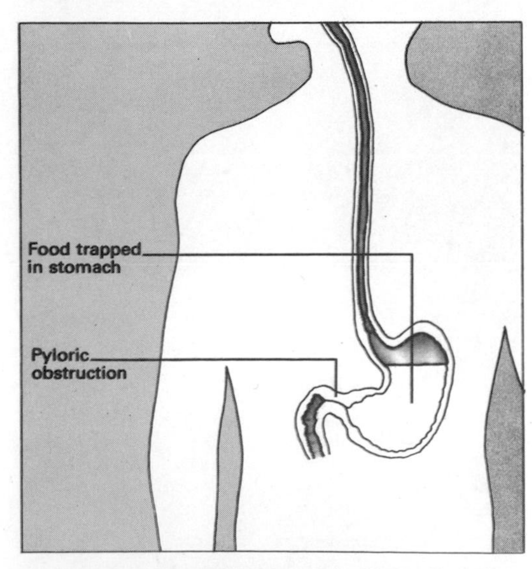

Pyloric stenosis is thickening in the wall of the pylorus causing intestinal obstruction.

Q

Q fever is an infectious disease, caused by the microorganism *Coxiella burneti,* a variety of RICKETTSIA. Q fever commonly occurs in sheep and cattle. Humans usually become infected by inhaling droplets from the milk, urine, or faeces of infected animals. The placenta of infected animals is particularly infectious. Rarely, the infection is transmitted by a tick bite, or from handling wild animals.

Q: *What are the symptoms of Q fever?*

A: After an incubation period of between nine and twenty-eight days, there is a sudden onset of fever, severe headache, shivering, muscle pains and, often, chest pains. A dry cough may develop after about a week. The fever may rise to about 40°C (104°F), and usually lasts for one to three weeks. Complications, such as PNEUMONIA and ENDOCARDITIS, also may develop. Despite the severity of the disease, death is rare, even in untreated patients.

Q: *How is Q fever treated?*

A: The disease is treated with antibiotics, usually tetracycline. A vaccine against Q fever has been developed, but it is still being tested.

Quadriceps is a muscle with four heads. The term usually is applied to the quadriceps femoris, the large muscle in front of the thighbone. It consists of a group of four muscles that share a common lower tendon. This tendon surrounds the kneecap (patella) and is attached to the front of the tibia (shinbone). Contraction of the quadriceps femoris straightens the lower leg.

Quadriplegia is paralysis of all four limbs. *See* PARALYSIS.

Quarantine is a period of isolation from public contact after exposure to an infectious disease so that the infection does not spread. The length of the quarantine period varies according to the incubation period of the infection. For example, the incubation period of mumps varies between ten and twenty-eight days. The quarantine period is twenty-eight days after the time of the last (not first) contact with an infected person.

Total isolation of potentially infected persons is not always necessary. It is often sufficient for them to be restricted in their movements or to be under medical supervision. If symptoms appear, total isolation may become necessary.

Quickening is the term used to describe a mother's awareness of her unborn baby's first movements. It usually occurs between the eighteenth and twentieth weeks of pregnancy but in subsequent pregnancies it usually occurs about two weeks earlier. *See* PREGNANCY AND CHILDBIRTH.

Quick's test is a blood test performed to measure the amount of prothrombin, an essential factor in the blood clotting process. Quick's test is used to monitor the effects of ANTICOAGULANT drugs.

Quinine is a bitter, white, crystalline alkaloid substance obtained from the bark of the cinchona tree. It is effective against MALARIA, but has largely been replaced by synthetic antimalarial drugs. However, it is still used to treat malaria in areas where strains of malaria have developed that are resistant to the synthetic drugs.

Quinine also is used to treat night cramps in the elderly.

Excessive doses of quinine may cause headaches, vomiting, noises in the ears (tinnitus), and visual disturbances which may result in blindness. This collection of symptoms is known as cinchonism.

Quinsy, known medically as peritonsillar abscess, is an infection of the tissue around the tonsils. It is usually caused by the spread of infection from TONSILLITIS.

Q: What are the symptoms of quinsy?

A: The symptoms include fever, severe pain on swallowing, even of saliva, and difficulty in opening the mouth (trismus). The patient's breath smells foul, and there may be earache (otalgia).

Q: How is quinsy treated?

A: Treatment with antibiotics usually is effective in the early stages of the infection. However, if the symptoms are severe, a surgical incision of the abscess may be necessary. This allows the pus to drain, and usually gives immediate relief. Quinsy tends to recur and a doctor may recommend that the tonsils be surgically removed (TONSILLECTOMY). This operation should be performed about four weeks after the abscess has healed.

Rabbit fever is an infectious disorder that is transmitted by the bite of an infected blood-sucking insect or tick. It is known medically as tularaemia. *See* TULARAEMIA.

A talk about Rabies

Rabies, also known as hydrophobia, is a virus infection transmitted to man and certain other mammals by the saliva of an infected animal. Infection is through a bite (usually from a dog) or by skin or mucous membrane contact with infected saliva. The incubation period of the disorder can be as short as two weeks or as long as a year; the usual time is one to two months. Death invariably follows within a week of developing symptoms. Anti-rabies injections usually prevent symptoms occurring if they are given as soon as possible contact has occurred.

Immunization is available for people who are particularly at risk. Because of strict control of the import of animals, rabies does not occur in the U.K.

Q: How can you tell if an animal has rabies?

A: The animal, including a wild animal, behaves abnormally, often without fear of humans. At first it is extremely agitated and vicious, but later this is followed by gradual paralysis which makes it move slowly.

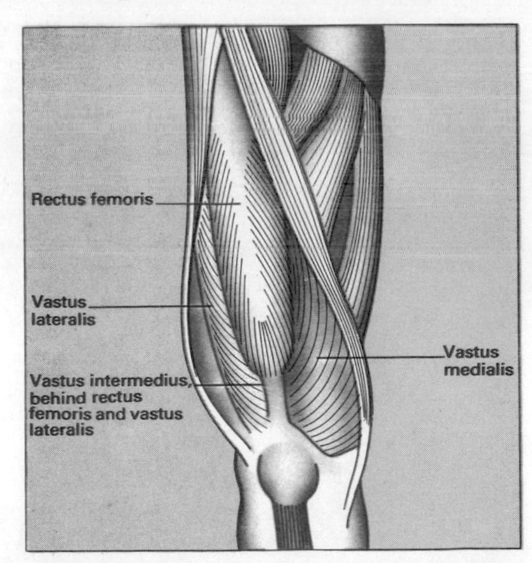

Quadriceps femoris is the strong muscle in the thigh with ligament attachments.

Q: What are the symptoms of rabies in humans?

A: The first symptoms are fever, depression, and increasing restlessness turning into uncontrollable excitement. There is agitation in which painful spasms of the throat muscles occur, accompanied by excessive saliva which froths and flows down the chin. Drinking even a sip of water produces spasms of the swallowing muscles, followed by saliva flow, hence the name hydrophobia (meaning fear of water).

Q: How is rabies treated?

A: The bite must be thoroughly cleaned, as this may prevent the spread of the virus. A person who has been in contact with rabies is given an injection of gamma globulin, which gives temporary protection until a series of rabies vaccine injections can be given.

Treatment of the symptoms involves complete isolation of the patient. Doctors and nurses must be immunized before contact with the patient. The patient is sedated, and mechanical artificial respiration is used to help control the symptoms. However, once the symptoms begin to appear, death follows within a week.

Radiation is any form of electromagnetic energy wave such as heat, light, or X-rays, or any stream of ions (electrically charged atoms or molecules) or subatomic particles. The earth is exposed to radiation from the sun's rays and from radioactive materials in the earth itself, much of which is harmless, low level radiation. Damage to human tissue and cell formation may be caused by high energy radiation. Low energy radiation scarcely penetrates the skin. A very high dosage of radiation causes RADIATION SICKNESS.

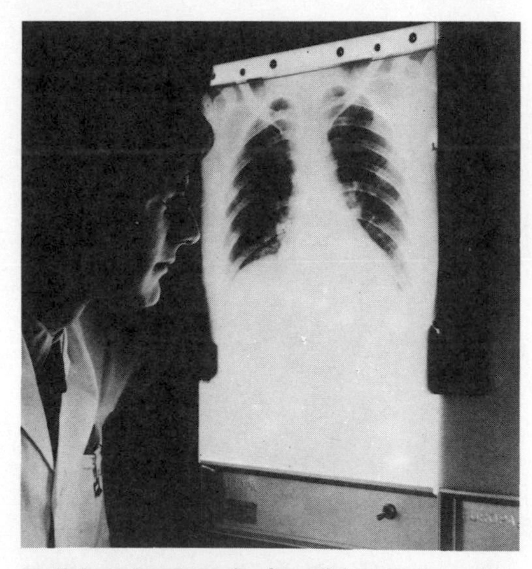

Radiology is a branch of medicine dealing with the understanding of X-ray photographs.

Q: How is radiation used in medicine?

A: The use of X-rays in radiology, including the use of isotopes such as radioactive dyes as tracers, is a normal diagnostic procedure in hospitals. Radiotherapy is a method of treatment that employs an intense source of radiation, as in cancer treatment.

Ultraviolet light is used to treat certain skin diseases, such as acne and psoriasis. Physiotherapists use infra-red heat and shortwave diathermy to treat rheumatic and muscular disorders.

Radiation sickness is an illness caused by over-exposure to ionizing RADIATION from radioactive substances, such as radium and uranium, or from X-rays. The symptoms depend mainly on the total dosage of radiation and the duration of exposure. Acute radiation sickness results from the absorption of a high dose of radiation over a short time. Delayed radiation sickness results from repeated or prolonged exposure to low doses of radiation. Adequate precautions can prevent the danger of radiation sickness in persons who might be exposed to the dangers of radiation in their work.

Q: What are the symptoms of acute radiation sickness?

A: The initial symptoms usually appear within a few hours of exposure and they include nausea, vomiting, diarrhoea, and burns. At a later stage there may be conjunctivitis, loss of hair, disorientation, a staggering gait, and convulsions. Anaemia and a severe, often fatal form of gastroenteritis also may develop. The body's immune system may be affected, thereby making the person vulnerable to infection.

Radiation may damage the foetus in a pregnant woman. This may result in a natural abortion, or the foetus may suffer from any of a variety of congenital defects, such as mental retardation or skull damage.

Q: What are the symptoms of delayed radiation sickness?

A: There may be cataracts, HYPOTHYROIDISM, and a reduction in fertility. People who have been exposed to low levels of radiation for a long time have an increased likelihood of developing cancer and leukaemia. Such effects may not become apparent for several years.

Radiculitis is a form of NEURITIS in which

there is inflammation of the spinal nerves in the spinal canal.

See also SLIPPED DISC.

Radiography is the use of radiation, usually X-rays, for studying the internal structures of the body as an aid to diagnosis. The X-rays are recorded on photographic plates, or they may be projected "live" on a fluoroscope or a television screen so that a doctor can study the movement of various structures within the body.

See also RADIOTHERAPY.

Radiology is the study of the techniques used in RADIOGRAPHY and RADIOTHERAPY, both of which require a degree of specialization.

Radiotherapy is the treatment of disorders using RADIATION. The machinery used is similar to X-ray equipment, but contains a source of high energy radiation, such as radium or a radioactive isotope of cobalt. An injection of a radioactive isotope, such as iodine, is another technique of radiotherapy.

Q: What conditions can be treated by radiotherapy, and is the treatment effective?

A: Conditions treated vary from rodent ulcers to cancer anywhere in the body. It is often used in conjunction with surgery, or cytotoxic drugs, so there is a higher degree of success than if one form of treatment is used alone.

Radium is a rare, naturally occurring radioactive element. It produces alpha, beta, and gamma rays, which can be used in RADIOTHERAPY.

Radius is the outer of the two bones of the forearm; it forms part of the elbow joint and the wrist joint. It rotates round the other forearm bone, the ULNA, allowing the hand to rotate at the wrist.

See also COLLES' FRACTURE.

Rale is the abnormal sound heard by a doctor when listening to air passing into or out of a diseased lung. The rattling rale produced when there is a partial blockage of an air passage is called a rhonchus.

Ranula is a small cyst under the tongue, commonly caused by the blockage of a salivary duct. Although not serious, a ranula should be examined and treated by a doctor.

Rash is a temporary discoloration or eruption of the skin, usually caused by an infection or an ALLERGY.

Rauwolfia is a drug obtained from the dried roots of the oriental shrub *Rauwolfia serpentina.* It contains a number of alkaloids, formerly used to treat high blood pressure.

Raynaud's phenomenon is an intermittent spasm of small arteries, usually in the fingers and toes, occurring in bad weather. It is most frequent in young women. It usually occurs without obvious cause, but may occasionally be caused by pressure on the nerves supplying the arteries, rare blood disorders, or SCLERODERMA. The fingers become white and numb and then, as circulation improves, swollen, painful, and blue-red in colour. In severe cases gangrene and ulceration of the fingertips may occur. Treatment with drugs to dilate the blood vessels is often effective. If known, the cause itself is treated.

See also ACROCYANOSIS; CHILBLAINS.

RBC is an abbreviation for red blood cell. *See* RED BLOOD CELL.

Recessive is a term used to describe certain genes in HEREDITY. It is the opposite of DOMINANT.

Rectal fissure, also known as anal fissure, is a tear in the mucous membranes that line the anus. It may extend into the lower part of the rectum, and commonly accompanies CONSTIPATION. *See* FISSURE.

Rectocele is a relaxation of the tissues that support the rectum so that it forms a type of hernia into the rear wall of the vagina. A rectocele occurs with PROLAPSE of the uterus. It may be accompanied by a similar prolapse of the front wall of the vagina, and may involve the bladder and urethra, causing stress incontinence (sudden loss of urine on straining). The symptoms and treatment are those associated with prolapse.

Rectum is the final portion of the large intestine, extending through the pelvis from the end of the colon to the anus. Situated in front of the sacrum and behind the bladder, the rectum is about 12cm (five inches) long. The upper part is covered by the peritoneum,

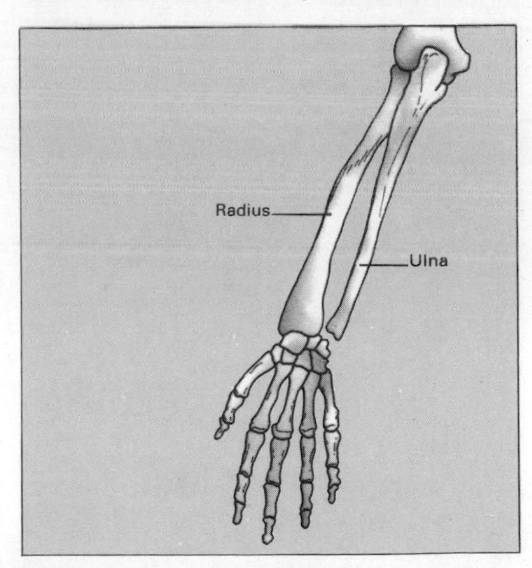

Radius is the outer bone of the forearm. It is shorter but stronger than the ulna.

the membrane that lines the abdominal cavity, and the lower part is supported by the muscles and ligaments of the pelvic floor.

The desire to defecate is caused by the feeling that occurs when faeces are passed from the colon into the rectum. Failure to defecate reduces the desire to do so, and chronic constipation may then develop.

Q: What conditions can affect the rectum?

A: Conditions that affect the rectum include infections such as amoebic dysentery, schistosomiasis, ulcerative colitis, and Crohn's disease of the rectum.

The rectum may undergo a prolapse, in which its internal mucous membranes become detached from the underlying wall and protrude from the anus. This usually corrects itself in infants, but in adults an operation probably is necessary.

Tumours of the rectum may be either benign (noncancerous) or malignant (cancerous). Such tumours are similar to those elsewhere in the colon, except that they produce bleeding, rectal pain, and spasmodic anal contractions. *See* CANCER.

Red blood cell (RBC), also called an erythrocyte, is one of the various types of cells in blood. An RBC is shaped like a biconcave disc and contains the red colouring matter haemoglobin. Its function is to transport oxygen from the lungs to the tissues in the form of oxyhaemoglobin. In the tissues, the oxygen is exchanged for carbon dioxide, which the blood carries back to the lungs, where it is exhaled.

Red blood cells are formed in the bone marrow contained in the ends of the long bones, vertebrae, breast-bone, and pelvis bones.

Underproduction of RBCs causes ANAEMIA, and overproduction POLYCYTHAEMIA. Some kinds of anaemia may be the result of abnormal formation of blood cells, such as THALASSAEMIA and SICKLE CELL ANAEMIA.

See also BLOOD; HAEMOGLOBIN.

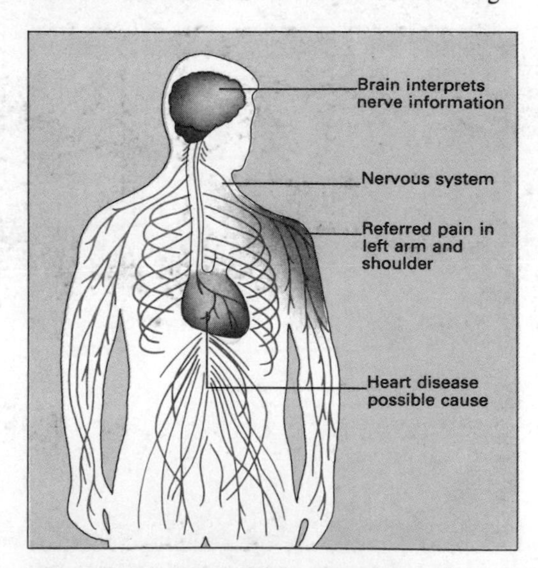

Referred pain is pain felt in an area away from the site of a disorder or previous injury.

Red eye is a condition in which there are brilliant red patches across the white of the eye. Occasionally the entire white of the eye is involved. Red eye is usually painless and is caused by bleeding under the conjunctiva (a subconjunctival haemorrhage). A subconjunctival haemorrhage may occur following a minor injury to the eye or following vigorous nose blowing. Red eye also may occur in more serious conditions, such as PINK EYE, IRITIS, and GLAUCOMA.

Referred pain is felt in one part of the body (usually on the surface), although the place of origin is elsewhere in the body.

Reflex is an involuntary muscular response to a stimulus, also known as a reflex action. The automatic muscular response is triggered by a nerve pathway between the point of stimulation and the responding muscle, without the involvement of the brain. For example, a person who touches something hot immediately recoils and pulls his or her hand away from the source of heat, even before the brain registers pain. A more commonly known example is the knee jerk reflex, produced in a test that is part of a doctor's basic examination of the nervous system (*see* KNEE JERK).

A conditioned reflex is any reflex not inborn or inherited. For example, a soldier can be trained to fall flat at the first sound of gunfire.

Refractory means failing to respond, or responding slowly, to treatment.

Regional ileitis. *See* CROHN'S DISEASE.

Regression, in medicine, is a return to an earlier stage of a disorder (which could be favourable or unfavourable). Biologically, filial regression is a return to the normal or average in inherited conditions. Psychologically, regression is a return to an earlier type of behaviour, such as childish behaviour.

Regurgitation is a backflow of fluid. The term usually applies to the passing back of food from the stomach to the mouth, usually because of eating too quickly with insufficient chewing. Various disorders of the oesophagus also can cause regurgitation.

Regurgitation also describes the backflow of blood in the heart, caused by damage or diseased heart valves and sometimes leading to heart failure.

Reiter's disease, or Reiter's syndrome, is

thought to be a form of venereal disease, a combination of NONSPECIFIC URETHRITIS (NSU), conjunctivitis, and arthritis. It sometimes follows a period of diarrhoea or, more commonly, a urethral discharge. The disorder is more common among young men than among women.

Relapse is the return of the symptoms of a disorder after an apparent recovery.

Relapsing fever, also known as recurrent fever or tick fever, are diseases carried by ticks or lice. The patient has a high fever for about ten days, then the temperature returns to normal. However, a relapse follows in a day or two. This pattern is repeated until immunity is built up by the patient.

Q: What causes relapsing fever?

A: The disorder is caused by a spirochaete organism (*Borrelia duttoni*) which can be transmitted from infected animals to humans by ticks. The ticks commonly are found in West Africa, the western U.S.A., and various other tropical and sub-tropical regions of the world.

Q: What are the symptoms of relapsing fever?

A: After an incubation period of seven days, the patient has shivering attacks, headache, high fever, rapid heartbeat, vomiting, muscle and joint pain and, possibly, a rose coloured skin rash. Delirium may occur. The fever rises to a peak during the following five to ten days and then suddenly falls.

After a short period of a day or two, a relapse occurs, often accompanied by jaundice, and the pattern of symptoms is repeated. Most patients respond to treatment with antibiotic drugs.

Relaxant is any agent that causes mental or physical relaxation when tension is present because of a mental or physical disorder. Physiotherapy often includes relaxation exercises, as do most antenatal classes. A simple hot bath also can relax tense muscles.

Special groups of drugs can be prescribed, usually with painkillers, to relax muscles after an injury or an operation. During surgery, similar drugs are used to produce complete muscle paralysis, which helps the surgeon while operating.

Remission is a period, during the course of an illness, during which a patient's symptoms become less severe or may even disappear completely.

Renal refers to anything having to do with, or shaped like, a kidney. *See* KIDNEY.

Renal calculus is a stone in the kidney. *See* CALCULUS; NEPHROLITHIASIS.

Renin is a hormone that is released by the kidney to maintain normal blood pressure if it should fall. *See* KIDNEY.

Rennin is an enzyme, produced in a baby's stomach, which curdles milk and aids in its digestion.

Replacement surgery, also known as spare-part surgery, concerns the replacement of diseased or damaged parts of the body with natural or artificial substitutes. Materials used range from plastic and metal to donated human tissue, so that many parts of the body, such as arteries, tendons, joints, and the cornea of the eye can receive some form of surgery. *See* TRANSPLANT SURGERY.

Reportable diseases are those which, in most countries or states, must be reported to the community health officer, who can then take action to control the spread of disease. *See* INFECTIOUS DISEASES.

Repression is a psychiatric term used to describe the transfer of unpleasant memories from the conscious to the unconscious mind. It can affect a person's attitude to situations in later life that force him or her to confront the past memory. Examples of repression related situations include a fear of heights (acrophobia) and a fear of strangers (xenophobia).

Resection is the removal of a part of an organ or a bone. Usually, it means that the remaining undamaged sections are joined together. *See* SUBMUCOUS RESECTION.

Reserpine is the principal alkaloid obtained from the root of the rauwolfia plant. *See* RAUWOLFIA.

Resolution has two medical meanings: (1) the ability of the eye to distinguish between two separate but close objects; and (2) a return to normal, or an improvement, of any

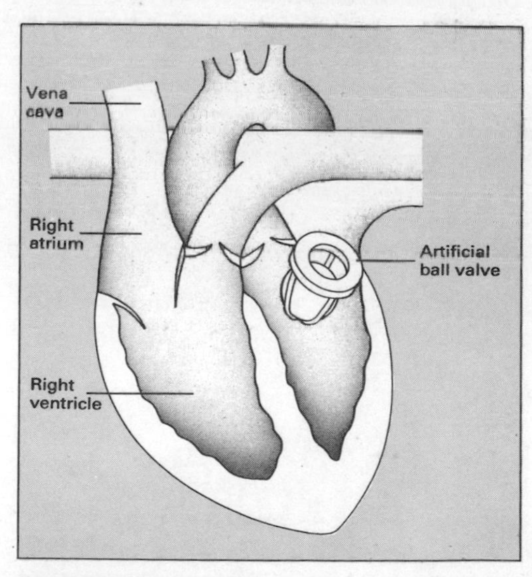

Replacement surgery may be performed to replace a damaged heart valve.

inflammatory condition, such as a boil.

Respiration, or breathing, is the process by which oxygen from the air is exchanged for carbon dioxide from the body cells. The physical process of breathing involves the inspiration of air into the lungs, from where oxygen is carried by the blood to the tissues. Here it is exchanged for carbon dioxide, a waste product. *See* LUNG DISORDERS; LUNG.

Respirator is an apparatus used to purify the air a person inhales. It may be a simple gauze mask or a complex piece of machinery which extracts dusts and gases from all the air in a building.

An artificial respirator is also a machine that is used in medicine to aid or maintain breathing. It commonly is used during general anaesthesia when the patient's breathing muscles have been paralyzed by muscle-relaxant drugs.

See also ARTIFICIAL RESPIRATION.

Respiratory disorders. *See* LUNG DISORDERS.

Respiratory distress syndrome is a lung disorder of the newborn, particularly of premature babies. Other predisposing factors include poorly controlled diabetes mellitus in the mother and maternal haemorrhage before the onset of labour. The second baby of a twin birth is liable to have respiratory distress syndrome.

Q: *What causes respiratory distress syndrome?*

A: The condition may be caused by a failure in the foetus of the immature lung to produce a substance that prevents the lung from collapsing once air has been inhaled immediately after birth. In a premature baby, areas of the lung may remain collapsed. These areas become inflamed, producing an abnormal membrane. Provided the baby can survive a few days, the necessary substance that keeps the lungs open is produced and the baby survives.

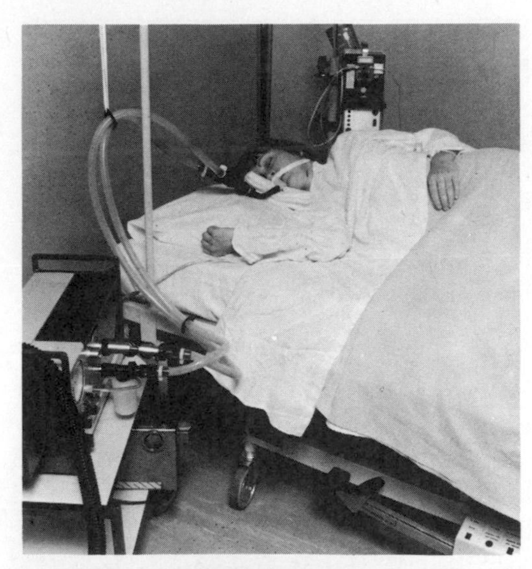

Respirator is used to help a patient breathe – most commonly during surgery.

Q: *What are the symptoms of respiratory distress syndrome?*

A: Usually the symptoms begin immediately after birth, although they may not be apparent for two or three hours. Symptoms include rapid breathing, often with an expiratory grunt, a bluish tinge to the skin (cyanosis) and, sometimes, respiratory arrest.

Q: *How is respiratory distress syndrome treated?*

A: Treatment is carried out in a neonatal special care unit or a neonatal intensive care unit, depending on the severity of the condition. Mild cases may be treated with just supplemental oxygen; severe cases may be treated with mechanical ventilation.

Respiratory stimulants are drugs or other substances used to stimulate the physical action of breathing.

Respiratory stimulants may be used in the respiratory failure that occurs during barbiturate or other forms of poisoning.

Restless legs is a common complaint of the elderly in which there is a feeling of general discomfort that compels a person to move his or her legs, sometimes almost involuntarily, when sitting at rest or lying down.

The condition may be associated with iron deficiency anaemia, varicose veins, or polyneuritis. It may follow a partial gastrectomy. Tranquillizers (such as the phenothiazines) used in the treatment of mental illness may also be a factor. Treatment with muscle relaxant drugs is sometimes effective.

Resuscitation is any one of various methods used to restore breathing and heart action. *See* First Aid, p.518.

See also ARTIFICIAL RESPIRATION; CARDIAC MASSAGE.

Retention is the inability to pass urine. The term also is used for a method of keeping false teeth in their correct position, and it is a psychological term meaning the ability to retain past memories.

Q: *What causes urinary retention?*

A: Retention may result if normal sensations from the bladder are disturbed by anaesthetic or painkilling drugs. Antispasm drugs and antidepressants also may cause retention.

Physical causes of retention include nervous disorders such as polyneuritis, multiple sclerosis, and the effects of a stroke. Bladder disorders, prostate problems, stricture (narrowing) of the urethra, or pregnancy also can cause sudden retention. Gradual retention when a person has a full bladder results in overflow INCONTINENCE. Treatment is directed at the cause.

Retina is the light-sensitive area at the back of the eyeball. It consists of a layer of cells called rods and cones. Rod cells are sensitive to various intensities of light, and cone cells are sensitive to colour. *See* DETACHED RETINA; EYE; RETINITIS.

Retinitis is inflammation of the retina, the light-sensitive surface inside the back of the eye. Retinitis is a symptom of a wide variety of conditions, including tuberculosis, kidney disease, arteriosclerosis, syphilis, eclampsia, leukaemia, congenital toxoplasmosis, hypertension, diabetes mellitus, and some diseases of the brain. Retinitis also may be caused by damage to the retina through excessive exposure to light (photoretinitis). Other forms of retinitis, such as RETINITIS PIGMENTOSA and retinitis proliferans, may be caused by an inherited disorder or by scarring following repeated retinal haemorrhages.

Retinitis pigmentosa is a degenerative condition of the retina of unknown cause (*see* RETINITIS). Degeneration of the light-sensitive rod cells in the retina occurs first, and night blindness is generally the first symptom. This usually begins in early adult life. The colour sensitive cone cells become involved more gradually, daytime vision deteriorates, and the field of vision is reduced from the edges inwards (telescopic vision). Although the cause of retinitis pigmentosa is unknown, it shows a hereditary tendency and is often associated with other congenital anomalies.

Q: How is retinitis pigmentosa treated?

A: There is as yet no treatment for the condition.

Retrobulbar neuritis is an inflammation of the part of the optic nerve that is within the eye socket. It may be caused by the spread of infection from the sinuses; bleeding into the nerve from an injury; a generalized illness, such as MULTIPLE SCLEROSIS or DIABETES MELLITUS; or infections of the nervous system, such as POLYNEURITIS and ENCEPHALITIS. Often, however, there is no apparent cause for the condition.

Q: What are the symptoms of retrobulbar neuritis?

A: The main symptoms are a rapid and progressive loss of vision; pain when the eye is moved; and a headache. The condition usually affects only one eye. There may be a spontaneous, almost complete recovery. However, further attacks are common.

Q: How is retrobulbar neuritis treated?

A: An eye specialist should be consulted to diagnose and treat the cause. Sometimes, retrobulbar neuritis is treated with corticosteroid drugs. Smoking is usually forbidden.

Retrograde amnesia is a loss of memory for events that occurred before a trauma, such as a head injury. *See* AMNESIA.

Retroversion is a backward displacement of an organ. The term most often is applied to the womb (uterus).

See also PROLAPSE.

Rhesus factor. *See* RH FACTOR.

Rheumatic diseases stem from a wide group of disorders. They include various forms of arthritis and various inflammatory disorders of muscles and ligaments. Symptoms of most rheumatic diseases include muscle stiffness, aching and, sometimes, joint pain. Continued discomfort requires medical investigation.

Q: How are rheumatic diseases treated?

A: Drugs based on aspirin are used when the complaint is mild. Various antirheumatic drugs also may be prescribed. Sometimes, in extremely painful cases, a local anaesthetic and a corticosteroid drug are injected directly into the area of pain to relieve the immediate local symptoms.

Heat, hydrotherapy, shortwave diathermy, ultrasonic treatment and joint exercises are often given by physiotherapists as short-term relief.

The following table lists rheumatic disorders and related diseases; each has a

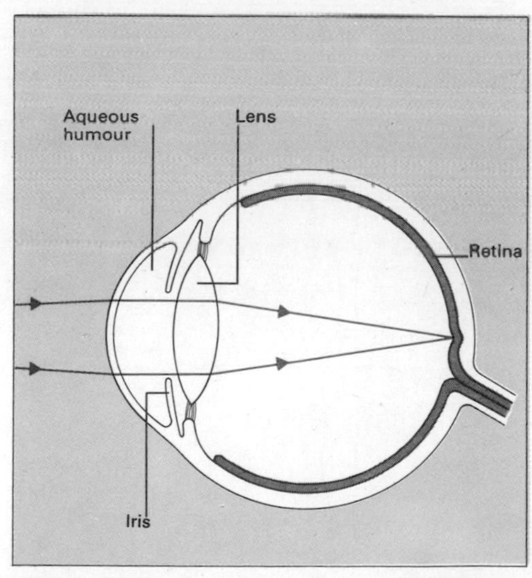

Retina receives light stimuli through the iris and lens, and transmits the image to the brain.

separate article in the A-Z section of this book.

Rheumatic type	Related disease
Arthritis	
(a) Unknown cause	ANKYLOSING SPONDYLITIS
	OSTEOARTHROPATHY
	PSORIASIS
	REITER'S DISEASE
	RHEUMATOID ARTHRITIS
	SPONDYLITIS
	STILL'S DISEASE
(b) Osteoarthritis	OSTEOARTHRITIS
(c) Infective arthritis	PYELONEPHRITIS
(d) Metabolic arthritis	ACROMEGALY
	GOUT
	HAEMOCHROMATOSIS
	HAEMOPHILIA
	HYPERPARA-THYROIDISM
	HYPOTHYROIDISM
	OSTEOMALACIA
	SCURVY
	SICKLE CELL ANAEMIA
(e) Cartilage disorders	CHONDROMALACIA
	MENISCUS
	OSTEOCHONDRITIS
	SLIPPED DISC
Generalized diseases often involving joints	CROHN'S DISEASE
	SARCOIDOSIS
	ULCERATIVE COLITIS
Rheumatic fever	RHEUMATIC FEVER
Disorders of connective tissue	ALLERGY (particularly to drugs)
	LUPUS ERYTHEMATOSUS
	POLYARTERITIS NODOSA
	POLYMYALGIA RHEUMATICA
	SCLERODERMA
Rheumatism	BACKACHE
	BURSITIS
	CAPSULITIS
	CARPAL TUNNEL SYNDROME
	FEVER
	FIBROSITIS
	MYALGIA
	MYOSITIS
	POLYNEURITIS
	TENDINITIS
	TORTICOLLIS
Miscellaneous	PARKINSON'S DISEASE
	various psychological disorders

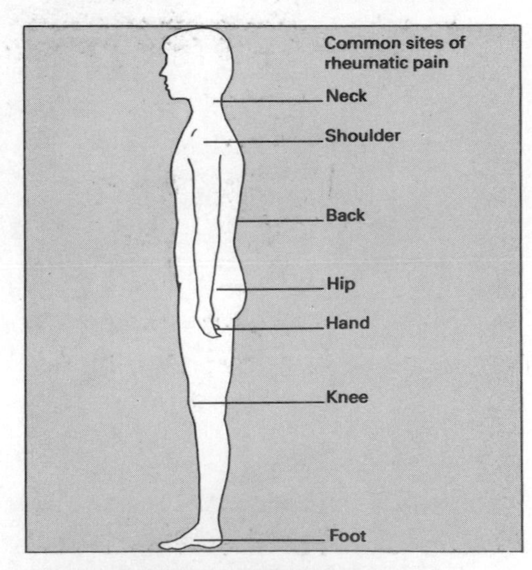

Rheumatic disease most commonly affects muscles and joints of the body.

A talk about Rheumatic fever

Rheumatic fever is a form of allergic reaction by the body to a particular kind of streptococcal infection. The infection usually occurs with tonsillitis. Rheumatic fever causes damage to the body's tissues, and this damage is most serious when it involves the tissues of the heart. Fever-related damage can also involve the central nervous system, the joints, skin, and subcutaneous tissues.

Rheumatic fever most commonly occurs in children between the ages of five and fifteen years, but it may also affect young adults.

Q: What are the symptoms of rheumatic fever?

A: Usually the patient has tonsillitis or a severe sore throat. This may have improved by the time the symptoms of rheumatic fever appear, which is usually about two weeks later. The most common symptom of rheumatic fever is a form of arthritis in which the joints become tender, swollen, and red.

Typically, as the swelling of one joint seems to settle, another joint becomes swollen and inflamed. The patient appears unwell, flushed, and has a moderate fever.

Less commonly, symptoms of

breathlessness, fever, or mid-chest pain due to underlying rheumatic pericarditis cause the patient to consult a doctor. It is then that the doctor, when examining the heart, detects the abnormal murmurs produced by inflammation of the heart valves.

Another possible symptom is CHOREA. It is caused by inflammation of the brain, which causes the victim to twist and turn the limbs involuntarily, become clumsy and irritable, and have facial contortions. The sufferer also may grunt and have difficulty in speaking normally.

Q: *What other symptoms may occur with rheumatic fever?*

A: Painless nodules may develop under the skin, particularly over the surface of the large joints, such as the knee and elbow. Transient rashes are also common, but seldom last for more than a day or two.

Abdominal pains are a common occurrence in young children and are probably caused by a combination of a swollen liver, slight heart failure, and inflammation of the lymph glands behind the peritoneum, the membrane that lines the abdominal cavity.

Q: *What is the progress of rheumatic fever?*

A: Usually the fever and joint pains subside within two or three weeks. A patient with chorea may take some months before losing all the symptoms. Skin rashes usually disappear by the end of the fever, and any nodules around the joints gradually become smaller and disappear in a matter of weeks.

The only permanent damage that can be caused by rheumatic fever is to the heart valves. Any pericarditis or rheumatic myocarditis disappears, but scarring occurs on the lining of the heart (endocardium) causing distortion of the heart valves, and eventually resulting in VALVULAR DISEASE of the heart.

However, at least half of all patients who develop the cardiac form of rheumatic fever make a recovery without any valve damage.

Q: *How is rheumatic fever treated?*

A: The most effective and still the basic form of therapy is aspirin. In patients with arthritis, the inflamed joints are rested, often in splints padded with cotton. Corticosteroid drugs are usually prescribed if aspirin is found to be ineffective. Bed rest is essential for those patients with heart involvement until the acute stages of the illness have passed.

It is essential that all patients with rheumatic fever are given antibiotics, preferably penicillin, to kill any residual streptococcal infection.

Q: *For how long should rheumatic fever be treated?*

A: Because the diagnosis usually is made while the patient is in hospital, treatment is started immediately and the patient allowed to return home only when symptoms have improved to such a degree that relatively normal activity can take place. Continued treatment with aspirin is necessary for some weeks or months. Antibiotic treatment should be continued for some years.

Any patient who has had rheumatic fever, particularly if the heart has been involved, must have antibiotics for any dental surgery.

Q: *Can a patient have a second attack of rheumatic fever?*

A: Yes. At present a second attack of rheumatic fever is extremely unusual because the continued daily use of antibiotics prevents further streptococcal infections. Some doctors recommend the use of antibiotics at the onset of any acute throat infection occurring in anyone who has had rheumatic fever. This may further reduce the chances of another attack.

Rheumatism is a general term for any condition that is characterized by stiffness and pain in the muscles and joints. *See* RHEUMATIC DISEASES.

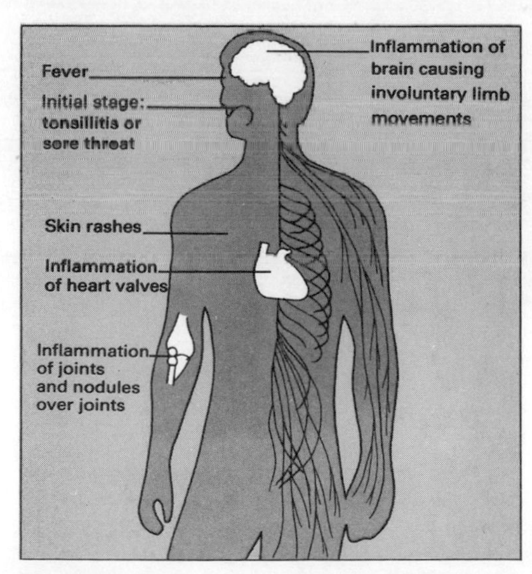

Rheumatic fever begins with a throat infection but progressively causes other symptoms.

A talk about Rheumatoid arthritis

Rheumatoid arthritis is a common disorder of the joints, usually symmetrically involving the body. There is a loss of the joint surface and degeneration because of inflammation of the surrounding tissues. The cause is not known, but it is a common condition affecting one per cent of the population. It is more common in women than in men, and usually affects people between the ages of thirty and forty.

Q: What are the symptoms of rheumatoid arthritis?

A: The small joints of the hands and feet usually are involved, but larger joints also may become stiff and swollen, with the corresponding joints on both sides of the body being affected. The stiffness and swelling tend to be worse in the mornings or after exercise, and there may also be tenderness. Frequently, nodules can be felt over joints or bones where they are near the skin surface. The patient frequently feels unwell and easily becomes fatigued. The onset may be sudden (acute) or gradual (chronic).

The joints become deformed, partly because of damage to the surrounding tissues and partly because of shortening of the tendons. Patients with an acute onset of the disorder are obviously ill, with a fever and considerable joint pain. Those with a milder form of rheumatoid arthritis complain more of stiffness and lethargy.

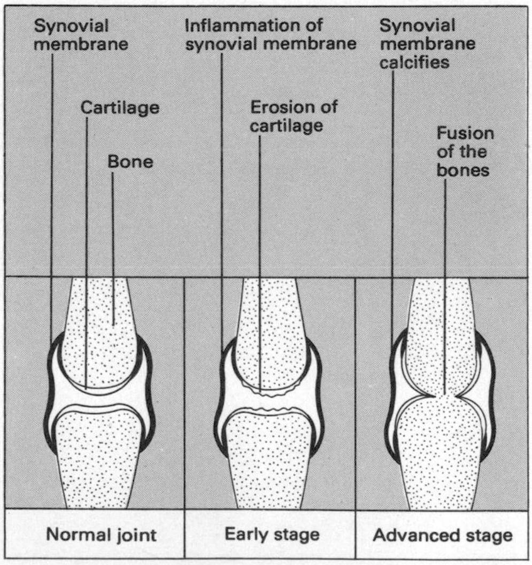

Rheumatoid arthritis begins with inflammation that eventually leads to calcification.

Q: How is rheumatoid arthritis treated?

A: Bed rest in hospital often produces an improvement in the acute form of rheumatoid arthritis while treatment is begun. Treatment can be started at home for less severely ill patients.

Drug treatment for rheumatoid arthritis consists mainly of adequate dosage of aspirin or aspirin-like drugs. If these do not seem successful, some of the newer antirheumatic drugs can be used; however, such drugs do not seem to have many major benefits in comparison to aspirin. In severe forms of rheumatoid arthritis, indomethacin or phenylbutazone may be prescribed. Other forms of drug treatment include injections of gold salts, d-penicillamine, and chloroquine.

Use of corticosteroid drugs results in dramatic improvement in the symptoms of rheumatoid arthritis. But their use has to be closely controlled, because they may have to be taken for many years, with an increasing likelihood of adverse effects, without preventing the gradual progress of the underlying disorder.

Diet should be normal and the patient should have frequent nutritious meals and take additional vitamins. Splints may be worn during the day or only at night if one or two joints are more severely affected than the others. Physiotherapy using gentle movements and exercises helps to maintain a full range of movement of the joints until the disorder naturally improves.

Q: Do many patients become disabled?

A: Most patients with rheumatoid arthritis make a complete recovery. But about thirty per cent are left with some disability, and a further ten per cent progress to a severely disabling form of rheumatoid arthritis, regardless of the treatment.

Q: What other forms of treatment are there for rheumatoid arthritis?

A: Various forms of orthopaedic surgery may be performed on joints that have become seriously deformed but in which the active disease has ceased. Minor operations to relieve adhesions or to remove the synovial membrane (which lines the capsule of a joint and secretes lubricating fluid) may produce considerable improvement. Dramatic progress in replacement surgery now enables surgeons to insert plastic joints in fingers and to carry out total joint replacement in the hips and knees.

However, many patients cannot benefit from these procedures, and may have to rely on specially designed appliances and equipment that can make everyday life easier.

Rh factor (rhesus factor) is the basis of the Rh system of blood groups, which is independent of the ABO system. The Rh factor was first discovered in the blood of the rhesus monkey.

Eighty-five per cent of the population is Rh positive. People without the Rh factor are Rh negative. If Rh positive blood is transfused into an Rh negative person, rhesus antibodies (agglutinins) are formed. There is no adverse reaction the first time this occurs. But subsequent transfusions of Rh positive blood will result in a transfusion reaction in which the red blood cells of the Rh positive person are destroyed. For this reason, it is essential that blood is grouped for A, B, O, and Rh factors before a transfusion is carried out.

Haemolytic disease of the newborn results from the incompatability of an Rh positive foetus and an Rh negative mother. *See* BLOOD GROUPS; BLOOD TRANSFUSION; HAEMOLYTIC DISEASE OF THE NEWBORN.

Rhinitis is inflammation of the mucous membrane that lines the nose, producing a watery discharge. It may be caused by an infection, such as the COMMON COLD; by an allergy, such as HAY FEVER; or the cause may be unknown, for example as with VASOMOTOR RHINITIS. Persistent inflammation may result in gross swelling of the mucous membrane and the formation of a POLYP.

Rhinophyma is a form of ROSACEA in which there is swelling of the sebaceous (grease-producing) glands in the nose, which becomes large, red, and misshapen. Antibiotics given at an early stage may be effective. In severe cases, plastic surgery may help.

Rhinoplasty is plastic surgery of the nose to correct its shape. *See* COSMETIC SURGERY; DEVIATED NASAL SEPTUM; SUBMUCOSAL RESECTION.

Rhinorrhoea is the medical term for a thin, watery discharge from the nose. *See* RUNNING NOSE.

Rhonchus. *See* RALE.

Rhythm method is a method of contraception which depends for its effectiveness on abstaining from sexual intercourse for that part of a woman's menstrual cycle during which she is fertile (*see* OVULATION). *See* CONTRACEPTION.

Rib is one of the twelve pairs of thin, curved bones that form the wall of the chest and surround the lungs and heart. The movement of the rib-cage and the diaphragm controls the flow of air into and out of the lungs.

The ribs are joined at the back to the thoracic vertebrae of the spine. The upper seven pairs are called the true ribs, because they are connected in front to the breastbone (sternum). The remaining five pairs of ribs are called the false ribs. The eighth, ninth, and tenth pairs of ribs are connected to the breastbone by cartilage.

Q: What is a cervical rib?

A: It is a rarc additional rib, joined to the seventh cervical vertebra in the neck. A cervical rib may cause pressure on the nerves and blood vessels serving the arm, and produce symptoms of neuralgia or Raynaud's phenomenon. Surgical removal of the rib cures the symptoms.

Q: Can the ribs be broken?

A: Yes. A fracture is the most common injury to a rib. It is most likely to occur in the middle ribs. Although painful, a broken rib is seldom serious. The usual treatment is to give the patient painkilling drugs, but sometimes a surgeon will inject the area of the fracture with a local anaesthetic.

A complete fracture sometimes pierces the chest wall. This causes air to collect in the chest cavity (pneumothorax) or allows bloody fluid to accumulate (haemothorax). Hospital treatment and surgery are necessary if either condition occurs.

Riboflavin, or vitamin B_2, is a water-soluble vitamin of the B complex group. It is found in many foods, particularly beef, fish, liver, kidney, leafy green vegetables, milk, and milk products, such as cheese.

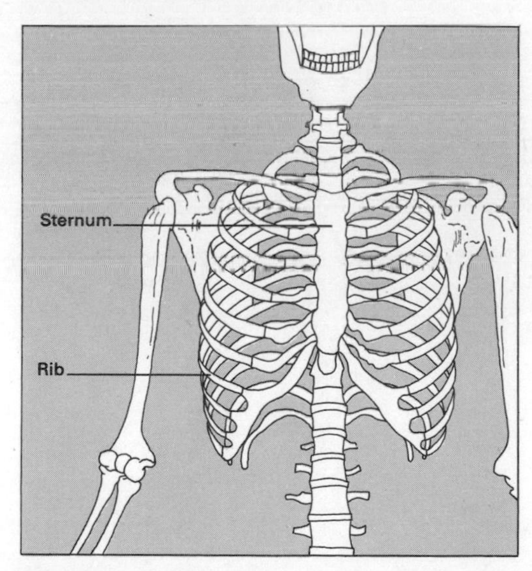

Rib is one of twenty-four bones forming a cage for the chest cavity.

Riboflavin is essential for the production of energy in the body. Deficiency results in eye disorders, forms of dermatitis, and cheilosis (in which there are small sores at the corners of the mouth).

Rickets is a bone disease of children that is caused by a lack of vitamin D. Vitamin D deficiency in adults causes OSTEOMALACIA. Vitamin D is formed in the skin when it is exposed to sunlight. It also may be obtained from some foods, such as fish and eggs. Lack of vitamin D affects the kidneys and disrupts the calcium and phosphorus metabolism in the body. This in turn affects the deposition of calcium in the bones, resulting in deformity (*see* CALCIUM).

Q: What are the symptoms of rickets?

A: Infants with rickets are sometimes restless, grow more slowly than normal, and do not crawl or walk until older than usual. If the condition continues, the ends of the long bones become enlarged. When the infant starts to walk, the legs may bend, resulting in either bow-legs or knock-knees. The chest also may be deformed, producing a pigeon breast, and small knobs may develop on the ends of the ribs. Occasionally, there may be spasms (tetany) due to the low level of calcium in the body.

Q: How is rickets treated?

A: Rickets is treated by giving a concentrated supply of vitamin D in addition to an adequate diet. Calcium supplements may also be prescribed to help to restore the normal calcium metabolism. Any deformities usually disappear if the condition is treated in the early stages.

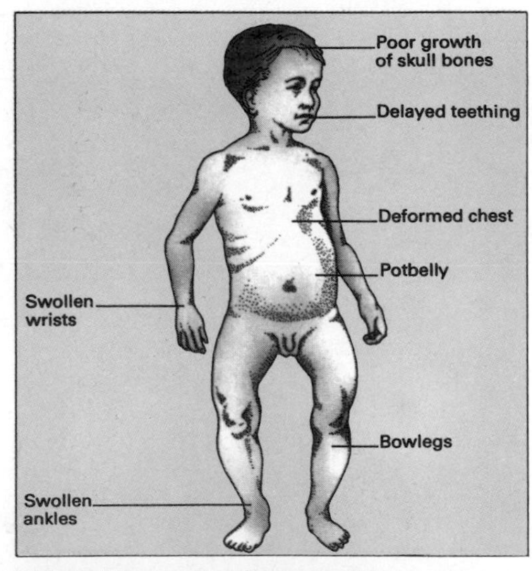

Rickets (vitamin D deficiency) affects bone formation, producing a variety of symptoms.

Rickettsia is a group of microorganisms that have characteristics of both bacteria and viruses. Rickettsia cause many diseases and usually are transmitted by parasites, such as fleas, lice, mites, and ticks. Rickettsial diseases tend to be of sudden onset and produce various symptoms, which are usually the result of blockage of the blood vessels by the rickettsia.

There are four main groups of rickettsial disease: the TYPHUS group; the spotted fever group, including ROCKY MOUNTAIN SPOTTED FEVER; Q FEVER; and trench fever, which is transmitted by lice and causes an illness that is similar to a mild form of Rocky Mountain spotted fever.

Rigor is a sudden attack of shivering with a high fever, followed by excessive perspiration. It is most commonly associated with the onset of an acute infectious illness, such as malaria or pneumonia.

Rigor mortis is the stiffening of the body after it dies. It may last for several hours before the body becomes relaxed again.

Ringing ears denotes a disorder of the ear. It is medically known as tinnitus. *See* TINNITUS.

Ringworm is an infection of the skin caused by a fungus from the group called dermatophytes. The three main types of these fungi are *Epidermophyton, Microsporum*, and *Trichophyton*. Typically they produce raised reddened rings or scaling of the skin as they feed on the dead skin tissue (epidermis), and affect the live tissue underneath.

Q: What areas of the body are likely to be affected by ringworm?

A: The feet may pick up the fungi *Trichophyton* in public places such as swimming pools or changing rooms. This form of the infection is known as ATHLETE'S FOOT (tinea pedis). Sometimes a secondary infection develops, causing CELLULITIS. The toenails develop a gnarled, thickened appearance if they become infected with tinea.

Ringworm of the nails (tinea unguium) is commonly caused by either the *Epidermophyton* or *Trichophyton* fungi. Jock itch (Dhobie itch) is a skin infection by the fungi *Epidermophyton* caused by a combination of tight underwear, obesity, and hot weather. Ringworm of the scalp (tinea capitis) usually is caused by the fungi *Microsporum*, and sometimes a variety of *Trichophyton*.

Q: How is ringworm treated?

A: A number of antifungal creams can be used to treat ringworm of the body, athlete's foot, and jock itch.

Ringworm is a contagious disease,

especially among children, so patients should avoid contact with other individuals wherever possible. Athlete's foot is extremely common and patients should not walk barefoot.

Rinne's test is a hearing test in which a vibrating tuning fork is placed alternately with its prongs near the auditory canal of the ear (air conduction), then with its base on the bone behind the ear (bone conduction). Normally the sound is heard for some time longer when the tuning fork is placed by the auditory canal. This is a positive result. In conductive deafness, the sound is heard longer through the bone. This is a negative result.

See also DEAFNESS.

Rio Grande fever is a local name for brucellosis. *See* BRUCELLOSIS.

Rocky Mountain spotted fever is an infectious rickettsial disease caused by the microorganism *Rickettsia rickettsii*, which is transmitted by ticks. It occurs in the western states of the U.S.A. and also in South America.

Q: *What are the symptoms of Rocky Mountain spotted fever?*

A: After an incubation period of about a week there is the sudden onset of a severe headache, muscle pains, and a high fever. Within four days, a rash appears on the arms and legs, and spreads rapidly to the rest of the body. Areas of the rash may coalesce and ulcerate. A dry, unproductive cough also may develop. In severe cases, the patient becomes delirious or comatose. The fever lasts between two and three weeks.

If untreated, various complications may develop, such as pneumonia, brain damage, and heart damage.

Q: *How is Rocky Mountain spotted fever treated?*

A: Immediate treatment with antibiotics, such as tetracycline, usually produces a rapid improvement. Hospitalization may be necessary in severe cases.

A vaccine against Rocky Mountain spotted fever is available.

Rodent ulcer is a form of skin cancer, sometimes called a basal cell carcinoma. It usually appears on the face, tip of the nose, eyelids, or ears. Although it is classified as a cancer, it spreads only by local ulceration and not by metastasis (spread of malignancy through the blood and lymph). Most patients are over the age of fifty.

At first a rodent ulcer appears as a small, pearl-like nodule which slowly grows and ulcerates in the centre to form a small scab. Early treatment produces a cure rate of over ninety-five per cent.

Romberg's sign is the inability to maintain balance when the feet are together and the eyes are shut. If the sense of balance is disturbed, as may occur with TABES DORSALIS, the person sways and may fall.

Rosacea, also called acne rosacea, is a skin inflammation associated with disorders of the sebaceous (oil secreting) glands in the skin. It usually affects the forehead, cheeks, nose, and chin.

Q: *What are the symptoms of rosacea?*

A: The chief symptom is frequent flushing of the skin, with residual redness. The sebaceous glands produce acne-like lumps, giving the skin a rough reddish appearance. Sometimes, there are also symptoms of seborrhoeic dermatitis with scurf on the scalp, and inflammation of the eyelids.

Q: *How is rosacea treated?*

A: Tetracycline drugs and other broad-spectrum antibiotics usually are effective. Corticosteroid creams should not be used for any length of time because they may damage the skin. Solutions containing sulphur may be beneficial.

See also RHINOPHYMA; SEBORRHOEA.

Roseola (roseola infantum), also known as exanthema subitum, is a disease of young children. The cause is not known, but it is thought to be a viral infection.

Q: *What are the symptoms of roseola infantum?*

A: After an incubation period of between four and seven days, there is the sudden onset of high fever, which may reach

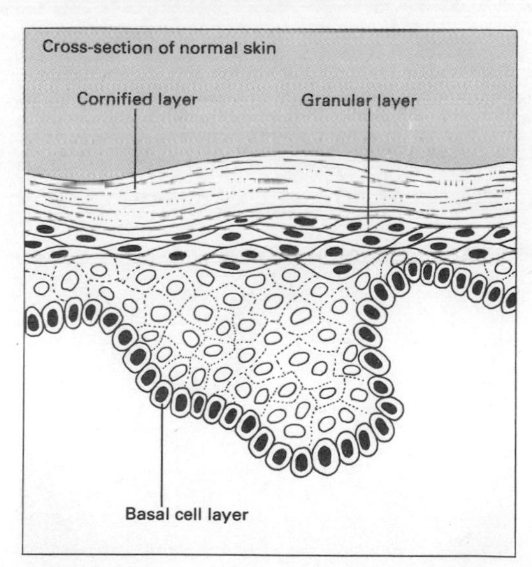

Rodent ulcer is a malignant growth that begins in the basal cells, usually on the face.

40.5°C (105°F). The fever usually lasts for three or four days, and may cause convulsions. The fever then disappears suddenly, and a pink rash appears. This occurs mainly on the body, but the limbs and face also may be mildly affected. The rash usually disappears within two days.

Q: How is roseola infantum treated?

A: Treatment is directed towards alleviating the symptoms. Aspirin or paracetamol may be prescribed to reduce the fever, and a doctor may also advise that the child is sponged with tepid water.

Anticonvulsant drugs may be given if the child has previously had convulsions.

Roundworms, also called nematode worms, are a group of parasitic worms. Members of this group that parasitize humans are found in most parts of the world. In some areas, usually those with poor sanitation, up to 90 per cent of the population may be infested. Roundworm infestations include ascariasis, enterobiasis, ankylostomiasis, strongyloidiasis, and trichuriasis.

Ascariasis is infestation of the small intestine with the giant intestinal roundworm (*Ascaris lumbricoides*). The adult worm produces eggs that pass out in the faeces. The infestation is transmitted by eating food that is contaminated by these eggs. When the eggs are swallowed, they develop into the adult ascaris worm. Ascariasis seldom causes symptoms. In some cases, there may be abdominal pain; fever; and coughing. Rarely, worms may block the bile or pancreatic ducts, causing jaundice or pancreatitis. The appendix may also become blocked. Treatment with drugs is usually effective.

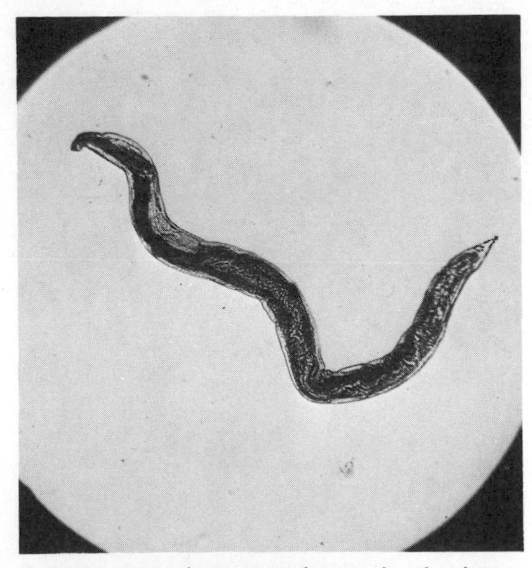

Roundworms: the eggs or larvae develop into adult worms in the intestine.

Enterobiasis and strongyloidiasis are infestations with *Enterobius vermicularis* and *Strongyloides stercoralis* respectively. These roundworms are commonly known as pinworms, seat worms or threadworms. The life cycles of both worms are similar. The adult worms infest the large intestine and the female emerges from the anus to lay eggs on the skin. The worms are spread either by direct contact between contaminated hands and the mouth, or by eating contaminated food. Treatment with piperazine, thiabendazole, or smilar drugs is usually effective. A doctor may advise treatment for the whole family.

Ancylostomiasis is infestation with hookworms (*Ancylostoma duodenale* and *Necator americanus*). The adult worms live in the intestines and discharge eggs in the faeces. The eggs develop into larvae in the soil, then penetrate the skin and travel in the blood to the lungs and then into the intestine, where they develop into adults, attach themselves to the intestinal wall and suck blood. Ancylostomiasis may cause a skin rash; a cough; anaemia from loss of blood; and occasionally, abdominal pain. In children, infestation with a large number of worms may cause malnourishment, which may affect the child's growth. Treatment with bephenium hydroxymaphthoate or thiabendazole is usually effective. Anaemia may be treated with iron tablets.

Trichuriasis is infestation with the whipworm (*Trichuris trichiuria*), which lives in the intestine. It is caught by eating food infected with eggs, or larvae that have developed in moist soil. Trichuriasis may not produce any symptoms. Occasionally, there may be abdominal pain and bloodstained diarrhoea. In children, prolapse of the rectum may occur. Trichuriasis is often difficult to cure, but drugs, such as mebendazole, may be effective.

See also OXYURIASIS; STRONGYLOIDES; TOXOCARIASIS; TRICHINOSIS; TRICHURIASIS.

Rubella is the medical term for German measles. *See* GERMAN MEASLES.

Rubeola is the medical term for measles. *See* MEASLES.

Running nose is a discharge from one or both nostrils. It results from any condition that causes inflammation of the lining of the nose (rhinitis). The most common cause is the COMMON COLD, although it also may be caused by an ALLERGY or SINUSITIS. A running nose following a head injury may be a sign of a fractured skull in which the cerebrospinal fluid leaks into the nose. The fluid may then become infected, and the condition can result in MENINGITIS.

Q: How is a running nose treated?

A: Decongestant nasal drops and sprays may relieve a running nose, but they should not be used for more than about three days. Antihistamines may also help by reducing the amount of mucus produced. A doctor should be consulted if a running nose persists for more than three or four days.

See also CATARRH; NOSEBLEED; RHINITIS.

Rupture is the bursting of an organ or tissue, such as an inflamed appendix. It also is a common term for a hernia. *See* HERNIA.

Ryle's tube is a thin rubber tube that is used to administer test meals and to empty the stomach after surgical operations. It is one of the many types of naso-gastric tubes. It may be inserted through the nose or through the mouth. One end of the tube is slightly enlarged so that it can be swallowed easily.

S

Sabin's vaccine is a vaccine against POLIOMYELITIS. It is a preparation of one or a combination of the three poliomyelitis viruses, which have been modified so that they confer immunity without causing any symptoms. Sabin's vaccine is taken orally and is considered to be the most effective form of poliomyelitis immunization.

Sacroiliac is the area of the body related to the sacroiliac joint that connects with the two large ilium bones on each side of the sacrum at the base of the spine. Strong ligaments surround the joint; these can become strained, causing backache and pain related to the movement of the joint. Inflammation of the sacroiliac joint is a symptom of ANKYLOSING SPONDYLITIS and other RHEUMATIC DISEASES of the joints.

Sacrum is a triangular bone that forms the rear part of the PELVIS. It binds the two hip bones together, and transmits the weight of the body from the spine to the pelvis.

The sacrum is made up of five sacral vertebrae, which are fused together to form a single bone. At the lower end it forms a joint with the COCCYX. The upper end is joined to the fifth lumbar vertebra with an intervening disc. On each side are the SACROILIAC joints with the two ilium bones of the pelvis.

SPONDYLOLISTHESIS, a congenital condition in which the lumbar vertebra tends to slip forward onto the sacrum, may occur. The result can be chronic backache.

Sadism is a sexual practice by individuals who enjoy inflicting pain upon others.

In normal love play, sexual partners quite often inflict slight pain upon each other and this may form part of the mutual pleasure. But extreme forms of sexual activity in which sadism plays a part is considered to be abnormal.

See also MASOCHISM.

Safe period is the period during a woman's menstrual cycle when conception is least likely to occur. *See* CONTRACEPTION.

Saint Vitus's dance is another name for Sydenham's chorea. *See* CHOREA.

Salicylate is a salt of salicylic acid. The most common compound of salicylic acid is acetylsalicylic acid (aspirin).

See also ASPIRIN.

Saline commonly refers to a solution containing salt (sodium chloride). Physiological saline is a solution of sodium chloride that is of the same concentration as the body fluids (isotonic). This solution may be given by intravenous infusion to replace salt that is lost either during surgery or as a result of shock.

Saliva is a watery, slightly alkaline fluid that is secreted by the three pairs of salivary glands in the mouth. Saliva helps to keep the mouth clean, aids speech, lubricates food, and makes taste possible (because the sensory nerves for taste respond only to dissolved substances). It contains various salts and the enzyme ptyalin that begins the digestion of starch.

Salivary glands are located in the mouth. They produce saliva. The two parotid glands are in front of each ear; the two submanr-

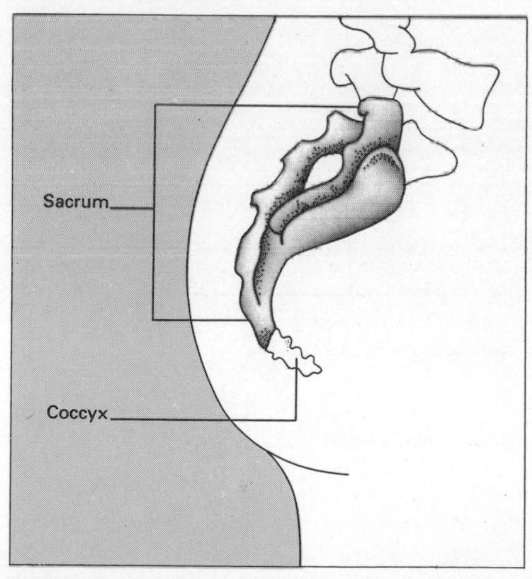

Sacrum is a triangle of five fused bones at the lower end of the spine, above the coccyx.

dibular glands are, like the two sublingual glands, situated mainly on the floor of the mouth beneath the tongue; and the small buccal glands are in the mucous membranes of the cheeks and lips. The salivary glands can be affected by viral infection (such as mumps), bacterial infection, stone formation (SIALOLITHIASIS), or cancer.

Salk vaccine is a vaccine against poliomyelitis. It contains three types of dead poliomyelitis virus. It has to be injected and has now been largely superseded by the orally administered SABIN'S VACCINE.

Salmonella is a genus of rod-shaped bacteria, some species of which can cause disease in humans. The most serious salmonella bacteria cause TYPHOID and PARATYPHOID fevers. Other salmonella infections may cause gastroenteritis, which may vary from a mild to a severe, and occasionally fatal, form of food poisoning.

Q: What are the symptoms of salmonella gastroenteritis?

A: The symptoms may vary from mild abdominal pain with occasional diarrhoea, to extremely severe vomiting and persistent diarrhoea. They usually occur within about two days of eating contaminated food. The severe form may result in shock due to fluid loss, requiring immediate hospitalization. In some cases, a fever develops, but this rarely lasts for more than about a day.

Occasionally, the infection may spread into the bloodstream (septicaemia) and cause localized abscesses in other parts of the body. Deaths from salmonella gastroenteritis are usually confined to the young, the elderly, and those who already have a serious underlying physical disorder.

Q: How is salmonella gastroenteritis treated?

A: Treatment is directed toward alleviating the symptoms and includes plenty of fluids, a bland diet, and antispasmodic drugs to relieve abdominal cramps. Generally, antibiotic drugs are not prescribed because they may prolong the course of the illness. However, antibiotics become necessary if the patient develops septicaemia.

If a large amount of fluid has been lost by vomiting and diarrhoea the patient may be given fluids intravenously to replace the lost fluid. If the patient has localized abscesses, surgery may also be necessary.

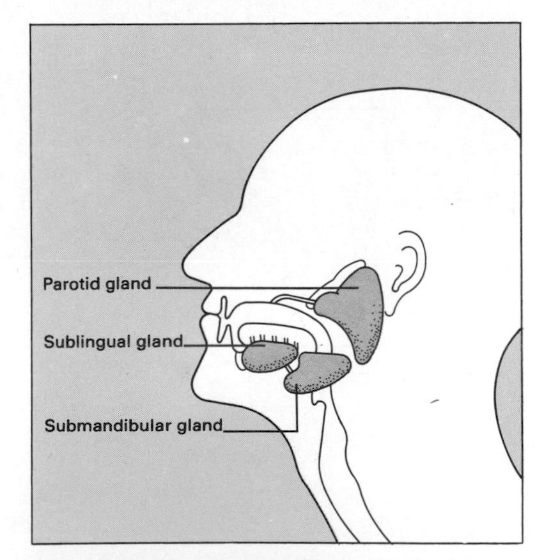

Salivary glands secrete saliva to moisten the mouth and help begin the digestion of food.

Salpingectomy is the surgical removal of a fallopian tube (oviduct). One tube may have to be removed because of an ECTOPIC PREGNANCY. Both tubes may have to be removed if continued abdominal pain occurs because of chronic salpingitis (*see* SALPINGITIS). The operation also is performed as a means of sterilization. *See* STERILIZATION.

Salpingitis is inflammation of the fallopian tubes. It may affect only one tube, but usually both are involved. The surrounding tissues and the ovaries also may become infected and inflamed.

Salpingitis most commonly is caused by the spread of infection following sexual intercourse. A venereal disease such as gonorrhoea is one such infection. It may also occur following childbirth, an abortion, or sometimes after the insertion of an IUD (intrauterine device). Rarely, salpingitis occurs in young girls and adolescents as a result of tuberculosis.

Q: What are the symptoms of salpingitis?

A: Acute salpingitis occurs suddenly and produces severe abdominal pain; a purulent vaginal discharge; fever; and, occasionally, vomiting. Chronic salpingitis may occur after treatment for the acute form of the disease. With chronic salpingitis, there may be a dull abdominal ache, irregular and painful periods, and pain while having sexual intercourse. Many women also feel vaguely ill, with backache, fatigue, and weight loss.

Q: How is salpingitis treated?

A: Immediate treatment with antibiotics is nearly always successful in curing the infection. Severe cases may need surgical removal to avoid infertility.

Chronic salpingitis is difficult to treat because the fallopian tubes become scarred, inflamed, and blocked. A long course of antibiotics is usually prescribed, and the patient may also be advised to abstain from sexual intercourse for several weeks. The sexual partner of a woman with salpingitis should also be examined and, if necessary, treated.

Sandfly fever is a virus infection, with high temperature, transmitted by the sandfly (*Phlebotomus papatasii*) and similar species that are common around the Mediterranean and the Asian subcontinent in hot, dry weather.

Saphenous vein is one of the two long surface veins in the leg.

The great saphenous vein runs from the inner side of the ankle to the groin, where it dips down to join the femoral vein. The small saphenous vein runs from behind the outer part of the ankle to join the popliteal vein in the tissues behind the knee.

See also VARICOSE VEIN.

Sarcoidosis is a condition of unknown origin in which areas of scar tissue are formed in many parts of the body, most commonly in the lungs, liver, eyes, skin, and the lymphatic system. It is also known as sarcoid.

Q: What are the symptoms of sarcoidosis?

A: Frequently there are no symptoms at all. Diagnosis is often made from a routine chest X-ray or a physical examination in which the patient's lymph nodes are found to be enlarged. Some patients, however, have symptoms of fever, breathlessness, vague muscle aching, joint pains, and skin lesions (ERYTHEMA NODOSUM). The liver may become affected in a minor way and, rarely, cardiac involvement may result in heart failure.

Q: How is sarcoidosis treated?

A: The aim of treatment is to prevent further damage to body tissue. If the patient has no symptoms and there is no evidence of damage, regular examination is all that is necessary. Corticosteroid drug treatment may have to be given for patients with severe symptoms.

Sarcoma is a malignant (cancerous) tumour formed from connective tissue. The usual treatment for sarcoma is surgical removal, often followed by radiotherapy or, in the case of bone tumours (Ewing's sarcoma), by a combination of radiotherapy and multiple-drug chemotherapy. *See* TUMOUR.

Scab is a protective layer of dried serum and blood, usually discharged from a wound. The tissues beneath the scab, thus protected, are allowed to heal; the scab falls off when healing is complete.

Scabicides are drugs used in the treatment of scabies. Benzyl benzoate and gamma benzene hexachloride are commonly used scabicides. *See* SCABIES.

Scabies is a contagious skin infestation, caused by the itch mite *Sarcoptes scabiei.* The female mite burrows beneath the skin and lays eggs. These in turn produce larvae which mature and mate, and the females form tunnel-like nests. The victim's body suffers an allergic reaction to the mite in the form of an itching rash of the eczema type, which may be widespread. The mite burrows in the hands, fingers, wrists, pubic areas and, sometimes, the soles of the feet.

Q: What are the symptoms of scabies?

A: For the first month following contact, there are no symptoms. During this period, the eggs of the mite hatch and develop into adults. The female lays several eggs a day for several weeks, so that by the end of the month many more females have burrowed beneath the skin. A rash and intense itching then occur as an allergic reaction.

Q: How is scabies treated?

A: The patient takes a bath and is painted over the whole body surface (excluding the eyes, nose, and mouth) with SCABICIDES. This treatment is repeated twice at daily intervals. A doctor may prescribe antihistamine drugs to relieve the allergic reaction. Usually the patient's family has to be treated as well, because the infection spreads very easily.

Scald is a burn to skin or flesh by hot vapour or liquid. *See* First Aid, p.524.

Scalene node biopsy is a diagnostic proce-

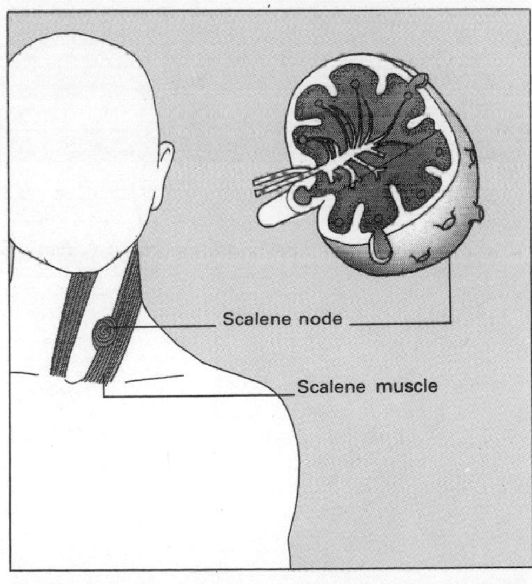

Scalene node, a lymph node in the neck, may be examined by a scalene node biopsy.

dure. It is an operation to remove part or all of a lymph gland from behind the scalene muscles in the neck. The gland is then subject to microscopic examination.

Scalp is a part of the covering of the skull consisting of hair, skin, and underlying layers of muscle and fibrous tissue (fascia).

Scalpel is a knife with a short, thin blade used during a surgical operation.

Scaphoid is one of eight small bones in the WRIST. It is jointed to the radius bone in the forearm, and is one of the bones most likely to be fractured in a fall.

See also COLLES' FRACTURE.

Scapula, or shoulder blade, is one of a pair of flat triangular bones that, together with the upper bone of the arm (humerus), forms the SHOULDER joint. The ball-and-socket joint at the shoulder allows a wide range of movement, activated by muscles at the front and back of the chest wall, as well as those from the scapula.

Scar, known medically as cicatrix, is a healed wound, burn, or incision. It is composed of tough fibrous tissue.

Scar tissue inside the body seldom causes any problems. But adhesions (long strips of scar tissue) in the abdomen may distort the intestine and lead to intestinal obstruction.

Scar tissue on the skin may become abnormally thickened, raised, or red. This is known as a KELOID scar. Most unsightly scars can be removed or treated by PLASTIC SURGERY.

Scarlatina. *See* SCARLET FEVER.

Scarlet fever, or scarlatina, is an infectious disease caused by bacteria called group A beta haemolytic streptococci. It may develop after a sore throat or acute tonsillitis. Scarlet fever can be spread by contaminated food or by infected droplets in the air.

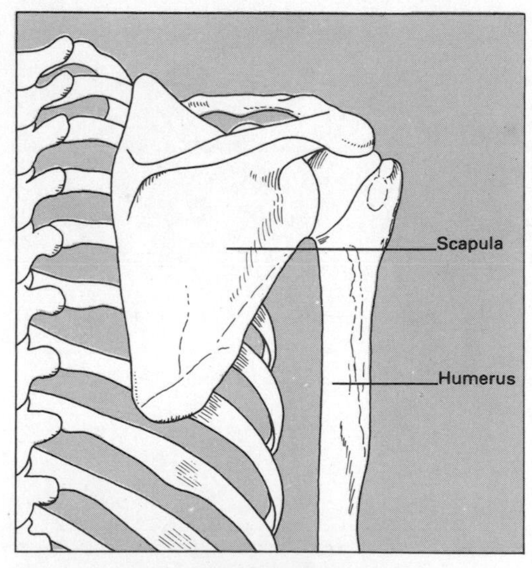

Scapula is a flat, triangular bone that forms the posterior part of the shoulder.

The symptoms usually take from three to five days to appear. The patient is contagious while the bacteria are still in the nose and throat, which may be for two or three weeks. Some persons become carriers of the infection for several months.

Q: What are the symptoms of scarlet fever?

A: There is usually a sudden fever and a sore throat. There may also be vomiting, diarrhoea, and a severe headache. About two days after infection, a rash of small red spots appears, initially on the neck and chest but spreading rapidly to the rest of the body and limbs. Typically the face is flushed, with a pale area around the mouth. The surface of the tongue is coated with small red spots protruding from a milky white background. The rash usually lasts for three or four days, after which the other symptoms gradually disappear. Often the skin flakes off after an attack, and sometimes there is considerable, temporary loss of hair.

Q: How is scarlet fever treated?

A: Penicillin or other antibiotics are usually given for ten days. The full course recommended by a doctor must be completed to prevent complications, such as ear infections and pneumonia, from developing. Aspirin may also be prescribed to relieve the fever, headache, and sore throat.

Schick test is a method of testing immunity to diphtheria. A small amount of diphtheria toxin is injected into the skin. If immunity to diphtheria is not present, a small red inflamed area develops on the skin.

Schistosomiasis, also known as bilharzia, is a parasitic disease that occurs mostly in Africa, South America, and the Far East. It can be caught by swimming in infected water.

The worm responsible for schistosomiasis is a species of fluke (*Schistosoma*), which uses freshwater snails and humans as hosts.

The symptoms are fever, cough, muscle pains, and skin irritation, followed by blood in the urine or faeces.

Schistosomiasis is difficult to treat. Special drugs are available but can be given only by intravenous or intramuscular injection, and must be used with care because of their many toxic effects. Surgery may be needed if internal organs are severely scarred.

Schizoid is a psychological term that describes a personality type. Schizoid persons are often considered to be emotionally withdrawn, preferring to keep their feelings to themselves.

Some people believe that being schizoid is a personality disorder similar to SCHIZOPHRENIA, but this is not necessarily so.

Schizophrenia, previously known as dementia praecox, is a complex group of related, but poorly defined, psychotic disorders. It occurs most commonly in young adults.

In schizophrenia, there is a disorganization of the thought processes so that abnormal emotional responses result. Logical thought is disrupted and socially unacceptable conclusions are reached. Normal life becomes complicated, and the patient enters a secret world of hallucinations and deluded thoughts, which may manifest itself as PARANOIA.

Often the individual who ultimately develops schizophrenia is shy, withdrawn, and finds difficulty in making friends. But such characteristics do not automatically imply that such a person is schizophrenic.

Hospitalization is needed for the acute form of schizophrenia. Prolonged drug treatment and sometimes ECT can control the disorder.

Sciatica is pain along the course of the sciatic nerve, which serves the buttock and the back of the thigh and leg. It is usually caused by pressure on the sciatic nerve which may be the result of a slipped disc; osteoarthritis of the spine; congenital anomalies of the spine, such as spondylolisthesis; or tumours of the spinal canal. *See* SLIPPED DISC.

Scirrhus is a hard, cancerous TUMOUR.

Sclera is the white, fibrous, outer coat of the eyeball. It forms the visible white of the eye, and surrounds the optic nerve at the back of the eyeball.

Scleroderma is an uncommon progressive disease that involves the fibrous tissue of the skin, joints, and internal organs, particularly the lungs, kidneys, and intestine. The cause of scleroderma is not known, but is thought to be a form of autoimmune disease. It is more common in women than men, and most cases occur during middle age.

Q: What are the symptoms of scleroderma?

A: The symptoms usually develop gradually. Initially, the fingers and toes become pale and painful when cold (RAYNAUD'S PHENOMENON). There may also be tightening and thinning of facial skin, difficulty in swallowing, pain in the joints, swelling of the hands, and muscle weakness. If the lungs or the heart are affected, PLEURISY, PERICARDITIS, or HEART FAILURE may occur.

Q: How is scleroderma treated?

A: There is no specific treatment. Scleroderma may occur in a mild form that is compatible with a long life, but it often causes early death because of the involvement of the internal organs. The symptoms can often be alleviated. Corticosteroid drugs may be prescribed to reduce the pain and swelling in the joints. Physiotherapy may help to preserve muscle strength.

Sclerosis is hardening of any body structure.

See also ARTERIOSCLEROSIS; MULTIPLE SCLEROSIS.

Scolex is the head end of a tapeworm, by which the worm attaches itself to the intestinal wall using small hooks or suckers. *See* TAPEWORMS.

Scoliosis is a curvature of the spine to one side. It may be caused by an alteration in the position of the underlying bones or by a reaction of the spinal muscles, both of which make the spine temporarily change position.

Treatment depends on the cause.

See also KYPHOSIS; LORDOSIS; VON RECKLINGHAUSEN'S DISEASE.

Scotoma is a loss of part of the field of vision, often experienced as a blind spot. Causes include a lesion within the eyeball, choroiditis, or haemorrhage. Migraine may cause flashes of light to be seen. Treatment depends on the cause.

Scrofula is an old term for tuberculosis of the lymph glands in the neck. It is often accompanied by ulceration of the overlying skin. *See* TUBERCULOSIS.

Scrotum is the bag of skin that contains the testicles, epididymides, and part of the spermatic cords. The skin of the scrotum contains muscles that can raise or lower the testicles, thereby keeping them at the optimum temperature for sperm production.

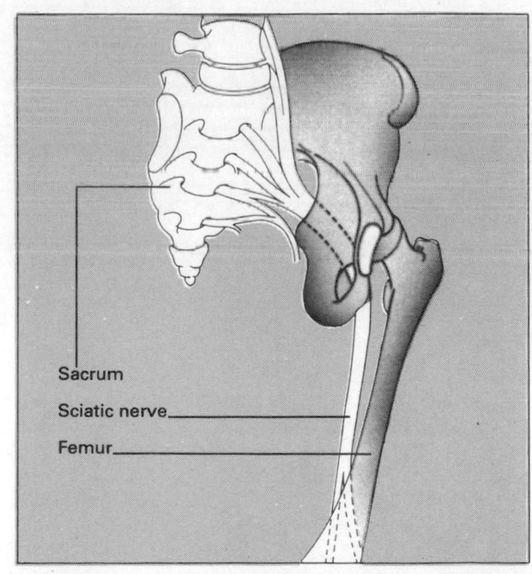

Sciatica is pain anywhere along the path of the sciatic nerve that runs down the leg.

Any skin condition may affect the scrotum. The commonest disorders are a SEBACEOUS CYST and tinea cruris (*see* RINGWORM).

See also TESTIS.

Scurvy is a deficiency disease that is caused by a lack of vitamin C (ascorbic acid) in a person's diet. Vitamin C is essential for the maintenance of the normal structure of the connective tissues. Vitamin C deficiency results in weakening of the blood capillaries, with subsequent bleeding, and defects of the bones.

Unboiled tomato juice, orange juice, or fresh fruit can be taken regularly to prevent scurvy.

Q: What are the symptoms of scurvy?

A: Scurvy in infants may cause irritability, fever, loss of appetite, and failure to gain weight. The infant may keep his or her limbs motionless because of pain caused by bleeding under the periosteum (the tissue layer covering the bones). The infant may also be anaemic.

In adults, there may be a delay of between three and twelve months after the onset of severe vitamin C deficiency before any symptoms appear. Initially there may be lethargy, irritability, weight loss, and aching of the joints. As the disease develops, there may be bleeding under the skin, particularly under the nails; the gums swell and bleed; bruising may occur spontaneously; and wounds may not heal.

Q: How is scurvy treated?

A: Treatment involves the administration of large amounts of vitamin C until the symptoms have disappeared. In addition to a balanced diet, vitamin C supplements may also be necessary for several months after the symptoms have disappeared.

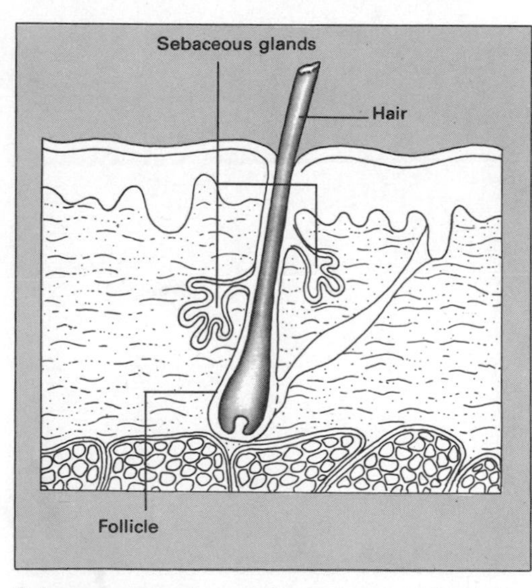

Sebaceous glands are situated around the hair shafts, which they lubricate with sebum.

Seasickness. *See* MOTION SICKNESS.

Sebaceous cyst, sometimes called a wen, is a swelling in the skin. It occurs when the duct of a sebaceous gland becomes blocked. The gland continues to produce waxy sebum, and becomes enlarged. Sebaceous cysts can occur on any hair-covered part of the body, but are most common on the scalp. They grow slowly, and only very rarely become malignant (cancerous).

See also CYST.

Sebaceous gland is a small gland in the skin. Sebaceous glands occur most commonly on the face, nose, scalp, over the shoulders, and in the genital area, but do not occur on the palms of the hands or on the soles of the feet. The glands produce SEBUM, a greasy secretion that conditions the skin.

Seborrhoea is a skin disorder caused by overactivity of the sebaceous glands. It results in dandruff (scaling of the skin of the scalp), often accompanied by blepharitis (scaling and redness of the eyelids) and slight greasiness of the face. In infants, the crusting of the scalp (cradle cap) is a form of seborrhoea. Seborrhoea is not serious, and tends to occur more in winter than in summer.

Q: How is seborrhoea treated?

A: Various commercial shampoos, some containing selenium, are available. These should be used two or three times a week. Scalp solutions containing corticosteroid drugs may be prescribed to control the condition until there is improvement. An infant's scalp needs only oiling and baby shampoo.

See also DANDRUFF.

Sebum is a thick, slightly greasy secretion that is produced by the SEBACEOUS GLANDS in the skin.

Secretion is the release of any substance produced by body cells. For example, hormones are secreted into the bloodstream, and saliva is secreted into the salivary ducts.

Sedatives are drugs that are used to reduce excitement or irritability. In small doses, they usually calm a patient; larger doses may produce sleep.

See also HYPNOTICS; TRANQUILLIZERS.

Sedimentation rate, or erythrocyte sedimentation rate (ESR), is a type of blood test. It is performed by placing blood containing an anticoagulant in a long, narrow glass tube and observing the speed at which the red blood cells settle and form a sediment at the bottom.

Faster sedimentation rates occur in the

presence of any serious infection, malignancy, or inflammatory disorder. The test does not diagnose any particular disorder, but indicates that one may be present.

Seizure is the sudden onset of a condition or illness. The term is, however, most commonly used to mean a convulsion of epilepsy, but can also refer to the rigor (shivering attack) that may accompany the start of an acute feverish illness, such as malaria. *See* CONVULSION; EPILEPSY.

Semen is the thick, creamy secretion produced by the male on ejaculation. It consists of sperm and the fluids secreted by the prostate gland and seminal vesicles. *See* SPERM.

Semicircular canal is one of the three fluid-filled tubes that form part of the inner ear. They are arranged at right angles to each other, one for each plane of movement. The canals are the body's organs of balance (*see* BALANCE). Disorders that affect the semicircular canals, such as LABYRINTHITIS and MÉNIÈRE'S DISEASE, usually cause vertigo and disturb the patient's sense of balance.

Seminal vesicles are two small pouch-like structures in which the SPERM of a male is stored. They are situated next to the prostate gland and at the end of the vas deferens. They produce secretions that keep the sperm active and alive.

Seminoma is the most common form of cancer of the testicle. It usually occurs in males between the ages of thirty and forty. *See* CANCER.

Senescence is the process of growing old. It usually refers to the later stages, when aging causes a failure of the normal functioning of the body.

Senility is, like senescence, the aging process of the body and mind, and is commonly associated with people of great age. Senility also involves a gradual deterioration of physical strength and co-ordination, accompanied by mental deterioration.

Sepsis is the presence in the body or bloodstream of disease-producing microorganisms, such as bacteria or viruses. It may result in abscesses throughout the body or blood poisoning. *See* ABSCESS; BLOOD POISONING; PUS.

Septal defect is a hole or some other defect in a septum or membranous wall dividing an organ or structure. Usually, the term refers to an anomaly present at birth in the septum between the two sides of the heart. *See* CONGENITAL HEART DISEASE.

The diagnosis may be confirmed, either in infancy or later in life, by passing a catheter (a pliable tube) into the heart and observing that it can pass through the septal defect into the other side of the heart. Septal defects of the heart may be accompanied by other congenital anomalies of the valves, and they are repaired by heart surgery.

Septic is any condition that produces pus, and is caused by sepsis. *See* PUS; SEPSIS.

Septicaemia is SEPSIS occurring in the blood. *See* BLOOD POISONING.

Septum is a thin layer of membranous tissue that forms a dividing wall between the two parts of an organ. There are septa between layers of muscle, between various parts of the brain, and between the two halves of the scrotum. Most commonly, the term refers to the division between the two halves of the heart, the atrial septum and the ventricular septum. A septum is also present between the two halves of the nose, formed partly by cartilage and partly by bone. *See* DEVIATED NASAL SEPTUM.

Serology is the study of SERUM and the investigation of IMMUNITY to disease.

Serum is the clear, watery fluid that remains after blood has clotted; it is blood plasma without the clotting components. Serum from persons or animals that are immune to a particular disease (antiserum) can be injected into a patient to confer temporary, passive IMMUNITY.

Q: Are there any possible dangers from the use of an antiserum?

A: Yes. Until recently, many antisera were prepared from animals, and these often produced an allergic reaction known as SERUM SICKNESS. Now, however, many antisera are prepared from humans, which greatly reduces the likelihood of producing serum sickness.

Serum sickness is a form of allergic reaction

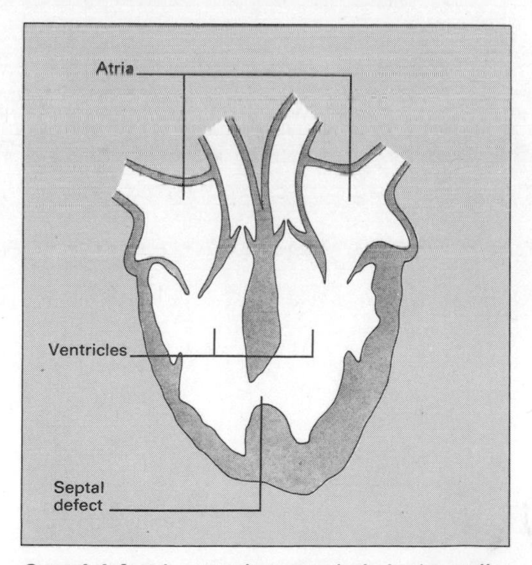

Septal defect is a weakness or hole in the wall that separates the two ventricles of the heart.

that may occur one to two weeks after the injection of a serum. Many drugs, including penicillin, occasionally produce a condition indistinguishable from serum sickness.

Q: What are the symptoms of serum sickness?

A: A skin rash and intense irritation (urticaria) are usually the first signs. These are commonly accompanied by joint stiffness, swelling, and a mild fever that lasts several days. Frequently the lymph glands enlarge, particularly near the site of the injection, causing a generalized aching.

In severe forms of serum sickness, the heart muscles may be involved (myocarditis), and very rarely the kidneys are affected. Kidney involvement causes a form of nephritis, with ankle swelling and high blood pressure. Occasionally polyneuritis occurs, and recovery from this form of the disorder is seldom complete. However, most patients with serum sickness make a rapid and complete recovery within four weeks.

Q: How is serum sickness treated?

A: Treatment depends on the doctor. Injections of antihistamines followed by doses of antihistamines by mouth usually control the irritation and joint stiffness. If these measures fail, corticosteroid drugs may be given to decrease the symptoms. Drug treatment is usually continued until the symptoms cease. *See* ANAPHYLAXIS.

Sex hormones are the hormones produced by the gonads: the ovaries in females and the testicles (testes) in males. Their production is under the control of the pituitary gland at the base of the brain. The main hormones produced by the ovaries are oestrogens (*see* OESTROGEN) and PROGESTERONE; the testes produce TESTOSTERONE. Small amounts of sex hormones are also produced by the adrenal glands.

See also HORMONES.

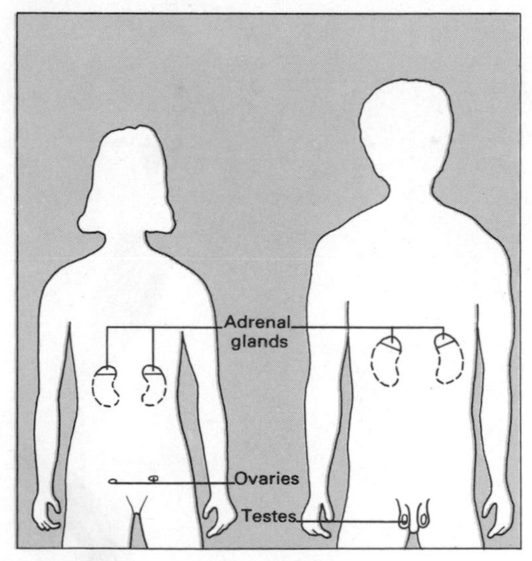

Sex hormones are produced by the ovaries, testes, and adrenal glands.

Sexual intercourse, also known as coitus, is the physical act of sexual union between a man and woman. It begins with the insertion of the man's penis into the woman's vagina and the beginning of physical movements, partly voluntary and partly reflex. The act usually ends with the male orgasm and ejaculation of semen and may be accompanied by the female orgasm.

See also SEXUAL PROBLEMS.

Sexually transmitted diseases. *See* VENEREAL DISEASES.

A talk about Sexual problems

Sexual problems. There is some dispute as to what is normal in sexual experience and what is abnormal. Much depends on individual sexual development, which can be affected by various factors, including genetic inheritance.

Healthy sexuality depends on age, culture, individual desire, and physical and psychological attitudes to sex. Feelings of sexuality begin in infancy and develop along with physical, social, psychological, and instinctive characteristics, all of them unique to a particular individual.

Sexual problems may arise because of a physical disorder, or because of psychological disturbances during growth and development, or in a relationship with another person or persons. The causes are varied and complex.

Q: What physical disorders cause sexual problems?

A: Sexual precocity, a very rare form of early puberty and sexual development, can give rise to sexual problems. It is caused by hormone disorders in childhood. Some people are born as hermaphrodites, with a combination of the sexual characteristics of both sexes. There may also be other genetic anomalies that result in abnormal physical or sexual features. This makes it difficult for them to have a normal sex life (*see* HERMAPHRODITE).

Painful intercourse (DYSPAREUNIA) is a disorder that can be caused by a tight hymen, vaginitis (inflammation of the vagina), or salpingitis (inflammation of the fallopian tubes). After menopause, painful intercourse may occur because vaginal secretions dry up slightly.

Painful intercourse in a man is often caused by balanitis, an infection of the end of the penis. Polyneuritis and diabetes mellitus can cause some men to fail to achieve an erection.

Q: What psychological disorders cause sexual problems?

A: Psychological disorders are the most common causes of sexual problems. They usually arise when there is difficulty in the relationship between the two people concerned. There is often a failure to understand each other's needs and desires, and this can become combined with feelings of guilt or anxiety that cause impotence in men and frigidity in women. Once sexual intercourse has failed, the symptoms tend to get worse.

Vaginismus is a severe form of frigidity in which the woman's vaginal muscles go into spasm, preventing penetration by the man's penis (*see* VAGINISMUS).

A common male problem is premature ejaculation, in which a man has an orgasm before the woman has become sexually satisfied. Thus, the man may feel he has failed, and the woman is left unsatisfied and frustrated.

Q: How are frigidity, impotence, and premature ejaculation dealt with?

A: The key to mutual pleasure is to relax and not to be overconcerned with orgasm. More time should be spent in pre-intercourse love play. Some women always fail to reach an orgasm, and this is usually because of psychological factors, such as the fear of becoming pregnant, or feelings of guilt or inferiority.

It is necessary for a man and a woman to have consideration for each other if impotence or frigidity are not to interfere with their sex life. Practice of gentle stimulation by the woman may help the man to control his orgasm. Giving a frigid woman gentle massage and sexual foreplay help the woman to experience sexual pleasure and even orgasm. *See* FRIGIDITY; IMPOTENCE.

Q: What other sexual problems may have a psychological basis?

A: Many sexual problems arise because of a failure in normal psychosexual development. Many variants of sexual behaviour are thought to develop from early childhood. Most people enjoy the touch of soft materials, such as fur, and these certainly encourage sexuality. But when a person is obsessed with materials such as rubber or leather, for example, and it is the sole source of sexual gratification (fetishism), it is a marked abnormality.

Some people, particularly men, remain at an infantile stage of sexuality. They are usually terrified of any form of physical sexual relationship with the opposite sex. But they still have a sex drive, and the only way they can get satisfaction is by frightening, as opposed to loving, the opposite sex. For example, some men get sexual gratification by indecently exposing themselves to unsuspecting women. Another form of retarded sexual development is paedophilia, in which loving and often sexual relationships develop between an adult and a child.

The problem of homosexuality is discussed elsewhere (*see* HOMOSEXUALITY). Everyone has some degree of homosexual feeling, but it may become increased to such an extent in some people that they appear entirely homosexual. But this also means that a few people fall in the centre of sexual feelings, halfway between homosexual and heterosexual.

Q: How can such psychological causes of sexual problems be treated?

A: It is important to discuss the problems with someone who has an understanding of sexual disorders, and who can offer reassurance. A couple who fear that they are in some way abnormal may be relieved to find that problems of this kind are fairly common and that they are relatively easy to treat.

Q: Can problems resulting from a failure of psychosexual development be treated?

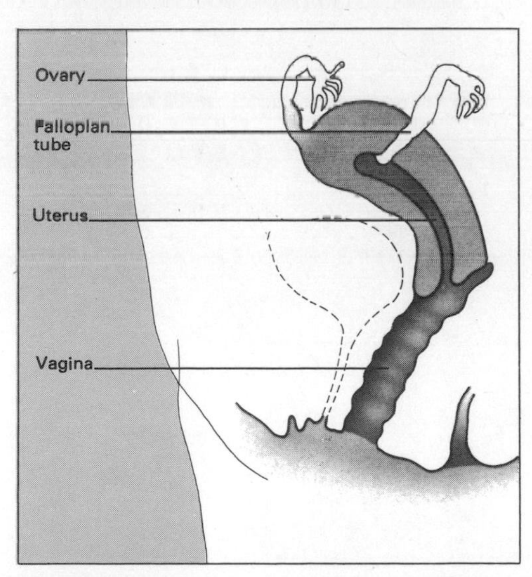

Sexual problems in women may be caused by infection of the genitalia.

Sexual problems

A: It is often extremely difficult to treat developmental sexual problems because they have become deep-seated by the time of adulthood. They are unlikely to be detected early enough in adolescence for psychotherapy and psychoanalysis to have much effect. Sexual problems can cause great distress to the individual concerned, and various forms of treatment (including types of behaviour therapy, such as aversion therapy and hypnotherapy) are often unsuccessful. Treatment with female sex hormones can reduce the sex drive in men who have committed sex crimes, although there are certain risks to the patient.

Q: Can excessive sex drive be a problem?

A: Yes. Increased libido (sex drive) can be associated with psychotic disorders, such as manic-depressive illness and some personality disorders, as well as with psychotic illness. This can lead to violently antisocial behaviour, including rape. In most people, however, an increase in libido accompanies a feeling of well-being and is controlled by normal social constraints.

Promiscuity is not necessarily the result of an increase in libido, and it usually indicates that the individual has problems maintaining any form of secure relationship.

Q: What sexual problems occur in adolescence?

A: The sexual problems of adolescence usually centre on sexual ignorance, fear of venereal disease, and anxiety about sexual success. Masturbation is a common form of sexual outlet that may induce fears and anxieties (*see* MASTURBATION). Most adolescents also go through a homosexual phase, and may fear that the feeling is going to be permanent (*see* HOMOSEXUALITY). Such problems can be helped by discussion with parents, and by routine education about the basic biological facts of life.

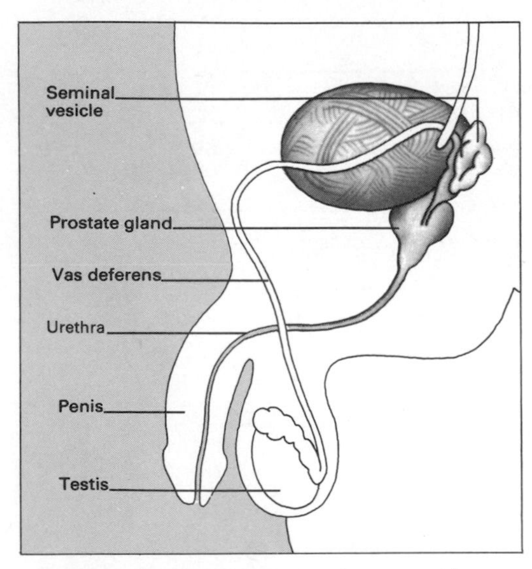

Sexual problems in men may be caused by infection of the genitalia.

Q: What sexual problems occur in the elderly?

A: Sexual intercourse may continue into old age provided the partners are healthy. The most common problems arise after an illness or operation; the break from regular sexual intercourse may be sufficient to stop it completely. This may not be a problem to the person who has had the illness, but it may create frustration in the healthy partner.

The best way to deal with this situation is frank discussion between the partners in the hope that either sexual intercourse will be resumed or the less fit partner will realize that some form of sexual stimulation is still necessary.

If regular intercourse has been maintained, there are seldom any problems, apart from a slight dryness of the vagina after menopause. Lubricant jellies or a cream containing oestrogens can be prescribed by a doctor.

Q: Does any form of drug treatment help in treating sexual problems?

A: Yes. There are drugs that reduce the sex drive, and they are sometimes used in the treatment of sexual deviants, such as paedophiles and psychopaths.

Depressed individuals can have their libido increased by antidepressant drugs. Small amounts of the male sex hormone testosterone are sometimes prescribed during menopause to increase a woman's sex drive. However, it is more usual for hormone replacement therapy to be used for some months during menopause.

Sheehan's syndrome is a rare condition in which there is a reduction in the production of pituitary hormones as a result of shock or bleeding following childbirth. This is caused by thrombosis of the blood vessels supplying the pituitary gland, which causes the tissues to die. Prolactin, the milk-stimulating hormone, is not produced, and breast-feeding cannot take place. *See* HYPOPITUITARISM; PITUITARY GLAND.

Shigella is a genus of rod-shaped bacteria that are closely related to SALMONELLA; they can cause diseases of the intestine, such as bacillary dysentery (*see* DYSENTERY). The bacteria are spread by infected faeces, contaminated food, or flies.

Shingles, known medically as herpes zoster, is an acute inflammatory infection of part of the central nervous system that produces pain and blisters on the skin over the ends of nerves. It is most common in people over age 50 years, although it can occur in children. The virus *Varicella zoster,* which also causes chickenpox, is the infecting agent.

Q: What are the symptoms of shingles?

A: The patient feels unwell, often with a headache, and has a fever, chills, and sometimes pain in the area where the infection is occurring. After three to five days, a red rash appears, which rapidly develops into the clear blisters typical of shingles. As new blisters erupt, the old ones form pus and then scabs, which fall off between seven and ten days later. The blisters appear on the area supplied by the infected nerves, and may cover any part of the body. The chest is a common site. It is usual for the affected area to be sensitive to touch, and the patient often suffers severe pain. As the blisters heal, the central part of the affected area may be without sensation at all.

Q: How is shingles treated?

A: In most cases, the infection is not severe and can be treated with painkilling drugs and a soothing lotion, such as calamine lotion. Once the blisters heal, the patient often feels weak and tired, and needs a long convalescence. Extra vitamins should be added to the diet.

A special antiviral lotion can be applied to the painful area before the blisters appear to stop them spreading. Painkilling drugs during the acute phase of the disorder reduce the chance of prolonged pain (post-herpetic neuralgia), which is difficult to treat.

Shivering is an uncontrollable trembling caused by rapid, involuntary muscle contractions, which produce a large amount of heat. It may be a response to cold, emotional shock, or fear. Extremely severe shivering is known as RIGOR.

Shock (for EMERGENCY treatment, *see* First Aid, p.566) is separable into two categories: emotional shock and physical, or organic, shock.

Emotional shock, caused by any frightening experience, makes the patient feel faint, dizzy, and possibly confused.

Physical shock can be an immediate or a delayed reaction. It follows physical damage and loss of blood, such as from a severe injury, or electric shock. It also occurs after surgery. Finally, physical shock can occur as a form of ANAPHYLAXIS or following a heart attack.

Shock therapy is a form of treatment for certain types of mental illness. *See* ELECTROCONVULSIVE THERAPY.

Shortness of breath. *See* BREATHLESSNESS.

Shortsightedness (myopia) is a visual defect in which distant objects cannot be seen clearly. It occurs because light entering the eye is focused in front of the retina instead of on it. Distant objects are out of focus because either the lens of the eye is too curved (and bends the light rays too much), or the eyeball is too long, a condition that is usually inherited. Close objects can be seen sharply, and even in old age shortsighted people may be able to read easily without glasses.

Shortsightedness can be corrected by wearing spectacles with concave (converging) lenses. *See* SPECTACLES.

Shoulder is the junction of the arm and the trunk. The ball-and-socket shoulder joint is located between the humerus (upper arm bone) and scapula (shoulder blade). It is held in place by strong muscles and ligaments, and supported by the clavicle. The shoulder muscles control a wide range of movement.

Q: What disorders can affect the shoulder?

A: Dislocation of the shoulder joint is the most common complaint. It mainly results from weakness of the ligaments, although it is also common in certain contact sports. Repeated shoulder dislocation may need surgical treatment to tighten the ligaments.

The shoulder joint can be affected by

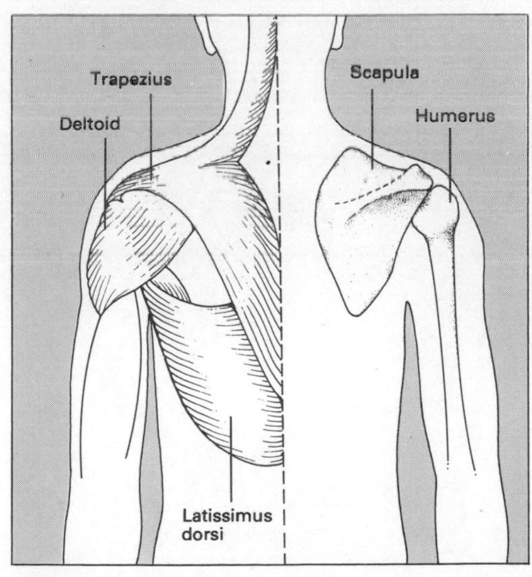

Shoulder joint between the humerus and the scapula is moved by strong muscles.

any JOINT DISORDERS, particularly rheumatoid arthritis.

Pain in the shoulder may be the result of inflammation of the shoulder membrane, ligaments, or tendon (FROZEN SHOULDER) although it may be a referred pain from such disorders as arthritis in the neck (spondylosis), pleurisy and angina pectoris.

Shoulder blade. *See* SCAPULA.

Shunt is an abnormal junction between two body passages that allows the contents of one to pass to the other, by-passing the normal channel. The term usually refers to a junction between two blood vessels, such as an arteriovenous shunt in which an artery is connected directly to a vein, so by-passing the capillary network.

Sialolithiasis is the presence of a stone (calculus) in the duct of a salivary gland. It prevents the escape of saliva, which accumulates in the affected gland and causes it to swell.

The stone is made of calcium salts, and can usually be detected by an X-ray. But, in some cases, a special radiopaque dye may have to be injected into the duct to reveal the presence of the stone.

Q: What are the symptoms of sialolithiasis?

A: Painful swelling of one salivary gland when eating. The swelling settles when the meal ends, only to begin again at the next meal.

Q: How is sialolithiasis treated?

A: In some cases the stone escapes spontaneously, and no treatment is required. Usually, a minor operation is necessary to remove the stone.

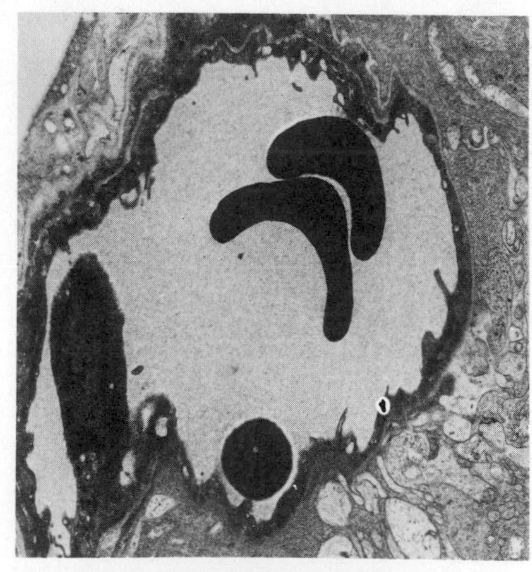

Sickle cell anaemia is characterized by the presence of deformed red blood cells.

Siamese twins are identical twins (which are formed from a single egg) that are still joined at birth, most commonly at the hip, chest, or head. Siamese twins are known medically as conjoined twins (*see* TWINS). They are extremely rare and often difficult to deliver so that a Caesarean operation is usually necessary.

The likelihood of both twins surviving a surgical separation is greater when only superficial tissues are shared.

Sickle cell anaemia is a hereditary form of ANAEMIA characterized by the presence of abnormal, sickle-shaped red blood cells. It occurs almost exclusively in black people. The abnormal cells are unable to pass easily through the capillary blood vessels, and this may lead to widespread thrombosis. They are also more fragile than normal blood cells, so they are easily destroyed by the buffeting in the circulation. This may lead to severe anaemia, which may be made worse by infection.

Q: How is sickle cell anaemia treated?

A: There is no curative treatment for the condition. Therapy is directed toward alleviating the symptoms as they arise. Blood transfusions are usually given only when the anaemia is severe enough to cause serious illness.

Siderosis, or haemosiderosis, is any condition causing excess iron in the tissues. It is usually caused by breathing in dust or fumes containing iron particles, hence its common name is welder's disease.

If siderosis affects the lungs, which is more common in young children, haemoptysis (the coughing up of blood) eventually can lead to death. If it occurs in the kidneys, it may lead to a condition similar to HAEMOCHROMATOSIS.

SIDS (sudden infant death syndrome), also known as cot death, is thought to be a respiratory disorder that usually affects infants under the age of six months.

Q: Are some babies more likely than others to succumb to SIDS?

A: Such deaths are more likely to occur in families living in crowded conditions, during the winter months, and in bottle-fed infants. SIDS is more common at night than in daytime. Boys of low birth weight succumb more often than do girls under similar conditions.

Q: What causes SIDS?

A: During sleep, the respiration of all infants is irregular, with brief periods when breathing stops completely. But if respiration stops for longer than 15 or 20 seconds, death can occur.

In most cases SIDS cannot be prevented, because obvious warning symptoms have not yet been discovered. In all cases of SIDS, it is the parents who suffer grief and shock, often blaming themselves. The family needs social and psychological support at this time. Help can be provided by the paediatrician, the family's doctor, and family counsellors. The family can also be helped by their religious adviser, or by contacting the Foundation for the Study of Infant Deaths, which can give immediate counselling and support.

Sigmoidoscopy is an examination of the S-shaped part of the colon (the sigmoid colon), the lower part of the colon that joins the rectum. It is performed using a sigmoidoscope, a lighted tube that can be inserted up to about ten inches beyond the anus.

Q: Why is a sigmoidoscopy performed?

A: A sigmoidoscopy may be done in a routine examination, to exclude any local disease or cancer of the rectum and sigmoid colon, or in the investigation of tropical diseases, such as amoebiasis and schistosomiasis, and in conditions such as ulcerative colitis and Crohn's disease.

A small piece of tissue (biopsy) may be taken. A sigmoidoscopy is commonly performed before a barium enema, or before the full length of the colon is examined with a flexible fibrescope (*see* BARIUM).

Silicosis is a form of pneumoconiosis caused by inhaling silica. It is an occupational hazard of coal miners, quarry workers, and stone workers, as well as anyone who is exposed to silica dust. The fine particles of silica cause scarring within the lungs, impairing lung function and causing increasing shortness of breath.

Over a period of years, a person with silicosis suffers frequent attacks of chronic BRONCHITIS that increase the development of the chronic pulmonary disorder emphysema. There is an increased incidence of tuberculosis and spontaneous pneumothorax, a collection of air in the pleural cavity. Death usually results from pneumonia or heart failure.

See also PNEUMOCONIOSIS.

Sinus is a cavity, usually filled with air or blood. There are many sinuses throughout the body. The term usually refers to the cavities in the bone behind the nose. These sinuses reduce the weight of the skull, and act as resonant chambers for the voice.

Sinus is also the medical term for a drainage channel formed from an abscess to the surface of the skin or to an internal organ.

See also SINUSITIS.

Sinusitis is inflammation of the mucous membranes that line the sinuses of the skull (the cavities within the skull bones that open into the nose). Acute sinusitis may be caused by a nasal infection (RHINITIS) in which the sinuses become blocked, or by the common cold, or any feverish respiratory illness, such as influenza. Sometimes, acute sinusitis may be caused by a dental abscess; a fracture of a bone in the face; or sudden pressure changes (*see* BAROTRAUMA). Chronic sinusitis may be caused by an allergy, such as hay fever; repeated attacks of acute sinusitis; or inadequate treatment of acute sinusitis combined with nasal obstruction, as may occur with a POLYP, a DEVIATED NASAL SEPTUM, or chronic dental infections.

Q: What are the symptoms of sinusitis?

A: The area over the affected sinus may be painful and tender, and there is usually a severe headache. The nose may be blocked on the affected side with a thick, sometimes bloodstained discharge causing the patient to breathe through the mouth. The patient may also have a fever, chills, and a sore throat.

Q: How is sinusitis treated?

A: Painkilling drugs may be used to relieve the pain. Decongestant nose drops and inhaled steam may help to open the sinuses and promote drainage of mucus that has accumulated within the affected sinus. A doctor may also prescribe antibiotics and advise bed rest.

In severe cases, surgery may be necessary to wash out the infected sinus. *See* CALDWELL-LUC OPERATION.

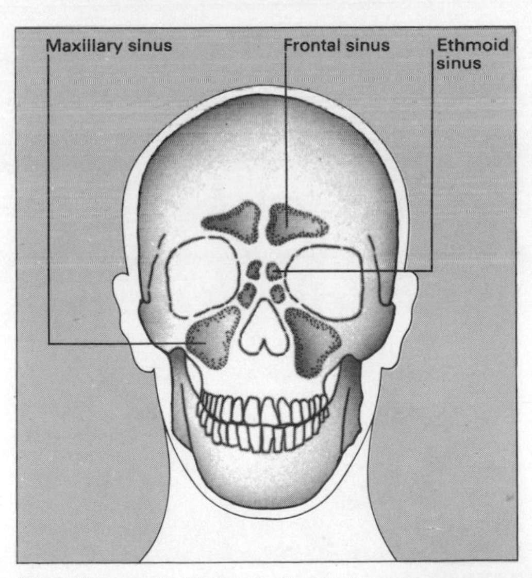

Sinus is a cavity in bone. Eight of these are located in the bones of the face.

Skeleton

Skeleton is the bony framework of the body; it consists of about 206 bones. The bones can be classified into two groups: the axial skeleton and appendicular skeleton. The skeleton has three functions: it protects the internal organs; it supplies support for the substance of the body; and, through the action of muscles, it allows movements of the body.

Q: What is the axial skeleton?

A: The axial skeleton is the main supporting framework of the body. It consists of the skull, spine, and rib-cage. The spine consists of seven cervical, twelve thoracic, and five lumbar vertebrae. The five sacral vertebrae and the four bones of the coccyx at the base of the spine are joined together to make a solid bone at the back of the pelvis. The thorax is composed of twelve pairs of ribs, joined at the back to the thoracic vertebrae; the upper ten pairs are joined by cartilage at the front to the breastbone (sternum). Some people have an extra rib or an extra vertebra.

Q: What is the appendicular skeleton?

A: The appendicular skeleton consists of the limbs. The upper limbs are composed of the shoulder girdle, collar-bone, and shoulder blade, as well as the bones of the arms and hands.

The lower limbs consist of the pelvis, which is joined to the sacrum, and which provides support for the bones of the legs and feet.

Q: How does the skeleton protect the internal organs?

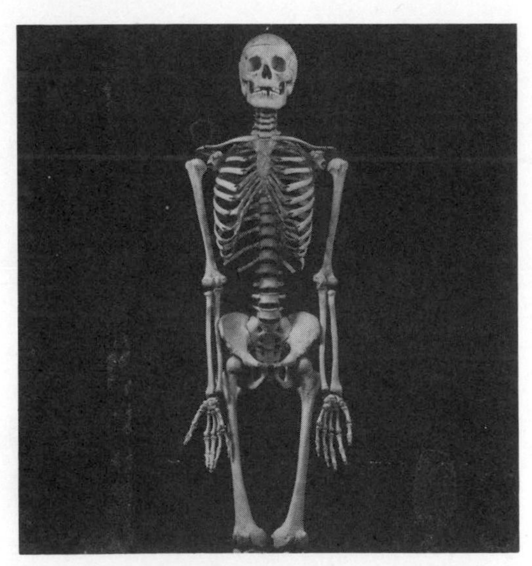

Skeleton is the framework to which muscles, ligaments, and other structures are attached.

A: The skull is the most protective part of the skeleton because it completely surounds the brain and the internal organs of the ear, and supplies a major form of protection for the eyes. The thorax (chest) protects the heart, lungs, liver, and spleen. The spine and pelvis help to protect the abdominal organs, such as the intestine, kidneys, bladder, and, in females, the womb.

Skin, known medically as integument, is the largest "organ" in the body, weighing about 3kg (7lbs) and covering about 1.7sq metres (18sq ft) in an adult. It is a waterproof covering, a defence against damage and infection, a regulator of body temperature, and a sensory organ.

Specialized areas of the skin constitute particular organs. For example, the female breast is composed of about twenty modified sweat glands and the nails are developed from a special layer of hard keratin (a tough protein substance) that grows over the outer skin at the ends of the fingers and toes.

Certain areas of the skin, such as the scalp, armpits, and pubic areas, are more thickly covered with hair than are others. A finer growth of hair covers the rest of the body, except for the soles of the feet and the palms of the hands.

Q: What is the structure of the skin?

A: The outer layer of the skin consists of dead cells that break away continually. They are formed as the underlying layer of living cells gradually grow outward to form the protective substance keratin. These two layers are known as the epidermis.

Beneath the epidermis is the dermis. It consists of supporting connective tissue surrounding blood and lymph vessels, sweat and sebaceous glands, nerve endings, and hair follicles. Fat storage cells lie beneath the dermis.

Skin complaints are not always easy to treat, and it is important that attempts at self-treatment do not make the condition worse and a doctor's diagnosis more difficult.

The symptoms of most skin complaints can be considered as various forms of lesion, dry or moist skin, or skin that itches. A combination of these symptoms is quite common.

Primary lesions should not cause difficulty unless they are blisters that break (as with chickenpox), when the skin should be kept clean, and a soothing lotion applied.

Dry skin is helped by moisturizing creams, and moist skin with calamine lotion. Itching is particularly distressing; clothes made from artificial fibres often aggravate the complaint. Antihistamine drugs are moderately effective, and a change to a natural fibres can help. If itching is severe, regular bathing gives relief. Sometimes a doctor may prescribe a local anaesthetic to help the patient over the worst of the symptoms.

Both corticosteroid and antibiotic creams should be used with caution and only on medical advice, because they can be dangerous if used for the wrong condition. Corticosteroids prevent the normal biological reaction to infection, thus an infection may spread. Antibiotics should be used only if the condition is a bacterial infection; used for any length of time, they can cause skin allergy.

Secondary lesions are caused by natural development of the disease, or because the patient interferes with the normal healing process by scratching the skin. This often leaves an ulcerated or eroded region.

Most individual skin disorders have separate articles in the A-Z section of this book.

Skin grafts are layers of skin transferred surgically from one part of a patient's body to another part. Skin grafts are of two main types: (1) a full-thickness graft, which includes the underlying layer of fat and is usually employed for only small areas of skin; and (2) a Thiersch's, or split-skin graft, a thinner layer of skin taken from a healthy part of the patient's body.

For a full-thickness graft, surgeons leave one end of a flap of skin attached to the donor (healthy) area, and the free end attached to the area to be grafted. This allows the blood supply to continue while the graft and its blood supply is becoming established. When the graft has taken, the end still attached to the donor area may be removed and stitched to the recipient area. This is known as a pedicle graft.

In patients with severe burns, it may not be possible to take sufficient skin from donor areas of the patient's body. Temporary grafting, using skin from another person or even that of a pig, can give protection while the patient recovers from the burn.

See also GRAFT.

Skull. *See* CRANIUM.

Sleep. Little is known about why sleep is essential for good health. It seems that the central nervous system needs a regular period of rest from waking activities. But it is not known why about a third of every twenty-four hours has to be spent in this recovery phase. People who go without their normal amount of sleep lack concentration and may ultimately have hallucinations.

Normal sleep consists of two types. The first is known as slow-wave sleep because during it there is reduced electrical activity in the brain. It is also known as non-REM (rapid eye movement) sleep, because the eyes do not move rapidly during this phase. During slow-wave sleep, there is a decrease in the basal metabolic rate, blood pressure, and respiratory rate so that the person lies still and is totally relaxed.

The second type of sleep is known as paradoxical or REM sleep, because of the rapid eye movement that takes place behind the closed eyelids. Also during this phase, dreaming takes place, the heartbeat and respiration become irregular, and there may be limb movement. An electroencephalogram shows electrical brain activity similar to that which occurs when a person is awake.

There is a period of normal wakefulness as a person falls asleep, followed by a state of relaxation that becomes light sleep, before the body enters the phase of slow-wave (non-REM) sleep. Slow-wave sleep initially lasts about two hours before the first episode of REM sleep begins. Sleep then alternates between periods of slow-wave and REM sleep lasting ten to twenty minutes and occurring every hour and a half until the patient awakes refreshed.

REM sleep is now known to be essential, because waking a person repeatedly at the beginning of each period of REM sleep produces depression, anxiety, and fatigue out of proportion to the amount of sleep that has been lost. Dreaming is a necessary part of normal sleep, and is also probably necessary for the well-being of the mind. Everyone dreams, even if he or she cannot remember the dreams on waking.

See also DREAMS; INSOMNIA; SLEEP PROBLEMS.

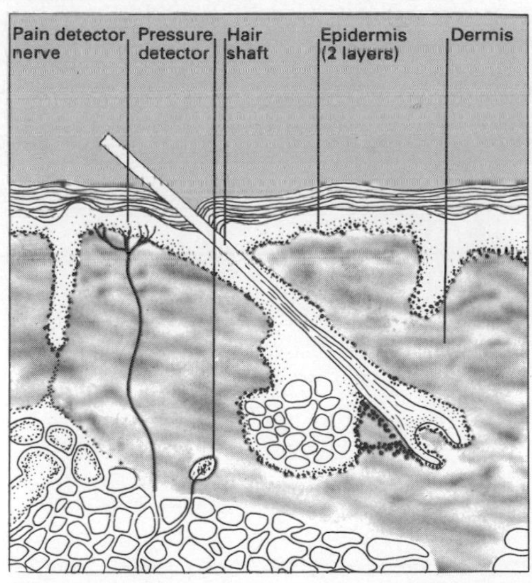

Skin is sensitive to a wide range of outside stimuli, including pressure and pain.

Sleeping sickness

Sleeping sickness, or African trypanosomiasis, is a disorder caused by protozoans called trypanosomes. They enter the blood of a human by the bite of an infected tsetse fly. Sleeping sickness occurs in tropical and subtropical regions of Africa where infected cattle and wild animals complete the disease's cycle by infecting the fly.

Sleeplessness. *See* INSOMNIA.

A talk about Sleep problems

Sleep problems. Insomnia (the inability to sleep) is the most common sleep problem and one that causes a lot of distress (*see* INSOMNIA). But other sleep problems commonly occur, particularly in children.

Q: *What sleep problems occur in children?*

A: Sleep problems may be associated with behaviour problems in children. For example, a child may refuse to settle down at night and may constantly get up or make excuses about some minor discomfort. Such children are often worried about something and need a set ritual, without overexcitement, at bedtime. Another problem is the young child, usually aged between three and five, who wakes in the early hours of the morning. A solution that can be tried by the parents is to stop afternoon naps and put the child to bed later in the evening. SLEEPWALKING and SLEEPTALKING are two problems that are common in childhood and tend to improve with the approach of puberty.

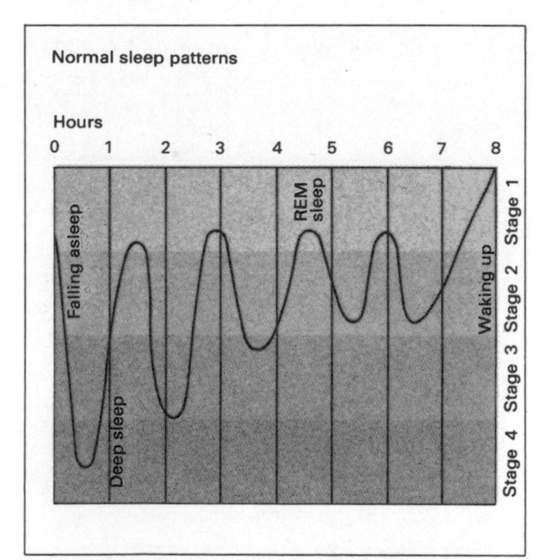

Sleep problems occur if the normal depth and rapid eye movement (REM) pattern is broken.

Q: *Can excessive amounts of sleep be a serious symptom?*

A: This is not usually a serious condition. Hypersomnia, as it is sometimes called, may develop after serious illnesses during the convalescent period. It may also be a factor in anaemia and depression, and sometimes occurs in adolescence as normal behaviour. Hypersomnia can, however, be a symptom of narcolepsy, a form of epilepsy in which the person suddenly falls asleep and may continue to sleep for hours and even days. It is more common in women than in men and may coincide with menstruation.

Sleep reversal, in which a person sleeps all day, is always a serious symptom when there is no obvious cause. It can happen in disorders such as Alzheimer's disease, encephalitis, and sleeping sickness.

Q: *How can sleep problems be treated?*

A: A full understanding of how the sleep disorder occurs is most important to the doctor, although diagnostic tests such as an electroencephalograph test may be of help. Drugs of the hypnotic and amphetamine group and, sometimes, one of the anti-depressant drugs can help to control some of the problems.

Q: *Can the use of drugs create its own problems?*

A: The amphetamine group of drugs is useful in treating many of the excessive sleep problems such as narcolepsy and hypersomnia. But amphetamines are addictive and so the doctor must take great care to ensure that excessive amounts of drugs are not being used.

A much greater problem is the use of sedative and hypnotic drugs in the treatment of insomnia. Although it is not known exactly how these drugs work, it seems that there is a reduction in the length and number of periods of REM sleep (*see* SLEEP) during their administration. This can cause mild depression for reasons that are not fully understood. When the drugs are stopped, sleep may be disturbed for ten to fourteen days. REM sleep increases, and the person feels that the insomnia is worse than before. After about two weeks, natural sleep patterns return.

Another problem with sleep-inducing drugs is the slight daytime sedation that may occur and reduce a person's speed of reaction. This is particularly relevant when driving a vehicle, using machinery or, most important of all, taking alcohol. Alcohol in combination with barbiturates, for example, is extremely dangerous and can be fatal.

See also BARBITURATES; DREAMS; MANIC-DEPRESSIVE ILLNESS; NARCOLEPSY; SLEEP-TALKING; SLEEPWALKING.

Sleeptalking is a common occurrence in children. It may consist of no more than a few grunts or an occasional word, or it may be a whole sentence. It is even possible to hold a brief conversation with a sleeptalker. Sleeptalking is probably the result of a vivid dream or a nightmare. *See* SLEEP PROBLEMS.

Sleepwalking, or somnambulism, is most common between the ages of four and fourteen and more frequent in boys than girls. It seldom lasts for more than about half an hour, and is more likely to occur when the child is sleeping in a strange room.

The individual may appear normal and can perform complex movements, such as opening and shutting doors and walking down stairs. The eyes may be closed or open, and may appear to be looking at something.

The sleepwalker may grunt or speak, but returns to bed with no memory of the episode in the morning (*see* SLEEPTALKING).

Q: Is it dangerous to wake someone who is sleepwalking?

A: No. However, it is better not to try because the sleepwalker may be frightened to wake in a strange place. It is best to attempt to lead the sleepwalker back to bed.

Q: Why does sleepwalking occur?

A: The cause is not known. It is associated with the dreaming stage of sleep, or with underlying fears and anxieties.

See also SLEEP.

Slimming. *See* WEIGHT PROBLEMS.

Slipped disc, also known as a prolapsed intervertebral disc, is a disorder of the spine. The discs between the bones of the spine (vertebrae) are composed of gristle-like fibrous tissue with a soft centre. A disc can rupture as a result of strain, allowing its soft centre to pass through the ruptured outer fibre. The soft tissue protrudes into and compresses the spinal canal, which contains the spinal cord and nerves. Pressure on the spinal nerves produces pain, felt either locally (backache and lumbago) or as referred pain in another part of the body, as in sciatica. Muscle weakness; paralysis; and loss of sensation is possible in severe cases.

In childhood and adolescence, the discs are flexible and pliable, and so strain at this stage is unlikely. The discs harden in later life, and the soft centres gradually solidify. By the age of forty-five or fifty, the centre is of the same tough composition as the outer edge.

The discs of the neck (cervical region) and those of the lower spine (lumbar region) are the most likely to rupture because they are the most mobile. A slipped disc in the thoracic spine, behind the chest, can occur in some people.

Q: What are the symptoms of a slipped disc?

A: In the neck, it is usually the result of a twisting injury that develops into a stiff neck. The pain is intense when the patient tries to move or cough. Gradually the pain spreads as the disc presses on the nerves that affect one shoulder and arm. Loss of sensation in the skin and muscle weakness may develop because of nerve damage. If the disc protrudes deeply into the spinal cord, there is loss of sensation or paralysis lower down the body. It may cause disruption in the nerves controlling walking, or cause difficulty in urinating.

The symptoms in the lower spine are usually caused by a slipped disc either between the fourth and fifth lumbar vertebrae, or between the fifth lumbar and first sacral vertebrae. There is severe pain in the back, making it difficult for the patient to move. The pain gradually improves over a matter of days.

The back pain may be followed by sciatica, with pain in one buttock, the thigh, leg, and foot. A tingling sensation is common, and is aggravated by coughing, sneezing, or bending. The patient limps, because of spasms in the back muscles, and is unable to raise the affected leg at right angles to the body.

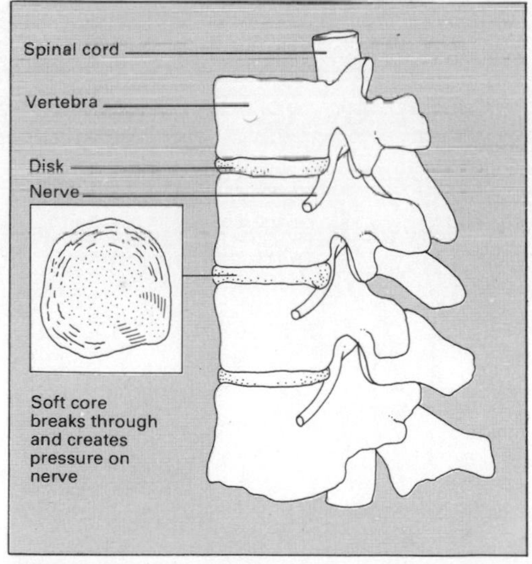

Slipped disc is a section of intervertebral disc that protrudes onto a nerve.

A slipped disc higher up in the lumbar region results in pain in the groin and in the front of the thigh.

Q: How is a slipped disc treated?

A: Painkilling drugs may be prescribed in mild cases; spinal manipulation may also help. A slipped disc in the neck usually involves immobilizing the neck with a stiff collar. This helps the patient sleep or to drive a car without too much pain. In addition, antirheumatic drugs, physiotherapy in the form of short-wave diathermy and massage, and, in severe cases, hospitalization and continuous TRACTION may be recommended.

A slipped disc in the lumbar region is treated with rest, painkillers, and antirheumatic drugs. Traction and a plaster-of-Paris jacket or a surgical corset that immobilizes the spine are commonly used for several months in severe cases. Occasionally, surgical removal of the disc may be necessary.

Q: Are there any other disorders that have symptoms similar to those of a slipped disc?

A: Osteoarthritis, tumours of the spinal cord, and secondary tumours of the vertebrae produce similar symptoms. Cervical rib trouble may produce disc-like pains down an arm. Spondylolisthesis, in which one vertebra slips forward on another, and ankylosing spondylitis cause similar back pains.

Smallpox occurs in two forms, variola major or variola minor, and is a serious, infectious disease. It produces blisters which, after healing, leave scars. Death occurs in fifteen per cent of patients with variola major, but in only 0.2 per cent of variola minor (alastrim) cases. The disease is transmitted mainly by direct contact with a smallpox patient or by contact with contaminated clothing.

The World Health Organization has declared that, from 1st January 1980, the world is free of smallpox. However, some countries, particularly in Africa, still require travellers to be vaccinated against smallpox.

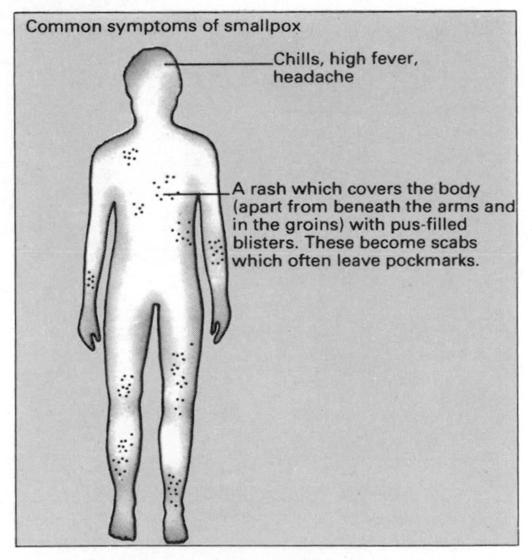

Smallpox is an acute contagious disease with a variety of characteristic symptoms.

Q: What are the symptoms of smallpox?

A: After an incubation period of ten to fourteen days, the patient has a high fever, headache, chills, and often muscle pains and vomiting. These symptoms last for two to three days, resulting in shock, when a diffuse pink skin rash may occur.

After the second day small pink spots appear on the face and, within twenty-four hours, they cover the body. The spots become blisters filled with a clear fluid and, after three days, contain pus; the blisters then form into scabs. After eight to ten days, improvement begins and the scabs drop off, leaving small pitted areas where the blisters formed.

Q: What is the treatment for smallpox?

A: The first step is isolation of the patient and, sometimes, the medical staff giving treatment; the medical staff also must be vaccinated. Quarantine lasts for a period of two weeks from last contact with the infection. All of the patient's clothing and bed linen should be sterilized. Intravenous fluids are given to maintain the level of body fluids; antiviral drugs can reduce the severity and the mortality rate in an epidemic.

Antibiotics should be used only if secondary infection occurs.

Q: Can vaccination prevent smallpox?

A: Yes. The vaccine against smallpox has been so successful that the disease has been officially eradicated.

Smear is a technique of preparing tissue for examination with a microscope. *See* CERVICAL SMEAR.

Smegma is a thick, greasy secretion produced by the sebaceous glands under the foreskin of the penis. In uncircumcised males it is thought to be a factor, if the glans (end of the penis) is not kept clean, in cancer of the penis.

Smell, sense of, is the ability to detect odours. The organ of smell consists of a group of sensitive cells situated in the upper part of the nasal cavity, which is connected to the brain by the olfactory nerve. The sense of smell is not well developed in humans. It is limited to the sensation of seven basic odours and their combinations. It is, however, an important contributory factor to the sense of taste (*see* TASTE). And like the sense of taste, it becomes less acute as a person becomes older.

Inflammation or blockage of the nasal passages, as with a common cold, dulls the sense of smell. The sense is also less acute in persons who smoke. A skull fracture can destroy the sense of smell completely (anosmia).

A talk about Smoking

Smoking of tobacco, in cigarettes, cigars, or a pipe, is a habit that meets many of the criteria that define an addiction. For some smokers, it provides a relief from anxiety and tension; but for others, it becomes a physical and psychological burden. Cigar and pipe smoking, although they present some hazards to health, are thought to be less dangerous than cigarette smoking.

Ten times as many deaths are caused by cigarette smoking as by road accidents. Cigarette smoking damages the lungs, blood vessels and, to a lesser extent, other organs such as the heart.

Cancer of the lung is the most publicized hazard, and the peak of its incidence in men is just before retirement in the fifty-five to sixty-five age group (when one in seven deaths results from lung cancer). Two out of every five heavy smokers die before the age of sixty-five.

In women who smoke, the highest mortality rate occurs ten years earlier than in men, but only one death in twenty is caused by lung cancer.

Every cigarette that is smoked reduces the life expectancy by about ten minutes. A person of thirty-five who smokes a packet of cigarettes a day can expect to live at least five years less than a person of the same age who does not smoke.

People who smoke not only damage their own health, but also harm others. Studies have shown that people who have to live or work in smoky environments, although non-smokers themselves, have an increased risk of developing respiratory ailments.

Q: What are the harmful substances in tobacco and what do they do?

A: There are four main groups of dangerous substances in tobacco smoke. Nicotine is the substance that causes addiction. It stimulates the release of adrenaline and other substances in the body that cause an increase in pulse rate, rise in blood pressure, and narrowing of the blood vessels in the skin. Adrenaline also causes an increase in fatty substances in the blood, and makes blood platelets (factors in blood clotting) stickier and therefore more likely to form blood clots.

Carbon monoxide is a poisonous gas produced by the incomplete burning of tobacco. In the lungs, it combines with haemoglobin in the blood and thus prevents the haemoglobin from carrying its full quota of oxygen through the circulation. It reduces a person's athletic ability, and also acts as a poison.

Various substances in tobacco irritate the lining of the bronchi, inducing spasm and increasing bronchial secretions. At the same time, these irritants damage cells that usually sweep the secretions out of the lungs. This increases the likelihood of developing bronchitis.

Cancer-producing substances are present in the tar in cigarette smoke.

Q: Is there any way of reducing the dangers of cigarette smoking?

A: Yes. Obviously, the best way of avoiding the dangers of cigarette smoking is to give up the habit. If this seems impossible, the smoker can use brands with low nicotine and tar content. Cigarettes, preferably with filters, should be smoked to a long and not a short stub. (The greatest concentration of tar and other irritants is in the stub of the cigarette.) Removing the cigarette from the mouth between puffs helps to reduce the amount of smoke that is inhaled.

Q: What effect does smoking during pregnancy have on the baby?

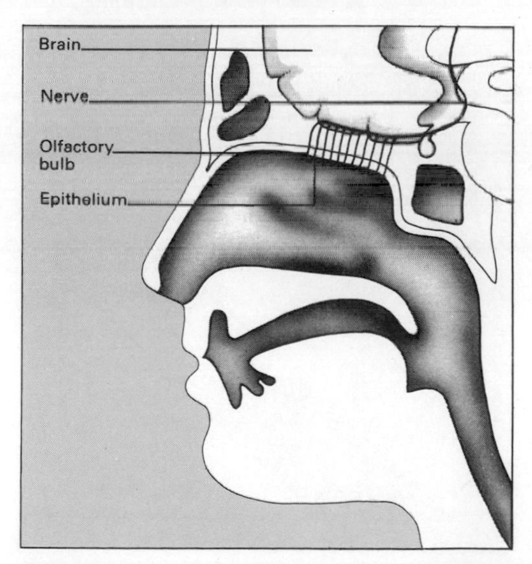

Smell stimuli entering the nose pass through the olfactory bulb up to the brain.

A: Babies born to mothers who smoke are 140-360 grams (5-13 ounces) lighter on average than those born to mothers who do not smoke. Also, pregnant women who smoke are more likely to have a miscarriage, a stillborn baby, or an infant that dies soon after birth. Twice as many premature babies are born to smoking mothers than to mothers who do not smoke. There is also evidence to suggest that by the age of eleven the children of mothers who smoked more than ten cigarettes a day during pregnancy are slightly shorter and slightly below the average in reading, mathematics, and general ability than are the children of nonsmoking mothers.

Q: What are the effects of smoking on the lungs?

A: There are two main effects of smoking on the lungs. Chronic bronchitis and, eventually, emphysema commonly occur in heavy smokers, and a morning cough, which clears the bronchi, is a common feature of all smokers. Early lung damage can be detected by pulmonary function tests before there is any obvious shortness of breath.

Among people who smoke a packet of cigarettes a day, lung cancer occurs twenty times more frequently than in nonsmokers. The risk is increased in those who smoke high tar cigarettes, who inhale deeply, and who began smoking in adolescence.

Q: Can smoking cause other cancers of the body?

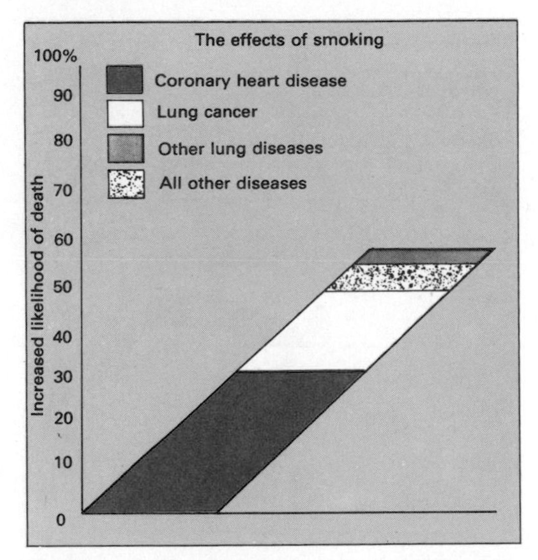

Smoking of tobacco increases the likelihood of death from various diseases by 57 per cent.

A: Yes. There are more cancers of the bladder and pancreas in smokers than in nonsmokers. Cancer of the mouth, tongue, larynx, and oesophagus are also more common in smokers of all kinds of tobacco, including pipe smokers and cigar smokers.

Q: Can smoking affect the heart?

A: Yes. Cigarette smoking increases the likelihood of ARTERIOSCLEROSIS, and there is twice the risk of CORONARY thrombosis than in those who do not smoke. The risk of developing other blood vessel disorders, such as BUERGER'S DISEASE, is also increased.

Q: Are other diseases more likely to occur in smokers?

A: Yes. Dental disorders, gingivitis, and other infections of the gums more commonly occur in smokers. Smokers are also more likely to develop tuberculosis, probably because the damaging effect of the irritants in tobacco lowers the resistance of the lungs.

Although smoking does not cause peptic ulcers, the continued habit prevents them from healing. Consequently, complications are more common and mortality from perforated ulcers is greater.

Q: What are the benefits from stopping smoking?

A: Within a few days or weeks there is an improvement in the sense of taste and smell, a gradual reduction in the amount of morning coughing, and less shortness of breath during exercise.

Although lung damage, such as that caused by chronic bronchitis and emphysema, cannot be reversed once it has occurred, it no longer gets worse.

However, the greatest long term benefit is the steady decrease in the chances of getting cancer. If a person who stops smoking cigarettes lives for ten years, his chance of developing lung cancer is no more than for someone who has never smoked.

Q: How may a person stop smoking?

A: For most people, stopping smoking is a goal that can be achieved only by gradual stages. First, only light a cigarette when there is a definite desire to smoke one. This should reduce the total amount of cigarettes smoked in a day, because it eliminates all the cigarettes that are smoked merely out of habit, and without positive intention. Next, decide when the next cigarette is to be smoked, and do not smoke until then. Each time you survive a period, of, say two or three hours without a cigarette, you will feel a definite sense of achievement. The gap between cigarettes can gradually be increased until you have reduced your total amount of cigarettes smoked in a day to about ten.

The next stage, in which you decide not to smoke until the following day, is the most difficult. For your first complete day without cigarettes, choose a day when you are constantly busy or physically active. After you have not smoked for two weeks your physical addiction to nicotine will have been cured, and any continued desire to smoke will be caused by nervous tension only.

Q: Are there any other ways of stopping smoking?

A: Yes. Often people decide that they cannot give up smoking on their own. Some doctors run smoking clinics or group therapy, or recommend aversion therapy as methods of giving up smoking. Some people may be helped by hypnosis. Injections of drugs similar to nicotine have been tried, but have not been successful.

Those who are unable to stop smoking should at least attempt to reduce smoking, or change to cigars or a pipe.

Snakebite. For EMERGENCY treatment, *see* First Aid, p.514. The only poisonous snake in the U.K. is the adder, which is not found in Ireland.

Snake venom is a complex protein substance that varies in its effect from species to species. Some venoms cause mainly tissue damage, others principally affect the nerves, and some cause destruction of blood cells and act as an anticoagulant. It is usually impossible to tell from the marks of a bite which species of snake has bitten a person. If possible, the snake should be killed, because this provides a positive identification, which is an important factor in treatment.

Sneezing is a sudden, involuntary, explosive expulsion of air resulting from irritation of the nose. A sneeze may project infected droplets 3 to 4 metres (10 to 12ft) so a sneeze should be blocked by a handkerchief or hand.

Snellen's chart is a chart of letters of decreasing size used to test a person's eyesight.

See also SPECTACLES.

Snoring is noisy breathing during sleep that is caused by vibration of the soft palate. It usually occurs when the soft palate falls backward, thus partly blocking the nose, while sleeping on the back with the mouth open. Snoring may be habitual, or it may result from an underlying condition that blocks the nose, such as swollen adenoids; mucus; a DEVIATED NASAL SEPTUM; or a nasal POLYP.

Snow blindness occurs when the eyes are directly exposed to intense ultraviolet light reflected off snow. It can also occur from exposure to arc welding flames, high-voltage electric sparks, and artificial sun lamps. The light causes severe eye pain and photophobia, a dislike of bright light. It may result in conjunctivitis, and sometimes inflammation of the retina.

Sodium is a metallic chemical element. Its salts, particularly the chloride, form the principal salts within the body. Most people get sufficient sodium in the food they eat.

Q: What happens if the body's level of sodium is incorrect?

A: Any condition that causes excessive loss of sodium from the body, such as severe vomiting and diarrhoea, kidney disease, a disorder of the adrenal glands (Addison's disease), or excessive use of diuretic drugs, produces signs of dehydration and shock.

Less commonly, lack of sodium occurs in the body fluids because of diabetes insipidus or excessive sweating. An excess may occur when a patient is recovering from acute kidney failure (when there is an imbalance of sodium and water). This may lead to symptoms of mental confusion, thirst, and high blood pressure.

Sodium bicarbonate is a white, odourless, crystalline powder that is used medically as an ANTACID to neutralize the stomach's acid

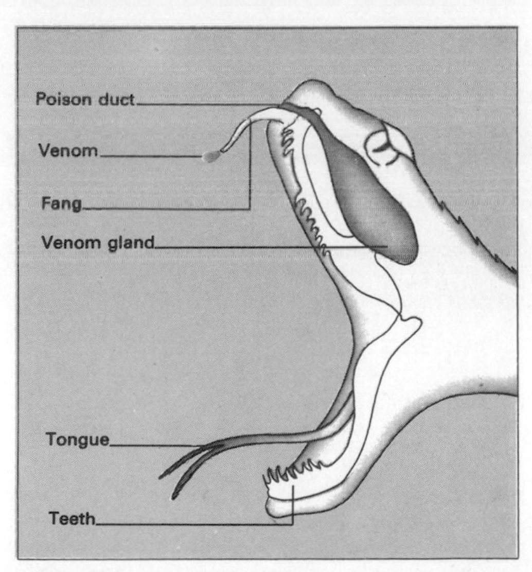

Snakebite may inject venom through a groove in the poison fang as the snake bites.

secretions and in weak solution as intravenous infusions in the treatment of certain disorders.

Soft sore. *See* CHANCROID.

Solar plexus. *See* PLEXUS.

Somatotype is a particular type of physique. For example, an ectomorph is tall and thin with poorly developed muscles; an endomorph is short and rounded; and a mesomorph is muscular and well-built.

Somnambulism. *See* SLEEPWALKING.

Sonne dysentery. *See* DYSENTERY.

Sonography. *See* ULTRASOUND TECHNIQUES.

Soporific is anything that causes drowsiness.

Sordes is a foul crust on the lips, teeth, and gums often found in patients with a fever.

Sore is any tender or painful lesion or ulcer on the skin, especially in the mouth or throat. *See* BEDSORE; MOUTH ULCER; SORE THROAT.

Sore throat is a symptom of many disorders, including the COMMON COLD, DIPHTHERIA, GLANDULAR FEVER; INFLUENZA, LARYNGITIS, MEASLES, PHARYNGITIS, QUINSY, and TONSILLITIS.

Temporary relief may be obtained by sucking medicated throat lozenges, and by taking aspirin or paracetamol. It is also advisable to stop smoking; to drink plenty of fluids; and to eat soft foods. A doctor should be consulted if a sore throat persists.

Spare part surgery is any form of surgery that uses artificial parts to replace diseased or injured parts of a patient's body. *See* REPLACEMENT SURGERY; TRANSPLANT SURGERY.

Spasm is a sudden involuntary contraction of a muscle or group of muscles, usually accompanied by pain and movement.

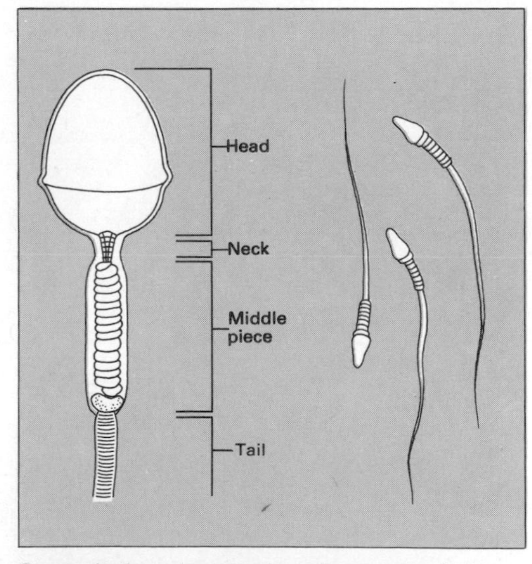

Sperm is the microscopic male gamete that fertilizes the female gamete, the ovum.

Spastic describes a condition in which a recurrent muscular contraction occurs. This condition is present in neurological disorders that affect the brain, such as those that follow a STROKE, or in CEREBRAL PALSY resulting from congenital brain damage.

Spastic colon. *See* MUCOUS COLITIS.

Spectacles, or eyeglasses, may be prescribed to correct visual defects. Recently, CONTACT LENSES have become a common alternative.

Common defects for which spectacles may be prescribed are ASTIGMATISM (distortion of the lens); hyperopia (LONGSIGHTEDNESS); myopia (SHORTSIGHTEDNESS); and PRESBYOPIA (loss of elasticity in the lens because of age). Glasses may also be required to correct a congenital disorder or a birth injury to the eyes.

Spectacles do not make the eyes lazy nor worsen a person's eyesight. But the eyes should be tested yearly.

Q: What types of spectacle lens are available?

A: As well as the usual concave or convex lenses (available in specified shapes and sizes under the National Health, subsidized), there are three main other types of lens. Dark lenses are used especially by albinos; by those with certain eye disorders in which light may cause pain; and in conditions of extremely bright light. Bifocals are glasses with divided lenses for each eye, correcting vision for both far and near objects. And trifocals correct vision for middle distance as well.

Some modern lenses are of variable darkness according to light intensity.

Speculum is an instrument used for examining the interior of the body, usually through one of the normal openings such as the ear, nose, rectum, or vagina.

Speech defects include any condition that results in a failure to speak normally. Most are first detected in childhood, when a baby fails to begin talking at the usual age.

Probably the most common cause of delayed speaking is some form of mental retardation. But hearing problems also cause difficulty in learning to speak. A rare cause of failure to speak is AUTISM.

Q: Are there any other conditions that may cause failure to develop normal speech?

A: Yes. Children with CEREBRAL PALSY or a CLEFT PALATE have difficulty in pronouncing words clearly.

Some children, who are in other ways normal and intelligent, develop a kind of word deafness. Sounds are not understood, although they are heard, and this results in disordered speech.

Stuttering or stammering, however,

may be the result of severe emotional disturbances.

Q: When should a parent become concerned about speech defects in a child?

A: A parent who notices that a baby is not reacting to sounds (by moving the eyes or head) between the ages of four and six months should discuss the matter with a doctor, because the infant may have a hearing problem. If an infant of eight to nine months is not able to repeat sounds, then a thorough assessment is needed.

The age at which a child learns to speak varies. But, on the average, a child of two-and-a-half should be able to understand simple speech and be speaking reasonably well.

Q: How can speech defects in children be treated?

A: Treatment of speech defects depends on the cause. Speech defects that are the result of deafness may be overcome by the use of a hearing aid or an operation. Lisping or stuttering can often be improved if the child is encouraged by the family to speak slowly and correctly. More complicated speech problems need help from a speech therapist. Autistic children require special training.

Q: What speech disorders occur in adults?

A: Once speech has been learned, the onset of deafness has no effect on the ability to speak, although speech may be louder than normal because the person cannot hear his or her own voice. Loss of speech (aphasia) may occur after any form of brain damage that involves the speech area of the brain. Recovery may be complete, or it may leave some degree of disability involving the use of incorrect words or phrases (dysphasia).

Extreme hoarseness may occur if the laryngeal muscles are partially paralyzed or destroyed. Dysarthria, speech that is correct but altered, may be the result of muscular or neurological disorders, such as Parkinson's disease.

Q: How can speech defects in adults be treated?

A: Treatment depends on the cause. Cancer of the larynx may require surgery. If necessary, the patient may be taught OESOPHAGEAL SPEECH. Drug treatment may help in neurological or muscular disorders. A speech therapist can help a patient with dysphasia after a stroke.

Sperm is the male sex cell, known also as a spermatozoon. It is produced in the testicles and ejaculated in SEMEN. After sexual intercourse, fertilization may occur if a sperm from the male combines with an ovum (egg) from the female. Both sperm and ovum each contain half the normal number of chromosomes that are required to form a single cell.

Infertility in men may be caused by an absence of sperm. One cause of this is a blockage of the vas deferens between the testicle and the prostate gland. Another cause is failure to produce sperm, or deficiency of healthy sperm.

Infection of the reproductive tract, epididymitis, and prostatitis cause defective sperm. Mumps causing orchitis may stop production of sperm. Other factors include obesity, smoking, drinking alcohol, and serious illness. Sperm production takes place only if the temperature of the testicles is two degrees below that of the rest of the body.

Spermatic cord consists of blood vessels; nerves; fibrous tissue; and the tube (VAS DEFERENS) that carries sperm from the EPIDIDYMIS of the TESTIS to the PROSTATE GLAND.

Spermatocele is a cyst in the epididymis and contains spermatic fluid. *See* CYST.

Spermicide is a substance that kills sperm. *See* CONTRACEPTION.

Sphincter is a ring of muscle that closes or constricts an opening or passage in the body when the muscle contracts.

Sphygmomanometer is an instrument that measures blood pressure. A rubber cuff is placed round the upper arm, or sometimes the thigh, and inflated with air to a pressure greater than that of the blood in the arteries. This temporarily stops the flow of blood. The air pressure is then gradually released while a stethoscope is used to listen for the sound of the pulse over the artery as the blood starts

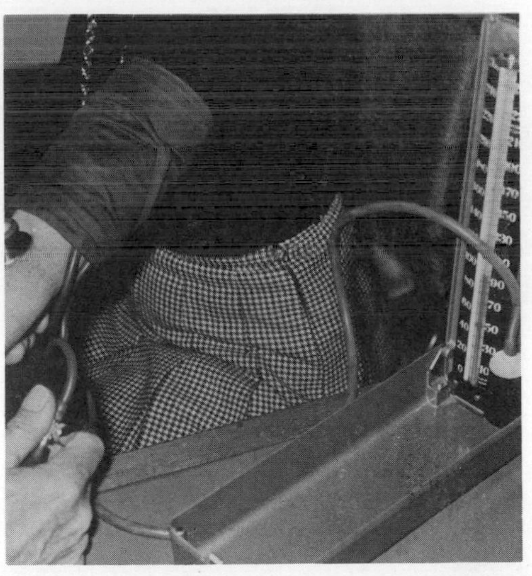

Sphygmomanometer is an instrument used to measure blood pressure.

to flow again. When this sound is heard, the air pressure in the cuff equals the upper blood pressure, known as the systolic blood pressure. The pressure is further reduced in the cuff until the sounds disappear. This is known as the diastolic pressure. The blood pressure is expressed in millimetres of mercury. *See* BLOOD PRESSURE.

Spina bifida is a congenital anomaly of the spine in which one or more vertebral segments are not joined together. The defect may extend over a number of vertebrae, usually in the lumbar or sacral regions.

The disorder is classified as either spina bifida occulta, in which few signs define its presence; or spina bifida cystica, in which there is a protruding sac that contains either membranes (meningocele) or the spinal cord (myelocele) or both (myelomeningocele). Spina bifida is commonly associated with HYDROCEPHALUS. If the protruding sac is damaged, meningeal infection or death may result.

Spina bifida occulta seldom produces neurological symptoms. But in cases in which the spinal cord is involved, the patient's legs may be paralyzed and urinary and faecal incontinence is common, although congenital anomalies such as CLUBFOOT may be the only outward sign of the disorder.

Q: What is the treatment for spina bifida?

A: Only for meningocele and myelocele is an immediate operation required. In such cases, surgery is needed to cover the area with skin to prevent meningitis.

In paralyzed children with myelocele or myelomeningocele, a decision must be made by the specialists and the family whether or not to operate, since surgery usually cannot prevent lifelong disability. These conditions occur in only one out of eight hundred live births.

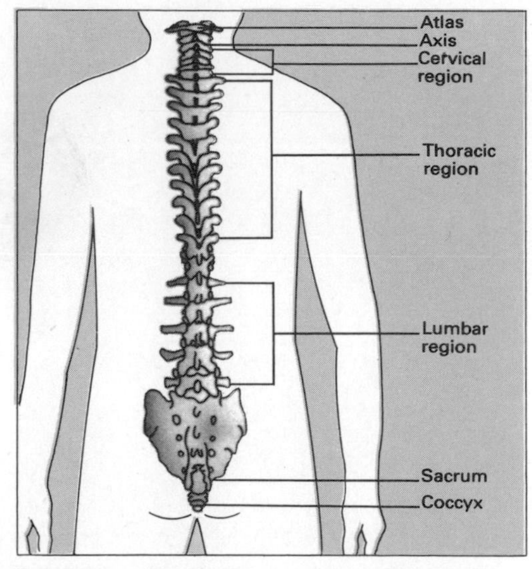

Spine consists of thirty-three vertebrae that encase and protect the spinal cord and nerves.

Q: Can spina bifida be detected in a foetus before birth?

A: Spina bifida can be detected by ULTRASOUND, by checking the mother's blood for a high level of alpha-feto protein, or through measuring the amount of this protein in the amniotic fluid surrounding the foetus (*see* AMNIOCENTESIS).

Spinal cord is the part of the central nervous system that extends along the spinal column from the base of the brain to the second lumbar vertebra in the small of the back. It is covered by the three membranes (pia, dura, and arachnoid) that make up the meninges and is bathed with cerebrospinal fluid.

The spinal cord is composed of 31 bundles of nerves, formed of sensory and motor fibres that carry impulses from the brain and relay messages from various parts of the body back to the brain. At the lower end of the spinal cord is the cauda equina, a fan-shaped network of nerves running in the spinal canal and supplying the lumbar, sacral, and coccygeal nerves that serve the lower part of the body.

See also NERVOUS SYSTEM.

Spinal curvature is any abnormal shape of the spine. A normal spine appears straight when viewed from the front, and from the side has an elongated double S-shape, with four curves.

Abnormal sideways curvature of the spine, when viewed from the front, is called SCOLIOSIS. LORDOSIS is an increased curvature of the lumbar spine, and KYPHOSIS is abnormal curvature of the thoracic spine.

Spinal fluid. *See* CEREBROSPINAL FLUID.

Spine, also called the spinal column or backbone, is a part of the axial skeleton (head and trunk). It is made up of seven cervical (neck) vertebrae; twelve thoracic (chest) vertebrae; five lumbar vertebrae; and the sacrum and coccyx.

The vertebrae are separated by tough, intervertebral discs of fibrocartilage and held together by ligaments. In addition, there are muscles that extend up and down, supporting the spine and the body, and producing movement. Some of these muscles extend up to the back and side of the skull to help to support the head.

Q: What disorders may affect the spine?

A: Many spinal disorders cause pain in the back (*see* BACKACHE). SPONDYLOLISTHESIS, a common cause of low back pain, affects the joint between the fifth lumbar vertebra and the sacrum. Fusion of the small joint between the sacrum and the coccyx can cause stiffness in this region, particularly in the elderly.

Congenital anomalies of the spine may include additional vertebrae, usually in the lumbar region; half vertebrae in the thoracic spine; fusing of the fifth lumbar vertebra with the sacrum; or the opposite effect, in which the first sacral vertebra is separated from the rest of the sacrum.

See also SLIPPED DISC; SPINA BIFIDA; SPINAL CURVATURE; VERTEBRA.

Spinal puncture. *See* ANKYLOSING SPONDYLITIS; BACKACHE; LUMBAR PUNCTURE.

Spinal tap. *See* LUMBAR PUNCTURE.

Spirochetes are spiral-shaped bacteria. *See* BACTERIA.

Spirometer is an apparatus used in lung function tests for measuring the volume of air that is breathed in and out. The patient breathes through a tube connected to the instrument, which produces a record on a moving strip of paper. *See* LUNG FUNCTION TESTS.

Splanchnic describes anything concerned with the intestines or internal organs, such as the liver and spleen.

Splay foot is another term for flatfoot (pes planus). *See* FLATFOOT.

Spleen is an abdominal organ that stores blood and plays a part in the body's immune system. It is about the size of a man's fist and varies in weight between 140 grams (5 oz) and 280 grams (10oz), depending on the amount of blood it contains. It lies in the upper left part of the abdominal cavity, above and behind the stomach, and is protected by the lower ribs. It has a large blood supply through the splenic artery.

The spleen is composed of sponge-like tissue (splenic pulp), consisting of white lymphoid tissue scattered throughout the reddish mass that makes up the basic substance of the spleen.

The white pulp produces lymphocytes (white blood cells), and the red pulp stores excess red blood cells and filters out any damaged cells, debris, and bacteria in the circulation.

Q: What disorders may affect the spleen?

A: The most common disorder is enlargement of the spleen, which may have various causes. It occurs in forms of chronic haemolytic ANAEMIA, such as sickle cell anaemia; malignant conditions of the lymphatic system, such as HODGKIN'S DISEASE, LEUKAEMIA and POLYCYTHAEMIA vera; in CIRRHOSIS of the liver, when there is an increase in venous pressure; in various inflammatory diseases, such as mononucleosis, hepatitis, malaria, brucellosis and kala-azar; and in conditions such as SARCOIDOSIS.

If the spleen is damaged by injury, such as a blow to the abdomen in a motor accident, it can be removed in an adult with little or no effect on the patient's general health (*see* SPLENECTOMY).

Splenectomy is the surgical removal of the spleen. There may be various reasons for this operation, including rupture of the spleen; enlargement of the spleen, often accompanying cirrhosis of the liver; and varicose veins in the oesophagus that cause internal bleeding.

Splenic anaemia is a type of ANAEMIA associated with enlargement of the spleen. It is a form of Banti's disease, which combines anaemia, splenic enlargement, and haemorrhage, and is caused by cirrhosis of the liver.

Splenomegaly is enlargement of the spleen (*see* SPLEEN; SPLENECTOMY).

Splint is a device that is used to immobilize and support an injured part of the body, usually a fractured limb.

For EMERGENCY treatment, *see* First Aid, p.546.

Splinter is a slender piece of wood, metal, or similar material embedded in the layers of the skin. It can also be a fragment from a fractured bone.

If the splinter enters or is the cause of a wound, it may be difficult to find or remove. This should be done by a doctor.

For EMERGENCY treatment of splinters, *see* First Aid, p.589.

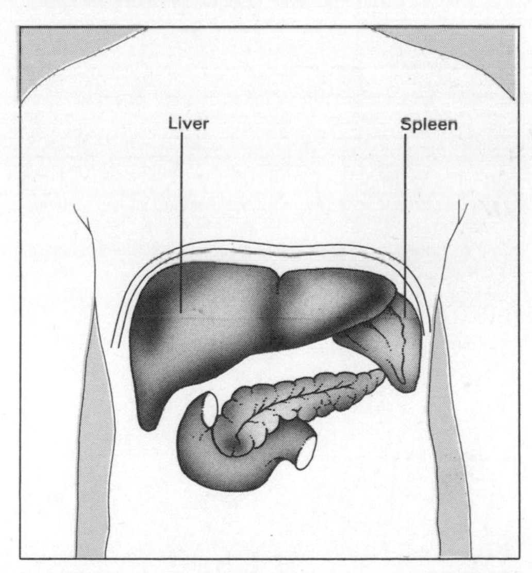

Spleen is mainly responsible for the production of white blood cells during adult life.

Spondylitis is inflammation of the vertebrae. The most common form is ANKYLOSING SPONDYLITIS, which is a rheumatoid disorder. There are various possible causes, including tuberculosis of the vertebrae.

Symptoms of spondylitis include back pain, pain on movement, a stiff back, and occasionally fever. Diagnosis is confirmed by an X-ray, white blood cell count, and raised sedimentation rate (ESR). Treatment usually involves rest, spinal support, improvement of posture and therapy specifically directed at the cause of the inflammation. Occasionally surgery may be necessary to prevent pressure on the spinal cord or nerves.

Spondylolisthesis is a deformity of the spine in which one vertebra slides forward over the top of another. It can occur in the neck or, more commonly, in the lumbar spine.

Q: What are the symptoms of spondylolisthesis?

A: The main symptoms of spondylolisthesis in the neck are weakness and pain in the arms, caused by compression of the spinal cord. Later symptoms are paralysis in the lower part of the body, with disorders of the bowel and bladder.

Spondylolisthesis in the lumbar spine is one of the causes of backache and SCIATICA.

Q: How is spondylolisthesis treated?

A: Treatment of spondylolisthesis in the neck depends on the severity of the condition. Often, the initial treatment is traction, which can only be applied to a patient in bed. A metal frame is attached to the skull and weights are attached to stretch the neck. Following this treatment, a neck cast may be necessary. Sometimes an operation is required to correctly reposition the vertebrae.

There is no need to treat spondylolisthesis of the lumbar region unless the symptoms are severe. If they are, a surgical corset and muscle-strengthening exercises may be sufficient; in some cases, an operation is necessary.

See also SLIPPED DISC.

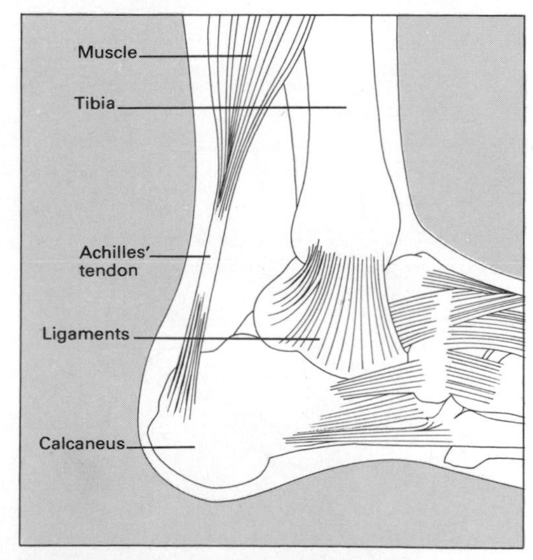

Rupture of the Achilles' tendon can occur if a person takes sudden exercise.

Spondylosis is osteoarthritis that affects the spine. It involves a degeneration of the joints, frequently accompanied by breakdown of the intervertebral discs (*see* SLIPPED DISC).

Spondylosis in the neck usually affects the lowest three vertebrae. It causes aching and stiffness in the back of the neck and a grating sound when turning the neck. The patient may also have a headache, and pain or muscle weakness in the arm. Spondylosis of the lower spine most commonly occurs in people who have done heavy manual labour or who have a history of either injury or degenerative changes following slipped disc or osteochondritis (inflammation of bone and cartilage). Backache with muscle spasm are the usual symptoms. The condition may cause pressure on local nerves resulting in pain in the legs or round the ribs.

Q: Does spondylosis always produce symptoms?

A: No. X-ray examination of the spine shows many of the characteristics of spondylosis in people as they get older, but symptoms may not occur. Symptoms may occur, however, if there is some minor injury to the spine, such as that caused by a fall or sudden twist.

Q: How is spondylosis treated?

A: Treatment depends on the severity of the symptoms. Aspirin or antirheumatic drugs are usually helpful, but sometimes temporary immobilization of the spine in a neck splint or spinal support is necessary. Physiotherapy, with heat, massage or manipulation may also be used.

Spore is the reproductive cell of a primitive organism, such as a fungus or bacterium. It is usually protected by a thick membrane, which makes it resistant to the effects of heat, chemicals, and dehydration. As a result, prolonged boiling or intense heat is usually required to kill spores.

Sports injuries are many and varied, depending on the physical demands of each individual sport and on the fitness, stamina, and strength of the athlete. Many of the injuries occur because of repeated movements or stresses on particular joints, bones and muscles. Training for a particular sport is aimed at increasing the stamina and strength of the participant in line with the stresses to be met.

The first requirement before a person takes part in any sport is physical fitness. This requires the slow development of physical capacity in all areas, so that it is possible for the body to withstand the initial strain of training. Too much exercise too soon can produce muscle and ligament strain, inflamed tendons (tenosynovitis) inflamed bursae (bursitis), and stress fractures of bones.

Stamina implies an increase in reserve capacity, especially of the heart and the lungs. The heart has to pump blood at an increased rate, and the lungs have to take in oxygen more rapidly. Strength develops by building muscle power, a slow process of using muscles a little harder over a period of time. When an individual has developed to a required peak, he or she is less likely to suffer injury and, if injured, finds that increased fitness aids the healing process.

Sprain (for EMERGENCY treatment, *see* First Aid, p.592) is an injury to a joint in which some of the ligaments are severely stretched or even partly torn, producing swelling, pain, and tenderness. These symptoms disappear when the joint is rested.

Sprue is an intestinal disorder characterized by impaired absorption of food (particularly fats) in the small intestine. It is common in the tropics but also occurs in temperate countries, where it is known as idiopathic or nontropical sprue.

Q: What causes sprue?

A: There are many disorders that may cause sprue or the similar symptoms produced by malabsorption of food in the intestine. The disorders include COELIAC DISEASE, which may appear spontaneously at any age, or which may result from intestinal infections that are common in the tropics and which impair normal digestion. A different condition, the malabsorption syndrome, may produce identical symptoms. This may be the result of PANCREATITIS, in which there is insufficient secretion of the enzymes necessary for digestion, or of other factors that interfere with normal intestinal activity, for example, the metabolic disorder AMYLOIDOSIS; worm infestations; irradiation treatment; or operations in which part of the stomach or small intestine are removed.

Q: What are the symptoms of sprue?

A: The patient usually appears unwell, is underweight, and has a dry, pale skin. Soreness at the corners of the mouth (cheilosis) and a red tongue are present because of vitamin B deficiency. There may be clubbing of the fingers and swelling of the ankles (oedema); the abdomen may also swell. The patient may complain of weakness, fatigue, and frequent cramps in the muscles.

Bruising may occur easily, and diarrhoea, with large pale, fatty stools that float, may be an obvious feature.

Q: How is sprue treated?

A: Treatment depends on the cause. Coeliac disease is treated with a gluten-free diet and the avoidance of all wheat and rye protein. Tropical sprue is treated with vitamins and antibiotics.

Sputum is the material that is coughed up from the windpipe, bronchi, and lungs. A small amount of clear mucus is produced by the lungs each day, and this is swept through the windpipe (trachea) and over the larynx by the hair-like cells that keep the lungs free of dust and other particles. The amount of sputum increases in any minor respiratory infection.

Bloodstained sputum may be an indication of an underlying condition, such as severe infection or cancer. It requires prompt investigation.

Squint. *See* STRABISMUS.

Stammering. *See* STUTTERING.

Stapedectomy is an operation to remove the stapes (one of the small bones in the middle ear). The stapes is replaced with a plastic or metal equivalent, which transmits sounds to the round window of the inner ear.

A stapedectomy may be necessary in the treatment of DEAFNESS due to OTOSCLEROSIS.

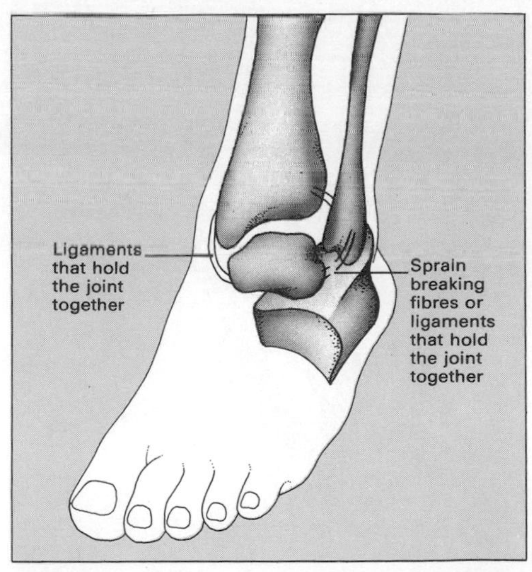

Sprain of the ankle is painful because the fibres and ligaments become stretched or torn.

Stapes is one of the three small bones (ossicles) in the middle ear; it is shaped like a stirrup iron. The stapes transmits sound vibrations to the round window of the inner ear. *See* EAR; OTITIS; OTOSCLEROSIS.

Staphylococcus is one of a group of BACTERIA that grow in clumps and, on microscopic examination, appear like bunches of grapes. Staphylococci are extremely common microorganisms and cause boils and other forms of skin sepsis characterized by pus.

Some staphylococci have the ability to resist antibiotics; for this reason doctors take particular care when treating staphylococcal infections. Staphylococci may also contaminate food and cause FOOD POISONING.

Startle reflex, also known as Moro's reflex, is the reflex reaction in infants under the age of three months to sudden movement or loud noise. The startle reflex can be seen if a baby is gently lifted a short way from a bed or table and then released, or if the table is hit hard. The infant throws his or her arms outward and then moves them slowly inward in a grasping movement as the legs are stretched out. This is usually accompanied by a cry.

A symmetrical movement is an indication that the central nervous system is functioning normally. An asymmetrical movement, in which one arm or leg seems to lag behind the other, can be one indication that brain damage (cerebral palsy) may have occurred.

Starvation is the physical change that the human body undergoes if there is a long and continued lack of sufficient nutrition. Provided fluids are available, a person can usually survive complete starvation for six to eight weeks finally dying.

In infants, starvation may cause marasmus or kwashiorkor. *See* KWASHIORKOR; NUTRITIONAL DISORDERS.

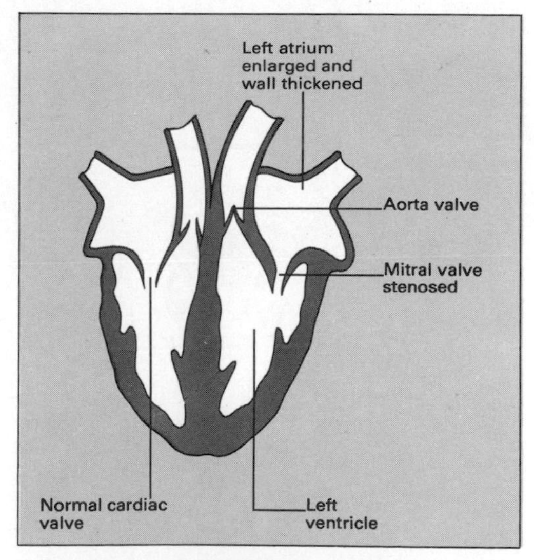

Stenosis of a valve produces muscle thickening in the part of the heart behind it.

Steatorrhoea is excessive fat in the faeces. It usually indicates a failure of fat absorption in the small intestine, and commonly occurs in SPRUE, but it may also accompany severe JAUNDICE.

Stenosis is a narrowing of a duct or tube within the body. It may develop in various places, such as at a heart valve (aortic or mitral stenosis); at the exit of the stomach from spasm of the muscle (pyloric stenosis); or in the duct of a salivary gland following infection or the passage of a small stone. Stenosis may also develop in the carotid artery or arteries of the leg, producing symptoms of reduced blood flow, such as transient minor strokes or intermittent claudication (*see* INTERMITTENT CLAUDICATION; STROKE).

Sterility is the inability to produce offspring. Sterility also refers to the stage of being free from living microorganisms, such as bacteria and viruses. *See* INFERTILITY; STERILIZATION.

Sterilization is any method by which various microorganisms, such as bacteria and viruses, are killed. Forms of sterilization include: boiling; dry heat; exposure to steam at high pressure; exposure to various gases or liquids; or exposure to radioactivity.

Sterilization is also the term used to describe an operation to make a man or woman infertile.

Q: How is a man sterilized?

A: A man can be sterilized by having a vasectomy, a simple operation that can be performed under a local anaesthetic, and which usually takes less than half an hour. Each vas deferens (the duct that carries sperm from the testicle) is cut and the ends tied off. For details, *see* VASECTOMY.

Q: How is a woman sterilized?

A: The corresponding procedure in a female is known technically as a tubal ligation. Each fallopian tube (the duct that carries eggs from an ovary to the womb) is cut and the ends tied. The operation is usually done under a general anaesthetic, and the woman may have to remain in hospital for four or five days. Nowadays many women are sterilized with a laparoscope (a type of ENDOSCOPE), and the tubes clipped or electrically burnt. This treatment requires only two days in hospital.

Q: Can sterilization be reversed in men or women?

A: Yes, but the chances of success are about 20% in women and 60% in men.

Q: In what circumstances should a couple consider sterilization?

A: A couple may consider sterilization if two or more children have been born with congenital anomalies (*see* GENETIC COUNSELLING). More usually, sterilization may be carried out for social reasons: for example, a woman aged over thirty who has already had children may dislike other forms of contraception, or find that they fail.

Sternum, or breast-bone, is a flat, dagger-shaped bone that forms the front part of the chest wall. It is about 17cm (7 inches) long in men and about 13cm (5 inches) long in women, and about 4cm (1.5 inches) across at its widest part.

The sternum is made up of three segments: the widest, top part (the manubrium), also known as the handle; the body of the sternum; and the tip (the xiphoid process or xiphisternum). In children the three parts of the sternum are jointed, but in adults they are fused to form one continuous bone.

Anomalies of the sternum may produce a protuberant, pigeon-chested appearance, or a sunken, funnel-chested appearance. These relatively common anomalies do not cause any major problems. *See* PIGEON CHEST.

Steroid is a class of chemical compounds. The term is commonly applied to the corticosteroid hormones produced by the adrenal glands. Other steroids include the hormones progesterone, the oestrogen group, and testosterone, as well as bile salts and cholesterol. *See* CHOLESTEROL; CORTICOSTEROID.

Stethoscope is an instrument for listening to the internal sounds of the body.

Stevens-Johnson syndrome is a rare skin disorder in which there are painful blisters in the throat and mouth, the conjunctiva of the eyes, and the anal region. Other reddish nodules, and sometimes blisters, may appear on the arms and legs. Blisters in the throat may be so painful as to prevent swallowing. Treatment with corticosteroid drugs may be necessary.

Stiff neck involves either difficulty in moving the neck from its normal position, or an abnormality known medically as torticollis that forces the neck to remain in an unusual position.

Q: What causes a stiff neck?

A: The most common cause is a twisting or whiplash injury suffered from jerking the neck too hard, as in a car accident or in a sports injury. It may also occur after sleeping with the neck in an awkward position. In infancy, stiff neck may be caused by muscle spasm; in the elderly it is usually caused by spondylosis.

Q: How is a stiff neck treated?

A: Usually with painkilling drugs and, if inflammation is present, with antirheumatic drugs. Treatment depends on the cause. If the stiffness is caused by local injury then heat, massage, and traction may be required.

Diagnosis before treatment is important because the stiffness may result from a slipped disc or other abnormality in which manipulation may cause further damage or delay before correct diagnosis. *See* SLIPPED DISC.

Stiffness is a common symptom of disorders of the muscles and joints. It can be accompanied by aching pain. Aspirin will relieve the pain, as will massage. Recurrent morning stiffness is a characteristic of rheumatoid arthritis.

Stigma is any physical mark on the body characteristic of a disorder or an occupation, or any mark, spot, or wound that appears for no apparent physical or psychological reason.

Stillbirth is the birth of a dead foetus after twenty-eight weeks of pregnancy. It can result from various disorders, such as congenital anomalies in the foetus, haemolytic diseases of the newborn, placental insufficiency, or maternal disorders such as diabetes mellitus, anaemia, or heart disease.

See also MISCARRIAGE.

Still's disease is a juvenile form of RHEUMATOID ARTHRITIS. Initial symptoms include a sudden high fever, vague rashes that appear and disappear all over the body, and enlargement of the lymph glands and spleen. The fever may continue for several weeks

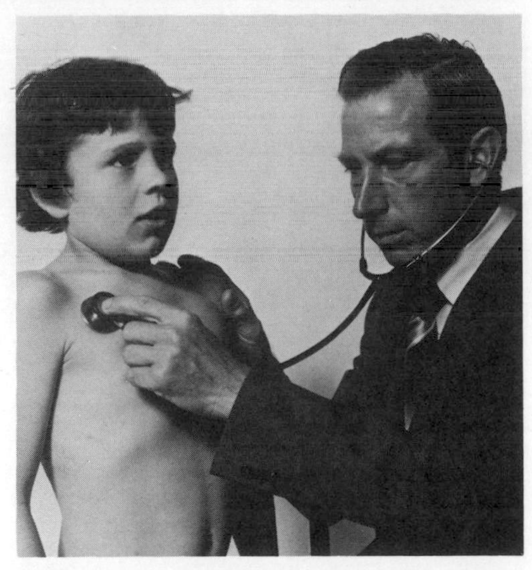

Stethoscope is used to listen to the heart beat, and to detect lung irregularities.

before any joint pain occurs, or the joints may become swollen and tender within a few days.

Aspirin-type drugs are usually prescribed until spontaneous improvement occurs, and corticosteroids may be given to treat severe cases.

Relapse is common, but eventually there is full recovery in most cases.

Stimulant is a drug or other agent that increases the activity of an organ or other part of the body.

See also AMPHETAMINES.

Sting is the damage and pain caused by contact with the poison from a plant or insect. For EMERGENCY treatment, *see* First Aid, p.514.

Stitch is a term popularly used to refer to a severe pain in the abdomen, usually under the rib-cage, that occurs with physical exertion. It is caused by a cramp in the muscles of the abdominal wall.

In surgical practice, the term stitch is equivalent to suture. *See* SUTURE.

Stokes-Adams attack is a form of heart block. The normal electrical impulses that regulate the heartbeat are blocked, and the heart first stops contracting and then continues at a much slower rate than normal. The rate may spontaneously return to normal. Stokes-Adams attacks are characterized by a sudden loss of consciousness, sometimes with immediate recovery, but often followed by a period of faintness, dizziness, and nausea when the patient tries to sit up. The length of these episodes may vary from periods as short as a few seconds to a few minutes. Occasionally a complete heartblock may persist.

A mechanical pacemaker is the most effective form of treatment, although drug treatment may sometimes be used. Stokes-Adams attacks are most common in the elderly and are associated with coronary heart disease. *See* HEARTBLOCK; PACEMAKER.

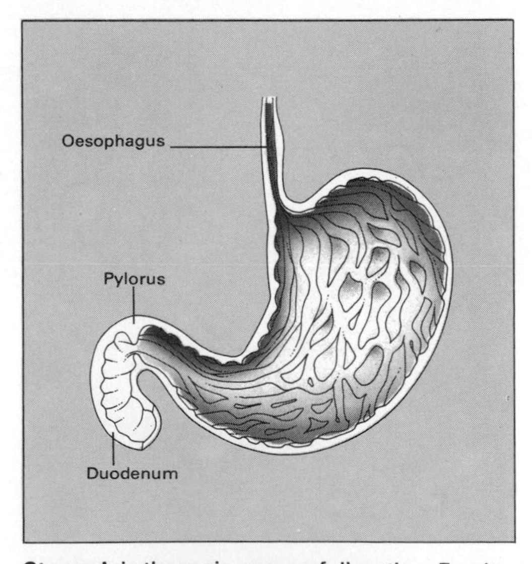

Stomach is the main organ of digestion. Food enters it through the oesophagus.

Stomach is the muscular storage organ of the intestinal tract. It lies in the upper part of the abdomen, under the liver and below the left side of the diaphragm.

Food and liquid from the mouth enter the stomach from the oesophagus (gullet). The stomach can hold up to 1.5 litres (three pints) of fluid.

The three chief activities of the stomach are: contracting and squeezing the food it contains; digestion and sterilization of the food by the gastric secretions; and intermittent and gradual release of the contents into the duodenum so that digestion can continue. The stomach is also able to absorb some substances, such as alcohol, and this explains the rapid effect if drunk when the stomach is empty.

The stomach is composed of three layers of muscle covered with a membrane (the peritoneum). The inner surface is lined with mucosa that secrete gastric juices. The lower and narrow end of the stomach is formed of tough muscle fibre ending in the pyloric sphincter, which closes the exit to the duodenum.

See also DIGESTIVE SYSTEM.

Stomachache is a vague feeling of upper abdominal discomfort often accompanied by distention. It is one of the symptoms of INDIGESTION. *See* ABDOMINAL PAIN.

Stomach disorders. Relatively few disorders directly involve the stomach, but these include some of the most common complaints, such as gastroenteritis and peptic ulcers. Many disorders that primarily involve other parts of the body can also affect the stomach. *See* ABDOMINAL PAIN; BELCHING; BILIARY COLIC; BLOOD, VOMITING OF; CANCER; COLIC; DIARRHOEA; FLATULENCE; FOOD POISONING; GASTRITIS; GASTROENTERITIS; HYPERCHLORHYDRIA; HYPEREMESIS; INDIGESTION; LOSS OF APPETITE; MOTION SICKNESS; NAUSEA; PEPTIC ULCER; PYLORIC STENOSIS; PYLOROSPASM; VOMITING.

Stomatitis is inflammation of the mouth. It may be caused by a local disorder in the mouth, or it can occur as the result of generalized disease of the body.

A doctor or dentist should be consulted to obtain treatment for the cause of the problem. The mouth must be kept clean with mouthwashes, and any deposit must be cleaned off the teeth and lips. Dehydration may have reduced the amount of salivation, and plenty of fluids should be drunk.

Infection of the SALIVARY GLANDS may occur with stomatitis, and sometimes infected material may enter the lungs and cause PNEUMONIA.

Stone. *See* CALCULUS.

Stool is the common name for faeces. *See* FAECES.

Strabismus, also called a squint, is a condition in which the axes of the eyes are not parallel even when a person is looking at a distant object. It is usually the result of an imbalance in the movement of the two eyes. In convergent strabismus (cross-eye), the axes of the eyes converge; in divergent strabismus (lazy eye) they diverge.

Q: *What symptoms may develop with strabismus?*

A: If only the unaffected eye is used, the other eye may get worse and defective vision or blindness (amblyopia) may occur in that eye. Paralytic strabismus, caused by paralysis of an eye muscle, results in double vision (diplopia). This may be accompanied by giddiness, vertigo, and a tendency to incline the head to one side.

Q: *What is the treatment for strabismus?*

A: The most important aspect of treating strabismus is first to correct defective vision by wearing spectacles all the time. If this fails, a patch over the good eye or atropine drops to produce blurred vision ensures that the patient uses the eye with poor vision. Occasionally, eye exercises may be used to teach the patient to co-ordinate movements. If vision is equally good in both eyes, an operation may be performed to move the eye muscles, thereby positioning the eyes normally.

Strain is a term that is used to describe either an emotional or a physical disorder.

An emotional strain causes symptoms of fatigue, anxiety, and sometimes slight depression. This may result in irritability, difficulty in sleeping, and loss of weight.

Physical strain can cause tearing of muscle fibres, resulting in local pain and stiffness. It is different from a sprain, which is more serious, and may involve tearing of the ligaments around a joint. Rest, painkilling drugs, and physiotherapy with infrared heat treatment and gentle exercise help a physical strain to heal.

Strangulation is the constriction of a tube or passage within the body. It may result in partial or complete obstruction of the affected part. Strangulation is one of the causes of INTESTINAL OBSTRUCTION.

Strangury is extremely painful urination. It is most commonly caused by CYSTITIS (inflammation of the bladder) or by a stone (calculus) in the bladder.

Streptococcus is a genus of bacteria that appears to grow in straight strings or chains, as seen under a microscope. Many streptococci are harmless and are normally found in the body without causing any disorder. Some types, however, cause conditions such as sore throat and tonsillitis, scarlet fever, impetigo, erysipelas, rheumatic fever, acute nephritis, puerperal fever; others may infect wounds.

Q: *Can streptococcal infections have complications?*

A: Yes. Infection by streptococcus may be followed by an allergic reaction involving other tissues of the body. This can lead to disorders such as acute nephritis, rheumatic fever, chorea, and scarlet fever.

Q: *How are streptococcal infections treated?*

A: Almost all streptococcal infections respond to large doses of penicillin, and this treatment usually produces a cure if used for long enough.

A talk about Stress

Stress is a physical and psychological reaction to excessive stimulus. It is considered by some experts to be a psychological disorder caused by constant mental strain; but it is also a physiological response.

Physical stress on various parts of the body

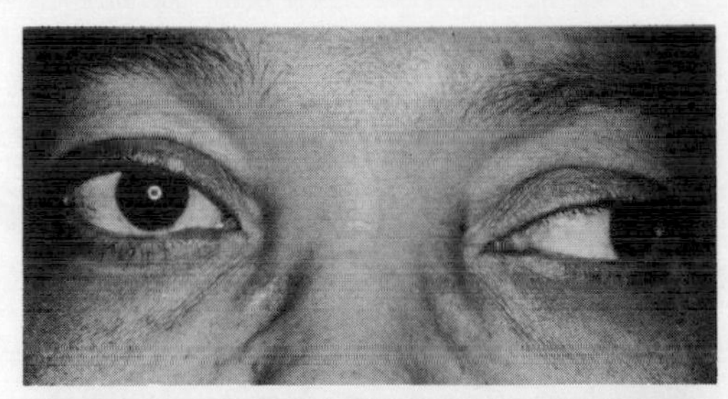

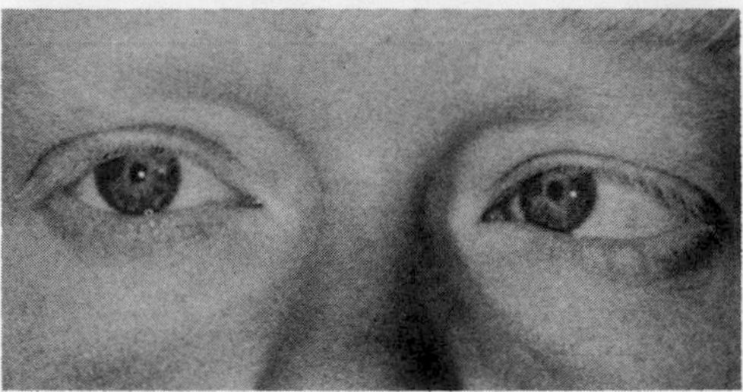

Strabismus is the misalignment of the axes of the eyes whichever way they look.

can cause damage. For example repeated minor injuries to a bone, such as one in the leg or foot of a runner, may cause a stress fracture in that bone.

Psychological stress, to a minor degree, is necessary for normal alertness and awareness, but excessive stress can have the opposite effect. The most common cause of psychological stress is fatigue, and a state of stress may be aggravated by a physical illness or by a mental disorder such as DEPRESSION.

Q: What are the symptoms of stress?

A: Symptoms of stress vary. Some people appear on the outside to be calm, but are inwardly in turmoil; others panic. Some people experience great discomfort in acute stress; they become hot and sweaty, have a rapid heartbeat, or even vomit or faint. Others may react with hysterical amnesia (loss of memory).

Q: What physical disorders can stress produce?

A: Disorders produced by stress vary greatly, but there are many disorders that can be triggered off or made worse by psychological stress, particularly when it is combined with anxiety or depression. Asthma and migraine are likely to occur more frequently with stress, and stress is a factor in causing peptic ulcer, irritable bowel syndrome, and ulcerative colitis.

In some people, the onset of hyperthyroidism (overactivity of the thyroid gland) is associated with a period of stress. Neurodermatitis, a skin condition accompanied by intense irritation, is often a stress disorder, and hyperhidrosis, or excess sweating, is thought to be affected by stress.

Heavy, prolonged menstrual periods (menorrhagia) occur in some women as a result of continued stress, and may even lead to a cessation of periods (amenorrhoea) in younger women.

Q: How is stress treated?

A: A person who suspects that he or she is suffering from stress should consult a doctor. The doctor will be able to decide whether external stress is the main factor or whether the condition is caused by depression or a phobic anxiety state. The doctor will also be able to give medication or advice that may help to relieve the symptoms of stress.

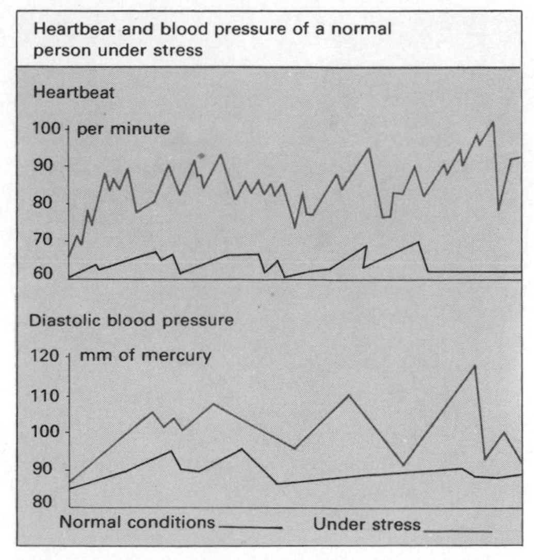

Stress can be measured in terms of specific physiological responses to external factors.

Stress incontinence is the inability to prevent loss of urine during physical stress, such as coughing, laughing, or sudden movement. It may be caused by a structural abnormality, such as a PROLAPSE of the womb. In such cases, the womb may pull the bladder from its normal position, and weaken the muscle that closes the bladder.

Women who suffer from stress incontinence should consult a doctor in order to diagnose the cause.

Stricture is an abnormal narrowing of a duct or passage within the body. It may be caused by inflammation; injury, with subsequent scarring of the tissues; a muscle spasm; or pressure, as from a growth or tumour. Strictures may also be caused by a congenital anomaly, such as HIRSCHSPRUNG'S DISEASE.

Stridor is a high pitched rasping sound produced by partial obstruction of the vocal cords. It is a common condition in children with croup. Stridor may also be produced by inflammation or tumours of the larynx or vocal cords.

A talk about a Stroke

Stroke (for EMERGENCY treatment, *see* p.554), also known as apoplexy, is a stoppage of the blood supply to part of the brain. The blockage can have one of three causes: (1) a blood clot, from somewhere else in the body (embolus), obstructing an artery; (2) clotting within an artery (cerebral thrombosis); or (3) the bursting of a blood vessel (cerebral haemorrhage). A stroke may be a relatively minor occurrence, and temporary strokes that are followed by complete recovery also occur.

Transient, temporary strokes may occur as

a result of disturbances in blood flow to the brain. This may be caused by constriction of the carotid and vertebral arteries in the neck by patches of arteriosclerosis in their walls. These constrictions reduce the blood supply so that a slight drop in blood pressure, from any cause, may produce a stroke. This is particularly likely to occur in an elderly person, and may be the result of illness, coronary thrombosis, or cardiac irregularities such as atrial fibrillation, as well as anaemia, sudden blood loss, or pressure on the neck from a tight collar. Temporary strokes may also occur from small emboli, usually blood clots, that form on the arteriosclerotic areas of the arteries, or sometimes from damaged heart valves that have been caused by subacute endocarditis. These small particles cause a momentary blockage of a small artery in the brain, which produces symptoms that disappear without loss of consciousness.

Q: *What are the symptoms of a stroke?*

A: The symptoms depend on the area of the brain that is involved. In an acute apoplectic stroke, breathing is difficult, and there is paralysis of part of the body, often affecting one whole side of the body, including the face, trunk, and one leg and arm. The skin feels clammy to the touch, and speech may be affected. Loss of consciousness may occur extremely rapidly, but occasionally a patient may remain conscious but confused. A temporary stroke may produce all the symptoms of a severe stroke, but the person usually recovers completely after a short time.

Q: *What can be done to help someone who has a stroke?*

A: An ambulance must be called immediately. Keep the patient quiet and warm (with a rug or blanket), either sitting up or lying down with the head and shoulders raised. An unconscious patient should be placed in the recovery position (*see* First Aid, p.573). The patient should not be moved until professional help arrives, unless it is essential. Do not give the patient anything to eat or drink. In most cases, the patient will be taken directly to hospital.

Q: *What is the hospital treatment for stroke patients?*

A: Careful nursing is necessary, including constant exercise of the limbs, to prevent stiffening or contraction of the muscles. Many routine actions (such as walking and sitting down) may have to be learned again. This is the task of a physiotherapist. A speech therapist may help the patient to speak again. Recovery from a stroke is never quick because retraining, a long and slow process, may take several months.

It is rare that the cause of a stroke can be actively treated. Anticoagulants will make a cerebral haemorrhage worse, therefore they can only be given if the neurologist considers that a slowly progressing stroke is due to cerebral thrombosis. Occasionally a neurosurgeon will operate if an aneurysm has been found to be the cause of subarachnoid haemorrhage or, less commonly, to remove a large clot following a cerebral haemorrhage. Rarely, haemorrhage occurs underneath (subdural) or outside (epidural) the dural layers that surround the brain. These haemorrhages can be diagnosed by the appropriate neurological investigations and can be treated surgically.

Q: *What are the patient's chances of making a full recovery from a stroke?*

A: Each case must be judged on the severity of its symptoms. In the most severe cases, patients fail to regain consciousness at all and die shortly after an attack.

Many patients return to normal health, however, with only a slight speech defect and perhaps some awkwardness in walking or handling objects. In some cases, people are left paralysed on one side (hemiplegia) with a speech disorder (aphasia) and an inability to control bladder and bowel functions (incontinence).

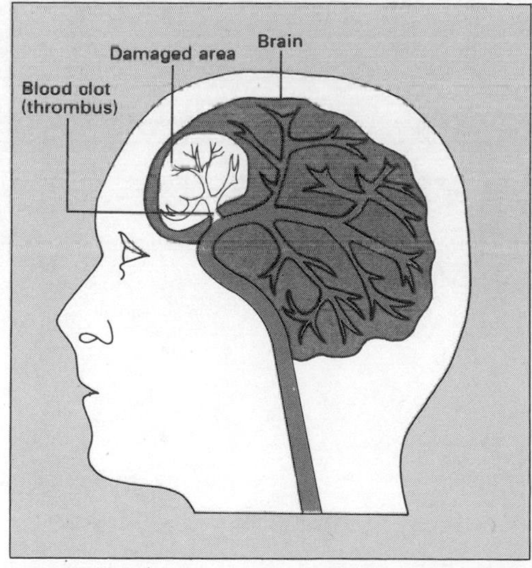

Stroke is caused by a blood clot that stops the blood supply to an area of the brain.

Q: Can strokes be prevented?

A: In the majority of people there is no way of preventing a stroke. Exceptions include those with arteriosclerosis, who may be helped by regular doses of aspirin under the supervision of a doctor, and people with high blood pressure or diabetes in whom these conditions can be controlled. Transient strokes are often a warning that a major stroke will occur. If the cause, such as a constriction in a carotid artery, can be found, an operation to remove the affected part of the artery may be a cure. Control of cardiac irregularities is necessary to prevent a sudden drop in blood pressure, and damage to the heart valves by endocarditis must be treated at once.

The majority of strokes occur in elderly people and are the consequence of arteriosclerosis, which cannot be treated effectively once it has occurred.

Strongyloides is a genus of roundworms, one species of which (*Strongyloides stercoralis*) is a common intestinal parasite in people who live in hot climates. Infestation with this roundworm is called strongyloidiasis.

There may be no symptoms if the infestation is light. But migration of larvae through the lungs usually produces a cough. Heavy infestations may also cause abdominal pain, vomiting, and diarrhoea. In most cases, drug treatment with thiabendazole is effective. It is advisable to have regular drug treatment in areas where the parasite is common.

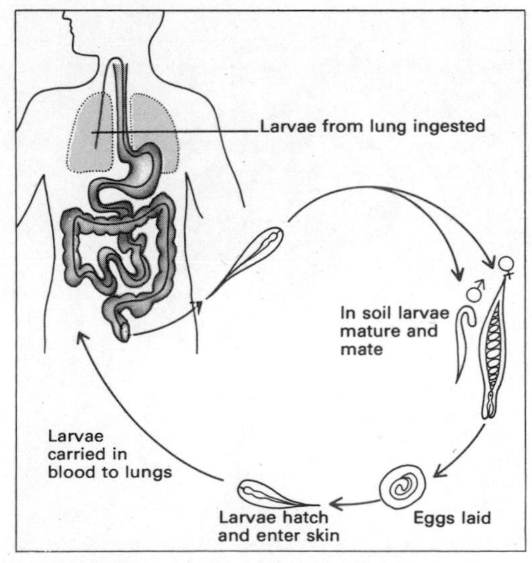

Strongyloides is a roundworm that enters the bloodstream through the skin of the foot.

Strychnine is a poisonous alkaloid obtained from the seeds of the tree *Nux vomica.* Strychnine poisoning causes extreme activity of the central nervous system, leading to repeated muscle spasms that end in death unless the victim's stomach is immediately washed out, and an injection of muscle relaxant drug given.

Stuffy nose is a common term for the blockage of one or both nostrils, resulting in difficulty in breathing. It is common in infections that cause inflammation of the nose, but may be caused by a POLYP or a DEVIATED NASAL SEPTUM.

See also CATARRH.

Stupor is a state of semicoma, with suppression of the senses and of the normal thought processes.

Stuttering, or stammering, is a speech disorder in which speech is faltering or hesitant, and the initial sounds of words are repeated. It usually starts between the ages of two and five years, and is more common in boys than in girls.

In many children, stuttering is caused by psychological factors, and may be aggravated by parental anxiety. If there is no sign of improvement after the child is seven years old, or if the stuttering gets worse, a speech therapist should be consulted.

Stye, medically known as a hordeolum, is an abscess of an eyelash hair follicle. It is caused by a bacterial infection, and is commonly associated with blepharitis (inflammation of the eyelid).

The symptoms of a stye include swelling, redness, and pain. But when the stye bursts, there is relief from pain and an immediate improvement.

Treatment is to bathe the stye with a cottonwool swab soaked repeatedly in hot water. Removing an affected eyelash sometimes helps to produce immediate discharge.

See also BLEPHARITIS.

Styptic is a substance such as alcohol, silver nitrate, or alum, that stops bleeding by its astringent action.

Subacute bacterial endocarditis is inflammation of the lining of the interior of the heart, especially the heart valves. Severe inflammation of rapid onset is called acute bacterial endocarditis. More usually, infection is of slow onset, known as subacute bacterial endocarditis. It is most likely to occur in people whose heart valves are deformed or damaged as a result of a congenital anomaly, rheumatic fever, or following heart surgery. People who inject themselves with opiates or other drugs, risk infection from septicaemia (blood poisoning), which may cause subacute bacterial endocarditis.

Q: What are the symptoms of subacute bacterial endocarditis?

A: In the early stages, the patient may feel unwell, with occasional slight fever, and aching muscles and joints. The aching is commonly accompanied by tender spots in the fingertips and a particular kind of fine rash (petechiae).

The patient becomes ill and weak as the disease progresses, with intermittent high fever and sometimes heart failure.

Q: How is the disorder diagnosed and treated?

A: A doctor may become suspicious if the patient has a heart murmur with a vague onset of intermittent fever. Blood samples, taken on several occasions, can be cultured to reveal the presence of bacteria. In such patients, the urine contains blood because of damage to the kidneys.

Without treatment, the disease is fatal, but with antibiotics, about three-quarters of patients affected survive. The penicillin group of antibiotics are the most frequently used and are given by intravenous or intramuscular injection for four to six weeks. The patient usually starts to feel better within a week.

Subarachnoid haemorrhage is bleeding into the space between the membranes that surround the brain, in which cerebrospinal fluid circulates. It most commonly occurs in people between the ages of twenty-five and forty-five, and is caused by the bursting of a blood vessel that was abnormally weak at birth. In the older age group, subarachnoid haemorrhage may occur when arteriosclerosis causes damage to an artery, or it may be associated with a bleeding disorder.

Q: What are the symptoms of a subarachnoid haemorrhage?

A: Most patients have a sudden and severe headache. There is also a temporary or prolonged loss of consciousness. After the patient recovers consciousness, he or she is confused, may vomit, and may have convulsions. Temporary weakness of the muscles may follow, or complete paralysis of one side of the body, and the neck becomes stiff.

Q: How is subarachnoid haemorrhage treated?

A: About a third of all patients die from the initial haemorrhage, and a further fifteen to twenty per cent die within the next month. It is therefore necessary to find the area of bleeding as quickly as possible. Neurosurgery may prevent further bleeding.

Subclavian describes anything that lies beneath the clavicle (collar-bone).

Subconjunctival haemorrhage is bleeding between the conjunctiva (the thin, transparent membrane that covers the outside of the eye) and the sclera (the fibrous tissue that forms the white of the eye). A subconjunctival haemorrhage causes the white of the eye to become red. *See* RED EYE.

Subconscious describes mental activity that occurs beneath the levels of normal conscious awareness. Psychoanalysts define it as a level between the conscious and the unconscious.

Subcutaneous means beneath the skin and above the underlying layers of tissue, such as muscle. The subcutaneous layer contains fat and connective tissue, and varies in thickness in different parts of the body.

Subdural describes the space between the dura and arachnoid mater, two of the membranes that cover the brain.

Haemorrhage into the subdural space may occur as the result of a head injury. In an acute haemorrhage, the patient is usually in coma and the bleeding results in extensive damage to the brain.

Sublingual gland is the smallest of the salivary glands. There are two sublingual glands located between the side of the tongue and the jawbone, one on each side of the face. *See* SALIVARY GLANDS.

Subluxation is a partial or incomplete dislocation. It may occur in a joint or in the lens of the eye. *See* DISLOCATION.

Submandibular gland is one of the salivary glands. There are two submandibular glands, one in each side of the mouth under the jawbone and below the back teeth. *See* SALIVARY GLANDS.

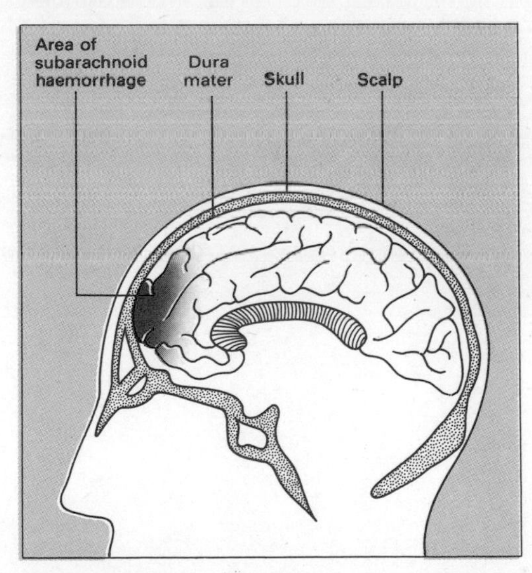

Subarachnoid haemorrhage into the tissues of the brain increases intercranial pressure.

Submucosal resection

Submucosal resection is a common operation on the nose, carried out under a general anaesthetic, to correct a DEVIATED NASAL SEPTUM. The operation removes the deformed part of the nasal septum (the cartilage and bone that divide the nostrils), allowing the two layers of mucous membrane to take up a straight position along the midline.

Subphrenic means beneath the diaphragm.

Succus entericus is the secretion of the glands that line the small intestine. It contains various enzymes essential for the digestion of food. *See* DIGESTIVE SYSTEM.

Sudden infant death syndrome. *See* SIDS.

Suffocation, or asphyxiation, is the result of blockage of the air passage, or a reduction or absence of oxygen in the air breathed in. For EMERGENCY treatment, *see* First Aid, p.518.

Brain damage occurs within five minutes if the condition is not treated, because of the shortage of oxygen. Treatment is to clear the airway, if it is obstructed, and give artificial respiration.

Sugar is a sweet-tasting carbohydrate that occurs in many foods. The sugar commonly used to sweeten food is sucrose. But there are many other sugars. They are either simple monosaccharides (such as dextrose, glucose, and fructose) or complex polysaccharides (such as sucrose and lactose).

Sugars are a good source of energy and can be broken down by the body to form glucose (blood sugar). Glucose can be reconstructed by the liver and body cells into various other forms of carbohydrates.

Excess intake of sugar causes obesity, and may be a contributory factor in arteriosclerosis.

See also CARBOHYDRATES; GLUCOSE; INSULIN.

Deaths by suicide in England and Wales

Male	Year	Female
2523	1969	1803
2271	1970	1669
2263	1971	1682
2198	1972	1572
2250	1973	1573
2280	1974	1619
2184	1975	1509
2330	1976	1486
2360	1977	1581
2436	1978	1586

Suicide attempts are more often successful by men than they are by women.

A talk about Suicide

Suicide is the taking of one's own life. It is a common cause of death between the ages of twenty and forty, second only to accidents. Attempted suicide is responsible for about twenty per cent of all emergency hospital admissions.

Q: Why do people try to commit suicide?

A: The reasons are usually complex, and may be part of a wider personality disorder. There may be a history of antisocial behaviour, delinquency, alcoholism, poor school attendance, poor work record, depression, loneliness, or indications of problems with social relationships. Many people who attempt suicide do not really want to kill themselves at all. Their attempts are desperate acts to draw attention to their plight.

The major reason for suicide, however, is mental illness. An elderly or chronically ill person may take his or her life in a state of acute depression, misery, and pain. A person with a personality disorder, unable to cope with stress, depression, or a physical disorder, is a typical potential suicide.

Q: How can suicide be prevented?

A: Seek professional help, if it is thought that a person is likely to commit suicide. If there is time, seek help from the family doctor. Or there are many groups, such as the Samaritans, which specialize in helping the suicidal individual.

A doctor may suggest psychotherapy or prescribe antidepressant drugs. Seriously depressed people should, however, be hospitalized immediately for observation.

Q: What should be done if someone has already attempted suicide?

A: Get the suicide victim to hospital as quickly as possible. In the meantime, give appropriate first aid (*see* the First Aid section). Collect and keep any bottles, and look for a suicide note.

If a person telephones to say that he or she has attempted suicide, find out the exact location and address, keep the person talking, and get someone else to call for the police and other emergency aid. Continue talking until help arrives.

Sulpha drugs are drugs of several related

types that are used in the treatment of infection. Sulphonamide, which is an antibiotic, is an example of one type.

Possible side effects of sulpha drugs include nausea, diarrhoea, vomiting, skin rashes, and, very rarely, STEVENS-JOHNSON SYNDROME, although modern preparations have largely eradicated the likelihood of this happening.

Sulphones are a group of drugs used in the treatment of leprosy. These include dapsone and sulfoxone. Possible side effects include allergic dermatitis, loss of appetite, nausea, vomiting, and giddiness.

Sunburn occurs after exposure to ultraviolet light. For EMERGENCY treatment, *see* First Aid, p.594. Mild sunburn usually occurs a few hours after exposure as red skin that eventually peels away. Severe sunburn, however, results in extreme pain, swelling, and blistering a few days after excessive exposure, accompanied by fever, weakness, and symptoms suggestive of mild shock. The blisters are second-degree burns and may become infected.

Q: How is sunburn prevented?

A: Those who are vulnerable to sunburn, particularly those with fair skins, should sunbathe for only short periods. For example, twenty minutes in the morning and twenty minutes in the evening for the first few days. Sunburn lotions and creams, if used, should be regularly applied. Ultraviolet rays that are reflected off water, sand, or snow have particularly strong effects.

Q: Are there any long-term hazards of sunburn?

A: Yes. Constant exposure to sunlight damages the skin and causes wrinkles. It also alters skin structure, producing warty lumps called keratoses that may ultimately form RODENT ULCERS or cancer of the skin.

Sunstroke (for EMERGENCY treatment, *see* First Aid, p.567) is a form of heatstroke that is caused by overexposure to the sun. *See* HEATSTROKE.

Superfluous hair is an excessive growth of hair, or the presence of hair in an unusual place. *See* HIRSUTISM.

Supine describes the position of lying on the back with the face upward.

Suppository is a cone-shaped or cylindrical medication that is inserted into the rectum for therapeutic purposes. Suppositories usually consist of glycerin or cocoa butter that contain medication and liquefy at body temperature. Suppositories for insertion into the vagina are called pessaries. *See* PESSARY.

Suppuration is the formation and discharge of pus. It may occur when an abscess or a wound becomes infected with pyogenic (pus-forming) microorganisms.

See also PUS.

Suprapubic means above the pubic bone in the pelvis. The suprapubic region is the lowest area of the abdomen.

Suprarenal gland. *See* ADRENAL GLAND.

A talk about Surgery

Surgery is the branch of medicine that treats disorders by surgical operation. For example, a surgeon can remove a diseased part of the body, correct deformities, repair injuries, or carry out internal examinations.

There are many different specialties within surgery, but every surgeon is trained in certain basic techniques and skills before starting further specialized training.

Q: What are some of the common surgical specialties?

A: Some surgeons specialize in dealing with certain age groups, such as children (paediatric surgery); or particular conditions, such as cancer, when the surgeon is part of a team including other doctors and radiotherapists. Common specialties include abdominal surgery or surgery of the gastrointestinal tract; accident surgery or the immediate treatment on emergency hospital admission; cardiac surgery or treatment of heart conditions; and cosmetic surgery, which is really a subspecialty of plastic surgery. Other specialist areas include

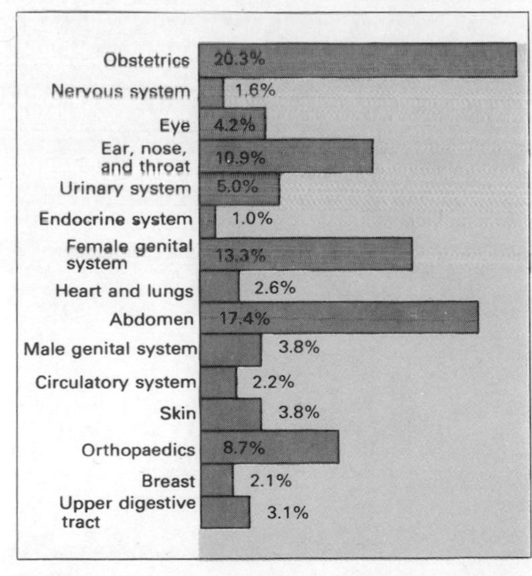

Surgery is used to treat many different kinds of conditions and disorders.

dental surgery, which includes facio-maxillary surgery, used in the treatment of teeth and damage to facial bones; genitourinary surgery for treatment of urinary disorders and male genital problems; gynaecological surgery, treatment of disorders of the female reproductive system; and neurosurgery, treatment of the brain and nervous system.

There is also obstetric surgery, the specialty of dealing with childbirth; ophthalmic surgery, treatment of eye disorders; orthopaedic surgery, treatment of bone and joint disorders; otorhinolaryngological surgery (ENT), treatment of ear, nose, and throat disorders; and plastic surgery to reform and replace damaged tissues.

There are three other common specialities: rectal surgery, a subspecialty of abdominal surgery; thoracic surgery, treatment of the chest, particularly the lungs; and vascular surgery, treatment of the blood vessels.

Q: *Are there certain procedures that are used in all forms of surgery?*

A: Yes. The surgeon ensures that the patient is as fit as possible before an operation. Even in a serious accident or emergency, time spent in resuscitation gives the patient a better chance of recovery.

Asepsis (the absence of infection) is essential to prevent microorganisms from entering the patient's body. This is achieved by careful sterilization of all surgical instruments, and by all medical staff wearing masks and special sterile clothing. The patient's skin is sterilized with antiseptic fluid before an operation.

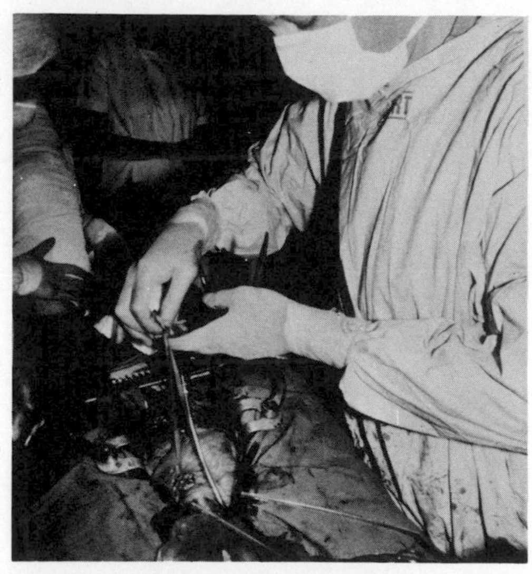

Surgery is a branch of medicine that deals with manual diagnosis, repair, or correction.

Q: *Are special surgery techniques necessary in some operations?*

A: Yes. Surgeons operating on the eye or ear may perform microsurgery, using a microscope. Eye surgeons may also use laser beams in the treatment of certain disorders. Cryosurgery, a freezing technique, can be used by eye surgeons as well as in surgery on other parts of the body. Cautery, or the use of heat or chemicals to destroy tissue, is another surgical technique. In replacement surgery, damaged body tissues, such as arthritic joints or damaged heart valves, may be replaced by artificial ones.

Avascular surgery is a technique used to prevent excessive bleeding in the limbs. This technique must be performed within a certain time to prevent tissue death. The patient is anaesthetized and the limb tightly bandaged, squeezing the blood out from the hand or foot upward, and then a tourniquet is left in place. This stops blood entering the limb and makes surgery simple and clean. The tourniquet must be released after about thirty minutes.

In heart surgery, special kinds of anaesthesia, which reduce the patient's body temperature, allow the heart to cease working and thus protect the brain from damage for longer than would normally happen. A heart-lung machine may be used while the heart is repaired or replaced.

Q: *Are there any risks in having an operation?*

A: Yes. There is always some risk in surgery, although the surgeon takes every precaution possible when operating. Risks include atelectasis (collapse of part of the lung because of the anaesthetic), postoperative pneumonia, or some rare or unexpected reaction to the anaesthetic drugs.

Immediately after the operation, the main danger is a sudden haemorrhage from the operated area, producing shock. A common problem in the immediate recovery period following all abdominal operations is paralytic ileus, or failure of the intestine to work. Continued paralytic ileus may result in abdominal swelling that opens the wound or the area of operation in the intestine. Breakdown or bursting of any wound may occur if the patient is ill or debilitated.

Lung infections, such as pneumonia,

and urinary retention are common problems. But a problem that can occur suddenly and unexpectedly is a pulmonary EMBOLUS from a blood clot formed in a deep vein, usually in the legs or pelvis.

Wound infections may develop from the cause of the original operation, such as in appendicitis, or they sometimes occur, despite all precautions, during the operation.

Late complications of any operation may occur from the scar tissue or adhesions that are formed. In the abdomen, these may cause obstruction.

Q: Do all operations have to be performed in a hospital?

A: No. Minor surgery can frequently be performed in the doctor's surgery under local anaesthetic. Operations such as the incision of an abscess, or the suturing of a wound do not require the facilities of a hospital.

Nevertheless, it is usually advisable to have even minor operations performed in an operating theatre of a hospital. The patient can then have access to professional care during the recovery phase. Operations such as removal of skin cysts, D and C (dilation and curettage), and many dental operations are performed on a day admission basis. But all hospitals require written consent before surgery is undertaken.

Q: How is consent given for an operation?

A: The surgeon explains what the operation entails, and asks for a Consent for Operation form to be signed. The form states that the patient agrees to the operation and that the details of the operation have been explained. The form also gives the surgeon permission to carry out any further procedure necessary if there is an unexpected complication.

Permission for an operation should be given by the patient if he or she is over the age of consent, or by a parent or guardian if the patient is under this age. But if the patient is unconscious or mentally ill, consent must be obtained from the nearest relative or legal guardian.

A surgeon may also be faced with an unconscious patient who is in need of urgent treatment and for whom permission cannot be obtained. This may be because the identity of the patient is not known or the next of kin is not available. In this situation, the surgeon has to make every effort to find someone who can give permission. If no one is available, the surgeon is under a moral, if not legal, duty to undertake any life-saving surgery.

Q: What treatment is given to a patient before an operation in hospital?

A: The patient usually goes into hospital the day before an operation, so that any tests can be performed and medical and nursing staff can make sure the patient is in good health.

The patient is usually given sedation the night before an operation, and is not allowed to eat or drink for at least four hours before the operation. This ensures that the stomach is empty and that solid food will not appear if vomiting occurs.

An hour before the operation, an injection, usually of a mild sedative opiate drug combined with an atropine-like drug, is given to dry the secretions. The patient is then taken to the anaesthetic room. In this room the anaesthetist usually gives an intravenous injection of a short-acting barbiturate drug. This puts the patient to sleep before any further form of anaesthetic is given.

Q: What can a patient expect to occur after an operation?

A: After an operation, the patient is usually kept in a recovery room or, in the case of major surgery, taken to an intensive care unit. As soon as the patient's general condition is good enough, he or she is returned to the ward or room.

On recovering consciousness from a

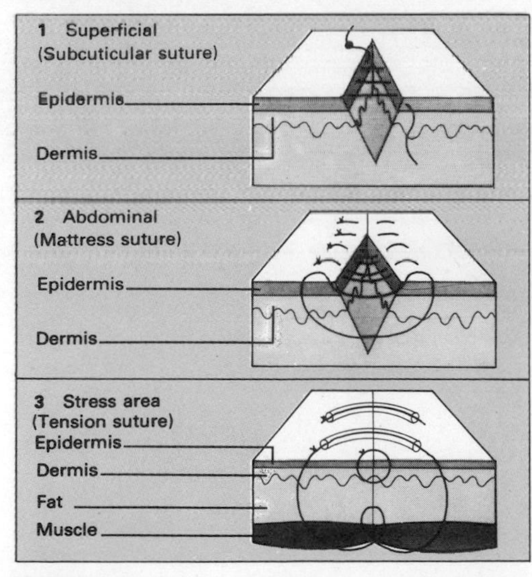

Sutures used to close incisions: (1) superficial, (2) abdominal, and (3) stress areas.

major abdominal operation, the patient is given an intravenous infusion of salts or blood into the vein of one arm. A naso-gastric tube may have been passed through one nostril and into the stomach to keep it empty of fluid. In addition to a dressing over the wound, a drain (frequently a tube) may extend from it to a suction bottle. This prevents the collection of blood or serous fluid in the operation area. In patients who have gynaecological or genitourinary operations, a catheter has usually been put in the bladder. This is connected to a bottle at the side of the bed.

During the first few hours after an operation, a nurse takes frequent recordings of blood pressure and pulse rate as well as keeping close observation of the amount of intravenous fluid and the measurement of urinary flow.

As soon as the intestine is starting to work again, the patient is allowed to have sips of liquid and the naso-gastric tube and intravenous infusion are removed.

Q: *How quickly does a patient recover after surgery?*

A: This depends on the type of operation and the patient's previous state of health. But even with major surgery, most patients are able to leave hospital within two weeks.

Q: *Are there any general precautions that a patient should take after surgery?*

A: Yes. It is important that patients who have had abdominal or thoracic surgery should not lift heavy weights for at least two months, and should not drive a car until the surgeon has given permission. It is advisable to avoid crowded situations, such as parties or theatres, where respiratory infections may be caught, because coughing can impose a strain on wounds.

A high protein diet is necessary, with additional vitamins as well as adequate rest, both at night and during the day.

Q: *Do all operations leave a scar?*

A: Any operation that involves an incision leaves a scar; there is no way of avoiding it. However, many surgeons try to position the scar to run in the natural skin folds so that it is not obvious when the scar has fully healed.

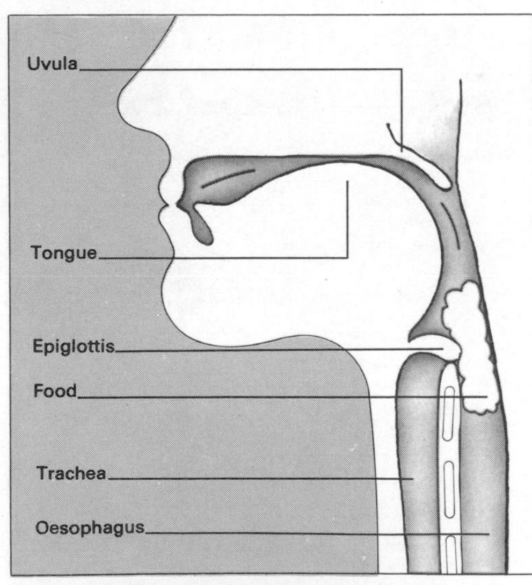

Swallowing closes the epiglottis over the trachea to prevent food entering the windpipe.

Suture is the technique of uniting parts of the body by stitching them together. The term has several other meanings, including the material with which a wound is stitched together, or the stitch that is left after the wound has been sutured. A suture is also a joint between two bones formed by fibrous tissues, as between the bones of the skull.

The materials most commonly used for surgical sutures are silk, cotton, or nylon, but steel wire may also be used for additional strength. Some sutures are made of materials such as catgut or synthetic substances that are slowly destroyed by the body. The tissues are finally held together by scar formation.

Swab is a piece of cotton on a stick that is used to collect pus or fluid for bacteriological culture and examination, or the gauze used by a surgeon to soak up blood and body secretions when cleaning a wound during an operation.

Swallowing is the movement of food from the mouth, through the pharynx, into the upper part of the oesophagus, and down to the stomach. It is a complex, co-ordinated movement of various muscles. The tongue forces the food backwards and the glottis closes, blocking the windpipe and preventing food from passing into the lungs. The food passes down the oesophagus by peristalsis, a series of waves of muscular contractions.

Q: *What disorders cause difficulty in swallowing?*

A: Difficulty in swallowing is known medically as dysphagia. It may be caused by a disorder of the throat, or it may be a symptom of a more general disease.

Q: *What disorders of the throat produce dysphagia?*

A: A common cause is a foreign body, such as a bone or fruit stone, that blocks the oesophagus and prevents swallowing. If the pharynx becomes infected, it results in pain as well as dysphagia. TONSILLITIS and QUINSY are examples of such infection.

ACHALASIA, a lack of the normal muscle co-ordination of swallowing, can produce dysphagia.

Occasionally, cancer of the pharynx, larynx, or oesophagus is the cause of problems with swallowing.

Q: What general diseases cause dysphagia?

A: It may be caused by a muscle disorder, such as MYASTHENIA GRAVIS; a neurological disorder, such as MOTOR NEURON DISEASE or POLIOMYELITIS; or an infection, such as DIPHTHERIA, which causes both muscle weakness and nerve damage. Sometimes iron deficiency ANAEMIA can be associated with dysphagia.

Q: How is dysphagia treated?

A: The treatment depends on the cause, which must be diagnosed by a doctor.

Sweat. *See* PERSPIRATION.

Swelling is an abnormal enlargement of any part of the body. *See* OEDEMA.

Sydenham's chorea. *See* CHOREA.

Sympathectomy is an operation in which the nerves of the SYMPATHETIC NERVOUS SYSTEM are inactivated, either by surgically cutting them or by destroying them chemically.

Sympathectomy may be performed on the sympathetic nerves in the neck to relieve the symptoms of RAYNAUD'S PHENOMENON. It may also be done in the lumbar region to improve the blood circulation in the legs. This may be used to treat INTERMITTENT CLAUDICATION or GANGRENE of the feet.

Sympathetic nervous system is part of the autonomic nervous system. It operates in conjunction with the parasympathetic nervous system. The sympathetic nervous system prepares the body for action by dilating the pupils of the eyes, cooling the skin, and raising the blood pressure and pulse rate. The blood is diverted from the intestines to the skeletal muscles, and the adrenal glands are stimulated to produce the hormone adrenaline, which enhances these actions.

The smooth muscle in the bronchi relaxes, allowing more air to enter the lungs; muscular movement in the intestines slows down; and sweating occurs.

All of this activity increases the basic metabolic rate of the body, increasing the use of glucose released from the liver, and prepares the body for immediate physical and mental activity.

See also AUTONOMIC NERVOUS SYSTEM; NERVOUS SYSTEM; PARASYMPATHETIC NERVOUS SYSTEM.

Symphysis is a cartilage joint between two bones. An example is the joint between the two bones at the front of the pelvis (pubic symphysis).

Symptom is a disruption of the normal functioning of the body that a patient notices, and which may indicate an underlying disorder. A pathognomonic symptom is characteristic of one specific disorder.

See also SYNDROME.

Syncope is a sudden, temporary loss of consciousness that is caused by an inadequate flow of blood to the brain. It is the medical term for a faint. *See* FAINTING.

Syndactyly is webbing between the fingers and toes. In most cases the condition is inherited, and usually affects both hands or feet. Syndactyly of the toes does not require treatment. Syndactyly of the fingers can be corrected by surgery.

See also POLYDACTYLISM.

Syndrome is a group of signs and symptoms that collectively indicate a particular disease or disorder.

Synovitis is inflammation of the synovial membrane, the layer of smooth, slippery membrane that lines the joints, surrounds tendons, and forms protective bags over bony protuberances (bursa).

Synovitis may be caused by injury to a joint; infection; or by various joint disorders, such as arthritis. The affected joint becomes swollen and painful, especially when the joint is moved. Treatment is directed toward the underlying cause.

See also ARTHRITIS; BURSITIS; CAPSULITIS; TENOSYNOVITIS.

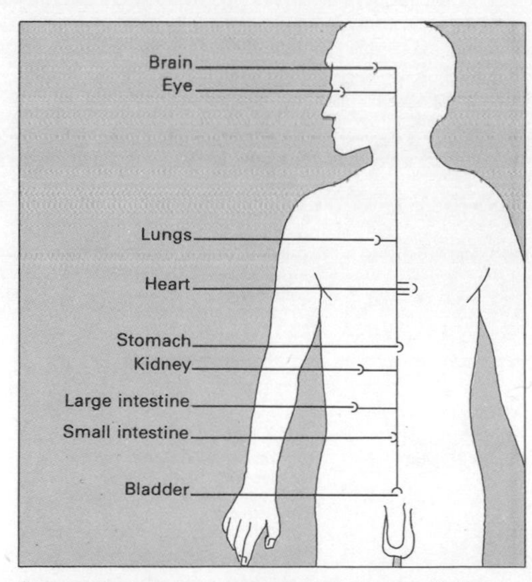

Sympathetic nervous system controls all the involuntary movements of the body.

Syphilis

A talk about Syphilis

Syphilis, also known as lues, is a contagious venereal disease that is caused by infection with spiral-shaped bacteria called *Treponema pallidum.* It can affect any tissue in the body, causing a wide variety of symptoms and complications.

The infection enters the body through the mucous membranes, such as the vagina and male urethra, or through grazes in the skin. It is usually transmitted by sexual intercourse. The infection can also pass through the placenta to a foetus, causing syphilis in the unborn child.

After infection, there is an incubation period before any symptoms appear. This may vary from a week to three months, but is usually about three or four weeks. Then the disease progresses through three stages, known as primary, secondary, and tertiary syphilis.

Q: What are the symptoms of primary syphilis?

A: A small red spot appears at the site of infection and ulcerates to form a CHANCRE that has a hard base. The chancre is usually painless and does not bleed but, when cut, exudes a clear fluid that contains the syphilis bacteria. The local lymph glands may become swollen. The chancre usually occurs on the penis, anus, or rectum in men, and on the vulva, cervix, or anal area in women. Occasionally, the chancre may appear on the lips, tongue, or even the tonsils.

Characteristic symptoms of syphilis	
Primary stage 2 to 4 weeks	Chancres appear on lip, tongue, nipples, or genitals. Painless swelling of lymph glands near genitals.
Secondary stage 6 weeks	Mild rash appears. Eruption of skin, reddish brown coppery spots, recurring possibly at a later stage.
Latency period	No obvious symptoms
Tertiary stage up to 20 years later	Heart, blood vessels, and central nervous system may be involved. Insanity and various types of psychoses may develop.

Syphilis is characterized by various symptoms at different stages of its development.

The chancre heals spontaneously in about one or two months, often leaving a scar. In a few cases, there is no chancre and the disease passes directly to secondary syphilis.

Q: What are the symptoms of secondary syphilis?

A: The symptoms of secondary syphilis usually appear about two months after infection. There is generalized illness with fever, headache, tiredness, aching of limbs, and a rash. Flat ulcers with raised edges often form in the mouth, vulva, penis, or rectum at the junction of the mucous membranes and the skin. These ulcers are known as condylomata lata and are extremely infectious.

Secondary syphilis may also cause enlargement of the liver, spleen, and lymph glands.

Secondary syphilis may persist for several months before the symptoms disappear. It is followed by a latent stage, after which tertiary syphilis may develop.

Q: What are the symptoms of tertiary syphilis?

A: It may take as long as twenty years before tertiary syphilis develops, or it may never occur. It may affect any part of the body, and may simulate almost any disease.

Tertiary syphilis may affect the central nervous system (neurosyphilis); the heart and blood vessels (cardiovascular syphilis); or it may produce swelling in the skin, bones, and intestinal organs (benign tertiary syphilis).

Neurosyphilis may cause general paralysis of the patient, with delusions, personality deterioration, and insanity, or it may cause TABES DORSALIS in which the normal reflexes are lost. If the spinal cord is affected, there may be sudden paralysis of the legs, and either urinary retention or incontinence.

Cardiovascular syphilis damages the aorta, causing it to become dilated (aneurysm). This swelling may compress adjacent organs, resulting in difficulty in swallowing, difficulty in talking, or collapse of part of the lungs. The aneurysm may rupture, causing sudden death. The heart valves may also be damaged, causing angina pectoris or heart failure.

Benign tertiary syphilis is characterized by the formation of gummas, which are swollen areas of firm, scar-like tissue. They may affect any part of the body, but usually produce only minor symptoms caused by localized swelling.

Q: How is syphilis treated?

A: Penicillin is effective in treating all stages of syphilis. Primary and secondary syphilis can be completely cured, but tertiary syphilis can only be arrested because the tissue damage cannot be repaired.

It is important for the patient to have regular medical checks to ensure that the treatment has been effective. The sexual contacts of the patient should be traced, and treated for syphilis if necessary.

Q: What are the symptoms of congenital syphilis?

A: Some infants with congenital syphilis never develop any symptoms throughout their lives. Others show symptoms at or shortly after birth, with blisters on the palms and soles; thickened, raised patches around the mouth and nappy area; and bloodstained nasal discharge. Within the first three months of life, the child's bones may become infected, causing weakness or apparent paralysis in one or more limbs. There may also be meningitis, epilepsy, or mental retardation.

In some children, the symptoms do not develop for several months or even years. When the symptoms do become apparent, there may be abnormalities of the incisor teeth (Hutchinson's teeth); infection of the eye (keratitis); gradual deafness; and neurosyphilis. Gummas may also develop particularly in the nose, producing a flattened nose because of the destruction of the nasal septum.

Q: How is congenital syphilis treated?

A: Congenital syphilis is usually treated with penicillin. If the mother is treated before the fourth month of pregnancy, the foetus is not affected. Treatment later in pregnancy usually cures both the mother and the foetus but, in some cases, the child may be born with some indication of infection.

If syphilis is not diagnosed until the child has been born, treatment prevents any further damage from occurring. It is important that other children in the family are examined to ensure that they do not have congenital syphilis. Both the mother and the child should be regularly examined after the infection has been treated.

Syringe is an instrument for injecting fluids into the body, or for washing out cavities or wounds. A hypodermic syringe consists of a glass or plastic tube, a fine nozzle, and a tightly fitting plunger. A needle is attached to the nozzle, and the complete assemblage is sterilized before use.

An irrigating syringe has a large rubber bulb instead of a plunger. It is used to wash out wax from the ears, and to cleanse wounds and body cavities.

See also INJECTION.

Syringomyelia is a rare congenital anomaly of the spinal cord or the lower part of the brain involving the central canal. Cavities slowly form in the substance of the cord in the region of the lower neck, but do not produce symptoms until late adolescence or early adulthood.

Q: What are the symptoms of syringomyelia?

A: The area involved is in the centre of the spinal cord, and the nerve fibres that are closest to the cord are the ones that are first affected. These fibres carry pain and temperature sensations, so that the first symptom may be a painless cut or burn on the hands or arms.

There is a gradual loss of sensation over the shoulders and arms, accompanied by weakness of the legs, as the disorder slowly progresses. If the lower part of the brain is involved, dizziness (vertigo) and problems with speech (dysarthria) and swallowing (dysphagia) may occur.

The condition slowly progresses over many years, causing increasing loss of sensation and paralysis, first of the legs and later of the rest of the body.

Q: What is the treatment for syringomyelia?

A: There is no effective form of treatment.

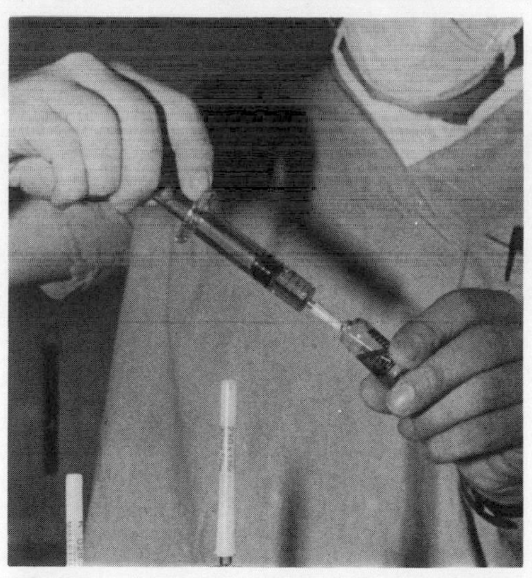

Syringe is an instrument used to draw up fluid and inject it into tissues or vessels.

Surgery has been attempted and may, in very few cases, be successful.

Systole is the contraction of the heart muscle that causes the forceful ejection of blood into the arterial system.

See also DIASTOLE.

T

Tabes dorsalis, also known as locomotor ataxia, is a syphilitic infection of the nerves in which there is progressive degeneration of the nerve fibres of the spinal cord. Tabes dorsalis may not develop until ten or twenty years after the original infection and is more common in men than in women.

The initial and the most characteristic symptom is an intense stabbing pain in the legs; this is known as a lightning pain. There may also be a loss of sensation in the limbs and a lack of awareness of their position.

As the disease progresses, the patient may walk unsteadily, with a typical high-stepping gait. There may also be a loss of sensation in the bladder, causing retention of urine and, eventually, incontinence. In the late stages of the disease, there may be lightning pains in the abdomen, and vomiting.

The treatment for tabes dorsalis is the same as that for syphilis. *See* SYPHILIS.

TAB vaccine is a combined vaccine that provides partial immunity to typhoid, paratyphoid A and paratyphoid B fevers. A single vaccine of typhoid alone is now advised.

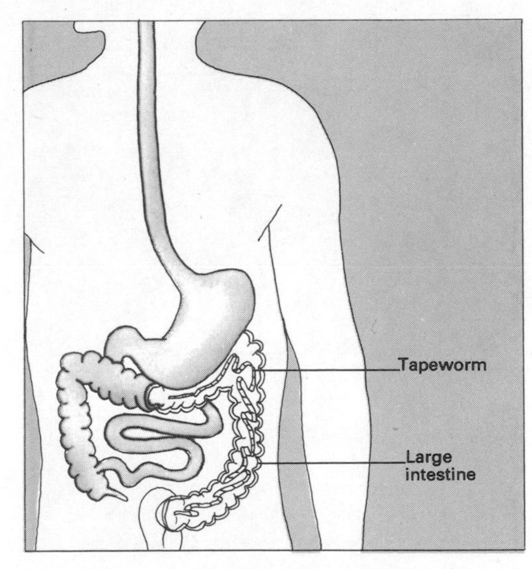

Tapeworm infests the descending section of the large intestine, where it rapidly grows.

Tachycardia is a rapid heart rate of more than one hundred beats a minute when the patient is at rest. Tachycardia may be caused by excessive exercise; an emotional response, such as fear; or an increase in the metabolic rate, which may occur with hyperthyroidism, fever, or infection. Tachycardia may also result from anaemia, haemorrhage, or the use of certain drugs.

See also ARRHYTHMIA; BRADYCARDIA.

Talipes is the medical term for clubfoot. *See* CLUBFOOT.

Talus is one of the seven tarsal bones of the foot. It articulates with the lower ends of the tibia and fibula to form part of the ankle joint. *See* FOOT.

Tampon is a plug of absorbent material, such as cotton wool or gauze, that may be inserted in the vagina to absorb menstrual bleeding. *See* MENSTRUATION.

Tapeworms (cestodes) are parasitic worms that are shaped like long, flat pieces of tape. Three main species of tapeworm infest human beings: *Taenia saginata* (beef tapeworm); *Taenia solium* (pork tapeworm); and *Diphyllobothrium latum* (fish tapeworm). Occasionally, another species, *Echinococcus granulosus,* may infest people, causing cysts to form in the liver (*see* HYDATID CYST).

The adult worms live in the human intestine. At one end of the worm is a head (scolex) with small hooks that attach it to the intestinal wall. Behind the scolex are hundreds of segments in which eggs develop. The segments break off, pass out of the body in the faeces, and are eaten by the primary host (cattle, pigs, or fish). The eggs hatch into larvae in the primary host. The larvae penetrate the intestinal wall and are carried by the blood circulation to the muscles, where they form cysts.

People become infested when they eat undercooked meat. The cysts mature into adult worms in the human intestine, thereby perpetuating the cycle.

Q: What are the symptoms of an infestation with tapeworms?

A: The most common symptom is the presence of tapeworm segments in the faeces. If a person is heavily infested, there may also be abdominal pain and loss of weight.

Q: How are tapeworm infestations treated?

A: In most cases, treatment with worm-killing drugs such as niclosamide is effective. Tapeworm infestation can be prevented by thoroughly cooking all meat and fish.

See also CYSTICERCOSIS.

Tarsus is the back of the foot between the metatarsal bones and the tibia and fibula.

The tarsus consists of seven tarsal bones. One of these, the TALUS, forms part of the ankle joint. *See* FOOT.

Tartar is a deposit on the teeth that consists of calcium salts and the remains of food. If the layer of tartar is allowed to accumulate, it may irritate the gums and cause GINGIVITIS or PERIODONTITIS.

Taste is the sensation that is obtained when specialized sensory nerve endings (the taste buds) detect soluble substances. The taste buds can register four fundamental tastes, either singly or in combination: sweet, bitter, sour, and salty. The sense of taste can be affected by a disorder of the mouth or nose.

Taste buds are sensory nerve endings on the surface of the tongue. They detect tastes and send impulses to the brain, where the perception of taste occurs. *See* TASTE.

Tay-Sachs disease is an inherited disorder in which there is a deficiency of a specific enzyme that breaks down fatty substances called lipids in the nervous system. The lipids accumulate in the brain cells, which gradually degenerate. The disease is more common in families of Jewish descent than in others.

Q: What are the symptoms of Tay-Sachs disease?

A: An affected child appears to be normal for the first few months after birth. But as the brain cells degenerate, there is a gradual onset of spasticity; convulsions; blindness; and a progressive loss of physical and mental abilities. Tay-Sachs disease is invariably fatal; the child usually dies before the age of four years.

Q: Can Tay-Sachs disease be prevented?

A: Yes. All potentially affected parents should obtain genetic counselling. Screening tests can be performed that can identify carriers of Tay-Sachs disease.

It is also possible to detect the disorder in a foetus by using AMNIOCENTESIS.

TB is an abbreviation for TUBERCULOSIS.

Tears are watery, slightly alkaline secretions that protect and lubricate the eyes. They contain salt and also an antibacterial enzyme (lysozyme) that prevents the eye from becoming infected. Tears are secreted by special glands around the eye (*see* LACRIMAL APPARATUS).

Teeth. Adult humans have thirty-two teeth, sixteen in each jaw; children have twenty milk, or deciduous, teeth. The outer layer of a tooth consists of hard, white enamel. Under the enamel is dentine, which is an ivory-like substance. Dentine forms the major part of a tooth. In the centre of a tooth is a soft pulp layer, which contains blood vessels, nerves, and odontoblasts (cells that can form more dentin if a tooth is damaged).

Q: What are the functions of the teeth?

A: There are four different types of teeth: incisors, canines, premolars, and molars. The incisors are used for cutting; the canines are used for gripping and tearing; and the back teeth, the premolars and molars, are used for grinding and chewing.

Q: How should teeth be cared for?

A: The teeth can be kept healthy by careful diet, with as little sugar as possible; regular brushing; and visits to the dentist every six months.

See also DENTAL DISORDERS; FLUORIDE; TEETHING; TOOTH DECAY.

Teething is the natural process by which a baby's teeth erupt through the gums. Teething may cause a slight increase in salivation; rubbing of the gums; and general restlessness.

In most babies, there is no need for any specific treatment for teething.

Telangiectasis is a disorder in which the small blood vessels become abnormally dilated, producing a type of angioma (*see* ANGIOMA). Telangiectases usually occur as red spots on the face and thighs. They are more common in the elderly; people exposed to the sun; people with varicose veins; and people treated with corticosteroid drugs. In most cases, the cause of the disorder is unknown.

Temperature is a measurement of the amount of heat in an object. The normal body temperature of a healthy person (taken with a thermometer placed under the tongue) is 37°C (98.6°F). *See* BODY TEMPERATURE; FEVER.

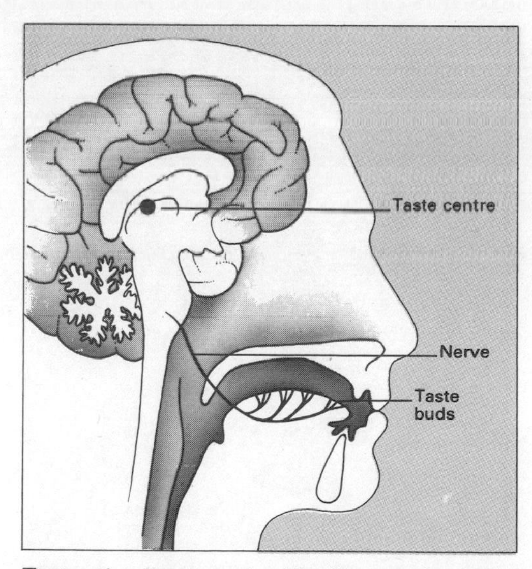

Taste stimuli are received by the taste buds on the tongue and transmitted to the brain.

Temper tantrum is a common occurrence in children between one and three years old, when the child is trying to assert his or her individuality. Temper tantrums usually last only a minute or two, but may recur if the child is unable to get what he or she wants.

Q: *How should a child with temper tantrums be treated?*

A: Parents should be firm and consistent in attitude toward the child, and should try to avoid any major conflict. It is advisable not to show anxiety and stress during a temper tantrum or, if possible, to ignore it.

Temporal lobe epilepsy is a form of epilepsy in which the seizures originate in the temporal lobe of the brain. *See* EPILEPSY.

Tendinitis is inflammation of a tendon. It is usually accompanied by tenosynovitis (inflammation of the membrane around a tendon). *See* TENOSYNOVITIS.

Tendon is the thick, strong, inelastic band of fibrous tissue that attaches a muscle to a bone. A tendon may be strained by excessive use, or, occasionally, ruptured. A tendon and its surrounding synovial membrane may also become inflamed (*see* TENOSYNOVITIS).

Tenesmus is painful straining to urinate or defecate. Straining to urinate may be a symptom of CYSTITIS; a bladder stone; or disorders of the prostate gland in which the flow of urine is obstructed. Straining to defecate may be a symptom of CONSTIPATION; an anal FISSURE; an anal FISTULA; an anal abscess; or, rarely, cancer of the rectum.

Tennis elbow is strain of the tendons of muscles to the forearm near the region of the outer side of the elbow. It is caused by repeated stress, particularly stress produced by sudden twisting movements.

Q: *What are the symptoms of tennis elbow?*

A: Pain on gripping, tenderness at the outer side of the elbow, and aching in the muscles of the outer side of the forearm, are the usual symptoms.

Q: *How is tennis elbow treated?*

A: Treatment may not be needed in mild cases. If the pain persists or becomes worse, injections of corticosteroid drugs and a local anaesthetic may be effective. If this fails, physiotherapy with massage and heat treatment may help.

Tenosynovitis is an inflammation of the synovial membrane that surrounds a tendon. It is often accompanied by inflammation of the underlying tendon (tendinitis). The cause of tenosynovitis is not known, but it may result from strenuous exercise; infection from an overlying wound; or from various diseases, such as rheumatoid arthritis, gout, or Reiter's disease.

Teratoma is a usually malignant tumour that consists of several different types of tissue, none of which originates in the area in which the tumour occurs. Treatment is by surgical removal, followed by radiotherapy and chemotherapy.

Termination means the end of an event. It commonly refers to the termination of a pregnancy (ABORTION).

Testicle. *See* TESTIS.

Testis is one of the two primary male reproductive organs (gonads) that lie in the scrotum. Each testis is about 4 centimetres (1.5 inches) long, and is partly surrounded by a protective bag that contains a small amount of fluid.

Q: *What are the functions of the testes?*

A: After puberty, the testes produce the male hormone TESTOSTERONE, and the reproductive cells (SPERM). From the testis, the sperm pass along special ducts to the EPIDIDYMIS. The epididymis leads to the VAS DEFERENS, through which the sperm are carried to the SEMINAL VESICLES where they are stored.

Q: *What conditions affect the testis?*

A: The testis may not reach the correct position after passing out of the abdomen and into the scrotum of a foetus; this condition is known as an UNDESCENDED TESTICLE. Excessive fluid may accumulate in the small bag next to the testis and form a HYDROCELE. The testis may become infected and inflamed (ORCHITIS) which may lead eventually to STERILITY. Occasionally, cancer of the testis (SEMINOMA teratoma) may develop.

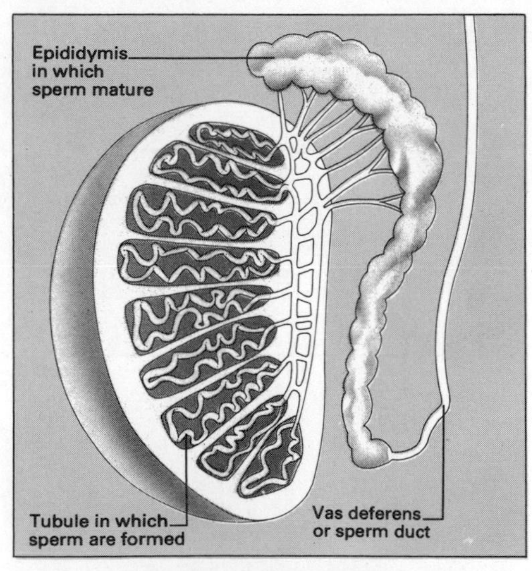

Testis manufactures sperm in the tubules, and they mature in the epididymis.

Test meal is a standardized meal that is given to test the gastric secretion of the stomach. A test meal may be used in the diagnosis of various disorders. Modern methods of testing acid secretion are done without giving a test meal.

Testosterone is the male sex hormone produced principally by the TESTIS. The amount of testosterone produced is controlled by the follicle-stimulating hormone (FSH), and luteinizing hormone (LH), both of which are secreted by the front lobe of the pituitary gland. At the onset of puberty there is an increase in the production of testosterone, particularly in boys.

Q: What are the effects of testosterone?

A: Testosterone stimulates the development of male secondary sexual characteristics. These include facial and pubic hair; enlargement of the larynx, which produces deepening of the voice; enlargement of the penis and testes; alteration of body shape; and an increase in muscle strength. Testosterone is also thought to influence the development of balding.

Although women produce only a small amount of testosterone, it occasionally affects hair growth after menopause. Rarely, overproduction of testosterone by the adrenal glands may result in the development of male secondary sexual characteristics in women (*see* VIRILISM).

Tetanus, also known as lockjaw, is caused by the toxin of the bacterium *Clostridium tetani.*

The bacteria are usually found in soil, and can remain alive for many years in the form of spores. The microorganisms grow in dead or damaged tissue that does not have an adequate blood supply and therefore has a low oxygen level. Infection may result from any wound that is contaminated by infected soil.

Q: What are the symptoms of tetanus?

A: There is an incubation period that may vary between four and fourteen days, but can last as long as seven weeks. The initial symptoms include stiffness of the jaw; slight difficulty in swallowing; restlessness; and stiffness of the arms, legs, and neck.

As the disease progresses, the patient may run a fever and may have difficulty opening the mouth (trismus or lockjaw). This may be accompanied by stiffness of the face muscles, which may contract to produce a characteristic fixed grin. As the stiffness of the muscles increases, there may be painful convulsions, which may be fatal.

Q: How is tetanus treated?

A: Hospitalization in a quiet room is necessary. A tracheostomy, a temporary opening in the windpipe, may be performed, and the patient may be given mechanical artificial respiration to aid breathing. An intravenous infusion may also be necessary to correct the patient's fluid balance.

Antitoxin in the form of gamma globulin is given to reduce the effect of the toxin. Muscle relaxant drugs will reduce the muscle spasms, and drugs that cause complete paralysis may be used when the patient is maintained on artificial respiration.

Q: Can tetanus be prevented?

A: Yes. An attack of tetanus itself does not confer immunity, but tetanus can be prevented by immunization.

See also IMMUNIZATION.

Tetany is a spasm of the muscles producing contractions in the hands, feet, and face (TRISMUS). Sometimes flexing of the arms and legs, with cramp-like pain may occur. Occasionally, seizures may occur.

Tetany may result from an abnormally low concentration of calcium in the blood (HYPOCALCAEMIA). Temporary hypocalcaemia may be caused by hyperventilation (resulting from temporary lowering of calcium when carbon dioxide is lost from the body); prolonged hypocalcaemia may be caused by a deficiency of the parathyroid hormones. Vitamin D deficiency may also cause tetany.

Q: How is tetany treated?

A: If tetany is caused by hyperventilation, the patient should breathe into a paper bag. This normalizes the carbon dioxide concentration of the blood. Tetany that is

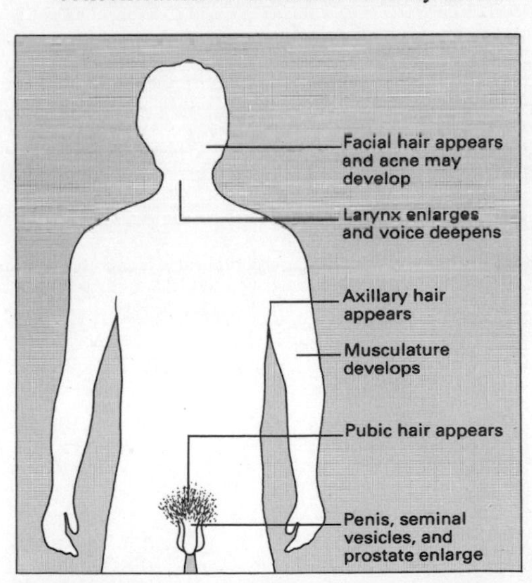

Testosterone stimulates the development of male sexual characteristics during puberty.

caused by prolonged hypocalcaemia may be treated with intravenous injections of calcium salts. Tetany resulting from vitamin D deficiency disappears when the deficiency is corrected.

Tetracyclines are a group of antibiotics that are produced by certain species of the fungus *Streptomyces.* Tetracycline drugs are effective against many bacterial infections. They are commonly prescribed to treat urinary infections; streptococcal infections; pneumonia; brucellosis; and rickettsial diseases, such as typhus. Tetracyclines may also be used to treat bacterial infections in patients who are sensitive to penicillin. Bacteria may become resistant to tetracyclines, but this does not usually occur during a short course of treatment.

Q: Can tetracyclines produce adverse side effects?

A: Yes. Treatment with tetracyclines may produce nausea, vomiting, and diarrhoea. Allergic reactions are extremely rare. Prolonged treatment may lead to moniliasis and deficiency of the B vitamins. Occasionally, the skin may become abnormally sensitive to light. In children, tetracyclines may discolour the teeth, so should not be taken by children under the age of seven.

Tetraplegia, also known as quadriplegia, is paralysis of all four limbs. *See* PARALYSIS.

Thalamus is a collection of nerve cells that is situated above the hypothalamus and is part of the forebrain. There are two thalami, one on each side of the midline of the brain. The thalami act as co-ordinating centres for nerve impulses from all of the senses. The impulses are then relayed to other areas in the brain, such as the cerebral cortex and hypothalamus.

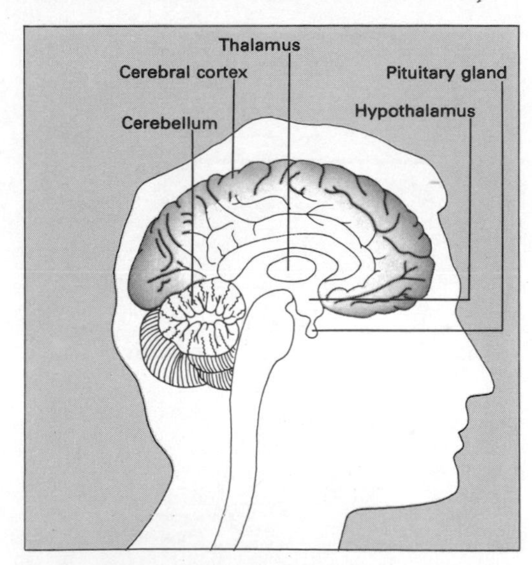

Thalamus receives all the sensory impulses except those from the nose.

Thalassaemia is the name given to a group of haemolytic anaemias, which are disorders that affect the red blood cells. Cooley's anaemia and Mediterranean anemia are types of thalassaemia.

Q: What are the symptoms of thalassaemia?

A: Symptoms of thalassaemia usually occur only in those who have inherited an abnormal gene from both parents; this is called thalassaemia major. When only one gene is inherited (thalassaemia minor), there are usually no symptoms.

The symptoms of thalassaemia major vary in severity. The common symptoms include breathlessness, pallor, and fatigue. There may also be jaundice; leg ulcers; enlargement of the spleen; and the formation of gallstones. The skull bones may thicken, and other bones may fracture easily.

Iron that is released from damaged red blood cells is deposited in the tissues (haemosiderosis), which may damage the heart muscle and ultimately result in heart failure.

Q: How is thalassaemia treated?

A: There is no effective treatment other than blood transfusion.

See also ANAEMIA; HAEMOCHROMATOSIS; SIDEROSIS.

Thalidomide is a sedative drug that was prescribed extensively in Europe during the late 1950s and early 1960s.

When it was taken by pregnant women thalidomide was found to cause foetal deformities, especially of the limbs, and the drug was withdrawn. It was also discovered that thalidomide caused a permanent form of peripheral neuritis.

Thermogram is a record of the infra-red heat waves that are emitted by the body. It gives a visual display of the hot and cold areas of the whole body. The technique of obtaining a thermogram is known as thermography; it involves photographing or televising the body with a special camera that is sensitive to heat.

Thermography may be used in detecting breast cancer because the tumour is slightly hotter than the surrounding body tissues. It may also be used to study the flow of blood throughout the body.

Thermometer is an instrument for measuring temperature. A clinical thermometer is used to measure body temperature; its range of measurement is from 34.5°C (94°F) to 42°C (108°F).

See also BODY TEMPERATURE.

Thiamine is a vitamin (vitamin B_1) that occurs naturally in such foods as dried yeast; wheat germ; liver; pulses; and brown rice. Thiamine is essential for the normal metabolism of fats and carbohydrates, and also the functioning of nerves and heart muscle. Thiamine deficiency may result from an inadequate diet; impaired absorption of nutrients, as may occur with sprue or alcoholism; or from increased bodily demands, which may result from hyperthyroidism or pregnancy. Thiamine deficiency may cause BERIBERI or, rarely, KORSAKOFF'S SYNDROME.

See also VITAMINS.

Thirst is the desire for fluid, especially water. The sensation of thirst is caused by, among many other factors, an increase in sodium concentration in the blood, and by loss of potassium from the body cells.

Thirst may be a symptom of various conditions, such as haemorrhage; profuse sweating; vomiting; diarrhoea; or excessive urination, as in diabetes mellitus or diabetes insipidus. Patients with heart failure may suffer from extreme thirst, but if they drink too much water, oedema of the legs may develop.

Thoracic duct is the largest lymphatic vessel in the body and joins the superior vena cava. It extends from the second lumbar vertebra up to the root of the neck. It receives lymph from all of the lower body, including the legs.

See also LYMPHATIC SYSTEM.

Thoracoplasty is a surgical operation in which several ribs are removed. The chest wall then collapses onto the underlying lung, causing the lung itself to collapse. This operation was frequently used in the treatment of tuberculosis.

Thoracotomy is any surgical operation that involves opening the chest wall.

Thorax (chest) is the part of the trunk between the neck and the abdomen. It is enclosed by the thoracic spine at the back; twelve pairs of ribs on either side; the breastbone (sternum) in front; and the diaphragm muscle at the bottom.

The thorax contains the two lungs; the heart; the main blood vessels – the aorta and pulmonary artery and their branches, and the venae cavae and pulmonary veins; and the oesophagus (gullet). Other structures include the thoracic duct; the thymus; the sympathetic ganglia and nerves; and the pleura (the membrane surrounding the lungs). The central part of the thorax that contains the heart and oesophagus is the mediastinum.

The muscles of the thorax include the intercostal muscles between the ribs; and the muscles that attach the shoulder girdle, the shoulder bone (scapula), the collar-bone (clavicle), and the bone of the upper arm (humerus) to the chest wall.

Threadworm is a small, parasitic nematode worm that infests the intestine. British authorities use this term to refer to the worm *Enterobius vermicularis* (*see* OXYURIASIS); Americans use it to refer to the worm *Strongyloides stercoralis* (*see* STRONGYLOIDES).

Throat is the common name for the pharynx and the fauces, the opening that leads from the back of the mouth into the pharynx. The front part of the neck is also referred to as the throat.

Throat, lump in, is a symptom of many disorders, such as a mild throat infection, and laryngitis. It is often accompanied by inflammation of the throat and slight discomfort on swallowing. A lump in the throat may also be caused by pressure on the throat from an enlarged thyroid gland (goitre) or from swollen lymph glands. Emotional states may cause the sensation of a lump in the throat that varies in severity, and this condition is known as globus hystericus.

If the sensation of a lump in the throat persists, a doctor should be consulted.

Throat abscess is a localized accumulation of pus in the throat. Throat abscesses occur most commonly around the tonsils. This condition is known as quinsy or peritonsillar abscess. *See* QUINSY.

Thromboangiitis obliterans, also known as Buerger's disease, is a chronic disease of the blood vessels in which there is a narrowing of the arteries and veins. *See* BUERGER'S DISEASE.

Thrombocytopenia is a decrease in the normal number of platelets, which are the

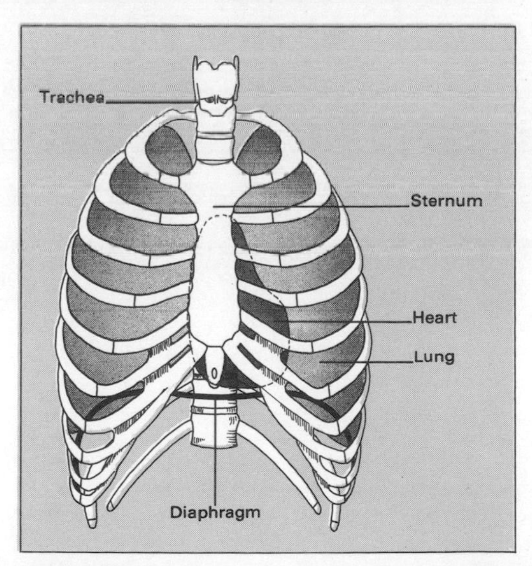

Thorax is the area of the body from the trachea to the diaphragm, including the lungs.

particles in the blood that are essential for clotting. The condition may result from decreased platelet production, caused by leukaemia, cancer, drugs, aplastic anaemia, or irradiation. Thrombocytopenia may also result from increased platelet destruction, which may be caused by drugs, such as sulphonamides, or poisons. Injuries and burns may cause the body to use platelets faster than they can be replaced, which may cause a temporary platelet deficiency. The commonest cause of thrombocytopenia is called idiopathic thrombocytopenic purpura (ITP). This is a type of autoimmune disease in which platelets are destroyed in the spleen.

Q: What are the symptoms of thrombocytopenia?

A: The main symptom is bleeding, which may occur in any part of the body. Usually, bleeding occurs just below the skin, producing bruises and small haemorrhages (petechiae). Anaemia may result from excessive bleeding.

Q: How is thrombocytopenia treated?

A: Treatment is directed toward the underlying cause. Transfusions of platelets may be given until the treatment takes effect or until the patient recovers naturally. In patients with idiopathic thrombocytopenic purpura, treatment with corticosteroid drugs may be effective. In severe cases, removal of the spleen may be necessary.

Thrombolysis is the destruction of a clot in a blood vessel (thrombus) by means of an intravenous infusion of enzymes that dissolve the thrombus. The technique involves a continuous infusion of enzymes into a vein for at least two days. This is followed by treatment with ANTICOAGULANT drugs to prevent further blood clots from forming.

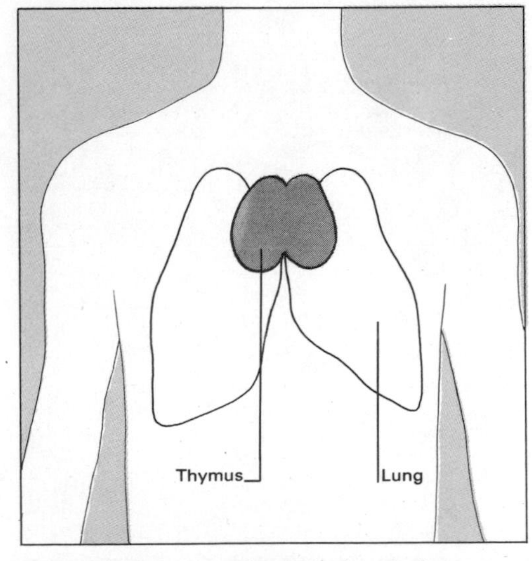

Thymus helps to combat infection during childhood by producing lymphocytes.

Thrombophlebitis. *See* VENOUS THROMBOSIS.

Thrombosis is the formation of a blood clot (thrombus) in an artery or vein. When a thrombus becomes detached from its original site of formation, it is called an embolus.

See also ARTERIOSCLEROSIS; EMBOLISM; GANGRENE; STROKE; VENOUS THROMBOSIS.

Thrombus is a blood clot in a blood vessel. *See* BLOOD CLOT; VENOUS THROMBOSIS.

Thrush is an infection caused by the fungus *Monilia albicans. See* MONILIASIS.

Thumb is the first digit of the hand. It contains only two bones (phalanges), unlike the fingers, which have three. *See* HAND.

Thumb sucking is a common habit in almost all babies and children. It occurs as frequently in breast-fed babies as in bottle-fed babies. Thumb sucking becomes less frequent after the age of three years and seldom continues after the age of ten.

Excessive thumb sucking may cause blistering of the thumb, which may lead to skin infection. Continual thumb sucking may also affect the normal position of the front teeth.

Usually it is safe to let a child suck a thumb. But, if problems such as skin damage or dental deformity develop, the child should be gently persuaded to stop. The child should not be punished.

Thymus is an organ in the upper part of the chest cavity lying just behind the breastbone (sternum). It is composed largely of cells similar to lymphocytes. The thymus grows until puberty, and then gradually shrinks and is replaced by fat.

The full function of the thymus is not known. It produces lymphocytes, a type of white blood cell, and plays a part in the development of immunity.

Q: What disorders may affect the thymus?

A: Disorders of the thymus are uncommon. Rarely, children are born without a thymus or with a defective one. This produces a defect in immunity and the child suffers from repeated infections. Tumours of the thymus are also rare, but many patients with MYASTHENIA GRAVIS have thymic tumours and usually recover when the tumour is removed. Most thymic tumours are benign (noncancerous).

Thyroidectomy is the surgical removal of part or all of the thyroid gland. A medical thyroidectomy is the destruction of part or all of the thyroid gland by the use of drugs.

A thyroidectomy may be performed to treat overactivity of the thyroid gland (hyperthyroidism), or to remove nodules or cancer forming on the gland. It may be necessary to remove part of the thyroid gland if it becomes greatly enlarged (goitre) and obstructs breathing.

Q: Are there any hazards associated with a thyroidectomy?

A: Yes, but these are rare. During surgery, great care has to be taken not to remove all four parathyroid glands, or to cut the nerves to the vocal cords. Removal of the parathyroid glands may cause HYPOCALCAEMIA and TETANY. If one of the nerves to the vocal cords is cut, hoarseness may result; if both nerves are cut, the patient will be unable to speak. If too much of the thyroid gland is removed, hypothyroidism eventually develops, and replacement of the deficient thyroid hormones will be necessary.

Thyroid gland is an endocrine gland in the front of the neck. It consists of two lobes, one on each side of the Adam's apple, which are joined across the front of the windpipe, just below the voice box.

The thyroid gland secretes two main hormones, thyroxine and triiodothyronine, into the bloodstream. These hormones stimulate all the cells in the body. The thyroid gland also secretes a hormone (calcitonin) that reduces the concentration of calcium in the blood.

The production of thyroid hormones is controlled by the thyroid stimulating hormone (TSH), which is secreted by the pituitary gland. This control is modified by the hypothalamus, which detects thyroid hormone levels in the blood and influences the secretion of TSH.

Q: What disorders may affect the thyroid gland?

A: The thyroid gland may become enlarged (goitre) because of a deficiency of iodine, overactivity (hyperthyroidism), or underactivity (hypothyroidism). Nodules may form in the thyroid gland and cause hyperthyroidism. The nodules may be either benign or malignant (cancerous).

Occasionally, the thyroid gland may become inflamed (thyroiditis). Rarely, this is caused by infection; more often, it is a form of autoimmune disease (Hashimoto's thyroiditis).

Thyroid preparations are drugs that are used to treat disorders of the thyroid gland, such as simple goitre; hypothyroidism (underproduction of thyroid hormones); hyperthyroidism (overproduction of thyroid hormones); and thyroiditis (inflammation of the thyroid gland).

Thyroid preparations are available as extracts of thyroid glands from animals, or as synthetic preparations of thyroxine or triiodothyronine.

Q: Can thyroid preparations produce adverse side effects?

A: Yes. Thyroid hormones may produce cramps; palpitations; and anginal pain. They may also permanently affect the heart. For this reason, thyroid hormones should be used with caution in those with heart disorders.

A talk about Thyrotoxicosis

Thyrotoxicosis, also known as Graves' disease, is a disorder caused by the overproduction of thyroid hormones by the thyroid gland (hyperthyroidism). Often the cause is not known. There seems to be a breakdown in the normal balance of the feedback mechanism between the pituitary gland and thyroid gland. This results in overstimulation of the thyroid gland by the hormone (thyroid stimulating hormone) that is produced by the pituitary gland. Rarely, the thyroid gland grows a benign tumour, and this can also cause an overproduction of thyroid hormones.

Occasionally, thyrotoxicosis starts after an emotional shock or prolonged period of anxiety.

Q: What are the symptoms of thyrotoxicosis?

A: The symptoms include sweating; nervousness; hunger; loss of weight; diarrhoea; trembling hands; and bulging of the eyes (exophthalmos). Often, there is a slight

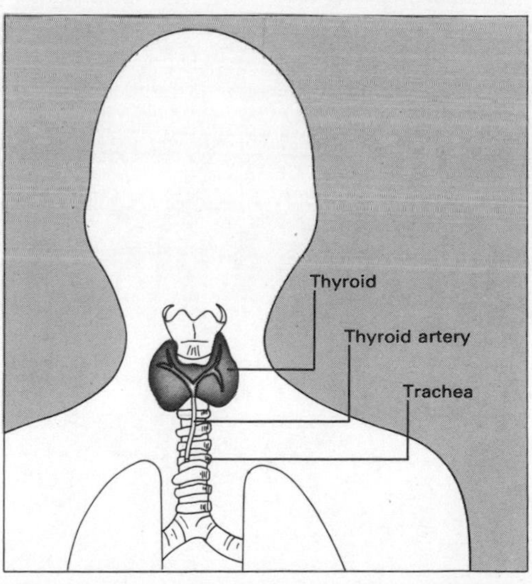

Thyroid gland is located below the Adam's apple and folds around the trachea.

swelling in the neck, just below the Adam's apple, because of enlargement of the thyroid gland. In older people, there may also be depression, atrial fibrillation, and heart failure.

Q: How is thyrotoxicosis treated?

A: While the condition is being diagnosed, drugs (beta-blockers) may be prescribed to control the symptoms. Once the diagnosis has been confirmed, there are three possible forms of treatment. The most suitable depends on expert medical advice.

Drugs that reduce thyroid activity are usually effective. Alternatively, the patient may undergo surgery to remove part of the thyroid gland or any active nodule in the gland (thyroidectomy).

Radioactive iodine treatment is simple and effective. Both surgery and radioactive iodine treatment tend to be followed, some years later, by diminished production of the thyroid hormones (*see* HYPOTHYROIDISM).

Q: Are there any complications of thyrotoxicosis?

A: Yes. Occasionally, the symptoms of thyrotoxicosis suddenly become much worse in a condition called a thyroid crisis, which may be brought on by acute anxiety, childbirth, or an operation. Thyrotoxicosis can develop into a fatal condition, with fever, rapid heartbeat, and worsening of all the other symptoms. This requires urgent hospital treatment.

A more common complication is that caused by protuberance of the eyes (exophthalmos). Such eye problems sometimes become worse after treatment for thyrotoxicosis, and result in swelling of the eyelids and tissues behind the eyeball. This condition requires skilled care to prevent eye infection. Another possible complication is ophthalmoplegia (paralysis of the nerves of the eye) that results in double vision (diplopia). This condition tends to improve on its own.

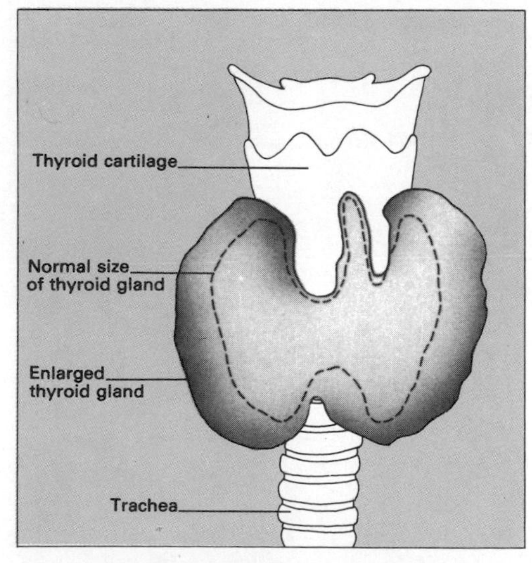

Thyrotoxicosis results from overactivity of the thyroid gland, which may become enlarged.

Thyroxine is one of the two principal hormones that are secreted by the thyroid gland; the other main thyroid hormone is triiodothyronine.

The effect of both hormones is similar: they increase the metabolic rate of the body cells. Preparations of these hormones may be given to treat thyroid gland deficiency disorders, such as hypothyroidism.

See also THYROID GLAND.

Tibia, also known as the shin-bone, is the innermost and largest of the two bones of the lower leg. The fibula is the outer bone.

The upper end of the tibia forms the knee joint with the femur and is covered by two semicircular cartilages (menisci). The lower end of the tibia forms the ankle joint with the fibula and the talus bone.

See also POTT'S FRACTURE.

Tic is an habitual, involuntary spasm or twitch that usually affects the face, head, neck, or shoulder muscles.

Tics often become more frequent when a person is under emotional stress, and disappear during sleep. For this reason, they are thought to be of psychological origin.

Childhood tics usually disappear spontaneously. But tics in adults may resist treatment. Psychotherapy may help some people but it is not always successful.

See also CHOREA; TRIGEMINAL NEURALGIA.

Tic douloureux, also known as trigeminal neuralgia, is a nervous disorder that causes severe facial pain. *See* TRIGEMINAL NEURALGIA.

Ticks are small, blood-sucking parasites that are related to the MITES. Soft-bodied ticks (*Argasidae*) may transmit the spiral-shaped bacteria that cause RELAPSING FEVER. Hard-bodied ticks (*Ixodidae*) may transmit the rickettsial bacteria that cause African tick typhus, Rocky Mountain spotted fever, and Q FEVER. Ticks may also play a part in the transmission of TULARAEMIA.

Some species of ticks can cause tick paralysis. This condition is characterized by lethargy; muscle weakness; loss of co-ordination; and paralysis, which may affect the respiratory muscles. Hospital treatment is necessary for tick paralysis.

Tietze's syndrome is a rheumatic disorder that is characterized by pain and tenderness on the front of the chest, although it is more common on the left side than on the right. The underlying cause of the condition is not known. The pain results from swelling of the rib cartilages where they join the breastbone.

Treatment for Tietze's syndrome is seldom necessary. It usually disappears spontaneously within about eight weeks. In severe cases, treatment with antirheumatic or painkilling drugs may be necessary.

Tinea is a fungal disease of the skin. The term usually refers to RINGWORM.

Tinea versicolor is a mild fungal skin infection that produces pale brown, slightly scaly areas on the chest, abdomen and neck. These affected areas may appear as pale patches on darker or sunburnt skins. Selenium shampoo usually cures the condition.

Tine test is a skin test for tuberculosis.

See also TUBERCULIN TEST.

Tingling is a sensation of pins and needles or prickling occurring in the skin, caused by hitting or prolonged pressure on a nerve, some neurological diseases, or cold. It is not usually a serious symptom; *see also* NUMBNESS.

Tinnitus is the subjective sensation of noises in the ear without there being any external sound. It may be experienced as a buzzing, ringing, hissing, or roaring noise, or as a series of more complex sounds. Tinnitus may be continuous or intermittent, and is usually associated with varying degrees of deafness.

Any disorder of the ear may cause tinnitus, such as wax in the outer ear; MÉNIÈRE'S DISEASE; OSTOSCLEROSIS; and OTITIS. It may also result from a head injury; nerve disorders; arteriosclerosis; smoking; and drugs.

Tocopherol is a general term for several compounds that are chemically related to vitamin E (alpha tocopherol). Vitamin E plays a part in the metabolism of fats in the body cells and also helps to maintain the stability of the cell membranes. It occurs naturally in wheat germ and can also be artificially synthesized.

See also VITAMINS.

Toe is a digit of the foot. Each toe has a protective nail at the end. The big toe (hallux) has two phalangeal bones; the other four toes each have three phalangeal bones. Movement of the toes is controlled by muscles in the foot and leg.

The toes help to distribute the weight of the body evenly along the heads of the main bones of the foot (the metatarsal bones). The toes also help to balance the body.

Q: What disorders can affect the toes?

A: Various generalized bone and joint disorders may affect the toes, such as osteoarthritis; rheumatoid arthritis; and gout, which usually affects the first joint of the big toe. These disorders may cause deformities of the toes, such as HALLUX VALGUS, HALLUX RIGIDUS, and HAMMER-TOE. Rarely, a child may be born with more than the normal number of toes (polydactylism).

See also SYNDACTYLY; TOE, CLAW.

Toe, claw, is a foot deformity in which one or more toes are abnormally curled. It is most commonly caused by poorly fitting shoes. In such cases treatment is seldom necessary until adulthood, when minor surgery to straighten the toes may be required.

Toilet training. Learning to control the bladder and bowels is an important stage in a child's development. Children cannot control their bladder and bowels until the nervous system has developed sufficiently. This normally occurs between the ages of eighteen months and two years. Bowel control is usually achieved first. But, by the age of about two-and-a-half years, most children have learned bladder control as well. Girls usually attain this stage before boys.

Q: How should a child be toilet trained?

A: There are no firm rules about toilet training. One method of toilet training involves gradually establishing a daily routine. The parent should sit the child on the potty immediately after breakfast. After a few minutes, the baby should be lifted from the potty. If there is anything in the potty, the parent should express obvious approval. If not, the parent should not punish the child.

See also BED-WETTING.

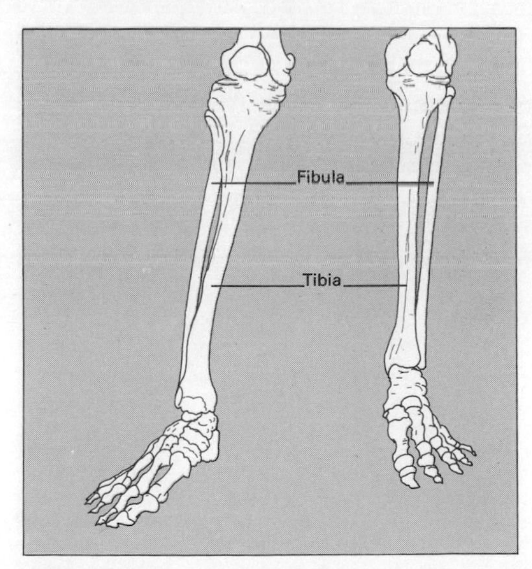

Tibia is the inner bone of the lower leg; it articulates with the ankle and the femur.

Tomogram is an X-ray image of one plane of the body, rather like a cross-sectional view. A tomogram is obtained by using a special technique in which the X-ray apparatus is rotated around the patient while the X-ray picture is being taken. *See* CAT SCANNER.

Tongue is the movable muscular organ that lies partly on the floor of the mouth and partly in the pharynx. It is attached to the hyoid bone above the larynx, to the base of the skull below the ears, and to the lower jaw. The tongue's surface is covered with a special mucous membrane that contains numerous TASTE BUDS which can detect salt, sour, bitter and sweet tastes. The tongue also manipulates food, and helps in the production of speech.

Q: What disorders can affect the tongue?

A: The most common disorder is inflammation of the tongue (*see* GLOSSITIS). Ulcers may form as a result of rubbing against broken teeth, or of the spread of a mouth ulcer (*see* COLD SORE).

An ulcer or a lump on the tongue may be caused by cancer; it occurs most commonly in those who smoke. Cancer of the tongue may be treated by inserting radioactive needles into the tongue, or by surgical removal of the cancer.

Q: Why may the tongue become discoloured or furred?

A: Discoloration or furring of the tongue is not always a sign of disease. It may result from smoking; a course of antibiotics; indigestion; a respiratory infection; or tonsillitis.

A bright red tongue may be a symptom of vitamin B deficiency, either PELLAGRA or PERNICIOUS ANAEMIA. A black tongue is often due to excessive smoking, but it may also appear for no apparent reason then disappear spontaneously.

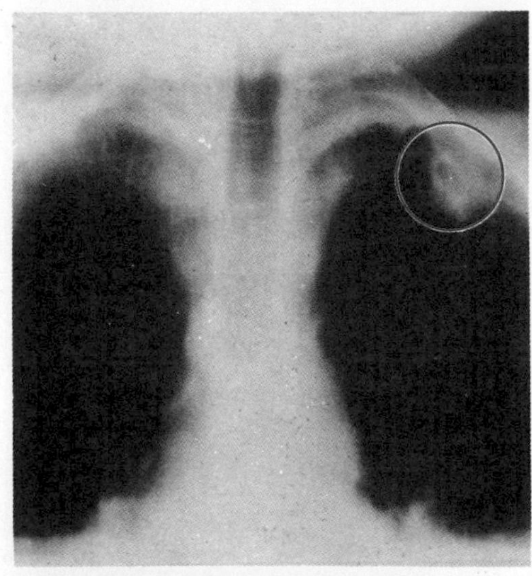

Tomogram is a type of X-ray used to study organs at certain depths within the body.

Tonic is the medical term for a continuous muscle contraction, as opposed to clonic contractions in which the muscles alternately contract and relax. As a general term, tonic refers to a preparation that is supposed to restore a person to normal health.

Tonsil is an almond-shaped mass of sponge-like lymphoid tissue. The two palatine tonsils are situated at the entrance to the pharynx, one on each side, below the soft palate and above the base of the tongue. The lingual tonsil is a similar mass of lymphoid tissue that is situated on the back of the tongue and which, with the adenoids and the tonsils, forms a ring of lymphoid tissue that protects the entrance to the throat. The tonsils and adenoids become smaller as children grow older.

Q: What are the functions of the tonsils?

A: The tonsils have two functions: they trap and destroy micro-organisms that enter the throat; and they play a part in the body's immune system by producing antibodies.

Q: What disorders may affect the tonsils?

A: The most common disorders that affect the tonsils are TONSILLITIS and GLANDULAR FEVER.

Tonsillectomy is the surgical removal of the tonsils. The adenoids are often removed (adenoidectomy) at the same time. The tonsils are not usually removed unless the patient has suffered several attacks of otitis media or tonsillitis. A doctor may also recommend a tonsillectomy if complications, such as QUINSY (peritonsillar abscess), develop from tonsillitis.

Q: Can a tonsillectomy cause complications?

A: Yes, but these are rare. Middle ear infections, such as otitis media, may occur, but the most serious complication is haemorrhage. For this reason it is advisable to stay in hospital until the surgeon is certain the area is healing well.

Q: What happens at the operation, and how long is it necessary to stay in hospital?

A: For four hours before the operation the patient must not eat or drink. Two hours later a sedative is given. Generally, a parent is allowed to stay with a child until the anaesthetist is ready to inject an anaesthetic into a vein in the arm.

After the operation the patient is sleepy for several hours, but apart from some bloodstained saliva there should be no painful complications. Next day the patient may complain of a sore throat. This is easily controlled with aspirin, iced drinks, ice cream, and jelly, which can be consumed without too much discomfort. In most cases the patient returns home within five days.

Tonsillitis is an inflammation of the tonsils. It is usually caused by a viral infection, but may also result from infection with streptococcal bacteria. Tonsillitis occurs most commonly during early childhood.

Q: What are the symptoms of tonsillitis?

A: Tonsillitis is characterized by a sore throat; difficulty in swallowing; headache; and high fever. In very young children, the main symptoms may be abdominal pain; vomiting; and diarrhoea.

Q: How is tonsillitis treated?

A: The treatment of viral tonsillitis is directed toward relieving the symptoms. It is not usually necessary to remove the tonsils surgically (tonsillectomy) unless tonsillitis recurs, or complications arise.

Tonsillitis that is caused by streptococcus infection is treated with antibiotics, usually penicillin. Aspirin may also be prescribed to relieve the symptoms. The patient should drink plenty of fluids to prevent dehydration.

Q: What complications can result from tonsillitis caused by streptococcus?

A: A type of allergic reaction may occur, causing RHEUMATIC FEVER, acute NEPHRITIS, SCARLET FEVER, or ERYTHEMA NODOSUM. OTITIS, middle ear infection, and QUINSY may complicate any kind of tonsillitis.

Toothache (for EMERGENCY treatment, see First Aid, p.595) is pain in a tooth, or in the area around a tooth. It can be a symptom of almost any dental disorder but is most commonly caused by caries (*see* TOOTH DECAY). Other common causes of toothache include GINGIVITIS; PERIODONTITIS; and an abscess at the root of the tooth.

A dentist should be consulted as soon as possible so that the underlying cause can be treated. Painkilling drugs, such as aspirin or paracetamol, may give temporary relief.

Tooth decay, also known as dental caries, is disintegration of a tooth because of bacterial action. Tooth decay begins with the formation of jelly-like PLAQUE on the surface enamel of the teeth. Bacteria in the plaque produce acid, which erodes the enamel and exposes the underlying dentine. The acid may also irritate the gums and cause GINGIVITIS. If the decay is not stopped by dental treatment, it spreads to the central pulp, and eventually reaches the root canals. Bacteria may penetrate the decayed teeth and produce a dental abscess, which may cause toothache.

Q: How is tooth decay treated?

A: Tooth decay requires expert dental treatment. If the decay is relatively minor, the damaged area of the tooth is drilled out, then filled with a special metal amalgam. Severely decayed teeth may need to be extracted.

Q: How may tooth decay be prevented?

A: Tooth decay may be prevented by a correct diet and good dental hygiene. The teeth should be cleaned thoroughly with TOOTHPASTE after every meal. Dental floss should also be used to remove plaque and food from between the teeth.

Toothpaste is a form of dentifrice that consists of a mild abrasive, a detergent, and, usually, flavouring and colouring.

Good dental hygiene depends more upon correct brushing than the type of toothpaste or dentifrice used. But toothpastes that contain fluoride help to prevent tooth decay.

Tophus is a gritty deposit that consists of the salts of uric acid. It may be found in the ears, and joints in people with gout. *See* GOUT.

Torn cartilage. *See* CARTILAGE; MENISCUS.

Torpor is a state of drowsiness or numbness in which there is no response to any stimulation except the most insistent or painful.

Torticollis is the medical name for wryneck. *See* STIFF NECK.

Touch, sense of, is the sense by which pressure on the skin is perceived. There are many thousands of sensory nerve endings throughout the surface of the skin that detect different levels of pressure and vibration. Some of the nerve endings are concentrated

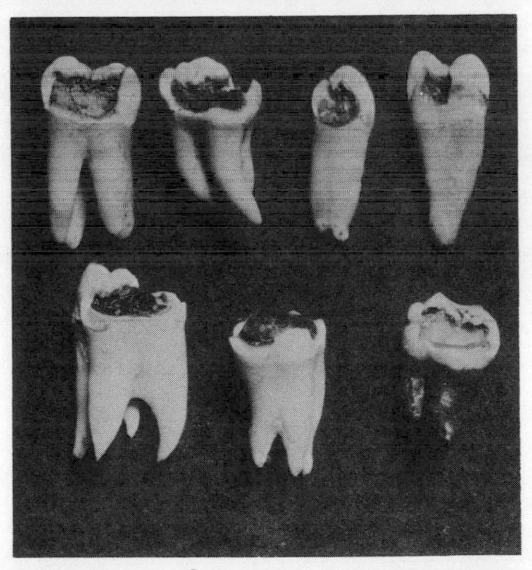

Tooth decay is a progressive breakdown of the structure of the enamel, dentine, and root.

in particular parts of the body, such as the fingertips and lips. The nerve endings send impulses to the brain, where they are deciphered into various touch sensations.

Tourniquet is a constricting band that is placed around a limb to stop the blood flow.

A tourniquet must be released at least every thirty minutes.

Toxaemia is a general illness that is caused by the absorption of poisonous bacterial toxins. Toxaemia may also refer to a complication of pregnancy that is commonly known as PRE-ECLAMPSIA.

Toxic means poisonous. The term is also used to describe an illness that is caused by poisonous substances.

Toxic shock syndrome is a form of BLOOD POISONING caused by staphylococcal bacteria, producing a rash, diarrhoea and sudden collapse. Originally it occurred only in children, but more recently it has been associated with a super-absorbent vaginal tampon (now no longer sold). Urgent treatment in hospital with large doses of antibiotics has reduced the mortality rate to about ten per cent.

Toxin is any poisonous substance of plant or animal origin. Venom is the toxin of a snake.

Many bacterial toxins can cause diseases, such as bacterial dysentery, diphtheria, food poisoning, gas gangrene and tetanus.

See also TOXOID.

Toxocariasis is a parasitic disease that is caused by infestation with the larvae of two species of roundworm, *Toxocara canis* or *Toxocara cati.* The adult worms live in the intestines of dogs and cats. The worms produce eggs, which are excreted in the faeces.

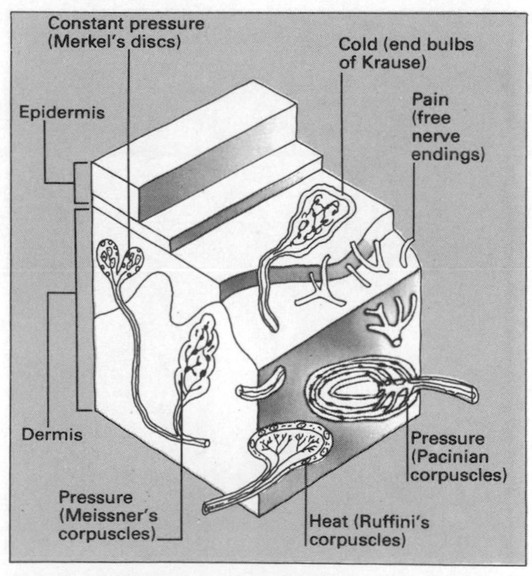

Touch is sensed by a combination of specialized nerves that relay information to the brain.

Humans become infested when they eat the eggs.

Toxocariasis occurs most commonly in children, as a result of sucking objects that are contaminated with the eggs. The eggs hatch into larvae in the intestine, penetrate the intestinal wall, and then spread throughout the body in the bloodstream. The larvae can affect most tissues in the body.

Q: What are the symptoms of toxocariasis?

A: The symptoms include fever; coughing or wheezing; and, occasionally, a skin rash. The liver and spleen may be enlarged, and there may be inflammation of the back of the eye. The larvae may affect the lungs, causing pneumonia. The disease is usually mild, and rarely causes prolonged illness.

Q: How is toxocariasis treated?

A: Toxocariasis may be treated with one of several drugs, such as thiabendazole or diethylcarbamazine.

Toxoid is a bacterial toxin that has been modified by chemical treatment so that it has lost its poisonous properties, but can still stimulate the formation of antibodies. Injections of toxoids can induce immunity against various diseases, such as diphtheria and tetanus (*see* IMMUNIZATION).

Toxoplasmosis is infection with the parasitic protozoan *Toxoplasma gondii.* This microorganism can infect any warm-blooded animal, but it requires a member of the cat family as its main host. In cats, the microorganism produces infectious cysts (oocysts), which are shed in the cat's faeces. In other animals, the microorganisms form cysts in the muscles. Humans become infected by exposure to oocysts in cat faeces, or by eating undercooked meat that contains the muscle cysts. The microorganisms then reproduce within the body cells. But, as immunity develops, reproduction stops and the parasites form cysts in the body tissues. The microorganisms can also infect an unborn child (congenital toxoplasmosis).

Q: What are the symptoms of toxoplasmosis?

A: In most cases, toxoplasmosis does not produce any symptoms. When symptoms do occur, they include slight fever; tiredness; muscle pains; and enlargement of the lymph glands.

Toxoplasmosis may cause prolonged illness in those whose resistance to infection is low. In such people, there may be weakness; headaches; diarrhoea; weight loss; and, sometimes, a severe eye infection (choroiditis). Rarely, it causes high fever and meningitis.

Congenital toxoplasmosis may cause a spontaneous abortion if the infection occurs early in pregnancy. Infection later in pregnancy may cause a miscarriage or stillbirth, or the child may be born with the infection.

At birth, the symptoms may be severe and rapidly fatal. Alternatively, symptoms may be absent at birth but may develop within a few months. In such cases, there may be choroiditis, which may lead to blindness; jaundice; skin rashes; and enlargement of the spleen and liver. There may also be brain damage.

Q: How is toxoplasmosis treated?

A: Drug treatment with a combination of pyrimethamine (an antimalarial drug) and sulphonamides is usually effective when the toxoplasmosis organisms are reproducing. There is no effective treatment for destroying organisms in the cyst stage. However, toxoplasmosis is rarely fatal in adults.

Trachea, also known as the windpipe, is the tube that extends from the voice box (larynx) to a point above the heart, where it divides into two tubes (bronchi) that lead to the lungs. The trachea is composed of C-shaped cartilage rings, which are held together by fibrous tissue. It is lined with a layer of moist, mucous membrane.

Food and liquid are both prevented from entering the trachea by a hinged flap of tissue (epiglottis) that diverts the food from the back of the tongue toward the oesophagus.

Tracheitis is an inflammation of the trachea (windpipe). It is commonly associated with an infection of the larynx (*see* LARYNGITIS) or bronchial tubes (*see* BRONCHITIS).

Tracheostomy is the surgical operation of cutting into the front of the trachea (windpipe) to relieve an obstruction and maintain a clear airway. The trachea is opened, and a double tube is placed in the hole. The outer tube remains permanently in place, but the inner tube can be removed for cleaning.

A tracheostomy may be performed if infection or injury causes problems with breathing in the throat (larynx), or after a patient has undergone a major operation on the lungs.

Tracheotomy is a surgical incision that is made through the skin and trachea (windpipe) when performing a TRACHEOSTOMY.

Trachoma is an infection of the thin membrane that covers the front of the eye (conjunctiva). It is a common cause of blindness in tropical countries.

Trachoma is caused by infection with the microorganism *Chlamydia trachomatis.* It is highly infectious and can be transmitted either directly by close contact, or indirectly by infested clothing.

Q: What are the symptoms of trachoma?

A: After an incubation period of about ten days, the symptoms of severe CONJUNCTIVITIS appear, with sore, watering eyes, and abnormal sensitivity to light (photophobia).

The symptoms gradually disappear but leave the conjunctiva red, inflamed, and covered with small lumps. These lumps eventually scar, causing blurring of vision and finally blindness. The scarring may also affect the eyelids, causing the edges to turn inward.

Q: How is trachoma treated?

A: Treatment with antibiotics is usually effective. Early diagnosis and treatment is essential to prevent scarring and possible blindness. If these have already occurred, a CORNEAL GRAFT operation may be necessary. Surgery may also be necessary to correct ingrowing eyelids.

Traction is the act of pulling or drawing. This is the method by which a baby may be delivered with forceps; a fracture reduced; or a fracture reduction maintained. Weight traction is a system of weights and pulleys that are attached to a fractured limb so that the broken bones remain in the correct position. Traction is also used in manipulative and osteopathic treatment.

A talk about Tranquillizers

Tranquillizers are drugs that are used to reduce mental stress without disturbing normal mental activities. There are two main

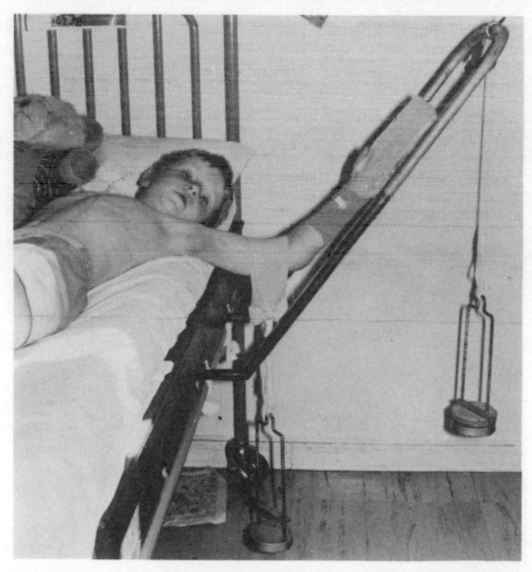

Traction is a method of treatment which holds fractured bones in position by using weights.

groups of tranquillizing drugs: minor tranquillizers and major tranquillizers. The minor tranquillizers are used to treat acute anxiety. They may also be combined with antidepressant drugs to treat patients who are both anxious and depressed. The major tranquillizers are used to treat psychotic mental illnesses, such as schizophrenia.

Q: *What are the different types of minor tranquillizers?*

A: The benzodiazepine group of drugs are the most commonly prescribed minor tranquillizers. They produce four main effects: sedation; alleviation of anxiety; prevention of convulsions; and muscle relaxation.

Various other drugs are also used as minor tranquillizers, such as hydroxyzine and loxapine.

Q: *Can minor tranquillizers produce adverse side effects?*

A: Yes. The main side effects include dizziness, drowsiness, and lack of co-ordination. Care should be taken when driving or operating machinery, and alcohol should be avoided. Minor tranquillizers may produce physical dependence during a long course of treatment, so a doctor may limit their use.

Q: *What are the different types of major tranquillizers?*

A: The major tranquillizers include the phenothiazines, thioxanthine derivatives, and butyrophenones. The phenothiazines are the most commonly prescribed of these drugs. All the groups of major tranquillizers produce similar effects, which include sedation; relaxation of the muscles; reduction of aggression; and prevention of nausea.

The major tranquillizers are extremely effective in controlling the symptoms of serious mental illnesses. Their use has enabled many patients to lead relatively normal lives.

Q: *Can major tranquillizers produce adverse side effects?*

A: Yes. Patients who are highly sensitive to these drugs may develop skin rashes and jaundice. The production of hormones may also be affected, which may cause irregular menstruation. Large doses may cause trembling and muscle rigidity.

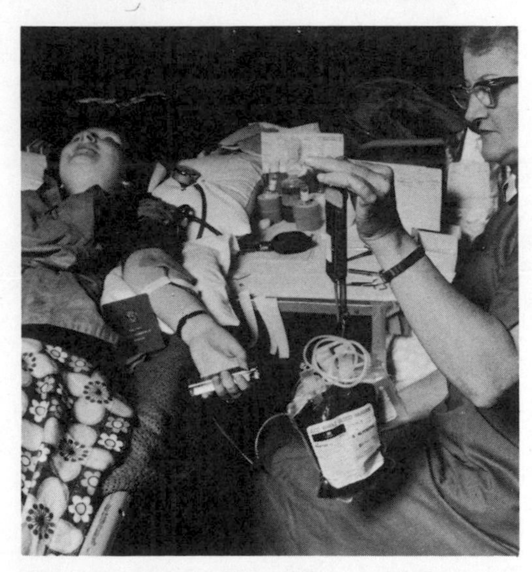

Donor gives blood that will be used in the future for a blood transfusion.

Transference is the redirection of emotion from important figures, such as parents, to another person, usually to a psychiatrist or a doctor who is treating the person.

Transfusion is the infusion of blood or plasma into the veins of a person. *See* BLOOD TRANSFUSION.

Transfusion reaction is a dangerous reaction that occurs between the blood of a donor and the recipient. Such reactions are rare when the blood types of the donor and the recipient are properly cross-matched. The severity of transfusion reactions varies greatly. The onset of the reaction is usually rapid, with breathlessness; chest pain; vomiting; and symptoms similar to those of shock.

Q: *What causes a transfusion reaction?*

A: A transfusion reaction is usually caused by an incompatability between the blood of the donor and that of the recipient. The recipient has antibodies that destroy the red blood cells of the transfused blood. This reaction may cause jaundice and disorders of the kidneys, which may become blocked, resulting in haemoglobin in the urine, and kidney failure.

In most cases, such complications are temporary, and are usually followed by a complete recovery.

See also BLOOD TRANSFUSION.

A talk about Transplant surgery

Transplant surgery is the transference of a tissue or organ from one person to another, or from one site to another in the same person. The main difficulty with transplantation is to prevent the body from treating the new organ as a foreign substance and destroying it (tissue rejection).

Q: When is transplant surgery performed?

A: Transplant surgery is performed when it is considered the most effective form of treatment. For example, a kidney transplant may be performed to stop the need for regular KIDNEY DIALYSIS. Corneal transplants may be performed to restore the sight of a person with severe corneal scarring. Heart valves may be transplanted to treat valvular heart disease. Diseased blood vessels may be replaced to treat arteriosclerosis. The technique has been performed successfully with tendons, nerves, bones, and skin.

Transplants between different people have been performed with the heart, liver, kidneys, and bone marrow. Other organs, such as the lungs, fallopian tubes, and pancreas have also been transplanted, but such transplants are still experimental.

Q: Are transplant operations successful?

A: There is no guarantee that a transplant operation will be successful. The success rate depends to some extent on the tissue being transplanted.

Up to seventy per cent of patients with heart and kidney transplants survive for at least two years after the operation.

Q: Why isn't transplant surgery always successful?

A: The relatively few transplantations that fail usually do so because of tissue rejection. Every person, unless an identical twin, has a characteristic set of proteins in the body (tissue type), rather like a fingerprint. The better the match between tissue types of the transplanted organ and the recipient, the lower the chances of rejection. Identical twins have the same tissue type, so rejection is extremely unlikely.

Q: Can rejection be prevented?

A: Yes, although the technique is not always successful. Several drugs reduce the ability of the transplant recipient to produce antibodies by suppressing the immune system of the recipient. These drugs are called immunosuppressive drugs.

Because these drugs suppress the immune system, they also prevent the body from reacting to infection so that even the mildest infection may be fatal. However, new immunosuppressive drugs are being developed, and rejection is becoming less of a problem.

Q: Which transplants need immunosuppressive drug treatment?

A: Kidney, heart, and liver transplants usually require immunosuppressive treatment for several years. The dosage is reduced slowly when a doctor is satisfied that rejection is unlikely.

Q: Which transplants do not need immunosuppressive drug treatment?

A: Corneal and tendon transplants can be performed without the problem of rejection. Transplantation of blood vessels and heart valves is usually successful without drug treatment because the transplanted tissues are replaced by the recipient's tissues.

Q: What happens if the transplanted organ is rejected?

A: The result of rejection depends, to some extent, on the organ that has been transplanted. If a vital organ, such as the heart or liver, is rejected, the patient usually dies unless another transplant can be performed. Most kidney transplant patients can be kept alive by kidney dialysis until another kidney is available for transplantation.

Transvestism is the desire to dress in the clothing of the opposite sex as a means of obtaining sexual excitement. A transvestite is not necessarily homosexual.

Trauma is the medical term for an injury. It usually refers to a physical injury but may also refer to a psychological shock.

Traveller's diarrhoea is a mild intestinal disorder that causes abdominal cramps, diarrhoea, and also vomiting. The combination of a bland diet, antispasmodic drugs, and kaolin usually controls the symptoms. *See* DIARRHOEA.

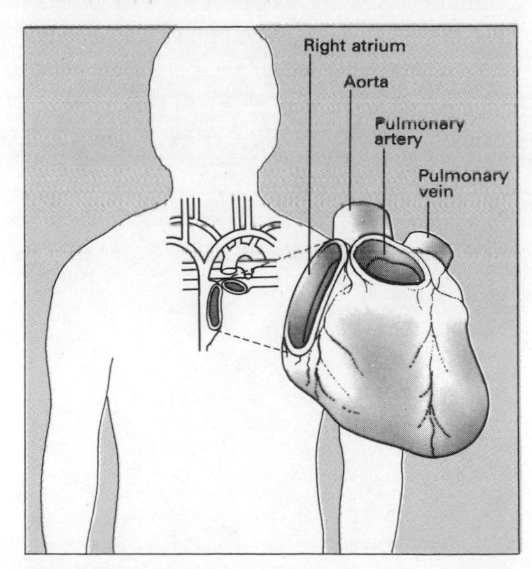

Transplant surgery involving the heart enables the surgeon to implant a healthy donor organ.

Travel sickness. *See* MOTION SICKNESS.

Trematodes, also known as liver flukes, are parasitic flatworms that require a member of the snail family as an intermediate host before causing various infections in man. *See* FLUKES; SCHISTOSOMIASIS.

Trembling. *See* TREMOR.

Tremor is an involuntary quivering of the muscles. There are several different types of tremor: a coarse tremor is one in which the movements are slow; a fine tremor produces rapid movements; and an intention tremor appears only when voluntary movements are attempted. Tremors may be present all the time or they may occur irregularly.

Tremors may be associated with shivering, excitement, or fear, or they may be a symptom of a more serious underlying disorder. Tremors may be caused by acute anxiety; poisoning; overactivity of the thyroid gland; or failure of the liver or kidneys. Other underlying causes of tremors include nervous disorders, such as Parkinson's disease; multiple sclerosis; Huntington's chorea; general paralysis of the insane (caused by syphilis of the brain); and Friedrich's ataxia, which is degeneration of the spinal cord.

Trench fever. *See* RICKETTSIA.

Trench foot. *See* IMMERSION FOOT.

Trench mouth is a painful ulceration of the mucous membranes of the mouth and throat. *See* VINCENT'S ANGINA.

Trephine is a small cylindrical saw that is used to make a circular hole in the skull, thereby exposing the brain for surgery.

Treponema is a genus of spiral-shaped bacteria. Many of these bacteria are parasitic, and cause various diseases, such as PINTA, SYPHILIS, and YAWS.

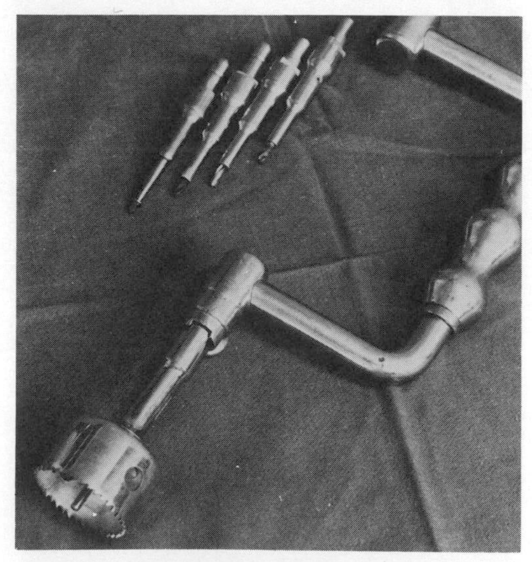

Trephine is a surgical instrument used for cutting circular pieces of bone from the skull.

Trichiasis is a condition in which the eyelashes grow inward and rub against the cornea of the eye. This causes irritation, watering of the eyes, and a feeling of a foreign body in the eye.

Trichiasis may result from various eye disorders, such as trachoma; inflammation of the eyelids (blepharitis); or entropion, in which the eyelids turn inward. It is treated by removing the inturned eyelash, or by surgical out-turning of the eyelids.

Trichinosis is a disorder that is caused by infestation with the parasitic roundworm *Trichinella spiralis.* People become infected by eating raw or undercooked pork that contains cysts of the parasite. The cysts break open in the stomach and they release larvae, which penetrate the wall of the small intestine, mature into adult males and females, and mate. After mating, the female worms discharge larvae which spread to the muscles and form small cysts that eventually calcify.

Q: What are the symptoms of trichinosis?

A: The symptoms vary according to the number of infecting larvae. Diarrhoea, nausea, and vomiting may occur within a few days of infection. About two weeks later there may be swelling of the eyelids; conjunctivitis; and abnormal sensitivity to light (photophobia). These symptoms may be followed by aching of the muscles, intermittent fever, and increasing weakness.

A variety of further symptoms develop, depending on the organs that are infected. Pneumonia and pleurisy, encephalitis and meningitis and sometimes heart muscle involvement (myocarditis) may all occur. If the myocarditis is severe, heart failure will develop. These severe and serious symptoms may last for between one and two months before gradually improving, leaving a vague aching of the muscles.

Q: How is trichinosis diagnosed and treated?

A: In the initial stages it is difficult to make a definite diagnosis, but the history of eating raw pork may be suggestive. The larvae may be found on muscle biopsy, and a skin test will become positive after about four weeks of the infection.

Treatment with thiabendazole is usually effective. Corticosteroid drugs may also be necessary to prevent an allergic reaction to the infection.

Trichinosis can be prevented by thoroughly cooking all pork.

Trichomonas vaginalis is a parasitic protozoan that is found in the vagina and in the male urethra. It seldom causes any symptoms in men, but the trichomonas may be transmitted to sexual partners. In women, it usually causes symptoms only after it has been disturbed by sexual intercourse, menstruation, or, rarely, vaginal surgery. The protozoan may cause VAGINITIS, with an offensive vaginal discharge and painful urination.

Treatment with drugs, such as metronidazole, is usually effective. The patient's sexual partner should also be treated.

Trichuriasis is infestation with the parasitic roundworm *Trichuris trichiura* (whipworm). It results from eating food that is contaminated with the worm's eggs. The eggs hatch into larvae in the small intestine, and migrate to the large intestine. By the time the larvae have reached the colon, they have matured into adult roundworms. The adults attach themselves to the lining of the colon and produce more eggs, which pass out of the body in the faeces.

Q: What are the symptoms of trichuriasis?

A: Symptoms usually appear only with heavy infestations. In such cases, there may be abdominal pain and diarrhoea. Extremely heavy infestations, particularly in children, may cause intestinal bleeding; anaemia; weight loss; and rectal prolapse.

Q: How is trichuriasis treated?

A: Treatment with mebendazole is usually effective. Trichuriasis may be prevented by careful personal hygiene.

See also ROUNDWORMS.

Trigeminal neuralgia, also known as tic doloureux, is a disorder of the trigeminal nerve, which supplies the face with sensory and some motor functions. The disorder occurs most commonly in the elderly. The cause is not known.

Q: What are the symptoms of trigeminal neuralgia?

A: The only common symptom is a severe, brief pain on one side of the face. This pain is often triggered by a light touch, cleaning the teeth, or by chewing.

Q: How is trigeminal neuralgia treated?

A: Treatment with some anticonvulsant drugs, such as carbamazepine and phenytoin, or with anti-migraine drugs is often effective. If such treatment is not successful, a doctor may recommend a surgical operation to cut the trigeminal nerve.

Triglyceride is a type of LIPID that is formed from a combination of fatty acids and glycerol. Most animal and vegetable fats are triglycerides.

The relationship between triglycerides, cholesterol, and lipoproteins is complex, but there is evidence to associate high levels of these three substances in the blood with an increased incidence of arteriosclerosis.

Excessive saturated animal fat in the diet causes a long-term increase in the concentration of triglycerides and cholesterol in the blood. A high triglyceride blood concentration may be associated with alcoholism; diabetes mellitus; the nephrotic syndrome; hypothyroidism; pregnancy; and also use of the contraceptive pill.

A diet that is low in animal fats and regular exercise can help to reduce the level of triglycerides in the blood.

Trismus is a spasm of the jaw muscles causing difficulty in opening the jaws. It may be caused by a fracture or dislocation of the jaw; a throat infection; or irritation of the nerves that control the jaw muscles, as occurs with tetanus. *See* TETANUS.

Trocar is a surgical instrument for piercing the walls of a cavity. It consists of a tube with a sharp, pointed central part, that can be removed, leaving the outer tube in place. A form of trocar is used for intravenous transfusions and for piercing the abdominal wall to remove ASCITES. TRACHEOSTOMY tubes often contain a central trocar.

Tropical diseases are those that occur almost exclusively in tropical climates. This is mainly because (1) the organisms that cause the diseases are able to survive only in tropical conditions; (2) the diseases are transmitted by insects or animals that are found only in the tropics; and (3) poor sanitation and health care are common in many tropical countries.

Travellers can be immunized against some

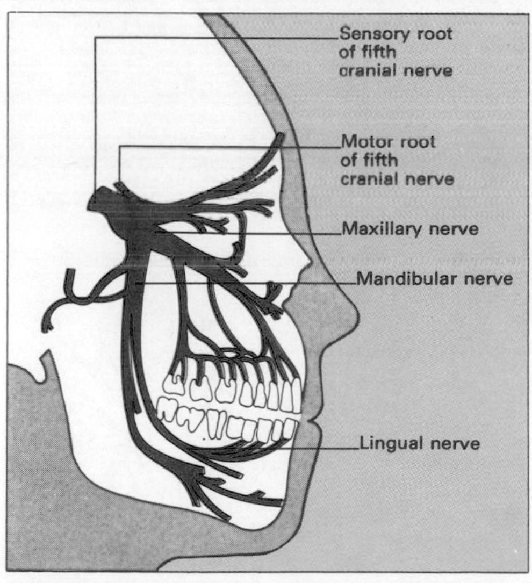

Trigeminal neuralgia can affect any part of the face supplied by the fifth cranial nerve.

tropical diseases. The use of insect-repellent creams may help to prevent insect-borne diseases. Diseases that are transmitted by body contact can usually be prevented by careful personal hygiene.

Air travel has introduced some tropical diseases to temperate climates where such diseases do not usually occur. Any fever or disorder that occurs within about two months of returning from the tropics should be reported to a doctor immediately.

Tropical sore, also known as Delhi boil and Oriental sore, is a skin ulcer that is caused by infection with parasitic microorganisms of the genus *Leishmania*. *See* LEISHMANIASIS.

Truss is a device that is used to hold a hernia (rupture) in place. A truss is usually used only when surgical treatment of a hernia is not possible. *See* HERNIA.

Trypanosomiasis is a general term for any of several related diseases that are caused by parasitic protozoa of the genus *Trypanosoma*. *See* CHAGAS' DISEASE; SLEEPING SICKNESS.

Trypsin is an enzyme produced by the pancreas that digests proteins in the small intestine.

Tsetse fly is a bloodsucking insect that transmits sleeping sickness. *See* SLEEPING SICKNESS.

TSH test is performed to assess the activity of the thyroid gland. It involves measuring the concentration of radioactive iodine in the thyroid gland both before and after the administration of thyroid-stimulating hormone (TSH).

Tubal pregnancy is a pregnancy that takes place in a fallopian tube instead of in the womb. *See* ECTOPIC PREGNANCY.

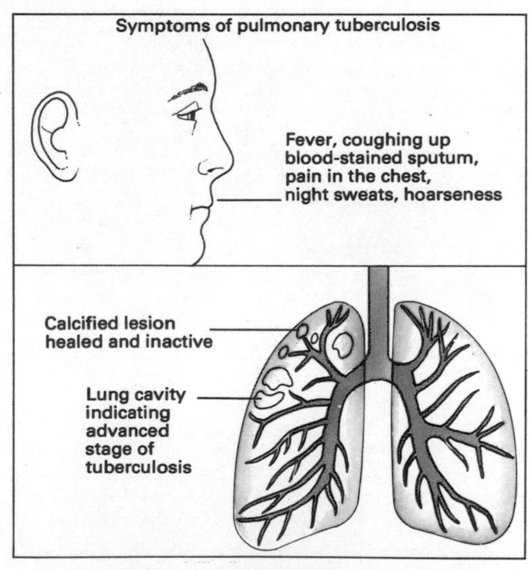

Tuberculosis can affect many parts of the body; pulmonary tuberculosis is the most common.

Tuberculin test is a skin test to determine whether a person has ever been infected with tuberculosis or related bacteria. A small amount of tuberculin, which is a preparation of dead tuberculous bacteria, is injected into the skin. A red swelling indicates previous infection with tuberculosis or immunization with BCG vaccine. A tuberculin test does not reveal whether the infection is active or inactive. *See* BCG; HEAF TEST; MANTOUX TEST; TINE TEST; TUBERCULOSIS.

A talk about Tuberculosis

Tuberculosis is an infectious disease that is usually caused by the bacteria *Mycobacterium tuberculosis.* Rarely, it may be caused by other species of *Mycobacterium,* such as *Mycobacterium bovis* which is found predominantly in cattle.

Infection may result from inhalation of minute droplets of infected sputum or, less commonly, from drinking infected milk. If the infected person is not immune, the bacteria grow freely within the body and spread from the lungs to other parts of the body.

Eventually the patient develops immunity and the bacteria stop spreading. They become surrounded by scar tissue and may not cause further tissue damage.

At a later stage, the protective layer of scar tissue may break down. This may be due to the development of another disorder; a reduction in immunity, which may occur with old age; the use of corticosteroid drugs; or malignant diseases, such as leukaemia and Hodgkin's disease.

Symptoms of tuberculosis occur when the body's immunity does not develop fast enough to prevent the infection from spreading to various parts of the body, or when immunity is interrupted by old age or certain drugs or diseases. The symptoms of tuberculosis in children usually differ from those in adults.

Q: What are the symptoms of tuberculosis in children?

A: The main symptoms of childhood tuberculosis include fever; weight loss; and swelling of the lymph glands. If the primary site of infection is in the lungs, the lymph glands in the chest become enlarged; if it is in the gastrointestinal tract, the lymph glands in the neck or abdomen are affected.

The enlarged lymph glands may ulcerate, causing bronchial irritation, with coughing and the collapse of parts of the lung. There may also be ulceration into the bronchial tubes, causing tuberculous pneumonia. If the lymph glands in the neck are affected, they may discharge pus through the skin. Swelling of the lymph glands in the abdomen may result in a slow form of PERITONITIS.

Q: What are the symptoms of tuberculosis in adults?

A: There is often a period of many months before symptoms appear. In most cases, the infection primarily involves the top of one of the lungs, although it may spread to other parts of the body. The initial symptoms include tiredness; weight loss; fever during the evening; and profuse sweating at night.

As the infection progresses, the patient begins to cough up blood-stained sputum, which may be infectious. If a large area of the lung is affected, pleurisy may develop, causing breathlessness and chest pain.

In some patients, particularly the elderly and those with silicosis, the progress of the disease is extremely slow and is accompanied by a large amount of lung scarring. In such cases, the main symptoms are usually breathlessness and coughing.

Q: In what other ways can tuberculosis affect the body?

A: Tuberculosis may affect any organ in the body. It may cause infection of the membranes round the brain (meningitis), which is characterized by headache, drowsiness, and intermittent vomiting. This usually affects children and is often fatal unless treated rapidly. In miliary tuberculosis, the infection spreads extremely rapidly, and small abscesses develop in most organs. Tuberculosis may also affect the bones, most commonly the spine (Pott's disease); the kidneys; or the epididymis. The infection may spread from the abdominal organs or the lungs, which may result in tuberculous peritonitis or inflammation of the fallopian tubes (salpingitis). Rarely, tuberculosis may affect the adrenal glands, causing ADDISON'S DISEASE.

More commonly, tuberculosis involves the membrane surrounding the lungs (pleura), causing an accumulation of tuberculous fluid between the layers of the pleura (pleural effusion). This may cause a serious illness, particularly if the fluid contains a large amount of pus.

Most people who become infected with tuberculosis do not develop symptoms of the disease: they become immune and the infection remains dormant in scar tissue.

Q: How is tuberculosis diagnosed?

A: Tuberculosis may be diagnosed with X-rays and examination of the sputum for the tuberculosis bacteria. Blood tests and a positive TUBERCULIN TEST may be used to confirm the diagnosis.

In children, X-rays are usually not helpful, and the doctor must obtain a history to determine if there has been exposure to tuberculosis.

Q: How is tuberculosis treated?

A: Most patients respond quickly to chemotherapy and are discharged from hospital after two or three weeks. Patients who are seriously ill may require hospitalization for two or three months.

Drugs are prescribed until the sensitivity of the bacteria to antibiotics and the response of the patient are determined. Thereafter, the drugs may be changed to suit the individual patient.They should be taken for many months. The drugs most commonly used are isoniazid (INH) in combination with rifampicin or ethambutol and, occasionally, streptomycin by injection.

Tuberculous meningitis requires specialized treatment. Early diagnosis is extremely important.

Q: Can tuberculosis be prevented?

A: Yes. Vaccination with BCG, which is a preparation of attenuated tuberculosis bacteria, has been shown to confer lifetime immunity in certain populations.

Q: What are the "open" and "closed" forms of tuberculosis?

A: "Open" tuberculosis refers to the stage in the disease when a person is producing

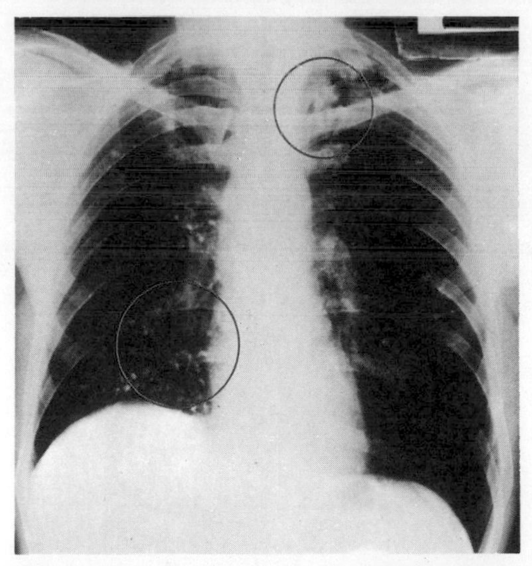

Tuberculosis affecting the lungs may be revealed by an X-ray examination.

infectious sputum. "Closed" tuberculosis refers to the noninfectious stage, in which the tuberculosis bacteria are surrounded by scar tissue. Patients with "open" tuberculosis should be isolated until sputum tests for the bacteria are negative.

Q: *What precautions should be taken by people who have been in contact with tuberculosis?*

A: Those who have been in contact with an infectious case of tuberculosis should be examined for infection by a doctor. If the person has been in very close contact, or has had a tuberculin test that indicates recent infection with tuberculosis, treatment with antituberculous drugs for at least a year is needed. Other contacts should be kept under regular observation, with chest X-rays, after being vaccinated with BCG if the tuberculin test is negative. Contacts of patients with "closed" tuberculosis should also be examined.

Tularaemia, also known as rabbit fever, is a disorder that is caused by the bacterium *Francisella tularensis.* The bacteria can penetrate unbroken skin, and most cases of tularaemia result from handling infected wild animals, particularly rabbits. Occasionally, infection may result from eating undercooked meat, or from the bite of an infected tick.

Q: *What are the symptoms of tularaemia?*

A: After an incubation period of about a week, there is a sudden onset of high fever; headache; nausea; vomiting; and extreme weakness. A day or two later, an inflamed nodule appears at the site of infection. The nodule ulcerates rapidly, and further ulcers may appear near the mouth or eye. The lymph glands around the site of infection may become swollen; they may also ulcerate and discharge pus.

The patient may develop a skin rash or pneumonia at any time during the illness, which usually lasts three or four weeks.

Q: *How is tularaemia treated?*

A: Treatment with streptomycin or tetracycline is effective in most cases. The patient should undergo the full course of treatment to prevent a relapse.

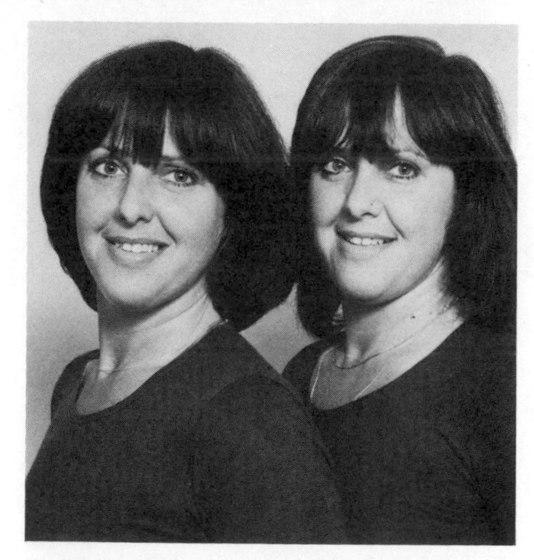

Twins formed from one fertilized ovum that splits are identical, or monozygotic.

Tumour is any swelling of the body tissues, such as an abscess, a cyst or a tissue growth. The term usually refers to a spontaneous new growth (neoplasm), which may be either malignant (cancerous) or benign (noncancerous). A malignant tumour is a neoplasm that grows and spreads throughout the body. A benign tumour is a neoplasm that does not spread or infiltrate other tissues of the body.

Most tumours are benign and are not life-threatening. However, malignant tumours may spread and cause extensive damage. *See* CANCER; SARCOMA.

Turner's syndrome is a CHROMOSOME anomaly of females in which one of the two X chromosomes is absent, so that there are forty-five instead of the normal forty-six chromosomes.

A person with Turner's syndrome has the physical appearance of an immature female. The characteristic features include short stature; webbing of the neck; multiple birthmarks; and underdeveloped or absent ovaries. There may be swelling of the hands and feet during infancy. Some patients have congenital heart defects, and a few are mentally retarded. At puberty, the breasts fail to develop normally, and menstruation does not occur.

There is no effective treatment for Turner's syndrome until the patient reaches puberty. After puberty, oestrogen and progesterone drugs can be given to replace the deficiency of ovarian hormones. Normal secondary sexual characteristics and menstrual periods can then occur.

Twilight sleep is a condition of impaired consciousness that is produced by a combination of painkilling drugs and inhaled anaesthetic gases. Twilight sleep is often induced in order to reduce the pain of childbirth, while keeping the mother sufficiently aware to be co-operative during labour (*see* PREGNANCY AND CHILDBIRTH).

Twins. There are two types of twins: fraternal twins (dizygotic or binovular twins), and identical twins (monozygotic or monovular twins).

Fraternal twins result from the fertilization of two separate eggs that are usually released simultaneously. They may be the same sex or different sexes. Each has a separate placenta within the womb, and each develops independently of the other.

Identical twins result from the fertilization of a single egg that later divides into two. They are the same sex, and share a single placenta. Rarely, the egg may not divide completely and the two foetuses remain joined (SIAMESE TWINS).

Twins occur in about one in eighty pregnancies, but the frequency varies slightly from country to country.

Fraternal twins are more common in families with a history of twins; in mothers who are older than average; and in mothers who have had more than the average number of babies.

Q: Can a twin pregnancy cause problems?

A: Yes. The initial difficulty is that of diagnosis. About one in ten twin pregnancies may go unnoticed until the onset of labour. A twin pregnancy may be confirmed by ultrasonic testing, or, if necessary, by an X-ray examination to show both foetuses.

Pre-eclampsia, anaemia, and premature labour occur more commonly with twin births. But, the main problem of a twin pregnancy is delivery. The first baby usually causes little difficulty, but the second may be in the wrong position and may require turning for a normal delivery. Another problem is survival of both twins without brain damage caused by a rapid delivery.

Due to the problems of pre-eclampsia and prematurity, there is a greater incidence of infant mortality during the latter half of pregnancy, during labour, or within a few days of birth. There is also a greater risk of haemorrhage in the mother after birth.

See also PREGNANCY AND CHILDBIRTH.

Twitching is an involuntary muscle contraction that produces a small, spasmodic jerking movement. It may occur as a TIC, as restless legs, or as a symptom of TETANY. Twitching may be a symptom of various neurological disorders, but occasional twitching in a healthy person is not serious.

Tympanum is the anatomical name for the eardrum. *See* EAR.

Typhoid fever, also known as enteric fever, is an intestinal disease that is caused by infection with the bacterium *Salmonella typhi.* Typhoid is the most serious of the salmonella infections. Similar, but milder infections with other salmonella bacteria cause PARATYPHOID fever.

Most cases of typhoid result from eating infected food or from drinking contaminated water. Food and water may become contaminated by direct contact with the urine or faeces of an infected person. Flies may carry the infection from faeces to food. When the bacteria have been swallowed, they penetrate the small intestine and spread throughout the body in the bloodstream.

Q: What are the symptoms of typhoid?

A: After an incubation period of about one or two weeks, there is a gradual onset of headache; loss of appetite; fatigue; and constipation.

During the following week, the patient's temperature rises gradually to about 40°C (104°F). This is accompanied by abdominal pain, nosebleeds, and slow pulse rate. Pale, rose-coloured spots may appear on the chest and abdomen; they usually last for about three or four days.

The high fever usually lasts for about a week, and the patient may become delirious. Diarrhoea may develop toward the end of the second week, by which time the fever starts to disappear. In most cases, the fever disappears completely by the end of the third week of illness.

Q: Can typhoid cause any complications?

A: Yes, pneumonia is the most common complication. More serious complications may occur in patients who develop diarrhoea. In such cases, the intestine may ulcerate and bleed. Severe bleeding from an ulcer may lead to anaemia, or may even

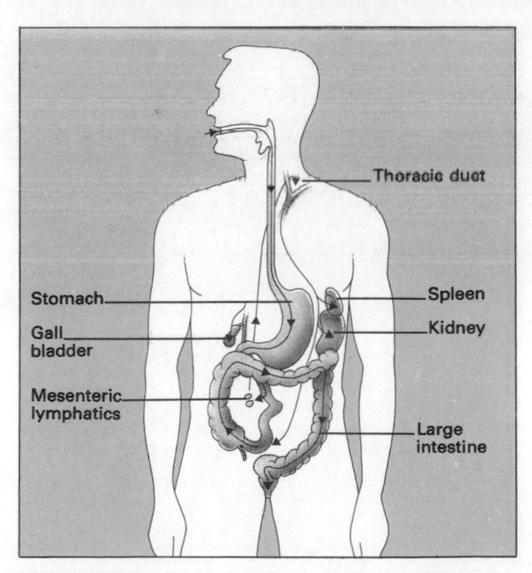

Typhoid bacteria enter the body orally then infect the bloodstream via the thoracic duct.

be fatal. Perforation of the ulcer will cause peritonitis. Relapses occasionally occur, but they are usually minor.

Q: How is typhoid diagnosed and treated?

A: A positive diagnosis may require a test to culture the bacteria spreading in the blood and to detect a rise in the antibodies (Widal test). The patient's urine and faeces may be cultured for the typhoid bacteria.

Typhoid is usually treated with antibiotics. Chloramphenicol is generally the most effective antibiotic, but bacterial strains have developed that are resistant to it. In such cases, ampicillin or trimethoprim-sulphamethoxazole drugs will be prescribed.

In addition to drug therapy, the patient may require a blood transfusion and intravenous infusions of fluid to prevent dehydration. Patients with perforation or haemorrhage of the intestine usually need an emergency operation to repair the ulcerated area. If the patient suffers a relapse, a further course of antibiotics is necessary.

It is essential that all patients who have had typhoid should have at least six specimens of faeces cultured and examined to ensure that the bacteria have been killed. Until this has been done, the patient should not be allowed to handle food, and should take great care with personal hygiene.

Q: What is a carrier of typhoid?

A: A typhoid carrier is a person who has made a complete recovery from the disease, but who continues to excrete typhoid bacteria in the urine and faeces. Such people can transmit the infection to others.

Q: Can typhoid be prevented?

A: No, but it is possible to reduce the likelihood of infection. All drinking water should be purified, if necessary by boiling, and milk should be pasteurized. Carriers of typhoid should not be allowed to handle food. Immunization with TAB VACCINE gives partial protection against infection, and may reduce the severity of the symptoms in those who contract typhoid.

See also IMMUNIZATION; SALMONELLA.

Typhus is a general term for any of several related diseases caused by various species of *Rickettsia,* which are microorganisms that resemble both bacteria and viruses.

The typhus group is generally considered to consist of a range of similar diseases, including epidemic typhus; endemic typhus; and scrub typhus. Some authorities consider Rocky Mountain spotted fever and Q fever to be forms of typhus. Although these diseases are also caused by *Rickettsia,* they are often classified as forms of spotted fever.

Epidemic typhus is caused by *Rickettsia prowazeki.* The infection may result from contamination of a bite by the faeces of the human body louse, or from inhalation of louse faeces. Endemic typhus is caused by *Rickettsia mooseri,* which is transmitted by fleas from infected rats or mice. Scrub typhus is caused by *Rickettsia tsutsugamushi,* which is transmitted by a mite that normally lives on rodents.

Q: What are the symptoms of epidemic typhus?

A: After an incubation period of between ten and fourteen days, there is a sudden onset of a severe headache and fever. The fever rises to about 40°C (104°F) and usually lasts for about two weeks. Between four and six days after the onset of symptoms, pink spots appear on all parts of the body except the face, hands, and feet. The spots may darken as a result of bruising. The patient may also vomit, and be in a state of delirium or shock. Epidemic typhus has a high mortality rate, particularly among untreated patients. Rarely, the symptoms of epidemic typhus may recur without the patient being reinfected. This is called Brill-Zinsser disease.

Q: What are the symptoms of endemic typhus?

A: The symptoms of endemic typhus are similar to those of epidemic typhus, but

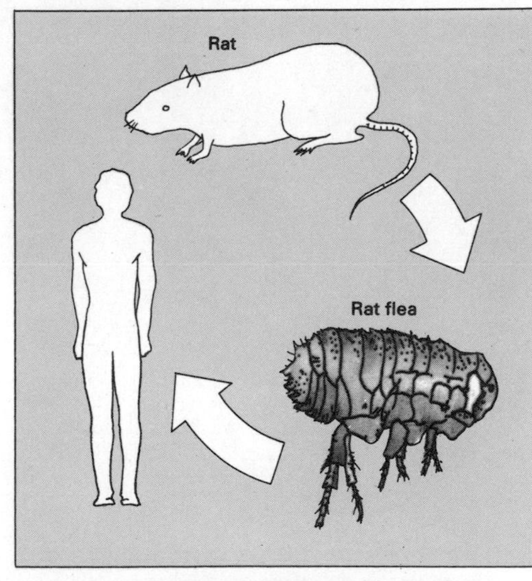

Endemic typhus is a disease transmitted by a flea that infests rats and humans.

are usually much milder. The mortality rate is low.

Q: What are the symptoms of scrub typhus?

A: The symptoms are similar to those of epidemic typhus, but scrub typhus may also cause a red nodule at the site of the mite bite. The nodule ulcerates and forms a black scab (eschar). A skin rash and cough may also develop. The rash is usually less clearly defined than the rash of epidemic typhus. Some patients may also develop complications, such as pneumonia and, rarely, inflammation of the heart muscle (myocarditis).

Q: How is typhus treated?

A: For all forms of typhus, treatment with antibiotics is usually effective. Patients who are seriously ill may also require hospitalization and treatment with intravenous infusions of fluid.

Q: Can typhus be prevented?

A: Yes. Effective vaccines are available against epidemic and endemic typhus, but not against scrub typhus.

The control of mites, lice, and rodents are also effective preventive measures. It is advisable to use insecticides and mite-repellent creams when visiting areas in which typhus is common.

See also RICKETTSIA.

U

Ulcer is an open sore that may occur on the skin or the internal mucous membranes of the body. For example, an ulcer may develop inside the mouth (aphthous ulcer); around the lips (cold sore); on the cornea; or in the stomach and duodenum (PEPTIC ULCER).

Q: What causes ulcers?

A: Ulcers may be caused by relatively minor disorders, such as a burn or abrasion. They also may result from more serious disorders. For example, ulcerative colitis produces ulceration of the colon; scrub typhus produces a skin ulcer called an eschar; and syphilis produces a chancre sore. Cancer may produce an ulcer in almost any part of the body.

Ulcers are particularly likely to develop in parts of the body where there is poor blood circulation, which may be caused by varicose veins. Reduced sensation in a particular part of the body may be caused by nervous disorders, and may also lead to ulceration.

See also BEDSORE; PEPTIC ULCER; RODENT ULCER; ULCERATIVE COLITIS.

Ulcerative colitis is a disorder of the large intestine in which the colon becomes inflamed and ulcerated. It usually occurs in people between fifteen and thirty-five years old. The underlying cause of the disorder is not known.

Q: What are the symptoms of ulcerative colitis?

A: The most common symptom is a series of attacks of bloody diarrhoea that vary in severity and duration from one person to another, and from one attack to another. They may start suddenly or gradually, and may occur as frequently as ten or fifteen times in twenty-four hours. The attacks are often accompanied by pain and spasms of the bowel (tenesmus). Attacks also may cause fever, loss of appetite, and weight loss.

With mild attacks, the symptoms are less alarming. The patient may feel tired but usually there are no signs of generalized illness.

The symptoms usually disappear between attacks, although some patients may suffer from mild diarrhoea.

Q: Can ulcerative colitis cause complications?

A: Yes. The most serious complications are associated with a sudden attack of bloody diarrhoea with perforation of the intestine, peritonitis, and intestinal bleeding.

People with ulcerative colitis also may develop anaemia; arthritis; inflammation of the eyes; or tender nodules under the skin. If ulcerative colitis persists for longer than about ten years, there is a much greater than average chance of

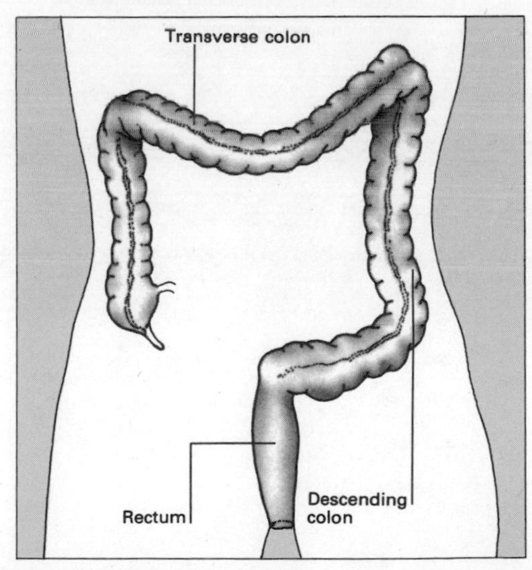

Ulcerative colitis may affect the rectum, then progresses to involve the colon.

developing cancer of the colon.

Q: *How is ulcerative colitis diagnosed and treated?*

A: A positive diagnosis may require an internal examination (endoscopy) of the colon and a barium enema X-ray.

Mild attacks of ulcerative colitis are usually treated with antidiarrhoeal drugs and rest. A special sulphonamide drug may control the symptoms of a severe attack and prevent recurrences. Treatment with corticosteroids, by mouth and as enemas, may also be necessary.

Persons who suffer an extremely severe attack may require hospital treatment. If complications develop, such as peritonitis or intestinal bleeding, emergency surgery may be necessary.

The outcome of ulcerative colitis is variable. However, most patients suffer repeated attacks over many years, and about thirty per cent eventually require some form of surgery. Patients with recurrent ulcerative colitis should have regular internal examinations of the colon to check for early signs of intestinal cancer. In many such cases, it is necessary to remove the colon and make an ILEOSTOMY, an opening in the abdominal wall for the small intestine.

Ulna is the slightly smaller of the two bones of the forearm. The other bone is the radius. At its upper end, the ulna articulates with the radius and humerus to form the elbow joint. At its lower end, the ulna joins with the radius to form the inner side of the wrist joint. *See* ELBOW; WRIST.

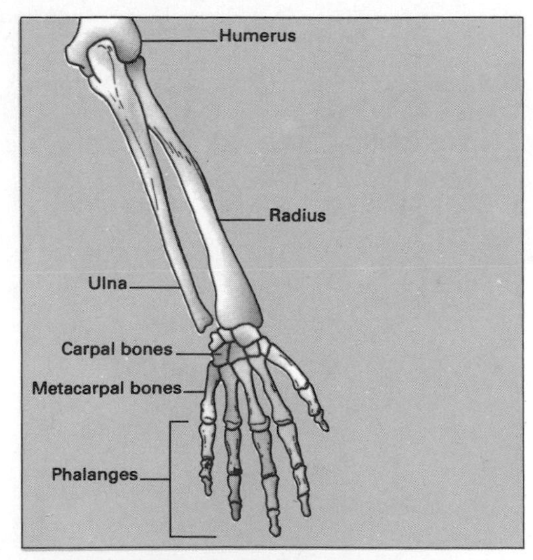

Ulna is able to twist round the radius, allowing a 180° turn of the wrist and hand.

Ultrasound techniques involve the use of high frequency sound waves (ultrasound) for diagnostic and therapeutic purposes.

Ultrasound is much too high-pitched to be audible (above about 20,000 cycles per second). It is focused into a thin beam, which is passed into the body. When ultrasound hits bone or air in the body, most of it is reflected while other tissues absorb the sound to varying degrees. When ultrasound is used for diagnosis, the echo is converted into a visual image. This image requires skilled interpretation by a specialist.

By using ultrasound techniques, it is possible to distinguish between different tissues in the body, measure the organs, and detect movement in the body.

Q: *Is ultrasound dangerous?*

A: No. It seems to be entirely safe. The amount of energy in ultrasound is too low to cause damage.

Q: *Can ultrasound techniques be used anywhere in the body?*

A: No. The skull reflects ultrasound, thereby preventing investigation of the brain. Ultrasound recordings of parts of the body that contain air, such as the lungs, are difficult to interpret.

Q: *Are there any special uses of ultrasound?*

A: Yes. Ultrasound is especially useful in investigating pregnancy because it does not harm the foetus or the mother. It may be used to measure the skull of a foetus, thereby giving an indication of the foetus's age; to detect foetal movements; to determine the position of the placenta; and to detect multiple pregnancies.

With ultrasound techniques, pregnancy can be detected as early as five weeks after conception. Abnormalities of the mother's womb, such as placental abnormalities or a hydatidiform mole, may be revealed. Foetal abnormalities, such as anencephalus, can also be detected early in pregnancy.

Ultrasound is particularly useful during AMNIOCENTESIS, because it can show the position of the placenta inside the mother's body.

Q: *What other uses of ultrasound are there?*

A: Ultrasound may be used to distinguish between a solid tumour and a cyst, to discover the cause of liver enlargement, to investigate kidney disorders, and to aid a biopsy of the liver. It may also help to diagnose thyroid, pancreatic, and gynaecological disorders, and to locate devices within the body, such as an intrauterine device.

Echocardiography is a form of ultrasound technique that may be used to diagnose heart disorders.

Ultrasound techniques may also be used to detect narrowing of the arteries and arterial thrombosis by recording alterations in the blood flow.

In the treatment of disease, a beam of ultrasound can be focused on a specific area within the body, where the energy of the beam changes into heat. This technique is used for relieving muscle and joint pains. A very powerful beam of ultrasound can be used to destroy small areas of body tissue.

Umbilical cord is the flexible, rope-like structure that connects the foetus with the PLACENTA. It is usually about 45cm (eighteen inches) long. The umbilical cord consists of two umbilical arteries and one umbilical vein, which are surrounded by a thick layer of jelly (Wharton's jelly) and a thin membrane. The umbilical vein transports oxygen and nutrients to the foetus. The umbilical arteries carry waste products from the foetus.

Soon after childbirth, the umbilical cord is tied and then cut by an obstetrician. The part of the cord that is still in the womb is expelled with the afterbirth. The stump that remains attached to the baby shrivels and falls off after a few days, leaving a small scar called the umbilicus (navel).

Unconsciousness (for EMERGENCY treatment, *see* First Aid, p.573) is a state of reduced awareness. It may vary in depth from a state of stupor, in which a person responds to painful stimulation, to a state of coma, in which a person cannot be roused by any form of stimulation.

The unconscious is a psychiatric term for the part of the mind that is believed to operate without the individual's immediate awareness or control.

See also COMA; STUPOR; TORPOR.

Undescended testicle is a condition in which a testis has not moved into the scrotum. *See* CRYPTORCHIDISM.

Undulant fever is another name for brucellosis. *See* BRUCELLOSIS.

Upper respiratory tract infection (URTI or URI) is any infection of the nose (rhinitis), throat (pharyngitis), or larynx (laryngitis). The most common form of upper respiratory tract infection is the common cold.

Uraemia is a toxic condition in which waste products of protein digestion, such as urea, are retained in the blood instead of being excreted in the urine. Uraemia is associated with kidney failure.

Q: *What conditions can cause uraemia?*

A: Uraemia may be caused by any condition that reduces the flow of blood through the kidneys, such as haemorrhage, vomiting, diarrhoea, or a serious illness. Kidney disease, such as nephritis, prevents the excretion of waste products which accumulate in the blood, causing uraemia. Disorders of the prostate gland or bladder stones block urine flow from the bladder and cause back pressure of urine into the kidneys, resulting in kidney failure and uraemia. Bacterial infections may also cause uraemia.

Q: *What are the symptoms of uraemia?*

A: The symptoms vary according to the underlying cause. Generally, the symptoms of acute uraemia include headaches, high blood pressure, confusion, dry mouth, and reduced urination.

The symptoms of chronic uraemia develop gradually. The first symptom is usually frequent urination (polyuria). Later, fatigue, loss of appetite, twitching muscles, confusion, and coma develop.

Because of the combination of illness, vomiting, and vitamin deficiency, the patient may also develop malnutrition.

Q: *How is uraemia treated?*

A: The treatment of uraemia is directed toward the underlying cause. A doctor may recommend a special diet that is low in protein, salts, and water to reduce the symptoms. Patients with high blood pressure may require special treatment to prevent heart failure.

If kidney failure is likely to develop, a specialist may advise kidney dialysis or, in suitable cases, a kidney transplant.

Q: *Can uraemia cause complications?*

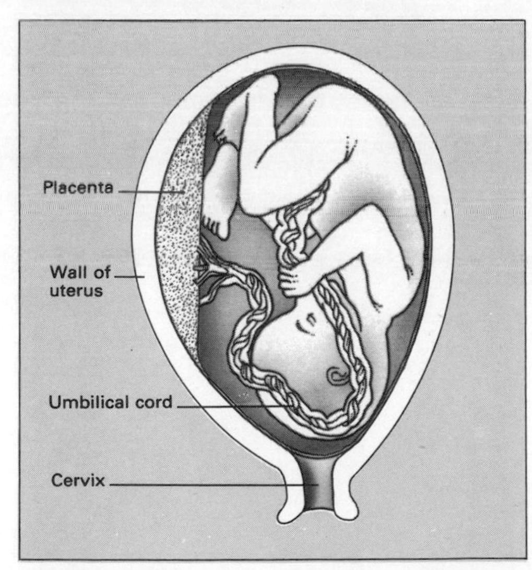

Umbilical cord carries nutrients and waste products between the mother and the foetus.

A: Yes. Uraemia may cause heart failure, disturbance of calcium metabolism, abnormal bone formation, nerve damage, and bleeding, which may occur anywhere in the body. Uraemia may also affect the immune system, leaving the patient vulnerable to infection.

If the condition is not treated, the patient becomes comatose and may die.

Ureter is one of a pair of thin, muscular tubes that drain urine from each kidney into the bladder. The urine is passed down the ureter by alternate contraction and relaxation (peristalsis) of the muscles in the ureter.

Several disorders may affect the ureter. For example, HYDRONEPHROSIS, which is accumulation of urine in the pelvis of the kidney, may be caused by obstruction of the ureter, or by a failure of normal peristalsis. The ureter may also become blocked by a stone (NEPHROLITHIASIS) or a tumour.

Urethra is the tube through which urine is discharged from the bladder.

In women, the urethra is short; it opens between the vagina and clitoris. The urethra is longer in men and also serves as the passage for semen. It passes through the prostate gland where it is joined by the sperm ducts, and opens at the end of the penis.

Various disorders may affect the urethra. It may open on the lower surface (hypospadiasis) or on the upper surface (epispadiasis) of the penis. Both these abnormalities are relatively common birth defects in boys.

The urethra may become infected and inflamed (URETHRITIS), which may result in scarring and narrowing of the urethra in men, or CYSTITIS in women. PROSTATE PROBLEMS may also deform the urethra, which may lead to difficulty in urination.

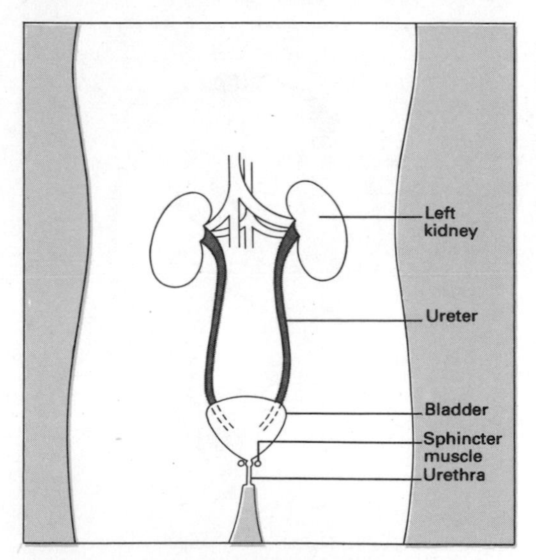

Ureter conveys urine to the bladder, from where it is expelled through the urethra.

Urethritis is inflammation of the urethra, the tube through which urine passes from the bladder and out of the body. It may be caused by venereal disease, such as GONORRHOEA or NONSPECIFIC URETHRITIS, or by the spread of infection from the local skin, as in honeymoon CYSTITIS.

The symptoms of urethritis include a painful discharge from the penis in men or from the urethra in women, and frequent urination.

Treatment depends upon the underlying cause. Usually, antibiotics are curative.

Uric acid is one of the waste products of the metabolism of certain proteins that is usually excreted in the urine. Uric acid crystallizes in the tissues when it is present in excessive amounts, resulting in GOUT.

Other conditions that increase the production of uric acid include blood disorders; psoriasis; and lymphomas (growths in the lymphatic system). Excessive uric acid in the body does not always result in gout, but the greater the excess, the greater the likelihood of developing gout.

Too much uric acid in the urine may result in the development of kidney stones.

See also URICOSURIC AGENTS.

Uricosuric agents are drugs that reduce the amount of uric acid in the body. They are used to treat GOUT.

Probenecid is a uricosuric agent that works by increasing the excretion of uric acid in the urine. It is usually necessary to continue treatment with probenecid for life. Another drug, called allopurinol, works by preventing the formation of uric acid. Allopurinol is among the safest of the urincosuric agents for the long-term treatment of gout.

Most uricosuric agents should be used with caution during an acute attack of gout. They may temporarily aggravate the condition by causing crystals of uric acid in the body tissue to dissolve in the blood.

See also URIC ACID.

Urinalysis is the detailed analysis of urine. It may be performed to detect alterations in the composition of the urine, which may help in the diagnosis of many disorders, particularly those of the kidney and urinary tract.

Q: What tests may be performed in a urinalysis?

A: Various chemical tests may be performed on the urine to detect abnormal substances. For example, the presence of glucose is a typical, but not conclusive, sign of DIABETES MELLITUS.

The urine may also be tested for acidity and the presence of ketones to confirm a preliminary diagnosis of diabetes mellitus. Albumin in the urine (albuminuria) may indicate NEPHRITIS. Bilirubin in the urine may be a sign of JAUNDICE. The presence of blood in the urine (HAEMATURIA) may be caused by a urinary tract infection, a stone, polyp, cancer, or some other abnormality. An abnormal protein in the urine may be a feature of MYELOMA.

The specific gravity, concentration, and volume of urine produced in twenty-four hours may be measured to assess kidney function.

Most of these tests can be performed in a doctor's surgery. Special tests may require laboratory analysis of the urine, for example, to detect hormones, and the concentration of various other chemicals.

Urinary abnormalities are usually symptoms of disorders of various parts of the urinary system. The following table lists urinary abnormalities with their possible underlying disorders. Each abnormality has a separate entry in the A–Z section of this book. Any of these abnormalities should be reported to a doctor.

Disorder	Abnormality
Bladder disorder	DYSURIA (painful urination)
	INCONTINENCE
Cystitis	Nocturnal enuresis (*See* BED-WETTING)
	STRANGURY (extremely painful urination)
Kidney disease	ALBUMINURIA (albumin in the urine)
	ANURIA (lack of urine)
	GLYCOSURIA (sugar in the urine)
	HAEMATURIA (blood in the urine)
	HAEMOGLOBINURIA (haemoglobin in the urine)
	MELANURIA (dark urine)
	NOCTURIA (urination at night)
	OLIGURIA (reduced production of urine)
	POLYURIA (excessive production of urine)
	RETENTION (inability to urinate)

Urinary acidifiers are drugs or chemicals, such as ammonium chloride and ascorbic acid, that make the urine acidic. They may be used to increase the effectiveness of certain drugs, or to increase the rate at which the kidneys eliminate some drugs from the body.

Urinary tract consists of all the organs and ducts that are involved in the production and elimination of urine. It comprises the two kidneys (*see* KIDNEY) and ureters (*see* URETER), the BLADDER, and the URETHRA.

Urine is a fluid that is produced by the kidneys, carried to the bladder by the ureters, and out of the body through the urethra. Urine consists mainly of water, but it also contains waste products that are filtered from the blood by the kidneys. The elimination of waste products in the urine helps to keep the body fluids at the optimum concentration.

The principal waste products are urea, uric acid, creatine, and other nitrogen compounds that are produced by various metabolic processes, mainly by the digestion of proteins. Urine also contains sodium chloride and other salts, and a few body cells.

Normal urine is amber in colour and has a faint but distinctive odour. Occasionally, urine contains abnormal substances, such as sugar or blood. Analysis of the urine may help to diagnose a large number of disorders.

See also URINALYSIS.

Urogenital means concerning the urinary and reproductive systems.

Urology is the branch of medicine that is concerned with the male and female urinary tract, and the male genital organs.

Urticaria, also known as hives or nettle rash, is a skin condition that is characterized by the eruption of welts and itching. *See* HIVES.

Uterus is the medical name for the womb. *See* WOMB.

Uveitis is inflammation of the uveal tract,

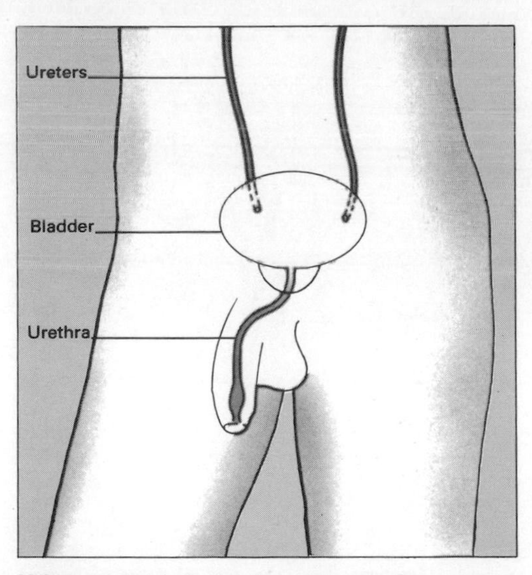

Urinary tract includes the ureters to the bladder, the bladder, and the urethra.

which is the part of the eye that comprises the iris, the ciliary body, and the choroid. In most cases, uveitis occurs without apparent cause. The symptoms differ according to whether the front or the back of the eye is affected. Uveitis that affects the front of the eye causes IRITIS; uveitis that affects the back of the eye causes CHOROIDITIS.

Uvula is a small, fleshy mass of tissue. The term usually refers to the structure that hangs from the soft palate at the back of the mouth. This is called the palatine uvula.

V

Vaccination is inoculation with infectious microorganisms or some part of them (a vaccine) to confer immunity against a specific disease.

See also IMMUNIZATION.

Vaccine is a preparation of disease-producing (pathogenic) microorganisms, or some part of them, that is given to induce immunity. There are three main types of vaccine: those that contain specially treated living organisms, such as measles vaccine; those that contain dead organisms, such as whooping cough vaccine; and those that contain specially prepared toxins, such as diphtheria vaccine.

See also IMMUNIZATION.

Vaccinia is a contagious viral disease that primarily affects cattle, but which also may cause a mild pustular infection in humans. *See* COWPOX.

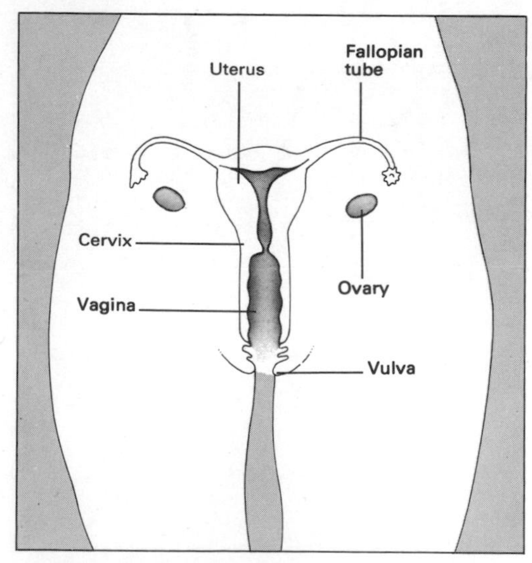

Vagina is the passage between the uterus and the external surface of the body at the vulva.

Vacuum extractor (ventouse) is an alternative to FORCEPS for use in assisting the delivery of a baby. It is a suction cap that is placed over the baby's head. The suction allows an obstetrician to gently pull the child during delivery. It is easier to attach than forceps, and pressure is applied over a larger area of the skull. There is no evidence that this reduces the chances of brain damage to the baby, but it does cause less damage to the mother than the use of forceps.

Vagina is the part of a female's genital tract that extends upward and backward from the vulva to the cervix (neck of the womb). The walls of the vagina are composed of fibrous and elastic tissue, so that it is normally a closed, flattened structure lying between the urethra in front and the rectum at the back.

An adult's vagina is about 7cm (three inches) long when relaxed, but it can stretch considerably during sexual intercourse. The size of the vagina is controlled by the surrounding muscles. During intercourse and childbirth, the muscles relax and contract. The ridged skin lining the vagina (epithelium) changes with the hormonal variations that occur during the menstrual cycle. The amount of mucous secretions also varies during the cycle.

Vaginal discharge, known medically as leucorrhea, is not necessarily abnormal; many women experience a slight discharge. However, it may be a symptom of VAGINITIS (inflammation of the vagina) or cervicitis. Other causes include a foreign body in the vagina, such as a bead in an infant girl or a forgotten tampon in a woman.

The discharge usually consists of secretions from the cervix (neck of the womb) and vagina. The amount of these varies from time to time during the menstrual cycle, because of the hormonal response of the cells that line the vagina and cervix. A day or two after menstruation has ended there is a slight increase in secretions. Another noticeable increase occurs in the middle of the cycle at about the time of OVULATION.

Sexual stimulation, physical or psychological, also causes an increase in secretions.

Newborn females usually have a swollen vulva and a slight vaginal discharge because of the presence of maternal hormones in their bloodstream. *See* LOCHIA.

Vaginismus is an extreme spasm of the muscles surrounding the lower end of the vagina, which causes pain and makes sexual intercourse extremely difficult (dyspareunia).

Q: What causes vaginismus?

A: The cause is usually of psychological origin, often fear. Other causes include inflammation of the vagina.

Q: How is vaginismus treated?
A: A doctor checks for any physical cause of pain before psychiatric treatment is recommended. Overcoming fear of intercourse may take a long time.
See also SEXUAL PROBLEMS.

Vaginitis is inflammation of the vagina. It produces vaginal discharge.

Q: What causes vaginitis?
A: Many women, probably fifteen to twenty per cent, have infectious organisms in the vagina that can cause inflammation, but only a sudden change in environment triggers them into action. Such infection may be stimulated by such diverse factors as the use of antibiotics, the contraceptive pill, vaginal douching, or sexual intercourse. The common microorganisms that infect the vagina are MONILIASIS (thrush) and TRICHOMONAS VAGINALIS.

Q: What are the symptoms of vaginitis?
A: Vaginitis causes soreness and a discharge. Typically, moniliasis causes an intense irritation, soreness, and a thick, white discharge, whereas trichomonas produces a more offensive, greenish watery discharge with less irritation.

Q: How is vaginitis treated?
A: Moniliasis is more common in women who are pregnant or who are taking contraceptive pills (because of their hormonal effect on the vaginal cells), but it is seldom necessary to stop taking the pills. Patients who develop moniliasis following a course of antibiotics treatment for some other condition, usually improve rapidly once the appropriate treatment is given.
Moniliasis is treated with suppositories or creams inserted into the vagina each night for at least a week. Trichomonas is treated with pills taken orally. The patient's sexual partner also should be treated. Other forms of vaginitis, such as nonspecific bacterial vaginitis, can be treated with a combination of suppositories, creams, or appropriate antibiotic drugs by mouth.

Q: Is vaginitis sexually transmitted?
A: Moniliasis may be sexually transmitted. If the woman has recurrent attacks, it is often advisable for the man to use a cream to be applied to the end of the penis at night. *See* CERVICITIS; SALPINGITIS; VAGINAL DISCHARGE; VULVITIS.
In cases of trichomonas, the man usually has the infection without any symptoms, and he should be given treatment at the same time as the woman.

Vagotomy is an operation to cut the VAGUS NERVE. Usually both branches of the nerve are cut at a point adjacent to the oesophagus where they pass through the diaphragm muscle. This greatly reduces the secretion of hydrochloric acid by the stomach. The operation frequently is done at the same time as a partial gastrectomy in the treatment of a PEPTIC ULCER, or a pyloroplasty, used to repair the pylorus.

Vagus nerve (tenth cranial nerve) is the principal nerve of the parasympathetic nervous system. It arises from the lower part of the brain stem (the medulla oblongata), passes through the base of the skull, down the neck, and through the chest to the abdomen.

The vagus nerve sends out branches to various parts of the body, including the outer ear, the throat, the vocal cords, the heart and lungs, and the digestive organs. The sensory fibres of the vagus nerve transmit sensations of stretch from the lungs, and of pressure from the heart. The motor fibres constrict the bronchi and stimulate the digestive organs. Both these types of fibres are part of the parasympathetic nervous system. The vagus nerve also contains fibres that are not part of this system. These ordinary fibres help to control speech and swallowing.

See also AUTONOMIC NERVOUS SYSTEM; PARASYMPATHETIC NERVOUS SYSTEM.

Valgus is any deformity in which part of the body is bent outwards from the midline. For example, talipes valgus is a form of clubfoot in which the heel is turned outwards.

See also VARUS.

Valley fever, also known as coccidioidomycosis, is an infectious disease that is caused by the fungus *Coccidioides immitis.*

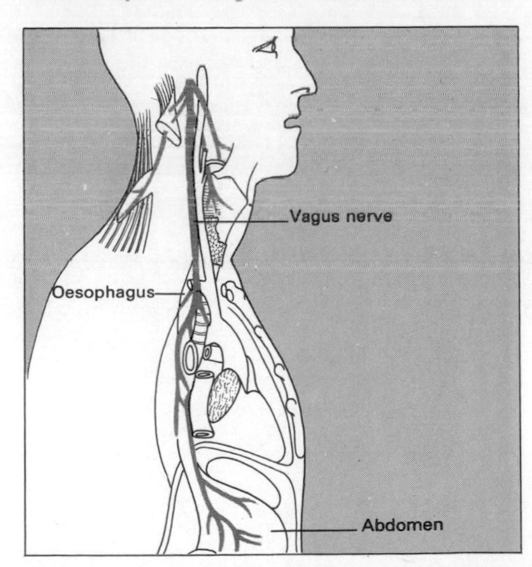

Vagus is one of the most widely distributed nerves with a motor and sensory function.

It occurs mainly in the southwest United States. Valley fever usually produces relatively mild symptoms that are similar to those of a feverish cold or acute bronchitis. Rarely, it may cause a form of pneumonia in which the brain also may be affected, producing a form of meningitis.

Treatment of the mild form of valley fever usually is not necessary because most patients recover spontaneously. The severe form of the disease is treated with the antifungal drug amphotericin, but even with treatment, the mortality rate is high in severe cases.

Valve is a fold of tissue within a tube in the body that prevents the backflow of fluid. Valves occur in the heart, veins, and lymphatic vessels. The ileocaecal valve is situated between the caecum and the small intestine. It helps to prevent digested food from moving backward in the intestine.

Valvotomy is a surgical operation in which a valve is cut. It most commonly is performed to repair a heart valve that has become deformed by scarring.

Valvular disease is a relatively common disorder of the heart in which there is deformity of the heart valves, lack of the usual number of flaps that form the valves, or constriction or dilation of the opening.

RHEUMATIC FEVER causes scarring of the valves and may lead to narrowing (stenosis) or dilation of the passages. It usually affects the mitral valve between the left atrium and left ventricle of the heart, but other valves, such as the tricuspid, aortic, and pulmonary valves, also may be damaged. Sometimes more than one valve is affected.

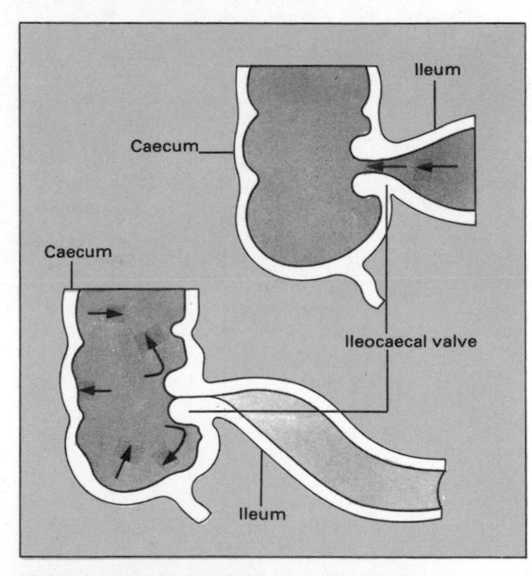

Valve between the ileum and the caecum allows food to pass in one direction only.

Valvular disease causes additional strain on the heart muscle and frequently leads to HEART FAILURE later in life. The distortion of the heart valves causes an alteration in blood flow through the heart, resulting in a HEART MURMUR. The type, timing, and position of the murmur help a doctor to determine the particular valve that is affected. Special diagnostic techniques, such as echocardiography and angiocardiography, may be necessary.

Apart from heart failure, the major complication of valvular disease is infection of the damaged valves resulting in SUBACUTE BACTERIAL ENDOCARDITIS.

In most cases, the deformed valves can be corrected surgically, either by a VALVOTOMY to remove the scarred tissue, or by replacement of the defective valve.

See also HEART DISEASE; HEART SURGERY; MITRAL VALVE DISEASE.

Vaporizer is a device that converts a fluid into a vapour spray. This is an effective method of administering medication for disorders of the lungs and bronchial tubes, such as asthma, bronchitis, and croup.

Varicella is the medical name for chickenpox. *See* CHICKENPOX.

Varicocele is varicose veins around the testes. The enlargement of the veins of the spermatic cord, which causes varicocele, is more common on the left side than the right in adolescent males. It seldom causes more than a slight ache that can be relieved, if necessary, by a scrotal support.

The increased blood flow and warmth in a varicocele occasionally may be a factor in reducing sperm production, leading to sterility in a man.

A varicocele may sometimes occur in a woman's vulva.

A talk about a Varicose vein

Varicose vein is a vein that is abnormally swollen and twisted. Varicose veins result from increased blood pressure in the veins, and damage or absence of the normal valves.

Damage to the valves may be caused by VENOUS THROMBOSIS. Absence of the normal valves may be due to a congenital defect. Increased blood pressure may result from an abdominal tumour, such as a fibroid in the womb, an ovarian cyst, pregnancy, or obesity. Varicose veins are more common in women than men. The condition also occurs in some families more than others, which suggests a hereditary factor.

Q: Where do varicose veins occur?

A: Varicose veins usually occur in the legs, but they also may occur around the anus, causing piles (haemorrhoids); around the testes (varicocele); or in the vulva of a pregnant woman.

The veins at the lower end of the oesophagus may also become enlarged as a result of CIRRHOSIS of the liver when there is an increase in venous pressure in the hepatic portal vein.

Q: What are the symptoms of varicose veins?

A: The most obvious symptom is the appearance of the affected veins. Varicose veins are blue and snake-like. They occur near the skin in the legs and may stand out from the legs. The patient also may suffer from aching of the legs and swelling of the ankles at the end of the day.

Q: How are varicose veins treated?

A: In the early stages, or for those who are elderly or unfit, an elastic stocking may relieve the aching and swelling. But it does not cure the condition.

Varicose veins also may be treated by injecting a fluid that inflames the vein wall, and then bandaging the leg tightly for about six weeks to keep the walls of the vein close together. The resultant scarring causes the walls of the vein to stick together.

Surgical treatment involves cutting and tying the varicose veins, passing a wire instrument down the length of the vein, and then removing the vein by pulling on the wire. This technique is known as stripping.

Q: What complications occur with varicose veins?

A: The most common complication is phlebitis, which has the same inflammatory effect on the vein as injection treatment. The vein becomes tender and eventually scarred, resulting in a nodule under the skin. Severe phlebitis may require antibiotics and tight bandaging. Rarely, anticoagulants may be necessary if a deep vein has also become thrombosed.

Bleeding from a varicose vein may result from injury (for EMERGENCY treatment, *see* First Aid, p.516).

Variola is the medical name for smallpox. *See* SMALLPOX.

Varus is a deformity in which a part of the body bends inwards from the midline.

Vas deferens, or sperm duct, is the tube that carries the sperm from the epididymis of the testes to the seminal vesicles (alongside the prostate gland), where sperm is stored. *See* TESTIS; VASECTOMY.

A talk about Vasectomy

Vasectomy is a form of sterilization for men in which a section of each of the two sperm ducts (vas deferens) is removed surgically. This operation prevents sperm from reaching the urethra.

Q: How is a vasectomy performed?

A: The operation can be done under a local or general anaesthetic. An incision is made at a site that overlies the point at which each sperm duct leaves the scrotum. The two sperm ducts are cut, and the ends are tied firmly with a material that does not dissolve, such as silk. The two incisions are then closed.

Q: How soon after a vasectomy does a man become sterile?

A: The man is fertile for about two or three months after the operation until sperm that were in the seminal vesicles when the operation was performed have either died or been ejaculated.

Q: Are there any immediate problems with a vasectomy?

A: There may be slight local discomfort over the groin wounds for two or three days, but this should not interfere with normal activities. Sexual intercourse may be uncomfortable, so it is advisable to abstain until the stitches are removed or are absorbed by the body, which normally takes about four or five days.

Q: Can a vasectomy cause long-term problems?

A: Long-term problems are extremely rare.

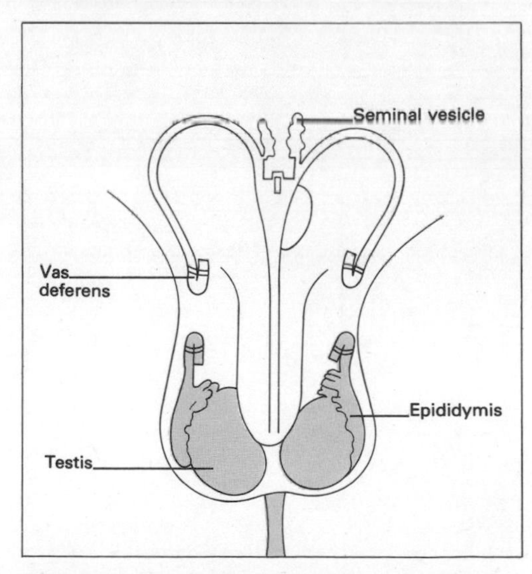

Vasectomy is a surgical operation in which parts of the two sperm ducts are removed.

There may be a dull ache in the testes for several weeks after the operation, but this slowly disappears.

The most common long-term problems usually are psychological in origin. The only difference a vasectomy makes is to stop the production of sperm. A man's sex drive (libido) usually is undiminished after the operation; it may even increase because the fear of an unwanted pregnancy is removed. A vasectomy does not reduce the production of sex hormones, nor should it affect a man's feelings of masculinity.

See also STERILIZATION.

Vasoconstrictor is any agent that causes constriction of the blood vessels. This effect usually is brought about by drugs, but it also may be the result of nervous stimulation.

Vasodilator is any agent that produces a dilatation of the blood vessels. It usually is a drug but also may be the result of nervous stimulation.

Vasomotor rhinitis is a condition affecting the mucous membranes that line the nose. It causes symptoms of runny nose, sneezing, postnasal drip and, occasionally, headache. The symptoms are similar to those of hay fever, but no allergic cause can be found.

Q: What causes vasomotor rhinitis?

A: In most cases, there is no obvious cause. Sometimes anxiety, changes in room temperature, or hormonal changes associated with adolescence, menstruation, or menopause may be factors.

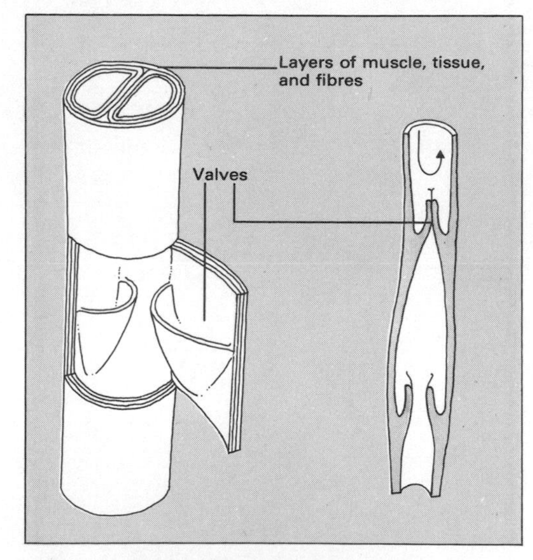

Veins frequently contain valves that prevent the backward flow of blood.

Occasionally, a similar condition occurs as a side-effect of some drugs used to treat high blood pressure, or as a result of overuse of nasal sprays or drops.

Q: How is vasomotor rhinitis treated?

A: Treatment is difficult. The symptoms are thought to be caused partly by overactivity of the parasympathetic nervous system, and so loss of weight, regular exercise, and the stopping of smoking may all help. Treatment with corticosteroid nasal sprays is often effective.

Vasopressin. *See* DIABETES INSIPIDUS.

Vasopressor is anything that stimulates the contraction of blood vessels, causing an increase in blood pressure. *See* VASOCONSTRICTOR.

Vasovagal syncope is the medical name for fainting induced by the sudden dilatation of the blood vessels (vasodilatation). This can happen because of either nervous stimulation, or a fall in heart rate because of vagal effects on the heart. *See* FAINTING.

VD. *See* VENEREAL DISEASES.

Vector is a person or an animal, but usually an insect, that carries an infection from one person to another, or from an infected animal to a person. For example, mosquitoes may be vectors of malaria and yellow fever. *See* FLEAS; MITES; MOSQUITO; TICKS.

Vegan is a person who does not eat meat, fish, or any type of animal or fish products. Vegans may suffer from vitamin B_{12} deficiency unless the vitamin is obtained from yeast. *See* PERNICIOUS ANAEMIA; VITAMIN.

Vegetarian is a person who does not eat meat or fish. Most vegetarians, however, do eat some animal products, such as milk, eggs, and cheese. A carefully-planned vegetarian diet can provide all the nutrients that are essential for good health.

See also DIET; VEGAN; VITAMINS.

Vein is a thin-walled blood vessel that carries blood from the body tissues back to the heart. All veins, except the pulmonary veins and the umbilical vein, carry blood with a low concentration of oxygen and a high concentration of carbon dioxide.

Like the arteries, the walls of the veins consist of three layers, but the muscle and middle layers are thinner than in the arteries and cannot keep the vein open if the blood pressure is low.

Veins start as capillaries within the body tissues. The capillaries unite to form veins, which themselves ultimately join to form two major veins (the venae cavae) that drain into the heart. The four pulmonary veins drain directly into the left atrium of the heart.

There are two veins that begin and end in

capillaries. These are known as portal veins. The hepatic portal vein drains blood from the gastrointestinal tract to the liver. The hypophyseoportal vein connects the hypothalamus in the brain to the anterior lobe of the pituitary gland and conveys hormones that stimulate the production of pituitary hormones.

See also PORTAL VEIN; VARICOSE VEIN; VENA CAVA; VENOUS THROMBOSIS.

Vena cava is one of the two veins (superior vena cava and inferior vena cava) that drain venous blood from all parts of the body, except the heart, into the right atrium of the heart. The superior vena cava returns blood from the head, neck, and arms to the heart. The inferior vena cava returns blood from the chest, abdomen, and legs to the heart.

A talk about Venereal diseases

Venereal diseases, known as VD, are infections that are contracted through sexual intercourse or by close body contact.

Q: *What symptoms are indicative of venereal disease?*

A: Any discharge from the penis or vagina, painful urination, or development of an ulcer on the sexual organs following intercourse may indicate venereal disease. These symptoms usually are obvious in men, but in women they may be so mild as to be unnoticeable. People who notice these symptoms should inform their sexual partners and both should consult a doctor immediately.

Q: *What are the different types of venereal disease?*

A: The different venereal diseases have separate entries in the A-Z section of this book. *See* CHANCROID; GONORRHOEA; GRANULOMA INGUINALE; LYMPHOGRANULOMA VENEREUM; NONSPECIFIC URETHRITIS; SYPHILIS.

Q: *Are there other diseases that may be transmitted by sexual intercourse?*

A: Yes. Scabies commonly is transmitted during sexual intercourse. Trichomonas vaginalis often is transmitted to women by men, although it usually does not produce symptoms in men.

A virus infection known as HERPES GENITALIS is probably the most common cause of painful ulceration of the genital organs. The ulcers may take a long time to heal and may reappear several times.

Genital warts are caused by a virus infection that commonly occurs in conditions of poor hygiene. The genital area becomes covered with moist, pink swellings which have a tendency to recur, despite treatment.

Moniliasis, a fungal infection, is a common problem in women. It may be stopped, only to return after intercourse with a partner who has penile moniliasis.

Q: *What should a person do who may have a venereal disease?*

A: It is important to consult a doctor or to attend a venereal disease clinic. A definite diagnosis of venereal disease may require a physical examination and samples of any penile or vaginal discharge. Blood tests to detect the presence of antibodies to syphilis also may be performed.

If the patient has a venereal disease, appropriate treatment is needed. The patient must regularly attend a clinic, usually every two weeks at first, then once a month for six months. This is necessary to ensure that the disease has been cured and that more than one venereal disease was not contracted at the same time.

Q: *Should a patient with VD take any other precautions?*

A: Yes. It is essential to abstain from sexual intercourse until it is certain that the infection has been cured. All sexual contacts of an infected person should receive medical attention.

Q: *Can venereal disease be cured?*

A: Yes. The common forms of venereal disease usually can be cured with antibiotics. However, people with nonspecific urethritis or herpes genitalis

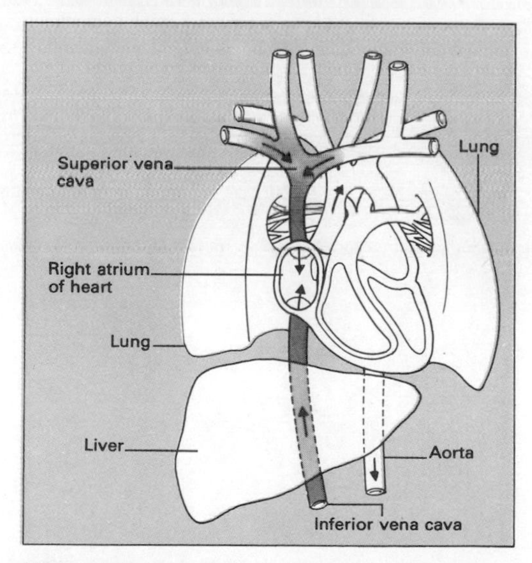

Vena cava connects the right atrium with the lungs and the body's venous system.

may have to wait for the condition to improve naturally, which may take several months.

In order to cure venereal disease, it is essential that the patient's disease should be diagnosed early and treated correctly. People who suspect that they have the symptoms of venereal disease must consult a doctor as soon as possible.

Q: Can venereal disease be prevented?

A: Yes, but only by complete sexual abstinence. In men and women the use of a condom may help to reduce the likelihood of catching a venereal disease.

Q: Is it possible to immunize against VD?

A: No. There are no vaccines that are effective against any form of venereal disease.

Venerology is the specialty of medicine concerned with the diagnosis and treatment of venereal diseases. The doctor who practises this specialty is called a venerologist.

Venipuncture is the act of puncturing a vein with a needle. It may be done to obtain a sample of blood for testing, or during an intravenous infusion, when the needle is left in the vein.

Venogram is a procedure in which a dye is injected into a vein so that an X-ray photograph will reveal the shape, size, and extent of the vein. *See* ANGIOGRAM.

Venom is a poisonous substance from a snake, insect, or other animal that can be injected through the skin by a bite or sting. It contains a variety of poisons and toxic enzymes. *See* ANTIVENIN; SNAKEBITE.

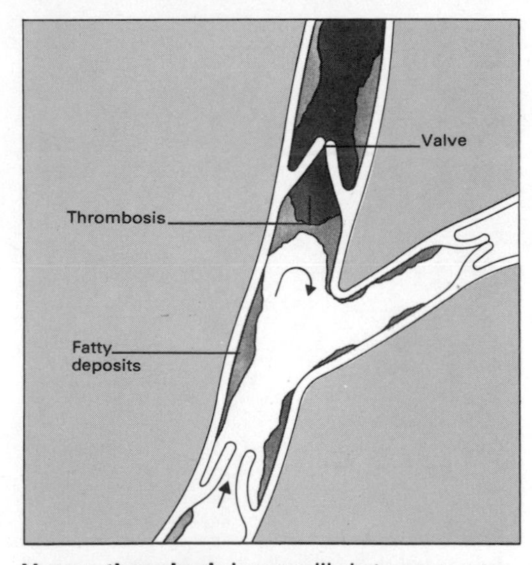

Venous thrombosis is more likely to occur near a valve where the flow of blood is sluggish.

A talk about Venous thrombosis

Venous thrombosis is the formation of a blood clot (thrombus) in a vein. Clotting that is associated with inflammation of a vein (phlebitis) is known as thrombophlebitis; clotting that occurs without venous inflammation is called phlebothrombosis.

Q: What causes venous thrombosis?

A: Venous thrombosis may be caused by any of several factors. These include damage to the wall of a vein, either as a result of injury, infection, or some form of autoimmune disorder in which the body reacts against itself, causing venous inflammation. Sometimes thrombosis may develop because of the combination of an increase in the clotting factors within the blood and slowing of the normal blood circulation.

The use of hormones, particularly oestrogen, may predispose a person to blood clotting.

Q: What are the symptoms of venous thrombosis?

A: Symptoms vary according to whether a superficial or deep vein is involved. The most common type of venous thrombosis is associated with superficial veins. With varicose veins, a combination of poor blood circulation, mild skin inflammation and, sometimes, ulceration may cause thrombophlebitis of the leg. This may result in local tenderness and swelling of the vein, and redness and swelling of the nearby skin.

If a deep vein has thrombosed, the symptoms may include swelling of the ankles, slight tenderness when the calf is pressed, and discomfort when the foot is pulled upwards. Deep vein thrombosis in areas other than the leg may be impossible to detect, and the diagnosis of deep vein thrombosis may require special techniques such as X-rays of the veins (*see* VENOGRAM), ultrasound techniques, and a variety of blood tests.

Q: Can venous thrombosis cause complications?

A: Yes. The most serious complication occurs when a piece of the blood clot breaks off to form an embolus (*see* EMBOLISM). This is potentially fatal. Emboli, however, are relatively rare.

The long-term consequence of venous thrombosis is usually degeneration of the valves in the affected veins. This may result in swelling of the ankles, and skin disorders, such as dermatitis and ulcers.

Superficial venous thrombosis seldom causes serious complications.

Q: How is venous thrombosis treated?

A: If a deep thrombosis is diagnosed, hospital treatment with anticoagulant (blood-thinning) therapy is required. Initially, injections of heparin usually are given. Later, other anticoagulant drugs are administered orally.

Anticoagulant treatment usually is continued for about six months. If an embolus develops, surgery may be necessary to tie off the affected vein.

Superficial venous thrombosis usually is treated with painkillers and tight bandaging of the leg to maintain an adequate blood supply.

If ankle swelling or other complications develop after deep vein thrombosis, the patient should wear elastic support stockings for his or her lifetime.

Q: Can venous thrombosis be prevented?

A: Yes. Some persons are more likely than others to develop venous thrombosis. Those at risk include the elderly; those with diabetes; those with blood disorders, such as polycythaemia vera; women who take contraceptive pills that contain oestrogens; people with a history of thrombosis; and patients who have undergone gynaecological surgery. In such cases, anticoagulant treatment may be necessary before surgery is performed. This may prevent venous thrombosis from occurring.

Before surgery is performed, the patient should do special calf and leg exercises. After surgery, he or she should resume physical activity as soon as possible. Such measures reduce the likelihood of venous thrombosis.

See also BUDD-CHIARI SYNDROME; WHITE LEG.

Ventral is the front (abdominal) surface of the body, also called the anterior surface, as opposed to the dorsal, or posterior, surface.

Vermiform appendix is the full anatomical name for the appendix. *See* APPENDIX.

Verruca is a wart on the foot. Verrucas commonly are called plantar warts; they are caused by a virus. *See* WART.

Vertebra is any of the thirty-three bones of the spinal column. The flexible part of the spinal column consists of seven cervical vertebrae in the neck; twelve thoracic vertebrae at the back of the chest; and five lumbar vertebrae in the small of the back. The five vertebrae below the lumbar vertebrae are fused to form the SACRUM. The lowest four vertebrae form the COCCYX.

Q: What is the structure of a vertebra?

A: A typical vertebra consists of two main parts: an inner, front part called the body; and an outer, back part called the vertebral arch. These two parts surround a central space through which the spinal cord passes.

The body is roughly cylindrical in shape, with flattened upper and lower surfaces. The bodies of adjacent vertebrae are separated by tough discs of fibrocartilage (intervertebral discs). The vertebral bodies increase in size down the length of the spine.

The vertebral arch consists of seven bony outgrowths. There are two pedicles that project backward from the body. The two laminae form connecting processes between the pedicles. The spinous process is a bony outgrowth that projects backward and downward. The two traverse processes project sideways and provide sites for the attachment of muscles and ligaments.

On the lower surfaces of the pedicles of each vertebra are two areas that form joints with similar surfaces on the upper parts of the pedicles of the vertebra below.

The seven cervical vertebrae differ from the others. The cervical vertebrae are smaller; the spinous process divides into two parts; and the transverse processes each contain a hole through

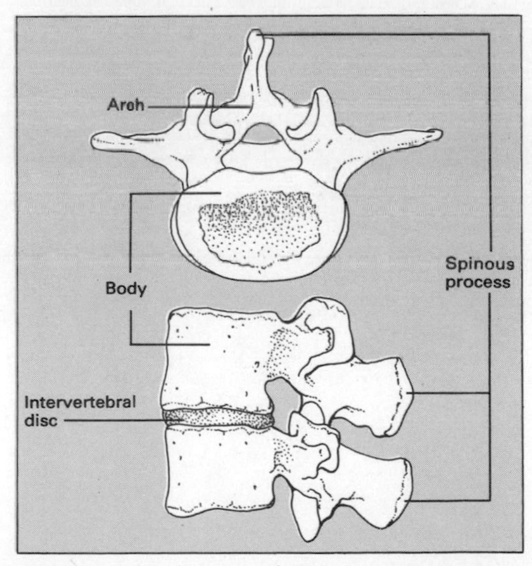

Vertebrae are separated by intervertebral discs, which allow the spinal cord to bend.

which the vertebral arteries to the brain pass. The top two bones of the cervical spine are completely different from typical vertebrae. The top bone, called the atlas, articulates with the skull. The atlas is a ring-like structure, without a vertebral body. This shape makes nodding movements of the head possible. The second cervical vertebra is called the axis. It has an upwards projection (the odontoid process) that fits into the part of the atlas where its vertebral body normally would be. The odontoid process enables the head to rotate.

The twelve thoracic vertebrae each bear a pair of ribs, which articulate with the sides of the vertebral bodies and the transverse processes.

See also SLIPPED DISC; SPINE; SPONDYLITIS; SPONDYLOSIS.

Vertigo is a disorder of balance which gives a person the sensation of spinning around in space when at rest. Alternatively, objects may appear to be spinning around the person. It is different from DIZZINESS, which is a vague sensation of unsteadiness.

Q: *What causes vertigo?*

A: Any disorder that affects the ear, the auditory nerve, or the centre in the brain concerned with balance may be responsible. Other causes include toxic compounds such as drugs, alcohol, or food poisoning, and also sudden disturbances of eye function.

Q: *What ear disorders cause vertigo?*

A: Blockage of the Eustachian tube or wax in the external ear may cause vertigo.

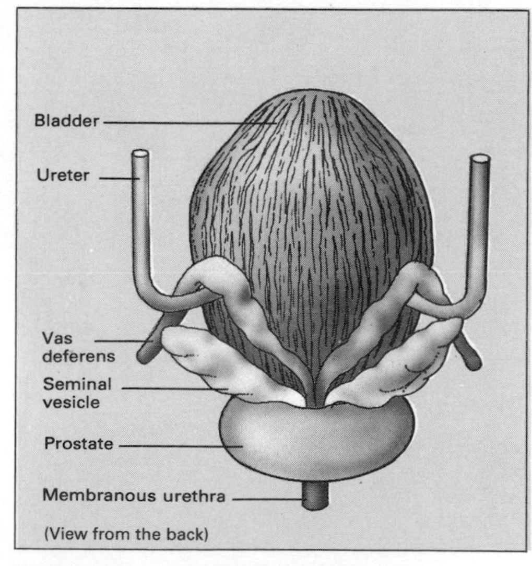

Vesicle is a pouch-like sac or bladder that contains fluid, such as the seminal vesicle.

Infections of the middle ear and inner ear, such as OTITIS media and LABYRINTHITIS or involvement by other disorders, such as OTOSCLEROSIS and MÉNIÈRE'S DISEASE, also cause vertigo.

Q: *How does the auditory nerve become involved?*

A: Vestibular neuronitis infections, in which the nerve cells become inflamed, are the most common cause. A tumour of the auditory nerve may produce vertigo as well as increasing deafness.

Q: *What conditions affecting the brain cause vertigo?*

A: The centres that co-ordinate balance are in the brain stem, and have connections with the cerebellum and temporal lobes of the cerebral hemispheres. These may be disturbed by a STROKE or ARTERIOSCLEROSIS, particularly in the elderly. Disorders such as MULTIPLE SCLEROSIS, EPILEPSY, and a brain TUMOUR may cause vertigo.

Q: *What is benign paroxysmal positional vertigo?*

A: Symptoms of vertigo may occur when the head is moved quickly, but they last for only a few seconds. It is thought to be a minor disturbance of the organ of balance and often spontaneously improves after several months.

Q: *Are there any other symptoms that may accompany vertigo?*

A: Yes. Nausea and vomiting commonly accompany vertigo, and walking may be difficult with a tendency to fall over sideways. The eyes may flicker (nystagmus), and there may be buzzing in the ears (tinnitus).

Q: *How is vertigo treated?*

A: The immediate treatment is to lay the person down, in a comfortable position, with the eyes closed. A doctor must be consulted, because antinauseant drugs can be prescribed to help to control the symptoms until a diagnosis is made.

Vesicle is either (1) a bladder or sac containing fluid, such as the gall bladder or urinary bladder; or (2) a blister on the skin containing serous fluid, as occurs in chickenpox and shingles.

See also BLISTER; PAPULE; RASH.

Vestibulitis. *See* LABYRINTHITIS.

Viable means capable of living. A foetus is considered to be viable when it has reached a stage at which it can be kept alive outside the womb. Usually this is when the foetus is at least twenty-eight weeks old.

Vibrio is a genus of motile, curved, rod-shaped bacteria. There are more than thirty different species of *Vibrio* of which three cause disease. *Vibrio cholerae* causes CHOLERA. There are two strains of this species – the normal strain, and a more resistant strain that is known as the El Tor strain. *Vibrio fetus* and *Vibrio parahemolyticus* rarely cause disease.

Villus is a small finger-like protrusion from the surface of a membrane in the body. The lining of the small intestine is covered with millions of villi that provide a large surface area for the secretion of intestinal enzymes and the absorption of digested food. Chorionic villi help the placenta to adhere to the lining of the womb.

Vincent's angina, also known as trench mouth, is a form of STOMATITIS (inflammation of the mouth). It is caused by bacteria which infect the gums, mucous membranes, tonsils, and pharynx. This disorder may develop when oral hygiene is neglected, if nutrition is poor, or in some serious illness such as leukaemia.

Q: What are the symptoms of Vincent's angina?

A: The chief symptom is a sudden onset of painful, bleeding gums (GINGIVITIS), with ulceration inside the cheeks and on the tongue. The patient has a foul-smelling breath and sometimes develops a fever.

Q: How is Vincent's angina treated?

A: Antiseptic oxygenating mouthwashes and dental care produce a rapid improvement. A dentist or doctor may prescribe an antibiotic drug and, if necessary, extra vitamins. Smoking should be avoided.

Virilism is the development of masculine characteristics in women or children. In boys, it is associated with the bodily changes of puberty. The early development of male secondary sex characteristics is caused by excessive secretion of the male sex hormone testosterone by the adrenal glands.

Q: What symptoms may occur in women?

A: Male-type distribution of body hair develops, with deepening voice and the onset of baldness. Acne may appear, and the woman's periods may become irregular or cease (AMENORRHOEA). There is usually an increase in sex drive (libido).

Q: How is the condition diagnosed and treated?

A: A diagnosis is made after examination of the patient's urine for breakdown products of testosterone, and X-rays to detect the presence of an adrenal gland tumour. Corticosteroid drugs will reduce the adrenal gland activity in mild cases. But an operation usually is necessary to remove a part of the adrenal glands, or a tumour if it is present.

Virulent means extremely poisonous. The term is applied to any infection that causes a rapid onset of severe symptoms because of its poisonous effects. Virulent infections are more likely to be fatal than indolent, benign infections.

Virus is one of a group of minute infectious organisms that are visible only under an electron microscope. They are much smaller than bacteria. Viruses consist only of a strand of either DNA or RNA, which are complex proteins that carry genetic information, and an outer coat of protein. Viruses cannot provide their own energy, nor can they grow outside living cells. For this reason, all viruses are parasitic. They alter the functions of the cells they infect so that these cells supply the viruses with energy and with the means of reproducing themselves.

Q: Do viruses infect all of the body tissues?

A: Yes, but individual viruses show a preference for particular tissues. For example, the poliomyelitis virus preferentially infects part of the nervous system, the rabies virus infects the brain, and the chickenpox virus infects the skin. Any viral infection may cause generalized symptoms of muscle aching and fever.

Not all viruses cause disease. Some remain within the body cells without disordering them, but can be activated by an alteration in the body.

Q: What diseases do viruses cause?

A: Many common diseases are caused by viruses; for example, chickenpox, German measles, influenza, measles, mumps, and many respiratory diseases.

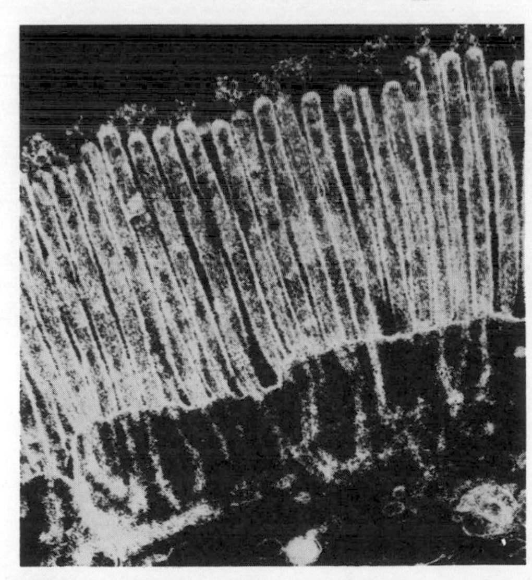

Villus, a short, finger-like projection, increases the absorbing surface of the gut.

Other viral diseases include dengue fever, encephalitis, shingles, smallpox, and yellow fever. At least thirty different viruses can cause the symptoms of the common cold.

Some diseases are caused by slow viruses that remain in the body for several years before producing any symptoms. Multiple sclerosis may be caused by an alteration in a person's immunity to a slow virus.

Q: *How does the body react to viral infections?*

A: At the onset of a virus infection, the body has little resistance to the virus, apart from the presence of lymphocytes, which are a type of white blood cell, and a small amount of INTERFERON, which is a substance that helps to destroy viruses. Within a few days of infection, the body's immune system is stimulated by the viruses to produce antibodies and larger amounts of interferon.

Q: *Is it possible to prevent virus infections?*

A: Yes. Vaccines have been produced against some of the common virus infections. Vaccines to combat German measles, measles, and poliomyelitis usually are given routinely in early childhood. It also is possible to vaccinate against influenza, rabies, smallpox, typhus, yellow fever, and mumps.

Antibiotics are ineffective against most virus infections, but new drugs are available to help to combat smallpox and shingles.

Q: *Can viruses cause tumours?*

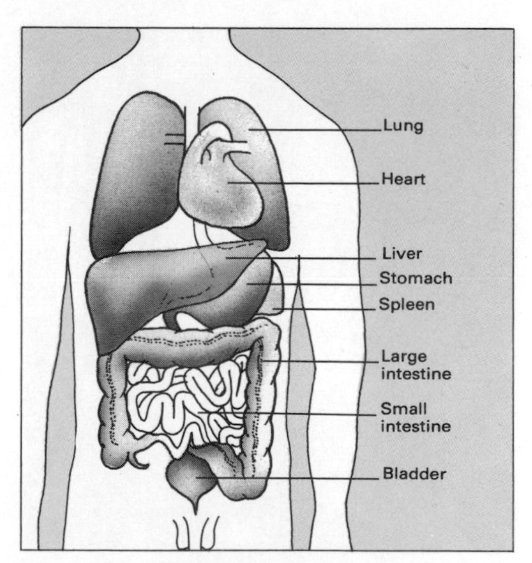

Viscera is a collective term for the internal organs of the chest and abdomen.

A: Yes. Viruses may cause benign (non-cancerous) growths, such as warts and the skin tumours that occur with molluscum contagiosum.

See also IMMUNITY; IMMUNIZATION.

Viscera is a general term for the internal organs in the abdominal and chest cavities. The viscera includes the heart, lungs, liver, spleen, gastrointestinal tract, womb, and bladder.

Visceroptosis is a downward displacement of the visceral organs. In most cases, no cause for the condition can be found. Visceroptosis may affect any of the internal organs, but it most commonly occurs in the abdomen.

Vision. *See* EYE.

Vitamins are chemical substances that are essential for the normal working of the human body. They are effective in extremely small amounts and act mainly as regulators of the body's metabolic processes. Most vitamins must be obtained from food but some, such as biotin and vitamin K, can be synthesized in the body by intestinal bacteria. Vitamin D can be synthesized directly by the body from the action of sunlight on the skin.

Vitamins are classified as either water-soluble or fat-soluble. Fat-soluble vitamins are vitamin A (retinol), vitamin D (calciferol), vitamin E (tocopherol), and vitamin K (phytomenadione). Water-soluble vitamins are vitamin C (ascorbic acid) and the vitamin B group: vitamin B_1 (thiamine), vitamin B_2 (riboflavine), vitamin B_6 (pyridoxine), vitamin B_{12} (cyanocobalamin), biotin, folic acid, and pantothenic acid.

Q: *Is a daily intake of vitamins essential?*

A: No. The body can store fat-soluble vitamins for many months and water-soluble vitamins for several weeks. A balanced diet should contain sufficient vitamins to maintain these stores. Growing children need proportionately more vitamins than adults. The body's vitamin requirements are also increased during illness, pregnancy, and breast-feeding.

Q: *What are the effects of excessive vitamins in the diet?*

A: Most vitamins do not produce any effects when taken in large amounts. But, vitamins A, D, and K may produce adverse effects if excessive amounts are taken continually for a long period. An overdose of vitamin A may cause hair loss, peeling of the skin, joint pains, and liver damage. Excessive vitamin D may cause kidney damage and the formation of calcium deposits in the body tissues. Excessive vitamin K in the newborn may cause kernicterus, which is a form of

Name	Source	Functions	Effects on deficiency	Additional information
Vitamin A (retinol)	Fish liver oils, eggs, butter, milk, cheese, liver, apricots, broccoli, cabbage, carrots.	Essential for night vision, healthy skin, and mucous membranes.	Night blindness, dry eyes (xerophthalmia), dry skin.	Excessive intake may cause hair loss, peeling of the skin, joint pains, and liver damage.
Vitamin B_1 (thiamine)	Yeast, whole grains, pork, liver, nuts, peas and beans, potatoes.	Essential for normal functioning of nerve cells, heart muscle, and carbohydrate metabolism.	Beriberi.	Increased amount needed during growth, pregnancy, and breast feeding.
Vitamin B_2 (riboflavine)	Yeast, eggs, milk, cheese, liver, kidney, green vegetables.	Essential for normal protein and carbohydrate metabolism, and for maintaining mucous membranes.	Cracked lips (cheilosis), skin rashes, dim vision.	Increased amount needed during growth, pregnancy, and breast feeding.
Vitamin B_6 (pyridoxine)	Yeast, whole grains, fish, liver, peas and beans.	Essential for general functioning of body cells and amino acid metabolism.	Convulsions in infants, anaemia, nerve disorders.	Increased amount needed during growth, pregnancy, breast-feeding.
Vitamin B_{12} (cyanocobalamin)	Eggs, milk, cheese, butter, liver, beef, pork.	Essential for growth of red blood cells and normal functioning of nerve cells.	Pernicious anaemia, dim vision, peripheral neuritis.	Deficiency is especially likely in total vegetarians (vegans), and persons with sprue, or following a total gastrectomy.
Niacin (nicotinic acid)	Yeast, meat, fish, whole grains, peas and beans.	Essential for cell metabolism, absorption and carbohydrates, and healthy skin.	Pellagra.	Resists most cooking and preserving processes.
Biotin	Present in all common foods.	Essential for energy production from fats and carbohydrate, and for formation of hormones.	Deficiency does not occur naturally.	Biotin can be produced by bacteria in the intestine.
Folic acid	Yeast, liver, kidney, green, leafy vegetables; fruit.	Essential for growth of red blood cells.	Anaemia and peripheral neuritis.	Increased amount needed during growth, pregnancy, and breast-feeding. Deficiency is particularly likely in people with sprue.
Pantothenic acid	Whole grains, eggs, liver, kidney, peanuts, cabbage.	Essential for normal functioning of enzymes inside the body cells.	Deficiency does not occur naturally.	Pantothenic acid can be produced by bacteria in the intestine.
Vitamin C (ascorbic acid)	Citrus fruits, tomatoes, potatoes, green vegetables.	Essential for normal tissue growth and repair, and normal functioning of blood vessels.	Scurvy.	Vitamin C is easily destroyed by cooking and ultraviolet light.
Vitamin D (calciferol)	Fish liver oils, eggs, butter, liver, yeast.	Essential for normal absorption of calcium and phosphorus, and for normal bone formation.	Rickets in children, osteomalacia in adults.	Increased amount needed during growth, pregnancy, and breast-feeding. Excessive intake may cause kidney damage and calcium deposits in the body tissues.
Vitamin E (tocopherol)	Eggs, vegetable oils, wheat germ, green vegetables.	Essential for stability of cell membranes.	Decreased resistance to rupture of red blood cells.	May also play a part in fertility. Produced by intestinal bacteria.
Vitamin K (phytomenadione)	Vegetable oils, pork, liver, leafy vegetables.	Essential for normal blood clotting.	Bleeding, particularly in premature babies.	Vitamin K can be produced by intestinal bacteria. Deficiency is rare in adults.

jaundice that occurs in children and which damages the brain.

Q: What are the effects of insufficient vitamins in the diet?

A: Prolonged vitamin deficiency leads to depletion of the vitamin stores in the body. This, in turn, results in various deficiency diseases (*see* DEFICIENCY DISEASES).

Q: Are vitamin supplements necessary?

A: Additional vitamins are unnecessary if a person is healthy and is eating a balanced diet. Certain vitamins, particularly the fat-soluble vitamins, may be harmful if taken in excessive amounts.

Additional vitamins may be needed during an illness or following a surgical operation. Those with disorders in which there is insufficient absorption of vitamins in the intestine may require vitamin supplements until the underlying disorder has been cured. Other disorders that increase the metabolic activity of the body's cells, such as an overactive thyroid gland, may increase the body's vitamin needs. A doctor will recommend vitamin supplements if they are necessary.

Q: Are vitamins affected by cooking and storing?

A: Yes. Some vitamins are unstable substances and can easily be destroyed by incorrect storing and cooking of food.

The fat-soluble vitamins can withstand normal cooking, but vitamins A and E are gradually destroyed by exposure to the air.

The amount of water-soluble vitamins is greatly reduced by boiling food because the vitamins dissolve in the water. Vitamin B_1, vitamin B_6, folic acid, and pantothenic acid are destroyed by heat; vitamin B_2 is destroyed by light; and vitamin C is destroyed by heat, light, and air. For these reasons, food should be used when fresh and should not be overcooked.

Certain food preservatives also destroy the vitamins in food. This may affect the vitamin content of canned foods.

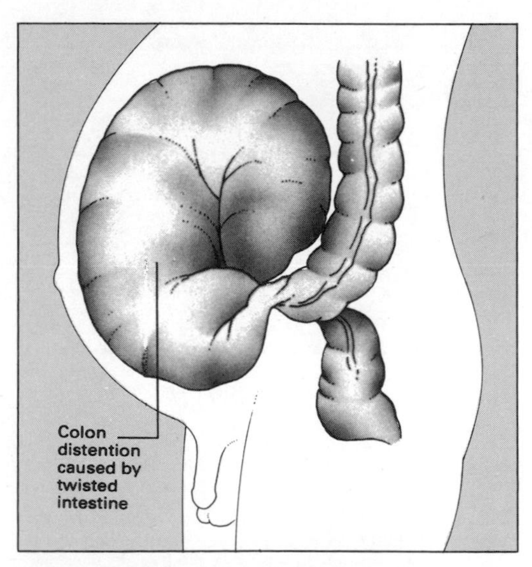

Volvulus occurs when the intestine twists over itself, causing abdominal distention.

Vitiligo is a relatively common skin disorder that affects about one per cent of the population. It involves the loss of normal skin pigment in irregular patches because melanin (the chemical that produces pigment) fails to be produced. About ten per cent of those affected recover spontaneously.

The condition may start at any age, but it commonly appears before the age of twenty. It generally is thought to be an auto-immune disease with an inherited component.

Vitiligo is more common in patients with some form of auto-immune disorder, such as pernicious anaemia, diabetes mellitus, and alopecia areata.

Q: How is vitiligo treated?

A: There are few drugs available to aid patients with vitiligo. Methyoxy psoralen has been found to help recolouring of the skin if it is exposed to sunlight. People with small patches of vitiligo can use special make-up to camouflage the area.

Vitreous humour is the jelly-like substance that fills the part of the eye behind the lens. *See* HUMOUR.

Voice box is a common name for LARYNX.

Volvulus is a twisting of the intestine around itself. This not only creates an intestinal obstruction, but also blocks the blood vessels that serve it. A volvulus most commonly occurs in the small intestine, caecum, and the sigmoid colon.

Q: Why does a volvulus occur?

A: A volvulus may be the result of a fault present at birth. One loop of bowel is larger than usual, and there is a longer membranous fold (mesentery). Another cause may be the looping of part of the intestine around an adhesion, a scar left by inflammation or surgery.

Q: What are the symptoms of a volvulus?

A: The symptoms of a volvulus are similar to the symptoms of intestinal obstruction: abdominal pain, and vomiting. A volvulus of the large intestine causes vomiting, and invariably involves complete constipation and abdominal pain, with swelling of the abdomen.

Q: How is a volvulus treated?

A: In most cases, an abdominal operation is needed to untwist the volvulus and, if the intestine has become gangrenous, to remove the damaged part of the intestine. It often is necessary to have a temporary colostomy while the intestine returns to normal.

See also INTESTINAL OBSTRUCTION.

A talk about Vomiting

Vomiting, known medically as emesis, is the forceful throwing up of some or all of the stomach contents by reversal of peristalsis, the normal muscular contractions of the stomach. For EMERGENCY treatment, *see* First Aid, p.597.

Vomiting may be a symptom of various disorders, some local to the stomach and some more generalized disorders. It usually is preceded by a loss of appetite and nausea.

Q: What are the local causes of vomiting?

A: The most common cause of vomiting is acute or chronic GASTRITIS (inflammation of the stomach). Vomiting sometimes occurs with a PEPTIC ULCER, particularly if there is PYLORIC STENOSIS (narrowing of the stomach exit). Vomiting also is a symptom of any form of INTESTINAL OBSTRUCTION.

Babies may vomit for a great variety of reasons. Some babies vomit more easily than others but, provided there is a general weight gain and the baby is obviously well, it is not a serious symptom.

Q: What generalized disorders may cause vomiting?

A: The onset of high fever and any condition that affects the sense of balance, such as a virus infection of the inner ear (labyrinthitis) result in vomiting.

Vomiting is a common symptom if the vomiting centre in the thalamus of the brain is disturbed by a MIGRAINE or by increased brain pressure associated with a brain TUMOUR. This takes place also in MENINGITIS and ENCEPHALITIS. Hormone changes in pregnancy alter the sensitivity of the vomiting centre, and this accounts for MORNING SICKNESS and also the excessive vomiting that may occur with HYPEREMESIS gravidarum.

Vomiting can occur for psychological reasons, such as an emotional shock or a nauseous sight or smell.

Vomiting also occurs in serious metabolic disorders; for example kidney failure and the onset of diabetic coma.

Q: Is vomiting always a serious symptom?

A: No. Occasional vomiting at the start of a generalized illness is part of that disorder. But prolonged and continued vomiting is a serious symptom because it leads to dehydration, which is usually an indication of a severe underlying disorder.

Q: How should vomiting be treated?

A: Until medical help is available, lay the patient down, supported by one or two pillows. Do not allow the patient to drink anything. Bathing the patient's face with a cool, damp flannel is often soothing.

Vomit should be collected in a bowl or other receptacle, in case the doctor wishes to examine it.

If vomiting ceases with these simple measures, and if there are no other symptoms, it may not be necessary to call a doctor. Keep the patient lying still for at least an hour, and do not allow any fluid to be drunk for two hours. Begin drinking by taking small sips of liquid to avoid starting another attack of vomiting.

Continued vomiting always is a more serious problem in small babies than in adults, because dehydration occurs more quickly. This is particularly the case if there also is diarrhoea.

Von Recklinghausen's disease, also known as neurofibromatosis and molluscum fibrosum, named after the German pathologist, is an inherited condition in which multiple freckle-

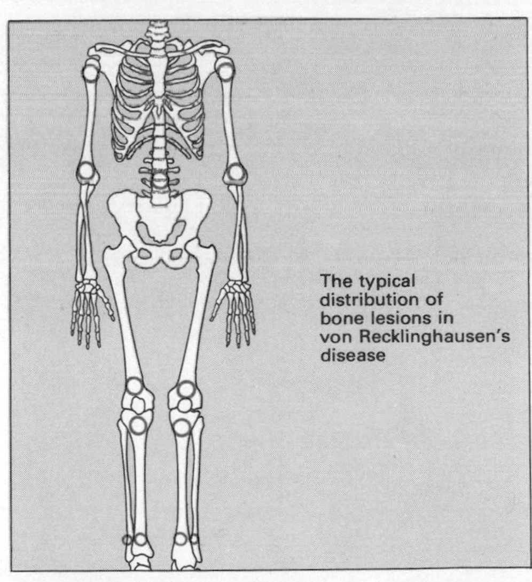

Von Recklinghausen's disease is associated with destructive lesions of the bones.

like spots appear on the skin. Nodules (fibromas) also occur and can be felt through the skin. The nodules also occur on nerves (neurofibroma).

Von Recklinghausen's bone disease is also an alternative name for hyperparathyroidism (*see* PARATHYROID GLANDS.)

Q: What are the symptoms of von Recklinghausen's disease?

A: The nodules may be noticeable at birth or may gradually develop later. Often, the skin spots are present at birth. As the child grows, curvature of the spine (scoliosis) may develop and, occasionally, become severe.

The nodules may occur anywhere in the body and cause pressure on adjacent tissues. The neurofibroma cause neurological symptoms, such as neuralgia and paralysis. Therefore, a variety of symptoms may occur. Any symptoms that do develop need careful assessment by a specialist familiar with this disease.

Q: How is von Recklinghausen's disease treated?

A: Treatment is necessary only if the symptoms are severe. Scoliosis may need orthopaedic treatment, and nodules may require surgical removal.

Vulva is the female external genital organ that surrounds the outside opening of the vagina and clitoris. In front, there is a soft padded area covered with hair (mons pubis), and sweeping back from this are the two large folds of the labia majora enclosing two smaller folds, the labia minora. These folds contain lubricating glands, the largest of which (Bartholin's glands) lie at the back.

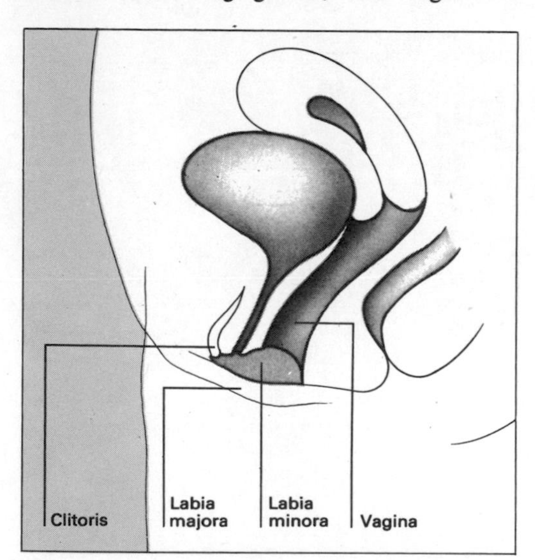

Vulva, the female external genital organ, includes the clitoris and the labia.

The vulva extends into the firm, fibrous tissue of the perineum, which is in front of the anus. Between the labia minora lies the fold of skin called the hymen, which partly closes the entrance to the vagina until it is broken by sexual intercourse or by the use of internal tampons.

Inflammation of the vulva is common (*see* VULVITIS). Other disorders are rare.

Vulvitis is inflammation of the VULVA. Its symptoms are soreness and itching.

Q: What causes vulvitis?

A: Any of the causes of inflammation of the vagina (VAGINITIS) may produce vulval itching. These commonly result from moniliasis (thrush) or trichomonas vaginalis infections, but vulvitis also may occur in diabetes mellitus or general skin diseases such as psoriasis and scabies.

In about one third of cases with vulval irritation, the cause is psychological. But continued scratching produces inflammation that may become infected and cause vulvitis.

Q: What other vulval infections may occur?

A: Other vulval infections include venereal diseases such as syphilis, granuloma inguinale, chancroid, lymphogranuloma venereum, and a viral infection producing warts that may develop on any part of the vulva. Infection with a herpes virus may develop into painful, shallow ulcers.

Q: How is vulvitis treated?

A: The patient must be examined to discover the cause of the irritation. Swabs may be taken for culture to identify an infection; the appropriate treatment can then be given.

Corticosteroid creams usually are soothing and often are prescribed until a firm diagnosis has been made.

See also BARTHOLIN'S CYST; LEUKOPLAKIA; MONILIASIS; TRICHOMONAS VAGINALIS; VAGINITIS; VENEREAL DISEASES; WARTS.

Vulvovaginitis is inflammation of both the vulva (vulvitis) and the vagina (vaginitis). It commonly is caused by moniliasis (thrush) and trichomonas vaginalis infections. *See* VAGINITIS; VULVITIS.

W

Warts are skin growths caused by virus infection. They are most common in children between seven and twelve years of age.

Q: Are there different kinds of warts?

A: Yes. The common wart is a small, raised rough lump on the skin made up of small columns of tissue arising from the base. They vary in colour from normal flesh tint to dark brown-black. Common warts usually occur on the hands, knees, and less frequently on the face or eyelids. They may also appear around the edges of the nails.

Plantar warts (verruca) are the same as the common wart, but are flat because of the different texture of the skin of the sole of the foot. They may be painful because the nodule presses into the flesh.

Venereal or genital warts (condylomata acuminata) are a typical wart infection, sometimes transmitted by sexual intercourse (*see* VENEREAL DISEASES).

Q: How are warts treated?

A: Warts usually disappear spontaneously. Treatment with solid carbon dioxide (dry ice) or liquid nitrogen destroys the wart and the surrounding tissue, leaving a small blister. There are various chemical solutions that can destroy warts, but these have to be used with care. It is advisable to remove any skin application after one or two days and then to rub away the dead tissue before reapplying the medication.

More radical methods of removing warts, such as by cautery, surgery, or X-rays, frequently leave a small scar which may itself produce a small, tender nodule.

Genital warts require special treatment due to their position and possible association with other venereal diseases.

Q: Are there any other kinds of warts?

A: Yes. Many people describe any small lump or nodule on the skin as a wart. Although these are not necessarily true warts, the appearance may be similar.

Changes in the skin, occurring with age, may produce slightly raised pigmented areas (senile keratosis), frequently in people who have spent years in the sun.

Seborrhoeic keratosis causes slightly raised darkened areas in the skin that appear as though stuck on the skin surface. These occur most commonly on the trunk but do not need treatment unless they are disfiguring.

See also CYST; RODENT ULCER; MOLLUSCUM CONTAGIOSUM.

Wasp sting venom is composed of various proteins and enzymes (for EMERGENCY treatment, *see* First Aid, p.515). The venom is rarely fatal unless the victim is allergic to it. In this case, ANAPHYLAXIS closely followed by death may occur.

Wasserman Reaction (W.R.) is a blood test that is used in the diagnosis of SYPHILIS.

Wasting, known medically as phthisis, is a gradual loss of body tissue and bulk. *See* STARVATION.

Watering eyes usually are caused by an emotional state, although blockage of the LACRIMAL APPARATUS or inflammation of the eyes also cause excessive production of tears.

See also EYE DISORDERS.

Water on the knee is a form of bursitis. *See* BURSITIS.

Wax, known medically as cerumen, is a soft substance produced by special glands in the ear canal. There is a large variation in the amount of wax produced by different people. Wax usually drains out by itself.

This production and discharge of wax is responsible for the continual cleansing of the ear canal of potentially harmful organisms and debris.

Q: What conditions cause increased wax production?

A: Two conditions that may cause increased production are chronic otitis externa and Parkinson's disease.

Q: How is hardened wax removed?

A: It should first be softened with warm olive oil or bicarbonate of soda solution for a few days before visiting a doctor. It may then be syringed out with warm water. Do not use any object to scrape out the wax, because of the danger of damaging the eardrum.

Q: Can wax formation be prevented?

A: No. It is a perfectly normal secretion.

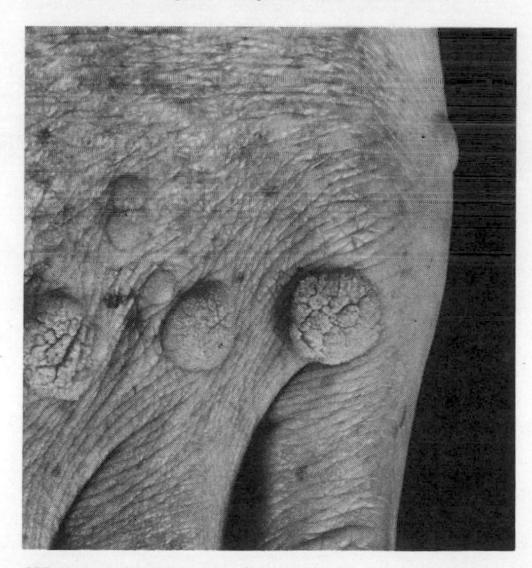

Warts on the hands usually form as many small growths.

Hard wax can be prevented by using warm olive oil once every two to three weeks to keep the wax soft.

Q: Are commercial wax softening mixtures safe to use?

A: Yes, provided they are used with care, especially by people who have had OTITIS externa. Some mixtures may soften the skin and allow infection to occur.

Weakness, or debility, is the sensation of loss or partial loss of strength and vigour. It is a symptom of a number of conditions and disorders, and a person who continues to feel weak should consult a doctor.

Weal is a red, swollen area of skin.

Weaning is the period in infancy when feeding gradually is changed from being entirely milk-based to include other foods, such as cereal, fruit, and vegetables. It also is used as an expression to describe the time at which a baby is taken off the breast and given milk feeding by bottle.

The age at which the weaning takes place varies widely from mother to mother, and is a matter for discussion between the mother and the doctor. New foods usually are introduced for the first time between the ages of two to three months, but this is often delayed until later. Breast-feeding may continue for many months, even when other foods are being given.

Weight problems. Many people may think that they are overweight when, in fact, their weight may be normal for their height, age, and sex. They are worried because their own shape or figure does not conform to the currently fashionable ideal. But very few people are able to achieve this shape, and it may even be abnormal in a biological and anatomical sense for some individuals.

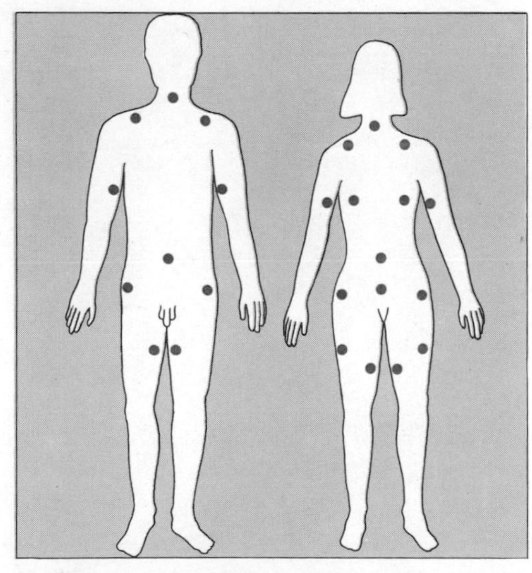

Excess fat tends to accumulate in certain areas, which differ between men and women.

Apart from such shape problems, there are genuine weight problems. A person may be overweight or underweight compared to the average or desirable weight. This can cause a physical disorder or anxiety.

Q: How is average weight calculated?

A: Weight tables are compiled by taking the weights of a large number of people and working out an average. The average weight varies because of many factors. For example, races vary in physical proportions; and some families are heavier than others, and their children inherit this characteristic. Weight also varies with occupation. Manual workers, athletes, and military personnel, for example, tend to be better developed and heavier than those who do light work.

Q: How does the body normally regulate weight?

A: Most people stay about the same weight throughout adult life, or gain weight only slowly. The appetite centre, in the hypothalamus of the brain, regulates the amount that is eaten. A slight imbalance results in a gradual weight gain. Even an extra slice of bread a day may cause a gain of 0.25kg (half-a-pound) a month, and about 3kg (seven pounds) in a year.

Q: When should a person consider there is a weight problem?

A: Average expected weights should not be considered ideal weights. The correct weight varies from ten per cent below to ten per cent above the average weight, and is still normal. Weight well above or below this is probably abnormal.

Q: What should be done if a person is below the normal weight?

A: A person may decide that he or she is underweight, but this may be because of racial or inherited characteristics. If, however, there has definitely been a weight loss, a doctor should be consulted and the cause found.

Q: How do underweight people gain weight?

A: This is a matter for a doctor, who first makes sure that there is no disorder that needs treatment. Some people become dangerously underweight by starving themselves. ANOREXIA NERVOSA is an extreme form of self-starvation common in adolescent girls and needs specialized drug and psychiatric treatment. Depression, anxiety, and general fatigue are other factors in weight loss.

Q: Why do people become overweight?

A: Nearly always because they eat too much.

When people eat more than they need for the amount of energy they expend, they tend to get fat.

But some people may be overweight because of a physical disorder, and some gain weight because of compulsive eating, often a sign of underlying anxiety or depression. Weight gain also may follow long illness. *See also* BULIMIA NERVOSA.

Q: Why do some people gain weight much more easily than others?

A: The reasons for weight gain are not fully understood, but the answer may lie in an individual's metabolism. Babies who are fed excessive amounts of food become fat babies and often grow into fat adults.

Q: Are some foods more likely to produce obesity than others?

A: Yes. Foods rich in carbohydrates, particularly those containing sugar, that exceed the body's carbohydrate requirement, get converted into fat. Proteins, such as meat and fish, fruit, and vegetables, are less likely to cause obesity. Alcohol has a high calorie content and, apart from other damage it may cause, is a factor in obesity.

Q: Are there any hazards in being overweight?

A: Yes. Overweight people have a greater chance of getting coronary thrombosis and strokes because of arteriosclerosis. Such people are more likely to develop diabetes mellitus; are more likely to hurt themselves seriously in accidents; develop osteoarthritis, particularly of the knees, hips, and ankles; and have more complications following surgery, such as venous thrombosis and chest infections.

Q: How should an obese person lose weight?

A: Anyone who is more than twenty per cent over the expected average weight for his or her age, sex, and height should discuss weight loss and dieting with a doctor. Sudden weight changes may cause extreme fatigue and exhaustion. Crash diets can be dangerous and may lead to vitamin deficiency diseases.

A gradual reduction in the amount of food eaten can result in a weight loss of 1 to 1.5kg (two to three pounds) a week, an overall loss of 5kg (ten pounds) a month. The doctor will probably recommend fewer carbohydrate foods, alcohol, and wheat products, and more protein foods and fresh salads.

Regular exercise is of value because it increases the body's metabolic rate and gives the person a sense of well-being and relative freedom from fatigue.

Once the ideal weight has been achieved, there can be a slight relaxation in the detail of the diet so that the ideal weight is maintained. It is, however, essential to keep to the same basic diet for life, to avoid a return to the original eating habits that caused obesity.

Q: Can drugs help in the treatment of obesity?

A: Yes. If obesity is caused by anxiety or depression, treatment with tranquillizers and antidepressant drugs can be a great help in reducing compulsive eating. Diuretic drugs, however, help to lose only 1 to 1.5kg (two to three pounds) of water from the body. Appetite suppressant drugs are only moderately effective, and do not help the obese person to learn new ways of eating. When such drugs are stopped, the weight usually increases again. Hormones, such as thyroid pills, have little effect unless taken in excessive amounts. Pep pills, such as amphetamines, reduce the appetite but are dangerous, not only because of the hazard of addiction, but also because of the effect on blood pressure and increased mental activity.

Q: Should vitamins be taken while dieting?

A: No. There should be no need for additional vitamins if the person is in good health and keeps to a sensible, balanced new diet.

Q: How can people help themselves if their weight is normal and they are dissatisfied with their shape?

A: Regular exercise helps to increase muscle tone and decrease waist measurements, as well as producing a slight slimming of

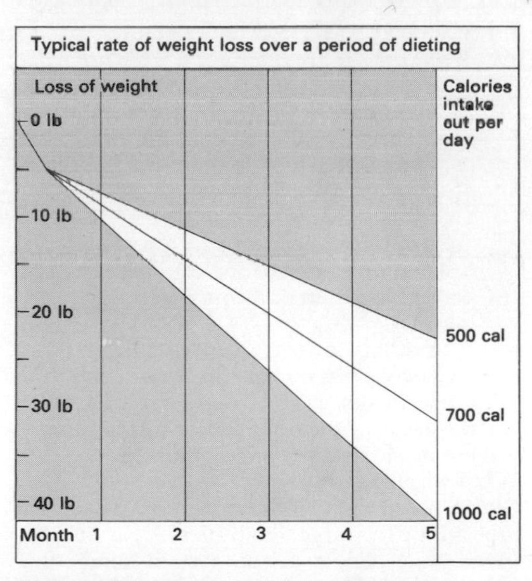

Dieting often causes weight to decrease dramatically at first, then more gradually.

the thighs. Weight may increase slightly due to extra muscle, but the figure will improve.

Q: Can disorders reduce body weight?

A: Yes. Any long-term illness, such as tuberculosis, sprue, untreated diabetes, or cancer, is accompanied by loss of weight. Fevers, operations, or accidents cause an increase in metabolic rate. Thus the body tissues are used faster than they can be replaced, and there is a loss of weight. Another cause of increased metabolic rate is hyperthyroidism.

Q: Can any disorders produce an increase in weight?

A: Yes. Heart, kidney, and liver failure are accompanied by retention of fluid in the body (oedema), and this results in a weight gain. An underactive thyroid gland (hypothyroidism) is often accompanied by an increase in weight.

Drug treatment of some mental disorders may be associated with a weight gain because of an effect on the hypothalamus.

Weil's disease. *See* LEPTOSPIROSIS.

Wen. *See* SEBACEOUS CYST.

Wharton's jelly is a layer of jelly-like substance that surrounds the umbilical arteries and veins in the UMBILICAL CORD.

Wheezing is a rasping or whistling sound heard with some breathing disorders.

See also STRIDOR.

Whiplash injury occurs when a sudden jerking forward of the body throws the head backward, resulting in injury to the neck. A whiplash injury commonly occurs in a car accident or as a sports injury. All such injuries must be treated by a doctor.

Q: What are the symptoms of a whiplash injury?

A: Momentary loss of consciousness may occur, usually followed by acute spasm and pain in the long muscles in the back of the neck. Almost always the victim has a STIFF NECK.

Sometimes there may be a partial dislocation of one of the cervical vertebrae, or an acute prolapsed intervertebral disc (*see* SLIPPED DISC).

In rare cases, a fracture occurs, or a disc may press on the spinal cord and cause weakness and loss of sensation in the areas of the body below this level in the neck. Paralysis may follow.

Whipworm. *See* WORMS.

White blood cells, also known as leucocytes, are relatively large, colourless cells in the blood that play a major part in combating infection. Unlike RED BLOOD CELLS, white blood cells contain a nucleus. There are three main categories of white blood cells: polymorphonuclear leucocytes, which have granules in the cell fluid; monocytes; and lymphocytes. Polymorphonucleocytes (polymorphs) are also known as granulocytes.

Polymorphs are subdivided into neutrophils, eosinophils, and basophils according to their reaction to a special dye. They are produced in the bone marrow.

The other leucocytes are subdivided into monocytes and lymphocytes. They are produced in the bone marrow, lymph nodes, spleen, and thymus gland.

There are between 4,000 and 10,000 white blood cells per cubic millimetre of blood in a healthy person. Bacterial infections usually result in an increase in the number of white blood cells; viral infections may result in a decrease in the number of white blood cells.

Q: How do white blood cells combat infection?

A: When the body is injured or infected, white blood cells pass through the walls of the capillary blood vessels and congregate at the site of injury or infection. Then they engulf and destroy invading bacteria and other foreign bodies. In doing so, the white blood cells themselves are destroyed, and form pus.

The lymphocytes also produce antibodies (*see* IMMUNITY). Lymphocytes are found in most body tissues and play a major part in the body's reaction to prolonged infections, such as tuberculosis. *See* AGRANULOCYTOSIS; LEUKAEMIA; PLATELET; RED BLOOD CELL.

Whiteleg is a condition that occurs after deep vein thrombosis in a leg. *See* THROMBOSIS.

Whitlow. *See* PARONYCHIA.

Whooping cough, or pertussis, is a disease of the respiratory tract. Infection is by the microorganism called *Bordetella pertussis*; the microorganism is transported by droplets. The disease is commonest in infancy. Incubation period is ten to twenty-one days, and the infectious period from the onset of symptoms until three weeks after the beginning of the paroxysmal stage.

Q: What are the symptoms of whooping cough?

A: The three stages of the disease begin with (1) the catarrhal. The patient develops common cold symptoms, slight fever, sneezing, rhinitis, irritability with loss of appetite, and a dry cough which increases in violence after two weeks, becoming a series of short coughs followed by a long dragging in of breath, during which the "whoop" is heard.

Vomiting is common in (2) the paroxysmal stage. As this is the most serious stage, a watch must be kept for complications such as pneumonia, possibly leading to bronchiectasis and emphysema in later life. Severe coughing can cause haemorrhage of membranes in the nose and eyes. Mental retardation can result from cerebral haemorrhage, as can spastic paralysis.

The third stage (3), the decline, begins after about four weeks. The coughing bouts subside and food intake improves. Recovery may take several months.

Q: How is whooping cough treated?

A: The antibiotic erythromycin may prevent the onset of paroxysmal coughing if given early in the catarrhal stage. If not arrested at this stage, isolation and normal cough treatment combined with sedatives for sleep are recommended.

Q: Can whooping cough be prevented?

A: Yes. A vaccine of killed *Bordetella pertussis* organisms must be given to an infant in three doses, usually at the age of 5, 6, and 12 months, and combined with diphtheria and tetanus vaccine.

Whooping cough is uncommon and a milder disease in later life.

Widal test is a blood test performed in the investigation of TYPHOID FEVER.

Wilson's disease is a rare, hereditary disorder in which there is an abnormal accumulation of copper in the body, particularly in the liver and brain. This causes cirrhosis, anaemia, and a form of chorea. Wilson's disease is caused by an abnormal recessive gene that controls copper metabolism in the body. Death usually occurs unless treatment with penicillamine, a drug which increases the excretion of copper, is successful.

Wind. *See* FLATULENCE.

Windpipe. *See* TRACHEA.

Wisdom teeth are the third and last molar teeth on each side of the upper and lower jaw. They may not come through until after the age of twenty-five. *See* TEETH.

If the jaw is not large enough to accommodate them, the wisdom teeth may become impacted. When this happens, they are extracted by a dentist under a general or a local anaesthetic.

Witches' milk is a common name for the small amount of rather watery milk produced for a few days after birth by the breasts of a newborn baby of either sex. This action is stimulated by maternal hormones in the baby's bloodstream.

Womb, or uterus, is a thick muscular organ about the size of a clenched fist located in the abdomen of females. It is lined with a layer of cells (the endometrium) that respond to the varying hormonal stimulus of the menstrual cycle (*see* MENSTRUATION). During pregnancy the womb is the organ that surrounds the developing foetus.

The womb is a pear-shaped organ with two fallopian tubes (oviducts) that extend from each side of the upper end to the ovaries. At the lower end, the cervix (neck of the womb) leads into the vagina. The womb is supported below by a combination of ligaments that stretch from the side of the cervix to the pelvic bones.

See also CERVICITIS; ENDOMETRITIS; FIBROID; GYNAECOLOGICAL DISORDERS; HYSTERECTOMY; MENSTRUAL PROBLEMS; POLYP; PROLAPSE.

Woolsorter's disease is a fatal lung disorder caused by ANTHRAX.

Worms are primitive animals, many species of which cause parasitic infections. Worms are classified into three main groups: tapeworms (Cestoda); roundworms (Nematoda); and flukes (Trematoda).

Tapeworms that infest the intestine include the beef tapeworm (*Taenia saginata*) and the fish tapeworm (*see* DIPHYLLOBOTHRIUM LATUM). The most common tapeworm that infests human beings is the sheep tapeworm (*Echinococcus granulosus*), causing hydatid disease (*see* HYDATID CYST). The pork tapeworm (*Taenia solium*) can cause CYSTICERCOSIS.

Roundworms that infest the intestine include *Ascaris lumbricoides* (*see* ROUNDWORMS); threadworms, such as *Enterobius vermicularis* (*see* OXYURIASIS); hookworms, such as *Ancylostoma duodenale* (*see* ANCYLOSTOMIASIS); other worms, such as *Strongyloides stercoralis* (*see* STRONGYLOIDES); and whipworms, such as *Trichuris trichuria* (*see* TRICHURIASIS). Roundworms that infest the body tissues include *Wuchereria bancrofti*, which causes Bancroftian filariasis (*see* ELEPHANTIASIS); *Brugia malayi*, which causes Malayan filariasis (*see* ELEPHANTIASIS); *Dracunculus medinensis*, which causes dracontiasis (*see* GUINEA WORM); *Loa loa*, which causes loiasis (*see* LOA LOA); *Onchocerca volvulus*, which causes river blindness (*see* ONCHOCERCIASIS); *Toxocara canis* and *Toxocara cati*, which cause TOXOCARIASIS; and *Trichinella spiralis*, which causes TRICHINOSIS.

Flukes that infest the body tissues include various species of *Schistosoma* (*see* SCHISTOSOMIASIS); *Clonorchis sinensis*; *Fasciola hepatica*, also known as the liver fluke; and the lung fluke, *Paragonimus westermani* (*see* PARAGONIMIASIS).

See also FLUKES; ROUNDWORMS; TAPEWORMS.

Wound is any injury that causes damage by cutting or tearing tissues. A surgeon's incision is an aseptic (without infection) wound.

A contusion (bruise) is a wound in which the skin is not broken. A penetrating wound is small, but the underlying structures are damaged far more than the punctured layer.

See also BLEEDING.

Wrist, known medically as the carpus, is the joint between the arm and the hand. There are eight bones in the wrist, located in two rows. The SCAPHOID, lunate, triquetral, and pisiform bones form a joint with the radius and ulna bones of the forearm. The trapezium, trapezoid, capitate, and hamate bones form joints with the five metacarpal bones of the hand. Each of the wrist bones forms a joint with each of the others. All of the bones are surrounded by synovial membranes and ligaments.

See also CARPAL TUNNEL SYNDROME.

Wrist drop is caused by paralysis of the muscles of the forearm, so that the wrist remains flexed ("dropped") and is unable to extend backward. Wrist drop usually follows injury to the radial nerve in the upper arm, or paralysis of muscles in the forearm.

Writer's cramp is stiffness of the thumb, first two fingers, and forearm muscles.

Wryneck. *See* STIFF NECK.

Xanthelasma is a condition in which small, yellow flat spots form in the inner corners of the upper and lower eyelids. It is most commonly seen in the elderly.

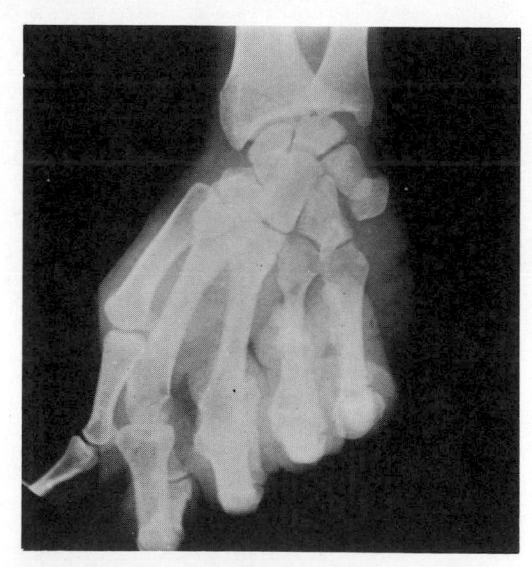

Wrist, the area between the forearm and the hand, contains eight carpal bones.

Q: What causes xanthelasma?

A: It may occur spontaneously for no obvious reason. But the condition often is associated with increased amounts of CHOLESTEROL in the blood, with LIPAEMIA, and with the appearance of a XANTHOMA elsewhere in the body.

Q: What is the treatment of xanthelasma?

A: Xanthelasma does not cause discomfort or disease, and so does not require treatment other than any that may be prescribed for lipaemia.

Xanthoma is a deposit or lump of yellow fatty substance (lipids) in the skin and tendons. The condition is most common in the ACHILLES TENDON, in the tendons of the hand and foot, and it occurs with LIPAEMIA, an inherited disorder in which there are excessive amounts of lipids in the blood. XANTHELASMA, a yellowish tumour on the upper and lower eyelids found in elderly people, also may occur. Individuals with xanthoma have an increased chance of developing coronary heart disease.

Q: How is xanthoma treated?

A: Treatment includes a low cholesterol diet (without saturated fats) and drugs that further decrease the lipids in the blood. The nodules of fatty substances sometimes ulcerate through the skin and have to be removed surgically.

X chromosome is one of the two types of human sex chromosomes. The other is called the Y chromosome. If two X chromosomes are present, the person is a female. If an X and a Y chromosome are present, the person is a male. The X chromosome usually is of a shape and size similar to the other twenty-two pairs of chromosomes present in the nucleus of every cell in the human body. *See* CHROMOSOME; GENE; Y CHROMOSOME.

Xenophobia is a psychiatric term for an abnormal dread or hatred of strangers or foreigners.

See also PHOBIA.

Xenopus test is a PREGNANCY TEST in which a female African toad (*Xenopus laevis*) is injected with urine from a woman who suspects that she is pregnant. If the woman is pregnant, the toad produces eggs within twelve hours of the injection. The xenopus test may give false results in some cases, and has been replaced by more reliable tests.

Xeroderma is a condition in which the skin is abnormally dry and rough.

Q: Why does the skin become abnormally dry?

A: The skin may become abnormally dry because of sunburn; the gradual dryness that occurs with increasing age; vitamin A deficiency; or ichthyosis, a mild type of dry skin disorder present at birth.

Q: How is xeroderma treated?

A: Often the problem is a minor one and it is only the mild irritation that makes the patient visit a doctor. The doctor usually prescribes a cream to keep moisture and fat in the skin, and advises against using soap. Vitamin A is prescribed only if there is evidence of deficiency.

See also ICHTHYOSIS.

Xerophthalmia is a disorder that results in dry eyes and reduced tear production, or a roughness of the conjunctiva often associated with night blindness.

Q: What causes xerophthalmia?

A: Vitamin A deficiency may be one cause; HYPOTHYROIDISM or a form of SARCOID also may be responsible for the condition.

Q: How is xerophthalmia treated?

A: Vitamin A produces an immediate improvement, and hypothyroidism can be treated with THYROXINE. If dryness continues, special eye solutions containing cellulose preparations can be used as artificial tears.

X-rays are a form of electromagnetic radiation that can penetrate body tissues to varying degrees. This variation in the amount of X-rays absorbed by different tissues can be recorded on film to produce an X-ray photograph.

See also RADIATION; RADIOGRAPHY; RADIOLOGY; RADIOTHERAPY.

Yaws is an infectious tropical disease caused by the spiral-shaped bacterium *Treponema pertenue.* This bacterium is indistinguishable from that which causes syphilis (*Treponema pallidum*) and pinta. Yaws is spread by direct contact between the infectious swellings of a diseased person and a break in the skin of another person. The bacterium that causes yaws cannot penetrate unbroken skin, nor can it pass through the placenta.

Q: What are the symptoms of yaws?

A: After an incubation period of about a month, a swelling appears at the site of infection; this may ulcerate and then heal. While it is healing, further soft swellings appear on the lips, elbows, buttocks, and knees. They are highly infectious, but rarely produce any irritation. Occasionally, the soft swellings may affect the underlying bones, particularly in the hands and feet. This may cause a limp in children.

When the soft swellings have healed, there often is an interval of several years before any further symptoms occur. After this interval, nodules appear on the skin. They may ulcerate and often affect underlying tissues. The ulcers heal slowly, forming scars that may be greatly disfiguring. The bones also may become distorted, and there may be shortening of the ligaments in the joints.

Q: How is yaws treated?

A: Yaws can be cured by treatment with penicillin. Surgery also may be necessary to correct any disfigurement or bone deformity.

See also PINTA; SYPHILIS; TREPONEMA.

Y chromosome is one of the two types of human sex chromosomes; the other is called the X chromosome. If a Y chromosome is paired with an X chromosome, the person is a male. If two X chromosomes are paired, the person is a female. The Y chromosome is so called because its shape is markedly different from the other forty-five chromosomes, which all resemble the X chromosome. *See* CHROMOSOME; GENE; X CHROMOSOME.

Yeast is a general term for any of the single-celled fungi of the genus *Saccharomyces.* Yeast is used for leavening bread and for brewing (brewer's yeast). Brewer's yeast is a rich source of vitamin B. Some species of yeast may cause disorders (such as MONILIASIS) or may be poisonous.

Yellow fever is a virus infection transmitted to humans by the bite of the mosquito *Aedes aegypti.* The disorder is common in tropical climates, particularly in Africa and South

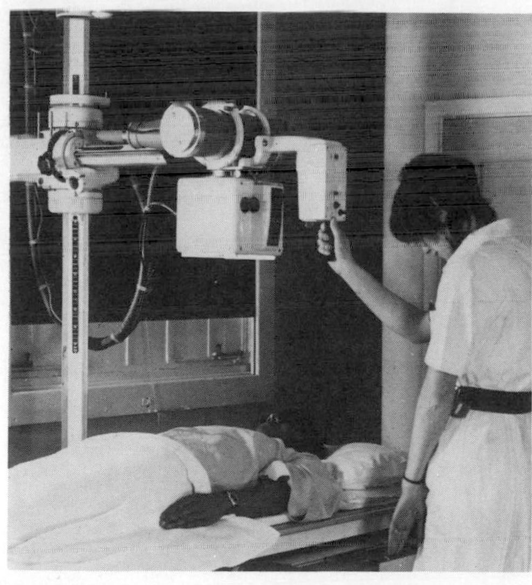

The patient lies over a photographic plate as the radiographer adjusts the X-ray equipment.

America. There is an incubation period of three to six days after infection and then symptoms appear.

Q: What are the symptoms of yellow fever?

A: Symptoms appear suddenly and include a shivering attack (rigor), high fever, severe headache and bone pains, vomiting, mild confusion, signs of meningitis, and photophobia (sensitivity to bright light).

The patient's temperature returns to normal in about four days and he or she appears to be recovering. But after a few hours, jaundice begins to appear, the fever returns, and there is bleeding into the urine, from the mouth, and into the skin.

The organs that are particularly involved are the liver (causing hepatitis), kidneys (kidney failure) and, to a lesser extent, the heart (heart failure), as well as the brain (encephalitis). The symptoms become increasingly severe, and death may occur within a week after a few hours in coma.

In people who live in the endemic areas and who have some immunity, the illness is much less severe and of shorter duration. In such people, yellow fever does not cause any permanent damage to the body, but full recovery may be attained only after several weeks or even months.

Q: What is the treatment for yellow fever?

A: There is no cure for yellow fever. The only treatment available is the administration of intravenous fluids, antinauseant drugs and, if necessary, kidney dialysis, as well as skilled medical and nursing care in hospital.

Q: Is there any protection against yellow fever?

A: Yes. Immunization with an extremely mild yellow fever virus gives protection for ten years. It should not be done within three weeks of a smallpox vaccination, and not given to children under the age of one year because there is a slight risk of causing encephalitis. It also is advisable not to immunize during pregnancy, even though foetal damage has not been detected.

An international certificate stating that a person has received immunization against yellow fever is valid from ten days after the injection for ten years. Such a certificate is legally required of travellers to countries where the disease is prevalent.

Preventive measures include mosquito control by screening, spraying, and destruction of breeding areas. Mass immunization also helps to decrease the incidence of the disease.

Yellow jaundice. *See* JAUNDICE.

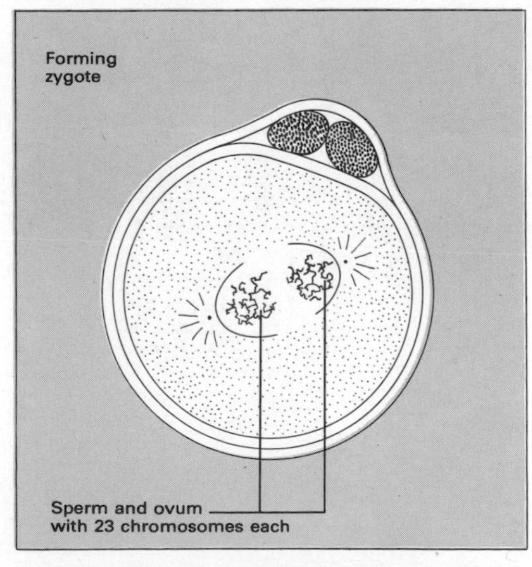

Zygote is formed when a sperm passes into an ovum and a new cell nucleus is formed.

Z

Zinc oxide is a white odourless powder that may be prepared in paste, lotion, cream, or powder form. It is used alone or combined with other substances as a soothing preparation in the treatment of eczema, varicose veins, and haemorrhoids, and around colostomies and ileostomies. It also is used as dusting powder for prickly heat and, combined with mild antiseptics, as a cement used as a temporary packing for holes in the teeth (caries).

Zinc oxide often is used in preparations on special bandages that are applied to ulcerated or eczematous areas of the skin. The bandages are left in place for some days, or even weeks, for as long as it takes for the underlying condition to heal.

Zoonosis is any disease of animals that can be transmitted to humans under natural conditions. *See* PETS AND DISEASE.

See also ANTHRAX; BRUCELLOSIS; CAT-SCRATCH FEVER; DENGUE; ENCEPHALITIS; GLANDERS; LASSA FEVER; MALARIA; PLAGUE; PSITTACOSIS; RABIES; ROCKY MOUNTAIN SPOTTED FEVER; SLEEPING SICKNESS; TYPHUS.

Zygote is the cell that is formed when a sperm fertilizes an egg (ovum). *See* FERTILIZATION.